HIGHER LEVEL 2023

This is Poetry

Brian Forristal & Billy Ramsell

FORUM PUBLICATIONS LTD.

Published by
Forum Publications Ltd
Unit 1703, Euro Business Park,
Little Island, Cork
Tel: (021) 4232268 | Fax: (01) 6335347
www.forum-publications.com

Copyright © Brian Forristal MA and Billy Ramsell MA 2021

Additional questions and annotations by Tom Dwyer

The moral right of the authors has been asserted

ISBN: 978-1-906565-50-3

© All rights reserved.
No part of this publication may be reproduced, copied or transmitted in any form or by any means without the written permission of the publishers or else under the terms of any licence permitting limited copying issued by the Irish Copyright Licensing Agency, The Writer's Centre, Parnell Square, Dublin 1.

ACKNOWLEDGMENTS

Poems by Elizabeth Bishop are from The Complete Poems 1927–1979 by Elizabeth Bishop; copyright © 1979, 1983 by Alice Helen Methfessel. Reprinted by permission of Farrar, Straus and Giroux, LLC; The poems by W. B. Yeats are reproduced by kind permission of Henry Holt and Company; Poems by Patrick Kavanagh are reprinted from Collected Poems, edited by Antoinette Quinn (Allen Lane, 2004), by kind permission of the Trustees of the Estate of the late Katherine B.Kavanagh, through the Jonathan Williams Literacy Agency. Poems by Paula Meehan are reproduced by kind permission of Dedalus Press; Poems by Derek mahon are reprinted by kind permission of Gallery press; 'The Uncle Speaks in the Drawing Room', 'Our Whole Life' from *Collected Early Poems 1950–1970* by Adrienne Rich. Copyright © 1993 by Adrienne Rich. Copyright © 1967, 1963, 1962, 1961, 1960, 1959, 1958, 1957, 1956, 1955, 1954, 1953, 1952, 1951 by Adrienne Rich. Copyright © 1984, 1975, 1971, 1969, 1966 by W.W. Norton & Company, Inc. Used by permission of the author and W.W. Norton & Company, Inc. 'Aunt Jennifer's Tigers', 'Storm Warnings', 'Living in Sin', 'The Roofwalker', 'Trying to Talk with a Man', 'Diving into the Wreck', 'From a Survivor' and 'Power' from *The Fact of Doorframe: Selected Poems 1950–2001* by Adrienne Rich. Copyright © 2002 by Adrienne Rich. Copyright © 2001, 1999, 1995, 1991, 1989, 1986, 1984, 1981, 1967, 1963, 1962, 1961, 1960, 1959, 1958, 1957, 1956, 1955, 1954, 1953, 1952, 1951 by Adrienne Rich. Copyright © 1978, 1975, 1973, 1971, 1969, 1966 by W.W. Norton & Company, Inc. Used by permission of the author and W.W. Norton & Company, Inc.

Contents

Glossary of Poetry Ideas and Terms — 06

Elizabeth Bishop — 08
- The Fish — 10
- The Bight — 12
- At The Fishhouses — 14
- The Prodigal — 18
- Questions of Travel — 20
- The Armadillo — 24
- Sestina — 26
- First Death in Nova Scotia — 28
- Filling Station — 30
- In the Waiting Room — 32

Emily Dickinson — 36
- "Hope" is the thing with feathers — 38
- There's a certain Slant of light — 40
- I felt a Funeral, in my Brain — 42
- A Bird came down the Walk — 44
- I Heard a fly buzz - when I died — 46
- The Soul has Bandaged moments — 48
- I could bring You Jewels - had I a mind to — 50
- A narrow Fellow in the Grass — 52
- I taste a liquor never brewed — 54
- After great pain, a formal feeling comes — 56

John Donne — 58
- Song: Go, and catch a falling star — 60
- The Flea — 62
- The Dream — 64
- The Sun Rising — 66
- Song: Sweetest love, I do not go — 68
- A Valediction Forbidding Mourning — 70
- The Anniversary — 72
- Batter my heart — 74
- Thou hast made me — 76
- At the round earth's imagined corners — 78

Patrick Kavanagh — 80
- Inniskeen Road: July Evening — 82
- Shancoduff — 84
- Epic — 86
- *from* The Great Hunger: Section 1 — 88
- Advent — 92
- A Christmas Childhood — 94
- On Raglan Road — 98
- The Hospital — 100
- Canal Bank Walk — 102
- Lines Written on a Seat on the Grand Canal — 104

Derek Mahon — 106
- Grandfather — 108
- Day Trip to Donegal — 110
- After the *Titanic* — 112
- Ecclesiastes — 114
- As It Should Be — 116
- A Disused Shed in Co. Wexford — 118
- The Chinese Restaurant in Portrush — 122
- Rathlin — 124
- Antarctica — 126
- Kinsale — 128

Paula Meehan — 130
- Buying Winkles — 132
- The Pattern — 134
- The Statue of the Virgin at Granard Speaks — 138
- Cora, Auntie — 142
- The Exact Moment I Became a Poet — 146
- My Father Perceived as a Vision of St. Francis — 148
- Hearth Lesson — 150
- Prayer for the Children of Longing — 152
- Death of a Field — 154
- Them Ducks Died for Ireland — 156

Adrienne Rich — 158
- Aunt Jennifer's Tigers — 160
- Uncle Speaks in the Drawing Room — 162
- Storm Warnings — 164
- Living in Sin — 166
- The Roofwalker — 168
- Our Whole Life — 170
- Trying to Talk with a Man — 172
- Diving Into the Wreck — 174
- From a Survivor — 178
- Power — 180

W.B. Yeats — 182
- The Lake Isle of Innisfree — 184
- September 1913 — 186
- The Wild Swans at Coole — 188
- An Irish Airman Foresees his Death — 190
- Easter 1916 — 192
- The Second Coming — 196
- Sailing to Byzantium — 198
- The Stare's Nest by My Window — 200
- In Memory of Eva Gore-Booth and Con Markiewicz — 202
- Swift's Epitaph — 204
- An Acre of Grass — 206
- *from* Under Ben Bulben: V and VI — 208
- Politics — 210

Poetry Notes

Elizabeth Bishop — 212
- The Fish — 219
- The Bight — 222
- At The Fishhouses — 225
- The Prodigal — 229
- Questions of Travel — 232
- The Armadillo — 236
- Sestina — 239
- First Death in Nova Scotia — 241
- Filling Station — 244
- In the Waiting Room — 246

Emily Dickinson — 250
- "Hope" is the thing with feathers — 252
- There's a certain Slant of light — 254
- I felt a Funeral, in my Brain — 257
- A Bird came down the Walk — 260
- I Heard a fly buzz - when I died — 263
- The Soul has Bandaged moments — 266
- I could bring You Jewels - had I a mind to — 269
- A narrow Fellow in the Grass — 272
- I taste a liquor never brewed — 274
- After great pain, a formal feeling comes — 277

John Donne — 280
- Song: Go, and catch a falling star — 282
- The Flea — 285
- The Dream — 287
- The Sun Rising — 290
- Song: Sweetest love I do not go — 293
- A Valediction Forbidding Mourning — 296
- The Anniversary — 299
- Batter my heart — 302
- At the round earth's imagined corners — 305
- Thou hast made me — 308

Patrick Kavanagh — 310
- Inniskeen Road: July Evening — 313
- Shancoduff — 315
- Epic — 318
- *from* The Great Hunger: Section 1 — 320
- A Christmas Childhood — 324
- Advent — 327
- On Raglan Road — 330
- The Hospital — 332
- Canal Bank Walk — 334
- Lines Written on a Seat on the Grand Canal — 337

Derek Mahon — 340
- Grandfather — 342
- Day Trip to Donegal — 345
- After the *Titanic* — 348
- Ecclesiastes — 351
- As It Should Be — 354
- A Disused Shed in Co. Wexford — 357
- The Chinese Restaurant in Portrush — 361
- Rathlin — 363
- Antarctica — 366
- Kinsale — 368

Paula Meehan — 370
- Buying Winkles — 373
- The Pattern — 376
- The Statue of the Virgin at Granard Speaks — 380
- Cora, Auntie — 384
- The Exact Moment I Became a Poet — 386
- My Father Perceived as a Vision of St. Francis — 388
- Hearth Lesson — 390
- Prayer for the Children of Longing — 393
- Death of a Field — 396
- Them Ducks Died for Ireland — 399

Adrienne Rich — 402
- Aunt Jennifer's Tigers — 406
- Uncle Speaks in the Drawing Room — 409
- Storm Warnings — 412
- Living in Sin — 414
- The Roofwalker — 417
- Our Whole Life — 420
- Trying to Talk with a Man — 423
- Diving Into the Wreck — 427
- From a Survivor — 432
- Power — 435

W.B. Yeats — 438
- The Lake Isle of Innisfree — 442
- September 1913 — 445
- The Wild Swans at Coole — 447
- An Irish Airman Foresees his Death — 450
- Easter 1916 — 452
- The Second Coming — 457
- Sailing to Byzantium — 461
- The Stare's Nest by My Window — 465
- In Memory of Eva Gore-Booth and Con Markiewicz — 468
- Swift's Epitaph — 472
- An Acre of Grass — 473
- *from* Under Ben Bulben: V and VI — 476
- Politics — 480

How to Answer the Poetry Question — 482

GLOSSARY OF POETRY TERMS AND IDEAS

Rhyme

Rhyme Schemes

Since time immemorial, rhyme has been deeply associated with poetry. The poem's rhyme scheme describes how rhymes are arranged in each stanza. When we describe a rhyme scheme, we refer to lines that rhyme with one another by the same letter.

In 'Inversnaid' by Gerard Manley Hopkins, for example, the first line of each stanza rhymes with the second line, while the third line rhymes with the fourth. We say, therefore, that the poem has an AABB rhyme scheme:

> This darksome burn, horseback brown **A**
> His rollrock highroad roaring down, **A**
> In coop and in comb the fleece of his foam **B**
> Flutes and low to the lake falls home. **B**

In 'Design' by Robert Frost, the first 8 lines follow an ABBA rhyme scheme:

> I found a dimpled spider, fat and white, **A**
> On a white heal-all, holding up a moth **B**
> Like a white piece of rigid satin cloth - **B**
> Assorted characters of death and blight **A**
> Mixed ready to begin the morning right **A**
> Like the ingredients of a witches' broth -**B**
> A snow-drop spider spider, a flower like froth **B**
> And dead wings carried like a paper kite. **A**

Half-rhyme

An important technique to watch out for is half-rhyme. This is where two lines end in words that almost rhyme.

In 'Day Trip to Donegal' by Derek Mahon, for example, the poet rhymes 'deck' with 'heartbreak'.

Elizabeth Bishop makes use of half-rhyme in 'The Armadillo'. In the eight stanza, the poet rhymes 'alone' and 'down', while in the sixth stanza she rhymes 'fire' and 'pair'.

Metaphor and Simile

Metaphors and similes are incredibly common in poetry, and many poems owe their most vivid and memorable moments to these techniques.

A metaphor is when one thing is compared to something else. A simile is very similar to a metaphor in that it also compares one thing to something else. The big difference is that a simile uses the words 'like' or 'as'.

Each of the following phrases compares the hurler D.J. Carey to a lion:

- 'D.J. was like a lion in attack.'
- 'D.J. played as if he was a lion in attack.'
- 'D.J. was a lion in attack.'

The first two comparisons are similes because they use the words 'like' or 'as'. The third comparison is a metaphor because it does not feature the words 'like' or 'as'. Very often a metaphor is referred to as a 'strong' or 'direct' comparison, while a simile is referred to as a 'weak' or 'indirect' comparison. As a general rule, similes tend to occur more often than metaphors, especially in modern poetry.

Consider the following phrases, and in the case of each say whether it is a metaphor or a simile:

- 'The words are shadows' **(Eavan Boland)**
- 'One tree is yellow as butter' **(Eavan Boland)**
- Suspicion climbed all over her face, like a kitten, but not so playfully' **(Raymond Chandler)**
- 'A leaping tongue of bloom' **(Robert Frost)**
- 'Love set you going like a fat gold watch' **(Sylvia Plath)**
- 'a dump of rocks/ Leftover soldiers from old, messy wars' **(Sylvia Plath)**
- 'The mists are … Souls' **(Sylvia Plath)**
- 'He stumbles on like a rumour of war' **(Eavan Boland)**
- 'My red filaments burn and stand, a hand of wires' **(Sylvia Plath)**
- 'I thought of London spread out in the sun/ Its postal districts packed like squares of wheat' **(Philip Larkin)**
- 'The sky is a torn sail' **(Adrienne Rich)**

Personification

This is a technique whereby an inanimate object is described as if it had the qualities of a living thing. In 'A Disused Shed in Co. Wexford', for example, Mahon personifies the mushrooms that have been trapped in the shed for decades, presenting them as capable of thoughts, feelings and emotions.

Glossary of Poetry
Ideas & Terms

Hyperbole

This is where we deliberately exaggerate to make a point. For example:

- These books weigh a ton. (These books are heavy.)
- I could sleep for a year. (I could sleep for a long time.)
- The path went on forever. (The path was very long.)
- I'm doing a million things right now. (I'm busy.)
- I could eat a horse. (I'm hungry.)

Metonymy

This is a technique whereby we describe something without mentioning the thing itself; instead, we mention something closely associated with it.

For example, we use the phrase 'White House', to refer to the President of the US and his advisers, or 'Hollywood' to refer to the film industry.

Synecdoche

In this technique we identify something by referring to a part of the thing, instead of naming the thing itself.

A good example is the phrase 'All hands on deck'. In this instance, the sailors are identified by a part of their bodies, i.e. their hands. Similarly, we might use the word 'wheels' to refer to a car or 'head' to refer to cattle.

Sound Effects

One of the features that most distinguishes poetry from ordinary language is its 'musical' quality. Much of this 'word music' is generated by assonance, alliteration and onomatopoeia.

Alliteration

Alliteration occurs when a number of words in close proximity start with the same sound.

We see this in the repeated 'h' sounds in line 3 of 'The Lake Isle of Innisfree' by Yeats: 'will I have there, a hive for the honey-bee'.

Alliteration also occurs in line 5 of 'Aunt Jennifer's Tigers', with the repeated 'f' sound in 'fingers fluttering'.

Assonance

Assonance occurs when a number of words in close proximity have similar vowel sounds.

Patrick Kavanagh uses assonance in 'Canal Bank Walk'. In line 9 he uses repeated 'o' sounds: 'O unworn world'. A similar repetition of the 'o' sound is evident in line 13: 'For this soul needs to be honoured with a new dress woven'.

Onomatopoeia

Onomatopoeia occurs when a word or a group of words sounds like the noise it describes. Examples of onomatopoeic words include buzz, murmur and clang.

It features in 'Lake Isle of Innisfree' by Yeats. In the phrase, ' noon a purple glow,/ And evening full of the linnet's wings', we can almost hear the fluttering sound of song-birds' wings.

Onomatopoeia is also a feature of 'A Disused Shed in Co. Wexford' by Derek Mahon. In the phrase, 'the cracking lock/ And creak of hinges', we can almost hear the sound of the lock breaking and the door opening.

Euphony and Cacophony

Euphony and cacophony are also important concepts. Euphony can be defined as any pleasing or agreeable combination of sounds. Cacophony, meanwhile, is a harsh, jarring or discordant combination of sounds.

Euphony features in 'The Prodigal' by Elizabeth Bishop in the line 'the sunrise glazed the barnyard mud with red', where the soft 's' and 'r' sounds create a pleasant and soothing musical effect.

Cacophony features in 'Our Whole Life' by Adrienne Rich. The lines 'Words bitten thru words// meanings burnt-off like paint' creates an unpleasant music suitable to the difficult experience being described.

GLOSSARY OF POETRY TERMS AND IDEAS

Other Useful Poetic Terms

Allegory A story in which the characters and events are symbols that stand for ideas about human life or for a political or historical situation.

Allusion Where a poem makes reference to another poem or text.

Anaphora The repetition of words or phrases at the beginning of lines.

Antithesis A figure of speech in which words and phrases with opposite meanings are balanced against each other. An example of antithesis is 'To err is human, to forgive, divine'.

Ballad A poem that tells a story. Ballads are traditionally rhymed ABAB.

Beat The rhythmic or musical quality of a poem. In metrical verse, this is determined by the regular pattern of stressed and unstressed syllables.

Couplet A unit comprising of two lines.

Elegy Poem written to lament the dead.

Ellipsis The omission of words whose absence does not impede the reader's ability to understand the expression.

Enjambment When a single sentence is spread across two or more lines of verse.

Form The structural components of a poem, e.g. stanza pattern, metre, syllable count, etc – as opposed to the content.

Free verse Verse without formal metre or rhyme patterns.

Imagery The mental pictures created by a piece of writing.

Internal rhyme Rhyme that occurs within a single line of verse. Also refers to rhyme between internal phrases across multiple lines.

Irony The expression of one's meaning by using language that normally signifies the opposite.

Neologism The coining of new words.

Oxymoron Figure of speech containing two seemingly contradictory expressions, e.g. a happy funeral.

Paradox Seemingly absurd or contradictory statement which, on closer examination, reveals an important truth, e.g. Wordsworth's 'The child is father of the man'.

Pathetic Fallacy Occurs when human emotions or behaviours are attributed to the natural world.

Pun A humorous way of using a word or phrase so that more than one meaning is suggested. For example: 'She's a skilful pilot whose career has really taken off.'

Quatrain A stanza comprising of four lines.

Refrain A line or phrase that recurs throughout a poem – especially at the end of stanzas.

Sonnet A fourteen line poem usually in iambic pentameters. Typically, it consists of an octave (eight lines) and a sestet (six lines). Usually, the octave presents or outlines a problem, situation or dilemma. The sestet mediates on this issue or attempts to resolve it. There is usually a 'volta', a turn or change in tone or outlook, that occurs between the octave and the sestet.

- **Italian or Petrarchan Sonnet** The sonnet was originated by the Italian poet Guittone of Arezzo and then popularised by Petrarch (1304-74). The term sonnet derives from the Italian for 'little song'. The Italian sonnet has the following rhyme scheme: ABBA ABBA CDE CDE.

- **Shakespearean or English Sonnet:** The Shakespearean or English sonnet employs an ABAB CDCD EFEF GG rhyme scheme. Essentially, therefore, it consists of three quatrains and a final couplet. Sometimes the volta or change of direction only occurs in the last two lines.

Elizabeth Bishop

Elizabeth Bishop was born in 1911 in Worcester, Massachusetts. Her life was blighted by strife and tragedy from a very young age, starting with the death of her father, William Bishop, who passed away when Elizabeth was just eight months old. This loss had a catastrophic impact on her mother, Gertrude Bulmer Bishop, who suffered a series of breakdowns and was permanently institutionalised when Elizabeth was five. Elizabeth would never see her mother again.

The tragedies that clouded Bishop's early life never truly left her. They contributed not only to her greatest personal battles but also to some of her most powerful poetry. Her mother's absence left its mark and explains the prominence of motherhood or maternity that features in her work. Echoes of this formative trauma can be found in such poems as 'Sestina'.

Following her mother's hospitalisation, Bishop was initially raised in a loving environment by her maternal grandparents in Nova Scotia, until her paternal family brought her back to Worcester, Massachusetts. Bishop was deeply unhappy with this turn of events, which she described as a 'kidnapping'. She later stated in a biographical piece: 'I had been brought back unconsulted and against my wishes to the house my father had been born in, to be saved from a life of poverty and provincialism'.

Bishop attended Vassar College in the late 1920s, studying music at first, before settling on English. Bishop struggled with low self-esteem and depression throughout her university years, and she drank heavily. She battled ongoing ill health, including chronic asthma, which was far less manageable at the time. It was, however, during this phase that Bishop's poetic talent began to blossom. The great American poet Marianne Moore became her friend and mentor. She took Bishop on as something of a poetic apprentice, and helped her to publish her first poems and stories.

Bishop also developed an enduring friendship with the esteemed poet Robert Lowell, to whom she was introduced in the late 1940s. They corresponded for years, right up until Lowell's death in 1977. They influenced one another's work in equal measure. After Lowell's death, Bishop remarked upon the warmth of their relationship: 'Our friendship was kept alive through years of separation only by letters, remained constant and affectionate, and I shall always be deeply grateful for it.' She wrote the poem 'North Haven' in Lowell's memory.

After finishing her education, Bishop spent a great deal of time travelling. A small inheritance from her deceased father ensured she could satisfy this restlessness without worrying about employment. She spent many years shuttling on a shoestring'

> "All my life I have lived and behaved very much like the sandpiper just running down the edges of different countries and continents, looking for something."

between France, New York and Key West in Florida. In Florida, in particular, she cultivated an appreciation for fishing, which is reflected in a poem entitled 'The Fish'. However, it was also during these nomadic years that her alcoholism festered.

Some academics have suggested that Bishop's drinking stemmed from a desire to fill the parental void in her life as well as from her feelings of inadequacy. Surprisingly, given her obvious talent, Bishop had little confidence in her own artistic ability, and felt overwhelmed by her equally gifted contemporaries and the edgy New York literati. She binged destructively, and alcohol came to dominate her life, as indicated in the poem 'The Prodigal'.

In 1951, Bishop travelled to Brazil. She intended to stay for two weeks, but instead settled there for almost two decades, during which time she won a Pulitzer Prize. She maintained a relationship with Lota Soares, a Brazilian woman she had known for many years. By all accounts, these were the most contented years of Bishop's life. The time that Bishop spent in Brazil influenced her poetry. She became fascinated with Brazilian culture and translated many poems and stories from Portuguese into English. Her appreciation of Latin American literature is evident in 'Questions of Travel' and 'The Armadillo'.

While much of Bishop's personal life was marked with tragedy and personal torments, it was not the focal point of her work. She was not inclined to use writing to complain and was not drawn to the confessional style of her contemporaries, who laid bare many dark and sordid details from their personal lives. Instead, Bishop devoted her poetry to celebrating and exploring the terrors and beauties of the physical world, as well as the mystery and complexity of the human psyche. Her work seems to concentrate intensely on small details, possibly because she perceived such details to be the only concrete (and, therefore, most important) things in life.

Bishop sometimes spent months, or even years, attempting to finish a poem. She would write the poem out in big letters on cardboard sheets above her desk, leaving gaps for the perfect words that she struggled to pin down. She explained this succinctly in one of her many letters to Robert Lowell: 'My passion for accuracy may strike you as old-maidish – but since we do float on an unknown sea I think we should examine the other floating things that come our way very carefully; who knows what might depend on it?'

Bishop's final years were difficult. She was devastated by the suicide of her partner, Lota, in 1967. She had returned to the US and landed teaching positions at the University of Washington, Harvard University and Massachusetts Institute of Technology. She also supplemented her income by giving public readings of her work.

Bishop famously refused to appear in female-only anthologies, a fact that has been interpreted by some as an unspoken censure of the feminist movement, which gained significant traction in 1960s America – just when Bishop was reaching her literary zenith. However, in a 1978 interview, Bishop explicitly identified herself as a feminist and explained that her aversion to being included in women-only anthologies arose rather from a deeply held conviction that she should be judged purely as a writer, not according to gender.

Bishop's literary celebrity increased, and her poetry was recognised with a glut of prestigious awards, including a National Book Award (1970), a Neustadt International Prize (1976) and a Guggenheim Fellowship (1978). Despite her success, these sometimes proved to be difficult and lonely years, as she continued to deal with alcoholism and depression. She died suddenly in 1979. Her reputation has grown steadily in the decades since her death. She is now recognised as the greatest American poet of her generation.

The Fish

I caught a tremendous fish
and held him beside the boat
half out of water, with my hook
fast in a corner of his mouth.
He didn't fight. [5]
He hadn't fought at all.
He hung a grunting weight,
battered and venerable
and homely. Here and there
his brown skin hung in strips [10]
like ancient wallpaper,
and its pattern of darker brown
was like wallpaper:
shapes like full-blown roses
stained and lost through age. [15]
He was speckled with barnacles,
fine rosettes of lime,
and infested
with tiny white sea-lice,
and underneath two or three [20]
rags of green weed hung down.
While his gills were breathing in
the terrible oxygen
– the frightening gills,
fresh and crisp with blood, [25]
that can cut so badly –
I thought of the coarse white flesh
packed in like feathers,
the big bones and the little bones,
the dramatic reds and blacks [30]
of his shiny entrails,
and the pink swim-bladder
like a big peony.
I looked into his eyes
which were far larger than mine [35]
but shallower, and yellowed,
the irises backed and packed
with tarnished tinfoil
seen through the lenses
of old scratched isinglass. [40]
They shifted a little, but not
to return my stare.
– It was more like the tipping
of an object toward the light.
I admired his sullen face, [45]
the mechanism of his jaw,
and then I saw
that from his lower lip
– if you could call it a lip –
grim, wet, and weaponlike, [50]
hung five old pieces of fish-line,
or four and a wire leader

Annotations

[4] *fast:* snagged, secured, locked in place
[8] *venerable:* worthy of respect
[9] *homely:* plain, not particularly attractive
[17] *rosettes:* fake, decorative roses
[32] *swim-bladder:* an organ that allows a fish to control buoyancy
[33] *peony:* a red or pink flower
[40] *isinglass:* a jelly obtained from fish bladders
[53] *swivel:* mechanism on a fishing rod
[59] *crimped:* wavy, bent
[68] *bilge:* dirty water
[71] *bailer:* device used to bail out (remove) water from a boat
[72] *thwarts:* timber benches that run across a boat
[73] *oarlocks:* U-shaped device for holding an oar in place
[74] *gunnels:* the upper edges of the side of a boat

with the swivel still attached,
with all their five big hooks
grown firmly in his mouth. [55]
A green line, frayed at the end
where he broke it, two heavier lines,
and a fine black thread
still crimped from the strain and snap
when it broke and he got away. [60]
Like medals with their ribbons
frayed and wavering,
a five-haired beard of wisdom
trailing from his aching jaw.
I stared and stared [65]
and victory filled up
the little rented boat,
from the pool of bilge
where oil had spread a rainbow
around the rusted engine [70]
to the bailer rusted orange,
the sun-cracked thwarts,
the oarlocks on their strings,
the gunnels – until everything
was rainbow, rainbow, rainbow! [75]
And I let the fish go.

Tease It Out

1. Describe the manner in which the poet holds the fish while she observes it.
2. The fish did not put up any fight when it was caught. Why do you think it did not struggle or resist? Is the poet surprised at its behaviour? Give a reason for your answer.
3. The poet uses three adjectives to describe the fish: 'battered', 'venerable' and 'homely'. In pairs, discuss (with the aid of a dictionary) what each word means. What does each adjective suggest about the fish and the poet's feelings about the creature?
4. Why do you think that the oxygen the fish breathes is 'terrible' to him?
5. Lines 27 to 33: The poet imagines what the fish's flesh and internal organs must look like. To what does she compare the flesh? To what does she compare the fish's swim bladder?
6. The poet provides a detailed description of the fish's eye, comparing aspects of it to foil and isinglass. Can you describe the appearance of the eye in your own words?
7. What is it about the fish's jaw that the poet first finds fascinating? What does the term 'weaponlike' suggest about this aspect of the fish?
8. The poet suddenly notices five hooks lodged in the fish's lower lip. Why are the threads and wires connected to the hooks 'frayed' and 'crimped'?
9. The poet compares the hooks and broken lines to soliders' medals and to a 'beard of wisdom'. What do these comparisons suggest about the fish's character?
10. The poet says that 'victory filled up' the boat. What sort of 'victory' do you think the poet has in mind here?
11. How does the poet describe the inside of the boat? What objects does she mention? What sort of condition is the boat in?
12. The poet says that 'oil had spread a rainbow/ Around the rusted engine'. What is she describing here?
13. Bishop says that suddenly 'everything/ was rainbow, rainbow, rainbow!' What do you understand her to mean by this? How would you describe her mood at this moment? What has caused her to feel this way?
14. Why do you think the poet repeats the word 'rainbow' in line 75? What effect does this have?
15. By the end of the poem, the poet discovers a way to relate to the fish? In what ways, do you think, might their experiences or their lives be similar?
16. Write a short paragraph explaining why, in your opinion, the poet 'let the fish go'?

The Bight
(On my Birthday)

At low tide like this how sheer the water is.
White, crumbling ribs of marl protrude and glare
and the boats are dry, the pilings dry as matches.
Absorbing, rather than being absorbed,
the water in the bight doesn't wet anything, [5]
the color of the gas flame turned as low as possible.
One can smell it turning to gas; if one were Baudelaire
one could probably hear it turning to marimba music.
The little ocher dredge at work of the end of the dock
already plays the dry perfectly of -beat claves. [10]
The birds are outsize. Pelicans crash
into this peculiar gas unnecessarily hard,
it seems to me, like pickaxes,
rarely coming up with anything to show for it,
and going of with humorous elbowings. [15]
Black-and-white man-of-war birds soar
on impalpable drafts
and open their tails like scissors on the curves
or tense them like wishbones, till they tremble.
The frowsy sponge boats keep coming in [20]
with the obliging air of retrievers,
bristling with jackstraw gaffs and hooks
and decorated with bobbles of sponges.
There is a fence of chicken wire along the dock
where, glinting like little plowshares, [25]
the blue-gray shark tails are hung up to dry
for the Chinese-restaurant trade.
Some of the little white boats are still piled up
against each other, or lie on their sides, stove in,
and not yet salvaged, if they ever will be, from the last bad storm, [30]
like torn-open, unanswered letters.
The bight is littered with old correspondences.
Click. Click. Goes the dredge,
and brings up a dripping jawful of marl.
All the untidy activity continues, [35]
awful but cheerful.

Annotations

Bight: a large, curved and shallow bay
[1] sheer: having a thin or transparent texture
[2] marl: deposits of silt or clay
[3] pilings: wooden struts that support decks and piers
[7] Baudelaire: Charles Baudelaire (1821–67), a French poet who often used the sea as an image in his verse and who strongly emphasised the importance of sound in poetry
[8] marimba: a xylophone-like musical instrument
[9] ocher: yellowish red in colour
[9] dredge: a digger-like machine that removes deposits from the seabed
[10] claves: an irregular rhythmic pattern
[16] man-of-war birds: seabirds, similar to pelicans
[17] impalpable: unable to be felt by touch; difficult to understand
[20] frowsy: untidy or dishevelled
[20] sponge boats: boats that gather sponge from the seabed
[21] retrievers: a class of dog known for its obedience
[22] gaffs and hooks: barbed instruments used to gather sponge
[22] jackstraw: a table game that involves a messy, random arrangement of sticks
[25] plowshares: the cutting blades of a plough
[29] stove in: having a breach in the hull

Tease It Out

1. **Get in Gear:** Watch Video 1, which depicts Key West Harbour. What three adjectives would you use to describe the harbour? Is it a place you would like to visit? Give a reason for your answer.
2. What is the seabed composed of? What does the poet see emerging up through the shallow water? What colour is this material? How does the poet convey the manner in which this substance reflects the sun?
3. What colour is the 'dredge'? What task is it performing? Is it noisy or quiet? How does the poet characterise the sound it makes?
4. What simile does the poet use to describe the diving pelicans?
5. **True or false:** The pelicans are excellent at catching fish.
6. **Class Discussion:** The pelicans, according to the poet, fly off with 'humorous elbowings'. What do you envisage the pelicans doing? Why do you think the poet finds their behaviour humorous?
7. What technique do the man-of-war birds use to soar into the sky?
8. The sponge boats remind the poet of golden retrievers. What is it about the boats that prompts this comparison?
9. What items are stacked on the decks of the sponge boats? Are these arranged in a stable manner? Give a reason for your answer.
10. What colour are the shark tails? What simile does the poet use to describe them? What will happen to them when they are finally dry?
11. The poet describes some of the 'little white boats' on the shore. What condition are these boats in? How did they end up like this?
12. To what does the poet compare the damaged boats? Is this comparison an effective one in your opinion?
13. Consider the following adjectives: 'tidy', 'awful' and 'cheerful'. What do they suggest about the poet's attitude towards the bight? Is this a place she loves or hates?

Exam Prep

1. **Class Discussion:** The poet says that the 'bight is littered with old correspondences'. What aspects of the bight's 'untidy activity' might correspond with the poet's life? Bishop saw fit to indicate that the poem was written on her birthday. Can you suggest why conveying this information was important to her?
2. **Theme Talk:** Bishop's poems often feature moments of awareness, where the poet suddenly gains an insight or understanding after carefully studying a scene or a particular object. Do you think such a moment of awareness occurs in 'The Bight'? Discuss the question in small groups.
3. **Personal Response:** Think of a location that means a lot to you. It could be your back garden, a relative's house or a favourite holiday destination. Write a poem or short prose text in which you capture as many details of the location as you possibly can.
4. **Exam Prep:** 'Bishop uses highly detailed observation, of people, places and events, to explore unique personal experiences in her poetry.' Discuss this statement, with reference to 'The Bight', 'Filling Station' and 'Questions of Travel'.

Language Lab

1. Bishop's description of the water in the bay is particularly memorable. Discuss the following questions in pairs and then share your answers with the class:
   - Consider the adjective 'sheer'. Does this suggest the water is cloudy or easy to see through?
   - Pick two adjectives that describe the colour of the flame on a gas cooking hob.
   - Bishop compares the water to such a flame. Is this a good comparison in your opinion?
   - Baudelaire is a poet associated with the literary device known as 'synaesthesia'. Describe this device in your own words.
   - The poet uses synaesthesia to describe the water. What two comparisons does she make?
2. **Class Discussion:** The bight's water interacts with the land in a most unusual fashion. Name three strange behaviours it exhibits. Would you agree that these lines contain hyperbole or deliberate poetic exaggeration?

At the Fishhouses

Although it is a cold evening,
down by one of the fishhouses
an old man sits netting,
his net, in the gloaming almost invisible
a dark purple-brown, [5]
and his shuttle worn and polished.
The air smells so strong of codfish
it makes one's nose run and one's eyes water.
The five fishhouses have steeply peaked roofs
and narrow, cleated gangplanks slant up [10]
to storerooms in the gables
for the wheelbarrows to be pushed up and down on.
All is silver: the heavy surface of the sea,
swelling slowly as if considering spilling over,
is opaque, but the silver of the benches, [15]
the lobster pots, and masts, scattered
among the wild jagged rocks,
is of an apparent translucence
like the small old buildings with an emerald moss
growing on their shoreward walls. [20]
The big fish tubs are completely lined
with layers of beautiful herring scales
and the wheelbarrows are similarly plastered
with creamy iridescent coats of mail,
with small iridescent flies crawling on them. [25]
Up on the little slope behind the houses,
set in the sparse bright sprinkle of grass,
is an ancient wooden capstan,
cracked, with two long bleached handles
and some melancholy stains, like dried blood, [30]
where the ironwork has rusted.
The old man accepts a Lucky Strike.
He was a friend of my grandfather.
We talk of the decline in the population
and of codfish and herring [35]
while he waits for a herring boat to come in.
There are sequins on his vest and on his thumb.
He has scraped the scales, the principal beauty,
from unnumbered fish with that black old knife,
the blade of which is almost worn away. [40]

Down at the water's edge, at the place
where they haul up the boats, up the long ramp
descending into the water, thin silver
tree trunks are laid horizontally
across the gray stones, down and down [45]
at intervals of four or five feet.

Cold dark deep and absolutely clear,
element bearable to no mortal,
to fish and to seals … One seal particularly
I have seen here evening after evening. [50]
He was curious about me. He was interested in music;
like me a believer in total immersion,
so I used to sing him Baptist hymns.
I also sang 'A Mighty Fortress is Our God.'
He stood up in the water and regarded me [55]
steadily, moving his head a little.
Then he would disappear, then suddenly emerge
almost in the same spot, with a sort of shrug
as if it were against his better judgement.
Cold dark deep and absolutely clear, [60]
the clear gray icy water … Back, behind us,
the dignified tall firs begin.
Bluish, associating with their shadows,
a million Christmas trees stand
waiting for Christmas. The water seems suspended [65]
above the rounded gray and blue-gray stones.
I have seen it over and over, the same sea, the same,
slightly, indifferently swinging above the stones,
icily free above the stones,
above the stones and then the world. [70]
If you should dip your hand in,
your wrist would ache immediately,
your bones would begin to ache and your hand would burn
as if the water were a transmutation of fire
that feeds on stones and burns with a dark gray flame. [75]
If you tasted it, it would first taste bitter,
then briny, then surely burn your tongue.
It is like what we imagine knowledge to be:
dark, salt, clear, moving, utterly free,
drawn from the cold hard mouth [80]
of the world, derived from the rocky breasts
forever, flowing and drawn, and since
our knowledge is historical, flowing, and flown.

Annotations

[4] *gloaming:* dusk, twilight

[6] *shuttle:* tool used to repair nylon fishing nets

[10] *cleated gangplanks:* ridged wooden walkways with projecting strips of metal or rubber to provide traction

[11] *gables:* the triangular part of a wall that attaches to the roof

[15] *opaque:* not transparent

[18] *translucence:* having the quality of being semi-transparent

[24] *iridescent:* varying in colour when seen in different lights or from different angles

[28] *capstan:* a revolving cylinder around which rope or cable is wrapped. Used for hoisting heavy weights such as anchors

[32] *Lucky Strike:* a brand of cigarette

[37] *sequins:* small shiny discs used for ornamentation; in this case, the term is used as a metaphor for the fish scales that fall onto the old man's hands and clothes as he scrapes the fish with his knife.

[53] *Baptist:* a member of a Protestant Christian denomination that believes in baptising its adult members by total immersion

[54] *A Mighty Fortress Is Our God:* a popular Protestant hymn

[74] *transmutation:* the process of changing from one form or state to another

Tease It Out

Lines 1 to 40

1. What physical features of the fishhouses are mentioned by the poet?
2. How are fish transported into the fishhouses?
3. What task is the 'old man' performing? What instruments is he using? Why is he described as being 'almost invisible'?
4. What effect, in lines 13 to 17, does the twilight have on the landscape of Great Village?
5. **Class Discussion:** In what way does the 'silver' of the sea differ from the 'silver' of the landscape?
6. The poet describes the 'fish tubs' and the 'wheelbarrows'. Does she present these objects as a) ugly b) strangely beautiful or c) boring and banal? Give a reason for your answer?
7. What does the poet offer the old man? What personal connection do they establish? What do they talk about?
8. What is the old man waiting for as he sits outside the fishhouses?
9. What work does the old man do on a daily basis?
10. What phrases suggest that he has been doing this work for a very long time?
11. What inventive metaphor does the poet use for the fish scales on 'his vest and on his thumb'?

Lines 41 to 65

12. Describe, in your own words, the ramps used by the fishermen to 'haul up the boats'.
13. The poet has seen a seal that, she believes, is 'interested' in her. Suggest how the seal might convey this interest.
14. What songs does the poet sing to the seal? How does the seal respond to her singing?
15. The seal is presented as being oddly human in its behaviour. Identify three words or phrases that convey this.
16. Look up the term 'total immersion'. What does it suggest about the poet's religious upbringing? How might the seal, in its own way, be described as 'a believer in total immersion'?
17. The poet uses personification to describe the forest of fir trees. What phrases contribute to this effect? What are the trees portrayed as doing?
18. The trees seem to blend with their own shadows. What phrase does the poet use to describe this effect? Would you agree that this phrase, too, contains an element of personification?

Lines 63 to 83

19. The poet describes how the sea comes 'swinging'. What does this suggest about the movement of its waves?
20. **True or false:** The poet believes the sea never changes.
21. The poet feels that the sea could flow anywhere, that it's unbound by the laws of physics. Identify three different phrases that suggest this.
22. According to the poet, what would happen if you were to 'dip your hand in' the sea?
23. The poet compares the sea to a very strange form of fire. What features of this fire does she mention? What does this comparison suggest about her attitude to the ocean?
24. What does she imagine 'feeds' this fire?
25. 'The poet imagines that tasting the sea water would be like ingesting acid'. Write three or four sentences in response to this statement.
26. The poet imagines the sea issuing from springs deep within the rocky seabed. What metaphors does she use to describe these springs?

Exam Prep

1. **Personal Response:** Imagine you are the old man described in the poem. Write a letter in which you describe your daily routine. You might also include some of your memories of growing up in Great Village. You might also mention how the community has changed and declined over the years.
2. **Group Discussion:** Working in groups of four, take a large piece of paper and create a placemat. The poet suggests that we imagine knowledge to be 'dark', 'salt', 'clear', 'moving' and 'utterly free'. Take each term in turn and, in your section of the placemat, jot down every association it has for you. Then, as a group, discuss each term. How might each be an accurate and effective description of self-knowledge?
3. **Class Discussion:** The poet draws a comparison between the sea and 'what we imagine knowledge to be'. Is the poet referring a) to general knowledge, b) to a specific set of skills or c) to knowledge of the self and the unconscious mind.
4. **Theme Talk:** 'The self, like the sea, is always in flux. Therefore, our self-knowledge is always out of date. For no sooner have we understood ourselves than our minds and personalities have changed again'. Can you identify two phrases in the poem that support this statement?
5. **Exam Prep:** 'Bishop's carefully judged use of language aids the reader to uncover the intensity of feeling in her poetry.' Write a short essay in which you discuss this statement in relation to 'At the Fishhouses' and two other poems on by Bishop on your course.

Language Lab

1. Would you agree that the poem's opening forty lines create an effective atmosphere? Which of our senses are appealed to in this rich descriptive passage?
2. Bishop is a poet known for her detailed description. Pick two aspects of this 'cold evening' that Bishop described well in your opinion. Give a reason for your choice. Can you identify one piece of description that didn't work for you?
3. Twice the poet begins to describe the sea. (In lines 47 to 49 and in lines 60 and 61). And twice she allows herself to be distracted. How can we explain this reluctance to directly contemplate the ocean? Consider the following explanations and rank them in order of plausibility.
    - The poet is afraid of water.
    - The poet thinks the ocean looks menacing and unpleasant on this particular evening.
    - The poet associates the sea with her unconscious mind and traumatic self-knowledge.
    - The poet is bored of looking at the ocean.
4. Do you consider 'At the Fishhouses' to be a realistic poem or an unrealistic one? Give a reason for your

The Prodigal

The brown enormous odor he lived by
was too close, with its breathing and thick hair,
for him to judge. The floor was rotten; the sty
was plastered halfway up with glass-smooth dung.
Light-lashed, self-righteous, above moving snouts, [5]
the pigs' eyes followed him, a cheerful stare –
even to the sow that always ate her young –
till, sickening, he leaned to scratch her head.
But sometimes mornings after drinking bouts
(he hid the pints behind a two-by-four), [10]
the sunrise glazed the barnyard mud with red;
the burning puddles seemed to reassure.
And then he thought he almost might endure
his exile yet another year or more.

But evenings the first star came to warn. [15]
The farmer whom he worked for came at dark
to shut the cows and horses in the barn
beneath their overhanging clouds of hay,
with pitchforks, faint forked lightnings, catching light,
safe and companionable as in the Ark. [20]
The pigs stuck out their little feet and snored.
The lantern – like the sun, going away –
laid on the mud a pacing aureole.
Carrying a bucket along a slimy board,
he felt the bats' uncertain staggering flight, [25]
his shuddering insights, beyond his control,
touching him. But it took him a long time
finally to make his mind up to go home.

Annotations

Prodigal: a spendthrift; someone who wastes his or her money in an extravagant fashion; refers to Jesus' parable of the Prodigal Son, which appears in the Gospel of Luke
[7] **sow:** a female pig
[10] **two-by-four:** a plank of wood
[11] **pints:** refers to pint bottles of whiskey, rum or other alcoholic spirit
[20] **companionable:** sociable, suited to the company of others
[20] **Ark:** refers to the biblical tale of Noah's Ark
[23] **aureole:** a halo of light

Tease It Out

1. **Get in Gear:** Watch Video 2, which features the biblical story of the Prodigal Son. Were you familiar with this story? Do you think that the father's treatment of his two sons was fair? Give a reason for your answer.
2. The prodigal no longer notices the foul stench of the pigsty where he lives and works. Which lines indicate this?
3. **Class Discussion:** Which literary device is used in the description of this odour? (Hint: it starts with an 's').
4. Describe the condition of the sty's floor and walls.
5. Describe in your own words the pigs' facial expressions. How does the prodigal react to the way they stare at him?
6. Which lines indicate that the prodigal is an alcoholic?
7. Where does he hide his pint bottles of gin or whiskey?
8. **Class Discussion:** Some mornings the sunrise has a particular effect upon the surface of the farmyard. Describe, in your own words, what the prodigal sees on these hungover dawns.
9. Consider lines 13 to 14. What indications are there that the prodigal is unhappy with his current way of life?
10. The prodigal feels a sense of dread as night approaches. Which line conveys this?
11. What does the prodigal's employer do each evening?
12. Describe in your own words the cows' and horses' sleeping conditions. What indication is there that the pigs, too, sleep in a cosy and comfortable fashion?
13. While the animals sleep, the prodigal completes his work for the day. What task is depicted in line 24?
14. Can you suggest what 'insights' or moments of comprehension the prodigal might experience as night falls?
15. Why might these 'insights' cause him to shudder? What indication is there that he usually tries to suppress or ignore these insights?
16. Which phrase indicates that the bats are guided by instinct rather that sight?
17. Do the bats proceed in a smooth or jerky manner as they hover through the air? Give a reason for your answer.

Exam Prep

1. **Personal Response:** Elizabeth Bishop struggled with alcohol addiction throughout her life. How does this effect your reading and understanding of the poem?
2. **Class Discussion:** 'But it took him a long time/ finally to make his mind up to go home'. The prodigal has a miserable existence in the pigsty. Yet he's reluctant or hesitant to change his life and return to his family. Suggest reasons why this might be the case.
3. **Theme Talk:** 'Bishop's poetry is marked by her sense of permanent exile, of properly belonging to no country or community'. Discuss this statement in relation to 'The Prodigal', 'At the Fishhouses' and 'Questions of Travel'.
4. **Exam Prep:** 'Bishop skilfully uses language and imagery to confront life's harsh realities'. Discuss this statement in relation to 'The Prodigal' and at least three other poems on your course.

Language Lab

1. The second stanza creates an atmosphere of heart-breaking loneliness. Which lines and images contribute to this atmosphere?
2. Did your knowledge of the Gospel story affect your understanding of this piece? Do you think you'd have understood the poem differently without this background knowledge? Say why.
3. Do you think that this poem is set in the past or in the present day? Support your answer with reference to the poem.
4. Which phrase indicates that the prodigal identifies with the bats as he sees them hovering overhead? In what sense is the prodigal, like the bats, guided by 'uncertain' instincts? Where are those instincts leading him?

Questions of Travel

There are too many waterfalls here; the crowded streams
hurry too rapidly down to the sea,
and the pressure of so many clouds on the mountaintops
makes them spill over the sides in soft slow-motion,
turning to waterfalls under our very eyes. [5]
– For if those streaks, those mile-long, shiny, tearstains,
aren't waterfalls yet,
in a quick age or so, as ages go here,
they probably will be.
But if the streams and clouds keep travelling, travelling, [10]
the mountains look like the hulls of capsized ships,
slime-hung and barnacled.

Think of the long trip home.
Should we have stayed at home and thought of here?
Where should we be today? [15]
Is it right to be watching strangers in a play
in this strangest of theaters?
What childishness is it that while there's a breath of life
in our bodies, we are determined to rush
to see the sun the other way around? [20]
The tiniest green hummingbird in the world?
To stare at some inexplicable old stonework,
inexplicable and impenetrable,
at any view,
instantly seen and always, always delightful? [25]
Oh, must we dream our dreams
and have them, too?
And have we room
for one more folded sunset, still quite warm?

But surely it would have been a pity [30]
not to have seen the trees along this road,
really exaggerated in their beauty,
not to have seen them gesturing
like noble pantomimists, robed in pink.
– Not to have had to stop for gas and heard [35]
the sad, two-noted, wooden tune
of disparate wooden clogs
carelessly clacking over
a grease-stained filling-station floor.
(In another country the clogs would all be tested. [40]
Each pair there would have identical pitch.)
– A pity not to have heard
the other, less primitive music of the fat brown bird
who sings above the broken gasoline pump
in a bamboo church of Jesuit baroque: [45]
three towers, five silver crosses.

– Yes, a pity not to have pondered,
blurr'dly and inconclusively,
on what connection can exist for centuries
between the crudest wooden footwear [50]
and, careful and finicky,
the whittled fantasies of wooden cages.
– Never to have studied history in
the weak calligraphy of songbirds' cages.
– And never to have had to listen to rain [55]
so much like politicians' speeches:
two hours of unrelenting oratory
and then a sudden golden silence
in which the traveller takes a notebook, writes:

'Is it lack of imagination that makes us come [60]
to imagined places, not just stay at home?
Or could Pascal have been not entirely right
about just sitting quietly in one's room?

Continent, city, country, society:
the choice is never wide and never free. [65]
And here, or there ... No. Should we have stayed at home,
wherever that may be?'

Annotations
[22] *inexplicable:* difficult to explain or account for
[23] *impenetrable:* difficult to understand
[34] *pantomimists:* performers in a pantomime
[37] *disparate:* different, not alike
[43] *primitive:* simple, unsophisticated
[45] *Jesuit baroque:* The baroque is a dramatic and complex style of architecture that was developed in 17th-century Europe; it was brought to South America by Jesuit priests
[51] *finiky:* fussy, attentive to small details
[52] *whittled:* wood that has been carved by repeatedly cutting small slices from it
[57] *calligraphy:* elaborate, decorative handwriting
[57] *oratory:* public speaking
[62] *Pascal:* Blaise Pascal (1623–62) was a French mathematician, philosopher and inventor. He famously suggested: 'All human evil comes from a single cause, man's inability to sit quietly in a room'

THIS IS POETRY   ELIZABETH BISHOP

Tease It Out

Lines 1 to 12

1. The mountains are so high that their peaks breach the cloud cover. What metaphor does the speaker use to describe this?
2. **Class Discussion:** '[I]n a quick age or so, as ages go here'. Does the speaker feel that time travels quickly in this location? Or does she feel that it travels slowly? Give a reason for your answer.
3. **Group Discussion:** Why does the poet repeat the word 'travelling' in line 10? What effect does this repetition create?
4. What simile does the speaker use to describe the mountains? Does it effectively capture their massiveness and stillness?
5. Would you agree that the speaker successfully creates a sense of hurry and pressure in the poem's opening three lines? Give a reason for your anwer.

Lines 13 to 29

6. What negative aspect of travel does the speaker identify in line 13?
7. The speaker suggests that it might be better to imagine a place than to actually visit it. Which lines convey this? Do you think is a reasonable or unreasonable one?
8. The poet compares travel and tourism to watching a play in a theatre. According to the poet, who are the performers and who are the audience members?
9. The speaker suggests that there's an element of 'childishness' in the behaviour of tourists. Which words and phrases convey this? Would you agree that she has a point?
10. The poet believes that tourists engage with the things they see on only the most superficial level. Which phrase suggests this?
11. The poet suggests that tourism is a form of gluttonous consumption. What phrases suggest this?

Lines 30 to 67

12. In this section, the speaker mentions a number of experiences that it would have been 'a pity' to miss out on. List them. Which of these experiences seems most appealing to you? Which seems least appealing? Give reasons for your answers.
13. What simile does Bishop use to describe the trees?
14. Describe, in your own words, the sound produced by the man's clogs as he walks around the filling station.
15. Why do the clogs produce this musical effect?
16. Why, according to the speaker, would you not find this effect in 'another country'?
17. Which phrases indicate that the cage is a complex construction crafted from wood?
18. Why do you think the bird's music is described as being 'less primitive' than than that of the clogs? Do you find this assertion surprising?
19. Describe in your own words what the speaker 'ponders' as she waits in the filling station. Do her thoughts lead to any definite conclusion?
20. The cage is described as a form of 'weak calligraphy.' What visual similarity might exist between handwriting and this woven wooden object?
21. **Class Discussion:** The speaker claims that she is 'studying history' when she looks at the songbird's cage. What might she mean by this? What might the cages tell her about Brazil's past?
22. What simile does Bishop use to describe the sound of the tropical rain?
23. What did Pascal suggest about sitting in one's room? Does the poet think he was correct? Does she wish that he wasn't correct'?
24. **Class Discussion:** 'the choice is never wide and never free'. What does Bishop mean by this rather enigmatic pronouncement?

Exam Prep

1. **Personal Response:** Can you think of a trip, holiday or excursion that didn't go according to plan? Write an account of what happened. Don't forget to mention any positive aspects of the experience!
2. **Class Discussion:** 'For Bishop, the concept of home is always temperary and uncertain'. Discuss this statement making reference to 'Questions of Travel', 'Sestina' and 'The Prodigal'.
3. **Theme Talk:** 'This poem is an extremely balanced meditation on travel. Every experience Bishop describes is shown to have both a negative and positive aspect. The poem, therefore, simply does not make up its mind on the question of whether travel is a good thing or a bad thing.' Write a paragraph in response to this statement.
4. **Exam Prep:** 'Bishop is often described as a poet of emotional restraint, one who communicates through images and description rather than direct statements of feeling'. Write a short essay in response to this statement in which you discuss 'Questions of Travel' and at least two other poems.

Language Lab

1. Consider the poem's title. Can you list every question or issue surrounding travel that Bishop addresses in the poem?
2. **Class Discussion:** The last eight lines of the poem are set apart by being printed in italics. Can you suggest why Bishop chose to present the lines this way? Could there be more than one reason for this choice?
3. 'Questions of Travel' sees Bishop's descriptive powers at their most refined. Identify two descriptive passages that you found impressive and say why.

THIS IS POETRY • **ELIZABETH BISHOP**

The Armadillo
for Robert Lowell

This is the time of year
when almost every night
the frail, illegal fire balloons appear.
Climbing the mountain height,

rising toward a saint [5]
still honored in these parts,
the paper chambers flush and fill with light
that comes and goes, like hearts.

Once up against the sky it's hard
to tell them from the stars – [10]
planets, that is – the tinted ones:
Venus going down, or Mars,

or the pale green one. With a wind,
they flare and falter, wobble and toss;
but if it's still they steer between [15]
the kite sticks of the Southern Cross,

receding, dwindling, solemnly
and steadily forsaking us,
or, in the downdraft from a peak,
suddenly turning dangerous. [20]

Last night another big one fell.
It splattered like an egg of fire
against the cliff behind the house.
The flame ran down. We saw the pair

of owls who nest there flying up [25]
and up, their whirling black-and-white
stained bright pink underneath, until
they shrieked up out of sight.

The ancient owls' nest must have burned.
Hastily, all alone, [30]
a glistening armadillo left the scene,
rose-flecked, head down, tail down,

and then a baby rabbit jumped out,
short-eared, to our surprise.
So soft! – a handful of intangible ash [35]
with fixed, ignited eyes.

Too pretty, dreamlike mimicry!
O falling fire and piercing cry
and panic, and a weak mailed fist
clenched ignorant against the sky! [40]

Annotations
[3] **fire balloon:** a small hot air balloon made of paper
[16] **Southern Cross:** a distinctive constellation visible in the southern hemisphere
[19] **downdraft:** downward current of air
[31] **armadillo:** a mammal with a protective leathery shell and long claws for digging
[35] **intangible:** something that cannot be touched; difficult to understand; vague and abstract

Tease It Out

1. Watch Video 3, which describes how to manufacture sky lanterns or fire balloons. Write a paragraph describing the main steps in this process.
2. The fire balloons are described as 'frail'. What does this suggest about the materials involved in their construction?
3. The fire balloons have been declared 'illegal'. Can you suggest why they might be banned by the authorities?
4. Why does light come and go within the balloons' 'paper chambers'? What simile does she use to describe this?
5. **True or false:** According to the poet, the balloons resemble stars when they are 'up against the sky'.
6. Would you agree that the poet corrects herself when making this comparison?
7. Which four verbs does the poet use to describe the balloons' movement on a windy night? In each case, can you come up with alternative verbs that have a similar meaning?
8. On 'still', windless nights the balloons move 'solemnly'. Working in pairs, consider this adverb and try to come up with three other words that it brings to mind.
9. Consider the phrase 'forsaking us'. Pick two adjectives of your own to describe the emotions felt by the spectators as they watch the balloons drift out of view.
10. The balloons, as they drift ever higher, seem to move among the stars themselves. What metaphor is used to describe this optical effect?
11. What's a 'downdraft'? What impact do such downdrafts have on the fire balloons?
12. Where did the fire balloon touch down on the previous night? What simile does the poet use to describe its impact?
13. What verbs are used to describe the movement of the owls? Would you agree that these verbs convey a sense of panic?
14. What has caused the armadillo to be 'rose-flecked'?
15. The armadillo's head and tail are 'down' as it flees. What does this suggest about its demeanour?
16. The rabbit's remains are described as 'intangible'. What would happen if you touched this rabbit-shaped 'handful of ash'?
17. The final lines refer to a clenched fist that is described as 'mailed', 'weak' and 'ignorant'. Who or what does this fist belong to?

Exam Prep

1. **Class Discussion:** 'This poem is about things that are dangerous but that we can't stay away from. Things like war, love and art exude a glamorous attraction despite – or perhaps because of – their danger.' Discuss this statement making reference not only to 'The Armadillo', but 'Questions of Travel' and 'The Prodigal' also.
2. **Theme Talk:** Bishop is well known as a poet of emotional restraint:
    - Can you identify three phrases in the poem that exhibit such restraint?
    - Would you agree that the poem's last four lines are more directly emotional? What emotions, in your opinion, are expressed here?
    - Why did Bishop choose to print the final stanza in italics? Do these lines come from the poet's point of view or from some other viewpoint?
3. **Exam Prep:** 'Bishop makes skilful use of a variety of poetic techniques to produce poems that are often analytical but rarely emotional'. Write a short essay in response to this statement, making reference to 'The Armadillo' and at least three other poems on your course.

Language Lab

1. **Class Discussion:** What do you understand by the expression 'Too pretty, dreamlike mimicry'? What precisely do the fire balloons mimic? Consider the following possibilities and rank them in order of likelihood:
    - They resemble bombs, being launched upwards then crashing back down again.
    - They resemble prayers, drifting upwards towards the heavens.
    - They resemble spacecraft. (Remember that Bishop was writing at the dawn of the Space Age.)
    - They resemble love poems; after all, they're made out of paper, just like books of poetry.
2. Identify three literary devices Bishop uses in this poem and provide an example of each one.

Sestina

September rain falls on the house.
In the failing light, the old grandmother
sits in the kitchen with the child
beside the Little Marvel Stove,
reading the jokes from the almanac, [5]
laughing and talking to hide her tears.

She thinks that her equinoctial tears
and the rain that beats on the roof of the house
were both foretold by the almanac,
but only known to a grandmother. [10]
The iron kettle sings on the stove.
She cuts some bread and says to the child,

It's time for tea now; but the child
is watching the teakettle's small hard tears
dance like mad on the hot black stove, [15]
the way the rain must dance on the house.
Tidying up, the old grandmother
hangs up the clever almanac

on its string. Birdlike, the almanac
hovers half open above the child, [20]
hovers above the old grandmother
and her teacup full of dark brown tears.
She shivers and says she thinks the house
feels chilly, and puts more wood in the stove.

It was to be, says the Marvel Stove. [25]
I know what I know, says the almanac.
With crayons the child draws a rigid house
and a winding pathway. Then the child
puts in a man with buttons like tears
and shows it proudly to the grandmother. [30]

But secretly, while the grandmother
busies herself about the stove,
the little moons fall down like tears
from between the pages of the almanac
into the flower bed the child [35]
has carefully placed in the front of the house.

Time to plant tears, says the almanac.
The grandmother sings to the marvellous stove
and the child draws another inscrutable house.

Annotations

Sestina: poetic form involving the use of six end-words that reappear according to a strict pattern

[4] *Little Marvel Stove*: a brand of stove

[5] *almanac*: an annual publication containing tide tables, astronomical data, weather forecasts and important dates for agriculture as well as stories, jokes and trivia

[7] *equinoctial*: occurring at an equinox (an equinox happens twice a year when day and night are equal in length)

[39] *inscrutable*: difficult to scrutinise or understand

Tease It Out

1. **Get in Gear:** As a preparation for reading this poem, research Bishop's childhood online and write a brief paragraph describing the tragic events that she experienced.
2. Describe the poem's setting in your own words. What time of day is it? What time of year? What is the weather like?
3. Where are the child and her grandmother? What is the grandmother doing at this moment?
4. What is the grandmother's emotional state? How does she attempt to conceal this from the child?
5. What, according to the grandmother, did the almanac predict?
6. **Class Discussion:** Consider the expressions 'known to' and 'foretold'. Is it fair to say that they represent two different types of knowledge or experience? What are the differences between the two?
7. What does the grandmother offer the child? How does the child react to this offering?
8. Why is the almanac described as 'clever'? What does this suggest about the grandmother's attitude towards this book?
9. What does the almanac 'do' after it's been hung up on its string? How does the grandmother react?
10. Why is the almanac described as 'birdlike'? What might function as its wings?
11. What metaphor is used the describe both the beads of perspiration on the side of the kettle and the tea in the grandmother's cup? How does this metaphor fit the poem's overall mood?
12. **Class Discussion:** What tragic event is referred to in lines 25 to 26?
13. Describe in your own words what the child draws with her crayons.
14. What falls from the pages of the almanac? Where do these objects settle? Does the grandmother notice this happening?
15. **Group Discussion:** Why does Bishop refer to the stove as the 'marvellous stove'?
16. The houses drawn by the child are described as 'inscrutable'. What might this suggest about the child's demeanour and psychological state at this moment?

Exam Prep

1. **Class Discussion:** 'The startling image of the almanac planting tears in the child's drawing is the poem's central image and emotional core'. Would you agree with this assessment, or is there another image that you found more memorable and effective? Say why.
2. **Theme Talk:** 'Sestina' has often been described as a poem where 'almost everything is left unsaid but where great feeling is conveyed indirectly'. Do you think this accurately describes the poem? Write a paragraph describing the emotions you experienced when you first read 'Sestina'.
3. **Exam Prep:** Like 'First Death in Nova Scotia' and 'In the Waiting Room', 'Sestina' is a poem of childhood. Write a pargraph comparing and contrasting the depiction of childhood in these three poems.

Language Lab

1. Look up the poem's title. What is a 'sestina'? Can you work out how this poem follows the rules of the sestina form?
2. How would you describe the poem's atmosphere? Is it sad, menacing, cosy or depressing? Would you agree that the atmosphere changes throughout the poem? Give reasons for your answers.
3. **Class Discussion:** Certain images in this poem are dreamlike or surreal. List as many as you can. Are these images haunting and memorable or silly and over the top?
4. Pick three words that in your opinion best describe the 'character' of the almanac as depicted in the poem. In each case, write a brief paragraph explaining your choice.
5. 'In 'Sestina', Bishop uses an adult vocabulary but skilfully captures a child's point of view'. Would you agree with this statement? Which lines, phrases and images suggest that we're witnessing events at least partly from a child's point of view?

First Death in Nova Scotia

In the cold, cold parlor
my mother laid out Arthur
beneath the chromographs:
Edward, Prince of Wales,
with Princess Alexandra, [5]
and King George with Queen Mary.
Below them on the table
stood a stuffed loon
shot and stuffed by Uncle
Arthur, Arthur's father. [10]

Since Uncle Arthur fired
a bullet into him,
he hadn't said a word.
He kept his own counsel
on his white, frozen lake, [15]
the marble-topped table.
His breast was deep and white,
cold and caressable;
his eyes were red glass,
much to be desired. [20]

'Come,' said my mother,
'Come and say good-bye
to your little cousin Arthur.'
I was lifted up and given
one lily of the valley [25]
to put in Arthur's hand.
Arthur's coffin was
a little frosted cake,
and the red-eyed loon eyed it
from his white, frozen lake. [30]

Arthur was very small.
He was all white, like a doll
that hadn't been painted yet.
Jack Frost had started to paint him
the way he always painted [35]
the Maple Leaf (Forever).
He had just begun on his hair,
a few red strokes, and then
Jack Frost had dropped the brush
and left him white, forever. [40]

The gracious royal couples
were warm in red and ermine;
their feet were well wrapped up
in the ladies' ermine trains.
They invited Arthur to be [45]
the smallest page at court.
But how could Arthur go,
clutching his tiny lily,
with his eyes shut up so tight
and the roads deep in snow? [50]

Annotations

Nova Scotia: a province of Canada that lies on the country's rugged eastern coast
[3] *chromograph:* an early form of colour photograph
[4] *Edward, Prince of Wales:* The picture depicts King Edward VII back when he was still Prince of Wales. That title is given to the heir apparent to the British throne.
[8] *loon:* short-tailed lake-dwelling bird
[14] *He kept his own counsel:* he kept his thoughts and ideas to himself
[19] *caressable:* inviting to the touch
[25] *lily of the valley:* a plant with white, bell-shaped flowers
[36] *Maple Leaf:* the national emblem of Canada; 'The Maple Leaf Forever' was a popular patriotic song
[41] *Jack Frost:* a personification of winter, usually depicted as a mischievous, sprite-like little boy. Said to be responsible for spreading frost and snow, and for painting foliage red when autumn comes.
[42] *ermine:* an expensive type of fur which comes from the rodent of the same name
[48] *page:* young attendant to a nobleman

Tease It Out

1. What has happened to Arthur? What family relationship does the speaker have with him?
2. Who has 'laid out' Arthur's body? Where has the body been placed?
3. Who is depicted in the images that hang on the wall?
4. 'Since Uncle Arthur fired/ a bullet into him'. Who or what had Uncle Arthur shot?
5. The speaker seems to find it noteworthy that the stuffed loon 'hadn't said a word'. Do you find this surprising? What does this suggest about the speaker's age?
6. What metaphor is used to describe the table on which the loon is situated?
7. **Class Discussion:** Does the phrase 'cold and caressable' refer to the stuffed loon or to little Arthur? Could it, on one level, refer to both?
8. What did Uncle Arthur use to replace the loon's dead eyes?
9. According to the speaker, these objects were 'much to be desired'. Do you think that they were really valuable?
10. What does the speaker's mother ask her to do?
11. What metaphor is used to describe Arthur's coffin?
12. In lines 31 to 32, the speaker uses an unusual comparison to describe her dead cousin. How do these lines reinforce our sense of the speaker's age?
13. How much of Arthur's body had Jack Frost painted? Why, according to the speaker, had he failed to paint the rest?
14. The young speaker uses this little story to explain the whiteness of Arthur's body. Do you think she came up with this fantastic tale herself?
15. **Class Discussion:** Comment on the repetition of the word 'forever' in the fourth stanza. What does it indicate about the young speaker's understanding of death?
16. Describe in your own words the clothing worn by the royal couples depicted in the chromographs.
17. Where, according to the speaker, is little Arthur going? What job has been offered?
18. Who might have told the speaker this story? Why?
19. Why does she fear that Arthur might not be able to complete this trip?
20. Do you think the speaker really believes that Arthur has received such an invitation?

Exam Prep

1. **Class Discussion:** 'This poem movingly recounts a child's first confrontation with death'. List the different ways in which the young speaker attempts to avoid thinking directly about Arthur's demise.
2. **Theme Talk:** 'By the end of the poem, the young speaker is on the verge of coming to terms with death – this strange new concept – and with her cousin's alien, altered state.'
   - Write a paragraph in response to this statement.
   - Write a short essay comparing this poem to 'The Prodigal' and 'In the Waiting Room', other poems that deal with moments of epiphany.
3. **Exam Prep:** 'Bishop is one of the great poet's of childhood'. Write an essay in response to this statement in which you refer to 'First Death in Nova Scotia' and at least two other poems.

Language Lab

1. 'This is a poem that creates a chilly, wintry atmosphere'. How many references to coldness can you identify? Can you identify any references to warmth and comfort? Would you agree that these, paradoxically, only increase the icy atmosphere of the poem as a whole?
2. 'This is a poem of white and reds'. Identify each reference to these colours. Are any other colours mentioned or referred to? How does this colour scheme contribute to the poem's atmosphere?
3. This poem attempts to capture a 'childhood mentality' and to depict the events it recounts from a child's point of view. Can you identify three phrases where such a mentality is conveyed?

Filling Station

Oh, but it is dirty!
– this little filling station,
oil-soaked, oil-permeated
to a disturbing, over-all
black translucency. [5]
Be careful with that match!

Father wears a dirty,
oil-soaked monkey suit
that cuts him under the arms,
and several quick and saucy [10]
and greasy sons assist him
(it's a family filling station),
all quite thoroughly dirty.

Do they live in the station?
It has a cement porch [15]
behind the pumps, and on it
a set of crushed and grease-
impregnated wickerwork;
on the wicker sofa
a dirty dog, quite comfy. [20]

Some comic books provide
the only note of color –
of certain color. They lie
upon a big dim doily
draping a taboret [25]
(part of the set), beside
a big hirsute begonia.

Why the extraneous plant?
Why the taboret?
Why, oh why, the doily? [30]
(Embroidered in daisy stitch
with marguerites, I think,
and heavy with gray crochet.)

Somebody embroidered the doily.
Somebody waters the plant, [35]
or oils it, maybe. Somebody
arranges the rows of cans
so that they softly say:
ESSO–SO–SO–SO
to high-strung automobiles. [40]

Annotations

[3] ***permeated:*** thoroughly saturated
[5] ***translucency:*** transparency
[8] ***monkey suit:*** refers to the father's overalls
[10] ***saucy:*** spirited, impudent
[18] ***wickerwork:*** furniture made from plaited or woven twigs
[24] ***doily:*** an ornamental tablemat
[25] ***taboret:*** a type of stool
[27] ***hirsute:*** hairy
[27] ***begonia:*** a tropical plant
[28] ***extraneous:*** out of place, not belonging
[32] ***marguerites:*** daisy-like flowers
[33] ***crochet:*** form of needlework

Tease It Out

1. What phrases convey that everything in the filling station is coated in oil?
2. What does the term 'transluceny' suggest about this layer of oil?
3. The poet finds this coating of oil 'disturbing'. Is she a) worried the place might go up in flames, b) disgusted by the lack of cleanliness or c) horrified that people work in such an environment?
4. The poet compares the owner's overalls to a 'monkey suit'. What does this suggest about the owner's behaviour and demeanour?
5. Do the overalls fit him properly? Give a reason for your answer.
6. **True or false:** The father's sons are a lot cleaner than he is.
7. In the third stanza the poet suspects that the owner and his sons not only work in the station but live there. What does she observe that suggests this?
8. **True or false:** The comic books are the only colourful items in the station.
9. Why do you think the doily has become 'dim'?
10. The poet is surprised by the presence of certain items. What are these?
11. **Class Discussion:** Can you suggest why these items might seem out of place in this squalid environment?
12. The poet considers the placing of these objects to be an act of love towards the station owner and his sons:
    - Why does she consider this to be an act of love?
    - Who is the 'Somebody' responsible for this act of love?
    - If the owner and his sons are capable of being loved, than anybody is capable of being loved. What phrase suggests this?
    - What does this suggest about her attitude towards the men who work in the filling station?
13. Describe in your own words how this person has arranged the cans of engine oil.

Exam Prep

1. **Personal Response:** What in your opinion does society consider to be typical masculine characteristics? What does it consider to be typical feminine characteristics? Is the filling station portrayed as a masculine or feminine environment? Support your answer with reference to the poem.
2. **Class Discussion:** Bishop's poetry is haunted by the early loss of her mother. Would you agree that her mother's presence or absence can be felt in 'Filling Station'? You might also wish to bring 'Sestina' and 'In the Waiting Room' into your discussion.
3. **Theme Talk:** 'Many of Bishop's poems feature a moment of insight or awareness that arises from the careful study or observation of a place or an object'. Is this statement true of 'Filling Station'? Give a reason for your answer. Write a short essay discussing this statement in relation to 'Filling Station' and two other poems on the course.
4. **Exam Prep:** 'Bishop is a poet whose keen eye for detail leads to an understanding of the human heart'. Write a short essay in response to this statement, making reference to 'Filling Station' and two other poems.

Language Lab

1. Bishop uses a chatty, immediate tone throughout this poem, as if the reader were standing beside her. Identify each phrase that contributes towards this effect.
2. The poet uses the terms 'saucy' and 'greasy' to describe the sons. What do each of these terms mean and what do they suggest about the young men?
3. Bishop describes the automobiles as 'high-strung'. Would you agree that there is an element of personification here? What does it suggest about the state of the automobiles' engines as they travel along the freeway? How do you imagine the personified automobiles responding to the cans of engine oil? Is this sight likely to make them more or less high-strung?
4. Draw a picture or diagram of the cement porch that features the following items: the taboret, the doily, the begoina, the dog and the sofa. Your drawing doesn't have to be life-like, but it should show where the various items are located in relation to one another.

In the Waiting Room

In Worcester, Massachusetts,
I went with Aunt Consuelo
to keep her dentist's appointment
and sat and waited for her
in the dentist's waiting room. [5]
It was winter. It got dark
early. The waiting room
was full of grown-up people,
arctics and overcoats,
lamps and magazines. [10]
My aunt was inside
what seemed like a long time
and while I waited I read
the National Geographic
(I could read) and carefully [15]
studied the photographs:
the inside of a volcano,
black, and full of ashes;
then it was spilling over
in rivulets of fire. [20]
Osa and Martin Johnson
dressed in riding breeches,
laced boots, and pith helmets.
A dead man slung on a pole
– 'Long Pig,' the caption said. [25]
Babies with pointed heads
wound round and round with string;
black, naked women with necks
wound round and round with wire
like the necks of light bulbs. [30]
Their breasts were horrifying.
I read it right straight through.
I was too shy to stop.
And then I looked at the cover:
the yellow margins, the date. [35]

Suddenly, from inside,
came an oh! of pain
– Aunt Consuelo's voice –
not very loud or long.
I wasn't at all surprised; [40]
even then I knew she was
a foolish, timid woman.
I might have been embarrassed,
but wasn't. What took me
completely by surprise [45]
was that it was me:
my voice, in my mouth.
Without thinking at all
I was my foolish aunt,
I – we – were falling, falling, [50]
our eyes glued to the cover
of the National Geographic,
February, 1918.

I said to myself: three days
and you'll be seven years old. [55]
I was saying it to stop
the sensation of falling off
the round, turning world
into cold, blue-black space.
But I felt: you are an I, [60]
you are an Elizabeth,
you are one of them.
Why should you be one, too?
I scarcely dared to look
to see what it was I was. [65]
I gave a sidelong glance
– I couldn't look any higher –
at shadowy gray knees,
trousers and skirts and boots
and different pairs of hands [70]
lying under the lamps.
I knew that nothing stranger
had ever happened, that nothing
stranger could ever happen.
Why should I be my aunt, [75]
or me, or anyone?
What similarities –
boots, hands, the family voice
I felt in my throat, or even
the National Geographic [80]
and those awful hanging breasts –
held us all together
or made us all just one?
How – I didn't know any
word for it – how 'unlikely' ... [85]
How had I come to be here,
like them, and overhear
a cry of pain that could have
got loud and worse but hadn't?
The waiting room was bright [90]
and too hot. It was sliding
beneath a big black wave,
another, and another.
Then I was back in it.
The War was on. Outside, [95]
in Worcester, Massachusetts,
were night and slush and cold,
and it was still the fifth
of February, 1918.

Annotations
[9] *arctics:* warm, waterproof overshoes
[14] *National Geographic:* official magazine of the National Geographic Society; primarily contains articles about geography, history and world culture
[20] *rivulets:* small streams
[21] *Osa and Martin Johnson:* an American couple who became famous in the early 20th century for their travels in Africa and other exotic locations; they wrote books and made films about their adventures.
[22] *riding breeches:* short trousers fastened just below the knee
[23] *pith helmets:* a hat made of cork worn in the tropics
[25] *Long Pig:* in certain Polynesian islands human flesh was referred to as 'long pig'
[95] *The War:* World War I

THIS IS POETRY — ELIZABETH BISHOP

Tease It Out

An Uncomfortable Wait

1. The young poet accompanies her aunt to the dentist. What time of year is it? What is the weather like?
2. **True or false:** The waiting room was full of adults and children.
3. **Class Discussion:** Are you familiar with the National Geographic magazine? What sort of stories and images do you associate with this magazine?
4. The young poet takes a copy of the National Geographic and reads it from cover to cover, studying the images very closely:
   - There are two images of a volcano. Describe in your own words what is happening in each picture.
   - How are Osa and Martin Johnson dressed? Why do imagine they are dressed like this?
   - What is being done with the 'dead man slung on a pole'? Why do you think the tribespeople might refer to this as 'Long Pig'?
   - What has been wound 'round and round' the heads of the babies in this tribe? What effect has this had on the shape of their heads?
   - What has been wound round the necks of the women in the tribe? What effect has this had on their necks? Why do you think that they do this?
5. How do you think the stories and images in the magazine make the young girl feel? What reason does she give for reading the magazine 'straight through'?
6. The young poet hears an 'oh! of pain'. Who does the young poet initially think uttered this cry? Why does she think this?

The Young Poet's Realisation

7. **Class Discussion:** '[It] was me: my voice in my mouth'. The realisation that it was she who uttered the cry and not her aunt takes the young poet 'completely by surprise'. What is it that surprises the young poet? Consider the following and say which is most likely:
   - She is surprised that she would ever make such a foolish sound
   - She is surprised that she initially thought it was her aunt who made the sound
   - She is surprised that her own voice sounds just like her aunt's
8. Does the realisation that she is, in some ways, just like her 'foolish aunt' take a while to dawn on the young poet or does it strike her suddenly? Give a reason for your answer.
9. **Class Discussion:** 'But I felt: you are an I,/ you are an Elizabeth,/ you are one of them'. Describe in your own words what the young poet is slowly beginning to realise. How did she think of herself before this moment? What has now changed about her self-understanding and her sense of identity?
10. What connection does the young poet suddenly realise she has with the other people in the waiting room? Why, do you think, she can scarcely [dare] to look' at them? What is she afraid of seeing or understanding?
11. **Class Discussion:** When the young poet first looked at the magazine, she felt that the people depicted were utterly different and alien to her. What 'similarities' does the poet now realise she shares with these people?
12. The poet suddenly gets a sense that everyone in the world is connected and that we are 'all just one'. What do you think she is describing here? Consider the following and say which ones are relevant:
    - We all need to visit the dentist on occasion
    - We are all human beings, with similar emotions, needs and desires
    - Despite our different shapes and sizes, our bodies are fundamentally the same
13. The poet characterises the 'oh! as a 'cry of pain'. Why do you think she describes it in this manner? What sort of 'pain' is she experiencing at this particular moment?
14. Bishop says that the cry 'could have/ got loud and worse but hadn't'. What do you think prevented this from happening? Was it the poet's own self-control or an inability to speak or cry out, or something else? Give a reason for your answer.

The Impact of this Realisation

15. These sudden realisations have a dramatic effect on the young poet. She describes the 'sensation of falling off/ the round, turning world,/ into cold, blue-black space'. What do you think she is describing here? Rank the following in order of plausibility:
    - The young poet is confused and disorientated
    - The young poet is experiencing a moment of intense clarity and focus
    - The young poet feels dizzy and thinks she is about to pass out
16. **Class Discussion:** Would you agree that lines 90 to 93 describe some form of a panic attack? What do you think the 'big black wave[s]' represent?
17. The young poet makes an effort to stop these sensations and regain control. What does she do and say in order to achieve this? Are her efforts a success? Give a reason for your answer.
18. 'Then I was back in it'. What is it that the young poet is back in? Consider the following and say which are relevant:
    - She is back in the waiting room
    - She is back in the everyday world
    - She is back to thinking about the world in a clear manner

Exam Prep

1. **Personal Response:** Based on the details that the poet provides us with, describe the waiting room in your own words. What sort of people are waiting with the young poet? Are they young or old? Are they interacting with one another or keeping to themselves? Is it a dimly or brightly lit room?
2. **Class Discussion:** 'I knew that nothing stranger/ had ever happened, that nothing/ stranger could ever happen'. How did the young poet think about herself and her relationship to the rest of the world prior to this moment in the waiting room? What similarities or connections does the young poet suddenly realise she shares with the following:
    - her family
    - the people living in her local community
    - women in general
    - the human race
3. **Theme Talk:** 'Bishop's poetry illustrates how we are capable of experiencing the most extraordinary realisations and emotions in the most ordinary places'. Write a short essay in response to this statement, referring to 'In the Waiting Room' and at least two other poems on your course.
4. **Exam Prep:** 'Bishop's attention to the small details is what makes her poems so extraordinary to read'. Write an essay in response to this statement, making reference to at least four poems on your course.

Language Lab

1. "In the Waiting Room' wonderfully captures a childhood mentality. Identify lines and phrases in the poem that convey this childlike outlook and mentality.
2. Consider the poem's title. Having the read the poem, do you think that the term 'Waiting Room' takes on greater significance and meaning given the young poet's experience?
3. How would you characterise the tone in the first sixteen lines of the poem? How do the tone and atmosphere change as the poem progresses?
4. Consider the images of the volcano which the young poet studies in the magazine. How might the young poet's experience in the waiting room be said to resemble the eruption of the volcano?

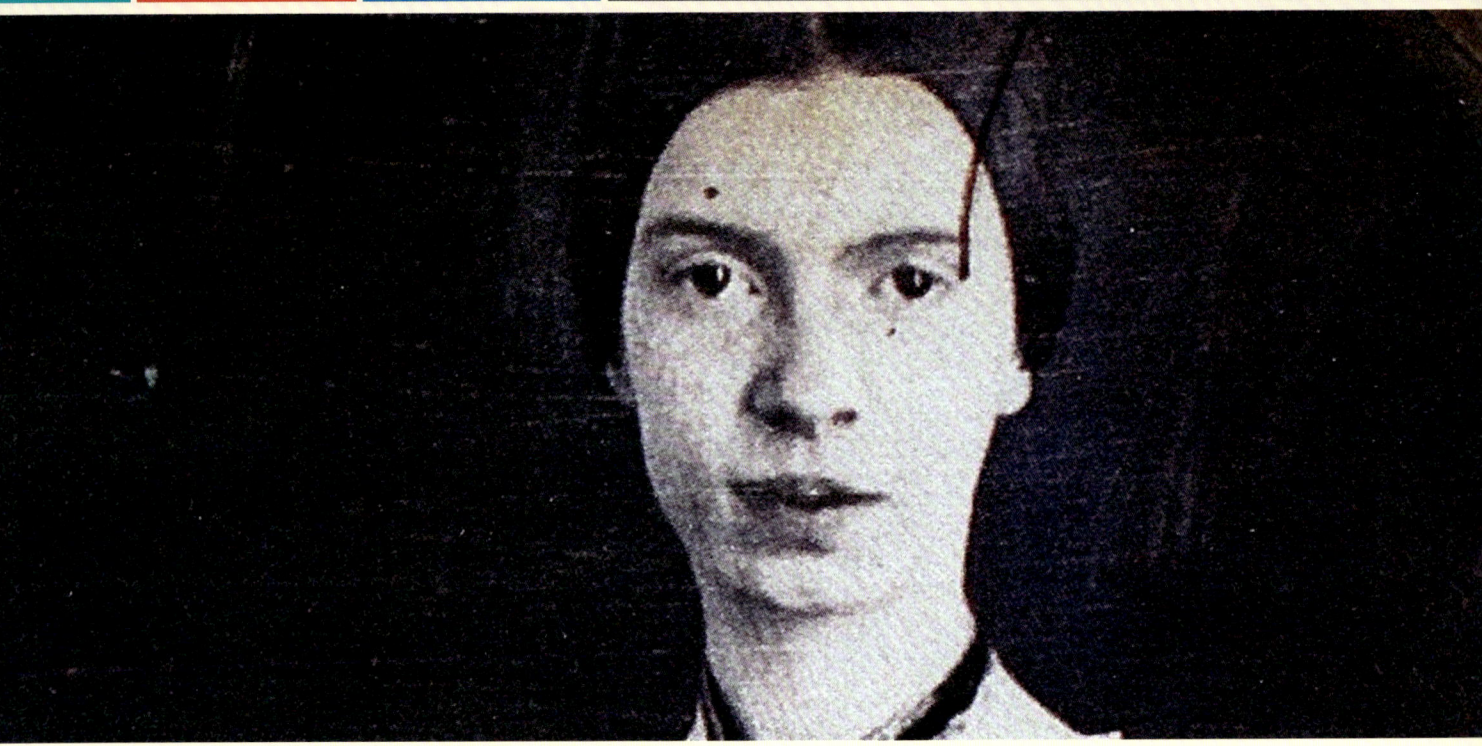

Emily Dickinson

Emily Dickinson was born in December 1830 in Amherst, Massachusetts. She had an older brother, Austin, and a younger sister, Lavinia. Her family had long been prominent in politics and local government. She was raised in 'Homestead', a mansion built by her grandfather on Amherst's main street. Her father, Edward, was a busy lawyer and a politician who served in the US congress in Washington. He provided a comfortable, thought not excessively wealthy, upbringing.

Dickinson, at her father's insistence, enjoyed a first class education. (Not all girls of the period, we must remember, were afforded such an opportunity). She first attended the local primary school – a two-room building that can still be seen on Amherst's Pleasant Street. Then in 1840, at the age of ten, she began her studies in Amherst Academy, a secondary college that had only begun to admit girls two years earlier.

Dickinson would spend seven years at the Academy, studying subjects such as history, literature and Latin. She was also introduced to botany, the study of plants, which became a life-long passion. Dickinson, in later years, loved to garden and developed an extraordinary collection of pressed flowers. She would often include pressed flowers with her letters and her work is marked by many botanical reverences. Her last years in the Academy were marked by a close friendship with Leonard Humphrey, the Academy's popular young principal who was only five years her senior.

Dickinson's fascination with the written word began to deepen in 1848, when she was 18 years old. It was around this time, scholars believe, that Dickinson began writing poetry in earnest. She became friends with Benjamin Franklin Newton, a young lawyer who worked with her father. It was Newton who introduced her to the latest trends in literature and poetry, lending her works by Wordsworth, Keats and Longfellow, and introducing her to the writings of Ralph Waldo Emerson, the great American poet, philosopher and nature writer. Emerson would prove an indispensable influence for Dickinson; his writings, she declared, had 'touched a Secret Spring' within her. His influence is especially palpable in 'I taste a liquor never brewed'.

Dickinson, having completed her education, lived the life of an ordinary young woman of the day. Her family's circumstances meant she had no need to work outside the home. Instead, she baked for the family and took care of various household chores. She enjoyed the social life of Amherst, attending concerts, festivals and other social events. 'Amherst is alive with fun this winter', she wrote in one of her letters, 'Oh, a very great town this is!'

Gradually, however, Dickinson began to confine herself more and more to the family home, where she lived with her mother and her sister Lavinia, who was also unmarried. This process began in the mid-1850's, when she was around twenty-five years old. By the early 1860's she had withdrawn almost entirely from social life. By 1866, when she thirty-six years old, she was effectively a recluse. She seldom left Homestead and preferred to speak to visitors from behind a door rather than face to face. It was around this time, too, that she began to dress only in white

> **"I have a brother and sister; my mother does not care for thought, and father, too busy with his briefs to notice what we do. He buys me many books, but begs me not to read them, because he fears they joggle the mind."**

clothing. Her family respected Emily's choice of a contemplative life: 'She had to think – she was the only one of us who had that to do'.

Scholars have long debated the cause of this retreat from the outside world. Her mother's ill-health was certainly a factor. In the mid-1850s Dickinson's mother became ill, and would go on to suffer from a variety of chronic ailments that would leave her bedridden for almost thirty years. Dickinson took on the responsibility of being her mother's primary carer, a role that necessitated she remain in and around the family home. Dickinson, it must be noted, had always been sensitive and melancholic, aspects of her personality that became more pronounced throughout her twenties and thirties. She was also deeply shaken by the deaths of several different friends; Leonard Humphrey, her former principal at Amherst College, passed away from 'brain congestion' while Benjamin Franklin Newton, her literary mentor, died from tuberculosis at only twenty-three years of age.

What's undeniable, however, is that Dickinson's seclusion brought with it an extraordinary surge of creativity. Between 1858 and 1866 she produced nearly 800 poems, which were carefully edited, rewritten and stitched into little booklets known as 'facsicles'. These poems – distinguished by a unique use of syntax, phrasing and punctuation – display an extraordinary originality. Dickinson's unconventional style is starting today and would have been utterly shocking to the tastes of the 1860's America.

Dickinson, though highly reclusive, wasn't completely shut off from the outside world. From time to time she received friends and relatives who came to visit her at Amherst. Through letter-writing she kept in touch with a range of correspondents. Her letters – which at times rival her poems in their brilliant use of language – reveal her to be witty, energetic and curious about the world around her. There are moments, too, when she reveals herself to be highly practical and insightful about the quirks of human behaviour.

One of Dickinson's correspondents was the newspaper editor Samuel Bowles, who provided her first appearance in print, publishing a number of her poems in the Spring field Republican. Another was the well-known writer Thomas Wentworth Higginson, who was disconcerted by her unconventional poetics and suggested that she 'regularise' the poems. Dickinson flatly refused his advice. Despite this disagreement, however, Dickinson remained friendly with Higginson for the rest of her life, valuing his advice and encouragement. They met face-to-face for the first time in 1870, eight years after beginning their correspondence.

In 1874 Dickinson's father passed away. Shortly after that, Dickinson's mother suffered a stroke, rendering her more dependent than ever on the poet's care and attention. Dickinson continued to write, though less prolifically. The poems from this period appear less carefully edited and were written on loose pages rather than stitched into 'facsicles'.

Dickinson's later years were marked by a close relationship with Otis Lord, an elderly judge from the nearby town of Salem. It's believed that in 1877, when Lord's wife died, this relationship blossomed into a romance, though one largely conducted through the medium of letters. The bulk of their correspondence, alas, has been destroyed. But their few surviving letters reveal an intense affection, one that endured until Lord's death in 1884.

Dickinson herself fell ill with Bright's disease in November 1885 and died on 15 May 1886. She was fifty-five years old. After the poet's death, a locked chest containing nearly 1800 poems and fragments, some stitched into 'facsiscles', hundreds of others on loose sheets, was discovered. Fewer than a dozen had been published in Dickinson's lifetime.

In 1890, four years after her death, Dickinson's first collection of poetry was published. The volume's editors 'regularised' her unusual punctuation and 'normalised' much of her unique phraseology. The book, featuring 115 poems, proved a literary sensation and Dickinson has never since been out of print. It was only in 1955, however, that an unedited version of her work appeared, one that preserves her unique style in all its eccentricity, force and power.

'Hope' is the thing with feathers –

'Hope' is the thing with feathers –
That perches in the soul –
And sings the tune without the words –
And never stops – at all –

And sweetest – in the Gale – is heard –   [5]
And sore must be the storm –
That could abash the little Bird
That kept so many warm –

I've heard it in the chillest land –
And on the strangest Sea –   [10]
Yet – never – in Extremity,
It asked a crumb – of me..

Annotations
[5] *Gale:* a very strong wind
[6] *sore:* severe, extreme
[7] *abash:* rattle, disconcert, to cause to feel ill-at-ease

Tease It Out

1. The poet presents life as a journey that we must each undertake. What different places does she imagine travelling through or across in the third stanza? What times or periods in life do you think these places represent?
2. In the second stanza, what sorts of weather conditions does the poet imagine encountering on this journey? Again, what sorts of experiences or moments do you imagine these represent?
3. The poet imagines 'Hope' accompanying her on this long and sometimes very arduous journey. How does she characterise 'Hope' in the opening stanza? What features or attributes does she ascribe to it?
4. Where does the poet imagine that 'Hope' is located? How does she describe the manner in which it abides there? How do you imagine or picture what the poet describes?
5. Based on the description given in the opening stanza, do you think that hope is something that has always been with us and will never leave us? Or do you think that hope is something that comes and goes? Give reasons for your answers.
6. The poet says that hope 'sings the tune without the words'. What sort of 'tune' do you imagine hope singing? What two adjectives do you think might best describe this tune?
7. When is Hope's tune 'sweetest … heard'? Why do you think the tune sounds sweetest at these times?
8. The poet says that it would have to be a severe or 'sore' storm to 'abash' this 'little Bird'. What does the word 'abash' mean? What do you think the 'storm' represents?
9. Why do you think this is 'the tune without the words'? Consider the following possibilities and rank them in order of likelihood:
   - The tune has no words.
   - Hope is described as a bird and, therefore, is incapable of singing words
   - The tune has words, but the bird chooses not to sing them because the effect is more powerful
10. Which of the following statements do you think best captures what the poet is saying in lines 6 and 7?
    - There are no occasions or circumstances that could damage our sense of hope.
    - Hope is vulnerable when it comes to particularly severe times in life.
    Give a reason for your answer.
11. What effect or impact does the poet describe hope having on 'so many' people in line 8? Describe in your own words what you think the poet has in mind here.
12. The poet describes being in the 'chillest land' and 'on the strangest Sea'. Describe in your own words the different landscapes and seascapes she has in mind. What do you think these different locations represent?
13. The poet describes being 'in Extremity'. Is this 'Extremity' the 'chillest land' and 'strangest Sea' or do you think the poet has an even more remote and inhospitable place in mind? Give a reason for your answer.
14. What does the poet say that hope asks for in return for all it does for her? Why do you think hope acts or behaves in this manner?

Exam Prep

1. **Personal Response:** The poet ascribes a number of characteristics to 'Hope'. Consider the following adjectives and rank them in order of their suitability for describing 'Hope', giving reasons for your decisions:
   - Constant
   - Fragile
   - Universal
   - Selfless
   - Changeable
   - Brave
   - Necessary
   - Foolish
2. **Class Discussion:** Out of all the creatures in the animal kingdom, why do you think Dickinson chose a bird to represent 'Hope'? What attributes does a songbird share with hope, if any?
3. **Theme Talk:** 'The poem suggests that hope and suffering are symbiotic; that one cannot exist without the other.' Do you agree or disagree with this statement? Write a few paragraphs in response.

Language Lab

1. 'By describing 'Hope' as a 'little Bird', Dickinson gives life to an abstract concept.' Write a few paragraphs in response to this statement.
2. Many Dickinson poems end in a dash, but 'Hope is the thing with feathers' ends in a full stop. What is the effect of this full stop on the closing lines? In your opinion, would a dash have been more or less effective here? Explain your answer.
3. Why do you think Dickinson refers to 'the thing with feathers' rather than using its more familiar name?
4. The poem features a number of metaphors. Can you say what metaphors the poet uses or suggests for the following:
   - Hope
   - Difficult circumstances in life
   - Periods of intense loneliness and hardship
   - Our individual lives

There's a certain Slant of light

There's a certain Slant of light,
Winter Afternoons –
That oppresses, like the Heft
Of Cathedral Tunes –

Heavenly Hurt, it gives us – [5]
We can find no scar,
But internal difference,
Where the Meanings, are –

None may teach it – Any –
'Tis the Seal Despair – [10]
An imperial affliction
Sent us of the Air –

When it comes, the Landscape listens –
Shadows – hold their breath –
When it goes, 'tis like the Distance [15]
On the look of Death –

Annotations
[3] *Heft:* weight
[10] *Seal:* an official stamp, often associated with a king or other royal personage; the Biblical Book of Revelation features a scroll bound with seven seals. The opening of each seal signals a terrifying or cataclysmic event
[11] *imperial:* having to do with an empire or emperor

Tease It Out

1. Identify two separate meanings of the word 'certain'. Would you agree that both meanings might be relevant here?
2. Which meaning of the word 'Slant' does the poet have in mind here? Rank the following options in order of plausibility:
   • A trait or quality
   • A tendency of someone or something to behave in a particular fashion
   • The angle at which something moves or is positioned
   • Crooked or untrustworthy
3. **Class Discussion:** Consider the poet's use of the term 'oppresses'.
   • In what sense might the light on 'Winter Afternoons' be said to differ from that at other times of the year?
   • Pick three adjectives that might describe the quality of such winter light?
   • Can you see why someone might find such light oppressive or depressing?
4. What type of music do you think of when you hear the term 'Cathedral Tunes'?
5. Would you agree that it's fair to describe such music as having 'Heft', as being weighty and somehow oppressive?
6. Do you think the poet enjoys attending church and listening to the music that accompanies religious services? Give a reason for your answer.
7. The oppressive winter light causes no physical or external damage to those it falls upon. Which phrase indicates this?
8. 'Where the Meanings, are'; What aspect of human nature is being referred to here?
9. What impact does the winter light have on this aspect of our selves?
10. Which phrase indicates that the light operates almost like an airborne disease?
11. Which phrase indicates that the light has a merciless, implacable quality?
12. **Class Discussion:** According to the poet, the light cannot be taught. What might the poet like to 'teach' the winter light? Does the light listen to those it falls upon?
13. What two entities are personified in lines 13 and 14?
14. Describe in your own words the impact that, according to the poet, the winter light has on the landscape when it appears.
15. The departure of this light brings a great relief. What simile does the poet use to describe this? Is it an effective one in your opinion?

Exam Prep

1. **Personal Response:** Pick three adjectives that in your opinion best describe the atmosphere of this poem. In each case, write three or four sentences explaining your choice.
2. **Class Discussion:** 'This poem presents a very negative view of religion, with God as a cruel emperor in heaven sending down an 'imperial affliction' to punish his subjects'. Do you agree with this reading?
3. **Theme Talk:** 'This poem is a powerful study of depression. It shows how when we're in a depressive state even light, something we usually associate with hope and optimism, strikes us as something cruel and oppressive'. Write a paragraph in response to this statement.
4. **Exam Prep:** 'Emily Dickinson's original approach to poetry results in startling and thought-provoking moments in her work'. Write a short essay in response to this statement, making reference to this poem and at least two others on the course.

Language Lab

1. **Class Discussion:** In the Bible's Book of Revelation, seven seals are broken, each revealing a judgement or apocalyptic event. Would you agree that Dickinson refers to or adapts these Bible verses in her poem?
2. Consider the phrase 'Heavenly Hurt' and pair with the person beside you to answer the following questions:
   • Does the light bring 'Heavenly Hurt' because it's been sent down form Heaven by God?
   • Does the light bring 'Heavenly Hurt' because it drifts down from the sky, often referred to as the heavens?
   • What's an oxymoron? Why might this phrase be considered an oxymoron?

THIS IS POETRY   **EMILY DICKINSON**

I felt a Funeral, in my Brain

I felt a Funeral, in my Brain,
And Mourners to and fro
Kept treading – treading – till it seemed
That Sense was breaking through –

And when they all were seated, [5]
A Service, like a Drum –
Kept beating – beating – till I thought
My mind was going numb –

And then I heard them lift a Box
And creak across my Soul [10]
With those same Boots of Lead, again,
Then Space – began to toll,

As all the Heavens were a Bell,
And Being, but an Ear,
And I, and Silence, some strange Race, [15]
Wrecked, solitary, here –

And then a Plank in Reason, broke,
And I dropped down, and down –
And hit a World, at every plunge,
And Finished knowing – then – [20]

Annotations

[3] *treading:* walk on, to press down or crush with the feet
[6] *Service:* a formal ceremony, often religious in nature
[12] *toll:* to sound a bell with a slow, uniform succession of strokes, as a signal or announcement

Tease It Out

1. The poet feels a funeral occurring inside her own brain. What does this suggest about her mental state? Rank the following statements in order of plausibility:
   - She is no longer in control of her own mental state.
   - She feels like her mind is being invaded.
   - She feels like she's having a nervous breakdown.
   - She is actually quite relaxed and curious about this strange psychological experience.
2. The funeral service proper has yet to begin. What are the mourners doing as they wait?
3. Suggest why the poet repeats the word 'treading' in line 3.
4. The poet can hear and feel the events taking place inside her own head. But can she see them? Give a reason for your answer.
5. **Class Discussion:** The speaker says that 'Sense' was 'breaking through'. What does the word 'Sense' signify in this particular context? Do you think that this 'breaking through' represents greater mental clarity or a loss of such clarity?
6. The funeral proper is called to order. What do the mourners do?
7. The poet compares the sound of the service to that of a drum. Is she suggesting a) that someone was hitting a drum throughout the ceremony or b) that the voice of the minister had a percussive drum-like quality?
8. How does the poet convey that the sound of the service was both intense and monotonous? If possible, provide two details.
9. Consider the phrase: 'My mind was going numb'. Write two or three sentences describing your impression of such numbness. Do you think of it as a pleasant or unpleasant mental state? Could it possibly be both?
10. What sound does the speaker hear as the mourners walk?
11. This ringing sound experienced by the speaker is so intense that it seems to emanate from the 'Heavens' themselves. Is she referring to a) outer space b) the afterlife or c) something else?
12. This sound is so intense that everything on Earth has no choice but to listen to it. What line conveys this?
13. The poet suggests that she and 'Silence' are closely related, are members of the same 'Race'. What does this suggest about her attitude towards noise and bustle?
14. The poet describes herself as 'Wrecked'. Can you think of at least two different meanings for this word? How might these different meanings be relevant here?
15. What does the speaker mean by 'Reason' in line 17?
16. The poet depicts herself falling down some kind of chute or shaft. What kind of mental state or event does this represent?
17. Does she plummet directly downwards, or does she collide against the sides of the shaft as she falls? Give a reason for your answer.
18. The poem ends with the speaker saying that she 'Finished knowing'. What does the poet mean by this? Rank the following statements in order of plausibility:
    - She gained some specific knowledge at this moment.
    - She gained some general insight and self-awareness at this moment.
    - Her ability to know or understand ceased at this moment.

Exam Prep

1. **Personal Response:** Would you agree that there's a sense of relief or release at the poem's conclusion? Give a reason for your answer.
2. **Class Discussion:** Based on your reading of the poem, do you think brain, mind and soul mean different things to the poet? Or does she use these terms interchangeably?
3. **Theme Talk:** 'This poem provides a powerful portrayal of a mind at the end of its tether'. Write two paragraphs in response to this statement.
4. **Exam Prep:** 'Dickinson's use of an innovative style to explore intense experiences can both intrigue and confuse'. Discuss this statement, supporting your answer with reference to 'I felt a Funeral' and two other poems on your course.

Language Lab

1. Consider the poet's use of the terms brain, mind and soul. Write one or two sentences describing your understanding of each concept.
2. Line 10 features a most unusual comparison, as the poet likens her soul to a floor on which the mourners walk. What kind of surface do you visualise?

A Bird, came down the Walk –

A Bird, came down the Walk –
He did not know I saw –
He bit an Angle Worm in halves
And ate the fellow, raw,

And then he drank a Dew [5]
From a convenient Grass –
And then hopped sidewise to the Wall
To let a Beetle pass –

He glanced with rapid eyes
That hurried all abroad – [10]
They looked like frightened Beads, I thought –
He stirred his Velvet Head –

Like one in danger, Cautious,
I offered him a Crumb,
And he unrolled his feathers, [15]
And rowed him softer Home –

Than Oars divide the Ocean,
Too silver for a seam,
Or Butterflies, off Banks of Noon,
Leap, plashless as they swim. [20]

Annotations
[3] *Angle Worm:* earthworm
[20] *plashless:* smoothly; fluidly; without splashing

Tease It Out

1. Watch Video 4, which is a trailer for the TV series *Emily*.
   - Mention three things it suggests about Dickinson's life.
   - Mention three things it suggests about her personality.
   - Did this portrayal fit with your own mental image of the poet?
2. Is there anything surprising or unusual about the phrase 'A Bird, came down the Walk'? What two worlds are colliding within this phrase?
3. Lines 3 to 4: Do you find the image of the 'Angleworm' being eaten 'raw' to be violent and disturbing or lighthearted? Give a reason for your answer.
4. In stanza 1, do you think the bird is aware he's being observed? Give a reason for your answer.
5. What do you understand by the phrase 'a convenient Grass'? How can grass be said to be convenient?
6. Lines 7 to 8: Do you think the bird really hops aside 'To let a Beetle pass'? What sort of behaviour is the speaker ascribing to the bird here?
7. How is the bird's fear and alertness suggested in stanza 3? What do you think he is on the look out for?
8. To what sort of materials does the speaker compare the bird's eyes and head? What does this suggest about her feelings towards the bird?
9. How does the speaker attempt to make contact with the bird? Why do you think she wants to do this?
10. Consider the questions below on your own for five minutes and jot down some ideas. Then compare notes with the person beside you. Finally, share your ideas with the class.
    - In line 13, who is being described as being 'in danger' and 'Cautious' – the speaker or the bird?
    - Is it possible that both the speaker and the bird are feeling 'Cautious' at this moment?
    - What reason has the speaker to feel 'Cautious' of the bird? How might the bird be 'in danger' from the speaker?
11. Why might the bird's feathers be said to be 'unrolled'? How do you picture this?
12. What 'Home' do you think the bird is returning to in line 16? Is there a broader meaning to the word 'Home' in this context?
13. Which action does the speaker say the bird's flight is 'softer' than?
14. Line 20: What does the poet mean when she suggests that the bird does not leave a 'seam' in his wake as he flies? What does this suggest about the manner of the bird's flight?
15. In lines 15 to 20, the poet makes two comparisons between flight and travelling on water. Describe these two images in your own words. Do you think this is an apt comparison? Why or why not?
16. The poet compares the bird's flight to that of butterflies. What similarities are there between these two images? What differences are there?

Exam Prep

1. **Personal Response:** Do you think the poem focuses more on the danger of nature or on the beauty of nature? Is there equal emphasis on both? Support your answer with reference to the poem.
2. **Class Discussion:** How would you characterise the tone of this poem? Is it serious or lighthearted? Is it strange or familiar? Does the tone shift from stanza to stanza?
3. **Theme Talk:** What does the poem suggest about humanity's place within nature? Support your answer with reference to the poem.
4. **Exam Prep:** 'Time and again, Dickinson shows a remarkable facility for zooming in on the small details of nature.' Discuss this statement with reference to 'A Bird, came down the Walk' and at least two other poems on your course.

Language Lab

1. As in many of her poems, Dickinson uses personification to describe an animal. What human characteristics does she ascribe to the bird? Explain your answer.
2. Consider the word 'plashless'. Could this be considered an example of onomatopoeia? Give a reason for your answer.
3. Suggest an alternative title for this poem and explain your choice.

THIS IS POETRY **EMILY DICKINSON**

I heard a Fly buzz – when I died –

I heard a Fly buzz – when I died –
The Stillness in the Room
Was like the Stillness in the Air –
Between the Heaves of Storm –

The Eyes around – had wrung them dry – [5]
And Breaths were gathering firm
For that last Onset – when the King
Be witnessed – in the Room –

I willed my Keepsakes – Signed away
What portion of me be [10]
Assignable – and then it was
There interposed a Fly –

With Blue – uncertain – stumbling Buzz –
Between the light – and me –
And then the Windows failed – and then [15]
I could not see to see –

Annotations
[4] *Heaves:* forceful, violent impacts
[6] *gathering firm:* preparing, readying
[7] *Onset:* attack, the beginning of something unpleasant
[9] *Keepsakes:* small items kept in memory of a person, place or event
[11] *Assignable:* transferable; capable of being given to another person
[12] *interposed:* placed between two people or objects

Tease It Out

1. List the different associations you have with flies. Is every association negative? Can you think of any positive traits we associate with these ubiquitous creatures?
2. 'I heard a Fly buzz – when I died'. This poem is spoken by someone who has already died. Can you think of any other poem, story or film you've come across that features a dead narrator?
3. As the speaker lay dying, the atmosphere in the room was very 'Still'. Do you think this was a pleasant stillness or a tense and uncomfortable one? Give a reason for your answer.
4. This stillness was only temporary. Describe in your own words the simile used to convey this?
5. What sounds and movements do you think might have preceded this stillness?
6. What sounds and movements will bring it to an end?
7. The speaker's relatives were present in the room and had been weeping a great deal. What metaphor is used to convey this? Is it an effective one in your opinion?
8. The relatives held their breaths. In fact they scarcely dared to breathe at all. How does the speaker convey this? What does it suggest about the relatives' mood?
9. The speaker braces herself for the 'last Onset' or attack of her illness. What will happen to her when this last assault on her mind and body finally occurs?
10. The speaker's relatives expected that a 'King' would be present at the moment of her death. What or whom does this King represent? Is it Jesus? An angel? Or is it Death itself? Give a reason for your answer.
11. **Class Discussion:** The speaker's relatives believed that this 'King' would be 'witnessed' in the room. Do they expect that the King will be physically visible? Or do they imagine that the King will make its presence felt in a more subtle manner?
12. What practical action does the speaker take before she dies?
13. The speaker refers to 'Keepsakes'. What kind of possessions does this term suggest to you? Do you imagine small items of sentimental value, larger goods like pieces of furniture or financial assets such as stocks and bonds? Give a reason for your answer.
14. The speaker says that one part of her is 'assignable', which implies that one part of her, presumably, is not. Which part of her might not be 'assignable' in this way? Give a reason for your answer.
15. Describe in your own words the manner in which the fly moved.
16. The fly positioned itself between the speaker and the 'light'. What verb is used to convey this?
17. **Group Discussion:** 'The Windows failed'. In small groups, try to work out what the speaker means by this:
    • Is the speaker referring to the actual windows in the room? If so, how might these be said to fail?
    • Or is the speaker referring to her own eyes? If so, how might these be said to fail?

Exam Prep

1. **Personal Response:** In your opinion, was the speaker ready to die when the moment of her death arrived? Refer to the poem in support of your answer.
2. **Class Discussion:** Would you agree that the speaker was hallucinating at the poem's conclusion? Consider this question in small groups, giving reasons for your answer.
3. **Theme Talk:** Would you agree that the speaker intended the moment of her death to be a solemn and peaceful one? What reduces the solemnity of this moment?
4. **Exam Prep:** 'Dickinson's poetry is a powerful exploration of the workings of the mind'. Discuss this statement in relation to this poem and at least two others on the course.

Language Lab

1. 'This is a surprisingly light-hearted poem, one that treats death with gravity'. Would you agree that the tone of this poem is somewhat playful? Write a paragraph in response, identifying two or three phrases that support your point of view.
2. What is the literary device known as synesthesia? Can you find an example in this poem?
3. The speaker says that the fly comes between her and the light, blocking it out.: What source of 'light', precisely, is the speaker referring to here?
    • Is she referring to the ordinary light of this world? What might it mean for the fly to block out this light source?
    • Or is she referring to the holy glow of the afterlife, which she glimpses (or thinks she glimpses) as she drifts towards death? What might it mean for the fly to block out this light source?

The Soul has Bandaged moments –

The Soul has Bandaged moments –
When too appalled to stir –
She feels some ghastly Fright come up
And stop to look at her –

Salute her, with long fingers – [5]
Caress her freezing hair –
Sip, Goblin, from the very lips
The Lover – hovered – o'er –
Unworthy, that a thought so mean
Accost a Theme – so – fair – [10]

The soul has moments of escape –
When bursting all the doors –
She dances like a Bomb, abroad,
And swings opon the Hours,

As do the Bee – delirious borne – [15]
Long Dungeoned from his Rose –
Touch Liberty – then know no more –
But Noon, and Paradise

The Soul's retaken moments –
When, Felon led along, [20]
With shackles on the plumed feet,
And staples, in the song,

The Horror welcomes her, again,
These, are not brayed of Tongue –

Annotations
[2] *appalled:* horrified, terrified, dismayed
[3] *ghastly:* horrifying, terrifying
[3] *Fright:* monstrous, goblin-like creature that personifies negative emotion
[9] *mean:* inferior in quality; nasty or malicious
[10] *Accost:* harrass, interfere with
[10] *Theme:* concept or idea; tune or melody
[13] *abroad:* outside, out and about
[15] *delirious:* in a state of wild excitement or ecstasy
[16] *Dungeoned from:* kept away from, excluded from
[20] *Felon:* a person who has committed a serious crime
[21] *shackles:* metal restraints connected by a chain
[21] *plumed:* decorated with long conspicuous feathers
[22] *staples:* metal fastening devices
[24] *brayed:* spoken of loudly or widely

Tease It Out

1. What sort of mental state do you think the first two lines of the poem describe? What do you think has given rise to this state of mind?
2. Does the term 'bandaged' suggest that the trauma is ongoing or that it has ended? Give a reason for your answer.
3. The speaker says that in the wake of what has happened, the soul is 'too appalled to stir'. What does it mean to be 'appalled'? What different meanings of the word might be relevant here?
4. The poet personifies her negative emotions, characterising them as a 'ghastly Fright' or 'Goblin'. How does this creature behave towards the soul? How does the soul react or respond?
5. The Goblin is said to 'Sip' from the soul's lips. What do you imagine the Goblin doing here? What does the term 'Sip' suggest about the manner in which this is done?
6. The Goblin's behaviour in line 7 is contrasted with the 'Lover' in line 8. Who or what do you imagine the 'Lover' represents? How does the Lover's behaviour compare and contrast with that of the Goblin's?
7. What sort of 'thought', do you think, can damage or tarnish the speaker's idea of romantic love? Why, do you think, such thoughts are 'Unworthy' of this kind of love?
8. What sort of image does swinging 'upon the Hours' bring to mind? What do you think the poet is suggesting here about the soul's attitude to time and routine when it is feeling so ecstatically happy?
9. Lines 15 to 18: The poet compares her soul's circumstances to a bee that has been 'Long Dungeoned from his Rose'. Why do you think the bee has been kept from visiting the flower it desires? What circumstances, do you think, make it possible for the bee to finally visit the flower again?
10. How does the poet characterise the manner in which the bee flies to the flower that it loves? What does this suggest about the bee's state of mind at this moment?
11. When the bee finally reaches the rose, it is said to 'Touch Liberty'. What sort of 'Liberty' do you think it experiences? From what is it free now that it has arrived at the flower it has been longing to visit?
12. Why do you think the soul's feet are described as 'plumed'? What special ability does this suggest the soul possesses?
13. The poet says that the 'Horror' is ready to greet the soul when it finally reaches the cell or dungeon. What do you think this 'Horror' represents? Do you think that the 'Horror' and the 'Goblin' are one and the same thing? Give reasons for your answer.

Exam Prep

1. **Personal Response:** Do you think the speaker has realistic expectations when it comes to love, or is she too idealistic? Support your answer with reference to the poem.
2. **Class Discussion:** What sort of person do you think the poem describes? Do you think that this person is experiencing a healthy range of emotions or do you think that there is something extreme or manic about their mood swings? Give reasons for your answer?
2. **Exam Prep:** 'Dickinson is a poet of hope and despair'. Discuss this statement in relation to this poem and two others on the course.

Language Lab

1. The poet says that these terrible moments are not 'brayed of Tongue'. What do you think it means to 'bray' about something? Why would someone not wish to 'bray' about the kind of experience described in these lines? What would prevent them doing so?
2. 'She dances like a Bomb'. What does this unusual comparison suggests about the manner in which the soul dances? Does it suggest energy and excitement, or is there a sense of danger and destruction evident here? Give reasons for your answer.

I could bring You Jewels – had I a mind to

I could bring You Jewels – had I a mind to –
But You have enough – of those –
I could bring You Odors from St Domingo –
Colors – from Vera Cruz –

Berries of the Bahamas – have I –   [5]
But this little Blaze
Flickering to itself – in the Meadow –
Suits Me – more than those –

Never a Fellow matched this Topaz –
And his Emerald Swing –   [10]
Dower itself – for Bobadilo –
Better – Could I bring?

Annotations

[3] ***Odors:*** odours, aromas

[3] ***St Domingo:*** a Caribbean island

[4] ***Vera Cruz:*** a Mexican port

[9] ***Topaz:*** a yellow gem; yellowish-brown in colour

[10] ***Emerald:*** a green gem, dark green in colour

[11] ***Dower:*** dowry, money or property brought by a woman to her husband at marriage

[11] ***Bobadilo:*** Francisco de Bobadilla (died in 1502). He was the Spanish governor of Santo Domingo and reputed to be the richest man in the world

Tease It Out

1. Watch Video 5, which provides a virtual tour of Homestead, the house where Dickinson spent her adult life. Based on your viewing of the video, pick three adjectives that, in your opinion, best describe the poet's personality.
2. **Get in Gear:** Look up St Domingo, Vera Cruz and the Bahamas on Google Maps. Write a short paragraph describing each location, saying which one you would most like to visit?
3. Who do you imagine the speaker of this poem to be? Who do you imagine he or she is addressing?
4. Is it significant that the word 'You' is capitalised in lines 1 and 3? What does this suggest about the importance of this 'You' to the poet?
5. What do you think might be meant by the 'Colors' referenced in line 4?
6. Why do you think the speaker rejects the idea of sending gems, perfumes, fruit and other traditional gifts?
7. What is the 'Blaze' referred to in line 7? Where is it located?
8. The 'Blaze' is described as 'Flickering to itself'. What sort of mood does this convey?
9. The 'Blaze' contains a 'Topaz' and an 'Emerald Swing'. What might these refer to?
10. What is the 'Dower' referenced in line 11? Why might the poet consider the 'Blaze' to be a suitable 'Dower'?
11. The speaker asks a question at the end of the poem. Rewrite this question in your own words. What effect does this question have on the poem's ending? Does it convey uncertainty or something else?

Exam Prep

1. **Class Discussion:** Compare and contrast St Domingo, Vera Cruz and the Bahamas with the location where the speaker finds her 'little Blaze'. How do these locations differ? What does it say about the poet that she would rather bring a gift from the nearby 'Meadow' than from an exotic destination?
2. **Theme Talk:** 'For Dickinson, the beauty of nature surpasses anything man-made.' Discuss this statement with reference to this poem and at least one other on your course.
3. **Exam Prep:** 'Dickinson isn't all about death and depression. She can also be a playful and witty poet.' Discuss this statement with reference to 'I could bring You Jewels', 'I taste a liquor never brewed' and 'A Certain Slant of Light'.

Language Lab

1. In your opinion, could this be described as a love poem? Support your answer with reference to the text.
2. Can you find any examples of hyperbole, or deliberate exaggeration, in the poem?
3. Pick out a phrase from the poem that strikes you as particularly memorable and say why you like it.
4. How would you characterise the overall tone of the poem?

A narrow Fellow in the Grass

A narrow Fellow in the Grass
Occasionally rides –
You may have met Him? Did you not
His notice sudden is –

The Grass divides as with a Comb, [5]
A spotted Shaft is seen –
And then it closes at your Feet
And opens further on –

He likes a Boggy Acre –
A Floor too cool for Corn – [10]
But when a Boy and Barefoot –
I more than once at Noon

Have passed I thought a Whip lash
Unbraiding in the Sun
When stooping to secure it [15]
It wrinkled And was gone –

Several of Nature's People
I know, and they know me
I feel for them a transport
Of Cordiality [20]

But never met this Fellow
Attended or alone
Without a tighter Breathing
And Zero at the Bone.

Annotations

[5] *as with a Comb:* as if it had been brushed with a comb
[6] *Shaft:* long, narrow pole-shaped object or part of an object
[10] *Floor:* ground, surface of the earth
[13] *Whip lash:* a whip, used in farming, especially to control livestock
[14] *Unbraiding:* unravelling, uncurling
[15] *stooping:* bending
[15] *secure:* claim, pick up
[17] *Several of Nature's People:* different creatures or animals
[19] *transport:* an overwhelmingly strong emotion
[20] *Cordiality:* affection, kindness, friendship
[22] *Attended or alone:* in the company of others or by myself

Tease It Out

1. **Get in Gear:** Can you think of any famous snakes in literature, pop culture or religion? What function do these snakes serve in their respective narratives? What do they represent?
2. **Class Discussion:** 'But when a Boy and Barefoot'. This poem, unusually for Dickinson, features a male speaker. It's easy to imagine that the speaker is based on one of the farmhands who worked in her home at Amherst. Why do you think Dickinson might have chosen to take on a male persona in this poem?
3. Consider the term 'Fellow'. Would you consider it a respectful or disrespectful form of address? What does it suggest about the farmhand's attitude to the snake?
4. 'You may have met Him'. Who do you imagine the farmhand is speaking to in this line? Is he addressing the reader directly? Or are we eavesdropping on a conversation between the farm-boy and some other local person?
5. What does the verb 'ride' suggest about the snake's movement through the grass? Consider the following statements and rank them in order of plausibility:
   - To travel in a horse-drawn carriage like a gentleman
   - To exhibit the speed and grace of a jockey on a thoroughbred horse
   - To cover a large area in a short period of time
   - To journey on the surface of the grasses, supported by the blades of grass themselves
6. The snake is excellent at concealing itself and can appear very suddenly. Which phrase conveys this?
7. What is the 'Shaft' referred to in line 6? Is the farm-boy able to study this shaft when it appears, or is it visible for only an instant?
8. 'The Grass divides as with a Comb'. Describe in your own words how the snake effects the grass it crawls through.
9. Describe in your own words the snake's preferred environment.
10. The farmhand recalls how in his younger days he came across an object lying in a field. What did he think this object was?
11. What happened when he bent to pick up this object?
12. The farmhand refers to 'Nature's People'. Who or what is he referring to? What poetic technique is being used here?
13. Which phrase suggests that the farmhand spends a great deal of time outdoors and is familiar with animals and their ways?
14. What physical reaction does the speaker experience whenever he glimpses a snake gliding through the grass? Which phrase suggests that the speaker experiences a chill on such occasions?

Exam Prep

1. **Personal Response:** Write a paragraph describing the farmhand's lifestyle as depicted in this poem. Do you think Dickinson would have pitied such a farmhand for the tough working conditions or envied him for his freedom?
2. **Class Discussion:** Which phrases suggest that the farmhand respects the snake? Which phrases suggest that he fears and mistrusts this creature? Do you think the speaker considers the snake to be one of 'Nature's People'? Give a reason for your answer.
3. **Theme Talk:** 'The farmhand regards the snake not only as dangerous and threatening, but also as noble and even beautiful in its colouring and movement'. Write a brief paragraph in response to this statement.
4. **Exam prep:** Dickinson, in one of her letters, wrote: 'and so I sing, as the Boy does by the Burying Ground – because I am afraid –'. Would you agree that fear rather than hope is the dominant emotion in her poetry. In your answer refer to this poem and at least two other poems on your course.

Language Lab

1. Why do you think Dickinson uses so many 's' sounds throughout the poem? Do you find this appropriate to the subject of the poem? What sort of atmosphere does it create?
2. The poet uses male pronouns to describe the snake throughout the poem, but refers to the snake as 'it' in stanzas 2 and 3. What, in your opinion, might be the reason behind this shift? Does it affect how we view the snake?
3. List all the various nouns the poet uses to describe the snake. Why, in your opinion, is the word 'snake' never used?
4. Discuss the phrase 'Zero at the Bone', highlighting in particular all the possible meanings of the word 'Zero'. Do you find this to be an effective or memorable phrase? Explain your answer.

THIS IS POETRY **EMILY DICKINSON**

I taste a liquor never brewed –

I taste a liquor never brewed –
From Tankards scooped in Pearl –
Not all the Vats upon the Rhine
Yield such an Alcohol!

Inebriate of Air – am I – [5]
And Debauchee of Dew –
Reeling – thro endless summer days –
From inns of molten Blue –

When 'Landlords' turn the drunken Bee
Out of the Foxglove's door – [10]
When Butterflies – renounce – their 'drams' –
I shall but drink the more!

Till Seraphs swing their snowy Hats –
And Saints – to windows run –
To see the little Tippler [15]
Leaning against the – Sun!

Annotations
liquor: alcoholic drink
[2] *Tankards:* cylindrical drinking cups
[2] *scooped in:* filled with
[3] *Vats:* vessels for storing liquid
[3] *Rhine:* a region in Germany famous for the production of alcoholic beverages
[5] *Inebriate:* someone who is drunk
[6] *Debauchee:* someone completely devoted to drinking alcohol
[8] *Molten:* vivid, having a burning intensity
[9] *Landlords:* publicans, innkeepers
[10] *Foxglove:* Common wildflowers known for their purple hue
[11] *renounce:* give up, promise to abstain from
[11] *drams:* small measures of liquor
[13] *Seraphs:* a type of angel
[15] *Tippler:* a drinker

Tease It Out

1. What substance does this speaker 'taste'?
2. What phrase indicates that this substance is naturally occurring and didn't have to be created?
3. What is a paradox? In what sense could the phrase 'a liquor never brewed' be considered a paradox?
4. With what type of alcoholic beverage do we associate the Rhine region?
5. Explain in your own words how lines 3 and 4 convey the potency of the liquor that the speaker drinks.
6. Explain in your own words what the terms 'Inebriate' and 'Debauchee' mean.
7. What has made the speaker inebriated? What has made her debauched?
8. Describe in your own words the nature of the speaker's movement as she travels through these 'endless summer days'.
9. Consider the phrases 'Tankards scooped in Pearl' and 'inns of molten Blue'. Is the speaker referring to actual pubs and drinking mugs? Or does it make more sense to view these terms as metaphors? Give a reason for your answer.
10. What substance do bees usually consume? Where has this particular bee been drinking? What impact has such consumption had?
11. With what type of establishment might you associate a landlord? Who or what might be the landlord of the Foxglove?
12. What does the landlord do to the drunken bee?
13. What does the term 'dram' mean? What substance might make up the drams enjoyed by butterflies?
14. Describe in your own words the personification that occurs in line 11.
15. Would you agree that there's a sense of playfulness and humour in these lines? Give a reason for your answer.
16. Will the speaker be deterred by the fates of the bee and the butterfly?
17. **Class Discussion:** How does line 13 suggest that the speaker will continue to be intoxicated by nature until she dies?
18. What are 'Seraphs'? What do the Seraphs do to celebrate in line 13?
19. What does the term 'Saints' mean, as it is used in line 14? What are the saints eager to see?
20. What is the setting for this last stanza?
21. Comment on the phrase 'little Tippler'. What does this suggest about the speaker?
22. How does the last line suggest that the speaker is exhausted from her exertions?
23. **Class Discussion:** What is meant by the poem's last line? In what sense could the speaker be 'Leaning' against the sun? Consider the following possibilities and rank them in order of plausibility:
    • The speaker is leaning against a fence at the end of the day while the sun goes down behind her.
    • The speaker has died and ascended to heaven.
    • The speaker is leaning against a mirror in which the sun is reflected.

Exam Prep

1. **Personal Response:** 'This poem emphasises Dickinson's ability to get 'high on life', to be rendered almost intoxicated by the delights of summer'. Think of an occasion that filled you with exhilaration and excitement and write two paragraphs recounting your experience.
2. **Class Discussion:** Read the poem again carefully. Who or what is speaking in this poem? Is it a human, an insect or a bird? Does it make sense to think of the speaker as sometimes human and on other occasions non-human?
3. **Theme Talk:** Describe in your own words the view of nature put forward in this poem. Is it a realistic view, in your opinion? Give a reason for your answer.
4. **Exam Prep:** 'Dickinson can be playful at times, but each of her poems has its serious side'. Discuss this statement in relation to at least three of the poems on your course.

Language Lab

1. Identify two examples each of assonance and alliteration in this poem.
2. What is the literary device known as a conceit? Explain how Dickinson uses a conceit, relating to alcohol, in the poem's first twelve lines.
3. Would you agree that there are several moments of hyperbole or deliberate exaggeration in this poem? If so, identify them.
4. List the poetic devices used by Dickinson in both 'I taste a liquor never brewed' and 'I could bring You Jewels'. How do these poetic devices contribute to the meaning and atmosphere of each poem?

After great pain, a formal feeling comes –

After great pain, a formal feeling comes –
The Nerves sit ceremonious, like Tombs –
The stiff Heart questions 'was it He, that bore',
And 'Yesterday, or Centuries before?'

The Feet, mechanical, go round – [5]
A Wooden way
Of Ground, or Air, or Ought –
Regardless grown,

A Quartz contentment, like a stone –
This is the Hour of Lead – [10]
Remembered, if outlived,
As Freezing persons, recollect the Snow –
First – Chill – then Stupor – then the letting go –

Annotations

[1] *formal:* marked by elaborate ceremony, obedient to convention, adhering to rules or constraints
[2] *ceremonious:* behaving in an extremely formal and polite manner
[3] *bore:* suffered, endured
[7] *Ought:* anything
[8] *Regardless:* unmindful, heedless
[9] *Quartz:* pertaining to or resembling the hard, transparent mineral
[9] *contentment:* a state of happiness and satisfaction
[11] *outlived:* survived
[13] *Stupor:* a state of near-unconsciousness

Tease It Out

1. Consider the term 'Nerves'. What is the scientific meaning of this term? We sometimes use the term 'nerves' in a more casual or everyday sense. Can you think of one such usage?
2. The speaker describes how her nerves 'sit'. Does this suggest that her mind is in an alert, active state or a drowsy, passive one?
3. In lines 3 and 4 the speaker personifies her heart:
   • The speaker's heart recently 'bore' or carried a great burden. What does this burden refer to?
   • Is the heart presented as male or female?
   • What has made her heart feel 'stiff'?
   • Is her heart sure about when this ordeal occurred?
   • Is her heart even sure that this ordeal occurred at all?
4. What does this personification suggest about the speaker's mental state? Rank the following adjectives in order of plausibility as descriptions of that mental state: she is a) exhausted b) confused c) numb d) empty e) relaxed
5. 'The Feet … go round'. The speaker finds herself walking around in circles again and again. What this does strange behaviour suggest about her mental state?
6. The speaker declares that she walks in a 'mechanical' and 'Wooden' manner. Can you think of three other adjectives that might describe this kind of movement?
7. 'The speaker feels compelled to keep walking. She would keep doing so even if the ground disappeared in front of her'. Can you identify two separate words or phrases that support this view?
8. **Class Discussion:** The speaker says that she experiences a form of 'contentment'. What do we mean when we say that someone is content? Is contentment the same as happiness? Do you think it's fair to describe the speaker, in this instance, as being in a happy state of mind?
9. 'A Quartz contentment, like a stone'. Consider the following adjectives, each of which we might associate with 'Quartz' and 'stone':
   • Cold   • Unfeeling   • Precious
   • Hard   • Indestructible   • Beautiful
   Which of these adjectives seems most appropriate to the 'contentment' experienced by the speaker? Rank them in order of plausibility.
10. **Class Discussion:** The element lead has many associations in the popular imagination. List at least three of these.
11. The speaker describes her post-traumatic period as the 'Hour of Lead'. What does this suggest about her thoughts and emotions in the wake of the great pain she has experienced?
12. The poet describes people 'Freezing' in the snows of an arctic environment. What three different stages do these 'Freezing persons' experience as they freeze to death? Write a sentence or two saying what you understand by each of these terms.
13. What do you understand by the phrase 'the letting go'? Are there a number of different things that the poet could mean here?

Exam Prep

1. **Personal Response:** 'The strangest thing about this poem is that the speaker finds a strange contentment in her numbness, the freedom of no longer caring, or thinking or feeling'. Do you agree with this statement? Write a short paragraph outlining your response.
2. **Class Discussion:** How will the speaker remember this post-traumatic period when she looks back on it? Is the speaker certain that she will actually survive or 'outlive' this difficult period in her life?
3. **Theme Talk:** 'This poem is a powerful study of post-traumatic stress, of the numbness and fatigue experienced in the wake of terrible trauma'. Write a few sentences in response to this statement.

Language Lab

1. How would you describe the atmosphere of the poem? What words and images capture or convey this atmosphere?
2. Consider the different references to stones, timber and metal in the poem. Why do you think the poet included these? What does each suggest about her emotional and physical condition?
3. Identify as many instances of personification as you can in the poem. In each case, say what is being personified and which human attributes have been assigned to non-human creatures or objects.

John Donne

When we look at the world today we see how religious differences cause tension everywhere from the Middle East to Northern Ireland. In 1572, when John Donne was born, things were little different. Both his parents were Roman Catholics, which made life difficult for them in an England that had recently converted to the Protestant religion. Catholicism was illegal and those who remained loyal to the Catholic faith were subject to punishments including fines, imprisonment, and even beheading on the grounds of treason. Several members of Donne's extended family were exiled or executed because of their loyalty to the Roman Catholic faith. The poet later asserted that no other family had 'suffered more in their persons and fortunes' for following Catholicism.

Donne was born in 1572, the son of a successful London merchant (also called John Donne) who died when he was only four years old. His mother, Elizabeth Heywood, came from a prominent and well-connected family. She did not long remain a widow, marrying Dr John Syminges only a few months after her husband's death. We don't know what the young poet made of this quickly acquired stepfather. Infant mortality was incredibly high in those days and though Donne had five siblings, only three of them made it to adulthood. It's clear that the young Donne possessed an extraordinary intellect, enrolling in Hart Hall at Oxford University when he was only eleven years old. He studied for six years – first at Oxford and later at Cambridge – but was unable to obtain a degree. To graduate each student had to sign an Oath of Supremacy, testifying that the King or Queen of England was a supreme religious leader. Donne, loyal to the Pope and Catholicism, was unwilling to do this.

Donne was an ambitious young man and was keen to pursue some kind of political or diplomatic career. Like many budding politicians – then as now – he chose to study law and attended a number of legal schools around London. In the 1590s London was buzzing. A growing and thriving metropolis, it was the centre of England's commercial, literary and intellectual life. Donne, in his late teens and early twenties, naturally responded to the excitement of the city. He enjoyed a colourful social life and earned a reputation as a womaniser. One friend described him as 'a great visitor of ladies, a great frequenter of plays, a great writer of conceited verses'. (In this instance 'conceited' means intellectually complicated and ingenious).

Religion continued to be a major issue. England was at war with Catholic Spain. The English government began to crack down even harder on its Catholic subjects, terrified that they might serve as agents of the Spanish enemy. It was in this climate that Donne's brother, Henry, was arrested for harbouring a Catholic priest. He

"No man is an island, entire of itself; every man is a piece of the continent, a part of the main ... Any man's death diminishes me, because I am involved in mankind, and therefore never send to know for whom the bells tolls; it tolls for thee."

contracted bubonic plague while incarcerated and died. (The priest, William Harrington, suffered an even worse fate, being hung, drawn and quartered.)

Donne, then, was faced with a major dilemma. Remaining loyal to Catholicism meant sacrificing any hopes of a successful career. However, it was equally difficult for him to contemplate abandoning the faith for which three generations of his family had suffered. Finally in 1595, on foot of his brother's death, Donne succumbed to religious pressure and relinquished the Catholic faith. Over the next few years Donne travelled widely. While we don't have the specifics of his 'grand tour' we do know that he visited France, Italy and Spain, returning home 'perfect in their languages'. This we must remember was at a time when few Englishmen travelled further than the next town. He also participated in several naval expeditions, fighting under Sir Walter Raleigh and the Earl of Essex. He saw battle against the Spanish navy at Cadiz in 1596 and in the Azores in 1597.

Donne's service on these voyages stood to him. He befriended a shipmate named Egerton, who recommended Donne to his father. On his return to England Donne ended up working as private secretary for Sir Thomas Egerton, the Lord Keeper and one of the highest-ranking officials in the English government. Sir Thomas was impressed by Donne and was influential in helping the young poet become Member of Parliament for Brackley in 1601. Now aged twenty-nine, Donne appeared to have every prospect of winning fortune and distinction – until he fell in love.

Egerton had been acting as guardian to Anne More, whose father, Sir George More, was also a high ranking government figure. Donne and Anne fell in love, and were married without the consent of either father or guardian. Sir George was furious about their secret marriage and had Donne thrown into prison. He was released after a number of weeks and used his legal training to have the validity of his marriage upheld. He was, however, dismissed from his position as Egerton's secretary and, under the circumstances, was unlikely to find another employer.

Donne and his seventeen-year-old wife moved to the town of Pryford, in Surrey, where the ambitious young poet must have deeply felt his exile from the bustle of the capital and its centres of power. Donne was extremely poor during these years. He repeatedly tried and failed to gain stable employment and was forced to eke out a living by practising law whenever he could. The family's financial situation wasn't improved by the fact that Anne gave birth to twelve children over sixteen years. With so many mouths to feed there were moments when Donne despaired and even contemplated suicide. Indeed if it hadn't been for Anne More's cousin Sir Francis Wolley, who provided the poet and his growing family with living quarters, Donne's circumstances would have been truly desperate.

Through it all, however, Donne continued to write poetry. His poems weren't formally printed but were circulated through 'coteries', informal circles of literary gentlemen. The brilliance and originality of his verse won him the admiration of lords, courtiers and even the King himself. One nobleman, Sir Robert Drury, became Donne's patron and benefactor, providing financial assistance when he needed it most. With Drury he undertook his final trip abroad, travelling through France and the Low Countries in 1611. It's generally believed that 'Sweetest Love, I do not go' and 'A Valediction: Forbidding Mourning' were prompted by this trip.

In 1615, under pressure from King James, Donne gave up his political ambitions and was ordained. The king was quick to make him an honorary doctor of divinity at Cambridge. But just as Donne's fortunes seemed to be improving, Anne Donne died. She passed away on 15 August 1617, aged thirty-three, after giving birth to their twelfth child, a stillbirth. According to Donne's friend Izaak Walton, Donne was thereafter 'crucified to the world'.

He continued to write poetry, notably his 'Holy Sonnets', but the time for love poems was over. In 1620 he returned to London where he was appointed Dean of Saint Paul's, an incredibly prestigious post he held until his death. In this last period of his life Donne achieved the distinction he had desired for so long, becoming the most eminent preacher of his generation. He died, aged fifty-nine, on 31 March 1631. The first edition of his poems was printed two years later. For some 250 years his reputation as a poet was uncertain, though he always had admiring readers. It was only in the 20th century that he became acknowledged as one of the major English poets.

Song: Go and catch a falling star

Go and catch a falling star,
   Get with child a mandrake root,
Tell me where all past years are,
   Or who cleft the devil's foot,
Teach me to hear mermaids singing, [5]
Or to keep off envy's stinging,
      And find
      What wind
Serves to advance an honest mind.

If thou be'st born to strange sights, [10]
   Things invisible to see,
Ride ten thousand days and nights,
   Till age snow white hairs on thee,
Thou, when thou return'st, wilt tell me,
All strange wonders that befell thee, [15]
      And swear,
      No where
Lives a woman true, and fair.

If thou find'st one, let me know,
   Such a pilgrimage were sweet; [20]
Yet do not, I would not go,
   Though at next door we might meet;
Though she were true, when you met her,
And last, till you write your letter,
      Yet she [25]
      Will be
False, ere I come, to two, or three.

Annotations
[2] *get with child:* impregnate
[2] *mandrake root:* a poisonous plant whose forked root resembles the lower half of the human body
[4] *cleft:* split, divided in two
[4] *the devil's foot:* the Devil's foot was believed to be shaped like a goat's hoof, with a 'cleft' or divide in the middle
[5] *mermaids singing:* the song of the mermaid was believed to enchant sailors and lure them to their death upon the rocks
[6] *envy's stinging:* the mental pain and torment of envy
[9] *advance:* benefit
[10] *If thou be'st born to strange sights:* If you have the gift or ability to see strange sights
[15] *befell thee:* happened to you
[18] *true:* faithful
[18] *fair:* beautiful
[20] *pilgrimage:* arduous physical and spiritual journey
[27] *False:* unfaithful
[27] *False, ere I come, to two, or three:* the poet is saying that the woman will have been unfaithful two or three times before he arrives

Tease It Out

Stanza 1

1. Watch Video 6, which features a reading of the poem by actor Richard Burton. Pick out three words or phrases to which he gives particular emphasis while he reads. Identify one place where he speeds up his reading and one place where he slows down.
2. The poet mentions a number of feats and tasks:
   - What is the scientific name for the phenomenon known as 'falling stars'?
   - The poet instructs the reader, somewhat bizarrely, to impregnate a plant. Suggest why he chose a 'mandrake root' rather than some other species of plant or flower.
   - Does the question in line 3 make any sense? Come up with the best and most imaginative answer you possibly can to this question.
   - **Group Discussion:** Who or what might be responsible for the devil's feet having a cloven, goat-like appearance? Working as a group can you come up with two or three suggestions? Is it possible to know for sure?
   - 'Teach me to hear mermaids singing'. Write a short story with this title. The story can be as realistic or unrealistic as you like.
3. What does the term 'stinging' suggest about the experience of envy? Do you think the poet believes it's possible to 'avoid or 'keep off' this negative emotion?
4. Would you agree that all the tasks mentioned above or by the poet are impossible or even nonsensical? Write a paragraph explaining your answer.
5. Finally, the poet asks us to find a circumstance that allows honest people to get ahead in life. What metaphor, related to ships and sailing, does he use to make this point?
6. **Class Discussion:** 'By lumping this last task in with the other nonsensical ones the poet presents a very cynical view of the world'. Does the class as a whole agree with this assessment?

Stanza 2

7. The poet imagines a woman who is both 'true, and fair'. What do you understand by each of these characteristics?
8. The poet imagines a man on horseback heading off to explore the world:
   - **True or false:** This rider would have strange, almost supernatural, abilities.
   - For how long would this rider explore the world?
   - What sign of aging would he display by the end of his journey?
   - What would he tell the poet about when he returned?
9. According to the poet, is the rider likely to encounter any woman who is both true and fair?

Stanza 3

10. In the unlikely event that the rider meets a true and fair woman, he must inform the poet. How will the rider do this?
11. The poet would set off immediately to meet such a woman. What does the term 'pilgrimage' suggest about this journey?
12. The poet then changes his mind about undertaking such a 'pilgrimage'. What phrase indicates this?
13. How would such a woman behave while the poet was on his way to meet her?

Exam Prep

1. **Personal Response:** What view of women and and femininity is presented in this poem? Write a few paragraphs outlining your own impression.
2. **Class Discussion:** 'Donne is a hateful and misogynistic poet'. Discuss this statement as a class, referring to the present poem and at least two others as a class.
3. **Exam Prep:** 'In Donne's poetry women are alternately celebrated for their perfection or damned for their insincerity, and sometimes both in the same poem'. Write an essay discussing Donne's view of women, referring to this poem and three others on your course.

Language Lab

1. **True or false:** The poet wouldn't go as far as next door in order to meet such a woman.
2. Donne's poetry is known for its outrageous claims and demands. Read the poem carefully. Identify three claims and three demands and state why each might be decribed as outrageous.
3. Which of the following terms best describe your reaction to the poem's opening stanza? Rank them in order:
   - Witty • Playful • Imaginative
   - Silly • Over-the-top • Irrelevant
4. 'This poem isn't meant to be taken too seriously. It's more a quip or a witticism than a genuine statement about women and the world'. Write a paragraph in response to this statement.

THIS IS POETRY **JOHN DONNE**

The Flea

Mark but this flea, and mark in this,
How little that which thou deniest me is;
It sucked me first, and now sucks thee,
And in this flea our two bloods mingled be;
Thou know'st that this cannot be said [5]
A sin, nor shame, nor loss of maidenhead,
   Yet this enjoys before it woo,
     And pampered swells with one blood made of two,
   And this, alas, is more than we would do.

Oh stay, three lives in one flea spare, [10]
Where we almost, nay more than married are.
This flea is you and I, and this
Our marriage bed, and marriage temple is;
Though parents grudge, and you, we're met,
And cloistered in these living walls of jet. [15]
   Though use make you apt to kill me,
   Let not to that, self-murder added be,
   And sacrilege, three sins in killing three.

Cruel and sudden, hast thou since
Purpled thy nail in blood of innocence? [20]
Wherein could this flea guilty be,
Except in that drop which it sucked from thee?
Yet thou triumph'st, and say'st that thou
Find'st not thy self, nor me the weaker now;
   'Tis true; then learn how false, fears be: [25]
   Just so much honour, when thou yield'st to me,
   Will waste, as this flea's death took life from thee.

Annotations
[1] *Mark:* note, notice
[6] *maidenhead:* virginity
[7] *woo:* courts and marries
[8] *pampered swell:* indulged, completely satisfied, lavishly treated
[10] *stay:* stop, refrain from action
[11] *nay:* no
[14] *we're met:* we are together or joined
[15] *cloistered:* being secluded in or confined to a monastery
[15] *jet:* black; a polished, black gemstone
[16] *apt:* have a tendency
[17] *self-murder:* suicide
[18] *sacrilege:* the destruction or violation of a sacred place
[20] *Purpled thy nail in blood of innocence:* the woman has swatted and killed the flea
[27] *waste:* waste away, disappear

Tease It Out

Stanza 1

1. Watch Video 7, which features a dramatised reading of 'The Flea'. Identify two emotions displayed by the female actor throughout the piece and two emotions displayed by the male actor. Did you find the performance effective or silly and over-the-top?
2. The woman is 'denying' the speaker some 'little' thing ('How little that which thou deny'st me is'). What is this little thing she refuses to give him?
3. What has the flea done to both the speaker and the woman?
4. What, according to the poet, is now mingled inside the flea's body?
5. **Class Discussion:** 'A sin, nor shame, nor loss of maidenhead'. What does this line suggest about the woman's reasons for denying the speaker?
6. The speaker asks the lady to 'mark' or pay attention to the flea. What lesson does he want her to learn from the flea's behaviour?
7. Why might the flea be described as 'pampered'?
8. And this, alas, is more than we would do'. What does the flea do that the speaker and the woman do not?

Stanza 2

9. The woman is about to do something but the poet asks her to 'stay', or stop. What is she about to do?
10. By killing the flea the woman will take 'three lives'. Who, according to the poet, will she kill?
11. The speaker suggests that he and the woman have become 'married' despite the objections of the woman herself and of her parents ('Though parents grudge, and you'). How and where have they become husband and wife?
12. What two striking metaphors does the speaker use to describe the flea in line 15?
13. What are the 'living walls of jet'? What has been 'cloistered' within them?
14. According to the speaker what three sins will the woman commit if she kills the flea?

Stanza 3

15. At the beginning of stanza 3 we learn that the woman has taken action. What has she done?
16. What effect has this had on her nail?
17. According to the speaker, did the flea deserve this treatment?
18. Why does the woman claim to have triumphed in their argument or debate?
19. **Class Discussion:** The woman's action, according to the speaker, has disproved her fears. Working as a class, restate the speaker's argument in your own words.
20. How much honour, according to the speaker, will 'waste' or drain from the woman if she yields to his advances?

Exam Prep

1. **Personal Response:** "'The Flea' has been described as a poem of seduction. Yet no woman could possibly be seduced by all this talk about a blood-sucking insect.' Do you agree with this opinion?
2. **Class Discussion:** Many critics have suggested that 'The Flea' is a poem of the head rather than of the heart, that it is designed to impress Donne's male readers with its clever comparisons rather than to win the affection of a lover. Do you agree?
3. **Theme Talk:** 'The Flea' is often compared to 'The Dream'. What similarities are there between the poet's situation in each of these poems? Which of them, in your opinion, do you think is most effective as a love poem? 'The Flea' can be contrasted with 'The Anniversary'. Can you identify two major differences between that poem and this?
4. **Exam Prep:** 'John Donne is a poet who celebrates love in all its aspects: sexual, emotional and spiritual'. Write an essay in response to this statement in which you mention 'The Flea' and at least three other poems on the course.

Language Lab

1. 'Use' or habit has made the woman 'apt' or expert at killing the poet. Can you suggest how the woman, in the poet's opinion, has been killing him slowly?
2. Each stanza of the poem introduces a different argument. Summarise each one in your own words. Which one do you find most convincing and which one least convincing?
3. **Group Discussion:** Discuss the poem as a group and identify as many metaphors as you can. How many of these might be described as 'conceits' or extended metaphors?

The Dream

Dear love, for nothing less than thee
Would I have broke this happy dream;
      It was a theme
For reason, much too strong for fantasy,
Therefore thou waked'st me wisely; yet [5]
My dream thou brok'st not, but continued'st it.
Thou art so true that thoughts of thee suffice,
To make dreams truths, and fables histories;
Enter these arms, for since thou thought'st it best,
Not to dream all my dream, let's act the rest. [10]

As lightning, or a taper's light,
Thine eyes, and not thy noise waked me;
      Yet I thought thee
(For thou lovest truth) an angel, at first sight;
But when I saw thou sawest my heart, [15]
And knew'st my thoughts, beyond an angel's art,
When thou knew'st what I dreamt, when thou knew'st when
Excess of joy would wake me, and cam'st then,
I must confess, it could not choose but be
Profane, to think thee any thing but thee. [20]

Coming and staying showed thee, thee,
But rising makes me doubt, that now
      Thou art not thou.
That love is weak where fear's as strong as he;
'Tis not all spirit, pure and brave, [25]
If mixture it of fear, shame, honour, have;
Perchance as torches, which must ready be,
Men light and put out, so thou deal'st with me;
Thou cam'st to kindle, goest to come; then I
Will dream that hope again, but else would die. [30]

Annotations

[3-4] *a theme/ For reason:* the dream was about something that should happen in reality not fantasy
[6] *brok'st:* broke
[7] *so true:* so real
[8] *make ... fables histories:* make fictitious tales reality
[11] *taper's light:* light from a candle
[16] *beyond an angel's art:* beyond the capabilities of an angel (only God can see into the hearts of humans)
[19] *it could not choose but be:* it would only be
[20] *Profane:* irreverent
[20] *to think thee any thing but thee:* to think of you as being anything but who you really are
[21] *show'd thee, thee:* showed the real you
[27] *Perchance:* perhaps
[27] *torches, which must ready be:* torches were lit and extinguished so that it would be easier to light them when needed
[28] *Men light:* Men get aroused
[29] *goest to come:* leave with the intention of returning
[30] *die:* 'to die' can also mean to reach sexual climax

Tease It Out

1. The poet is in bed. He was asleep and having a dream. Describe in your own words what the poet has been dreaming about.
2. The poet says that his lover came into the bedroom and woke him up. What does he say was just about to happen in his dream the moment he awoke? What lines in the poem tell us this?
3. **Class Discussion:** Donne says that his lover has 'brok'st not, but continued'st' his dream. How might her presence in the bedroom be a continuation of the dream he has been having?
4. Donne believes that his lover woke him deliberately. What, does he say, were her intentions or motivations for waking him? What lines in the poem tell us this?
5. 'Thine eyes, and not thy noise wak'd me'. To what does the poet compare his lover's eyes? How does he suggest his lover's eyes woke him up?
6. Donne says that he first thought his lover was an angel when he woke. But he quickly realised that it wasn't an angel because his lover managed to do something that is 'beyond an angel's art'. Explain in your own words what the lover can do that angels cannot?
7. 'Thou art so true'. What does the poet mean by this? Consider the following options:
   - His lover's existence or presence is so real that it cannot be doubted.
   - His lover is so honest and would never say anything false.
   - His lover is so faithful in love for the poet and would never betray him.
8. Create a two-columned table. One column will be headed 'Real' and the other 'Unreal'. Now place each of the following into one or both columns and give a reason for your decision:
   - Dreams • Fables • Histories • Angels
   - The poet's lover's presence in the room
   - The love that the poet feels for his beloved.
   - The love that the poet's lover has for him.
9. 'Coming and staying show'd thee, thee'. The poet says that entering the bedroom and staying revealed something about his lover. What does he say her presence showed?
10. However, the poet's lover is not in the room. He gets up and she is not there. Her absence tells him that 'now,/ Thou are not thou'. Consider the following and say which you think is the most relevant or correct:
    - She is not present. The poet was mistaken in thinking she was ever in the room.
    - She is not sincere in her love for him. Her absence shows that her feelings are false.
    - Her not staying in the room is out of character. She is not being herself or being true to herself when she behaves like this.
11. What does the poet 'hope' has happened at the end of the poem? What does he hope his lover has done or is doing?

Exam Prep

1. **Personal Response:** How would you characterise the poet's descriptions of his lover in the first two stanzas? Do you think he is being sincere or is he merely flattering his lover in order to get what he wants?
2. **Class Discussion:** The poet says that true love ought to be 'all spirit'. What do you think he means by this? Is he being hypocritical in making demands of his lover if this is what he truly believes? Give a reason for your answer.
3. **Theme Talk:** Donne associates love with being 'true', honourable and 'pure'. What do you think he means by each of these qualities? Based on your reading of this and other poems by Donne on the course, does the poet believe that men and women ought to be held to the same standard when it comes to love?
4. **Exam Prep:** 'Donne uses startling imagery and wit in his exploration of relationships'. Write a response to this statement, making reference to 'The Dream' and three other poems on the course.

Language Lab

1. How would you characterise the poet's tone and mood in the first two stanzas? How does his tone and mood change in the third stanza? What has happened to bring about this change?
2. Outline in your own words the argument that the poet puts forward in the opening stanza to convince his lover to come to bed with him. Do you think that the poet's argument is reasonable or crazy? Give a reason for your answer.
3. Donne uses a number of interesting comparisons in the poem. In what way does he say that a man's passion and arousal is similar to a 'torch' or candle? Explain in your own words the comparison he makes and say whether you think it is an effective one.

THIS IS POETRY   **JOHN DONNE**

The Sun Rising

Busy old fool, unruly sun,
        Why dost thou thus,
Through windows, and through curtains call on us?
Must to thy motions lovers' seasons run?
        Saucy pedantic wretch, go chide   [5]
          Late school boys and sour prentices,
   Go tell court huntsmen that the king will ride,
   Call country ants to harvest offices;
Love, all alike, no season knows nor clime,
Nor hours, days, months, which are the rags of time.   [10]

        Thy beams, so reverend and strong
          Why shouldst thou think?
I could eclipse and cloud them with a wink,
But that I would not lose her sight so long;
        If her eyes have not blinded thine,   [15]
          Look, and tomorrow late, tell me,
   Whether both th' Indias of spice and mine
   Be where thou left'st them, or lie here with me.
Ask for those kings whom thou saw'st yesterday,
And thou shalt hear, All here in one bed lay.   [20]

        She's all states, and all princes, I,
          Nothing else is.
Princes do but play us; compared to this,
All honour's mimic; all wealth alchemy.
        Thou, sun, art half as happy as we,   [25]
          In that the world's contracted thus.
   Thine age asks ease, and since thy duties be
   To warm the world, that's done in warming us.
Shine here to us, and thou art everywhere;
This bed thy center is, these walls, thy sphere.   [30]

Annotations

[1] ***unruly:*** disruptive, disorderly
[5] ***saucy:*** cheeky, brazen
[5] ***pedantic:*** very fussy and excessively concerned with minor detail
[5] ***wretch:*** miserable creature
[5] ***chide:*** scold
[6] ***prentices:*** apprentices
[8] ***country ants:*** farmers, those working in fields
[9] ***all alike:*** always the same, unchanging
[9] ***clime:*** climate
[17] ***both th'Indias:*** the East and West Indies
[17] ***mine:*** gold mines
[23] ***play:*** pretend, imitate
[24] ***mimic:*** imitation
[24] ***alchemy:*** false, not real. Alchemy was the medieval forerunner of chemistry, concerned particularly with attempts to convert metals into gold
[27] ***Thine age asks ease:*** Your advanced years require that you take it easy

Tease It Out

Stanza 1

1. Beams of sunlight are entering the poet's bedroom. What phrases indicate this?
2. Is he happy that the sun has come to 'call' on him in this manner? Give a reason for your answer.
3. The poet lists other people the sun should bother instead:
   - The poet imagines schoolboys. Why are these in need of chiding?
   - The poet imagines apprentices. What does the term 'sour' suggest about their mood? Why might they feel this way?
   - The poet imagines peasants in the countryside? What rather insulting metaphor does he use to describe them? What 'offices' or tasks does he imagine them performing?
   - The poet imagines 'court huntsmen'. Describe in your own words why these have a busy day ahead of them.
4. **Class Discussion:** What does it mean to be pedantic? What according to the poet is the sun being pedantic about on this particular morning?

Stanza 2

5. The sun believes that its beams of sunlight are extremely powerful. What phrase suggests this?
6. Does the poet agree with sun's assessment of its power?
7. The poet believes that he could 'eclipse' and 'cloud' these beams of light. How can he do this? Why is he reluctant to do so?
8. What according to the poet is capable of blinding the sun itself?
9. The poet uses the conceit of states and princes to describe the relationship.
   - The poet compares his lover to all the _____ in the world. He compares himself, meanwhile, to all the _____ in the world.
   - Will the islands of the East and West Indies be where the sun 'left' or last saw them' as it travelled around the earth? Where will they be instead?
   - What will the sun 'hear', according to the poet, if it asks about the kings of various lands around the world?
   - What does this conceit suggest about the poet's view of the relationship?

Stanza 3

10. Donne produces a typically weird and wonderful argument, declaring that his bedroom is now the whole world:
    - What phrase indicates that the world has shrunk?
    - What phrase indicates that nothing exists outside the bedroom?
    - What according to Donne is now at the centre of the world?
    - What now marks the limits of the world?

Exam Prep

1. **Personal Response:** 'This is yet another poem where Donne focuses on showing off his intellect rather than expressing genuine emotion'. Do you agree? Write a paragraph or two in response.
2. **Class Discussion:** Consider the following lines: 'compared to this, /All honour's mimic, all wealth alchemy'.
   - What does the term 'honour' mean in this context?
   - How does the poet suggest the worthlessness of conventional wealth?
   - What do these lines suggest about the value the poet places on his current relationship?
   - Can you think of any songs that make a similar point about love?
3. **Exam Prep:** 'The poetry of John Donne contains wit as well as wisdom'. Discuss this statement in relation to 'The Sun Rising' along with at least two other poems on your course.

Language Lab

1. Donne's tendency for making outrageous and unlikely claims is especially evident in 'The Sun Rising'. Can you identify one such claim from each of the poem's three stanzas?
2. 'The Sun Rising' is well known for its personification of the sun:
   - Describe the device known as personification in your own words.
   - Consider the following terms: busy, fool, wretch, call, chide, saucy, old, unruly. Which are verbs, which are adjectives and which are nouns?
   - What does each term suggest about the personality of the sun as the poet perceives it?
   - Mention two things that Donne imagines the sun doing in stanza 2.
   - How does stanza 3 add to this personification?
   - The sun is usually thought of as powerful and magnificent. Does Donne's personification fit with this view? Give a reason for your answer.

Song: Sweetest love, I do not go

Sweetest love, I do not go
    For weariness of thee,
Nor in hope the world can show
    A fitter love for me;
        But since that I   [5]
Must die at last, 'tis best
To use myself in jest
    Thus by feign'd deaths to die.

Yesternight the sun went hence,
    And yet is here today;   [10]
He hath no desire nor sense,
    Nor half so short a way:
        Then fear not me,
But believe that I shall make
Speedier journeys, since I take   [15]
    More wings and spurs than he.

O how feeble is man's power,
    That if good fortune fall,
Cannot add another hour,
    Nor a lost hour recall!   [20]
        But come bad chance,
And we join to it our strength,
And we teach it art and length,
    Itself o'er us to advance.

When thou sigh'st, thou sigh'st not wind,   [25]
    But sigh'st my soul away;
When thou weep'st, unkindly kind,
    My life's blood doth decay.
        It cannot be
That thou lov'st me, as thou say'st,   [30]
If in thine my life thou waste,
    That art the best of me.

Let not thy divining heart
    Forethink me any ill;
Destiny may take thy part,   [35]
    And may thy fears fulfil;
        But think that we
Are but turn'd aside to sleep;
They who one another keep
    Alive, ne'er parted be.   [40]

Annotations
[2] *weariness:* discomfort, dislike, mistrust
[4] *fitter:* better, more appropriate
[6-8] *'tis best/ To use myself in jest,/ Thus by feign'd deaths to die:* The poet considers his departure good preparation for the ultimate end (death)
[8] *feign'd:* fake
[9] *Yesternight:* last night
[21] *But come bad chance ... length:* we succumb to misfortune, which allows it to grow stronger; our misery in the face of bad situations simply begets more misery
[31] *waste:* lay waste to, destroy
[33] *divining:* intuitive, predictive
[34] *Forethink:* predict, anticipate

Tease It Out

Stanza 1

1. In the opening four lines the poet reassures his wife that he has not fallen out of love with her. Describe in your own words the specific claims that he makes.
2. The poet refers to a 'feign'd' or fake death. How might his departure be considered such a fake death? What do death and such a departure have in common?
3. 'But since that I/ Must die at last'. According to the poet, how should he and his wife prepare for his eventual death?
4. **Class Discussion:** 'To use myself in jest'. What does the poet mean by this phrase? Try to describe his meaning in your own words.

Stanza 2

5. What did the sun do last night? What did it do this morning?
6. What does the poet suggest about the sun in line 11? Does this strike you as a reasonable claim?
7. 'Nor half so short a way'. Which journey is shorter, that of the poet or that of the sun? Explain your answer.
8. In lines 15 and 16 the poet uses the metaphor of 'wings' and 'spurs', saying these will allow him to make 'speedier journeys' than the sun. What do these 'wings' and 'spurs' represent?

Stanza 3

9. In lines 17 to 20 the poet laments that man's 'power is feeble', that human beings are incapable of changing certain things. According to the poet, what aspects of our existence are we powerless over?
10. What are we incapable of doing on those occasions when we experience good fortune?
11. What does the poet say about the 'lost hours' of good fortune that are now in the past?
12. What do you understand by the expression 'bad chance'? According to lines 22 to 24, how do we facilitate such misfortune when it arises in our lives?

Stanza 4

13. According to the poet, his wife isn't sighing wind or air. What does he suggest she is actually sighing?
14. What substance, according to the poet, drains away with every tear she cries?
15. What consequences, according to stanza 4, will the wife's grief have for the poet's health?
16. The poet suggests that his wife may not really love him after all. Why does he suggest this? Do you think he really means this?

Stanza 5

17. In lines 33 to 36 the poet asks his wife to avoid thinking in a particular fashion. What kind of thoughts does he ask her to avoid?
18. Why does he ask her to do this? Would you agree that the poet is superstitious? Give a reason for your answer.
19. How does he ask his wife to think of their separation?
20. Why, according to lines 39 to 40, can he and his wife never be truly parted?

Exam Prep

1. **Class Discussion:** In this poem Donne uses several different arguments to comfort his lover. List them. Which did the class find most effective? Which did the class find least effective?
2. **Personal Response:** Imagine your boyfriend or girlfriend was leaving you for a long trip abroad and tried to make you feel better by using the type of statements put forward by Donne in this poem. How would you feel?
3. **Theme Talk:** 'Donne's poem is little more than a guilt-trip. He tries to make his partner feel guilty about crying over his departure so he doesn't have to face the reality of the pain he's causing her.' Do you agree with this statement? Write three or four paragraphs outlining your response.
4. **Exam Prep:** Donne wrote that 'to know and feel all this and not have the words to express it makes a human a grave of his own thoughts.' Write an essay describing three concepts or emotions that Donne knew, felt and expressed.

Language Lab

1. In this poem Donne makes a number of deliberately exaggerated comparisons. identify as many as you can. Which you think are witty, over the top, or just plain silly?
2. 'That art the best of me'. Describe in your own words what the poet means by this movingly simple statement.
3. The poet refers to his wife as 'unkindly kind'. What does he mean by this seemingly contradictory statement? How can his wife's behaviour be simultaneously both kind and unkind?
4. **Class Discussion:** This poem is described as a 'Song'. What song-like qualities does it have? Do you think it would work as lyrics to a modern day piece of music? Can you think of any recent songs that articulate a similar sentiment?

A Valediction: Forbidding Mourning

As virtuous men pass mildly away,
   And whisper to their souls to go,
Whilst some of their sad friends do say
   The breath goes now, and some say, No:

So let us melt, and make no noise, [5]
   No tear-floods, nor sigh-tempests move;
'Twere profanation of our joys
   To tell the laity our love.

Moving of the earth brings harms and fears,
   Men reckon what it did, and meant; [10]
But trepidation of the spheres,
   Though greater far, is innocent.

Dull sublunary lovers' love
   (Whose soul is sense) cannot admit
Absence, because it doth remove [15]
   Those things which elemented it.

But we, by a love so much refined,
   That our selves know not what it is,
Inter-assured of the mind,
   Care less, eyes, lips, and hands to miss. [20]

Our two souls therefore, which are one,
   Though I must go, endure not yet
A breach, but an expansion,
   Like gold to airy thinness beat.

If they be two, they are two so [25]
   As stiff twin compasses are two;
Thy soul, the fixed foot, makes no show
   To move, but doth, if the other do.

And though it in the centre sit,
   Yet when the other far doth roam, [30]
It leans and hearkens after it,
   And grows erect, as that comes home.

Such wilt thou be to me, who must,
   Like the other foot, obliquely run;
Thy firmness makes my circle just, [35]
   And makes me end where I begun.

Annotations

Valediction: farewell; a poem of farewell
[1] *virtuous men:* men who have not led sinful lives
[1] *pass mildly:* die in a calm manner
[6] *No tear-floods, nor sigh-tempests:* no floods of tears or heavy, mournful sighs
[7] *profanation:* a defilement or desecration
[8] *laity:* ordinary people
[9] *Moving of the earth:* an earthquake
[10] *reckon what it did, and meant:* consider the damage and significance
[12] *innocent:* harmless
[13] *sublunary:* earthly, and therefore prone to change
[14] *Whose soul is sense:* who rely on physical, sensual contact
[16] *elemented:* constituted
[19] *Inter-assured of the mind:* calm in the understanding that their love is not just a physical thing
[23] *breach:* break, separation
[24] *Like gold to airy thinness beat:* like gold beaten to a sheet of such incredible thinness that it resembles air
[26] *twin compasses:* two arms of a mathematical compass used for drawing circles
[31] *hearkens:* listens for
[34] *obliquely:* in a slanting direction, not straight

Tease It Out

1. The poet is about to embark on a lengthy trip to Europe. He tells his wife that they should 'melt' apart. What does this term suggest about the manner in which he would like them to part?
2. Donne uses the image of a virtuous man on his deathbed to illustrate how he would like he and his wife to behave as they separate.
   - What phrase does he use to suggest that such men die in a very peaceful manner?
   - **True or false:** The virtuous man desperately clings to his soul, not wishing it to leave his body.
   - Why are the friends who stand by his bedside unsure whether the moment of death has arrived?
3. To what does the poet compare tears and deep, mournful sighs in line 6?
4. What effect, according to the poet, would any public show of grief have on their love?
5. The poet uses religious terms to suggest that their love is something special and sacred. Identify these terms and explain them in your own words.
6. The poet describes how people react and respond when earthquakes occur? What impact does he say such events have on peoples' lives?
7. The poet says that a tremor or disturbance of planets in outer space has no impact on human lives. What word or phrase indicates this?
8. **True or false:** The shaking or tremor of the planets is of less significance than earthquakes.
9. The poet characterises the love that most couples share as 'Dull' and 'sublunary'. Describe in your own words what each of these terms suggests or implies.
10. **Class Discussion:** What 'elements' or constitutes the love that most couples share? What is of most importance to these peoples' relationship?
11. Donne says that he and his wife share a love 'so much refined':
    - What does the term 'refined' suggest about the nature or quality of their love?
    - **True or false:** Donne and his wife are capable of comprehending the nature of their love.
    - How does Donne convey the fact that their love is more than just physical?
12. Donne argues that he and his wife share the one soul. If this is the case, what will happen to this soul as he journeys away from his wife?
13. The poet uses an ingenious mathematical conceit, declaring their souls are joined together like the two legs of a compass. The wife's soul is compared to the _____ leg of the compass. The poet's soul, meanwhile, is compared to the _____ leg. The fixed leg _____ as the moving leg _____. This suggests how the wife will long for her husband while he is gone. The fixed leg remains at the _____ of the arc traced by the moving leg. This suggests how the poet's wife will remain at the forefront of his mind as he _____. Once the circle has been traced, the two legs are recombined. This suggests how _____.

Exam Prep

1. **Personal Response:** Compare the poem's opening lines with those of 'Sweetest love, I do not go'. How does the poet's style of address differ? Which poem do you find more convincing?
2. **Class Discussion:** 'But we, by a love so much refined'. Discuss the way in which the poet distinguishes the love that he and his wife share from the love that others experience. Do you think he is being honest about what matters most to his wife and himself?
3. **Theme Talk:** 'Donne is a great poet of sex and seduction, but his poems also deal with romantic love and the ups and downs of married life'. Discuss this statement in relation to 'A Valediction' along with at least two other poems on your course.
4. **Exam Prep:** 'John Donne's poetry is cold and unfeeling. It's all about ingenious metaphors rather than genuine emotion'. Write an essay in response to this statement, making reference to at least four poems on your course.

Language Lab

1. Donne uses a typically inventive simile when he compares the 'expansion' of their single soul to gold that is beaten to an 'airy thinness'. What does this simile suggest about their relationship as the poet journeys ever further away??
2. **Class Discussion:** Donne suggests that when most people part, it is like an earthquake has occured, but when he and his wife part it it like a disruption of the planets. What point is he trying to make with this analogy? Would you consider this to be a reasonable or crazy argument?
3. Donne is well known as a poet of paradox and contradiction. Would you agree that Donne's claim that their love is 'so much refined' but their parting should cause no disturbance or grief could be regarded as paradoxical? Give a reason for your answer.

THIS IS POETRY **JOHN DONNE**

The Anniversary

    All kings, and all their favourites,
       All glory of honours, beauties, wits,
The sun itself, which makes times, as they pass,
Is elder by a year now than it was
When thou and I first one another saw: [5]
All other things to their destruction draw,
       Only our love hath no decay;
This no tomorrow hath, nor yesterday,
Running it never runs from us away,
But truly keeps his first, last, everlasting day. [10]

    Two graves must hide thine and my corse;
       If one might, death were no divorce.
Alas, as well as other princes, we
(Who prince enough in one another be)
Must leave at last in death, these eyes, and ears, [15]
Oft fed with true oaths, and with sweet salt tears;
       But souls where nothing dwells but love
(All other thoughts being inmates) then shall prove
This, or a love increased there above,
When bodies to their graves, souls from their graves remove. [20]

    And then we shall be throughly blessed;
       But we no more than all the rest.
Here upon earth, we're kings, and none but we
Can be such kings, nor of such subjects be;
Who is so safe as we, where none can do [25]
Treason to us, except one of us two?
       True and false fears let us refrain,
Let us love nobly, and live, and add again
Years and years unto years, till we attain
To write threescore: this is the second of our reign. [30]

Annotations

[1] *favourites:* lords or courtiers especially favoured by a king
[2] *wits:* people known for their intelligence
[6] *all other things ... draw:* everything is drawn towards destruction
[11] *corse:* corpse
[16] *Oft:* often
[19] *there above:* in heaven
[20] *remove:* depart, leave
[26] *Treason:* betrayal
[27] *refrain:* control, restrain, hold back
[30] *threescore:* sixty

Tease It Out

1. Read the first stanza carefully. When did the poet and his lover see each other for the first time?
2. **Class Discussion:** Think about the phrase 'glory of honours'. What does it bring to mind? Is the poet talking about physical objects or about something more abstract?
3. Why might 'wits', 'beauties' and 'favourites' command the envy and admiration of those around them?
4. We use the sun's movements to regulate our concept of time. What lines indicate this?
5. What has happened to all these things – even the sun itself – in the year since the poet and his lover first met?
6. What makes the love between the speaker and his partner different from everything else in the world?
7. 'Running it never runs from us away.' What is the 'it' referred to in this line? What do you visualise or imagine here?
8. **Class Discussion:** In lines 9 to 10 Donne makes a typically outrageous claim about the nature of love. What does he suggest? Is he speaking literally or metaphorically?
9. The poet and his lover must be buried in two separate graves. Why do you think this is?
10. How might death be considered a form of divorce?
11. Under what circumstances would the poet consider death not to constitute divorce?
12. The poet and his lover must leave behind their bodies when they die. What lines indicate this?
13. According to line 20, what happens to our souls when our bodies are laid in the ground?
14. In heaven the souls of the poet and his lover will be free to continue their relationship. They will, he says, be 'thoroughly blessed'. Yet the speaker does not appear to be fully satisfied with this arrangement. Why is this?
15. The poet considers himself and his lover to be exceptionally 'safe'. Why is this?
16. The poet mentions the possibility of 'treason'. What does he have in mind here? Do you think he comes across as someone who is secure in his relationship?
17. The poet mentions fears that are 'true' and 'false'. What 'false' fears does he have in mind here? What might be an example of a 'true' fear that concerns him?
18. 'Let us love nobly, and live'. In the poem's final four lines the speaker advises his lover with regard to how they should live and continue their relationship. Summarise this philosophy in a few lines.
19. According to the poem's final line, for how long does the poet envisage their relationship lasting?

Exam Prep

1. **Personal Response:** Do you think 'The Anniversary' is successful as a love poem? Many of Donne's critics have suggested his verse lacked passion and romance. Would you describe 'The Anniversary' as a passionate poem or a poem of the intellect?
2. **Class Discussion:** The poem presents several different notions of what an 'everlasting love' might be. Think about these. Which of them do you find most realistic?
3. **Theme Talk:** 'This is a poem that begins with disgust at change but moves towards embracing our changing, living world with all its joys and challenges'. Write a paragraph in response to this statement.
4. **Exam Prep:** 'Donne writes about emotional, sexual and spiritual matters in a manner that is suited to his time but not to ours'. Write an essay in response to this statement, making reference to at least four poems on your course.

Language Lab

1. Donne uses a typically inventive metaphor when he compares himself and his lover to both kings and subjects. What does this metaphor suggest about his view of their relationship?
2. **Class Discussion:** According to the poet, why are souls more suited to love than bodies?
3. Donne is a poet famous for his conceits or extended metaphors. Identify a conceit in this poem. Say whether or not you think it is effective and why.
4. Donne is known for his weird and wonderful arguments. In 'The Anniversary' each stanza represents a different argument with regard to love. Summarise each argument in a few lines. Which argument did you find most convincing?

Batter my heart

Batter my heart, three-personed God, for you
As yet but knock, breathe, shine, and seek to mend;
That I may rise and stand, o'erthrow me, and bend
Your force to break, blow, burn, and make me new.
I, like an usurped town to another due, [5]
Labour to admit you, but oh, to no end!
Reason, your viceroy in me, me should defend,
But is captived, and proves weak or untrue.
Yet dearly I love you, and would be loved fain,
But am betrothed unto your enemy; [10]
Divorce me, untie or break that knot again,
Take me to you, imprison me, for I,
Except you enthral me, never shall be free,
Nor ever chaste, except you ravish me.

Annotations

[5] *usurped:* wrongfully seized; overthrown
[7] *viceroy:* a man who is the governor of a country, province or colony, ruling as the representative of a sovereign
[8] *captived:* captured, held captive
[9] *fain:* gladly
[10] *betrothed:* engaged
[13] *enthral:* capture, enslave
[14] *chaste:* virginal, pure, refraining from sexual intercourse
[14] *ravish:* to seize and carry away by force, to rape or violate, to overwhelm with emotion; to enrapture

Tease It Out

Line 1 to 4

1. **Class Discussion:** Consider the phrase 'Batter my heart':
    - What Christian idea does the term 'three-personed' refer to?
    - What kind of action is suggested by the verb 'batter'?
    - Is this choice of verb surprising in the context of a religious poem?
    - Is the poet referring to the physical organ or to something more abstract?
2. God has been seeking to 'mend' the poet. Can you suggest what these efforts by God might have consisted of?
3. The poet instead wants to be completely remade by God. What phrase indicates this?
4. What phrase suggests that such re-making will require a great effort on God's part?
5. Contrast the verbs 'knock, breathe, shine' with the verbs 'break, blow, burn'. Which set of verbs is more aggressive? Give a reason for your answer.
6. **Class Discussion:** These lines are influenced by pottery. There is a sense in which he compares God to a potter and himself to a defective vase. Can you identify words and phrases that support this view?

Lines 5 to 8

7. The poet compares himself to a town that has been 'usurped' or captured. Tease out this conceit or extended metaphor by filling in the gaps below:
    - The town owes its loyalty to its rightful lord, just as the poet owes his loyalty to _____.
    - But the town has been taken over by a foreign power, just as the poet's life has been taken over by _____.
    - The townspeople struggle to expel the foreign power and re-admit their rightful lord. The poet, similarly, struggles to _____ and _____.
    - The town's rightful lord appointed a 'viceroy' to 'defend' it on his behalf. _____, similarly, gave the poet the faculty of _____ with which to _____.

Lines 9 to 14

8. The poet presents his feelings towards God in what might be described as romantic terms. What phrase indicates this?
9. Who or what is god's 'enemy'? What does the term 'betrothed' suggest about the poet's relationship with this enemy?
10. **True or false:** The poet calls on God to break up this relationship.
11. **Class Discussion:** The poet calls on God to 'imprison' him. What action on God's part is being imagined here?

Exam Prep

1. **Personal Response:** Donne's poetry is known for its outrageous claims and demands. In this poem, for instance, he calls on God to 'make [him] new'. In what sense, do you think, Donne wants to be re-invented? In what sense would his life be altered by this remaking?
2. **Class Discussion:** The poet mentions the faculty of 'reason':
    - As a class, list three or four terms you might associate with this faculty.
    - What role did the poet expect 'reason' to play in his life?
    - Why according to the poet did reason fail to play this role?
3. **Theme Talk:** 'Donne always thinks of himself as special, even when it comes to sinning. He insists the normal path to redemption isn't good enough for him; he requires special treatment'. Write a short essay in response to this statement, referring to 'Batter my Heart' and the other 'holy' sonnets on the course.

Language Lab

1. Donne is poet well-known for paradox and contradiction:
    - What phrase indicates that the poet wants God to _____ or enslave him?
    - The poet claims there is only one way he can find freedom. What is this?
    - The term 'ravish' has multiple meanings. Which do you think is most relevant to line 14?
    - Describe in your own words why lines 13 and 14 are both examples of the literary device known as paradox.
2. What three words would you use to describe the poem's tone? Are you surprised that someone would use such a tone when addressing God?
3. In the Bible, the nation of Israel, when it sinned against God, was compared to a defective piece of pottery, a captured town and a woman trapped in an adulterous relationship. Suggest how these images might have influenced Donne's poem.

Thou hast made me

Thou hast made me, and shall thy work decay?
Repair me now, for now mine end doth haste,
I run to death, and death meets me as fast,
And all my pleasures are like yesterday;
I dare not move my dim eyes any way, [5]
Despair behind, and death before doth cast
Such terror, and my feebled flesh doth waste
By sin in it, which it towards hell doth weigh.
Only thou art above, and when towards thee
By thy leave I can look, I rise again; [10]
But our old subtle foe so tempteth me,
That not one hour I can myself sustain;
Thy grace may wing me to prevent his art,
And thou like adamant draw mine iron heart.

Annotations
[2] *doth:* does
[2] *haste:* hurry
[7] *feebled:* enfeebled, weakened, decayed
[8] *weigh:* lean, droop
[10] *leave:* permission
[11] *tempteth:* tempts
[14] *adamant:* magnet

Tease It Out

1. **Class Discussion:** Consider the 'work' mentioned in Line 1:
   - Does this term refer to the poet's soul, to his body or to both?
   - Who is responsible for this 'work'?
   - What has happened to this work in recent years?
   - What action the poet want God to undertake with regard to this work?
   - When must this task be undertaken?
   - Why is this a matter of some urgency for the poet?
2. What fast approaching event is mentioned in line 3?
3. What phrase suggests that the poet's 'pleasures' are a thing of the past? Suggest at last three different activities the poet might have in mind here.
4. The poet describes his eyes as being 'dim'? Is he referring a) to his power of vision, b) to the appearance of his eyes or c) to both?
5. Donne uses a conceit or extended metaphor to describe his predicament, declaring that he is unable to look in any direction:
   - What does the poet 'see' when he looks back? What does this suggest about his attitude towards the past?
   - What does the poet 'see' when he looks ahead? How does this prospect make him feel?
   - What is described as being below the poet? What weighs or drags him downwards?
   - Who or what is described as being 'above' the poet? Is it easy for the poet to look upwards? What kind of activity or behaviour would this looking upwards involve?
6. **Class Discussion:** Consider the phrase 'I rise again'. In what sense is the poet 'rising' at such moments? Is he referring to his body, his soul or his emotions?
7. What does line 6 suggest about the poet's physical condition? According to the poet, what causes this malaise?
8. The poet claims he cannot 'sustain' himself for even an hour. What does he mean by this? Who or what prevents him from doing so?
9. **Class Discussion:** What do you understand by the idea of God's 'grace'? What impact will this 'grace' have on the poet's life? What metaphor does he use to describe this impact?
10. Read the poem's final line carefully:
    - Who or what is compared to a piece of iron?
    - Who or what is compared to a magnet?
    - What does the poet envisage the magnet doing?
    - What activity or outcome is suggested by this metaphor?

Exam Prep

1. **Personal Response:** Do you think it is accurate to describe 'Thou hast made me' as a kind of prayer? What features might set it apart from more conventional prayers?
2. **Class Discussion:** Discuss the following questions as a class, then write your own response to each one:
   - Is Donne a poet of the intellect rather than of the emotions?
   - What emotion comes across most clearly in this poem? Is it fear, rage, self-disgust, desperation or something else entirely?
   - What view of God emerges from this poem? Does He come across as gentle and forgiving or as stern and vengeful?
3. **Theme Talk:** This poem is often compared to 'Batter my heart'. Do you think there is a similar attitude to religion in these poems? Which of them do you prefer? Give a reason for your answer.
4. **Exam Prep:** Donne presents a bleak and unappealing view of religion and spirituality'. Write an essay in response to this statement in which you refer to this poem, 'The Anniversary', 'Batter my heart' and 'A Valediction'.

Language Lab

1. How would you describe the poet's tone in 'Thou hast made me'? Does he address God in a haughty fashion or a humble one? Refer to specific words and phrases in your answer.
2. Consider the phrase 'old subtle foe'. What impression of the devil is created by this phrase? What according to the poem is the devil's' art'? What phrase indicates that the devil is exceptionally gifted at this art?
3. Try to identify each of the metaphors used by Donne in this poem. Which metaphor do you think is most effective? Give a reason for your choice.

At the round earth's imagined corners

At the round earth's imagined corners, blow
Your trumpets, angels, and arise, arise
From death, you numberless infinities
Of souls, and to your scattered bodies go;
All whom the flood did, and fire shall o'erthrow, [5]
All whom war, dearth, age, agues, tyrannies,
Despair, law, chance, hath slain, and you whose eyes
Shall behold God and never taste death's woe.
But let them sleep, Lord, and me mourn a space,
For if above all these my sins abound, [10]
'Tis late to ask abundance of thy grace
When we are there; here on this lowly ground
Teach me how to repent; for that's as good
As if thou hadst sealed my pardon with thy blood.

Annotations

The description of the angels at the earth's 'corners' comes from the Book of Revelation, the final book of the New Testament, which contains an account of how the world will end: 'And after these things I saw four angels standing on the four corners of the earth'

[5] *fire:* the fire that will accompany the world's end

[6] *dearth:* famine; poverty

[6] *agues:* fevers or illnesses

[6] *tyrannies:* cruel, oppressive regimes

[7] *hath slain:* has killed

[8] *and never taste death's woe:* those who are free of sin and still alive when God appears on the Day of Judgement. These people will go straight to heaven without dying

[9] *a space:* for a short time

[10] *my sins abound:* my sins are even more plentiful

[11] *abundance of thy grace:* God's generous blessing or forgiveness

[14] *sealed my pardon:* guaranteed my forgiveness

Tease It Out

1. A vast number of people have lived and died since the beginning of the world. What phrase indicates this?
2. The 'flood' killed many people. To what biblical story is the poet referring?
3. Describe in your own words three other causes of death described by the poet.
4. **Class Discussion:** Where have the souls of these dead people been residing?
5. What phrase suggests that their bodily remains are to be found all over the world?
6. How will angels signal that the end of the world has come?
7. What will the souls of the dead do at this moment?
8. **Class Discussion:** Some people will still be living when the angelic trumpets sound and the end of the world arrives.
    - According to Donne, will these people ever experience death?
    - Suggest what will happen to these bodies and souls now that the world has ended.
    - What phrase indicates that these individuals will experience God in a special way?
9. The poet in the first eight lines is eager for the end of the world to come. What phrases indicate this? Can you suggest why he is so eager?
10. In what line does the poet change his mind about wanting this to happen?
11. The poet considers himself to be a truly terrible sinner. What phrase indicates this?
12. **True of false:** It will be too late when the world ends to seek forgiveness for his sins.
13. What do you understand by the term 'lowly ground'?
14. What does the poet want to accomplish while he is still on this 'lowly ground'?

Exam Prep

1. **Personal Response:** Write a few lines describing your understanding of the term 'repent'. Why must Donne be taught how to do this? Rank the following in order of plausibility:
    - Donne knows little about Christianity and requires special instruction
    - Donne is asking God to grant him resolve and mental fortitude
    - Donne is a special person who requires God to enter his life in a special way
2. **Class Discussion:** 'Donne presents a very bleak view of religion, one obsessed with sin, death and damnation'. Discuss this statement as a class, referring to the three Holy Sonnets on your course.
3. **Exam Prep:** Write an introduction to the poetry of John Donne aimed at transition year students. You should mention two poems that focus on spirituality and two poems that focus on romantic and sexual love. Don't forget to mention Donne's use of metaphor and other literary devices.

Language Lab

1. Donne is well known as a poet of paradox and contradiction.
    - Would you agree that the poem's opening line contains such a contradiction?
    - What common expression is referred to in this line?
    - Search for images of 17th century maps of the world. Can you suggest how these might have influenced this line?
2. Donne's poetry is known for its outrageous claims and demands. Read the poem carefully. Identify one such claim and one such demand and state why each might be decribed as outrageous.
3. The poem's conclusion features a typically inventive simile. Repentence is compared to a legal document sealed in Christ's own blood. Come up with three similes of your own that compare an abstract concept (such as victory, sorrow, desire) to a physical object.

Patrick Kavanagh

Patrick Kavanagh was born in Inniskeen, in the townland of Mucker, Co. Monaghan in 1904. Kavanagh was one of ten children. His father was a shoemaker by trade and the family also had a small farm. Kavanagh's father worked hard, from six in the morning till nearly midnight each day, his kitchen alive with the talk of customers and journeyman cobblers. Kavanagh left school at thirteen, and it was expected that he would follow in his father's footsteps and become a shoemaker and part-time farmer.

The young Kavanangh spent his days working on the family farm or as hired hand on the farms of his neighbours. He would thin turnips, spray potatoes and haul dung in a cart. When the weather was too wet for farming he would spend his time learning his father's trade. There was always a sense, however, in which Kavanagh was not cut out for the life his parents chose for him. He was always something of a dreamer who tended to have his head in the clouds or stuck in a book. From the age of about twelve he began writing verses of his own. As he grew older he began sending his work to various journals, newspapers and literary magazines. Gradually, he began to see himself as a poet, as someone who was different from the other farmers in his parish.

When his father died in 1929, Patrick became the man of the house, his mother's mainstay and support. Antoinette Quinn describes what was for many years his daily routine: 'Rise at 6 to 7a.m. on weekdays, feed the hens, milk the cows, tend the fire, prepare the breakfast, work all day on the farm except in very wet or wintry weather, home at noon for dinner, finish work at sunset in time for tea. After tea he cycled to the village to buy the paper, practise football, visit a friend, gossip with the neighbourhood lads at the Chunk or play pitch and toss. Invariably, every evening, either before or after these leisure time activities, he would devote a couple of hours to literary pursuits, reading and scribbling by candlelight in an upstairs bedroom'.

Of course there was always the dances which he loved to attend, though he was an awkward and clumsy dancer. Quinn tells us that he 'generally joined a group of male wallflowers, middle-aged spectators who passed the time commenting on the merits and demerits of the dancing couples. One of their staple topics of discussion was the likely number of virgins among the women present. For him, as for most of his acquaintances, the draw of the dance place was the proximity of so many pretty young women; he would select the prettiest and then follow her progress, rarely approaching her but agonising over the possible success of those who did'.

He was better suited to the Gaelic-football field than the dance floor. He was taller than most of his companions and he became the Inniskeen goalkeeper in 1929. He was, however, a rather erratic and unreliable one. Easily bored with standing about when nothing was happening in his vicinity, he had a habit of deserting

"My advice is this, do whatever pleases yourself. These things don't matter. What does matter is that if you have anything worth while in you, any talent, you should deliver it. Nothing must turn you from that."

his goal to run up the field and take close-in frees, hot-footing it back before the action returned to his end of the pitch. On one occasion he left his goal to go and buy ice-cream.

In the late 1930s Kavanagh's life began to change. His first book, *The Ploughman and Other Poems*, was published in 1936, and an autobiography, *The Green Fool*, was published in 1938. In the wake of these publications, Kavanagh left Co. Monaghan and moved to Dublin in order to focus on his writing. In Dublin, Kavanagh worked as a journalist, columnist and film reviewer, but often experienced periods of grinding poverty. In 1952 he and his brother Peter founded *Kavanagh's Weekly*, a newspaper in which he scrutinised and criticised every aspect of Irish society. The paper folded after only thirteen issues.

During this time Kavanagh wrote 'Advent', 'A Christmas Childhood' and 'On Raglan Road'. Yet his poetry did not win him the fame and fortune he so desired. His two major works of this period, a long poem called 'The Great Hunger' and a novel called *Tarry Flynn*, were banned by the Irish state because of their grimly realistic portrayal of Irish rural life. These works frankly depicted the sexual and social repression common in rural Ireland of the time. This was a message the authorities were not ready or willing for the people of Ireland to hear.

Kavanagh became something of a fixture in the bars frequented by the city's literary community, acquiring a reputation as a wild, eccentric and unpredictable character. He could be gruff, rude and contrary but also kind and generous. Just as in Monaghan, Kavanagh felt like something of an outsider. In Monaghan he felt different to the other farmers because of his poetic leanings. In Dublin he felt different to the other writers because of what they saw as his humble country origins. He could be intensely critical of his fellow Dublin poets and writers, and in his satirical poem 'The Dunciad' portrayed the majority of them as talentless time-wasters.

In 1954 Kavanagh's life changed once again. He sued *The Leader* newspaper for libel but lost, an undertaking that left him in dire financial straits. He was also diagnosed with lung cancer and was admitted to hospital where he had a lung removed. Yet it was in this dark time that Kavanagh felt he was 'reborn' as a poet and a person. He recovered from this operation by relaxing on the banks of the Grand Canal in Dublin, where he wrote 'Canal Bank Walk', 'The Hospital' and 'Lines Written on a Seat on the Grand Canal, Dublin'. The negative experience of the past year filled him with a new sense of calmness and acceptance, and he vowed to appreciate the beauty in the 'habitual' and 'banal' things that surrounded him.

In his later years Kavanagh's poetry began to receive the acclaim he felt it had always deserved. His reputation began to grow, not only in Ireland but also in the United States and Britain. He won several awards and was invited to give lectures in UCD and in various American colleges. He also became a hero – if not a legend – to the younger generation of Irish writers. He represented Ireland at international literature conferences and became a judge of the Guinness Poetry Awards. Kavanagh died in a Dublin nursing home on 30 November 1967. Shortly before his death he had married Katherine Moloney, his long-time companion.

Inniskeen Road: July Evening

The bicycles go by in twos and threes –
There's a dance in Billy Brennan's barn tonight,
And there's the half-talk code of mysteries
And the wink-and-elbow language of delight.
Half-past eight and there is not a spot
Upon a mile of road, no shadow thrown
That might turn out a man or woman, not
A footfall tapping secrecies of stone.

I have what every poet hates in spite
Of all the solemn talk of contemplation.
Oh, Alexander Selkirk knew the plight
Of being king and government and nation.
A road, a mile of kingdom. I am king
Of banks and stones and every blooming thing.

Annotations

Inniskeen: the County Monaghan village where Kavanagh was born and is buried. The parish hall in Inniskeen was an important social venue in Kavanagh's time, and dances were regularly held there.

[11] ***Alexander Selkirk:*** (1676–1721) a famous Scottish sailor who spent over four years as a castaway on an otherwise uninhabited island in the South Pacific Ocean. Daniel Defoe's classic novel *Robinson Crusoe* was inspired by Selkirk's story.

Tease It Out

1. The poem is set on the evening of a local dance. What is the atmosphere like in the locality? Which words and phrases do you think help us to imagine the scene and feel what it was like to be there?
2. Why would a dance have been held in a barn rather than a dance hall or some other venue? What kind of community is the poem depicting?
3. Is the dance important to the local people? Which words or phrases tell us about their attitude to the dance?
4. What could the poet mean when he talks about 'the half-talk code of mysteries/ And the wink-and-elbow language of delight'?
5. Does Kavanagh fully share in the joyful mood that he senses all around him? Give reasons for your answer.
6. How has the poet's environment changed by half-past eight? What does he see around him? How do you think he feels at that point?
7. What do you think Kavanagh means when he says that Alexander Selkirk knew how difficult it was to be 'king and government and nation'?
8. Why do you think Kavanagh might have mentioned Alexander Selkirk? How is the poet's situation like Selkirk's?
9. What is it that Kavanagh has that 'every poet hates'? Why do you think every poet would hate it?
10. When Kavanagh draws a contrast between 'the solemn talk of contemplation' and the thing that every poet hates, what do you think he is telling us about the life and responsibilities of a poet?
11. We would usually associate being a king with a life of power and luxury, but in what sense is Kavanagh a king? What is his kingdom? How is the poet's life like that of a king?
12. How do you think the poet fits in with his community? Do you think that being a poet makes him feel different in any way? Give reasons for your answer.
13. How do you think Kavanagh feels about Inniskeen, the place in which he was born and grew up? Is there anything in the poem that helps us to answer this question?

Exam Prep

1. **Personal Response:** The place where he was born and raised obviously means a great deal to Kavanagh and is ever-present in his writing. Think about how you feel about the place where you live. What are the things about it that matter to you? What do you love about your location, and what bothers or irritates you about it?
2. **Class Discussion:** What do you think the poem as a whole says about the poet's life? Does it make that life sound attractive or difficult?
3. **Theme Talk:** How do you think rural life is portrayed in 'Inniskeen Road: July Evening'? What kind of society does the poem depict? Is it an attractive one? What do you think it would be like to be a poet or artist in an environment like that? Working together in small groups, look through the poem to find any evidence that might help to answer these questions?
4. **Exam Prep:** 'In Kavanagh's poetry, larger themes and questions can never be truly separated from local environments and very personal feelings about them'. Discuss this statement with reference to 'Inniskeen Road: July Evening' and two other poems by Kavanagh.

Language Lab

1. In the first stanza, Kavanagh uses repetition and parallel structures to intensify the rhythm of the poem and to evoke a mood. How well do you think he succeeds? Can you give some examples of how he uses repetition to depict the scene unfolding around him?
2. The mood of the poem seems to change as it moves into the second stanza and the poet begins to address us in the first person. Why do you think he does this? In your opinion, does the change to the first person work? Give reasons for your answers.
3. Look at the phrase 'every blooming thing' in the concluding line. Could it have a deeper meaning along with the obvious one? What might the phrase tell us about the poet's relationship to rural life?

Shancoduff

My black hills have never seen the sun rising,
Eternally they look north towards Armagh.
Lot's wife would not be salt if she had been
Incurious as my black hills that are happy
When dawn whitens Glassdrummond chapel. [5]

My hills hoard the bright shillings of March
While the sun searches in every pocket.
They are my Alps and I have climbed the Matterhorn
With a sheaf of hay for three perishing calves
In the field under the Big Forth of Rocksavage. [10]

The sleety winds fondle the rushy beards of Shancoduff
While the cattle-drovers sheltering in the Featherna Bush
Look up and say: "Who owns them hungry hills
That the water-hen and snipe must have forsaken?
A poet? Then by heavens he must be poor." [15]
I hear, and is my heart not badly shaken?

Annotations

Shancoduff: a townland in County Monaghan. In the 1920s, the Kavanaghs bought some boggy land there, and Patrick worked on it.
[3] Lot's wife: a biblical figure whose story is told in the Book of Genesis. She was warned by an angel not to look back as she fled from the city of Sodom, which God was about to destroy because of its legendary sinfulness. She disobeyed that warning and was turned into a pillar of salt.
[5] Glassdrummond: a townland in County Armagh
[8] Alps: Europe's highest and most extensive mountain range
[8] Matterhorn: one of the highest mountains in the Alps; it rises to 4,477 metres in height
[10] Rocksavage: an estate near Inniskeen, County Monaghan. The Kavanaghs rented land there.
[10] forth: a prehistoric hill forth; Kavanagh ironically compares this low mound to the Matterhorn
[12] cattle-drovers: people who brought cattle to market, usually on foot and often with the help of dogs
[14] water-hen: a water bird often found in marshes and lakes
[14] snipe: a wading bird found in marshes and wet meadows

Tease It Out

1. Why do you think Kavanagh twice uses the word 'my' to indicate his relationship to the black hills?
2. It seems odd to compare a set of hills to the biblical character Lot's wife. What was it about her that brought about her very unusual and harsh punishment?
3. What is it about the hills that makes them so different from Lot's wife and enables them to avoid her tragic fate? What do you think the poet is saying about his beloved landscape here?
4. How would you describe Kavanagh's attitude to the hills he describes? Is it personal or detached? Pick out some phrases and words that support your answer.
5. At the beginning of the second stanza, the poet says that his hills 'hoard shillings'. What is he referring to here?
6. The image of the hills having their pockets searched by the sun is striking and unusual. What do you think it means?
7. When he compares his black hills to the Alps, Kavanagh seems to be deliberately exaggerating. Why might he be doing this?
8. Is the poet aware that his own view of his hills is not shared by everyone? Which words and phrases help us to answer that question?
9. Why do you think the cattle-drovers might have seen the hills in different terms than Kavanagh did?
10. Although the poet looks at the hills in figurative, loving terms, there was clearly another, harsher, side to life in that environment. Which lines and phrases tell us about that aspect of life there?
11. How do you think the cattle-drovers might have regarded the life and work of a poet?
12. What insights might the poet have that the cattle-drovers are lacking? How do you think this might be connected to his poetic vocation?
13. At the end of the poem, Kavanagh suggests that his heart might be 'badly shaken'. Do you think that he would be shaken (a) because he sadly realises that what he has overheard is true, (b) because he fundamentally disagrees with what he hears or (c) because he feels torn between these two responses? Give reasons for your answer.
14. Do you think that Kavanagh likes being a farmer as well as a poet? How do think these two aspects of his life might relate to each other?

Exam Prep

1. **Personal Response:** Which images of nature do you find most effective in the poem? Give reasons for your answer.
2. **Class Discussion:** In what ways does the poet's attitude to the local landscape resemble that of a lover? What insights might this give us into Kavanagh's personality and his distinctive approach to poetry?
3. **Theme Talk:** Do you think that the depiction of rural life in 'Shancoduff' is a realistic one? Which details suggest that the poet was very familiar with this kind of life?
4. **Exam Prep:** 'In 'Shancoduff', as in so much of his poetry, Kavanagh finds magic in everyday things that others overlook.' Write a short essay in response to this statement, referring to at least three Kavanagh poems on your course.

Language Lab

1. In 'Shancoduff', as in other poems, Kavanagh makes clever use of repetition as he sets the scene for his readers. Pick out three examples of repetition in the poem. Explain why you think each one works effectively.
2. Kavanagh uses vivid words and phrases to contrast the great value he sees in his local environment with the drovers' dismissive attitude towards it. Which words and phrases express (a) Kavanagh's and (b) the drovers' respective attitudes to the landscape depicted in the poem? In your own words, describe these two contrasting attitudes.
3. The poet personifies his beloved landscape in various ways. Pick out three of the phrases and comparisons that he uses to do this. Write a brief note about what each of them tells us about the landscape and how the poet sees it.

Epic

I have lived in important places, times
When great events were decided; who owned
That half a rood of rock, a no-man's land
Surrounded by our pitchfork-armed claims.
I heard the Duffys shouting 'Damn your soul' [5]
And old McCabe, stripped to the waist, seen
Step the plot defying blue cast-steel –
'Here is the march along these iron stones.'
That was the year of the Munich bother. Which
Was most important? I inclined [10]
To lose my faith in Ballyrush and Gortin
Till Homer's ghost came whispering to my mind.
He said: I made the *Iliad* from such
A local row. Gods make their own importance.

Annotations

Epic: A long poem that narrates the deeds and adventures of heroic or legendary figures

[3] *rood:* an old measure of land area that was equivalent to a quarter of an acre

[4] *Duffys:* This name may have been chosen in part as an allusion to the Irish nationalist and fascist politician Eoin O'Duffy, who formed a right-wing paramilitary movement known as the Blueshirts and raised an Irish Brigade to fight for General Franco in the Spanish Civil War.

[8] *the year of the Munich bother:* In 1938 a European war was narrowly averted when Germany's annexation of part of Czechoslovakia was accepted by Britain and France in an agreement signed in Munich.

[9] *Ballyrush:* a townland near Kavanagh's birthplace, Inniskeen, in County Monaghan

[9] *Gortin:* another townland in rural County Monaghan

[10] *Homer:* author of the *Iliad* and the *Odyssey*, the two epic poems that were at the centre of ancient Greek literature and culture

[11] *Iliad:* epic poem that narrates part of the ten-year-long siege of the city of Troy (Ilium) by an alliance of Greek states

Tease It Out

1. When Kavanagh talks about having lived in places where great events is decided, how serious is he being? What point do you think he is making?
2. The poet may be alluding not only to purely local events that he has witnessed but also to then recent developments in Irish history. What larger events might he have in mind?
3. What is being disputed between the two rival families or clans?
4. **Class Discussion:** Why do you think the poet compares the local dispute over land to the big international quarrels that culminated in the Munich agreement of September 1938?
5. Why might Kavanagh be 'inclined' to 'lose faith' in the two local places mentioned?
6. Homer's ghost came to the poet to remind him of something important about the relationship between real-life events and poetry. What was it?
7. What is the 'local row' from which Homer made the *Iliad*?
8. Why do you think Kavanagh might have chosen to give Homer an important role in 'Epic'?
9. How does it compare to the local dispute that Kavanagh has in mind?
10. "Gods make their own importance." What does Kavanagh mean by this?

Exam Prep

1. **Personal Response:** Think of some local events that are important to your own family or community. Devoting a paragraph to each one, consider how each event might be compared to a larger story that you have heard about or seen in the news. Explain briefly how doing this might give you new insights into Kavanagh's 'Epic'.
2. **Class Discussion:** Land is deeply important both to Kavanagh as a poet and to the feuding families who are prepared to fight each other over a quarter acre. What might Kavanagh have thought about the quarrelling families? Would he have understood their struggle? Why does he think it deserves to be commemorated in a poem?
3. **Theme Talk:** In 'Epic', Kavanagh gives us a practising poet's insights into how the epic stories of great literature spring from the ordinary events of life as it is lived. In your own words, but with relevant quotations from the poem, explain the main points that Kavanagh is making about the origins of great poetry.
4. **Exam Prep:** 'For Kavanagh, the smaller things that shape our lives are just as important as the celebrated adventures of kings and legendary heroes'. Write a short essay in response to this statement, making reference to 'Epic' and at least three other Kavanagh poems.

Language Lab

1. 'Although he frequently uses irony when comparing smaller, local disputes with the great events of history, Kavanagh also wants to tell us that even the smaller events are important when seen from the perspective of those involved'. Write a few paragraphs in response to this statement.
2. Although it is called 'Epic' and alludes to lengthy accounts of the adventures of kings and heroes, this poem is written in the short form known as the sonnet. Why do you think Kavanagh may have chosen to write this poem as a sonnet? How might his choice of form relate to what he has to say in the poem?

from The Great Hunger

I

Clay is the word and clay is the flesh
Where the potato-gatherers like mechanised scare-crows move
Along the side-fall of the hill — Maguire and his men.
If we watch them an hour is there anything we can prove
Of life as it is broken-backed over the Book [5]
Of Death? Here crows gabble over worms and frogs
And the gulls like old newspapers are blown clear of the hedges, luckily.
Is there some light of imagination in these wet clods?
Or why do we stand here shivering?
   Which of these men [10]
Loved the light and the queen
Too long virgin? Yesterday was summer. Who was it promised marriage to himself
Before apples were hung from the ceilings for Hallowe'en?
We will wait and watch the tragedy to the last curtain,
Till the last soul passively like a bag of wet clay [15]
Rolls down the side of the hill, diverted by the angles
Where the plough missed or a spade stands, straitening the way.

A dog lying on a torn jacket under a heeled-up cart,
A horse nosing along the posied headland, trailing
A rusty plough. Three heads hanging between wide-apart legs. [20]
October playing a symphony on a slack wire paling.
Maguire watches the drills flattened out
And the flints that lit a candle for him on a June altar
Flameless. The drills slipped by and the days slipped by
And he trembled his head away and ran free from the world's halter, [25]
And thought himself wiser than any man in the townland
When he laughed over pints of porter
Of how he came free from every net spread
In the gaps of experience. He shook a knowing head
And pretended to his soul [30]
That children are tedious in hurrying fields of April
Where men are spanning across wide furrows.
Lost in the passion that never needs a wife
The pricks that pricked were the pointed pins of harrows.
Children scream so loud that the crows could bring [35]
The seed of an acre away with crow-rude jeers.
Patrick Maguire, he called his dog and he flung a stone in the air
And hallooed the birds away that were the birds of the years.
Turn over the weedy clods and tease out the tangled skeins.
What is he looking for there? [40]
He thinks it is a potato, but we know better
Than his mud-gloved fingers probe in this insensitive hair.

'Move forward the basket and balance it steady
In this hollow. Pull down the shafts of that cart, Joe,
And straddle the horse,' Maguire calls. [45]
'The wind's over Brannagan's, now that means rain.
Graip up some withered stalks and see that no potato falls

Annotations

[1] *Clay is ... the flesh*: An ironic allusion to the description in John's Gospel of the conception and birth of Jesus: "And the Word was made flesh and dwelt amongst us" [John, 1:14]. Kavanagh is contrasting this spiritual text with the materialistic values of rural Ireland in his time.

[11/12] *the queen/ Too long virgin:* probably alludes to the Virgin Mary, who was held up by the Catholic Church as a model of purity

[13] *apples were hung from the ceilings:* An old Halloween game required participants, whose arms were tied behind their backs, to take a bite from an apple hanging on a string.

[18] *heeled-up cart:* a cart lying on its tail-board so that its shafts face upwards

[32] *spanging:* a dialect word meaning moving quickly or in jumping motions

[34] *The pricks that pricked:* allusion to Acts 9:5 in the King James Bible: "It is hard for thee to kick against the pricks". The image refers to how cattle pointlessly kick out in protest when they are jabbed with pointed sticks to keep them moving.

[39] *skeins:* loosely coiled lengths of thread or yarn; metaphorically: parts of a complex network or system

[47] *Graip:* a long-handled fork for digging potatoes

[48] *ruckety:* a dialect word meaning uneven or bumpy

Over the tail-board going down the ruckety pass –
And *that's* a job we'll have to do in December,
Gravel it and build a kerb on the bog-side. Is that Cassidy's ass [50]
Out in my clover? Curse o' God –
Where is that dog?
Never where he's wanted.' Maguire grunts and spits
Through a clay-wattled moustache and stares about him from the height.
His dream changes like the cloud-swung wind [55]
And he is not so sure now if his mother was right
When she praised the man who made a field his bride.

Watch him, watch him, that man on a hill whose spirit
Is a wet sack flapping about the knees of time.
He lives that his little fields may stay fertile when his own body [60]
Is spread in the bottom of a ditch under two coulters crossed in Christ's Name.

He was suspicious in his youth as a rat near strange bread,
When girls laughed; when they screamed he knew that meant
The cry of fillies in season. He could not walk
The easy road to destiny. He dreamt [65]
The innocence of young brambles to hooked treachery.
O the grip, O the grip of irregular fields! No man escapes.
It could not be that back of the hills love was free
And ditches straight.
No monster hand lifted up children and put down apes [70]
As here.
          'O God if I had been wiser!'
That was his sigh like the brown breeze in the thistles.
He looks, towards his house and haggard. 'O God if I had been wiser!'
But now a crumpled leaf from the whitethorn bushes [75]
Darts like a frightened robin, and the fence
Shows the green of after-grass through a little window,
And he knows that his own heart is calling his mother a liar.
God's truth is life – even the grotesque shapes of his foulest fire.

The horse lifts its head and cranes [80]
Through the whins and stones
To lip late passion in the crawling clover.
In the gap there's a bush weighted with boulders like morality,
The fools of life bleed if they climb over.

The wind leans from Brady's, and the coltsfoot leaves are holed with rust, [85]
Rain fills the cart-tracks and the sole-plate grooves;
A yellow sun reflects in Donaghmoyne
The poignant light in puddles shaped by hooves.
Come with me, Imagination, into this iron house
And we will watch from the doorway the years run back, [90]
And we will know what a peasant's left hand wrote on the page.
Be easy, October. No cackle hen, horse neigh, tree sough, duck quack.

Annotations
[59] ***a wet sack flapping:*** when they had to kneel down in muddy fields, farmers sometimes wore a sack over their trousers
[61] ***coulter:*** a vertical cutting blade attached at the front of a ploughshare
[64] ***fillies:*** young female horses, especially ones under four years old
[85] ***coltsfoot:*** a plant of the daisy family; used in herbal medicine to treat coughs and respiratory problems
[86] ***sole-plate:*** horseshoe
[87] ***Donaghmoyne:*** a parish near Kavanagh's native Inniskeen

Tease It Out

1. **Class Discussion:** The poem opens with a strange, almost biblical, statement: 'Clay is the word and clay is the flesh'.
   - Having read the entire excerpt, what do you think this might mean?
   - What is being said about the values of rural Ireland at the time?
   - Why might the poet have decided to use a biblical phrase here?
2. What kind of work is being done at the beginning of the poem?
3. What sort of mood is the poet creating as he describes this work?
4. What month is it?
5. As we watch Maguire and his mean in the fields, we are asked what this might tell us about 'life at it is broken-backed over the Book of Death'. What could this mean? What are we being told to watch out for?
6. Who might the queen mentioned in Line 11 be? Give reasons for your answer.
7. Why would apples have been hung from the ceiling at Halloween?
8. Line 14 says that we will 'watch the tragedy to the last curtain'. This is one of several phrases that suggest we are looking at events taking place in a play. How might this perspective shape our attitudes to the characters and events we are reading about?
9. **Class Discussion:** What kind of tragedy is unfolding in 'The Great Hunger'? Working in pairs, see if you can describe it in your own words. Support your answer with references to the poem.
10. What promise did Patrick Maguire make to himself but fail to keep?
11. What reasons did he give to himself for his failure to keep this promise?
12. Maguire once 'thought himself wiser than any man in the townland'. Was he right? Give reasons for your answer.
13. Maguire 'trembled his head away and ran free from the world's halter'. To what kind of creature is he being compared here? How successful was he in his instinctive effort to be free from all ties and constraints?
14. Did Maguire think that it would have been good for him to have children? Give reasons for your answer.
15. The poet tells us that although Maguire thinks that he is looking in the clay for potatoes, 'we know better'. What do you think this means? What else could Maguire be looking for?
16. '[H]e laughed over pints of porter/ Of how he came free from every net spread/ In the gaps of experience'. In your own words, what do you think this means? What kinds of nets are we talking about?
17. From what did Maguire believe himself to have escaped?
18. Which words of phrases suggest (a) that he may have been mistaken in this and (b) that he was not entirely convinced by his own opinions about marriage and children?
19. In Maguire's life, what has taken the place of marriage?
20. Which important figure in his life discouraged him from getting married? Why?
21. **Class Discussion:** Because he was cynical and suspicious as a young man, Maguire could see only 'hooked treachery' in the 'innocence of young brambles'. How do you think this would have affected his life? Support your answer with references to the poem.
22. Why do you think Maguire was suspicious when he saw girls laughing? Of what was he afraid?
23. 'He could not walk the easy road to destiny'. Where would this road have taken Maguire? Why does the poet describe it as 'easy'?
24. What is Maguire saying about life in rural Ireland when he tells us that no man escapes 'the grip of irregular fields'?
25. What repeated phrase tells us that Maguire regrets the choices he made earlier in life?
26. Maguire's heart tells him that his mother lied to him. What lie did his mother tell him, and how did it affect him?
27. In what sense might morality be like the boulders that weigh down the bush in the gap?
28. Why do you think Maguire's 'own heart is calling his mother a liar' as he looks back over his life? What might the rather odd phrasing here suggest about how willing he is to consciously blame his mother? How do you think he looks back at his mother's influence on his life?
29. 'The fools of life bleed if they climb over [this boulder].' What might Kavanagh be saying here about the power of moral rules and customs in a rural society?
30. What will Maguire's imagination allow or compel him to do in the remainder of 'The Great Hunger'? Do you think this opening section of the poem has set the scene effectively? Give a reason for your answer.

Exam Prep

1. **Personal Response:** Imagine that you are Patrick Maguire. Relying on information provided in 'The Great Hunger', write a brief essay explaining what kind of relationship you have with the land you farm, what daily life is like for you, why you never got married or had children, how your mother influenced your opinions and how you now look back on the decisions you made in your life.
2. **Class Discussion:** When he was younger, Maguire told himself that he was wise to avoid marriage? What reasons did he give in support of this opinion? Does he now regret his choice? Why?
3. **Theme Talk:** The phrase 'The Great Hunger' (An Gorta Mór) was often used as a name for the catastrophic potato famine that caused mass starvation in Ireland between 1845 and 1849. Kavanagh alludes to this meaning but focuses rather on a different, metaphorical kind of hunger. Supporting your answer with quotations from the text, write two or three paragraphs explaining what kind of hunger Kavanagh is talking about.
4. **Exam Prep:** 'Kavanagh draws on his first-hand experience to give us a very realistic and unsparing picture of life in rural Ireland'. Write three or four paragraphs in response to this statement, referring to 'The Great Hunger' and at least two other poems on your course.

Language Lab

1. 'Although he gives us a very realistic and unsentimental picture of life in rural Ireland, Kavanagh also makes great use of surreal and bizarre imagery. Giving examples, explain how such imagery helps Kavanagh to set the scene in 'The Great Hunger'.
2. Give some examples of the use of the following literary techniques in the extract from 'The Great Hunger'. In each case, describe the effect that is created for the reader.
    - Alliteration (the repeated use of words beginning with the same letter)
    - Metaphor (drawing comparisons between apparently dissimilar things)
    - Onomatopoeia (where the sound of a word resembles its meaning

Advent

We have tested and tasted too much, lover —
Through a chink too wide there comes in no wonder.
But here in the Advent-darkened room
Where the dry black bread and the sugarless tea
Of penance will charm back the luxury [5]
Of a child's soul, we'll return to Doom
The knowledge we stole but could not use.

And the newness that was in every stale thing
When we looked at it as children: the spirit-shocking
Wonder in a black slanting Ulster hill [10]
Or the prophetic astonishment in the tedious talking
Of an old fool will awake for us and bring
You and me to the yard gate to watch the whins
And the bog-holes, cart-tracks, old stables where Time begins.

O after Christmas we'll have no need to go searching [15]
For the difference that sets an old phrase burning —
We'll hear it in the whispered argument of a churning
Or in the streets where the village boys are lurching.
And we'll hear it among decent men too
Who barrow dung in gardens under trees, [20]
Wherever life pours ordinary plenty.
Won't we be rich, my love and I, and please
God we shall not ask for reason's payment,
The why of heart-breaking strangeness in dreeping hedges,
Nor analyse God's breath in common statement. [25]
We have thrown into the dust-bin the clay-minted wages
Of pleasure, knowledge and the conscious hour —
And Christ comes with a January flower.

Annotations

Advent: the period in the Church calendar that leads up to Christmas; it includes the four preceding Sundays. Advent is a period of fasting, penance and renewal.
[6-7] We'll return . . . could not use: alludes to the account in the Book of Genesis of how Adam and Eve were expelled from Paradise because they disobeyed God's wishes and ate the apple from the Tree of Knowledge.
[13] whins: wild bushes with yellow flowers and sharp thorns, also known as gorse
[13-14] the whins . . . begins: the poet is picturing the surroundings in which Christ was born
[14] Time begins: because Christ's birth begins a new era and because Christmas is just before the start of a new year
[24] dreeping hedges: hedges that are dropping or bending down, and dripping with water

Tease It Out

1. At the beginning of the poem, the poet seems to be rather fed up with life. What has made him uneasy and discontented?
2. 'Through a chink too wide there comes in no wonder'. In your own words, try to explain what the poet is telling us in this famous but cryptic line.
3. Kavanagh talks about the fasting and penance that form part of the Advent season's preparations for Christmas. How does he think fasting and penance affect us?
4. What might the poet mean when he says that we 'have tested and tasted too much'?
5. A child's soul is presented as something precious, a 'luxury'. What do you think makes it precious?
6. The poem tells us that children see the world differently. How? [Hint: Look carefully at the second stanza.]
7. Kavanagh suggests that the loss of our childhood innocence is a sort of 'doom'. In what sense might growing old and knowing more be seen in this way?
8. What would happen if somehow we could give back the knowledge that got us into trouble? What would we be like then?
9. How might a child respond differently to 'the tedious talking/ Of an old fool' than an adult might do? Why?
10. Why will we no longer need to go searching after Christmas? What change will have taken place within us?
11. The phrase 'ordinary plenty' is a memorable one. What do you think it means? Why is it important to us?
12. In what sense will we be rich?
13. The poet says that, having been renewed, we will no longer 'ask for reason's payment' or 'the why'? What do you think he means by this?
14. Pleasure, knowledge and 'the conscious hour' are contrasted with wonder and 'ordinary plenty' and described as 'clay-minted'. What do you think 'clay-minted' means?
15. Why would Christ bring us 'a January flower'? What might this flower symbolise?

Exam Prep

1. **Personal Response:** As Christmas draws near, we become increasingly excited as we anticipate the fun that we will have, not to mention the presents we might get. Do you think that "Advent" captures that sense of excitement? Give reasons for your answer.
2. **Class Discussion:** Kavanagh suggests that there is a close connection between childhood and the season of renewal known as advent. In what ways do you think the two are related?
3. **Theme Talk:** "Advent' can be seen as a reflection on the need to recover a sense of innocence on the other side of experience.' Write a brief essay explaining why the poet thinks it is important for us as adults to recover the sense of innocent wonder we had when we were children.
4. **Exam Prep:** 'Kavanagh's poetry is so often concerned with how we might renew ourselves by casting off the burdens of adulthood and learning once again to enjoy life as children do.' Write an essay in response to this statement, referring to 'Advent' and at least three other poems on your course.

Language Lab

1. Reread the poem and find examples of Christian words and images to which Kavanagh gives new meaning. Explain how the poet uses these words and images to give us insights into the importance of wonder and imagination.
2. As it begins, 'Advent' uses apostrophe, a poetic technique which has the speaker turning to address another person. He identifies this person only as 'lover'. Do you think he is talking to another real person, or might he be addressing a different part of himself? Give reasons for your answer.

A Christmas Childhood

I

One side of the potato-pits was white with frost –
How wonderful that was, how wonderful!
And when we put our ears to the paling-post
The music that came out was magical.

The light between the ricks of hay and straw   [5]
Was a hole in Heaven's gable. An apple tree
With its December-glinting fruit we saw –
O you, Eve, were the world that tempted me

To eat the knowledge that grew in clay
And death the germ within it! Now and then   [10]
I can remember something of the gay
Garden that was childhood's. Again

The tracks of cattle to a drinking-place,
A green stone lying sideways in a ditch,
Or any common sight, the transfigured face   [15]
Of a beauty that the world did not touch.

II

My father played the melodeon
Outside at our gate;
There were stars in the morning east
And they danced to his music.   [20]

Across the wild bogs his melodeon called
To Lennons and Callans.
As I pulled on my trousers in a hurry
I knew some strange thing had happened.

Outside in the cow-house my mother   [25]
Made the music of milking;
The light of her stable-lamp was a star
And the frost of Bethlehem made it twinkle.

A water-hen screeched in the bog,
Mass-going feet   [30]
Crunched the wafer-ice on the pot-holes,
Somebody wistfully twisted the bellows wheel.

My child poet picked out the letters
On the grey stone,
In silver the wonder of a Christmas townland,   [35]
The winking glitter of a frosty dawn.

Cassiopeia was over
Cassidy's hanging hill,
I looked and three whin bushes rode across
The horizon — the Three Wise Kings.

And old man passing said:
'Can't he make it talk –
The melodeon.' I hid in the doorway
And tightened the belt of my box-pleated coat.

I nicked six nicks on the door-post
With my penknife's big blade –
There was a little one for cutting tobacco.
And I was six Christmases of age.

My father played the melodeon,
My mother milked the cows,
And I had a prayer like a white rose pinned
On the Virgin Mary's blouse.

Annotations
[17] *melodeon:* a small accordion
[37] **Cassiopeia:** a northern constellation of stars

Tease It Out

Part I

1. What sort of mood is the narrator in at the beginning of the poem?
2. Why might the sight of frost on the potato-pits have seemed wonderful to the child?
3. As you read through the poem, what kind of weather do we find? Do you think that the poet is successful in depicting the natural environment around him? Give reasons for your answer.
4. Name two things commonly seen on farms that he now remembers fondly.
5. When the children looked between the ricks of hay, what did the light they saw conjure up in their imaginations?
6. What would the children have heard as they put their ears up against the fence post?
7. Why do you think the poet mentions Eve? To what is he alluding?
8. How would you describe the child's attitude to the world as it is portrayed at this point in the poem?
9. What happened to the child that changed this attitude?
10. What was the later attitude to the world like and how did it differ from the child's one?
11. When the poet says that childhood was like a garden, which famous garden does he have in mind?
12. In what sense do you think childhood can be seen as a sort of Paradise?
13. **Class Discussion:** In what sense might knowledge be associated with mortality and a kind of death?
14. What was the child able to find in 'any common sight'?

Part II

15. What kind of music might the child's father have been playing at the gate? Would it have been solemn or joyful?
16. The music 'called/ To Lennons and Callans'. What kinds of people are represented by these names? In what sense did the music call them?
17. The young boy knows that 'some strange thing has happened' in his world. Is this a literal change in the world outside or a change brought about by his imaginative response to the Christmas season? Give reasons for your answer.
18. Why does the child now compare the ordinary sights and sounds of his parents' farm to the wonderful scene of the nativity at Bethlehem?
19. What memorable sounds does the child identify in the next verse after the one that mentions Bethlehem?
20. Of whom did the three whin bushes remind the young poet?
21. Why might the boy have hidden behind the doorway while a passer-by commented on his father's melodion playing?
22. Pick out three or four ordinary things or experiences that the child saw as wonderful or magical.
23. Why would the child's prayer be 'like a white rose pinned/ On the Virgin Mary's blouse'? What does this striking image say about childhood and its relationship to the spiritual side of life?
24. Does the poem as a whole suggest that we should be in a hurry to acquire knowledge and leave childhood behind? Give reasons for your answer.
25. **Class discussion:** The poem's title suggests that there is a profound connection between Christmas and childhood. Working in pairs, note down your ideas about what this connection might be. Explain why the poem's title might be more suitable than the seemingly more straightforward and obvious 'A Childhood Christmas'.

Exam Prep

1. **Personal Response:** Can you remember how you felt about Christmas, birthdays and other happy occasions when you were about the same age as the boy in the poem? Can you identify with the picture of a child's imagination that Kavanagh paints in this poem?
2. **Class Discussion:** Why do you think the poem is called 'A Christmas Childhood' rather than the more obvious 'A Childhood Christmas'? Does the poem offer us more than a straightforward account of what one Christmas was like for the child? What else does it offer?
3. **Theme Talk:** In what ways might a child like the one in 'A Christmas Childhood' be like a poet? Why do you think there might be a connection between childhood and the role of the poet? Support your answer with references to the poem.
4. **Exam Prep:** 'Kavanagh's poetry expresses a longing to see the world as though through a child's eyes and to rediscover the magic and mystery of everyday life'. Write an essay in response to this statement, making reference to 'A Christmas Childhood', 'Advent' and 'Canal Bank Walk'.

Language Lab

1. 'Although he gives us a very realistic and unsentimental picture of life in rural Ireland, Kavanagh also makes great use of surreal and bizarre imagery. Giving examples, explain how such imagery helps Kavanagh to set the scene in 'The Great Hunger'.
2. Give some examples of the use of the following literary techniques in the extract from 'The Great Hunger'. In each case, describe the effect that is created for the reader.
    - Alliteration (the repeated use of words beginning with the same letter)
    - Metaphor (drawing comparisons between apparently dissimilar things)
    - Onomatopoeia (where the sound of a word resembles its meaning

On Raglan Road

On Raglan Road on an autumn day I met her first and knew
That her dark hair would weave a snare that I might one day rue;
I saw the danger, yet I walked along the enchanted way,
And I said, let grief be a fallen leaf at the dawning of the day.

On Grafton Street in November we tripped lightly along the ledge [5]
Of the deep ravine where can be seen the worth of passion's pledge,
The Queen of Hearts still making tarts and I not making hay —
O I loved too much and by such and such is happiness thrown away.

I gave her gifts of the mind I gave her the secret sign that's known
To the artists who have known the true gods of sound and stone [10]
And word and tint. I did not stint for I gave her poems to say.
With her own name there and her own dark hair like clouds over fields of May

On a quiet street where old ghosts meet I see her walking now
Away from me so hurriedly my reason must allow
That I had wooed not as I should a creature made of clay — [15]
When the angel woos the clay he'd lose his wings at the dawn of day.

Annotations
Raglan Road: Kavanagh lived in 19 Raglan Road in Ballsbridge, Dublin, between 1946 and 1958
[5] ***Grafton Street:*** one of Dublin's main shopping streets

Tease It Out

1. Watch Video 8, which features legendary folk singer Luke Kelly.
   - What impression of Kavanagh emerges from Kelly's introduction?
   - Did you enjoy Kelly's performance of 'On Raglan Road'? Give a reason for your answer?
   - During which stanza, in your opinion, did his performance become most emotional in your opinion?
2. When he found himself beguiled by the young woman in the poem, the poet was already aware that he might regret being enchanted by her. Why?
3. The poet was aware of the risk involved in being in love, but how did he react to that risk?
4. 'I said, let grief be a fallen leaf': What do you think this memorable image says about the poet's attitude at the time? What might it mean?
5. What do you think is symbolized by the ledge mentioned at the start of the second stanza?
6. How careful is the poet as he makes his way along the ledge?
7. The poet talks about 'tripp[ing] lightly along the ledge' and above 'a deep ravine' in Dublin's Grafton Street. What do you think the poet means by this? Say which options you find true and which ones you think are false, giving reasons for your decision in each case.
   - He and his beloved were walking along the rooftop terrace of a tall building and had to be careful not to fall
   - Grafton Street is usually so busy and crowded that you need to be careful where you are walking
   - When you're in love, you behave in a carefree and easy way, tending to ignore the dangers that also come with being in love
   - The great value of love stems in part from the fact that it involves risk?
8. Why might the dangerous depth of a ravine symbolize the poet's passionate love for the young woman?
9. The poet confesses that he was 'not making hay'. In what respects was he failing?
10. Kavanagh tried to win the young woman's heart by impressing her with his knowledge of poetry and the other arts. To which arts does he allude? Which word or image related to which art form?
11. In the second and final stanzas, there are signs that the poet blames the young woman for her failure to love him in return. Which images or phrases might suggest this?
12. Towards the end of the poem, Kavanagh tells us how he now thinks he went wrong in his attempts to win the young woman's heart. What reason/s does he give?

Exam Prep

1. **Personal Response:** 'On Raglan Road' was set to the air of a famous traditional song called 'The Dawning of the Day'. Since then it has been voted Ireland's favourite folk song. Why do you think Kavanagh's poem provided the basis for such a popular song? What is especially attractive about the poem?
2. **Class Discussion:** What do you think about 'On Raglan Road' as a love poem? Is it fair to say that the poet tells us more about his own feelings, both at the time and afterwards, than he does about the young woman with whom he was in love?
3. **Theme Talk:** From the poet's retrospective viewpoint, how might his vocation as a poet have contributed to his failure to win the young woman's heart?

Language Lab

1. 'Before it was ever set to music, Kavanagh's 'On Raglan Road' was already very musical in its own right.' Pick out some of the qualities that might explain what this statement says about the poem. You might usefully focus on the poet's use of:
   - alliteration (the repeated use of words beginning with the same letter)
   - assonance (repeating a particular vowel sound)
   - rhyme, including internal rhyme (rhyming words within individual lines)

The Hospital

A year ago I fell in love with the functional ward
Of a chest hospital: square cubicles in a row
Plain concrete, wash basins – an art lover's woe,
Not counting how the fellow in the next bed snored.
But nothing whatever is by love debarred, [5]
The common and banal her heat can know.
The corridor led to a stairway and below
Was the inexhaustible adventure of a gravelled yard.

This is what love does to things: the Rialto Bridge,
The main gate that was bent by a heavy lorry, [10]
The seat at the back of a shed that was a suntrap.
Naming these things is the love-act and its pledge;
For we must record love's mystery without claptrap,
Snatch out of time the passionate transitory.

Annotations

[2] **chest hospital:** St James' Hospital (formerly the Rialto Hospital) in Dublin
[5] **debarred:** excluded from something; prohibited from doing something
[6] **banal:** obvious; commonplace; lacking in originality
[13] **claptrap:** silly or foolish talk or notions
[14] **transitory:** impermanent; lasting for only a short time

Tease It Out

1. Watch Video 9, which features a reading of the poem by the poet himself.
   - Would you describe Kavanagh's reading as highly performative or matter-of-fact?
   - Are there any words or phrases that he particulalrly emphasises as he reads?
   - What is the main emotion that comes across in the reading?
2. A 'functional' hospital ward seems an odd subject for poetry. In choosing this setting, what might the poet be telling us about how he understands the role of the poet?
3. What does the poet mean when he describes his hospital surroundings as 'an art-lover's woe'?
4. When the poet says that 'nothing whatever is by love debarred', what is he telling us about his attitude to everyday life?
5. Why would such an apparently boring place as a gravel yard be an 'inexhaustible adventure'?
6. What is it that 'love does to things'?
7. Quickly reread the poem. Find six things or places in which the poet finds magic although they appear very ordinary.
8. In what sense is naming such things an act of love?
9. We are not really told anything about the hardship and suffering that Kavanagh must have experienced while being treated for a very serious illness. Why might he have chosen not to focus on these things?
10. **Class Discussion:** To say the least, it seems odd to fall in love with a hospital ward. Did Kavanagh do so:
    - Because he had gone temporarily insane and thought the ward was a person?
    - Because he was so grateful to the hospital for successfully treating his illness?
    - Because anyone with real poetic sensibility can find wonder and magic even in the most apparently unpoetic and mundane places and things?
    - Because he had been so comfortable there that he would have liked to stay there for the rest of his life?
11. The poem concludes by telling us that we must 'snatch out of time the passionate transitory'. What might the phrase 'passionate transitory' mean?
12. Why should we '[s]natch [it] out of time'? How might we do so? How has Kavanagh achieved this?
13. What do these lines tell us about how Kavanagh thought about the role and vocation of the poet?

Exam Prep

1. **Class Discussion:** How does the poet now look back on his stay in hospital? What does his poetic insight allow him to see that others might miss or reject?
2. **Personal Response:** Can you think of any situation in which you have found beauty and inspiration in unpromising or difficult circumstances? Write a note setting out the circumstances and explaining how you were able to find something very positive in them.
3. **Theme Talk:** 'Although it recalls a time when Kavanagh was recovering from serious surgery, this poem nevertheless provides us with one of his greatest celebrations of the everyday and the ordinary.' Write a few paragraphs in response to this statement.
4. **Exam Prep:** The poem's final two lines tell us something important about how Kavanagh thought of a poet's work and responsibilities. Write two or three paragraphs explaining in your own words what these lines tell us. Refer also to the rest of the poem.

Language Lab

1. 'The Hospital' takes the form of a Petrarchan sonnet, in which an eight-line stanza (an octet) is followed by one of six lines (a sestet). The sestet often draws more general, philosophical conclusions from what has been described in the octet. In the present poem, how well do the images presented in the octet prepare us for the insights offered in the sestet?
2. In 'The Hospital', we find both elevated, fine language and more ordinary, conversational words and phrases. Write a few paragraphs about how this mixture reflects the general message that Kavanagh is imparting in the poem.

Canal Bank Walk

Leafy-with-love banks and the green waters of the canal
Pouring redemption for me, that I do
The will of God, wallow in the habitual, the banal,
Grow with nature again as before I grew.
The bright stick trapped, the breeze adding a third [5]
Party to the couple kissing on an old seat,
And a bird gathering materials for the nest for the Word,
Eloquently new and abandoned to its delirious beat.
O unworn world enrapture me, encapture me in a web
Of fabulous grass and eternal voices by a beech, [10]
Feed the gaping need of my senses, give me ad lib
To pray unselfconsciously with overflowing speech
For this soul needs to be honoured with a new dress woven
From green and blue things and arguments that cannot be proven.

Annotations

[2] *redemption:* being saved from sin, evil or error

[6] *the Word:* alludes to the Word of God, as set out in the Bible. Kavanagh is probably making a connection between his religious or spiritual feelings and his own poetic work with words.

[7] *delirious:* being wildly excited or in a state of incoherent rapture

[8] *enrapture:* give pleasure or intense delight to

[8] *encapture:* Kavanagh created this neologism to rhyme with "enrapture" and to expand on its meaning. To be enraptured by something is, figuratively speaking, to be captivated by it.

[9] *ad lib:* to improvise a speech or performance instead of preparing it beforehand

Tease It Out

1. Briefly describe the atmosphere of the place in which the poem is set. Is it a happy or sorrowful place?
2. What do the canal waters do for the poet?
3. In what sense might they be said to redeem him?
4. Who or what is the third party that joins the kissing couple?
5. What does 'the will of God' require the poet to do?
6. To 'wallow in the habitual, the banal' might sound a bit lazy and negative. What does the poet mean by this phrase? How might it fit in with his idea of spiritual rebirth?
7. How is God present in the poem's canal-bank setting?
8. Bearing in mind the poet's renewed sense of spiritual wonder, how might we interpret the idea of a bird building a nest 'for the Word'? [Hint: Note the capital "W" and think about Kavanagh's sense that God is present in nature.]
9. How might the urgent needs of the poet's senses be met by 'overflowing speech' and unselfconscious prayer?
10. What might be symbolised by the 'new dress' that the speaker wants to put on?
11. What is that dress made of?
12. When the poet mentions 'arguments that cannot be proven', is he talking about something negative like 'fake news'? What do you think he means?
13. Looking back at the opening lines of this poem, we can see that the imagery used recalls the Christian sacrament of baptism. Having worked your way through the poem, why do you think Kavanagh might associate his canal bank walks with baptism?

Exam Prep

1. **Personal Response:** Think of a place that makes you happy and content with life. It might be a local park, a path through some woods, a shopping street, a particular neighbourhood or somewhere else that is important to you. Explain how this location makes you feel and why you see it as a special place.
2. **Class Discussion:** 'In Kavanagh's eyes, God and nature are one'. Discuss this statement in light of the ideas and imagery that you find in 'Canal Bank Walk'. You may also refer to other poems by Kavanagh that are on your course.
3. **Theme Talk:** 'Having undergone and recovered from serious surgery, Kavanagh responded by innocently marvelling at the world once again'. Write a few paragraphs explaining how the poet's renewed sense of innocence and wonder is expressed in 'Canal Bank Walk'.
4. **Exam Prep:** The poet praises this natural setting for enabling him to grow again 'as before I grew'. What kind of growth is he talking about here? What might previously have stopped him from growing in this way? In your answer, you should refer also to other Kavanagh poems that you have studied.

Language Lab

1. 'Canal Bank Walk' depicts a spiritual rebirth in which nature and the divine are closely interwoven. Write a paragraph about how each of the following literary techniques helps Kavanagh to paint a compelling picture of new life.
    - alliteration (the repeated use of words beginning with the same letter)
    - assonance (repeating a particular vowel sound)
    - rhyme, including internal rhyme (rhyming words within individual lines)
2. In keeping with his belief that God and nature are intimately connected, Kavanagh uses imagery drawn from both religion and the natural world. Pick out examples of each kind of imagery and write a brief essay explaining how the blend of the two mirrors what the poem wants to tell us.

Lines Written on a Seat on the Grand Canal, Dublin

Erected to the memory of Mrs. Dermot O'Brien

O commemorate me where there is water,
Canal water, preferably, so stilly
Greeny at the heart of summer. Brother
Commemorate me thus beautifully
Where by a lock niagarously roars [5]
The falls for those who sit in the tremendous silence
Of mid-July. No one will speak in prose
Who finds his way to these Parnassian islands.
A swan goes by head low with many apologies,
Fantastic light looks through the eyes of bridges — [10]
And look! a barge comes bringing from Athy
And other far-flung towns mythologies.
O commemorate me with no hero-courageous
Tomb — just a canal-bank seat for the passer-by.

Annotations

[8] ***Parnassian islands:*** poetic islands; In Greek mythology, Mount Parnassus was the home of the muses, the goddesses who inspired poets and artists.

[11] ***a barge comes:*** This is poetic invention. By the time of the poem's setting (summer 1955) the canal was no longer used by commercial traffic.

Tease It Out

1. Who do you think the poet might be addressing in this poem?
2. Why might he address that person as 'Brother'?
3. What kind of instructions is he giving them?
4. What do you think Kavanagh means when he says that 'a lock niagarously roars'? What kind of comparison is he making? How literally does he mean it?
5. Why might people at the canal bank be sitting in "tremendous silence"?
6. What does the poet mean when he likens this apparently ordinary Dublin setting to Parnassian islands?
7. Why will nobody in this lovely, peaceful setting speak in prose?
8. In what other form will they speak?
9. What do you think the 'mythologies' that the barge brings from 'far-flung towns' might be?
10. What might a 'hero-courageous tomb' be? In what way would it typically portray its occupant or the person to whom it is dedicated?
11. Why might Kavanagh prefer a commemorative canal-bank seat to a more obviously glorious memorial? Pick out the answer/s that seems most accurate to you, and explain your choice/s.
    - He thinks the canal-bank seat is a very important place in the eyes of powerful and important people?
    - He is very shy and doesn't want his memorial to be too showy or pretentious?
    - He believes that ordinary places that heal or uplift us are at least as important as the typical sites of great tombs and memorials?
    - He believes that large crowds will pass along the canal bank, and that more people will therefore be likely to see his name on a seat plaque and remember him?

Exam Prep

1. **Theme Talk:** 'Kavanagh often celebrates the wonder and magic of everyday life and ordinary things and places.' Discuss this statement with reference to 'Lines Written on a Seat on the Grand Canal, Dublin'. Refer also to at least one other poem by Kavanagh.
2. **Class Discussion:** We hear a great deal nowadays about how best to commemorate important historical events. Think of some recent commemorations of important events from times gone by. What did you think was well and badly done in these commemorations? How does the kind of commemoration that Kavanagh has in mind differ from these larger public commemorations?
3. **Personal Response:** 'This poem seems to offer us some wise advice about how best to enjoy life'. Write a few paragraphs setting out your personal response to this statement. What do you think that advice might be? Say whether or not you agree with him, giving reasons for your answer.
4. **Exam Prep:** 'In 'Lines Written on a Seat on the Grand Canal, Dublin', Kavanagh once again takes an ordinary scene and makes it extraordinary.' Write a brief essay in response to this statement. Focus on the present poem, but also refer to two other poems by Kavanagh that you have studied.

Language Lab

1. In this poem Kavanagh cleverly picks out words and images that will help him to build up a picture of tranquillity and contentment. Pick out some of the words and images that you find especially effective in this respect. Give reasons for your answer.
2. Write a note explaining how Kavanagh uses assonance, personification, half-rhymes and a fluid rhythm to create a suitably laid-back atmosphere for this poem. Give examples of each of these techniques and say why you find them effective.

Derek Mahon

Derek Mahon was born in Belfast in 1941, the only child of Ulster Protestant parents. Like many only children Mahon had to make his own fun. He became something of a solitary dreamer, comfortable with his own company but intensely aware of the physical world around him. Certain objects in his parents' house seem to been especially important to him, for example an old 1940's radio set. These objects, he claims, were his 'best friends' during childhood, acting as spurs for his youthful imagination. Mahon's status as an only child was important to his development as a poet: 'I had time for the eye to dwell on things, for the brain to dream about things'. In his poem 'Courtyards in Delft' he describes himself, famously, as 'a strange child with a taste for verse'.

This 'strange child' attended Skegoneil Primary School and then the Royal Belfast Academical Institution ('Inst'), famous, among other things, for its rugby team. It is difficult to know whether Mahon's schooldays were happy or miserable. In an interview with the Paris Review he presents himself as something of a teenage misfit: 'I started moping, brooding; I didn't go in for sport'. Whereas elsewhere he claims to have been a decent rugby player (a 'mean scrum-half'). What is certain, however, is that Inst played an important role in the growth of Mahon's poetic gift. At Inst he encountered what he describes as other 'young sophisticates', fellow students who shared his interest in poetry and literature. His English teacher 'Basher' Boyle was familiar with the Dublin literary scene and with the circle of the great Irish poet W.B. Yeats. From Boyle, Mahon acquired his life-long fascination with Yeats's work: 'his idea of teaching five hundred years of English Literature was to race through Shakespeare and the rest in the first term and spend the remaining two terms on a close study of Yeats'. The Institution also had a well-produced school magazine to which Mahon contributed poems that, according to the critic Hugh Haughton, were 'fluent and extraordinary' for one so young.

Mahon's youth was shaped by his Protestant cultural background, what Haughton describes as the 'Protestant house-proud ethos', which involved a sober emphasis on hard work and religion above all else. His family was tied to industrial Belfast, with his father and grandfather both working in the famous Harland and Wolf shipyard, while his mother had worked at the York Street flax mills. As time went by Mahon developed a negative, or at least ambivalent, attitude toward both his hometown and his Protestant cultural inheritance. In 'Ecclesiastes', for instance, Belfast is presented as a grim, industrialised wasteland, with its 'shipyard silence' and 'dark doors', while its Protestant inhabitants are dismissed as 'puritan' and a 'credulous people'. Even in a

"I lie here in a riot of sunlight watching the day break and the clouds flying. Everything is going to be all right."

poem as bitter as 'Ecclesiastes', however, Mahon acknowledges that his Protestant upbringing is an important part of his identity. As Haughton puts it, 'that Protestant world is crucial to him though it's one that he could be seen to be in flight from, to some extent, in his later work'.

Mahon, then, seems to have been glad to leave behind what an early poem describes as 'this desperate city' and relocate to Dublin to study at Trinity College. The move to Dublin was important in expanding Mahon's horizons. As the poet Gerald Dawe puts it: 'It was a move from a city which was highly industrialised, full of the work ethic and an intense environment ... to the more open, cosmopolitan atmosphere of Trinity'. Here Mahon began to mature as a poet. Though he admits that he 'didn't go to lectures much' he had a good social life and formed friendships with many now well known writers, including Michael Longley, Eavan Boland and Brendan Kennelly. In 1960's Dublin, according to Dawe, he became intensely aware of the world beyond Ireland: 'They were picking up on a vibe that was coming from America and they found that very liberating'. Trinity College provided him with a link to European culture, something that was to be of huge importance to Mahon as a writer and as a person: 'it was a kind of bridgehead into Europe through the writers who'd gone before him, like Beckett'.

The poems selected for this course were written in the twenty years between his departure from Trinity in 1965, and the publication of his collection *Antarctica* in 1985. During this time Mahon led something of a nomadic existence. He studied for a year in Paris, worked his way through Canada and the United States, taught for a while in Dublin, and spent many years in London as a free-lance journalist. It is unsurprising, then, that Mahon is regarded as one of the great poets of place and travel, and that place names feature in the titles of so many of his poems. Throughout his wanderings, however, Mahon's Northern Protestant upbringing continued to exert a powerful pull on his work. Several of his poems are influenced, usually indirectly, by the Troubles that have dogged Northern Ireland from the late 1960's to the present day.

Mahon eventually settled in the Republic of Ireland and arguably began to identify more and more with that state rather than with the Ulster of his birth. America, too, especially New York, loomed large in some of his recent poetry. Mahon emerged as a fierce critic of contemporary life, of the shallowness, greed and stupidity he saw everywhere in today's society. As Hugh Haughton puts it 'These recent poems take on New York, homelessness, dereliction, and the new Celtic Tiger metropolis in Dublin'.

The last twenty years of Mahon's life were spent in Kinsale, Co. Cork. These years saw him strike up a new relationship with the artist Sarah Iremonger. They also saw a late harvest of poems, essays and translations, which gained him a range of literary awards and host of new admirers. In 2014, 'A Disused Shed in Co. Wexford' was shortlisted in a competition to find Ireland's favourite poem. While in 2020, another poem, 'Everything is Going to be Alright', went viral during the beginning of the Coronavirus pandemic. He passed away in October of that year. Tibutes to Mahon's life were led by the President of Ireland Michael D. Higgins, who compared the poet's passing to the falling of a great oak tree.

Grandfather

They brought him in on a stretcher from the world,
Wounded but humorous; and he soon recovered.
Boiler-rooms, row upon row of gantries rolled
Away to reveal the landscape of a childhood
Only he can recapture. Even on cold [5]
Mornings he is up at six with a block of wood
Or a box of nails, discreetly up to no good
Or banging round the house like a four-year-old —

Never there when you call. But after dark
You hear his great boots thumping in the hall [10]
And in he comes, as cute as they come. Each night
His shrewd eyes bolt the door and set the clock
Against the future, then his light goes out.
Nothing escapes him; he escapes us all.

Annotations

[3] ***Boiler-rooms:*** refers to the boiler rooms of various ships that were built in Belfast's famous shipyards. Mahon's grandfather worked as a boilermaker and was employed in the ship-building industry
[3] ***gantries:*** large bridge-like cranes used in shipbuilding; a travelling crane, used in the building of ships
[11] ***cute:*** clever
[12] ***shrewd:*** astute, sharp-witted

Tease It Out

1. Based on your reading of the poem, how old do you think the poet was when his grandfather came to live with him?
2. The grandfather was injured when he arrived at the poet's house? Based on your reading of the poem, can you suggest how this injury might have occurred?
3. Did it take the grandfather a long time to recover from this injury? What might this suggest about his personality?
4. In what industry had the poet's grandfather worked in all his life?
5. What does the phrase 'rolled away' suggest about the grandfather's memory of his working years? Rank the following in order of plausibility:
   - Those years no longer seemed important to him.
   - He was eager to think and talk about his career.
   - The grandfather's memory was failing.
6. What type of projects did the grandfather undertake while he was living with the young poet?
7. **Class Discussion:** Consider the phrase 'getting up to no good'. What does this suggest about the young poet's attitude towards these projects?
8. What phrase indicates that the grandfather made a lot of noise early in the morning?
9. What phrase indicates he was usually absent from the house most of the day?
10. When the grandfather came home in the evening was he eager to talk to the other members of the family? Give a reason for your answer.
11. The grandfather is described as 'bolting the door... against the future'. What does this suggest about the grandfather's attitude to the future? Rank the following in order of plausibility:
    - He is terrified of death.
    - He doesn't like the direction in which society seems to be headed.
    - He would rather relive memories of the past than think about the future.
12. **True or false:** The poet regards his grandfather as a highly observant person.

Exam Prep

1. **Personal Response:** Imagine you are the poet's grandfather. Write a diary entry describing an average day. Your entry should begin early in the morning and conclude late in the evening.
2. **Class Discussion:** 'This poem depicts an elderly man enjoying a second childhood'. Discuss this as a class, saying whether you agree or disagree with the statement.
3. **Theme Talk:** Mahon's poetry is deeply concerned with the theme of community and solitude. List the different ways in which the grandfather is part of the family's community. List the different ways in which he remains a solitary figure, one who keeps that community at a distance.
4. **Exam Prep:** 'Derek Mahon explores people and places in his own distinctive style'. Write a short essay in response to this statement, making reference to 'Grandfather' and at least two other poems on your course.

Language Lab

1. **Poet of Precision:** As a class, consider the poem's opening line. What does it suggest about the relationship between the grandfather and the outside world? How had the grandfather's social role and responsibilities changed with his retirement?
2. **Group Discussion:** The poem provides several hints about the poet's grandfather. Working in small groups, list as many as you can. Then come up with three adjectives that in your opinion best capture his demeanour and approach to life.

Day Trip to Donegal

We reached the sea in early afternoon,
Climbed stiffly out; there were things to be done,
Clothes to be picked up, friends to be seen,
As ever, the nearby hills were a deeper green
Than anywhere in the world, and the grave [5]
Grey of the sea the grimmer in that enclave.

Down at the pier the boats gave up their catch,
A writhing glimmer of fish; they fetch
Ten times as much in the city as here,
And still the fish come in year after year – [10]
Herring and mackerel, flopping about the deck
In attitudes of agony and heartbreak.

We left at eight, drove back the way we came,
The sea receding down each muddy lane.
Around midnight we changed-down into suburbs [15]
Sunk in a sleep no gale-force wind disturbs.
The time of year had left its mark
On frosty pavements glistening in the dark.

Give me a ring, goodnight, and so to bed …
That night the slow sea washed against my head, [20]
Performing its immeasurable erosions –
Spilling into the skull, marbling the stones
That spine the very harbour wall
Muttering its threats to villages of landfall.

At dawn I was alone far out at sea [25]
Without skill or reassurance – nobody
To show me how, no promise of rescue –
Cursing my constant failure to take due
Forethought of this; contriving vain
Overtures to the vindictive wind and rain. [30]

Annotations

[5] *grave:* dull, sombre

[6] *enclave:* a part of one country surrounded by another, an enclosed community that is distinct from the rest of society

[8] *writhing:* twisting and contorting

[12] *attitudes:* positions of the body indicating a particular mental state

[21] *immeasurable:* impossible to measure

[22] *marbling:* caressing a surface until it is as smooth as marble

[24] *landfall:* occurs when a storm that forms out at sea reaches land; can also refer a land slide

[29] *Forethought:* preparation, advance consideration

[29] *contriving:* devising, inventing

[29] *vain:* futile or useless, proud or conceited

[30] *Overtures:* attempts to open negotiations

[30] *vindictive:* malicious, vengeful

Tease It Out

1. What ordinary tasks have brought the poet and his friends to Donegal?
2. **True or false:** The sea off the Donegal coastline has a pleasant appearance.
3. **Class Discussion:** The poet refers to Donegal as an 'enclave'. What does this suggest about the county's geographical location?
4. What is happening 'Down at the pier'? Describe in your own words how you visualise this process.
5. The poet suggests that the bulk of each day's catch is transported to the city. Why is this?
6. What do the phrases 'flop about', 'agony' and 'heartbreak' suggest about the plight of live fish amid the catch?
7. At what time did the poet arrive back home? What phrase indicates that the suburbs are less exposed to the elements than the Donegal coastline?
8. At what time of year is the poem set? How has this season 'left its mark' on the area around the poet's home?
9. **Class Discussion:** What situation is suggested by the line 'the slow sea washed against my head'?
   - The poet depicts his body somehow merging with the Donegal coastline
   - The poet depicts himself as having been transported back to the coastline.
   - The poet depicts sea water somehow filling up his bedroom.
10. **Class Discussion:** In these lines is the poet dreaming, half-asleep or hallucinating?
11. 'Performing its immeasurable erosions'. What precisely is being eroded in this line?
12. **True or false:** The poet imagines water washing into his skull, just as it washes into a cave along the coastline.
13. What impact does erosion have on the stones in lines 22 to 23? How do you picture these stones?
14. Line 24 features an example of personification. What is being personified? What threat does it convey?
15. Where does the poet find himself at daybreak? Do you imagine him to be in the water or aboard some kind of vessel?
16. What is the weather like? What phrase indicates that the poet is alone?
17. **True or false:** The poet feels that he is perfectly capable of handling the situation in which he finds himself.
18. What does the word 'this' in line 29 refer to? How much planning or provision did the poet do to prepare for this?

Exam Prep

1. **Class Discussion:** Discuss the following questions as a class:
   - 'And still the fish come in year after year'. Is the poet surprised that the fish return each year to the fishing grounds?
   - Can you identify an instance in the poem of human beings exploiting the natural world?
   - Would you agree that Mahon presents the suffering of the fish in very human terms?
   - Can you find any evidence that the memory of this suffering stays with the poet for the rest of the day?
   - Is there a link between this suffering and the strange experience the speaker undergoes that night?
2. **Theme Talk:** 'This is a poem that highlights Mahon's sensitivity to the natural world. We must take 'due forethought' of nature or suffer the consequences'. Write a paragraph in response to this statement.
3. **Exam Prep:** 'Many of Mahon's poems feature individuals facing into extreme and hellish isolation.' With this statement in mind, write a paragraph comparing the present poem to either 'Antarctica' or 'After the Titanic'.

Language Lab

1. Mahon is a poet of the perfectly chosen phrase, one that works on several different levels. We see this with 'Writhing glimmer of fish'. What does this suggest about the movement of the fish? What else does it suggest about their appearance?
2. **Class Discussion:** Is this an example of euphony or cacophony? How does this verbal music fit with the image the line paints for us?
3. Mahon is a poet of precision, especially when it comes to verbs.
   - What verb indicates that the poet and his friends are moving further and further away from the sea?
   - What verb indicates that most people in the city are in a deep sleep?
   - What was 'glistening'? Can you suggest an alternative to this verb?
   - **Class Discussion:** When might someone 'change-down' when driving? Suggest how this verb might also refer to the car's passengers as they return to the suburbs.

THIS IS POETRY **DEREK MAHON**

After the *Titanic*

They said I got away in a boat
And humbled me at the inquiry. I tell you
    I sank as far that night as any
Hero. As I sat shivering on the dark water
    I turned to ice to hear my costly   [5]
Life go thundering down in a pandemonium of
    Prams, pianos, sideboards, winches,
Boilers bursting and shredded ragtime. Now I hide
    In a lonely house behind the sea
Where the tide leaves broken toys and hatboxes   [10]
    Silently at my door. The showers of
April, flowers of May mean nothing to me, nor the
    Late light of June, when my gardener
Describes to strangers how the old man stays in bed
    On seaward mornings after nights of   [15]
Wind, takes his cocaine and will see no one. Then it is
    I drown again with all those dim
Lost faces I never understood, my poor soul
    Screams out in the starlight, heart
Breaks loose and rolls down like a stone.   [20]
    Include me in your lamentations.

Annotations

The Titanic: the passenger liner that famously sank on 14 April 1912, while on its maiden voyage between Southampton and New York, with the loss of 1,500 lives. The speaker of the poem is Bruce Ismay. He was the manager of the White Star Line for which the *Titanic* sailed. He was one of the few men who survived the shipwreck and was later criticised heavily for neglecting to help the drowning passengers.

[6] **pandemonium:** confusion, disorder, uproar

[7] **winches:** hauling devices that consist of a rope or chain around a horizontal drum

[8] **ragtime:** a genre of jazz music popular in the early 20th century

[15] **seaward mornings:** mornings when the wind is coming from the sea

[16] **takes his cocaine:** in the early 20th century cocaine was prescribed for a wide range of psychological ailments

[21] **lamentations:** laments

Tease It Out

1. Ismay describes how he was 'humbled' at the inquiry into the *Titanic's* loss? What view of his actions did the inquiry conclude and publicise?
2. 'I sank as far that night as any/ Hero'. In what way did 'Heroes' sink that night? In what very different way did Ismay 'sink' that night?
3. The speaker says that as he sat in the lifeboat he 'turned to ice'. What different ways might we understand this? Rank the following in the order you consider most appropriate:
   - He turned to look at the iceberg that the *Titanic* collided with
   - He felt so cold that it was as if he was turning into ice
   - He felt utterly numb as he witnessed this loss and destruction of everything he had built
4. The speaker describes his 'costly' life 'thundering 'down' the night the *Titanic* sank. In what different ways might his life be considered 'costly'?
5. Ismay describes how he hides in a 'house behind the sea'. Who or what could he be hiding from? What does the verb 'hide' suggest about his daily life?
6. **Class Discussion**: It is odd that Ismay, given the loss of the *Titanic*, would choose to live by the sea. Do you agree with this statement.
7. The speaker says that the 'tide leaves broken toys and hatboxes/ Silently' at his door'. Do you think that the tide actually washes these objects up in front of his house, or is the poet speaking in a figurative or metaphorical way here?
8. Identify three phrases that indicate Ismay is suffering from some kind of depression.
9. Ismay describes how his depression is worse on 'seaward mornings'.
   - Can you suggest why this might be the case?
   - How does Ismay attempt to mitigate his depression on these mornings?
   - Ismay describes how he drowns again and again and again. What kind of mental state is being suggested by these lines?
   - According to Ismay, what happens to his 'heart' and 'soul' on such mornings? What does this suggest about his state of mind?
10. **Class Discussion:** [T]hose dim/ Lost faces I never understood'. Does this phrase refer to a) the ordinary workers on the ship, b) the wealthy passengers, or c) both. Can you suggest why Ismay might never have understood such people?

Exam Prep

1. **Personal Response:** What do you think has caused the speaker the most pain? Rank the following in the order you consider most appropriate:
   - The fact that so many people died when the *Titanic* sank
   - The fact that his illustrious career came to an end that night
   - The fact that his behaviour was deemed to be cowardly
   - The fact that he lives alone without any friends or family
2. **Theme Talk:** 'Mahon is a poet of real compassion. Here he gives voice to someone who is regarded as one of history's villains, asking us to mourn for him along with the passengers and crew who drowned'. Write a paragraph in response to this statement. Having read the poem, do you feel any sympathy for Ismay?
3. **Exam Prep:** 'Mahon's poetry provides a fascinating study of isolation and solitude and the effects these have on individuals'. Discuss this statement with reference 'After the *Titanic*' and four other poems on the course.

Language Lab

1. **Class Discussion:** Read lines 6 to 8. How do these lines capture the horrific din of the enormous ship breaking apart and sinking into the ocean? What different poetic devices does he utilise to achieve this? List and describe in your own words the different sounds that are mixed up here.
2. Define each of the following literary devices in your own words:
   - Metaphor • Hyperbole • Metonymy
   Now consider the following phrase: 'hear my costly/ Life go thundering down'. Which of the above devices features here? Is it possible that more than one features?

Ecclesiastes

God, you could grow to love, it, God-fearing, God –
   chosen purist little puritan that,
for all your wiles and smiles, you are (the
   dank churches, the empty streets,
the shipyard silence, the tied-up swings) and   [5]
   shelter your cold heart from the heat
of the world, from woman-inquisition, from the
   bright eyes of children. Yes, you could
wear black, drink water, nourish a fierce zeal
   with locusts and wild honey, and not   [10]
feel called upon to understand and forgive
   but only to speak with a bleak
afflatus, and love the January rains when they
   darken the dark doors and sink hard
into the Antrim hills, the bog meadows, the heaped   [15]
   graves of your fathers. Bury that red
bandana and stick, that banjo; this is your
   country, close one eye and be king.
Your people await you, their heavy washing
   flaps for you in the housing estates –   [20]
a credulous people. God, you could do it, God
   help you, stand on a corner stiff
with rhetoric, promising nothing under the sun.

Annotations

Ecclesiastes: a book of the Old Testament. It is known not only for its wisdom and poetic beauty but also for its bleak view of human existence

[1] ***God-fearing:*** extremely religious

[2] ***purist:*** a person who insists on traditional rules or structures, especially in matters of language or style.

[2] ***puritan:*** morally strict and judgemental, especially when it comes to luxury and pleasure. Also refers to a strict and severe form of Protestantism that emerged in the 16th and 17th centuries. The Protestantism with which Mahon grew up is descendant from these original puritans.

[3] ***wiles:*** strategies used to deceive or manipulate others

[4] ***dank:*** unpleasantly damp and cold

[5] ***shipyard silence:*** Belfast was famous for its shipbuilding industry. On Sundays the shipyards would be closed and silent

[5] ***tied-up swings:*** On Sundays, in the Northern Ireland of Mahon's youth, all work and play was forbidden. The public public parks would be closed and the swings would be tied up.

[9] ***locusts and wild honey:*** the Biblical prophet John the Baptist adopted an extreme and self-punishing diet, eating only locusts and wild honey

[12] ***afflatus:*** divine inspiration

[14-15] ***red/ bandana and stick:*** a symbol of travel. A wanderer would fold his belongings into a bandana, which he would carry tied to the end of his walking stick

[16] ***close one eye and be king***: a reference to the old proverb that 'In the land of the blind the one-eyed man is king'

[19] ***credulous:*** gullible

[21] ***rhetoric:*** the art of persuasive public speaking, also suggests language that while persuasive is also insincere

[21] ***Nothing under the sun:*** this line adapts a famous quote from the Book of Ecclesiastes: 'There is nothing new under the sun'.

Tease It Out

1. This poem describes the Protestant Belfast in which Mahon was raised:
   a. On Sundays, all forms of work and play were strictly forbidden. Find three phrases that suggest this.
   b. What phrase suggests that this community believed they had a special relationship with God?
   c. What does the phrase 'God-fearing' suggest about this community's attitude towards religion?
2. Consider the following phrases: 'dank churches', 'dark doors', "heavy washing/ flaps'. What impression of Belfast do they create? Is it a flattering or an unflattering one?
3. Describe in our own words the rain that falls in Belfast and its surrounding areas. What does it look like? What does it feel like?
4. **Group Discussion:** What does this depiction of the rain symbolise about the culture in which Mahon was raised?
5. What phrase indicates that Mahon's ancestors have lived in this landscape for hundreds of years?
6. **Class Discussion:** Mahon has left behind Protestant Belfast and adopted a new way of life, one represented by a banjo, a stick and a bandana. Working as a class, can you suggest what each of these objects might symbolise?
7. Mahon's personality, however, is still shaped by this upbringing. Can you identify two phrases that indicate this?
8. Mahon imagines life as a kind of prophet in his native Belfast. What kind of clothing would he wear? What kind of diet would he have?
9. **True or false:** Mahon imagines preaching a kindly, gentle faith.
10. What phrases suggest that as a prophet he would speak with absolute certainty?
11. What phrases suggest that such a prophet could become a leader of Belfast's protestant community?
12. Mahon would have to 'close one eye' in order to adapt such a role. Can you suggest what this phrase symbolises?

Exam Prep

1. **Class Discussion:** As a class, discuss the following questions:
   - Can you suggest what Mahon means by 'the heat of the world'?
   - Why might the prophet imagined by Mahon have to 'shelter' from such heat?
   - What attitude towards women and children must be exhibited by such a preacher?
2. **Personal Response:** 'You could grow to love it'. Based on your reading of Mahon's poetry, do you think that he actually could 'grow to love' the life of such a prophet?
3. **Exam Prep:** 'Mahon's poetry is all about the positive and negative aspects of community'. Write a short essay responding to this statement, in which you discuss 'Ecclesiastes' along with two other poems.

Language Lab

1. **Class Discussion:** 'In this poem, Mahon is actually talking to himself. He considers the possibility of abandoning poetry for religion because he realises that the poet and the preacher attempt to cast a spell by means of language'. Write a paragraph in response to this statement.
2. 'There is nothing new under the sun' is a famous quote from the Book of Ecclesiastes. What do you understand this Biblical quotation to mean?
3. In the poem's final line, Mahon adapts this quotation. What does he mean? Rank the following in order of plausibility:
   - You get nothing in this life, but will be rewarded in the next.
   - His is a religion that demands you stay indoors on sunny days.
   - His is a religion that seems to offer his believers a great deal but in the end gives them nothing.
   - His is a religion that despises fun, joy and brightness of all kinds.

As it Should be

We hunted the mad bastard
Through bog, moorland, rock, to the star-lit west
And gunned him down in a blind yard
Between ten sleeping lorries
And an electricity generator. [5]

Let us hear no idle talk
Of the moon in the Yellow River.
The air blows softer since his departure.

Since his tide burial during school hours
Our kiddies have known no bad dreams. [10]
Their cries echo lightly along the coast.

This is as it should be.
They will thank us for it when they grow up
To a world with method in it.

Annotations
[3] **blind yard:** a dead end, a yard with only one way in and out
[7] **the moon in the Yellow River:** the ancient Chinese poet Li Po is said to have died while drunkenly attempting to embrace the reflection of the moon in the Yellow River. The phrase describes those who grasp after romantic or poetic ideals
[9] **tide-burial:** his body was disposed of by being cast into the sea

Tease It Out

1. Watch Video 10, which depicts a scene from the 1982 film *Rambo: First Blood* and answer the following:
   - Pick two adjectives that describe the sheriff's attitude towards the drifter.
   - **True or false:** The sheriff would like to see a diverse range of people settling in his town.
   - Do you get a sense that the sheriff cares about his community?
2. What phrases indicate that the speaker and his companions were relentless in their pursuit of the 'mad bastard'?
3. **Class Discussion:** What hints do we get that their pursuit of their victim lasted for the entire night?
4. Where did they finally catch up with their victim? Describe this location in your own words.
5. What word or phrase indicates that the victim could not escape from this location?
6. What did the speaker and his companions do with their victim's body? At approximately what time of day did this occur?
7. The speaker viewed the 'mad bastard' as a disruptive presence in the community.
   - What impact did the victim's presence have on the community's children?
   - What impact did the victim's presence have on the weather?
   - Are these claims realistic in your opinion? What do they suggest about the speaker's attitude towards the victim?
8. According to the speaker, has life in the community improved since his victim was gunned down?
9. **Class Discussion:** Consider the different meanings of the word 'method'. Which of these meanings do you think the speaker has in mind? What kind of world does the speaker want to live in?
10. 'The speaker uses the welfare of the community's children to justify his actions'. Write a paragraph in response to this statement.

Exam Prep

1. **Personal Response:** Break into small groups and discuss the following questions. Then, working alone, write your personal response to each one:
   - The speaker feels that he's speaking on behalf of his entire community. What features of the poem indicate this?
   - Do you think the speaker and his companions are keeping the killing of the 'mad bastard' a secret, or are they open about what they've done? Give a reason for your answer.
   - Do you think the victim was actually 'mad', or was he simply different? Can you think of any other fictional characters who met with a similar fate?
   - We learn little about the 'mad bastard'. However, as a group, can you suggest two or three different ways in which he might have compromised or upset this world of rigorous method?
2. **Class Discussion:** Working as a class consider the phrase 'the moon in the Yellow River' and the story from which it comes. What concepts or ideas are suggested are suggested by this tale? In what ways might they be opposed to the 'method' so valued by the speaker?
3. **Theme Talk:** 'Mahon brilliantly captures the psychology of a murderer attempting to justify his actions to himself.' Discuss this statement as a class.
4. **Exam Prep:** 'As it should be', like much of Mahon's work, tackles the theme of community: The poem presents a stifling community that values structure, order and conformity above all else'. Discuss this statement as a class.

Language Lab

1. 'Even in a brutal poem like this one, Mahon presents us with sensual images of the natural world'. Write a paragraph in response to this statement.
2. What features of the sonnet form are present in 'As It Should Be'? Would you agree that the poem has an irregular rhyme scheme? Give a reason for your answer.
3. 'The speaker's tone mixes hatred with a surprising tenderness'. Write a paragraph in response to this statement.
4. Is the speaker convinced that the killing of the 'mad bastard' was justified? Does he betray any doubts about the rightness of his actions?

A Disused Shed in Co. Wexford

Let them not forget us, the weak souls among the asphodels.
— Seferis, *Mythistorema*

(for J. G. Farrell)

Even now there are places where a thought might grow —
Peruvian mines, worked out and abandoned
To a slow clock of condensation,
An echo trapped for ever, and a flutter
Of wildflowers in the lift-shaft, [5]
Indian compounds where the wind dances
And a door bangs with diminished confidence,
Lime crevices behind rippling rain barrels,
Dog corners for bone burials;
And in a disused shed in Co. Wexford, [10]

Deep in the grounds of a burnt-out hotel,
Among the bathtubs and the washbasins
A thousand mushrooms crowd to a keyhole.
This is the one star in their firmament
Or frames a star within a star. [15]
What should they do there but desire?
So many days beyond the rhododendrons
With the world waltzing in its bowl of cloud,
They have learnt patience and silence
Listening to the rooks querulous in the high wood. [20]

They have been waiting for us in a foetor
Of vegetable sweat since civil war days,
Since the gravel-crunching, interminable departure
Of the expropriated mycologist.
He never came back, and light since then [25]
Is a keyhole rusting gently after rain.
Spiders have spun, flies dusted to mildew
And once a day, perhaps, they have heard something —
A trickle of masonry, a shout from the blue
Or a lorry changing gear at the end of the lane. [30]

There have been deaths, the pale flesh flaking
Into the earth that nourished it;
And nightmares, born of these and the grim
Dominion of stale air and rank moisture.
Those nearest the door grow strong — [35]
'Elbow room! Elbow room!'
The rest, dim in a twilight of crumbling
Utensils and broken pitchers, groaning
For their deliverance, have been so long
Expectant that there is left only the posture. [40]

A half century, without visitors, in the dark —
Poor preparation for the cracking lock
And creak of hinges; magi, moonmen,
Powdery prisoners of the old regime,
Web-throated, stalked like triffids, racked by drought [45]
And insomnia, only the ghost of a scream
At the flash-bulb firing-squad we wake them with
Shows there is life yet in their feverish forms.
Grown beyond nature now, soft food for worms,
They lift frail heads in gravity and good faith. [50]

They are begging us, you see, in their wordless way,
To do something, to speak on their behalf
Or at least not to close the door again.
Lost people of Treblinka and Pompeii!
'Save us, save us,' they seem to say, [55]
'Let the god not abandon us
Who have come so far in darkness and in pain.
We too had our lives to live.
You with your light meter and relaxed itinerary,
Let not our naive labours have been in vain!' [60]

Annotations

[2] *worked out:* stripped of all its resources

[3] *a slow clock of condensation:* moisture drips from the roof of the mineshafts, producing a ticking sound like that of a clock

[12] *the bathtubs and the washbasins:* items that are stored in the disused shed

[13] *crowd to a keyhole:* the mushrooms growing in the shed are drawn towards the light

[14] *firmament:* the heavens or sky

[16] *rhododendrons:* flowers that are growing outside the shed

[20] *querulous:* complaining, whining; describes the sound of the rooks' call

[21] *foetor:* a strong, foul smell

[22] *civil war days:* refers to the Irish Civil War (1922-1923)

[23] *gravel-crunching:* the sound made by the mycologist's footsteps as he walked away

[23] *interminable:* endless, taking a long time

[24] *expropriated:* having had one's land or belongings taken away

[24] *mycologist:* an expert on mushrooms and other fungi, describes the property's original owner who planted the mushrooms before his property was taken away from him during the Civil War

[26] *flies dusted:* flies have died and turned to dust

[34] *Dominion:* supremacy, domination

[34] *rank:* unpleasant, foul-smelling, overgrown

[43] *magi:* plural of magus, sorcerers or magicians

[43] *moonmen:* depicts the mushrooms as alien beings from the moon

[44] *old regime:* the previous system of rule or government

[45] *stalked like triffids:* a plant-like alien species that invades earth in *The Day of the Triffids* by John Wyndham

[45] *racked:* tortured

[50] *gravity:* seriousness

[50] *in good faith:* operating on the assumption that fairness and honesty will be adhered to by all parties

[54] *Treblinka:* a Nazi concentration camp in Poland where thousands of Jews were put to death

[54] *Pompeii:* a city in Italy that was destroyed after the eruption of Mount Vesuvius in 79 BC

[59] *light meter:* a device used in photography to measure brightness

[59] *itinerary:* a list or plan of things to do during a trip

Tease It Out

1. What metaphor is used to describe the dripping sound of condensation in the abandoned mine?
2. What metaphor is used to describe the behaviour of the wind in Indian compounds?
3. What has happened to the limestone wall mentioned in line 8? What is responsible for this effect?
4. The poet imagines a remote corner of a field or garden. To what use might dogs put such a corner?
5. **Class Discussion:** What do each of the above locations have in common?
6. Why might a thought 'grow' in such places? Is the poet suggesting a) that such places are a source or inspiration or b) that such places might harbour intelligent life?

The mushrooms and the shed

7. Where is the disused shed located?
8. How many mushrooms, according to the poet, are growing in the shed? Do you think this is an exact number? Give a reason for your answer.
9. The mushrooms were cultivated by an amateur mycologist who once owned the grounds:
    - What sound did the mushrooms hear as the mycologist walked away from the shed?
    - What phrase indicates it took him a long time to do so?
    - **Class Discussion:** What happened to the mycologist's land?
    - Did the mycologist ever return, after that, to check on the mushrooms?
    - When, according to the poet, did these events occur? (Hint: it was during a major event in Irish history)
    - For how long, since then, have the mushrooms remained in the shed?
    - Has the shed door ever been opened in all that time? Give a reason for your answer.
10. The shed also contains various bits and pieces of bric-a-brac. Which items specifically are mentioned throughout the poem?
11. **Class Discussion:** 'What should they do there but desire?' Can you suggest two or three things that the mushrooms might have desired during their confinement in the shed?

Light

12. What is the shed's only source of light?
13. Can you suggest why the mushrooms 'crowd' towards this light source?
14. What happens to the mushrooms 'nearest the door'?
15. What phrase indicates that this occurs at the expense of the mushrooms who are further away from the door?

16. **Class Discussion:** The poet focuses on those mushrooms that are further away from the door:
    - Why are these mushrooms said to exist in a 'twilight'?
    - Suggest why they have been 'groaning'.
    - For years, according to the poet, these mushrooms have been 'expectant'. What were they hoping or waiting for?
    - What phrase indicates that the long wait has taken a terrible toll on these mushrooms?
    - Do these mushrooms still expect anything?

The suffering of the mushrooms

17. The mushrooms are covered in their own sweat. What phrase suggests that this has a terrible odour?
18. What phrases suggest that the shed is a dry and dusty environment? Is there any moisture at all? Suggest why the air here might have a 'stale' quality.
19. What has happened to the mushrooms that died over the decades?
20. The mushrooms endure a near constant silence. How often, according to the poet, is this interrupted? What sounds do the mushrooms typically hear?
21. The mushrooms endure terrible nightmares. Describe in your own words what causes these.

The poet enters the shed

22. **True or false:** The mushrooms' experience means they are untroubled by the sudden influx of light.
23. How do the mushrooms respond to being photographed?
24. What phrases indicate that the mushrooms have taken on a mutated, almost alien appearance?
25. What phrases indicate that mushrooms are on the verge of death?
26. **Class Discussion:** Consider the phrase 'Powdery prisoners of the old regime'. With what 'old regime' are the mushrooms associated? What does the term 'powdery' suggest about their physical state?

The mushrooms ask for help

27. What phrase indicates that the poet is a keen photographer? What phrase indicates that he is in no particular hurry?
28. **True or false:** The mushrooms view the poet as an almost godly figure.
29. Read lines 52 to 53 carefully. What three things do the mushrooms ask the poet to do?
30. In what sense have the mushrooms been labouring? Why might these labours be described as 'naive'?
31. What according to the mushrooms will prevent these labours from being 'in vain'?

Exam Prep

1. **Personal Response:** 'They are begging us you see'. Who is the 'us' referred to in this line? Could this be open to more than one interpretation?
2. **Class Discussion:** Mahon associates the mushrooms with the 'Lost people of Treblinka and Pompeii!'
   - What do the terrible events at Treblinka at Pompeii have in common? In what way are these tragedies very different?
   - In what sense are the victims of Treblinka and Pompeii 'lost'? Might they be lost in more ways than one?
   - What does the poem suggest about our duty towards these lost people?
   - The mushrooms are presented as a symbol or metaphor for these lost people. Is this an effective comparison in your opinion?
3. **Theme Talk:** 'In this poem the speaker realises the important of speaking out on behalf of the voiceless. The tragedy of history's 'lost people' is not only the 'darkness and pain' that they endure but also the fact that their suffering is so often forgotten about'. Write a short essay in response to this statement.
4. **Exam Prep:** 'Mahon uses inventive images to explore the tragedies of history'. Wrte an essay in response to this statement in which you refer to the present poem, as well as to 'Rathlin', 'Antarctica' and 'After the *Titanic*'.

Language Lab

1. This poem centres on the personification of the mushrooms'. List the different ways in which the poet presents the mushrooms as living and thinking personalities. Is this personification effective in your opinion, or did you finds it silly and over the top?
2. Consider the phrase 'cracking lock/ And creak of hinges'. What does it suggest about the state of the shed's door? What poetic device is Mahon using here? (Hint: is starts with an 'o'!)
3. **Class Discussion:** Lines 27 to 28 are almost achingly beautiful as they suggest not only the beauty of the natural world but also the agony of the mushrooms' confinement'. Discuss this statement as a class.
4. Mahon's use of polished forms is again evident in this poem. Is the poem's rhyme scheme regular or irregular? Can you identify any internal rhymes? Can you identify two instances each of assonance and alliteration?
5. Watch Video 11, which features a reading of the poem by actor Stephen Rea.
   - Pick out three words or phrases to which he gives particular emphasis while he reads.
   - Identify one stanza where the reading slows down.
   - Do you think the musical accompaniment suits the atmosphere of the poem? Give a reason for your answer.

The Chinese Restaurant in Portrush

Before the first visitor comes the spring
Softening the sharp air of the coast
In time for the first 'invasion'.
Today the place is as it might have been,
Gentle and almost hospitable. A girl [5]
Strides past the Northern Counties Hotel,
Light-footed, swinging a book-bag,
And the doors that were shut all winter
Against the north wind and the sea mist
Lie open to the street, where one [10]
By one the gulls go window-shopping
And an old wolfhound dozes in the sun.

While I sit with my paper and prawn chow mein
Under a framed photograph of Hong Kong
The proprietor of the Chinese restaurant [15]
Stands at the door as if the world were young,
Watching the first yacht hoist a sail
− An ideogram on sea-cloud – and the light
Of heaven upon the mountains of Donegal;
And whistles a little tune, dreaming of home. [20]

Annotations

Portrush: a seaside town in north Antrim

[3] ***first seasonal 'invasion':*** the first visitors of the tourist season

[5] ***hospitable:*** friendly and welcoming

[11] ***wolfhound:*** a species of large hunting dog originating in Ireland. It has featured in Irish songs, poetry and artworks and is sometimes used as a symbol of Ireland itself

[15] ***proprietor:*** owner

[17] ***the first yacht:*** it is the beginning of the sailing season

[18] ***ideogram:*** a symbol that indicates a concept; many of the symbols in the Chinese writing system are ideograms

Tease It Out

1. What time of year is it? What effect does this have on the coastal winds around Portrush?
2. **True or false:** Portrush receives a lot of visitors during the winter time.
3. What metaphor is used to describe the fast-approaching tourist season? Mention at least three things the metaphor suggests about this influx.
4. **Class Discussion:** Discuss the following question as a class:
   - The poet refers describes Portrush as 'Gentle'. Is he referring to the wreather conditions, to the people or to both?
   - '[T]he place is as it might have been'. Working as a class suggest what might have prevented Portrush fulfilling its potential.
   - **True or false:** Portrush is hospitable on this particular afternoon. What does the poet's phrasing here suggest about his feelings towards his native county of Antrim?
5. Consider the terms 'striding', 'light-footed' and 'swinging'. How do they cause you to visualise the young girl who comes walking past the hotel? Pick three other terms that might describe her attitude and demeanour.
6. Why were the doors of the town 'shut all winter'? Why are they open on this particular afternoon?
7. What metaphor is used to describe the behaviour of the gulls? Is it an effective one in your opinion?
8. What is the restaurant proprietor doing as the poet enjoys his lunch?
9. What phrase indicates that the sailing season is just beginning?
10. Google some Chinese characters or ideograms. Identify one that, in your opinion, resembles a sail. What does the ideogram you've chosen mean in English?
11. What phrase indicates that the sunlight is especially beautiful on this spring afternoon?
12. The proprietor, we're told, is 'dreaming of home'. Can you guess, based on your reading of the poem, where he might have been born?

Exam Prep

1. **Personal Response:** 'The poet on this sunny afternoon is filled with optimism. He feels that Portrush and Ireland are embarking on a new beginning'. Identify at least four phrases from the poem that support this statement. Can you identify any phrases that contradict this statement?
2. **Class Discussion:** Community and solitude are recurring themes in Mahon's work.
   - Do you think the poet is currently residing in Portrush, or is he just passing through?
   - Does the poet feel at one with the town's community, or does he consider himself more of a detached observer?
   - The restaurant owner is described as 'dreaming of home'. Is he dreaming of Hong Kong, where he came from, or Portrush, where he now resides?
   - What similarities are there between the poet and the proprietor?
3. **Theme Talk:** The wolfhound is a symbol of Ireland and Irish history. What might it represent, therefore, that the wolfhound is sleeping? In your discussion you may wish to reference Northern Ireland's history.

Language Lab

1. 'This tone of this poem is extremely light-hearted and playful'. Identify at least four phrases from the poem that support this statement. Can you identify any phrases that contradict this statement?
2. Mahon is a poet well-known for his polished and elegant verse. This poem is shaped by an irregular pattern of half-rhyme. Can you identify which lines rhyme with one another and which ones don't?
3. 'Mahon's poetry focuses on both the positive and negative aspects of the natural world'. Discuss this statement with reference to 'The Chinese Restaurant in Portrush' and three other poems on the course.

Rathlin

A long time since the last scream cut short –
Then an unnatural silence; and then
A natural silence, slowly broken
By the shearwater, by the sporadic
Conversation of crickets, the bleak [5]
Reminder of a metaphysical wind.
Ages of this, till the report
Of an outbound motor at the pier
Fractures the dream-time, and we land
As if we were the first visitors here. [10]

The whole island a sanctuary where amazed
Oneiric species whistle and chatter,
Evacuating rock-face and cliff-top.
Cerulean distance, an oceanic haze –
Nothing but sea-smoke to the ice-cap [15]
And the odd somnolent freighter.
Bombs doze in the housing estates
But here they are through with history –
Custodians of a lone light that repeats
One simple statement to the turbulent sea. [20]

A long time since the unspeakable violence –
Since Somhairle Buidh, powerless on the mainland,
Heard the screams of the Raithlin women
Borne to him, seconds after, upon the wind.
Only the cry of the shearwater [25]
And the roar of the outboard motor
Disturb the singular peace. Spray-blind,
We leave here the infancy of the race,
Unsure among the pitching surfaces
Whether the future lies before us or behind. [30]

Annotations

Rathlin: an island off the coast of County Antrim
[1] ***the last scream:*** refers to the massacre of 1575 (see note on line 22 below)
[4] ***shearwater:*** a long-winged seabird
[4] ***sporadic:*** occurring at irregular intervals
[6] ***metaphysical:*** ghostly or supernatural, relating to poetic metaphor
[7] ***report:*** a sudden loud noise like an explosion or gunfire
[9] ***dream-time:*** Australian Aboriginal concept referring to the far distant past
[12] ***Oneiric:*** relating to dreams or dreaming
[14] ***Cerulean:*** a deep shade of blue
[15] ***sea-smoke:*** fog that is formed when cold air moves over warm water
[16] ***somnolent:*** sleepy, drowsy
[17] ***Bombs doze:*** a reference to the many bombings that were carried out during the Troubles in Northern Ireland
[22] ***Somhairle Buí:*** a Scots Irish chieftain who opposed English rule in Ireland. His main castle was on Rathlin Island. In 1575 the Earl of Essex, who was Queen Elizabeth's viceroy in Ireland, captured the castle and massacred its inhabitants. During the massacre, Somhairle Bui was trapped on the mainland. He heard his people dying but could do nothing to prevent the slaughter.
[27] ***singular:*** extraordinary, remarkable
[29] ***pitching:*** rocking, swaying, tilting

Tease It Out

1. 'A long time since the last scream cut short'. When did this 'last scream' occur? Who do you imagine was screaming? Can you suggest why this scream was interrupted?
2. **Class Discussion:** Can you suggest what an 'unnatural silence' might sound like? How might it differ from a natural silence? What does this phrase suggest about the atmosphere that filled the island?
3. **True or false:** What sounds, according to the poet, were responsible for breaking this unnatural silence?
4. What 'bleak reminder' is carried on the wind? What poetic device is Mahon using here? (Hint: it starts with a 'p'!)
5. **Group Discussion:** 'Mahon knows that hundreds of people live on Rathlin but he presents the island as being uninhabited'. What words and phrases suggest this? What does this choice suggest about the poet's first impressions of the island?
6. What sound signals that the poet and his friends have reached the island?
7. 'As if we were the first visitors here'. The poet, of course, knows that Rathlin is an inhabited island. But he imagines that he's the first person to set foot there since the massacre. What does this suggest term suggest about his impression of the island?
8. What phrases suggest that the island's landscape is jagged and mountainous?
9. Mahon's careful word choice is again evident in the second stanza. What do the terms 'sea-smoke', 'cerulean' and 'oceanic haze' suggest about the weather conditions on the day he visited Rathlin?
10. **True or false:** The poet saw no ships at all when he looked out from the island's cliffs.
11. The poet finds himself thinking about 'bombs' that are ready to detonate on the mainland. What historical conflict is the poet referring to in these lines?
12. What phrase tells us that a lighthouse is located on the island?
13. **Class Discussion:** The lighthouse, according to the poet, 'repeats/ one simple statement'. Working as a class, can you suggest what the lighthouse is saying or trying to say? What code or language does it use in its effort to communicate?
14. What sound did the wind carry to Somhairle Buí? Describe in your own words why he found himself 'powerless' at this moment.
15. What sound accompanies the poet's departure from the island?
16. Describe in your own words why the poet found it difficult to see as he crossed back to the mainland?
17. What does the phrase 'pitching surfaces' suggest about the conditions at sea?

Exam Prep

1. **Personal Response:** 'Rathlin is presented as a 'sanctuary' in more ways than one'. Write a paragraph in response to this statement. How would you characterise the island's atmosphere? List the different words and phrases that contribute to this effect.
2. **Class Discussion:** As the speaker leaves Rathlin, he contemplates the future:
    - What phrases indicate the poet's uncertainty about the future of the Irish people?
    - What kind of future is represented by the mainland?
    - What kind of future is represented by Rathlin?
    - Do you think that Mahon, based on your reading of this and other poems, is optimistic about Ireland's future?
3. **Theme Talk:** 'The island is presented as a 'sanctuary' from history's violence and suffering, as a place where the passage of time has been suspended and nothing ever changes any more'. Write a couple of paragraphs responding to this statement.

Language Lab

1. Research the term 'dreamtime'. Write a paragraph describing your understanding of the term as it is used in the indigenous cultures of Australia.
2. **Class Discussion:** The poet suggests that 'For ages' Rathlin has existed in such a dreamtime. What impression does it give of the island and its atmosphere?
3. Mahon is a poet of precision, especially when it comes to verbs. Consider the verbs 'whistle', 'chatter' and 'evacuate'. What do they tell us about a) the sounds of the birds and b) the manner in which the birds move?
4. Mahon is a poet of polished surfaces and structures:
    - Comment on the poem's rhyme scheme. Is it regular or irregular?
    - What sounds are mentioned or described in the opening stanza?
    - How many of these sounds are referred to again in the closing stanza?
    - Can you identify any other parallels between the first and third stanzas?

Antarctica

'I am just going outside and may be some time.'
The others nod, pretending not to know.
At the heart of the ridiculous, the sublime.

He leaves them reading and begins to climb,
Goading his ghost into the howling snow; [5]
He is just going outside and may be some time.

The tent recedes beneath its crust of rime
And frostbite is replaced by vertigo:
At the heart of the ridiculous, the sublime.

Need we consider it some sort of crime, [10]
This numb self-sacrifice of the weakest? No,
He is just going outside and may be some time

In fact, for ever. Solitary enzyme,
Though the night yield no glimmer there will glow,
At the heart of the ridiculous, the sublime. [15]

He takes leave of the earthly pantomime
Quietly, knowing it is time to go.
'I am just going outside and may be some time.'
At the heart of the ridiculous, the sublime.

Annotations

Antarctica: In late 1912 the British Naval Officer Robert Falcon Scott lead an expedition that aimed to be the first ever to reach the South Pole. Scott and his party, including Captain Laurence Oates, reached the Pole on 18 January 1913 only to discover that the Norwegian explorer Roald Amundsen had beaten them to their destination. Scott and his men suffered a horrendous journey back across the frozen wasteland, finding themselves hindered by blizzards, bad luck, starvation and ill-health. On 16 of March, Oates, who was suffering from severe frostbite, walked out of his tent and into a snowstorm, sacrificing himself so that his companions might have a better chance of survival. Oates' efforts proved in vain, however. Scott and the remaining members of the team perished a few days later.

[1] ***'I am just going outside and may be some time.':*** Oates' last words as recorded in Scott's diary, which was later recovered from the Antarctic

[3] ***the sublime:*** a quality of greatness that is difficult to understand or express; the concept of the sublime is often opposed to that of the ridiculous

[5] ***Goading:*** driving, forcing

[7] ***recedes:*** disappears, is left behind

[7] ***rime:*** frozen water droplets

[8] ***frostbite:*** an injury caused by the freezing of the skin and underlying tissues

[8] ***vertigo:*** a sensation of whirling and loss of balance

[13] ***enzyme:*** a chemical that aids the transformation of another substance

Tease It Out

1. Are you surprised at Oates' choice of final words to his companions? Give a reason for your answer.
2. How do the others respond to Oates' announcement?
3. What do they 'know'? Why do they pretend not to know this?
4. **Class Discussion:** Oates leaves the tent and 'begins to climb'. What is his destination?
5. What does the term 'ghost' suggest about Oates' physical state? What does it suggest about his mental state?
6. Consider the phrase 'howling snow'. Is this an example of assonance or alliteration? In what different ways does it convey the conditions into which Oates wandered?
7. What substance has formed on the tent he leaves behind?
8. Oates must force himself to press on through these terrible conditions. What phrase indicates this?
9. What is vertigo? Can you suggest why Oates might experience this as he walks?
10. What phrase indicates that after a while Oates no longer feels any physical discomfort?
11. **True or false:** Mahon considers Oates' self sacrifice an almost criminal act.
12. What aspects of this entire situation might be considered ridiculous? Rank the following in order of ridiculousness as you see it:
    - The other men pretending not to know what Oates is up to
    - Oates pretending that he is going for a casual walk
    - The egotistical desire to be first to the South Pole
    - The various mishaps and misunderstandings that plagued Scott's expedition
    - The fact that Oates' colleagues died anyway in spite of his sacrifice
13. Have you ever heard the term 'sublime' used in conversation, on radio or on television? Who or what was being described?
14. **Group Discussion:** What characteristics do you associate with pantomime? What does Mahon's description of life as 'the earthly pantomime' suggest about his view of human existence?

Exam Prep

1. **Personal Response:** Why do you think Oates' colleagues responded the way they did to his departure? Rank the following options in the order you consider most relevant:
    - They are utterly exhausted and cannot muster up the strength to question or stop Oates.
    - They just don't care about Oates.
    - Oates is injured and it is best for everyone if he is gone.
    - They are too preoccupied with their own survival to care about what Oates is doing.

    Do you think that they should have behaved differently? Give a reason for your answer
2. **Class Discussion:** 'Oates' selfless act is sublime, but even more sublime, according to Mahon, is the manner in which he goes so quietly about it'. Discuss this statement as a class.
3. **Theme Talk:** 'Many of Mahon's poems deal with individuals who are willing to undertake extreme acts for the good of their community'. Discuss this statement in relation to 'Antarctica', 'As it Should be' and 'Ecclesiastes'.
4. **Exam Prep:** 'Mahon uses rich and vivid language to explore the twin themes of community and isolation'. Write an essay responding to this statement in which you refer to the present and poem and at least three others on the course.

Language Lab

1. Google the term 'villanelle'. What are the main features of this poetic form? How many of those features are present in 'Antarctica'?
2. **Class Discussion:** Consider the poem's two repeating lines. What do they suggest a) about Oates' thoughts as walks away from the tent and b) about the weather conditions as he does so?
3. 'Just as an enzyme transforms one substance into another, so Oates' sacrifice transforms a ridiculous situation into a sublime one'. Write a paragraph responding to this statement.

Kinsale

The kind of rain we knew is a thing of the past –
deep-delving, dark, deliberate you would say,
browsing on spire and bogland; but today
our sky-blue slates are steaming in the sun,
our yachts tinkling and dancing in the bay [5]
like race-horses. We contemplate at last
shining windows, a future forbidden to no-one.

Annotations
Kinsale: a harbour town in County Cork. A popular tourist resort, it is known for its restaurants, yachting, angling and golf. Mahon lived there from 2003 until his death in 2020.
[2] ***deep-delving:*** reaching deep into the earth
[5] ***tinkling:*** producing a series of short bell-like sounds

Tease It Out

1. The poet depicts a particular 'kind of rain':
   - Such rain, he says, was 'dark'. What mood or atmosphere is conjured by the idea of dark rain?
   - Mahon describes this kind of rain as 'deliberate'. Would you agree that there's an element of personification in this phrase? What action might the rain be undertaking in a 'deliberate' fashion?
   - What phrase indicates that this kind of rain seeped into the depths of the landscape?
   - **Class Discussion:** Mahon mentions church spires and boglands. Do you envisage a pleasant, cheery landscape, or a dreary depressing one?
2. **Class Discussion:** Mahon describes how 'we' were familiar with this kind of rain. Comment on his use of term 'we' here. Is he referring a) to his own friends and family b) to the population of Ireland or c) the inhabitants of Kinsale town?
3. Such rain, according to Mahon, is a 'thing of the past'. What does he mean by this?
4. Rain has recently been replaced by sunshine. Can you suggest why this might have lent the roof slates a 'sky blue' colour? What other effect has this change in weather had on the roof slates?
5. Consider the verbs 'tinkling' and 'dancing'. What do they suggest about the movement and appearance of the yachts in the harbour?
6. What simile is used to describe the yachts? Is it an effective one in your opinion?
7. What two things does the poet contemplate in the poem's final line?
8. Suggest why the windows might be shining.

Exam Prep

1. **Personal Response:** Do you think this poem depicts two different landscapes? Or does it depict the same landscape in very different sets of weather conditions? In each case give a reason for your answer.
2. **Class Discussion:** 'The poem's first three lines are associated with Ireland's past, while the second three are associated with Ireland's future'. Discuss this statement as a class.
3. **Theme Talk:** Working in pairs, discuss the following questions:
   - According to the poet, the 'future' was forbidden to certain people. Think about what you know of Ireland's past. Can you think of any groups who were excluded in such a fashion?
   - What phrase in the poem indicates that this negative situation went on for a long time?
   - Do you share the poet's belief that in Ireland the future is forbidden to no one?'
4. **Exam Prep:** Mahon's poetry is marked by a persistent desire to escape from the nightmare of history'. Discuss this statement with reference to 'Kinsale' and two other poems on the course.

Language Lab

1. "But today' is the pivotal phrase in this short poem'. Do you agree with this statement? Write a paragraph explaining your answer.
2. Would you agree that 'Kinsale' is optimistic in terms of tone and atmosphere? Support your answer with reference to the poem.

Paula Meehan

The eldest of six children, Paula Meehan was born in a working-class community in Dublin's inner-city tenements in 1955. With its rich heritage of storytelling and song, that community played a vital early part in the process that led Meehan to embrace the life of a poet. A dramatic change took place in 1968, when Meehan's neighbourhood was scheduled for development, and the local people were moved to the Dublin suburb of Finglas. Witnessing the break-up of her original, close-knit community was an important early experience that subsequently informed her attitude to poetry and art. Between 1972 and 1977, Meehan studied English, History and Classical Civilization at Trinity College Dublin. While she was studying at Trinity, she became actively involved in street theatre, beginning as a costuming assistant before moving on to become a dramatist.

Between 1981 and 1983, Meehan studied for an MFA (Master of Fine Arts) degree at Eastern Washington University in the United States. While attending Eastern Washington, she participated in writing workshops with some famous American writers. Among them was the poet and environmental activist Gary Snyder, who became a major influence on Meehan's thinking and writing. Meehan found herself especially drawn to Snyder's concern for nature, to his emphasis on the importance of communities and to the discipline that stemmed from his Zen Buddhist spiritual practice. In Snyder's understanding of the poet as a sort of dreamer and spiritual hero for the tribe, Meehan found an important conception of poetry that would underpin her resistance to aspects of Irish culture that she thought were harmful and oppressive. It's important to note that the influence of Snyder and other American writers didn't simply replace Meehan's earlier Irish inspirations. What really happened was far more interesting: American themes and influences fused with Meehan's highly original take on Irish culture to produce something new and unique. During her time in Washington, Meehan began to compose the poems that would feature in her first two collections, *Return and No Blame* (1984) and *Reading the Sky* (1986). Even in the first of these collections, Meehan's trademark blend of lyric poetry and more dramatic forms was already evident.

In Meehan's next two collections, *The Man Who Was Marked by Winter* (1991) and *Pillow Talk* (1994), the inner-city Dublin and American settings and themes of the first two volumes were joined by reflections on life in County Leitrim, where she lived between 1985 and 1989. Meehan's original focus on her native Dublin was revived when she moved back there in 1990, living first in the city's Merrion Square and subsequently in the north Dublin suburb of Baldoyle. In the poetry written between 1990

> "There are poems that tell stories but there are also poems that just give you a moment of vision or transcendence or colour even, or just an image that you can carry around with you. Two lines. Two lines can save a life, I believe it."

and the end of the twenty-first century's first decade, Meehan chronicled the dramatic changes that took place in Dublin, particularly during the period when a boom in property prices gave rise to intensive building and redevelopment. We can see Meehan's often critical and sorrowful attitude to these changes in such poems as "Death of a Field", which is set in a suburban building site and laments the harmful effects of the boom years on local communities.

Another form of oppression that becomes a major theme for Meehan is the subjugation and silencing of women's voices by Ireland's religious and secular authorities. Although she could draw inspiration from the powerful women poets who had emerged in Ireland during the 1980s and 1990s, Meehan once again followed a distinctive and original path in her poetic response to the oppression of women. For one thing, Meehan is less interested in private reflections on women's lives than she is in creating a form of public poetry that will resist the systemic oppression that restricts those lives. In "The Statue of the Virgin at Granard Speaks," for example, Meehan is consciously intervening in public debates about the status of women and commenting on Ireland's political and legislative battles about contraception, divorce and abortion. In doing so she is not only reflecting the influence of socially conscious poets from America and elsewhere but also placing herself in the tradition of the pre-Christian Irish bards, whose poetry had as much of a social function as it had a purely aesthetic or literary one.

In addition to her six collections of poetry, Meehan has written plays for both adult and young audiences. She has also authored *Music for Dogs*, a series of three radio plays that address the tragic subject of suicide during Ireland's boom years. Her poetry has been translated into French, Spanish, German, Galician, Japanese, Estonian and Greek. Meehan has been awarded numerous literary prizes, including the Butler Literary Award for Poetry, the Marten Toonder Award for Literature, the PPI Award for Radio Drama and the Denis Devlin Award. The famous folk singer Christy Moore is among the musicians who have set her poetry to music. This process of collaboration with other art forms has consistently played an important part in Meehan's artistic life, and she has frequently worked with dancers, visual artists and film makers. Meehan's commitment to social justice and communal values has inspired her to lead writers' workshops in communities, prisons and recovery programmes.

In February 2012, Meehan and her fellow poet and life partner, Theo Dorgan, co-hosted 'The Old Triangle – A Celebration for the Benefit of the Irish Penal Reform Trust' at the Abbey Theatre in Dublin. This event reflected Meehan's intense belief in the need for penal reform and greater awareness of the issues confronting prisoners in Ireland today. She has also acted as a mentor to emerging poets both within and beyond the universities.

Meehan has been publicly acknowledged by being elected as a member of Aosdána, an association of artists whose work is deemed to have made a particularly important contribution to the creative arts in Ireland. From 2013 to 2016, she served as Ireland Professor of Poetry, a position created following the award of the Nobel Prize for Literature to Seamus Heaney in 1995. In October 2020 a collections of Meehan's selected poetry was published under the title *As If By Magic*.

Buying Winkles

My mother would spare me sixpence and say,
'Hurry up now and don't be talking to strange
men on the way.' I'd dash from the ghosts
on the stairs where the bulb had blown
out into Gardiner Street, all relief. [5]
A bonus if the moon was in the strip of sky
between the tall houses, or stars out,
but even in rain I was happy – the winkles
would be wet and glisten blue like little
night skies themselves. I'd hold the tanner tight [10]
and jump every crack in the pavement,
I'd wave up to women at sills or those
lingering in doorways and weave a glad path through
men heading out for the night.

She'd be sitting outside the Rosebowl Bar [15]
on an orange-crate, a pram loaded
with pails of winkles before her.
When the bar doors swung open they'd leak
the smell of men together with drink
and I'd see light in golden mirrors. [20]
I envied each soul in the hot interior.

I'd ask her again to show me the right way
to do it. She'd take a pin from her shawl –
'Open the eyelid. So. Stick it in
till you feel a grip, then slither him out. [25]
Gently, mind.' The sweetest extra winkle
that brought the sea to me.
'Tell yer Ma I picked them fresh this morning.'

I'd bear the newspaper twists
bulging fat with winkles [30]
proudly home, like torches.

Annotations
Winkles: a species of edible sea snail

Tease It Out

1. What advice would the poet's mother give her before allowing her out to buy the winkles?
2. How does Meehan convey the fact that the winkles were a luxury that her family could rarely afford?
3. What did the young poet imagine dwelt in the stairwell leading down to the street? Why was this part of the building so dark?
4. Why would the young poet experience a sense of 'relief' when she reached the street?
5. Why would the young poet only see a 'strip of sky' when she looked up?
6. What term does she use to suggest that seeing the moon or the stars on these occasions afforded her additional pleasure?
7. Describe in your own words the effect that the rain would have on the appearance of the winkles? What simile does the poet use to describe the appearance of the wet winkles?
8. Why do you think the young poet jumped 'every crack' in the pavement?
9. The poet recalls how she would 'wave up' to the women in her neighbourhood.
    - Where would these women be located?
    - What do you imagine the women were doing?
    - Do you think these women were familiar to the poet? Give a reason for your answer.
10. Where was the woman selling the winkles located? What kind of premises was she outside?
11. Describe what the young poet would see and smell each time the bar door swung open.
12. What line suggests that the poet would be feeling the cold as she waited to buy the winkles?
13. **Class Discussion:** The young poet would ask the woman to show her 'again' the 'right way' to extract the winkle from its shell. Why did she do this? Consider the following and say which you think is most likely:
    - She could never remember how to do this.
    - It takes great skill to do this and was very difficult for the young poet.
    - She knew if she asked she would get to eat the winkle.
    - She just wanted to spend more time out on the evening streets.
14. Describe in your own words the method used to extract the winkle from its shell.
15. How does the poet convey the fact that she would return home with a great quantity of winkles?
16. How would the young poet be feeling as she walked back home? What do you think made her feel this way?

Exam Prep

1. **Personal Response:** Can you recall an occasion when you were young and were asked to do something that made you feel important? Describe the task that you were given and the feelings that you experienced when doing it.
2. **Class Discussion:** What impression does the poem give us of the men that lived in the neighbourhood?
3. **Theme Talk:** 'Although Meehan's poetry vividly documents the hardships of growing up in an impoverished neighbourhood, her poems are never gloomy'. Discuss this statement with reference to 'Buying Winkles' and two other poems on your course.
4. **Exam Prep:** 'Meehan's poetry presents us with a cast of memorable women who possess powerful personalities and great character'. Write a short essay in response to this statement, referring to 'Buying Winkles' and two other poems on your course.

Language Lab

1. How does this poem capture and convey a childlike view of the world? What words and phrases best illustrate this?
2. **Class Discussion:** Meehan describes how she would carry the packages of winkles home 'like torches'. Why do you think she makes this comparison? What does this simile tell us about the young poet's feelings as she made her way home?
3. 'Meehan's poetry provides us with wonderful snapshots of Dublin over the last seventy years'. Discuss this statement with reference to 'Buying Winkles' and two other poems on your course.

The Pattern

Little has come down to me of hers,
a sewing machine, a wedding band,
a clutch of photos, the sting of her hand
across my face in one of our wars

when we had grown bitter and apart. [5]
Some say that's the fate of the eldest daughter.
I wish now she'd lasted till after
I'd grown up. We might have made a new start

as women without tags like *mother, wife,*
sister, daughter, taken our chance from there. [10]
At forty-two she headed for god knows where.
I've never gone back to visit her grave.

   *

First she'd scrub the floor with Sunlight soap,
an arm reach at a time. When her knees grew sore
she'd break for a cup of tea, then start again [15]
at the door with lavender polish. The smell
would percolate back through the flat to us,
her brood banished to the bedroom.

As she buffed the wax to a high shine
did she catch her own face coming clear? [20]
Did she net a glimmer of her true self?
Did her mirror tell what mine tells me?

I have her shrug and go on
knowing history has brought her to her knees.
She'd call us in and let us skate around [25]
in our socks. We'd grow solemn as planets
in an intricate orbit about her.

   *

She bending over crimson cloth,
the younger kids are long in bed.
Late summer, cold enough for a fire, [30]
she works by fading light
to remake an old dress for me.
It's first day back at school tomorrow.

   *

Annotations
[17] *percolate:* to filter through the air
[18] *brood:* a family of young birds or animals
[19] *buffed:* polished

'Pure lambswool - Plenty of wear in it yet.
You know I wore this when I went out with your Da. [35]
I was supposed to be down in a friend's house,
your Granda caught us at the corner.
He dragged me in by the hair – it was long as yours then –
in front of the whole street.
He called your Da every name under the sun, [40]
cornerboy, lout; I needn't tell you
what he called me. He shoved my whole head
under the kitchen tap, took a scrubbing brush
and carbolic soap and in ice-cold water he scrubbed
every spick of lipstick and mascara off my face. [45]
Christ but he was a right tyrant, your Granda.
It'll be over my dead body anyone harms a hair of your head.'

*

She must have stayed up half the night
to finish the dress. I found it airing at the fire,
three new copybooks on the table and a bright [50]
bronze nib, St Christopher strung on a silver wire,

as if I were embarking on a perilous journey
to uncharted realms. I wore that dress
with little grace. To me it spelt poverty,
the stigma of the second hand. I grew enough to pass [55]

it on by Christmas to the next in line. I was sizing
up the world beyond our flat patch by patch
daily after school, and fitting each surprising
city street to city square to diamond. I'd watch

the Liffey for hours pulsing to the sea [60]
and the coming and going of ships,
certain that one day it would carry me
to Zanzibar, Bombay, the Land of the Ethiops.

*

There's a photo of her taken in the Phoenix Park
alone on a bench surrounded by roses [65]
as if she had been born to formal gardens.
She stares out as if unaware
that any human hand held the camera, wrapped
entirely in her own shadow, the world beyond her
already a dream, already lost. She's [70]
eight months pregnant. Her last child.

*

Her steel needles sparked and clacked,
the only other sound a settling coal
or her sporadic mutter
at a hard place in the pattern. [75]
She favoured sensible shades:
Moss Green, Mustard, Beige.

I dreamt a robe of a colour
so pure it became a word.

Sometimes I'd have to kneel [80]
an hour before her by the fire,
a skein around my outstretched hands,
while she rolled wool into balls.
If I swam like a kite too high
amongst the shadows on the ceiling [85]
or flew like a fish in the pools
of pulsing light, she'd reel me firmly
home, she'd land me at her knees.

Tongues of flame in her dark eye
she'd say, 'One of these days I must [90]
teach you to follow a pattern.'

Annotations

[41] *cornerboy:* a young man who hangs around on street corners looking for trouble; a mild term of abuse
[44] *carbolic soap:* a type of soap made from carbolic acid. It's known for its aggressive and abrasive qualities.
[51] *nib:* the tip of a fountain pen
[51] *St Christopher:* the patron saint of travellers
[55] *stigma:* a mark of disgrace
[63] *Zanzibar:* an island off the coast of east Africa
[63] *Bombay:* the Indian city known today as Mumbai
[63] *Land of the Ethiops:* Ethiopia
[74] *sporadic:* occasional
[82] *skein:* a loosely coiled and knotted length of wool
[89] *Tongues of flame:* the *Acts of The Apostles* describes how at Pentecost fire, described as 'tongues of flame', descended from heaven and landed on the twelve apostles, granting them the power to speak in all known languages, along with other abilities

THIS IS POETRY   PAULA MEEHAN

Tease It Out

Lines 1 to 12

1. What physical sensation does the poet recall? Can you suggest why this sensation lingered so visibly in the poet's memory?
2. **Class Discussion:** The poet presents the memory of this sensation as an heirloom she inherited. In what way is it different to the other heirlooms mentioned by the poet? In what ways is it similar?
3. The poet describes the relationship with her mother during her late teens and early twenties. Rank the following in order of plausibility:
   - She and her mother were best friends
   - They were close but argued
   - They had a love/hate relationship
   - They were completely estranged
   - They rarely conversed, and when they did it led to terrible arguments.
4. What age was the mother when she died?
5. What does the poet wish for?
6. **True or false:** The poet frequently visits her mother's grave. What does this suggest about her feelings towards her dead mother?

Lines 13 to 27

7. The poet remembers her mother polishing the floor of the family's flat on Sean MacDermott Street.
   - What hints do we get that the flat was a small one?
   - What phrases indicate that the mother went about this task in a systematic manner?
   - What phrases indicate that the mother was a hard worker who set out to perform the task well?
   - Where were the children while the mother performed the task?
8. **Class Discussion:** 'Did her mirror tell what mine tells me?' Suggest the thoughts and feelings the adult poet experiences when she looks in the mirror.
9. Did the mother study her reflection in a similar fashion? Does the poet know this for sure?
10. The poet describes how she and her siblings would skate around the room in a 'solemn' fashion. Does this choice of adjective surprise you? Give a reason for your answer.
11. The mother played a central role in the lives of her children. What comparison does the poet use to describe this? Is it a metaphor or a simile. Is it an effective comparison in your opinion?

Lines 34 to 63

12. Consider the phrase 'bending over crimson cloth'. What does this suggest about the manner in which the mother went about her work?
13. **True or false:** The mother was casual with her possessions and frequently threw things out.
14. The mother recalls when she herself wore the red dress. Describe what she was doing at the time.
15. Describe in your own words how the poet's grandfather punished the mother. Can you suggest why the grandfather was so angry? Does his reaction strike you as reasonable?
16. **True or false:** It took little effort for the mother to complete the alterations on the dress.
17. **Class Discussion:** Consider the term 'grace' in line 54. Does this suggest a) gratitude or b) physical deportment or c) something else entirely? Why did the poet react to the dress in this manner?
18. What phrases suggest that the young poet explored the 'world beyond [the] flat' in a deliberate and systematic manner?
19. **Group Discussion:** The poet would spend hours watching the river. Working in pairs, suggest two or three topics she might think about while she watched the river flow.

Lines 64 to 71

20. The mother seemed unaware that 'any human hand held the camera'. Does this suggest a) the mother is exhibiting great poise and lack or self-confidence or b) that she is distracted and distressed.
21. Consider lines 68 to 69 and rank the following in order of plausibility:
    - The mother seems self-reliant and independent
    - The mother seems troubled and depressed
    - It's a comment on the quality of the photography
22. Consider the poet's choice of the word 'wrapped' in these lines. Is it an effective one in your opinion? How does it relate to the poem's other images, especially those that relate to clothing?
23. **Class Discussion:** [T]he world beyond her/ already a dream, already lost'. Does this suggest the mother was a) a mindful person who lived in the moment or b) someone who resented lost opportunities or c) someone who is happy to live within the limits of their own area.

Lines 72 to 91

24. The poet describes her mother knitting by the fireside.
    - What sounds would be audible during these knitting sessions?
    - What indicates that the mother worked with intense conversation?
    - Suggest why the mother's needles 'sparked'.
    - **True or false:** The mother improvised a lot, adding stitches in an almost random fashion.
25. The poet also recalls helping her mother convert a 'skein' or hunk of wool into neat balls.
    - What position would the poet have to take up during this procedure?
    - How would she have to hold the skein of wool?
    - What indicates that she frequently lost concentration?
    - How did her mother react when she did so?
26. How did the young poet imagine interacting with the shadows on the ceiling?
27. The flames from the hearth were reflected in the polished floor. What metaphor does the poet use to describe this?
28. How did she imagine interacting with these reflections?
29. Comment on the poet's use of the verbs swim and fly in this passage. Does this surprise you? What does this suggest about her imagination when she was a child?

Exam Prep

1. **Personal Response:** Meehan paints a very vivid portrait of her mother in this poem. Pick out two or three lines that indicate the following:
   - The mother was a diligent worker
   - She was fiercely protective
   - She tried to do the best for her family
   - She had an angry side

   Which of the above characteristics are associated with the 'Tongues of flame' the poet sees in her mother's eyes? Is the mother, overall, presented as a strong and powerful woman or as a vulnerable one? Give a reason for your answer.

2. **Class Discussion:** Consider the following phrase for a moment: 'I dreamt a robe of a colour/ so pure'.
   - What do you visualise when you read these lines?
   - Would you agree that they are difficult to visualise precisely?
   - What do they suggest about the young poet's imagination?
   - Can you find two other phrases that suggest that even as a young person Meehan was evolving into a creative artist?
   - 'Knitting, like poetry, is presented as a creative act'. Can you identify any passages that support this claim?

3. **Theme Talk:** 'Meehan's concern with social justice is evident in this poem, as she describes how her mother had been brought 'to her knees' by a society that denied her freedom and opportunity'. Write a short essay in response to this statement.

4. **Exam Prep:** Meehan has described how poetry 'can be a tool for excavation'. Discuss how Meehan's own poetry excavates the past, making reference to 'The Pattern', 'Cora, Auntie' and 'Hearth Lesson'.

Language Lab

1. The poet imagines herself and her mother meeting as 'women without tags'.
   - Is the poet suggesting that society views women only in terms of their family roles rather than as individuals?
   - Is the poet suggesting that relations with her mother would have been easier when she was 'grown up' and no longer depended on her as a provider?
   - Would you agree that men are 'tagged' in a similar fashion by society?

2. "One of these days I must/ teach you to follow a pattern".
   - What does this suggest about the young poet's personality?
   - Which of Meehan's poems can be said to follow a pattern? Which have a freer and looser quality?
   - 'This poem presents each family as a pattern in which traits and characteristics are repeated across the generations'. Write a short essay in response to this statement.

3. Watch Video 12, which features a reading of the poem by the poet herself.
   - Mention three things we learn about the poet's mother from the introduction to the reading.
   - Pick out two or three words or phrases that Meehan particulalrly emphasises as she reads.
   - During what section of the poem did the poet's reading become most emotional? Give a reason for your answer.

The Statue of the Virgin at Granard Speaks

It can be bitter here at times like this,
November wind sweeping across the border.
Its seeds of ice would cut you to the quick.
The whole town tucked up safe and dreaming,
even wild things gone to earth, and I [5]
stuck up here in this grotto, without as much as
star or planet to ease my vigil.

The howling won't let up. Trees
cavort in agony as if they would be free
and take off — ghost voyagers [10]
on the wind that carries intimations
of garrison towns, walled cities, ghetto lanes
where men hunt each other and invoke
the various names of God as blessing
on their death tactics, their night manoeuvres. [15]
Closer to home the wind sails over
dying lakes. I hear fish drowning.
I taste the stagnant water mingled
with turf smoke from outlying farms.

They call me Mary — Blessed, Holy, Virgin. [20]
They fit me to a myth of a man crucified:
the scourging and the falling, and the falling again,
the thorny crown, the hammer blow of iron
into wrist and ankle, the sacred bleeding heart.
They name me Mother of all this grief [25]
though mated to no mortal man.
They kneel before me and their prayers
fly up like sparks from a bonfire
that blaze a moment, then wink out.

It can be lovely here at times. Springtime, [30]
early summer. Girls in Communion frocks
pale rivals to the riot in the hedgerows
of cow parsley and haw blossom, the perfume
from every rushy acre that's left for hay
when the light swings longer with the sun's push north. [35]

Or the grace of a midsummer wedding
when the earth herself calls out for coupling
and I would break loose of my stony robes,
pure blue, pure white, as if they had robbed
a child's sky for their colour. My being [40]
cries out to be incarnate, incarnate,
maculate and tousled in a honeyed bed.

Annotations

Granard: a town in Co. Longford. The statue is located in a grotto on the outskirts of the town
[7] *vigil:* a period of keeping awake during the time usually spent asleep, especially to keep watch or pray
[9] *cavort:* jump or dance around excitedly
[10] *ghost voyagers:* the statue imagines the trees being carried through the night by the wind
[11] *intimations:* indications; hints; communications
[12] *ghetto:* an impoverished part of the city, often occupied by a minority group
[18] *stagnant water:* water that has an unpleasnat odour due to having no current or flow
[37] *coupling:* sexual intercourse
[41] *incarnate:* made flesh; having a human form or body
[42] *maculate:* stained; imperfect; sexual. The Virgin Mary is usually thought of as being immaculate, as being stainless, perfect and asexual
[42] *tousled:* caressed
[43] *pageantry:* elaborate display or ceremony
[45] *scud:* to move fast in a straight line as if driven by the wind
[46] *windfalls:* fruit that has fallen from a tree's branches
[50] *All Soul's Night:* In the Catholic Church this is a day of remembrance for all the faithful sho have passed away. It is celebrated annually on 2 November.

Even an autumn burial can work its own pageantry.
The hedges heavy with the burden of fruiting
crab, sloe, berry, hip; clouds scud east [45]
pear scented, windfalls secret in long
orchard grasses, and some old soul is lowered
to his kin. Death is just another harvest
scripted to the season's play.

But on this All Souls' Night there is [50]
no respite from the keening of the wind.
I would not be amazed if every corpse came risen
from the graveyard to join in exaltation with the gale,
a cacophony of bone imploring sky for judgement
and release from being the conscience of the town. [55]

On a night like this I remember the child
who came with fifteen summers to her name,
and she lay down alone at my feet
without midwife or doctor or friend to hold her hand
and she pushed her secret out into the night, [60]
far from the town tucked up in little scandals,
bargains struck, words broken, prayers, promises,
and though she cried out to me in extremis
I did not move,
I didn't lift a finger to help her, [65]
I didn't intercede with heaven,
nor whisper the charmed word in God's ear.

On a night like this I number the days to the solstice
and the turn back to the light.
                     O sun, [70]
centre of our foolish dance,
burning heart of stone,
molten mother of us all,
hear me and have pity.

Annotations

[51] **keening:** wailing

[53] **exultation:** a state of elation or exhuberance

[56] **I remember the child:** refers to the tragic death of Ann Lovett, a 15-year-old schoolgirl from the town. Ann had become pregnant but had managed to keep the pregnancy secret from her family and friends. On 31 January 1984, knowing her baby was coming, she went to the grotto alone to give birth. Ann was discovered by some fellow school children, who noticed her schoolbag while passing the grotto. By then Ann's baby was already dead, and she passed away some hours later. The story became a national scandal and greatly influenced the debate on women, sexuality and pregnancy in Irish life, and the story of her death played a huge part in a seminal national debate on women giving birth outside marriage

[63] **in extremis:** in an extremely difficult situation at the death

[68] **solstice:** refers to 21 December, the shortest day of the year, when the sun appears furthest from the equator

THIS IS POETRY   PAULA MEEHAN

Tease It Out

The weather on All Soul's Night
1. The statue describes the wind on this particular November evening.
   - The wind carries particles of ice and sleet. What line indicates this?
   - How does the statue characterise the sound of the wind? Is this sound constant or intermittent?
   - What impact does the wind have on the nearby trees? What poetic device is used to describe this?
   - What can the statue taste when the wind blows into her mouth?
2. On this night the statue is the only person or creature exposed to these terrible conditions. What lines or phrases indicate this?
3. In lines 50 to 55 the statue suggests the wind is loud enough to wake the dead:
   - This suggestion might be considered an example of what poetic device?
   - What term suggests this exceptionally loud wind has a mournful quality?
   - Why is this image appropriate to the night in which the poem is set?
   - **True or false:** The risen corpses of the dead will move quietly through the land.
   - What does the statue imagine these risen bodies would demand?

Intimations from the North
4. It's time to refresh your knowledge of Irish history and geography:
   - How is the term 'garrison town' used in the context of Irish history?
   - Name one 'garrison town' in the northern part of the island.
   - Name one city that still has its city walls in the northern part of the island.
   - What phrases indicate that violent acts are carried out each night in these towns and cities?
5. Describe in your own words how the statue learns about these violent acts.
6. **Class Discussion:** '[I]nvoke/ the various names of God'. Discuss the Northern Ireland Troubles as a class. What role did religion play in this terrible conflict?

The statue's view of Christianity
7. What startling simile does the statue use to describe the prayers of the local people?
8. What does this comparison suggest about the statue's attitude to these prayers? Rank the following in order of plausibility:
   - Awe
   - Admiration
   - Pity and contempt
   - Puzzlement
9. **Class Discussion:** 'They call me Mary'. How does the statue feel about being addressed in such a fashion? Does she respond with puzzlement, pride, indifference or something else entirely?
10. What visitors - real or imagined - come to the statue's grotto in spring, summer, autumn and winter? What does this suggest about the role of the Catholic faith in Irish society?
11. The statue mentions different forms of suffering associated with the crucifixion. Describe each one in your own words.
12. The statue refers to the crucifixion as a 'myth'. What different meanings of the word 'myth' might be relevant here?
13. The statue seems to view Catholicism as a religion that focuses on misery and sorrow. What phrases support this?

The changing seasons
14. This poem features a great deal of imagery related to the seasons and the sun.
    - Consider the term 'riot'. What does this suggest about the wildflowers that fill the hedges in spring and early summer?
    - **True or false:** The whiteness of the wildflowers is less intense than the Communion frocks.
    - According to the statue, is the smell from rush covered fields pleasant or unpleasant?
    - What use will farmers make of these fields later in the year?
    - What causes the hedges to be weighed down in autumn?
    - In autumn, the scent of fruit hangs in the air. What phrase indicates this?
15. **Class Discussion:** In summer, according to the statue, what does the earth itself want people to do? What two poetic devices might be said to feature here? (Hint: they both start with a 'p').

The death of Ann Lovett
16. The statue remembers the tragic death of Ann Lovett in 1984.
    - What age was Ann when she so tragically passed away?
    - Did Ann have any assistance or medical attention while she was giving birth?
    - Suggest why Ann might have 'cried out' to the statue at this moment. What did the statue represent to her?

Language Lab

1. Read lines 38 to 42 carefully and answer the following questions:
   - In what sense does the statue want to break free? Is this possible?
   - What comparison does she use to describe the colour of her robes? Is this a simile or a metaphor?
   - The statue would like to become a living, breathing human being. What words and phrases indicate this?
   - What activity would the statue like to engage in once it has attained human embodiment?
2. The statue presents a very spritual view of nature.
   - Over the years the statue has watched funerals taking place. Does it feel any grief or sorrow for the people who have died?
   - **True or false:** The statue presents the earth itself as a goddess. Give a reason for your answer.
   - Describe in your own words why the statue is looking forward to the 21 December.
   - To whom or what does the statue pray at the close of the poem?
   - Does she present this entity as male or female?
   - What does she ask this entity to do? Do you find this request surprising? Give a reason for your answer.
   - **Class Discussion:** 'There is something pagan or almost pre-Christian in how the statue presents the changing of the seasons'. Discuss this statement as a class.
3. Watch Video 13, which is the first part of a documentary about the tragic death of Ann Lovett.
   - Mention three things you learned about Irish society in the 1980s.
   - Has Irish society changed completely since that time?
   - Are any aspects of irish society the same?

Exam Prep

1. **Class Discussion:** The statue refers to various 'scandals' that have occured in Granard.
   - Can you suggest two or three topics that these scandals might relate to?
   - According to the statue, are these scandals important in the greater scheme of things?
   - How do the local townspeople attempt to deal with these scandals? Do you get the impression they are dealt with openly and honestly?
2. **Personal Response:** Consider the phrase 'she pushed her secret out into the night'.
   - What literary device is being used here? (Hint: It starts with an 'm', but isn't a metaphor).
   - What does this suggest about how Ann behaved during her pregnancy? What does it suggest about the nature of the society in which she lived?
   - List two or three emotions you experienced while reading the statue's account of Ann's tragic passing.
   - 'There is a terrible irony in Ann's decision to give birth at the grotto'. Discuss this statement in small groups. Then write a paragraph outlining your own personal response.
3. **Theme Talk:** 'This poem presents a very negative view of the Catholic religion'. Write a short essay in reponse to this statement. Consider the statue's account of the Troubles in Northern Ireland, of the crucifixion and of the local peoples' prayers. Also consider the statue's response to Ann's prayers and cries.
4. **Exam Prep:** 'Again and again in her poetry, Meehan gives voice to the voiceless, to those who have been failed and forgotten by society at large'. Discuss this statement in relation to the present poem and three others on the course.

Cora, Auntie

Staring Death down
with a bottle of morphine in one hand,
a bottle of Jameson in the other;

laughing at Death-
love unconditional keeping her just this side
of the threshold

as her body withered
and her eyes grew darker and stranger
as her hair grew back after chemo

thick and curly as when she was a girl;
always a girl in her glance
teasing Death – humour a lance

she tilted at Death.
Scourge of Croydon tram drivers and High Street dossers
on her motorised invalid scooter

that last year;
bearing the pain,
not crucifixion but glory

in her voice.
Old skin, bag of bones,
grinning back at the rictus of Death:

always a girl in her name-
Cora, maiden, from the Greek Κορη,
promising blossom, summer, the scent of thyme.

Sequin: she is standing on the kitchen table.
She is nearly twenty-one.
It is nineteen sixty-one.

They are sewing red sequins, the women,
to the hem of her white satin dress
as she moves slowly round and round.

Sequins red as berries.
red as the lips of maidens,
red as blood on the snow

in Child's old ballads,
as red as this pen
on this white paper

Annotations

[2] **morphine:** a narcotic drug obtained from opium that's used to relieve pain
[3] **Jameson:** a brand of whiskey
[5] **love unconditional:** unconditional love
[9] **chemo:** chemotherapy
[12] **humour a lance:** humour was a lance
[13] **tilted at:** aimed at; attacked with a lance while on horseback
[14] **Scourge:** menace
[14] **Croydon:** an area of south London
[14] **dossers:** an idle person; a person who sleeps rough
[23] **Κορη:** can mean girl, maiden or daughter. In the latter sense it came to be an alternate name given to Persephone to denote her being the daughter of Demeter
[25] **Sequin:** a small piece of shiny coloured metal foil or plastic, usually round, used to decorate garments; an ancient coin of Italy and Turkey
[34] **Child's old ballads:** The Child Ballads are 305 traditional ballads from England and Scotland, and their American variants, anthologised by Francis James Child during the second half of the 19th century.
[46] **taking the boat to England:** emigrating to England
[65] **coinage:** coins that have been standardised for use as currency; a brand new word or phrase created by an author

I've snatched from the chaos
to cast these lines
at my own kitchen table —

Cora, Marie, Jacinta, my aunties,
Helena, my mother, Mary, my grandmother —
the light of those stars

only reaching me now.
I orbit the table I can barely see over.
I am under it singing.

She was weeks from taking the boat to England.
Dust on the mantelpiece,
dust on the cards she left behind:

a black cat swinging in a silver horseshoe,
a giant key to the door,
emblems of luck, of access.

All that year I hunted sequins:
roaming the house I found them
in cracks and crannies,

in the pillowcase,
under the stairs,
in a hole in the lino,

in a split in the sofa,
in a tear in the armchair
in the home of the shy mouse.

With odd beads and single earrings,
a broken charm bracelet, a glittering pin,
I gathered them into a tin box

which I open now in memory —
the coinage, the sudden glamour
of an emigrant soul.
.

Tease It Out

Lines 1 to 24

1. The poet mentions 'love unconditional':
    - For whom do we usually feel unconditional love?
    - Who do you imagine was giving the aunt such love?
    - How does the poet convey that it was such love that was keeping the aunt alive at this point?
2. What surprised the poet about the aunt's hair when it grew back after her chemotherapy?
3. **Class Discussion:** The poet describes how in her final year she heard '[N]ot crucifixion but glory// in her [aunt's] voice'. What does this tell us about the manner in which the aunt bore the great pain and suffering in her final years?
4. Where was the aunt living at this stage in her life? What line in this part of the poem makes this clear?
5. How did the aunt get around the city streets? What indication are we given that she was rather reckless and careless with the handling of this device?
6. '[G]rinning back at the rictus of Death'. What sort of facial expression does 'rictus' suggest? What emotions does it suggest the personified Death experienced when it came face to face with the poet's aunt? What does this line suggest about the aunt's attitude towards death?
7. The poet contemplates the aunt's name. What does she say that the name Cora means? What associations does the Greek form of the name Cora have?
8. **Class Discussion:** Based on your reading of lines 1 to 24, does the poet think that her aunt's name suit her?

Lines 25 to 51

9. The poet recalls a moment from 1961 when her aunt was 'nearly twenty-one'.
    - Why is the aunt 'standing on the kitchen table'?
    - Do you think that this is happening in the aunt's house or in the young poet's house? Give a reason for your answer.
    - Who are the 'women' who have gathered around the aunt? What are these women doing?
    - **True or false:** The aunt remains completely still while the women go about their work.
10. Do you think it was traditional to have such sequins sewn into the hem of a wedding dress or do you think that this was something that Cora wanted to do personally? Give a reason for your answer.
11. Lines 46 to 50: The poet shifts to the present moment, where she is at her own writing this very poem. Where is she seated? What colour pen is she using to write the poem? What colour paper is she writing on?
12. What is it that the poet has 'snatched from the chaos'? Is it a moment from her hectic life or is it some paper that she has retrieved from the mess of her kitchen?
13. The poet thinks of her three aunties, her mother and her grandmother. She compares them to stars whose 'light' is only now 'reaching' her. What do you think she means by this? Rank the following in order of plausibility:
    - These women always seemed so remote from her in terms of age and life experience, but now she can relate to them
    - The poet only now realises how important and special these women were
    - These were women that never cared about her
14. Lines 44 to 45: The poet returns to the occasion in 1961 when the sequins were being sewn onto the hem of Cora's wedding dress. How does the poet convey that she was a very young child at this time? What does she remember doing while the women were gathered around the kitchen table?
15. 'She was weeks from taking the boat to England. Why do you think Cora moved to England around this time?
16. **Class Discussion:** The poet recalls the cards that Cora received in the weeks leading up to her move to England. What sorts of images or pictures were on the front of these cards? What was the purpose of these cards and what sort of messages do you think they contained?

Lines 52 to 63

17. Did the young poet go in search of sequins around the house or did she come across them by accident? What word or phrase indicates this?
18. List the different places in the house that the poet found sequins.
19. What else did the young poet find as she searched for the sequins?
20. Where did the poet store the things she found? Why do you think she wanted to keep these items?
21. **Class Discussion:** Why do you think the poet refers to the items kept in the tin box as 'coinage'?
22. Whose soul is the poet referring to in the poem's last lines? Why do you think she uses the term 'emigrant' to describe this soul? Do you think there are a number of ways of interpreting this? Give a reason for your answer.

Exam Prep

1. **Personal Response:** The first twenty-one lines detail the manner in which Cora responded to and coped with the fact that she was close to death. List the different ways that Cora dealt with this uncomfortable truth. Do you think that the aunt was genuinely fearless or do you think she was just pretending to be? Give a reason for your answer.
2. **Class Discussion:** What three adjectives would you use to describe the poet's aunt, based on your reading of the poem? What do you think Meehan most admired about Cora?
3. **Theme Talk:** 'Meehan's poetry documents the formative role that strong female relatives played in her young life'. Write a short essay discussing this statement, making reference to 'Cora, Auntie' and at least two other poems on your course.
4. **Exam Prep:** 'Meehan's poetry wonderfully captures the the ups and downs, the joys and heartbreaks, of family life'. Discuss this statement with reference to 'Cora, Auntie' and at least two other poems on the course.

Language Lab

1. Consider the poem's title. Why do you think the poet used 'Cora, Auntie' as opposed to 'Auntie Cora'? Give a reason for your answer.
2. The poet imagines the aunt as a kind of gunslinger in the opening lines.
   - What is the aunt armed with?
   - Who is her enemy?
   - What immediate impression do these opening lines give us of the aunt?
3. What other metaphors does the poet use to describe the aunt's attitude to death? Describe them in your own words and say which you found to be the most effective and memorable.
4. The poet uses four similes to describe the vivid red colour of the sequins that were being sewn into the hem of the aunt's wedding dress. What are the four comparisons that she makes?
5. Meehan describes the 'sudden glamour' of the sequins in the tin box. What do you think these found sequins represent or symbolise for the poet? What does she think of when she sees them?

The Exact Moment I Became a Poet
for Kay Foran

was in 1963 when Miss Shannon
rapping the duster on the easel's peg
half obscured by a cloud of chalk

said *Attend to your books girls,
or mark my words, you'll end up* [5]
in the sewing factory.

It wasn't just that some of the girls'
mothers worked in the sewing factory
or even that my own aunt did,

and many neighbours, but [10]
that those words 'end up' robbed
the labour of its dignity.

Not that I knew it then,
not in those words – labour, dignity.
That's all back construction. [15]

making sense; allowing also
the teacher was right
and no one knows it like I do myself.

But: I saw them; mothers, aunts and neighbours
trussed like chickens [20]
on a conveyor belt,

getting sewn up the way my granny
sewed the sage and onion stuffing
in the birds.

Words could pluck you, [25]
leave you naked,
your lovely shiny feathers all gone.

Annotations
[2] **easel:** used for holding the blackboard in place
[20] **trussed:** having your legs and arms tied together

Tease It Out

1. How did Miss Shannon attempt to get the attention of the girls in her class?
2. Why for a moment or two was Miss Shannon difficult to see?
3. What advice did Miss Shannon give the girls?
4. What would happen to the girls, according to Miss Shannon, if they failed to follow this advice?
5. Why might Miss Shannon's words have made some of the girls feel awkward or embarrassed?
6. Did the poet herself experience such feelings? Give a reason for your answer.
7. **Class Discussion:** What does the word 'dignity' mean? What does it mean for labour to possess dignity? Would you agree that all jobs, when done well, possess dignity of a sort?
8. **True or false:** The young poet felt that work in the sewing factory possessed no such dignity.
9. Use the phrase 'end up' in three separate sentences. Does it suggest a good or a bad outcome?
10. Can you suggest why this phrase, as the young poet saw it, made work in the sewing factory seem undignified?
11. 'the teacher was right/ and no one knows it like I do myself'. In what sense, according to the poet, was Miss Shannon 'right' in her assessment of the sewing factory? Suggest how the poet came to this conclusion.
12. But: I saw them. The poet's imagination runs away with her and she is struck by an intensely vivid daydream:
    - Who does the poet see and where are these individuals?
    - The poet describes how these individuals have been 'trussed up'. What do you visualise here?
    - Describe in your own words what is happening to these poor 'trussed up' individuals.

Exam Prep

1. **Personal Response:** Pick an occasion from your time in primary school that stands out in your memory. Write a poem or short prose piece in which you describe that 'exact moment' in as much detail as possible.
2. **Theme Talk:** Meehan is well known for her depictions of childhood:
    - What do you understand by the term 'back construction' as Meehan uses it in this poem?
    - Compare this poem to 'Buying Winkles' and 'Hearth Lessons'. Which poem in your opinion most vividly captures the mentality of childhood?
3. **Class Discussion:** Consider the poem's title. What was so special about this moment in the classroom? In what sense did the young poet's understanding of language change on that day in 1963? In what sense did she become a poet at that very moment?
4. **Exam Prep:** 'Meehan is nothing if not outspoken when it comes to issues of poverty and social justice'. Write an essay responding to this statement in which you reference this poem and two others on the course.

Language Lab

1. The young poet realised for the first time that words are extremely powerful and can cause great psychological harm. What metaphor is used to describe this harm? Is it an effective one in your opinion?
2. Meehan is known for her playful, witty approach to the poetry. Is this playfulness in evidence in her depiction of the 'trussed up' mothers, aunts and neighbours? Or is this an image of pure horror? Give a reason for your answer.

My Father Perceived as a Vision of St Francis

for Brendan Kennelly

It was the piebald horse in next door's garden
frightened me out of a dream
with her drawn whinny. I was back
in the boxroom of the house,
my brother's room now,
full of ties and sweaters and secrets.
Bottles chinked on the doorstep,
the first bus pulled up to the stop.
The rest of the house slept

except for my father. I heard
him rake the ash from the grate,
plug in the kettle, hum a snatch of a tune.
Then he unlocked the back door
and stepped out into the garden.

Autumn was nearly done, the first frost
whitened the slates of the estate.
He was older than I had reckoned,
his hair completely silver,
and for the first time I saw the stoop
of his shoulder, saw that
his leg was stiff. What's he at?
So early and still stars in the west?

They came then: birds
of every size, shape, colour; they came
from the hedges and shrubs,
from eaves and garden sheds,

from the industrial estate, outlying fields,
from Dubber Cross they came
and the ditched of the North Road.
The garden was a pandemonium
when my father threw up his hands
and tossed the crumbs to the air. The sun
cleared O'Reilly's chimney
and he was suddenly radiant,
a perfect vision of St Francis,
made whole, made young again,
in a Finglas garden.

Annotations

St Francis: St Francis of Assissi (1182-1226) was an Italian monk, mystic and preacher. Known for his intense bond with animals in the natural world. He is Italy's patron saint and one of the most venerated figues in Christianity

[1] ***piebald:*** having irregular patches of black and white

[4] ***boxroom:*** small room used for storage or as a bedroom

[30] ***pandemonium:*** chaos; uproar

[34] ***radiant:*** shining; glowing

Tease It Out

1. Watch Video 11, which is a scene from *Brother Sun, Sister Moon*.
   - Who has St Francis come to visit and what does he want?
   - Do Francis and his followers seem to fit in in this location? Give a reason for your answer.
   - Pick three adjectives that best describe your impression of St Francis's personality.
2. The poet has returned for a brief stay at her family home in Finglas.
   - What room of the house is she staying in?
   - Who normally sleeps in this room nowadays?
   - What items of clothing are scattered around the room?
   - What secret items might the room's normal occupier have hidden in there?
3. What sound woke the poet from her dream?
4. What other two sounds does she hear as she lies in bed?
5. What indications do we get that it is still very early in the morning?
6. The poet listens to her father downstairs. What does she hear him doing?
7. The poet looks out an upstair's window. What are the weather conditions like outside?
8. **True of false:** It is so early that stars are still visible in the sky?
9. The poet is suddenly struck by the fact that her father is growing older. Mention three aspects of his appearance and demeanour that she finds startling?
10. Suddenly, the garden starts to fill with birds:
    - **True or false:** The birds all belong to a single species.
    - The poet imagines that the birds have travelled from all around the locality. Mention three locations that she thinks of.
    - What did the father toss into the air once the birds had assembled?
    - How did the birds respond to this event?
11. **Class Discussion:** How do we know that the father does this every morning?
12. What object has been blocking the light of the rising sun?
13. The poet's father seemed very different when the sunlight finally struck him. Pick out three phrases that suggest this.
14. What does the comparison with St Francis suggest about the poet's father at this moment? Rank the following in order of plausibility:
    - He seemed like a kindly and gentle person
    - He seemed like someone with a close kinship with the natural world
    - He seemed like a mystical figure, one capable of triggering miraculous events
    - He seemed like an extremely holy and moral person
    - He seemed capable of persuading, leading and influencing others

Exam Prep

1. **Personal Response:** Write a letter in which you describe your morning ritual. Describe the birds in as much detail as you can imagine them. What emotions do you imagine feeling as the flock of birds descend on your Finglas garden?
2. **Class Discussion:** 'All too often we fail to see close even family members for who they really are'.
   - Might this statement be applied to both family members mentioned in this poem?
   - Mention two ways in which the poet is surprised by her father on this particular morning.
   - Do you agree that at the end of the poem, the poet sees her father as he really is? Give a reason for your answer.
3. **Theme Talk:** 'Meehan uses her unique poetic style to explore the highs and lows of family relationships'. Discuss this statement in relation to this poem and two others on your course.
4. **Exam Prep:** 'Meehan has a uniquely spiritual view of the natural world'. Write a short essay discussing this topic.

Language Lab

1. **Class Discussion:** Take a moment to consider the poem's title:
   - How is the term 'vision' used in the context of religion?
   - Are 'visions' the same as hallucinations or do they reveal a deeper reality about the world?
   - In what sense is the poet's experience similar to such a religious 'vision'? In what sense is it different?
   - Is the poet's father really transformed at this moment, or does this transformation only occur in the poet's perception?
2. Meehan is a poet who makes skilful use of repetition in her poetry. Discuss this statement with reference to this poem, 'Death of a Field' and 'Prayer for the Children of Longing'.

Hearth Lesson

Either phrase will bring it back —
money to burn, burning a hole in your pocket.

I am crouched by the fire
in the flat in Seán MacDermott Street
while Zeus and Hera battle it out.

for his every thunderbolt
she had the killing glance;
she'll see his fancyman
and raise him the Cosmo Snooker Hall;
he'll see her ' the only way you get any
attention around here is if you neigh';
he'll raise her airs and graces
or the mental state of her siblings
every last one of them.

I'm net, umpire, and court; most balls
are lobbed over my head.
Even then I can judge it's better
than brooding and silence and the particular hell of the unsaid,
of 'tell your mother…' ' ask your father…'.

Even then I can tell it was money,
the lack of it day after day,
at the root of the bitter words
but nothing prepared us one teatime
when he handed up his wages.

She straightened each rumpled pound note, then
a weariness come suddenly over her,
she threw the lot in the fire.

The flames were blue and pink and green,
a marvellous sight, an alchemical scene.
'It's not enough,' she stated simply.

The flames sheered from cinder to chimney breast
like trapped exotic birds;
the shadows jumped floor to ceiling, and she'd
had the last, the astonishing, word.

Annotations

[5] Zeus and Hera: in Greek mythology Zeus and his wife Hera were the king and queen of the Gods and rulers of Mount Olympus. Many legends recount their tempestuous relationship

[8-9] see … raise: terms used in the game of poker. To 'see' is to match the amount being gambled by another player. To 'raise' is to increase the amount being gambled

[8] fancyman: a man that the mother fancies or finds attractive

[29] alchemical: relating to alchemy, which was the medieval forerunner of chemistry and focused on transforming one substance into another

[31] sheered: swerved

[31] chimney breast: portion of a chimney which projects forward from a wall to accommodate a fireplace

Tease It Out

1. Where did the young poet frequently find herself during the arguments between her parents?
2. What posture did the young poet adopt at these moments? What does this suggest about her emotional state as the argument raged above her?
3. **Class Discussion:** 'The poet's reference to Zeus and Hera is playful and amusing, but it also highlights the feelings of dread and powerlessness she felt during these rows'. Discuss this statement as a class.
4. What do the terms 'see' and 'raise' mean in the context of poker and similar card games? What does Meehan's use of these terms suggest about the arguments between her parents?
5. Working in pairs, answer the following questions:
    - What do you understand by the terms 'fancyman' and 'airs and graces'. What is the father suggesting about the mother when he uses these terms?
    - What phrase indicates that the father, in the opinion of the mother, spent too much time and money betting on horses?
    - Mention another of the father's pastimes that met with the mother's disapproval.
    - What phrase indicates that the father, as the mother saw it, paid the mother very little attention?
6. What sporting metaphor does the poet use to describe the argument between her parents? Is it an effective one in your opinion?
7. What phrase indicates that the young poet didn't understand much of what was said in these arguments? Do you think this was deliberate on the parents' part?
8. **True or false:** The poet preferred her parents' arguments to the periods when they silently ignored one another.
9. The poet describes how the father handed up his wages each week.
    - **True or false:** The father was paid by cheque.
    - What use do you imagine the mother made of this money?
    - Do you get the impression the father always handed over the entirety of his wages? Give a reason for your answer.
10. What did the mother do with the wages on one particular teatime?
11. '[N]othing prepared us'. Can you suggest why the family were so surprised by this gesture?
12. Describe the mother's demeanour as she did this. What mental or emotional state did it exhibit?
13. Why does the poet view this gesture as part of the argument between her parents? Why does she view it as the winning move in this argumentative game, the one to which there can be no response?

Exam Prep

1. **Theme Talk:** Meehan writes frequently about the theme of poverty and hardship. Consider the phrase "It's not enough" in this regard.
    - Is the mother referring only to money here?
    - Would you agree that this demeans the father's role as worker and provider?
    - Do you think this was deliberate on the mother's part?
    - In what sense is this gesture a self-defeating one?
    - 'The gesture is born of frustration and desperation'. Write a paragraph in response to this statement.
2. **Exam Prep:** Meehan uses her unique style to explore the positive and negative aspects of human existence'. Write a short essay in response to this statement.

Language Lab

1. **Personal Response:** 'Either phrase will bring it back'. Can you suggest why these phrases are linked in the poet's mind to this particular set of memories? Can you recall a time when your own memory was triggered by an overheard phrase, a scent or a piece of music? Write a paragraph describing your experience.
2. **Class Discussion:** 'Meehan's use of the present tense renders her memories immediate and vivid for the reader'. Discuss this statement as a class.
3. What impact did the burning notes have on the colour of the flames? What simile does Meehan use to describe the action of the flames at that moment? What other literary device is used in this passage?
4. Do you think the flames really behaved in this fashion, or is it just in the poet's memory?

Prayer for the Children of Longing

A poem commissioned by the community of Dublin's north inner city for the lighting of the Christmas tree in Buckingham Street, to remember their children who died from drug use.

Great tree from the far northern forest
Still rich with the sap of the forest
Here at the heart of winter
Here at the heart of the city

Grant us the clarity of ice [5]
The comfort of snow
The cool memory of trees
Grant us the forest's silence
The snow's breathless quiet

For one moment to freeze [10]
The scream, the siren, the knock on the door
The needle in its track
The knife in the back

In that silence let us hear
The song of the children of longing [15]
In that silence let us catch
The breath of the children of longing

The echo of their voices through the city streets
The streets that defeated them
That brought them to their knees [20]
The streets that couldn't shelter them
That spellbound them in alleyways
The streets that blew their minds
That led them astray, out of reach of our saving
The streets that gave them visions and dreams [25]
That promised them everything
That delivered nothing
The streets that broke their backs
The streets that we brought them home to

Let their names be the wind through the branches [30]
Let their names be the song of the river
Let their names be the holiest prayers

Under the starlight, under the moonlight
In the light of this tree

Here at the heart of winter [35]
Here at the heart of the city

Annotations
[12] ***track:*** track mark, a scar created by continuously injecting a needle into the same point in the body over and over again

Tease It Out

I

1. This entire poem is addressed to the 'Great Tree' on Buckingham Street. What is the name for the literary device by which a poet addressses an inanimate object?
2. The tree grew in a 'far northern forest'. Is the poet referring to a) The North of Dublin, b) Northern ireland or c) a country in Northern Europe.
3. How do we learn from the poet that the Christmas tree was only recently cut down?
4. The poet asks the tree to 'Grant' the community a moment of stillness and serenity.
5. The poet asks the tree to 'freeze' life, or, at least, certain aspects of life.
   - Line 11 describes three events associated with a murder. Describe each of these events in your own words.
   - What aspect of drug abuse is referred to in line 12?
   - What kind of crime is referred to in line 13?

II

6. **Class Discussion:** The poet refers to the young victims of drug use as 'the children of longing'. What did these young people long for? Is it possible that they longed for more than one thing?
7. The poet imagines it might be possible to hear these young victims. In what sense might the 'children of longing' be present, despite the fact that they have passed on?
8. **Class Discussion:** Metonymy occurs when we substitue something associated with a concept for the concept itself. What concept is the term 'streets' being substituted for?
9. The street's 'broke' these young victims in both body and spirit. Identify three phrases that suggest this.
10. What do the phrases 'spellbound' and 'blew their minds' suggest about the nature of drug addiction?
11. The 'streets', according to the poet, promised these young victims 'everything'. Can you suggest two or three specific promises the 'streets' might have made? Did any of these promises come true?
12. The relatives of these young victims felt guilty about their untimely deaths. What phrases indicate this?

III

13. The moment is approaching when the 'Great tree' will be illuminated.
    - What phrases indicate that it is a cloudless night?
    - What words or phrases, according to the poet, do those assembled now utter?
    - These words should be spoken like the 'holiest prayers'. What kind of speaking and tone of voice do you think the poet has in mind?
14. What does the poet imagine hearing in the wind and in the sound of the river? What does this suggest about how the young victims are remembered by those who love them?

Exam Prep

1. **Personal Response:** Imagine you were at the event where the poet read this poem aloud for the first time. Write a diary entry describing your experience.
2. **Class Discussion:** In life, these young victims were confined to the streets of the inner city. In death, however, the poet wishes them beauty, freedom and expanse. Discuss this statement as a class.
3. **Theme Talk:** 'Meehan presents nature as if it were a mystical, almost conscious entity that surrounds and nourishes human beings'. Write a short essay responding to this statement in whcih you compare this poem to 'Death of a Field' and 'My Father Perceived as a Vision of St Francis'.
4. **Exam Prep:** 'Meehan is a poet of social justice, someone who again and again speaks out on behalf of those who have been forgotten'. Write a short essay discussing this statement, making reference to this poem and three others on your course.

Language Lab

1. Consider the following common features of prayers and say which are present in the poem:
   - Asking for a grant, blessing or favour
   - Repetition
   - Admitting your faults and asking for help to do better
   - Praise
2. **Class Discussion:** Let's focus on the poet's depiction of the northern forest.
   - Consider the phrase 'clarity of ice'. Would you agree that the word 'clarity' has two different meanings here?
   - What might these woodland trees remember? Why do you think these memories might be described as 'cool'?
   - In what sense might snow, often considered to be a cold and unforgiving feature of the landscape, provide a form of comfort.

Death of a Field

The field itself is lost the morning it becomes a site
When the Notice goes up: Fingal County Council – 44 houses

The memory of the field is lost with the loss of its herbs

Though the woodpigeons in the willow
The finches in what's left of the hawthorn hedge [5]
And the wagtail in the elder
Sing on their hungry summer song

The magpies sound like flying castanets

And the memory of the field disappears with its flora:
Who can know the yearning of yarrow [10]
Or the plight of the scarlet pimpernel
Whose true colour is orange?

And the end of the field is the end of the hidey holes
Where first smokes, first tokes, first gropes
Were had to the scentless mayweed [15]

The end of the field as we know it is the start of the estate
The site to be planted with houses each two or three bedroom
Nest of sorrow and chemical, cargo of joy

The end of dandelion is the start of Flash
The end of dock is the start of Pledge [20]
The end of teazel is the start of Ariel
The end of primrose is the start of Brillo
The end of thistle is the start of Bounce
The end of sloe is the start of Oxyaction
The end of herb robert is the start of Brasso [25]
The end of eyebright is the start of Persil

Who amongst us is able to number the end of grasses
To number the losses of each seeding head?

                        I'll walk out once
Barefoot under the moon to know the field [30]
Through the soles of my feet to hear
The myriad leaf lives green and singing
The million million cycles of being in wing

That – before the field become solely map memory
In some archive of some architect's screen [35]
I might possess it or it possess me
Through its night dew, its moon white caul
Its slick and shine and its profligacy
In every wingbeat in every beat of time

Annotations

[3] **castanets:** small wooden percussion intruments that produce a clacking sound
[9] **flora:** plantlife
[10] **yarrow:** a wildflower
[11] **scarlet pimpernel:** a wildflower
[14] **tokes:** inhalations from a marijuana cigarette
[14] **first gropes:** earliest, somewhat awkward sexual experiences
[15] **mayweed:** a wildflower
[28] **seeding head:** describes how the top flowering part of a plant transforms into a dry cluster of seeds
[32] **myriad:** countless
[37] **caul:** a membrane or covering
[38] **profligacy:** extravagance; plentifulness; wastefulness

Tease It Out

1. A planning notice has been placed at a field near the poet's home. What does the local authority have planned for this site?
2. **Class Disucssion:** According to the poet, 'the field is lost' the moment this Notice is posted. How can the field be 'lost' before any construction has taken place?
3. The field, according to the poet, has a memory all of its own. What kind of things do you think the field might remember?
4. Where, according to the poet, do its memories reside? What causes its memories to be erased?
5. Describe, in your own words, the literary device known as personification. In what way is the field being personified in these lines?
6. **True or false:** The death of the field will cause the birds in the locality to stop singing.
7. **Class Discussion:** The birds' song is described as 'hungry'. Suggest what the birds might be hungering for. Why might such hunger lead to their constant singing?
8. Take a moment to visualise the 'hidey holes' referred to in line 13:
   - Write two or three sentences describing these little hideaways as you imagine them.
   - Which members of the community made use of these spaces?
   - Describe in your own words the activities that took place in them.
9. **True or false:** The poet views the arrival of the estate in a completely negative light. Give a reason for your answer.
10. **Group Discussion:** Read lines 19 to 26 carefully. Then, working in small groups, attempt to answer the following questions:
    - How many of the products or brand names do you recognise?
    - How many of the herbs or wildflowers would you recognise if you saw them growing wild?
    - What impact will the arrival of the estate have on local biodiversity?
    - What impact will the arrival of the estate have on soil and on the water table?
11. How does the poet intend to say goodbye to the field? At what time of day or night will she do this? What will she be wearing on her feet when she does so?
12. The field will live on as a 'map memory'. Where, according to the poet, will this memory reside? Does this thought bring the poet any comfort? Give a reason for oyur answer.
13. Consider the term 'profligacy'. What does it suggest about the kind of growth the poet has witnessed in the field over the years?
14. Every second spent barefoot in the field will be filled with sensation. How does the poet convey this?

Exam Prep

1. **Personal Response:** Discuss the following questions as a class:
   - The poet maintains that she will 'know' the field better by walking across it barefoot. Can you suggest why this might be the case?
   - 'I might possess it or it possess me'. In what ways might the poet possess the field? In what ways might she be possessed?
   Then, drawing on the discussion, write your own response to each question in your copybook.
2. **Class Discussion:** Meehan is a poet well known for her concern for social justice. In what sense might 'Death of a Field' be said to share this concern?
3. **Theme Talk:** 'In this poem Meehan emphasises the extraordinary richness and diversity of growth that can be found in even a modest patch of ground'. Identify at least four words or phrases that support this statement.
4. **Exam Prep:** 'Meehan's poetry emphasises an intense, almost spiritual bond between nature and human beings'. Write a short essay responding to this statement in which you discuss 'Death of a Field' and at least one other poem on the course.

Language Lab

1. 'Death of a Field', like many of Meehan's poems, is rich in metaphor and simile:
   - What very inventive simile is used to describe the sound of the magpies' singing?
   - In what sense might the 'night dew' that covers the field resemble a 'caul'? Is this an effective comparison in your opinion?
2. 'Death of a Field' has been described as an outpouring of emotion:
   - How many punctuation marks can you identify in the poem? How might the lack of punctuation contribute to this outpouring?
   - Identify two emotions that in your opinion the poet is attempting to convey. What is a litany? In what sense might lines 19 to 26 be described as a litany?
   - Litanies are associated with prayer. Is it reasonable to describe this poem as a kind of prayer? To who or what might the poet be praying?
   - Would you agree that the poem increases in intensity towards its conclusion?

Them Ducks Died for Ireland

'6 of our waterfowl were killed or shot, 7 of the garden seats broken and about 300 shrubs destroyed'.
- Park Superintendent in his report on the damage to St Stephen's Green, during the Easter Rising 1916

Time slides slowly down the sash window
puddling in light on oaken boards. The Green
is a great lung, exhaling like breath on the pane
the seasons' turn, sunset and moonset, the ebb and flow

of stars. And once made mirror to smoke and fire, [5]
a Republic's destiny in a Countess' stride,
the bloodprice both summons and antidote to pride.
When we've licked the wounds of history, wounds of war,

we'll salute the stretcher-bearer, the nurse in white,
the ones who pick up the pieces, who endure, [10]
who live at the edge, and die there and are known

by this archival footnote read by fading light;
fragile as a breathmark on the windowpane or the gesture
of commemorating heroes in bronze and stone.

Annotations

This poem comes from a series entitled 'Six Sycamores', which arose when the poet was commissioned by the Office of Public Works on St Stephen's Green in Dublin. Meehan set out to write about Georgian Dublin and its multiple, conflicting histories. During her research for this project, she visited the Irish Architectural Archive where she discovered the Park Superintendent's report which serves as the poem's epitgraph.

[1] **sash window:** window made up of two moveable panes or panels
[2] **The Green:** St Stephen's Green
[6] **Countess:** Countess Constance Markievicz (1867-1927). She was born Constance Gore-Booth into an aristocratic Anglo-Irish family in Co. Sligo. In 1900 she married a Polish Count. She was the only female leader in the 1916 Rising and, along with Michael Mallin, commanded the Rebel position on St Stephen's Green. After the Rising, she served as a minister in the First Dail, becoming the first woman in Europe to attain such a position.
[9] **stretcher-bearer:** St Stephen's Green served as a field hospital during the Rising

Tease It Out

1. The poet's breath forms a mist on the window of the Office of Public Works. What phrase indicates this? The Green, too, exhales. What features of the Green might be responsible for this 'exhaling'?
2. **True or false:** According to the poet, the Green exhales differently depending on the time of day and time of year.
3. What feature of the Green might be compared to a 'mirror'?
4. The poet remembers a time when this 'mirror' reflected smoke and fire. What historical event was responsible for this effect?
5. **Class Discussion:**
   - Consider the verb 'stride'. What does it suggest about the manner in which the Countess walked across the Green?
   - Consider the phrase 'Republic's destiny'. Does it suggest that the fate of the fledgling Irish Republic was a) already determined or b) very much in the balance?
   - **True or false:** The poet suggests that the actions and choices of the Countess are central to the outcome of the Rising.
6. An independent Irish Republic could only be established through war and bloodshed. What phrase indicates this?
7. **Class Discussion:** Consider the phrase 'summons and antidote to pride'.
   - The word pride has several different meanings. Is it possible that more than one meaning is being referred to here?
   - Whose 'pride' does the poet have in mind?
   - In what sense might this 'pride' be both a 'summons' and an 'antodote'?
8. Consider those who 'pick up the pieces' after an event like the Easter Rising. What kind of work do you imagine them doing?
9. These people, along with nurses and stretcher-bearers, 'live at the edge'. But at the 'edge' of what exactly? What does this phrase suggest about their role in history?
10. What phrase suggests that these people at the 'edge', no less than heroes like the Countess, exhibit strength and courage?
11. The poet is reading a note she found in an archive.
    - What does it say?
    - Who wrote it?
    - Is this person also one of those who '[picked] up the pieces'?

Exam Prep

1. **Personal Response:** The poem's opening lines depict time as if it were a physical substance. What precisely do you visualise when you read these lines? Is it an effective comparison in your opinion? What do these lines suggest about the nature of time's passage?
2. **Class Discussion:** 'Some heroes are commemerated by statue, others are recalled only in long lost footnotes, but all will be forgotten in due time'. Discuss this statement as a class.
3. **Theme Talk:** 'Meehan's poetry celebrates the strength and power of ordinary women as well as the strength and power of those recorded in the history books'. Discuss this statement in relation to 'Them Ducks', 'Cora, Auntie' and 'The Pattern'.
4. **Exam Prep:** 'Paula Meehan uses her uniquely playful style to explore topics of great importance'. Write an essay in response to this statement, referring to 'Them Ducks' and at least three other poems on your course.

Language Lab

1. **Class Discussion:** The poet compares St Stephen's Green to a 'great lung' at the centre of the city.
   - Is this comparison a metaphor or a simile?
   - In what sense might the Green be said to function like a lung?
   - In this an effective comparison in your opinion?
2. This poem comes from what the poet has described as 'a series of sonnets interspersed with what I would hear as living voices, snatches of conversation out of the flux of the city'. Consider the title of the poem.
   - Who do you imagine speaking these words?
   - Would you agree that they differ in tone from the poem itself?
   - How does the title relate to the theme of the poem as you understand it?
3. What features of the sonnet form can you identify in this poem?
4. Meehan described how she adopted this form in order to 'mirror the incredibly beautiful Georgian structures around St Stephen's Green'. Discuss this formal choice as a class.

Adrienne Rich

Adrienne Rich was born in Baltimore, USA, in 1929. Her family was wealthy, cultured and successful. Her father was a doctor and a professor at the prestigious Johns Hopkins University. Her mother, too, was extremely talented, having been a successful pianist and composer. She had given up this career, however, in order to devote herself to the rearing of her two daughters.

Rich was educated at home by her parents until she entered public school in the fourth grade. Her father was a major influence on her life, encouraging her interest in literature. In the long poem 'Sources', for instance, she recalls how she first began to write poetry under his tutelage.

Like many first-born daughters, Rich was desperate for her father's approval and continued to conform to his standards well past her early successes and publications. Eventually, however, Rich began to find his influence on her life and work somewhat suffocating, and tensions developed between them. According to several critics, it is possible to see the roots of Rich's later feminism in this complex relationship with her somewhat overbearing father.

Coming from such an intellectual background, it is unsurprising that Rich herself was a bright and precocious child. She was a star pupil at the prestigious Radcliffe College, and she graduated at the head of her class in 1951, which also resulted in her election as a member of the prestigious academic honours society known as Phi Beta Kappa. That same year, when she was only twentytwo, her first book of poems appeared. This volume, *A Change of World*, had been chosen by the famous poet W.H. Auden for the Yale Series of Younger Poets award. These early poems, including 'Aunt Jennifer's Tigers' and 'The Uncle Speaks in the Drawing Room', earned Rich a reputation as an elegant, controlled stylist, with their imaginative metaphors and carefully controlled rhyme schemes.

In 1953, Rich married Alfred Conrad, a Harvard economist, and moved to Cambridge, Massachusetts, where she bore three sons in the next five years. On the surface, Rich seemed to have it all. She had artistic success, a loving and successful husband and three healthy children. Yet she was not happy. As her journal from this period reveals, this was an emotionally and artistically difficult period.

Rich was gripped by an inner struggle between her need to be an artist and her desire to be a happy, contented 1950s 'all-American mom'. She didn't see how it could be possible to fill both of these roles. Sexual tensions also arose in her marriage over this time as Rich gradually became aware of her lesbian tendencies. Yet, in the late fifties and early sixties, these were issues she could not easily express or even understand. Rich's diaries reveal that these thoughts and emotions left her feeling guilty, even 'monstrous'.

> "I absolutely cannot imagine what it would be like to be a woman in a non-patriarchal society. At moments I have this little glimmer of it. When I'm in a group of women, where I have a sense of real energy flowing and of power in the best sense - not power of domination, but just access to sources - I have some sense of what that could be like. But it's very rare that I can imagine even that."

Rich's third book, *Snapshots of a Daughter-in-Law*, published in 1963, dealt with these issues in verse. This volume, which was written over a period of eight years, was one of the first attempts by a writer to explore explicitly what it meant to be a woman and an artist in the modern world. The collection was full of the doubts, fears and sexual tensions that had privately haunted Rich over the years of her marriage. In this volume, Rich rebels against the contemporary notions of marriage and motherhood and suggests that her marriage might have been a mistake, a way of life inflicted on her rather than chosen. As 'The Roofwalker' states: 'A life I didn't choose/ chose me'.

Snapshots of a Daughter-in-Law was poorly received by the critics and by Rich's fellow writers. (One can only imagine how her husband felt.) Rich would later remark that the crushingly negative response to this book was one of the most significant experiences of her life. America, it seemed, was not ready for an artist who addressed the concerns of modern women in such a frank and bitter way.

As the 1960's progressed, however, Rich's outlook seemed more and more in keeping with the times. This was a decade of revolution and upheaval, with America rocked by the civil rights, anti-war and women's rights movements. Rich 'came into her own' during this turbulent decade. She moved to New York in 1966, when her husband took a teaching position at City College. She taught in the SEEK program, a remedial English program for poor, African-American and third-world students entering college. This experience was to greatly influence her later thinking about outsiders, oppression and the relation of language to power, issues that have consistently been addressed in Rich's work.

Though Rich and her husband were both involved in movements for social justice, it was to the women's movement that Rich gave her strongest allegiance. Rich was strongly influenced by the women's movement's investigation of 'sexual politics'. She was inspired by the connection that the movement made between, as she phrased it, 'Vietnam and the lovers' bed'. Here, she found a firm basis for her future focus on issues of language, sexuality, oppression and power - issues that linked all the different liberation movements of the period.

According to many critics, Rich's involvement in the women's movement was the catalyst for her 'coming out' as a lesbian and the breakup of her marriage. At the time, this was a bold and risky move, as tolerance of 'alternative lifestyles' was not as widespread as it is now. Shortly after the break up of the marriage, Rich's husband committed suicide, a personal tragedy movingly recounted in Rich's poem 'From a Survivor'.

In the years to follow Rich went on to become one of the most influential figures in American literature. She published many books of poetry and essays and taught at some of America's finest colleges. In 1997, on political grounds, she turned down the National Medal for the Arts, one of the highest honours the American government can award an artist. Even into her seventies, Rich continued to write prose and poems that fearlessly addressed and recorded both personal and political difficulties. This mingling of the political and the personal is one of the most distinctive aspects of her poetic style. Though she died in 2012, Rich, through the legacy of her writing and political activism, remains a presiding spirit over American letters.

THIS IS POETRY | **ADRIENNE RICH**

Aunt Jennifer's Tigers

Aunt Jennifer's tigers prance across a screen,
Bright topaz denizens of a world of green.
They do not fear the men beneath the tree;
They pace in sleek chivalric certainty.

Aunt Jennifer's fingers fluttering through her wool [5]
Find even the ivory needle hard to pull.
The massive weight of Uncle's wedding band
Sits heavily upon Aunt Jennifer's hand.

When Aunt is dead, her terrified hands will lie
Still ringed with ordeals she was mastered by. [10]
The tigers in the panel that she made
Will go on prancing, proud and unafraid.

Annotations
[1] *prance:* to strut, to move in a confident, spirited manner
[2] *topaz:* a dark yellow colour, derived from the gemstone of the same name
[2] *denizens:* inhabitants
[4] *sleek:* smooth and glossy; elegant in shape
[4] *chivalric:* relating to medieval knights and the ideal qualities of knighthood, including grace, nobility and physical prowess
[5] *fluttering:* to shake or tremble
[7] *wedding band:* wedding ring

Tease It Out

1. Aunt Jennifer has knitted a screen depicting tigers. What colour are these animals?
2. **Class Discussion:** The tigers 'pace' and 'prance'. How do you visualise them moving? Can you find two other verbs that describe the tigers' motion?
3. What do the terms 'sleek' and 'chivalric' suggest in this context?
4. Which word suggests that the tigers have a calm, confident demeanour?
5. The tigers are described as 'denizens' or inhabitants of a world Aunt Jennifer has created:
   - What is the main colour of this environment?
   - What other elements feature in this embroidered image?
   - Where are the 'men' located? What do you imagine these men are doing?
   - What is the tigers' attitude to these men?
6. Why do her fingers flutter in this way? Rank the following terms in order of likelihood:
   - Old age
   - Fear
   - Ill-health
   - Exhaustion
   - Nervousness
7. What phrase suggests that Aunt Jennifer finds the act of knitting a great effort?
8. Aunt Jennifer's fingers are depicted as 'fluttering' as she knits. How do you visualise this?
9. Consider the phrase 'massive weight'. Is it best understood literally or metaphorically? Why do you think Rich uses this phrase?
10. Aunt Jennifer's wedding ring 'Sits heavily' on her hand. Does this suggest a) that Aunt Jennifer takes her wedding vows very seriously or b) that her marriage is unhappy and oppressive. Give a reason for your choice.
11. Consider the phrase 'terrified hands'. Suggest what might have frightened Aunt Jennifer so much while she was alive.
12. According to the speaker, Aunt Jennifer experienced various 'ordeals'. Suggest two different trials she might have undergone.
13. In what sense might she have been 'mastered' by these ordeals?
14. Did even death allow Aunt Jennifer to escape these ordeals?

Exam Prep

1. **Personal Response:** Do you think the poet liked and admired her aunt? Support your answer with reference to the text.
2. **Theme Talk:** 'Rich enjoys writing about women who are confident and empowered'. Write two paragraphs comparing this poem to 'Power' in light of this statement.
3. **Theme Talk:** 'This poem portrays a negative view not only of Aunt Jennifer's marriage but also of marriage in general'. Is there any evidence in the poem to support this view? Give a reason for your answer.
4. **Exam Prep:** Rich wrote, 'the desire to be heard, - that is the impulse behind writing poems, for me'. Would you agree that Aunt Jennifer too had such a desire to be heard? And, if so, how did she act on this desire? Discuss Rich's statement with reference to 'Aunt Jennifer's Tigers' and two other poems on the course.

Language Lab

1. Write a few lines contrasting Aunt Jennifer and the tigers she created. As you do so, consider the following concepts:
   - Fear
   - Physical Strength
   - Mastery
2. Describe the poem's rhyme scheme. How does its form differ from that of 'Power'. What is the major difference between them? Would you agree that each poem has the form most suited to it?
3. 'This poem celebrates the ability of art to provide an emotional and imaginative space into which the artist can retreat'. Would you agree that in knitting the tigers Aunt Jennifer created an image of how she would like to be rather than how she really was?

The Uncle Speaks in the Drawing Room

I have seen the mob of late
Standing sullen in the square,
Gazing with a sullen stare
At window, balcony, and gate.
Some have talked in bitter tones, [5]
Some have held and fingered stones.

These are follies that subside.
Let us consider, none the less,
Certain frailties of glass
Which, it cannot be denied, [10]
Lead in times like these to fear
For crystal vase and chandelier.

Not that missiles will be cast;
None as yet dare lift an arm.
But the scene recalls a storm [15]
When our grandsire stood aghast
To see his antique ruby bowl
Shivered in a thunder-roll.

Let us only bear in mind
How these treasures handed down [20]
From a calmer age passed on
Are in the keeping of our kind.
We stand between the dead glass-blowers
And murmurings of missile-throwers.

Annotations

Drawing Room: a space used to entertain guests before and after dinner

[2] ***sullen:*** silently resentful

[7] ***follies:*** acts or instances of foolishness

[16] ***grandsire:*** grandfather

[16] ***aghast:*** shocked, horrified

[23] ***glass-blowers:*** craftspeople who shape molten glass by blowing air through a tube

[24] ***murmurings:*** whispered or mumbled complaints

Tease It Out

1. **Get In Gear:** Watch Video 14. How would you describe the atmosphere of the crowd? What are they talking or complaining about? Do you imagine that they will take action to get what they want? What form do you imagine this action taking?
2. The uncle lives in a grand home. What lines and phrases indicate this?
3. What time of day do you imagine it is? Who do you imagine is present in the room?
4. What term does the uncle use to describe the people who have gathered outside his property? What does this term imply or suggest about the uncle's view of these people?
5. How does the uncle characterise the mood of the crowd? Do you think the uncle's appraisal is fair and reasonable? Give a reason for your answer.
6. How does the uncle characterise or describe the gathering and behaviour of the crowd in line 7? What, according to him, usually comes of such gatherings? What does he fear might happen if the crowd becomes more unruly?
7. What sort of 'glass' do you think the uncle has in mind in line 9?
8. What, according to the uncle in line 14, is preventing the crowd from throwing stones or 'missiles' at the house?
9. The uncle says that the scene outside the house is reminiscent of a time when their 'grandsire' or grandfather was a young man. What sort of event or occasion do you imagine the grandfather witnessed or experienced?
10. To what do you imagine the 'thunder-roll' in line 18 is a reference? What effect did this 'thunder-roll' have on the grandfather's 'antique ruby bowl'?
11. The uncle describes the precious glass bowls, vases and chandeliers as 'treasures'. How did the uncle and those present in the drawing room come to possess such 'treasures'?
12. Consider the phrase 'our kind'. What does the uncle mean by this?
13. In the poem's final stanza, the uncle describes what he considers the family's role or purpose to be. What great responsibility or duty does he believe they have?
14. What, according to the uncle in the last stanza, is the crowd's intention or objective?

Exam Prep

1. **Group Discussion:** In small groups, discuss the uncle's character. Pick three adjectives that in the opinion of the group best define his personality.
2. **Personal Response:** Let's imagine that the aunt described in 'Aunt Jennifer's Tigers' is present in the drawing room. How do you think she might behave as he speaks? What do you imagine her doing?
3. **Theme Talk:** What is the uncle's attitude towards the family's privileged position? Does he think it is fair and reasonable that they should possess so much? What is his attitude to those who have gathered outside? Do you think that the uncle has a good appreciation of their grievances?
4. **Exam Prep:** 'Rich explores the twin themes of power and powerlessness in a variety of interesting ways.' Write a response to this statement with suitable reference to 'The Uncle Speaks' and two other Rich poems on your course.

Language Lab

1. How would you characterise the speaker's tone? Does it change at any point throughout the poem? What does his manner of speech suggest about the kind of person he is?
2. What do the 'crystal vase and chandelier' represent or symbolise for the Uncle?
3. Can you identify the poem's rhyme scheme? How does this rhyme scheme affect the the mood of the poem?
4. Why do you think the uncle believes that the times in which these 'treasures' were made to be 'a calmer age'? Consider the following options:
    - It was a time of general peace and stability.
    - The world was quieter because there were no big cities and factories.
    - The working classes quietly accepted their lot in life and did not agitate for social change.

Storm Warnings

The glass has been falling all the afternoon,
And knowing better than the instrument
What winds are walking overhead, what zone
Of gray unrest is moving across the land,
I leave the book upon a pillowed chair [5]
And walk from window to closed window, watching
Boughs strain against the sky

And think again, as often when the air
Moves inward toward a silent core of waiting,
How with a single purpose time has travelled [10]
By secret currents of the undiscerned
Into this polar realm. Weather abroad
And weather in the heart alike come on
Regardless of prediction.

Between foreseeing and averting change [15]
Lies all the mastery of elements
Which clocks and weatherglasses cannot alter.
Time in the hand is not control of time,
Nor shattered fragments of an instrument
A proof against the wind; the wind will rise, [20]
We can only close the shutters.

I draw the curtains as the sky goes black
And set a match to candles sheathed in glass
Against the keyhole draught, the insistent whine
Of weather through the unsealed aperture. [25]
This is our sole defense against the season;
These are the things that we have learned to do
Who live in troubled regions.

Annotations

[1] *glass:* short for 'weatherglass', a type of a barometer

[2] *instrument:* refers to the barometer

[11] *undiscerned:* unnoticed

[20] *proof:* protection

[25] *aperture:* a gap or opening

Tease It Out

1. What does the 'glass' refer to in the poem's opening line?
2. What sort of conditions has the 'glass' been registering 'all the afternoon'?
3. Why do you think the poet knows 'better' than the instrument about the 'winds'? Is she speaking metaphorically or literally?
4. Why does the speaker move 'from window to window'? What does she see outside? How do you imagine she is feeling at this particular moment?
5. **Class Discussion:** The poet describes how the 'air/ Moves inward toward a silent core of waiting'.
   - What meteorological phenomenon is the poet describing here?
   - From where and to where is the 'air' moving?
   - What do you imagine this innermost or central space represents?
   - Who or what is 'waiting' here?
6. How does the poet imagine time travelling in lines 10 to 11? What are the 'secret currents' that carry it?
7. What do you think 'this polar realm' signifies or represents? Do you think it is where the poet is living or is it a different region entirely? Give a reason for your answer.
8. Rich says that 'Weather abroad' comes on 'Regardless of Prediction'. What do you think she means by this? What is she suggesting about the weather and the forecasts or predictions we make?
9. What does the 'weather of the heart' represent? In what way might such internal 'weather' be like the external weather?
10. According to Rich, is it easier to foresee dangerous changes in the weather or to stop such changes occuring?
11. What kind of 'mastery' is required to 'avert' these changes?
12. According to Rich, do our instruments and technologies provide us with such mastery?
13. **True or false:** According to Rich, in our modern age humans have nothing to fear from storms.
14. Why do you think the poet draws the curtains? Are her reasons for doing so practical or personal?
15. What practical reason might she have for lighting candles as the storm begins?
16. Where, according to the poet, is the wind blowing?
17. **Class Discussion:** Consider and discuss how the following phrases relate not only to the weather but to the poet's internal struggle:
    - 'the sky goes black'
    - 'set a match to candles'
    - 'troubled regions'

Exam Prep

1. **Theme Talk:** 'This poem is as much about the 'weather in the heart' as it is about 'Weather abroad".
   - What does the poem suggest about our ability to control the elements?
   - What does the poem suggest about our ability to control and regulate our own emotions and feelings?
   - In what way might the storm that the poet describes be read as a metaphor for depression?
   - Why do you think the poet connects the weather and time? What do these things have in common, according to the poem?
2. **Exam Prep:** Rich's poetry returns again and again to the theme of suffering and survival. Discuss this statement in relation to 'Storm Warnings', 'From a Survivor' and 'Aunt Jennifer's Tigers'.

Language Lab

1. How does the poet create a sense of unease in the opening stanza?
2. The poet describes how the 'winds are walking overhead' and a 'zone/ Of gray unrest'. Write three or four sentences describing the conditions these phrases conjour up?
3. Did you find the comparison that the poet makes between the external weather and our internal emotions to be effective? Give reasons for your answer.

Living in Sin

She had thought the studio would keep itself;
no dust upon the furniture of love.
Half heresy, to wish the taps less vocal,
the panes relieved of grime. A plate of pears,
a piano with a Persian shawl, a cat [5]
stalking the picturesque amusing mouse
had risen at his urging.
Not that at five each separate stair would writhe
under the milkman's tramp; that morning light
so coldly would delineate the scraps [10]
of last night's cheese and three sepulchral bottles;
that on the kitchen shelf among the saucers
a pair of beetle-eyes would fix her own –
envoy from some village in the moldings …
Meanwhile, he, with a yawn, [15]
sounded a dozen notes upon the keyboard,
declared it out of tune, shrugged at the mirror,
rubbed at his beard, went out for cigarettes;
while she, jeered by the minor demons,
pulled back the sheets and made the bed and found [20]
a towel to dust the table-top,
and let the coffee-pot boil over on the stove.
By evening she was back in love again,
though not so wholly but throughout the night
she woke sometimes to feel the daylight coming [25]
like a relentless milkman up the stairs.

Annotations

Living in Sin: a pejorative or negative term that was used to describe a man and woman living together as a couple without being married

[1] ***studio:*** a small apartment, an artist's workroom, or both

[3] ***heresy:*** a belief that is misguided, immoral or inappropriate

[6] ***picturesque:*** visually attractive, especially in a manner that's quaint, cute or charming

[8] ***writhe:*** to twist or contort

[10] ***delineate:*** indicate the exact position of something, show the outline of something

[11] ***sepulchral:*** resembling a tomb

[14] ***moldings:*** decorative fittings made of plaster or wood

Tease It Out

1. In lines 3 and 4, the young woman identifies two problems with the studio accommodation. Describe these two issues in your own words.
2. Such negative thoughts about life in the studio make the young woman feel guilty or uncomfortable. Which phrase suggests this?
3. **Class Discussion:** Describe in your own words the painting created by the young woman's partner. Consider the phrase 'had risen at his urging'. What does this suggest about the artistic process?
4. What does the young woman hear at five each morning?
5. Does the young woman find the morning light in the apartment pleasant or unpleasant?
6. What, according to the young woman, do the empty wine bottles resemble? What does this comparison suggest about her attitude to life in the studio?
7. What does the young woman see on the kitchen shelf? Pick two adjectives that in your opinion might describe her reaction to this sight.
8. In what sense might this creature be described as an 'envoy'? Where, according to the poet, is it an envoy from?
9. The young woman's partner is an artist of some kind. What suggests that he dabbles in various art forms rather than focusing on one medium in particular?
10. Read lines 15 to 18. Does the young woman's partner strike you as committed and hard-working? Give a reason for your answer.
11. What tasks does the young woman perform while her partner is 'out for cigarettes'? What suggests that he is gone a long time?
12. **Class Discussion:** Why does the coffee 'boil over' on the stove? Could there be more than one reason for this occurrence?
13. 'By evening she was back in love again'. Is the young woman 'back in love' with a) her partner or b) her life in the studio or c) both? Support your choice with reference to the poem.
14. Does the young woman sleep well in the studio? Give a reason for your answer.
15. Which phrase indicates that, slowly but surely, the young woman is becoming more and more disenchanted with life in the studio?
16. The young woman seems to be most unhappy in the morning and least unhappy in the evening. Identify every phrase that supports this point of view.

Exam Prep

1. **Personal Response:** What did the young woman imagine life in the studio would be like before she actually moved in? Write a diary entry she might have written on the night before she took up residence.
2. **Class Discussion:** Would you characterise the lifestyle of the young woman and her partner as conservative and conventional, on the one hand, or as rebellious and unconventional, on the other? Give a reason for your answer.
3. **Exam Prep:** 'Rich's poetry often explores inequality of the relationship between the genders'. Do you think the couple in this poem have an equal relationship? Discuss the above statement in relation to 'Living in Sin' and two other Rich poems.

Language Lab

1. Consider the phrases 'writhe', 'less vocal' and 'envoy'. In what sense might each one be described as an example of personification?
2. Describe in your own words the poem's closing simile. Is it an effective comparison in your opinion? Give a reason for your answer.
3. Consider the phrase 'jeered by the minor demons'. Take five minutes to jot down your responses to the questions below. Then discuss your findings with the person next to you and come up with the answer you both feel best fits the evidence:
    - In what sense might the young woman feel she's failed, that she deserves to be 'jeered at'?
    - Which emotion or emotions are suggested by this metaphor?

The Roofwalker
for Denise Levertov

Over the half-finished houses
night comes. The builders
stand on the roof. It is
quiet after the hammers,
the pulleys hang slack. [5]
Giants, the roofwalkers,
on a listing deck, the wave
of darkness about to break
on their heads. The sky
is a torn sail where figures [10]
pass magnified, shadows
on a burning deck.

I feel like them up there:
exposed, larger than life,
and due to break my neck. [15]

Was it worth while to lay –
with infinite exertion –
a roof I can't live under?
– All those blueprints,
closings of gaps, [20]
measurings, calculations?
A life I didn't choose
chose me: even
my tools are the wrong ones
for what I have to do. [25]
I'm naked, ignorant,
a naked man fleeing
across the roofs
who could with a shade of difference
be sitting in the lamplight [30]
against the cream wallpaper
reading – not with indifference –
about a naked man
fleeing across the roofs.

Annotations
[5] *pulleys:* a device consisting of a wheel over which a rope or chain is pulled in order to lift heavy objects
[7] *listing:* tilting or inclining to one side
[19] *blueprints:* technical drawings, especially prints of architectural plans

Tease It Out

1. How does the poet indicate that the builders have just stopped working for the day?
2. Who are the 'roofwalkers' that the poet mentions in line 6? Why do you think she describes them in this manner?
3. Why do you think the poet says that the 'roofwalkers' are 'Giants'. Consider the following and say which you think is most likely:
    - The roofwalkers are physically enormous.
    - They appear enormous from where she is positioned.
    - These are exceptionally brilliant individuals, 'giants' of their trade.
    - The men are like mythical creatures of superhuman size.
4. The poet imagines that the half-finished houses are a ship and that the roofwalkers are standing on the ship's deck. Why do you think she makes this comparison? In what ways might a half-finished house resemble a ship?
5. 'The sky/ is a torn sail where figures/ pass magnified'. Discuss this image in pairs. In what way might the darkening sky resemble a 'torn sail'? Why might the men on the roof appear 'magnified' against this backdrop?
6. Why do you think the poet describes the roof on which the men stand as a 'burning deck'? How might the time of day make it seem this way? Why do you think the men appear as 'shadows'?
7. Lines 13 to 15: What three things does the poet imagine these men on the roof might feel? What does it suggest about the poet's life at this moment that she feels the same way?
8. The poet says that she too has built a 'roof'. What phrase does she use to convey that this took a lot of time and effort?
9. Lines 19 to 21: Describe in your own words all the planning and preparation that occurred before construction of the 'roof' even commenced?
10. The 'roof' that the poet built is not an actual roof but a metaphor for some aspect of her life to which she devoted much time and effort. What aspect of her life do you think this 'roof' represents?
11. Why is it, do you imagine, that the poet 'can't live under' the 'roof' that she built?
12. The poet says that her 'tools are the wrong ones' for what she has to do in life. What do you imagine these 'tools' refer to? In what way can they be considered 'wrong'?
13. The poet imagines that she is a 'naked man fleeing across the roofs'. Why do you imagine she pictures herself in this manner? What does it suggest about the way she feels about life at this moment?

Exam Prep

1. **Theme Talk:** 'A life I didn't choose/ chose me'. Over what aspects of her life do you think the poet considers she did not have a choice? How might these aspects of her life have determined who and what she is?
2. **Theme Talk:** Why do you think the poet describes herself as a 'naked man' rather than a woman? What do you think the poem has to say about the difficulties and challenges that women experience in life?
3. **Exam Prep:** Rich, in one of her essays, wrote: 'Responsibility to yourself means refusing to let others do your thinking, talking, and naming for you; it means learning to respect and use your own brains and instincts; hence, grappling with hard work'. Write a statement in which you discuss this statement in light of three poems on the course.

Language Lab

1. How would you describe the atmosphere of the first twelve lines of the poem? Which words, phrases and images create or convey this atmosphere?
2. Consider the following two images:
   Image 1: A naked man 'fleeing' across the rooftops.
   Image 2: A person reading by 'lamplight' in a room with 'cream wallpaper'.
   - Pick two adjectives that, in your opinion, best describe the state of mind suggested by Image 1.
   - Pick two adjectives that in your opinion best describe the state of mind suggested by Image 2.
   - Which image, according to the poet, best describes her current state of mind?
   - The poet suggests that only luck or circumstance, only a 'shade of difference', has placed her in this mindset. Can you suggest what might have happened to place her in her current uncomfortable state of mind?

Our Whole Life

Our whole life a translation
the permissible fibs

and now a knot of lies
eating at itself to get undone

Words bitten thru words [5]

meanings burnt-off like paint
under the blowtorch

All those dead letters
rendered into the oppressor's language

Trying to tell the doctor where it hurts [10]
like the Algerian
who walked from his village, burning

his whole body a cloud of pain
and there are no words for this

except himself [15]

Annotations

[1] *translation:* the act of rewriting a text in another language; the act of altering an object's fundamental nature; the act of changing an object's position according to specific rules
[8] *dead letters:* letters that are undeliverable by the postal service
[9] *rendered into:* translated
[9] *oppressor:* someone who keeps others down by severe and unjust use of force or authority
[11] *the Algerian:* a victim of the Algerian War of Independence (1954-1962)

Tease It Out

1. **Class Discussion:** Consider the terms 'translation' and 'lost in translation'. Are phrases translated from one language to another always completely accurate? Have you ever encountered a mistranslation, while travelling or online, that might lead someone astray? Is it possible that certain thoughts and ideas are too complex to ever be properly translated?
2. Language, the poet believes, allows women to express themselves only in a way that is distorted and inaccurate, allows them to present only a false account of their 'whole life'. Identify three phrases from the poem that suggest this.
3. **Class Discussion:** Consider the phrase 'knot of lies'.
   - How does this image combine something concrete with something abstract?
   - How do we visualise such a 'knot'? Would you agree that it is difficult to visualise?
   - Is this image effective, or is it too abstract and outlandish?
4. Women, the poet suggests, are bound in such a 'knot of lies'. What does this suggest about their relationship with the language in which they're forced to speak?
5. The poet compares women's efforts at communication to 'dead letters'. What does this suggest about women's ability to communicate?
6. The poet depicts a child attempting to 'tell the doctor where it hurts'. Why might a child have difficulty explaining how he or she feels to a doctor?
7. The poet compares the situation of such a child to that of women attempting to communicate in the 'oppressor's language'. What does this suggest about women's ability to express themselves?
8. The poet depicts a victim of the Algerian War. Google this conflict. When did this war take place? Which countries were involved? How many people died over the course of this terrible conflict?
9. Consider the term 'burning'. Does it refer to the man or to his village? Might it refer to both?
10. What incident do you think the man has witnessed?
11. Can you suggest why the man is walking, rather than running, away from this attack? Might there be more than one reason?
12. 'and there are no words for this// except himself'. What does Rich mean by this rather cryptic conclusion? Consider the following possibilities and rank them in order of plausibility:
    - It is impossible to express the horror of this situation in words. Only a photograph or other image will convey the misery of the man's plight.
    - The man is so traumatised by what he's witnessed that he can no longer even express his fear and rage.
    - The man cannot communicate with those who attack and dominate his country; they will not listen to him or even learn to speak his language.

Exam Prep

1. **Class Discussion:** Rich draws a comparison between the situation of the Algerian people and that of women everywhere. What similarities exist between these situations? In what ways are these situations different?
2. **Theme Talk:** The poet believes that all languages are male-dominated systems that inevitably exclude and oppress women. Can you identify three images from the poem that support this view? Can you identify any images that suggest women might one day be free of a system? Does this notion of language seem reasonable to you? In each case give a reason for your answer.
3. **Exam Prep:** "Rich's poetry communicates powerful feelings through thought-provoking images and symbols." Discuss this statement in relation to 'Our Whole Life' and two other poems by Rich on your course.

Language Lab

1. This poem is replete with violent and aggressive imagery. Identify as many examples as you can.
2. How would you describe the mood of this piece? Is it relaxed and contemplative or angry and agitated? Pick three adjectives that in your opinion best describe its tone.
3. There is very little punctuation in the poem. Does this make it easier or more difficult to understand?
4. Would you agree that the poem might be described as a flow of images rather than as a sustained argument?
5. 'words bitten thru words'. What is happening to the 'knot of lies'? Is it destined inevitably to be 'undone'?
6. What impact does a blowtorch have when applied to a painted surface? What is happening to the 'meanings' in line 5?

Trying to Talk with a Man

Out in this desert we are testing bombs,

that's why we came here.

Sometimes I feel an underground river
forcing its way between deformed cliffs
an acute angle of understanding [5]
moving itself like a locus of the sun
into this condemned scenery.

What we've had to give up to get here –
whole LP collections, films we starred in
playing in the neighbourhoods, bakery windows [10]
full of dry, chocolate-filled Jewish cookies,
the language of love-letters, of suicide notes,
afternoons on the riverbank
pretending to be children

Coming out to this desert [15]
we meant to change the face of
driving among dull green succulents
walking at noon in the ghost town
surrounded by a silence

that sounds like the silence of the place [20]
except that it came with us
and is familiar
and everything we were saying until now
was an effort to blot it out –
coming out here we are up against it [25]

Out here I feel more helpless
with you than without you
You mention the danger
and list the equipment
we talk of people caring for each other [30]
in emergencies – laceration, thirst –
but you look at me like an emergency

Your dry heat feels like power
your eyes are stars of a different magnitude
they reflect lights that spell out: EXIT [35]
when you get up and pace the floor

talking of the danger
as if it were not ourselves
as if we were testing anything else.

Annotations
[5] *acute:* sharp, pointed or severe
[6] *locus:* a particular position or place; a curve along which an object moves
[7] *condemned:* marked for destruction; pronounced guilty
[8] *LP:* a vinyl record
[10] *playing:* being screened or shown
[17] *succulents:* plants with a thick, fleshy surface that are used to store water
[18] *ghost town:* a town that has been abandoned by its former inhabitants
[31] *laceration:* a deep cut or tear in the skin or flesh

Tease It Out

1. This poem describes how the poet and her husband venture into the Nevada desert to protest against a nuclear test that's being carried out by the United States government. Do some research online and determine the following:
   - What does the Nevada desert look like?
   - How many nuclear tests were carried out there in the 1960s and 70s?
   - What kind of public reaction did these tests provoke?
2. The poet uses the word 'we' in line 1. Is she referring to a) the United States military or b) herself and her husband? Give a reason for your answer.
3. The poet also uses the word 'we' in line 2. Who is she referring to in this instance?
4. In line 2, the poet declares, 'that's why we came here'. Describe in your own words why the couple have come to the desert. Do you think that there is more than one reason for their journey?
5. In lines 8 to 14, the poet remembers the life with her husband. Use this series of images to write a paragraph describing a typical day in the life of this couple.
6. What phrase suggests that they've sacrificed their comfortable lifestyle in order to devote themselves to protest and political campaigns?
7. How did the poet and her husband attempt to 'blot out' the silence at the heart of their relationship?
8. What do the poet and her husband talk about as they wait for the detonation to occur?
9. The speaker describes how she feels helpless. Rank the following statements in order of plausibility. Does she feel:
   - Helpless to respond to any emergencies that might occur if the test goes wrong?
   - Helpless to alter her government's destructive nuclear policy?
   - Helpless to fix her failing marriage?
10. What makes the speaker feel 'helpless'? What does this suggest about the relationship?
11. '[Y]ou look at me like an emergency'. List three adjectives you associate with the concept of an emergency. Based on this line, does the poet's husband have a positive or negative view of the poet and their marriage?
12. In the last line, the poet describes how she and her husband have been 'testing' themselves. What are the results of this test? What have they learned about their marriage? What do you think will happen to their relationship now?

Exam Prep

1. **Theme Talk:** Write a brief response (three or four paragraphs) to each of the following statements:
   - 'This poem movingly describes a marriage where communication has broken down'
   - 'This poem details a last, desperate effort to repair a failing relationship'.
2. **Theme Talk:** The poet feels the heat emanating from her husband's body and compares it to 'power'. Rank the following statements in order of plausibility.
   - Her husband, as a man in a male-dominated society, has power over her life.
   - Her husband, as a privileged white male, is associated with the government and the military elites that created the nuclear tests in the first place.
   - Her husband is a powerful and capable individual.
3. **Theme Talk:** Rich's poetry often deals with the theme of power and powerlessness. In this poem, it is the poet rather than the husband who exercises power in the relationship. Write a paragraph saying whether you agree or disagree with this statement.

Language Lab

1. 'The word 'EXIT' has two meanings, one relating to the observation post from which the couple watch the nuclear test, one relating to the failing state of their relationship'. Write four sentences in response to this statement.
2. **Class Discussion:** In lines 18 to 22 the poet mentions two different types of 'silences', the 'silence of the place' and another that 'came with us'. How are these silences different? To what specifically does each of these silences refer?

Diving into the Wreck

First having read the book of myths,
and loaded the camera,
and checked the edge of the knife-blade,
I put on
the body-armor of black rubber [5]
the absurd flippers
the grave and awkward mask.
I am having to do this
not like Cousteau with his
assiduous team [10]
aboard the sun-flooded schooner
but here alone.

There is a ladder.
The ladder is always there
hanging innocently [15]
close to the side of the schooner.
We know what it is for,
we who have used it.
Otherwise
it is a piece of maritime floss [20]
some sundry equipment.

I go down.
Rung after rung and still
the oxygen immerses me
the blue light [25]
the clear atoms
of our human air.
I go down.
My flippers cripple me,
I crawl like an insect down the ladder [30]
and there is no one
to tell me when the ocean
will begin.

First the air is blue and then
it is bluer and then green and then [35]
black I am blacking out and yet
my mask is powerful
it pumps my blood with power
the sea is another story
the sea is not a question of power [40]
I have to learn alone
to turn my body without force
in the deep element.

And now: it is easy to forget
what I came for   [45]
among so many who have always
lived here
swaying their crenellated fans
between the reefs
and besides   [50]
you breathe differently down here.

I came to explore the wreck.
The words are purposes.
The words are maps.
I came to see the damage that was done   [55]
and the treasures that prevail.
I stroke the beam of my lamp
slowly along the flank
of something more permanent
than fish or weed   [60]

the thing I came for:
the wreck and not the story of the wreck
the thing itself and not the myth
the drowned face always staring
toward the sun   [65]
the evidence of damage
worn by salt and sway into this threadbare beauty
the ribs of the disaster
curving their assertion
among the tentative haunters.   [70]

This is the place.
And I am here, the mermaid whose dark hair
streams black, the merman in his armored body.
We circle silently   [75]
about the wreck
we dive into the hold.
I am she: I am he

whose drowned face sleeps with open eyes
whose breasts still bear the stress
whose silver, copper, vermeil cargo lies   [80]
obscurely inside barrels
half-wedged and left to rot
we are the half-destroyed instruments
that once held to a course
the water-eaten log   [85]
the fouled compass

We are, I am, you are
by cowardice or courage
the one who find our way
back to this scene   [90]
carrying a knife, a camera
a book of myths
in which
our names do not appear.

Annotations
[9] ***Cousteau:*** Jacque Yves Cousteau (1910-1997), a famous French underwater explorer
[10] ***assiduous:*** careful, hard-working
[11] ***schooner:*** large sailing vessel
[20] ***maritime:*** relating to the sea
[21] ***sundry:*** miscellaneous
[48] ***crenellated:*** jagged, uneven
[58] ***flank:*** the side
[67] ***assertion:*** statement
[70] ***tentative:*** hesitant or cautious
[80] ***vermeil:*** bright red in colour
[85] ***log:*** a book in which the ship's captain records details of the voyage

Tease It Out

Lines 1 to 21

1. Watch Video 15, which contains footage from an expedition to the *Titanic* in 2004. Then answer the following questions:
    - What is the condition of the ship's hull?
    - What objects and details does the camera focus on?
    - In your opinion, what is the most striking and dramatic shot in this video?
2. What three things does the poet put on as she prepares for her dive?
3. What two pieces of equipment does she bring with her?
4. The speaker contrasts herself with the famous explorer Jacques Cousteau. In what way is her situation different to those experienced by Cousteau in his films?
5. How will the poet enter the water?
6. True or flase: The poet has never gone diving before.
7. This poem is very much about gender. Consider the phrase 'book of myths' in this context and then answer the following questions:
    - Can you think of two or three 'myths' that exist in the world about gender today?
    - Is the poet referring to an actual physical book, or is she speaking more metaphorically?
    - The term 'myth' has at least two different meanings. Which, in your opinion, do you think the poet is referring to? Is it possible she is referring to both?
8. This poem describes a journey into the unconscious mind. In this regard, what do you think might be represented by a) the camera, b) the diving mask, and c) the ladder?

Lines 22 to 74

9. It takes a long time for the poet to climb down the ladder. What phrases indicate this?
10. Does the poet find this descent a comfortable one?
11. Answer the following questions true or false. In each case support your answer with reference to the poem:
    - The poet almost loses consciousness when she finally enters the water.
    - Manouvering in the sea's 'deep element' can be accomplished by brute force.
    - The poet doesn't encounter any fish as she dives.
    - The poet never feels distracted from the ultimate objective of her dive.
12. '[M]y mask is powerful'. What capabilities does the mask possess?
13. Lines 55 to 66: The poet finally reaches the wreck that is the objective of her dive and runs or 'strokes' the beam of her flashlight along the ships 'flank'. What condition is the ship in? What is the diver's response or reaction to the wreck? Is she appalled by what she sees?
14. **Class Discussion:** The poet stresses that she came the wreck and not the story of the wreck ... and not the myth'. Why do you think it is so important to the poet that sees the actual wreck?
15. **Group Discussion:** The poet describes different features and aspects of the wreck. Discuss the following questions in pairs and share your answers with the class:
    - What aspect of the ship might the 'drowned face' represent.
    - What aspect of the ship do you think the 'ribs' represent?
    - What damage has the 'salt' and the 'sway' of the water caused?
    - Does the poet find the wreck to be a thing of beauty or something ugly?
16. As she approaches the wreck the poet finds herself changing and becoming both 'mermaid' and 'merman'. Consider this transformation in terms of the poet's journey into the unconscious mind and her exploration of gender. Who or what do you think these figures represent?

Lines 75 to 94

17. What condition are the instruments and tools in? What has caused them to be this way? What did these instruments once enable the ship to do or accomplish?
18. Lines 75 to 81: The merman and the mermaid enter the hold of the ship. As they do so, they fuse or become one with the ship itself. How is such a fusion evident in these lines?
19. **Class Discussion:** 'We can interpret the wrecked ship to represent the poet's earliest ungendered self - who she essentially was at the moment of birth'. Discuss this statement as a class and answer the following questions:
    - What do you think caused this self to be wrecked and, ultimately, lost in the depths of her unconscious mind?
    - What, do you think, the ship's cargo and its tarnished and 'half-destroyed instruments' might represent when it comes to an understanding of the self?
20. **Class Discussion:** Do you think that the discovery of such valuable items and instruments offers a sense of hope to the poet, a sense that something can be salvaged from this?
21. Who do you think the 'We' and the 'you' refer to in line 85? Consider the following and say which you think is most likely:
    - It is the self that the poet now experiences, an identity that fuses the masculine and feminine aspects, the 'you' and 'I' into a 'We'
    - The poet is extending her experience to all of us, suggesting that we are all capable of undertaking this inner journey and discovering the ungendered self
22. **Class Discussion:** The poet considers two very different motivations that might lead us to undertake such a journey: 'cowardice or courage'.
    - Why, do you think, cowardice might inspire us to explore the unconscious mind in an effort to discover a very different sense of who we are?
    - What do you think someone might be shying or backing away from?
    - Why might such an inner exploration be considered courageous?

Exam Prep

1. **Personal Response:** Did you find this the poet's description of a deep-sea dive to be an interesting method of imagining an exploration of the unconscious mind? What aspects of the analogy do you think work best? Give a reason for your answer.
2. **Class Discussion:** 'The poem suggests that gender - the norms, behaviours and roles associated with being a man or a woman - is a social construct. Rich imagines that deep in our psyche we can discover a memory of our ungendered self - of who we were before society taught us to think and identify as male or female'. Do you agree with this reading of the poem? Do you think that it is possible to imagine the kind of ungendered self that the poet imagines?
3. **Theme Talk:** 'Rich's poetry offers us an inspirational way to think about who we are and what we are capable of'. Write a short essay in response to this statement, making reference to 'Diving into the Wreck' and at least two other poems on your course.
4. **Exam Prep:** Adrienne Rich once wrote that 'this drive to self-knowledge, for women, is more than a search for identity: it is part of our refusal of the self-destructiveness of male-dominated society'. Write an essay discussing how Rich's poetry deals with the theme of the subjugation of women in society. Refer to at least three poems on your course.

Language Lab

1. 'The ladder is the most powerful symbol in the poem, allowing the speaker to utterly change her perspective by moving from one world to the next.' Do you agree or disagree with this statement? Support your answer with reference to the poem.
2. There are several instances of repetition throughout the poem. How does this affect our reading of it? Pick out an instance of repetition that you find particularly effective, and say why it works for you.
3. The poet compares the wrecked ship to a body that lies upon the ocean floor, describing both its 'face' and 'breasts'. What aspect of the ship, do you think, is being likened to a face? What aspect of the ship do you think the breasts represent?

From a Survivor

The pact that we made was the ordinary pact
of men & women in those days

I don't know who we thought we were
that our personalities
could resist the failures of the race   [5]

Lucky or unlucky, we didn't know
the race had failures of that order
and that we were going to share them

Like everybody else, we thought of ourselves as special

Your body is as vivid to me   [10]
as it ever was: even more

since my feeling for it is clearer:
I know what it could and could not do

it is no longer
the body of a god   [15]
or anything with power over my life

Next year it would have been 20 years
and you are wastefully dead
who might have made the leap
we talked, too late, of making   [20]

which I live now
not as a leap
but a succession of brief, amazing movements
each one making possible the next

Annotations
[1] *pact:* treaty, agreement

Tease It Out

1. Who is the speaker addressing in this poem?
2. What is the 'ordinary pact' to which the speaker refers?
3. What do you understand by the term 'the failures of the race'? Does it suggest that there are universal failures when it comes to marriage? What might these be?
4. Did the younger versions of the speaker and her husband know about these 'failures' when they were preparing to marry? Explain your answer.
5. Line 9: How would you describe the tone of this line? Do you think the poet blames her younger self for thinking of herself as 'special', or is her attitude more forgiving?
6. What do you think the speaker means when she says that her 'feeling' for her husband's body is 'clearer' than before? How might your feelings for a partner's body be unclear?
7. 'I know what it could and could not do'. What does this line suggest about the intimacy of marriage – even one that is not particularly happy?
8. 'Your body is as vivid to me/ as it ever was'. In what context do you imagine the poet is thinking of her husband's body here? Consider the following possibilities and rank them in order of likelihood, giving reasons for your decisions:
    - They are in bed together.
    - She is looking at him from across the room.
    - She is remembering his body from the early days of their marriage.
    - She is paying her respects to his body at his funeral.
9. What milestone would have occurred 'Next year'?
10. What does the phrase 'wastefully dead' suggest about the manner of her husband's death?
11. What do you understand by the phrase 'to take a leap'? What 'leap' do you think the speaker and her husband were discussing before his death?
12. The speaker says that she is now attempting to achieve this 'leap' but in 'brief, amazing movements' rather than in one big gesture. What does this suggest about the nature of grieving?
13. Why do you think the poet refers to these movements as 'amazing'? What meaning of 'amazing' do you think she is emphasising here?

Exam Prep

1. **Theme Talk:** 'Although the poet makes it clear that her marriage was far from perfect, she nevertheless displays real affection for her husband at several points in this poem.' Write a few paragraphs in response to this statement, referring to the poem to support your answer.
2. **Exam Prep:** 'Throughout her work, Rich presents marriage in a negative light as a force that oppresses and dominates women.' Discuss this statement with reference to 'From a Survivor' and at least one other poem by Rich on your course.
3. **Personal Response:** 'Like everybody else, we thought of ourselves as special.' Write a short story of a few hundred words, using this as your first line.

Language Lab

1. When someone dies, we often hear the phrase 'He is survived by his wife'. The title of this poem, 'From a Survivor', alludes to this terminology. However, do you think there is another sense in which the poet considers herself to be a survivor? Support your answer with reference to the poem.
2. Do you think that the tone of the poem is ultimately a hopeful one? Support your answer with reference to the poem.

THIS IS POETRY **ADRIENNE RICH**

Power

Living   in the earth-deposits of   our history

Today a backhoe divulged   out of a crumbling flank of earth
one bottle   amber   perfect   a hundred-year-old
cure for fever   or melancholy   a tonic
for living on this earth   in the winters of this climate.   [5]

Today I was reading about Marie Curie:
she must have known she suffered   from radiation sickness
her body bombarded for years   by the element
she had purified
It seems she denied to the end   [10]
the source of the cataracts on her eyes
the cracked and suppurating skin   of her finger-ends
till she could no longer hold   a test-tube or a pencil

She died   a famous woman   denying
her wounds   [15]
denying
her   wounds   came from the same source as her power

Annotations
[1] ***deposits:*** sediments and minerals that accumulate in the soil; things entrusted for safekeeping to be recovered at a later date
[2] ***backhoe:*** mechanical digger
[2] ***divulged:*** revealed
[3] ***amber:*** brownish yellow in colour
[4] ***tonic:*** a medicinal preparation designed to improves one's health and sense of well-being
[6] ***Marie Curie:*** (1867-1934) French chemist (born in Poland) who won two Nobel prizes; one for research on radioactivity and another for her discovery of the elements radium and polonium
[7] ***radiation sickness:*** sickness caused by exposure to radiation
[8] ***the element:*** radium
[11] ***cataracts:*** loss in the transparency of the lens of the eye, which reduces a person's ability to see
[12] ***suppurating:*** forming or discharging pus

Tease It Out

1. Watch Video 16. What most impressed you about the life of Marie Curie?
2. Consider the phrase 'crumbling flank of earth'. In what type of terrain precisely, do you imagine the backhoe to have been digging? Write three sentences describing this excavation site in your own words.
3. How old was the bottle? What colour was the liquid it contained?
4. Were the bottle – or its contents – damaged in any way?
5. The bottle's label described it as a 'tonic'. According to line 5, when might such a tonic prove especially useful.
6. Name two specific ailments that, according to its label, the tonic could relieve.
7. Such tonics or elixirs were extremely popular in 19th-century America. Do you think such tonics could best be described as a) a genuine scientific product b) a folk or herbal remedy c) a scam designed to con people out of their hard-earned money? Give a reason for your answer.
8. 'the element/ she had purified'. What substance is being referred to here? In what sense had Marie Curie 'purified' this element?
9. According to the speaker, what impact did exposure to this element have on Marie Curie's eyes? What impact did it have on her fingers.
10. Did Marie Curie know that her symptoms were caused by exposure to this element? Did she publicly accept that this was the case?
11. 'She died a famous woman'. Name two major accolades that Marie Curie received for her work.
12. 'denying/ her wounds/ denying/ her wounds'. Pair with the person next to you and try to work out why Rich chooses to repeat this particular phrase? Can you think of an effect this repetition has on the reader?
13. **Class Discussion:** Why might Marie Curie have been reluctant to accept that her illness was caused by exposure to the element she had 'purified'? Could there be more than one reason for this reluctance?
14. 'This is a poem where the long spaces between the words are as important as the words themselves; the gradual breakdown of the poem's lines reflects the breakdown of its subject's body'. Do you agree with this reading of the poem or do you think it's too fanciful? Give a reason for your answer.

Exam Prep

1. **Theme Talk:** 'This poem highlights the extreme lengths to which women must go in order to compete on the same playing field as men'. Write a paragraph in response to this statement.
2. **Class Discussion:** Consider and discuss the following statements regarding the relationship between the bottle of tonic and the story of Marie Curie's death.
    - The poet resents the fact that the 'quack' scientists who created the tonic got rich, while Marie Curie, a real scientist, suffered for her work.
    - The tonic and its creators have been forgotten, but Marie Curie will remain an inspiration forever.
    - If they could, the male-dominated scientific establishment would 'bury' the story of this great female scientist.
3. **Theme Talk:** 'It is a grim irony that the source of Marie Curie's power ultimately made her powerless'. Do you agree or disagree with this statement? Write a paragraph in response.

Language Lab

1. According to the speaker, Marie Curie enjoyed great power. What precisely does she mean by this? Consider the following possibilities and rank them in order of plausibility:
    - Her scientific discoveries made her extremely wealthy, a woman not to be crossed.
    - She was capable, through her discoveries, of literally changing the world.
    - Because she was famous in one field, she was listened to when it came to other matters and became an influential figure in terms of public policy.
    - Her undeniable brilliance allowed her to compete and succeed in what was (and, unfortunately, all too often still is) a 'man's world'.
    - She discovered elements that, when processed correctly, could power engines, weapon and entire electricity supplies.

William Butler Yeats

William Butler Yeats was born in Sandymount, Dublin on 13 June 1865 into an Anglo-Irish family. When Yeats was a child, his father, John Butler Yeats, gave up a career in law and moved the family to London to pursue his passion for painting. Although talented, John Butler Yeats was never able to make painting pay and the family struggled financially.

In 1872, when William was seven, the family travelled to Sligo for a summer holiday, staying with his mother's family. The holiday lasted the best part of two and a half years and proved to be a vital experience for Yeats. He fell in love with the landscape and listened intently to the servants' stories of fairies. From an early age, Yeats was fascinated by both Irish legends and the occult. These memories and stories of Sligo were to remain with the poet for the rest of his life.

Back in England, Yeats struggled at school. He was considered to be 'very poor in spelling', a weakness that persisted throughout his poetic career. It was in science that he excelled. While reading his son's school report, John remarked that William would be 'a man of science; it is great to be a man of science'.

In 1880 the family moved back to Dublin, settling first in Harold's Cross and later in Howth. Yeats didn't fare any better in school in Dublin, but spent a lot of time at his father's nearby studio, where he met many of the city's artists and writers. John Butler Yeats constantly encouraged his children in the world of ideas, philosophy and art. The entire family was highly artistic; William's brother Jack went on to become a famous painter, while his sisters Elizabeth and Susan were active in the arts and crafts world.

After finishing school in 1883, Yeats attended the Metropolitan School of Art in Dublin, now the National College of Art and Design. By then, Yeats had been writing poetry for a few years, beginning in his late teens. His early work was strongly influenced by Percy Bysshe Shelley, William Blake and other Romantic poets. His first publication, 'The Island of Statues', appeared in the Dublin University Review in 1885.

Despite their Anglo-Irish background, Yeats' parents were broadly supportive of Irish nationalism. Yeats, in turn, was passionate about the Irish cause. In 1885 he met the Fenian activist John O'Leary, whose romanticised view of the nation struck a chord with Yeats. O'Leary's twenty years of imprisonment and exile, his sense of patriotism, and his devotion to cultural rather than militant nationalism all held an attraction for the young Yeats. O'Leary embodied a sense of an older, romantic Ireland, one that was ancient and mysterious. Yeats termed this 'indomitable Irishry'. He would later lament O'Leary in the poem 'September 1913': 'Romantic Ireland's dead and gone,/ It's with O'Leary in the grave'.

The Yeats family moved back to London in 1887, where Yeats continued to write in earnest. In 1888 he wrote one of his most

"The creations of a great writer are little more than the moods and passions of his own heart, given surnames and Christian names, and sent to walk the earth."

famous poems, 'The Lake Isle of Innisfree'. When it was published in the *National Observer* in 1890, it received critical acclaim and brought Yeats' work to national attention. His first collection, The Wanderings of Oisin and Other Poems, was published in 1889. It drew heavily on Irish mythology and dealt with one of Yeats' most common themes: the tension between a life of action and a life of contemplation.

Yeats met the heiress and Irish nationalist Maud Gonne in 1889 when she visited the family home. He was immediately struck by her, and she would provide him with the inspiration for a lifetime of great love poetry and unrequited longing. He proposed to Gonne four times and was refused on each occasion, partly because Gonne believed that Yeats' unrequited love for her inspired his greatest poetry. Gonne went on to marry the republican icon John MacBride in 1903. The marriage soon fell apart, and though Gonne did have a fleeting romance with Yeats in 1908, it never became the committed relationship he hoped for.

In 1890 Yeats joined the Order of the Golden Dawn, a secret society with initiation rites, rituals and other occult practices. His membership of this society was reflective of his lifelong interest in mysticism and the supernatural. He attended séances and read widely the mystical literature of other belief systems, such as Buddhism and Judaism. He was fascinated by the ritual and mystery of the supernatural, something which also fuelled his interest in Irish legends. That sense of ceremony and symbolic importance in the revelation of truth never left Yeats and permeates his poetry.

In 1896 Yeats met Lady Augusta Gregory, and her estate at Coole Park in Galway was to become a summer retreat for Yeats for many years. Lady Gregory encouraged Yeats' nationalism and his playwriting. Together with other writers such as J.M. Synge and Sean O'Casey, Yeats and Gregory were instrumental in founding the movement known as the Irish Literary Revival. In 1899, they established the Irish Literary Theatre for the purpose of performing Irish and Celtic plays. This led in turn to the foundation of the Abbey Theatre in 1904. Yeats' play *Cathleen Ní Houlihan*, starring Maud Gonne, was performed on the opening night.

Yeats proposed to Maud Gonne one last time in 1916, soon after John MacBride was executed for his part in the 1916 Rising. When Maud refused him, Yeats proposed to her daughter, twenty-one-year-old Iseult Gonne. When Iseult also turned him down, Yeats eventually married twenty-five-year-old Bertha Georgie Hyde-Lees at the age of fifty-one. Georgie was involved in much of Yeats' writing, and like her husband was interested in the occult. With Georgie, Yeats experimentally wrote numerous poems by a process called automatic writing. Georgie considered herself a medium and claimed to channel the messages of spirits in the form of symbols. Together they produced hundreds of pages' worth of poetic material, eventually published in the 1925 book *A Vision*.

The couple bought a Norman castle, Thoor Ballylee, from Lady Gregory sometime in 1916 or 1917. Their first-born, Anne, arrived in 1919, the same year that Yeats published his seventh collection of poetry, *The Wild Swans at Coole*. Their second child, Michael, was born in 1921 while the family was living in Oxford.

Yeats was appointed to the first Senate of the Irish Free State in 1922, and was re-appointed for a second time in 1925. In 1923 Yeats was awarded the Nobel Prize for Literature, the first Irish person to achieve that honour. The Nobel Committee remarked on his 'inspired poetry, which in a highly artistic form gives expression to the spirit of a whole nation.' Yeats could not help but associate his win with Ireland's recently-won independence, saying: 'I consider that this honour has come to me less as an individual than as a representative of Irish literature; it is part of Europe's welcome to the Free State.'

Despite his ill health, Yeats remained a prolific writer. After reportedly going through an operation that restored his libido, Yeats even had several affairs with younger women in his later years, among them the actress Margot Ruddock and the novelist Ethel Mannin. He died in the town of Menton in the south of France in 1939, aged seventy-three. He was initially buried nearby in Roquebrune, before being exhumed in 1948 to be brought back to Drumcliff, Co. Sligo. His epitaph is taken from the last lines of 'Under Ben Bulben', one of his final poems: 'Cast a cold Eye/ On Life, on Death./ Horseman, pass by!'

The Lake Isle of Innisfree

I will arise and go now, and go to Innisfree,
And a small cabin build there, of clay and wattles made;
Nine bean-rows will I have there, a hive for the honey-bee,
And live alone in the bee-loud glade.

And I shall have some peace there, for peace comes dropping slow, [5]
Dropping from the veils of the morning to where the cricket sings;
There midnight's all a glimmer, and noon a purple glow,
And evening full of the linnet's wings.

I will arise and go now, for always night and day
I hear lake water lapping with low sounds by the shore; [10]
While I stand on the roadway, or on the pavements grey,
I hear it in the deep heart's core.

Annotations

Innisfree: a tiny uninhabited island on Lough Gill, Co. Sligo

[2] *Clay and wattles:* an ancient construction technique known as 'wattle and daub', whereby clay is smeared over a frame of interwoven branches

[7] *a purple glow:* Innisfree comes from the Irish *Inis Fraoich*, which means 'island of heather'. Here Yeats imagines the purple heather glowing in the noon sunlight

[8] *linnet's wings:* a linnet is a type of finch, typically brown and red-breasted

Tease It Out

1. The poet declares his intention to go and live on Innisfree. Is this a spontaneous decision or something he's been thinking about for a long time? Give a reason for your answer.
2. What ancient building process will the poet use to construct his cabin on Innisfree? Describe it in your own words.
3. The poet imagines living a self-sufficient life on the island. What different foodstuffs does he imagine growing in order to feed himself?
4. What metaphor does the poet use to describe the mist that drifts across the island each morning? Is it an effective one in your opinion?
5. What word or phrase describes the effect of starlight as it's reflected in the waters around the island?
6. What sound fills the island as evening comes?
7. Google the Irish language origins of the name Innisfree? What does this suggest about the purple glow that fills the island each noon?
8. What sound does the poet claim to hear 'night and day'?
9. Consider his description of this sound. Do you think he finds it a pleasant one? Do you think it bothers him that he 'always' hears this sound, seemingly everywhere he goes?
10. Is he really hearing this sound or does he experience it only in his own imagination?
11. What aspect of the mind or self is suggested by the phrase 'deep heart's core'?
12. In what sort of environment is the poet at this moment? Is he happy to be where he is?

Exam Prep

1. **Personal Response:** Take a moment to visualise your own perfect getaway. It could be a real place or an imaginary one. Write a poem or a short prose piece in which you describe its most important features.
2. **Class Discussion:** The poet states three times that he will 'go' and live on Innisfree. Do you think the poet is serious about changing his life in this way or is he merely trying to convince himself that he's actually capable of such a radical move? Do you think the poet is prepared for the challenges of living a solitary, self-sufficient lifestyle?
3. **Theme Talk:** 'Innisfree is a real place, but it's also an idea, a state of mind that the speaker can access any time'. Do you agree with this statement? Write a few paragraphs in response.
4. **Exam Prep:** 'Yeats's poetry is driven by a tension between the real world in which he lives and an ideal world that he imagines'. Write a short essay in response to this statement, referring to 'Lake Isle' and at least two other poems on your course.

Language Lab

1. 'In stanza 2, peace is depicted almost as a physical substance, 'dropping' like dew from veils of mist onto the grasses'. Do you agree with this interpretation? Write a few sentences in response.
2. 'The Lake Isle of Innisfree' uses repetition to great effect. In particular, the phrase 'I will arise and go now' has great power when repeated in the final stanza. Suggest how the meaning and tone of this line changes between stanza 1 and stanza 3.
3. This poem makes extensive use of assonance and alliteration to create a beguiling verbal music, such as in line 3: 'Nine bean-rows will I have there, a hive for the honey-bee'. Can you identify another example of assonance and another example of alliteration in the poem?
4. 'And I shall have some peace there'. Identify three words or phrases that emphasise the island's extreme tranquillity. Is the impression he creates of the island a realistic one, in your opinion?

September 1913

What need you, being come to sense,
But fumble in a greasy till
And add the halfpence to the pence
And prayer to shivering prayer, until
You have dried the marrow from the bone; [5]
For men were born to pray and save:
Romantic Ireland's dead and gone,
It's with O'Leary in the grave.

Yet they were of a different kind,
The names that stilled your childish play, [10]
They have gone about the world like wind,
But little time had they to pray
For whom the hangman's rope was spun,
And what, God help us, could they save?
Romantic Ireland's dead and gone, [15]
It's with O'Leary in the grave.

Was it for this the wild geese spread
The grey wing upon every tide;
For this that all that blood was shed,
For this Edward Fitzgerald died, [20]
And Robert Emmet and Wolfe Tone,
All that delirium of the brave?
Romantic Ireland's dead and gone,
It's with O'Leary in the grave.

Yet could we turn the years again, [25]
And call those exiles as they were
In all their loneliness and pain,
You'd cry, 'Some woman's yellow hair
Has maddened every mother's son':
They weighed so lightly what they gave. [30]
But let them be, they're dead and gone,
They're with O'Leary in the grave.

Annotations
[1] *being come to sense:* having achieved wisdom
[7] *Romantic:* passionate and idealistic; creative and imaginative; open to risk and adventure; pertaining to an earlier past
[8] *O'Leary:* John O'Leary (1830-1907) was an Irish patriot and a mentor to Yeats
[10] *stilled:* silenced, brought to a stop
[17] *the wild geese:* Irish soldiers who left the country, often after defeat in rebellion against English rule, and served in continental European armies during the 16th, 17th and 18th centuries
[20] *Edward Fitzgerald:* (1763-1798) Irish patriot and leader of the 1798 rebellion against British rule in Ireland. Died in captivity
[21] *Robert Emmet:* (1778-1803) Irish patriot who was hanged after leading an rebellion against British rule in 1803.
[21] *Wolfe Tone:* (1763-1798) Irish patriot and leader of the 1798 rebellion against British rule in Ireland. Died in captivity
[22] *delirium:* madness, overcome by excessive emotion
[28] *Some woman's yellow hair:* songs and stories often personified Ireland as a woman

Tease It Out

1. This poem is addressed to the leading businessmen of Dublin. What phrase indicates that in Yeats's opinion these are a mean-spirited, miserly lot?
2. What phrase indicates that these people pray a lot?
3. Consider the phrase 'prayer to shivering prayer'. Does it suggest that
   - These people pray in churches that are cold and draughty
   - They pray out of fear rather than true spiritual devotion
   - They count their prayers, adding them up like coins
4. According to line 6, what are the twin purposes of human existence and the only things the middle classes need to do?
5. Consider the poem's tone in these lines. Is it sarcastic or sincere?
6. Google the Fenian John O'Leary. What political goals did he strive for and what did his efforts cost him?
7. **Class Discussion:** Yeats associates O'Leary with a 'Romantic' vision of Ireland. What does the word 'Romantic' mean in this context?
8. How do the values embodied by O'Leary differ from those of the businessmen, as depicted in this stanza?
9. Yeats imagines these captains of industry playing as children. What, according to the poet, would interrupt their childhood games?
10. Yeats describes the great heroes of Irish history, declaring that 'They have gone about the world like wind'. Which of the following statements best sums up his meaning?
    - The heroes' names have travelled around the world, as their fame grew and word spread of their deeds
    - The heroes themselves have travelled around the world because they were exiled from Ireland
11. What phrase indicates that these heroes were more interested in revolution than religion?
12. What phrase indicates that in Yeats's opinion they were destined to die as soon as they embraced the cause of Irish freedom?
13. Does the poet feel that heroes like Emmet and Tone would be delighted with or horrified by the Ireland of 1913?
14. The poet imagines somehow calling these heroes from the past. What image does he use to describe this feat of time travel?
15. According to Yeats, how would the businessmen who now run Ireland react to these heroes, if the heroes were summonsed and turned up in 1913.
16. Consider line 30. What did the heroes give for Ireland? According to the poet, what was their attitude to this great sacrifice they were making?
17. 'But let them be'. The poet eventually decides it's better not to 'call' these heroes from the past. Why do you think he makes this choice?

Exam Prep

1. **Personal Response:** Try to identify the three main criticisms Yeats makes of Ireland in 'September 1913'. Express each one in your own words. How many of these criticisms might equally be applied to the Ireland of today?
2. **Class Discussion:** Consider the questions below on your own for five minutes and jot down some ideas, before comparing notes with the person beside you. Finally, share your ideas with the class.
   - Why does Yeats refer to the heroes as 'exiles'?
   - Might they have been exiled in more than one way?
   - Why might they have experienced 'loneliness'?
   - Why might they have experienced 'pain'?
3. **Theme Talk:** Consider Yeats's use of the term 'delirium'. Would you agree that Yeats's portrayal of these patriots isn't an entirely positive one?
4. **Exam Prep:** 'Yeats is both enticed and repelled by political violence'. Write a resonse to this statement, making reference to 'September 1913' and at least two other poems on your course.

Language Lab

1. Picture someone with his or her hands in a dirty, greasy till, fumbling to pick up a few coins. Write a few sentences describing precisely what you visualise. Is it a pleasant or an unpleasant image?
2. Who is the yellow-haired woman referred to in line 28? Is this an actual woman the heroes might have known when they were alive? Or is this woman a symbol or metaphor of some kind? Could it be a mixture of both?
3. **Class Discussion:** 'Until/ You have dried the marrow from the bone'. What precisely do we visualise happening here? What kind of approach to living does this image of a dried-up bone suggest?

The Wild Swans at Coole

The trees are in their autumn beauty,
The woodland paths are dry,
Under the October twilight the water
Mirrors a still sky;
Upon the brimming water among the stones [5]
Are nine-and-fifty swans.

The nineteenth autumn has come upon me
Since I first made my count;
I saw, before I had well finished,
All suddenly mount [10]
And scatter wheeling in great broken rings
Upon their clamorous wings.

I have looked upon those brilliant creatures,
And now my heart is sore.
All's changed since I, hearing at twilight, [15]
The first time on this shore,
The bell-beat of their wings above my head,
Trod with a lighter tread.

Unwearied still, lover by lover,
They paddle in the cold [20]
Companionable streams or climb the air;
Their hearts have not grown old;
Passion or conquest, wander where they will,
Attend upon them still.

But now they drift on the still water, [25]
Mysterious, beautiful;
Among what rushes will they build,
By what lake's edge or pool
Delight men's eyes when I awake some day
To find they have flown away? [30]

Annotations
Coole: Coole Park, near Gort in Co. Galway. Was the home of Yeats's friend, Lady Gregory, whom he visited often
[10] *mount:* take to the air
[11] *wheeling:* flying in wide circles or curves
[12] *clamorous:* noisy
[13] *brilliant:* bright, magnificent
[21] *Companionable streams:* streams where the swans can congregate and be togther
[23] *Passion or conquest:* Yeats personifies these qualities, suggesting that they follow the swans wherever they go

Tease It Out

1. What time of the year is it, and what time of day?
2. Through what type of landscape is the poet walking? What has the weather been like?
3. The water on the lake is very calm. What word or phrase indicates this? What does the word 'brimming' suggest about the level of water in the lake?
4. The poet describes the water 'among the stones'. How do you visualise this? Are the stones on the bank, or scattered across the lake surface?
5. How many swans are swimming on the lake, according to the poet?
6. This is not the first time the poet has counted the swans in this particular lake. How long ago did he first count them?
7. Back then the poet saw the swans 'suddenly mount'. What process is he describing here? How do we usually use the verb 'mount'? What does the poet imagine the swans mounting?
8. What does the word 'wheeling' suggest about the swans' motion as they took flight?
9. The swans' wings made a great ruckus as they ascended. What word suggests this?
10. What feature of the swans' appearance is suggested by the adjective 'brilliant'?
11. How does contemplating these 'brilliant' creatures make the poet feel? Pick two adjectives that best describe his mood or state of mind as he looks at the swans.
12. The poet declares that nineteen years ago he 'Trod with a lighter tread'. Why does he not move as lightly now? Is this a reference to mental changes or physical changes or both?
13. 'Their hearts have not grown old'. What does this suggest about the swans' mental vibrancy and vitality?
14. The poet imagines the swans being engaged in a series of long-term, loving relationships. What phrase indicates this?
15. The swans, according to the poet, are capable of romantic 'Passion' and sexual 'conquest'. Does he believe that this capacity will ever diminish?
16. The poet imagines the swans leaving the lake at some future time. Where does he imagine them going once they leave? What does he imagine them doing there?
17. The poet imagines other people in these locations watching the swans. How will they react to the sight of these creatures?
18. Lines 29 to 30: The poet imagines himself looking on the empty lake after the swans have left. How do you imagine he will feel when that moment comes?

Exam Prep

1. **Personal Response:** In this poem the poet grapples with the effects of reaching middle age. What do each of the following suggest about the stage of life in which the poet finds himself: the time of day; the time of year; the fullness of the lake; a sore heart; a heavy tread.
2. **Theme Talk:** The poet anticipates old age, which is associated with the departure of the swans. What does this image suggest about old age, as the middle-aged Yeats imagines it?
3. **Group Discussion:** The poet compares and contrasts himself with the swans throughout the poem. Get into groups of four. Draw two overlapping circles, labelling one 'The Poet' and the other 'The Swans'. Now categorise the following descriptions, placing those that are relevant to both where the circles overlap:
    - Imposing
    - Strong-willed
    - Untiring
    - Passionate
    - Free
    - Contented
    - Physically powerful
    - Self-pitying
    - Physically tired
    - Ageing
4. **Exam Prep:** 'Yeats uses powerful imagery to explore the harsh realities of ageing and death'. Discuss this statement in relation to this poem as well as 'An Acre of Grass' and 'Sailing to Byzantium'.

Language Lab

1. How would you characterise the atmosphere of the woodland lake the poem describes? Pick out three adjectives that in your opinion best describe this setting, and in each instance support your choice with a quotation from the poem.
2. Alliteration occurs when two words in close proximity begin with the same sound, for example the 't' sound in 'Trod with a lighter tread'. Can you find two other examples of alliteration in this poem?
3. Identify three words that are repeated throughout the poem. What effect does this repetition have?
4. Consider the phrase 'Unwearied still, lover by lover'. Yeats presents the swans as semi-immortal figures, as creatures somehow immune to time and change. Would you agree with this statement? Does Yeats really think that swans have such immunity? Or is he speaking in a symbolic or metaphorical fashion?

An Irish Airman Foresees His Death

I know that I shall meet my fate
Somewhere among the clouds above;
Those that I fight I do not hate,
Those that I guard I do not love;
My country is Kiltartan Cross, [5]
My countrymen Kiltartan's poor,
No likely end could bring them loss
Or leave them happier than before.
Nor law, nor duty bade me fight,
Nor public men, nor cheering crowds, [10]
A lonely impulse of delight
Drove to this tumult in the clouds;
I balanced all, brought all to mind,
The years to come seemed waste of breath,
A waste of breath the years behind [15]
In balance with this life, this death.

Annotations

An Irish Airman: the poem is spoken by an Irish pilot serving with the British forces during the First World War (1914-18). It was inspired by Major Robert Gregory, the son of Yeats's great friend Lady Gregory. Major Robert served with distinction in the Royal Flying Corps before being shot down and killed on a combat mission in Italy in 1918.

[3] ***Those that I fight:*** Germany and its allies
[4] ***Those that I guard:*** the British people; the army in which the airman serves is dedicated to their defence
[5] ***Kiltartan Cross:*** a crossroads near Lady Gregory's home in Gort, Co. Galway
[9] ***Nor law, nor duty:*** as an Irish person, the airman is under no legal or moral obligation to fight for Britain
[10] ***public men:*** politicians
[12] ***tumult:*** a state of confusion or disorder

Tease It Out

1. The speaker anticipates the moment of his death. What kind of death do you think he is imagining? Where does he imagine this taking place?
2. What does the word 'fate' suggest about his death?
3. How does the airman feel about those he is fighting? Why do you think he feels this way?
4. 'Those that I guard I do not love'. In which country's military is the airman serving? Why doesn't he love this country or its people?
5. Where is the airman from? What does he tell us about his native village?
6. **True or false:** The outcome of the war will have a great impact on the airman's 'countrymen'?
7. The airman mentions four different reasons why an individual might join the military. Explain each one in your own words.
8. **Class Discussion:** The airman finds delight in flying and in aerial combat. Can you suggest why these activities might bring him pleasure and excitement?
9. The airman's impulse to fly is a 'lonely' one. What do you think he means by 'lonely'? Consider the following possibilities and rank them in order of likelihood, giving reasons for your decisions:
    - He arrived at his decision alone, without consulting with others
    - It's the only impulse affecting him
    - Not many people share the impulse to fly, making it a lonely vocation
    - He is alone in the cockpit and can only rely on himself
    - He is motivated by a desire to ascend into the clouds alone, leaving the busy world of people behind
10. What does the word 'tumult' suggest about the nature of aerial combat?
11. 'I balanced all'. What does this suggest about the process that was involved in the speaker's decision to join the air force? Do you think it took him long to reach his decision?
12. The speaker feels that his life prior to becoming a fighter pilot was pointless; life only really began when he became a fighter pilot. What phrase captures this?
13. **True or false:** The airman is excited by the prospect of life after the war.
14. **Group Discussion:** Break into pairs and discuss the following statements:
    - The speaker feels that this dramatic, exciting death will make up for the boredom and the pointlessness of his existence up until then
    - The speaker feels that this pointless death is a fitting end for his pointless life
    - Which statement best captures the last line of the poem?

Exam Prep

1. **Personal Response:** Would you agree that the speaker is indifferent to the outcome of the war? If given the choice between going home and fighting for the other side, which do you think he would choose? Explain your answer.
2. **Class Discussion:** 'The speaker of the poem is essentially a thrill seeker; he has no other motivation for getting involved in the war'. Do you agree with this statement? Support your answer with lines or phrases from the poem.
3. **Theme Talk:** 'The speaker feels he has nothing but hatred and contempt for ordinary life and longs to die in order to escape it'. Write a paragraph agreeing or disagreeing with this statement. Support your answer with reference to the poem.
4. **Exam Prep:** 'Yeats, in both his life and work, exhibited great admiration for men of action'. Write a short essay in response to this statement, making reference to this poem and two other poems on your course.

Language Lab

1. 'Anaphora' is a literary device in which words at the beginning of lines or phrases are repeated. Can you identify any examples in this poem? What effect does this give?
2. Identify the rhyme scheme of this poem.
3. This is a very rhythmic poem. Is there any connection between this rhythmic effect and the relentless mechanical rhythm of an airplane's engine? What does this rhythm suggest about the airman's state of mind?
4. 'A lonely impulse of delight'. Do you think of impulses as being hard or easy to resist? Is an impulse like an addiction or a desire, or is it more like a whim? Explain your answer.

Easter 1916

I have met them at close of day
Coming with vivid faces
From counter or desk among grey
Eighteenth-century houses.
I have passed with a nod of the head [5]
Or polite meaningless words,
Or have lingered awhile and said
Polite meaningless words,
And thought before I had done
Of a mocking tale or a gibe [10]
To please a companion
Around the fire at the club,
Being certain that they and I
But lived where motley is worn:
All changed, changed utterly: [15]
A terrible beauty is born.

That woman's days were spent
In ignorant good-will,
Her nights in argument
Until her voice grew shrill. [20]
What voice more sweet than hers
When, young and beautiful,
She rode to harriers?
This man had kept a school
And rode our wingèd horse; [25]
This other his helper and friend
Was coming into his force;
He might have won fame in the end,
So sensitive his nature seemed,
So daring and sweet his thought. [30]
This other man I had Dreamd
A drunken, vainglorious lout.
He had done most bitter wrong
To some who are near my heart,
Yet I number him in the song; [35]
He, too, has resigned his part
In the casual comedy;
He, too, has been changed in his turn,
Transformed utterly:
A terrible beauty is born. [40]

Annotations
Easter 1916: refers to the Easter Rising, a rebellion by about 700 Irish volunteers against British rule in Ireland. The Rising lasted six days and sixteen of its leaders were executed in the aftermath
[1] ***I have met them:*** Yeats knew several leaders of the Rising and would have met them regularly on the streets of Dublin
[10] ***gibe:*** an insulting remark
[12] ***club:*** a gentleman's club
[14] ***motley:*** clothing created by combining patches of many different colours, traditionally worn by the court jester
[17] ***That woman:*** Countess Constance Markievicz (1867-1927), a leader of the Rising
[20] ***shrill:*** piercing, sharp
[23] ***rode to harriers:*** participated in a hunt with horse and hounds
[24] ***This man:*** Patrick Pearse (1879-1916), a leader of the Rising and one of those executed
[25] ***wingèd horse:*** Pegasus, a mythological winged horse and symbol of poetry
[26] ***This other:*** Thomas MacDonagh (1878-1916), a leader of the Rising
[27] ***Was coming into his force:*** Yeats feels that MacDonagh was coming into his own as a writer when he died
[31] ***This other man:*** Major John MacBride (1868-1916), a participant in the Rising and one of those executed
vainglorious: excessively vain, proud and boastful
[33-34] ***He had done ... heart:*** MacBride was married to Maud Gonne, the woman Yeats loved, and mistreated her throughout their marriage

Hearts with one purpose alone
Through summer and winter seem
Enchanted to a stone
To trouble the living stream.
The horse that comes from the road, [45]
The rider, the birds that range
From cloud to tumbling cloud,
Minute by minute they change;
A shadow of cloud on the stream
Changes minute by minute; [50]
A horse-hoof slides on the brim,
And a horse plashes within it;
The long-legged moor-hens dive,
And hens to moor-cocks call;
Minute by minute they live: [55]
The stone's in the midst of all.

Too long a sacrifice
Can make a stone of the heart.
O when may it suffice?
That is Heaven's part, our part [60]
To murmur name upon name,
As a mother names her child
When sleep at last has come
On limbs that had run wild.
What is it but nightfall? [65]
No, no, not night but death;
Was it needless death after all?
For England may keep faith
For all that is done and said.
We know their dream; enough [70]
To know they Dreamd and are dead;
And what if excess of love
Bewildered them till they died?
I write it out in a verse –
MacDonagh and MacBride [75]
And Connolly and Pearse
Now and in time to be,
Wherever green is worn,
Are changed, changed utterly:
A terrible beauty is born. [80]

[43] ***Enchanted to a stone:*** made stone-like, transformed into a stone
[46] ***range:*** wander, roam
[51] ***slides on the brim:*** slips at the edge of the stream
[52] ***plashes:*** splashes
[68] ***England may keep faith:*** in 1914 the British government had promised to grant Ireland 'Home Rule', a measure of independence. This promise had been put on hold. Yeats considers the possibility that it might still be kept
[76] ***Connolly:*** James Connolly (1870-1916), a leader of the Rising and one of those executed

Tease It Out

Lines 1 to 35

1. Watch Video 17 and explain in your own words why the Rising happened. What did those who organised it hope to achieve?
2. Yeats would run into nationalist revolutionaries on the streets of Dublin. At what time would these encounters typically occur?
3. Where do you imagine these revolutionaries worked during the day?
4. **True or false:** Yeats was always eager to stop and chat with the revolutionaries when he met them.
5. The poet thought the revolutionaries were rather ridiculous. What phrase indicates this?
6. The poet describes how he would attend a 'club'.
   - What sort of establishment do you imagine this is?
   - What does the poet imagine sharing with his companions there?
   - Do you think the revolutionaries would attend such an establishment?
7. What is 'motley' and who typically wears it? What is Yeats suggesting about Ireland when he describes it as a place 'where motley is worn'?
8. The first part of the poem ends with the poet stating that 'All changed, changed utterly'. What do you think has changed and what was it that brought about this change?

Lines 17 to 40

9. How has Constance Markievicz been spending her nights? What impact does this have on her voice?
10. What does the phrase 'ignorant good-will' suggest about the poet's attitude towards Constance's political beliefs?
11. Yeats knew Constance personally when she was younger. What activities does he recall her doing?
12. Lines 24 to 25 describe the rebel leader Padraig Pearse. What was his profession?
13. **Class Discussion:** Yeats associates Pearse with a 'winged horse'. Does this symbolise Pearse's career as a) a poet, b) a revolutionary soldier, or c) a journalist?
14. Yeats had a high opinion of Thomas MacDonagh's ability as a poet and writer in lines 29 to 30? How does he convey this?
15. Lines 31 to 34: How does Yeats characterise Major John MacBride?
16. **True or false:** Yeats has no personal reason to dislike MacBride.
17. **Class Discussion:** MacBride and the other leaders have left the 'casual comedy'. Does this phrase refer to a) human existence in general, b) life in Ireland or c) something else entirely?

Lines 41 to 56

18. Consider the scene the poet paints in lines 45 to 54:
    - List everything the horse and its rider do
    - Where, according to Yeats, do the birds 'range' or wander?
    - **True or false:** The shadow or reflection of the cloud is unchanging.
    - What behaviour is exhibited by the moorcocks and hens?
19. 'Minute by minute they change'. Would you agree that this scene presents the natural world as a place of constant change?
20. How does the stone differ from everything else depicted in the scene?
21. Yeats compares life itself to such a body of water, describing it as a 'living stream'. What does this suggest about his view of human existence?
22. Fanatical people, meanwhile, are compared to unbudging pieces of stone. What does this suggest about such an obsessive or fanatical mindset?
23. **Class Discussion:** What impact do fanatical people have on the 'living stream' of human existence?

Lines 57 to 80

24. The revolutionaries, according to Yeats, sacrificed much in their devotion to the cause of Irish freedom. Suggest two or three things they may have sacrificed?
25. What impact did this sacrifice have on their psyches?
26. **True or false:** Human beings always know when they sacrificed enough to when the goals they aim to achieve are finally in sight?
27. For a moment the poet denies to himself that the revolutionary leaders are actually dead. What phrase indicates this? Can he maintain this self-deception?
28. The poet worries that the deaths of the rebel leaders might have been needless. What political outcome might render their actions redundant?
29. 'We know their dream'.
    - What was the rebel leaders' 'dream'?
    - Who is the 'We' referred to in this line?
    - How do these people now 'know' or understand the dream of the rebel leaders?
30. **Class Discussion:** Yeats describes how the rebel leaders were 'Bewildered' by an 'excess of love'. What did the rebel leaders 'love'? In what sense might this have 'Bewildered' them?

Exam Prep

1. **Group Discussion:** The poet describes how 'All [has] changed, changed utterly' in Ireland since the Rising. Based on your knowledge of the period, can you suggest two ways in which the country has changed? Do you think that Yeats was pleased with these changes?
2. **Group Discussion:** What does Yeats mean when he says that the rebel leaders have been 'Transformed utterly'? Rank the following in order of possibility:
   - The will be regarded as figures of hate for bringing destruction to Dublin
   - They once were living, but now are dead
   - They have undergone a career change swopping the life of shopkeeper or school teacher for that of military leader
   - They have been transformed in the national imagination from obbsessives and oddballs into figures of heroism and majesty

   Do you think this transformation applies to the leaders who survived as well as those who were executed?
3. **Class Discussion:** Yeats viewed Irish society as being in permanent decline. Is this statement true of 'Easter 1916'. You might also compare the poem to 'September 1913' and 'Under Ben Bulben'.
4. **Theme Talk:** Yeats regards the reborn Irish patriotism as a thing of 'terrible beauty'.
   - The phrase 'terrible beauty' is an example of what literary device? (Hint: It starts with an 'o').
   - In what sense might it be terrifying? In what sense might it be beautiful?
   - How are the rebel leaders similar to the businessmen satirised in 'September 1913'? How are they different?
   - The rebel leaders, like the heroes in 'September 1913', are presented as somewhat crazed. Identify two phrases from each poem that supports this claim
   - Compare the treatment of patriotism in this poem with 'The Stare's Nest by my Window'.
5. **Exam Prep:** 'In Yeats's poetry he is both horrified and facinated by war, violence and social upheaval'. Write a response to this in which you discuss 'Easter 1916' and two other poems.

Language Lab

1. **Personal Response:** The poem is full of uncertainty and doubt. Create a two-column table. Label the first column 'Things the poet is sure of' and label the second column 'Things the poet is unsure of'. Now read through the poem and identify five things the poet is sure of and five things he is unsure of.
2. In lines 60 to 63, Yeats focuses on an image of a mother and her sleeping child.
   - What has the child been doing all day?
   - What has happened to the child now?
   - How does the mother comfort the child?
   - In what sense do the rebel leaders resemble the child?
   - The Irish people, according to Yeats, must behave like the child's mother. What exactly does he want the Irish people to do?
3. What do you understand by the phrase 'Wherever green is worn'? Rank the following in order of plausibility:
   - The poet is referring to the St. Patrick's day parades
   - The poet is referring to matches involving Ireland's national team
   - The poet is referring to parades by the Irish army
   - The poet is referring to any occasion where Irish people around the world take pride in their country.

The Second Coming

Turning and turning in the widening gyre
The falcon cannot hear the falconer;
Things fall apart; the centre cannot hold;
Mere anarchy is loosed upon the world,
The blood-dimmed tide is loosed, and everywhere [5]
The ceremony of innocence is drowned;
The best lack all conviction, while the worst
Are full of passionate intensity.
Surely some revelation is at hand;

Surely the Second Coming is at hand. [10]
The Second Coming! Hardly are those words out
When a vast image out of Spiritus Mundi
Troubles my sight: somewhere in sands of the desert
A shape with lion body and the head of a man,
A gaze blank and pitiless as the sun, [15]
Is moving its slow thighs, while all about it
Reel shadows of the indignant desert birds.
The darkness drops again; but now I know
That twenty centuries of stony sleep
Were vexed to nightmare by a rocking cradle, [20]
And what rough beast, its hour come round at last,
Slouches towards Bethlehem to be born?

Annotations

The Second Coming: a Christian belief that Jesus will return to Earth at some time in the future. Yeats's poem, however, is not Christian in its outlook. It adapts the term 'Second Coming' to describe the appearance, or reappearance, of a terrifying beast

[1] gyre: a spiral or a cone; describes the shape traced by the falcon's flight-path as it soars upwards and away from the falconer

[2] falconer: in the sport of falconry a hunter, known as a falconer, uses trained birds of prey to pursue small birds and animals

[4] anarchy: disorder, chaos, the collapse of political authority

[5] blood-dimmed tide: describes a body of water that runs red with blood, so much so that it is no longer transparent

[6] ceremony of innocence: refers not to a specific practice or ritual, but to a formal and ordered approach to living

[7] lack all conviction: lack firmly-held beliefs; lack faith and certainty regarding their own view of the world

[9] some revelation is at hand: something striking and important is about to be revealed or disclosed

[12] Spiritus Mundi: a Latin term meaning 'world spirit'; a vast universal mind or consciousness that contained the memory of everything experienced by mankind. Yeats believed that at certain moments poets and writers could tap into this supernatural consciousness. It would fill them with extraordinary inspiration, providing them with symbols and images for their writing

[17] indignant: annoyed, angry, irritated

[20] vexed to nightmare: describes how the beast's slumber becomes agitated until it experiences a nightmare

[22] Bethlehem: Yeats imagines the beast entering the world where Jesus was born two thousand years ago

Tease It Out

1. Watch Video 18. Based on your viewing of this video, what topics do you anticipate will be tackled by 'The Second Coming'?
2. What is the sport of falconry? Write a few lines describing this activity in your own words.
3. The poem describes a falcon whose flight path takes it spiralling upwards and outwards away from its falconer. What words and phrases indicate this?
4. How, according to the poet, does a falconer normally direct the falcon?
5. Is the falcon responding to the falconer's directions on this occasion? Why or why not?
6. The poet believes that sensible, balanced political opinion is being replaced by views that are extreme and unreasonable. What phrase suggests this?
7. What phrase suggests that in the poet's opinion the world is becoming a chaotic and unstable place?
8. Consider the phrase 'is loosed'. Does it suggest that this unwanted change is occurring quickly or slowly?
9. The poet imagines a rising tide of water. What has happened to this tide to make it 'dim'?
10. **Class Discussion:** Consider the phrase 'ceremony of innocence':
    - Does it suggest a particular ceremony or a ceremony in a more abstract sense?
    - What impact does the rising tide have on this ceremony?
    - What does this suggest about the state of the world as the poet sees it?
11. According to the poet, what is the attitude or demeanour of good people in these terrible times? Meanwhile, how are wicked, immoral people behaving?
12. The poet feels that some great upheaval, possibly even the end of the world as we know it, is fast approaching. What phrases indicate this?
13. **Class Discussion:** Consider the phrase 'vast image'. Do you think the poet is dreaming, day-dreaming or perhaps even hallucinating? Give a reason for your answer.
14. Is the poet thrilled or terrified by this image? Support your answer with reference to the poem.
15. The poet describes the creature he witnesses in this 'image'. Where is it located? What mythical monster does it resemble?
16. What phrase indicates the end of the poet's dream or vision?
17. For how many years has the creature been sleeping?
18. What phrase indicates that the creature rouses itself only slowly from its slumber, twitching gradually into wakefulness?
19. Where is the creature headed? What will happen when it reaches its destination?

Exam Prep

1. **Personal Response:** This is one of Yeats's most quoted poems, featuring in everything from political speeches to the lyrics of death metal songs. Can you suggest why such a seemingly strange text would have such broad appeal?
2. **Class Discussion:** 'Yeats's poetry laments the end of a particular innocence, the decline of the Anglo-Irish class and the social order they were associated with'. Discuss this statement with reference to 'The Second Coming', 'Under Ben Bulben' and 'In Memory'.
3. **Theme Talk:** 'Yeats's poetry reveals a complex attitude towards war, violence and social upheaval'. Compare and contrast how 'The Second Coming', 'Politics' and 'Easter 1916' deal with this topic.
4. **Exam Prep:** 'Yeats's poetry speaks with great clarity to our present moment'. Discuss this statement with reference to 'The Second Coming' and two other poems on the course.

Language Lab

1. Yeats had a number of occult beliefs. How many references to such beliefs can you find in the poem?
2. Yeats imagines this terrifying creature being 'born' in Bethlehem. What precisely does he mean by this? Consider the following options and, working in pairs, rank them in the order you consider most accurate or appropriate:
    - The 'rough beast' will physically enter the world; a vast lion-bodied creature will actually appear in Bethlehem.
    - The 'rough beast' is about to enter the world in the form of new born human being, an individual whose life will change the world and have terrible consequences for the rest of humanity.
    - The rough beast is only a metaphor, symbolising a sequence of traumatic events that will leave the world altered forever.
3. What simile does the poet use to describe the way the creature looks at him? What does this suggest about the creature's temperament?

Sailing to Byzantium

I
That is no country for old men. The young
In one another's arms, birds in the trees,
– Those dying generations – at their song,
The salmon-falls, the mackerel-crowded seas,
Fish, flesh, or fowl, commend all summer long   [5]
Whatever is begotten, born, and dies.
Caught in that sensual music all neglect
Monuments of unageing intellect.

II
An aged man is but a paltry thing,
A tattered coat upon a stick, unless   [10]
Soul clap its hands and sing, and louder sing
For every tatter in its mortal dress,
Nor is there singing school but studying
Monuments of its own magnificence;
And therefore I have sailed the seas and come   [15]
To the holy city of Byzantium.

III
O sages standing in God's holy fire
As in the gold mosaic of a wall,
Come from the holy fire, perne in a gyre,
And be the singing-masters of my soul.   [20]
Consume my heart away; sick with desire
And fastened to a dying animal
It knows not what it is; and gather me
Into the artifice of eternity.

IV
Once out of nature I shall never take   [25]
My bodily form from any natural thing,
But such a form as Grecian goldsmiths make
Of hammered gold and gold enamelling
To keep a drowsy Emperor awake;
Or set upon a golden bough to sing   [30]
To lords and ladies of Byzantium
Of what is past, or passing, or to come.

Annotations

Byzantium: an ancient city, renamed Constantinople in 330 AD and known today as Istanbul. It was the capital of an empire and a great centre of art and learning
[4] **salmon-falls:** waterfalls over which salmon leap as they swim up-river to spawn
[5] **commend:** praise, celebrate, glorify
[6] **begotten:** conceived
[8] **Monuments:** landmark achievements and permanent objects; creations that will outlast us
[9] **paltry:** pitiful, insignificant
[12] **mortal dress:** the soul's 'clothing', i.e. the body
[17] **sages:** men revered for their profound wisdom
[18] **mosaic:** a picture produced by arranging together small pieces of stone, metal or glass;
[19] **perne in a gyre:** Yeats believed that time is a stream that spirals in a 'gyre' or clockwise direction. He imagines the sages 'perning' or moving in a counter-clockwise direction, as if they were swimming against time's current
[24] **artifice:** workmanship; ingenuity; a cunning strategem
[27] **Grecian:** relating to Greece. Byzantium was a Greek-speaking city
[28] **enamelling:** a varnish, decorative paint
[30] **a golden bough:** Yeats writes that in the Imperial Palace in Byzantium there was 'a tree made of gold and silver, and artificial birds that sang'

Tease It Out

Stanza 1

1. Line 6 mentions three stages in the cycle of life. Describe each one in your own words.
2. The poet regards the summer as a time of fertility and sexuality.
   - What happens to shoals of mackerel at this time of year?
   - What indicates that it is mating season for the birds?
   - What journey do the salmon make?
   - For human beings too, summer is regarded as a time of passion and sexuality. What phrase indicates this?
3. **Class Discussion:** These creatures through their actions 'commend' the cycle of life. Discuss this statement as a class.
4. The poet himself feels incapable of commending this cycle. Suggest why this might be the case.

Stanza 2

5. **True or false:** The poet is quite comfortable with the reality of bodily ageing.
6. What metaphor does the poet use to describe his ageing body?
7. What do you understand by the term 'mortal dress'? Who or what is wearing this dress?
8. The poet imagines the soul responding with joy to the body's decline. What phrase indicates this?
9. **Group Discussion:** Can you suggest why the soul might respond to old age in such a fashion?
10. **True or false:** The singing of the soul can compensate for the paltriness of old age.
11. **Class Discussion:** According to the poet, there is only one 'singing school', only one way through which the soul can sing louder and better. As a class, describe this in your own words.
12. All magnificent and enduring artworks are a product of the soul. What phrase indicates this?

13. **Group Discussion:** What is it about Byzantium that so attracted the poet? Bear in mind your answers to the other questions about this stanza.

Stanza 3

14. The poet is contemplating a Byzantine mosaic.
    - Who is depicted in this mosaic?
    - What is happening to them?
    - What does he want the sages to do?
    - What role would they play in his life?
    - What kind of things could they teach his soul?
15. The 'heart' is the aspect of the self associated with love and longing.
    - Does the poet's 'heart', even in old age, still experience desire?
    - Is he capable of fulfilling these desires? Why is this the case?
    - What impact does this state of affairs have on the poet's 'heart'?
16. **Class Discussion:** What does the poet want the sages to do with his 'heart'?

Stanza 4

17. Yeats imagines taking the form of a Byzantine piece of art, specifically a decorative metal bird.
    - Who manufactured this bird?
    - From what material was it fashioned?
    - What phrase indicates that the bird was capable of producing musical tones?
    - Yeats imagines the decorative bird being placed by the Emperor's throne. What purpose would it serve?
    - **True or false:** Yeats imagines the bird resting upon an artifical tree branch.
18. How do you think the 'lords and ladies of Byzantium' would have reacted to this elaborate contraption? Give a reason for your answer.

Exam Prep

1. **Personal Response:** Yeats imagines being gathered up by the sages and being led 'out of nature'. Take a moment to consider these odd but striking images. Do you find these notions pleasant or unpleasant?
2. **Theme Talk:** 'In this poem Yeats rejects nature and the body in favour of art and the mind'. Write a short essay in response to this statement.
3. **Exam Prep:** 'Yeats's poetry is driven by a tension between the real world in which he lives and an ideal world that he imagines'. Write a short essay in reponse to this statement, making reference to 'Sailing to Byzantium' and three other poems on the course.

Language Lab

1. What does the phrase 'dying generations' suggest about the brevity of life?
2. What does the phrase 'dying animal' suggest about the poet's attitude towards his ageing body?
3. Yeats refers to sexuality as 'that sensual music'.
   - What kind of music do you imagine when you hear this phrase?
   - What phrase indicates that this 'music' bewitches people?
   - Does this 'music' bewitch young and old alike?
   - What, according to Yeats, does this bewitchment cause people to forget?

The Stare's Nest by My Window

The bees build in the crevices
Of loosening masonry, and there
The mother birds bring grubs and flies.
My wall is loosening; honey-bees,
Come build in the empty house of the stare. [5]

We are closed in, and the key is turned
On our uncertainty; somewhere
A man is killed, or a house burned.
Yet no clear fact to be discerned:
Come build in the empty house of the stare. [10]

A barricade of stone or of wood;
Some fourteen days of civil war:
Last night they trundled down the road
That dead young soldier in his blood:
Come build in the empty house of the stare. [15]

We had fed the heart on fantasies,
The heart's grown brutal from the fare,
More substance in our enmities
Than in our love; O honey-bees,
Come build in the empty house of the stare. [20]

Annotations

Stare: starling

Civil War: the Irish Civil War (1922-23), a bitter conflict fought between former comrades. On one side were those who accepted the Anglo-Irish Treaty (1921). On the other side were those who rejected this treaty.

[1] ***crevices:*** narrow openings or fissures in a wall

[2] ***masonry:*** stonework

[3] ***grubs:*** the larva or immature form of an insect

[9] ***discerned:*** recognised, perceived

[11] ***barricade:*** an improvised barrier

[17] ***fare:*** food, sustenance

[18] ***enmities:*** hostilities, rivalries

Tease It Out

1. Watch Video 19 and answer the following questions:
   - Why was Thoor Ballylee so important to Yeats?
   - In what year did he move from this tower?
   - What happened to the tower after he left it?
   - What happened to the tower in 2015?
2. The masonry that binds the stones of the tower together is 'loosening'. What use do the bees make of the gaps created by this process?
3. Birds also make use of these gaps. What do they use them for?
4. What do the 'mother birds' bring back to these 'crevices'?
5. One of the gaps in the wall is empty. What did this gap once house and why might its previous occupants have moved on?
6. What does the poet want to happen in this gap?
7. **Class Discussion:** Consider the phrase, 'My wall is loosening', and answer the following:
   - The poet uses the word 'loosening' twice in this stanza. What is the effect of this repetition?
   - Is the poet bothered by the deterioration of his tower's walls or does he view it as a positive development?
   - Can we read the 'crumbling' of the poet's walls on a symbolic or metaphorical level, perhaps as a description of something that's happening to the poet's life or psyche?
8. For how long has the Civil War been raging?
9. What has happened to the roads around the poet's home?
10. What phrase indicates that the poet and his neighbours feel like prisoners in their own homes?
11. Describe in your own words what happened to the dead young soldier's body. Do you think the poet personally witnessed this occurrence or merely heard about it? Give a reason for your answer.
12. Name two other terrible events that have occurred.
13. What phrase indicates that the poet is unable to learn the exact details of these terrible events? Suggest why this might be the case.
14. Suggest three different notions or ideals that had obsessed the Irish populace in the years after the 1916 rebellion.
15. Would you agree that the poet considers these 'fantasies' to be dangerous ones? Give a reason for your answer.
16. What impact has the obsession with these notions had on the psyches of the Irish people?
17. What phrase indicates that the twisted minds of the Irish people now thrive on and are motivated by hatred rather than love?

Exam Prep

1. **Personal Response:** Working in pairs, list everything the creatures of the natural world do in this poem. List everything human beings do. Together compose a paragraph contrasting these two sets of activities.
2. **Class Discussion:** 'This poem powerfully describes how an obsession with abstract ideals can twist the mind not only of an individual but of an entire population, leading to terrible consequences'. Write two paragraphs in response to this statement.
3. **Theme Talk:** 'This poem captures not only the violence of war but also the terrible 'uncertainty' it inflicts on a population, especially in a time before modern technology and communications'. Compare this poem's treatment of war and violence with that in 'September 1913' and 'Easter 1916'.
4. **Exam Prep:** 'Yeats uses evocative language to create poetry that includes both personal reflection and public commentary'. Write a short essay in response to this statement, referring to "The Stare's Nest' and at least two other poems on the course.

Language Lab

1. Again and again Yeats returns to the refrain 'Come build in the empty house of the stare'. How do you imagine his tone as he repeats this phrase? Do you think the poet is pleading or demanding? Why do you think he contrasts the activity of the bees with the destruction that rages in the countryside around him?
2. Do you think it's possible that the people of Ireland, locked in a 'brutal' conflict, could somehow learn from or be inspired by the activity of the bees? Support your answer with reference to the text.
3. **Class Discussion:** Consider the metaphor of feeding the heart. Would you agree it's an effective way of describing our obsessions, fixations and fascinations? Can you think of any other metaphors for the same process?
4. '[T]he key is turned/ On our uncertainty'. What is responsible for 'locking' the poet and his neighbours in this state of uncertainty? Do you think this metaphor of imprisonment is an effective one? Give a reason for your answer.

In Memory of Eva Gore-Booth and Con Markievicz

The light of evening, Lissadell,
Great windows open to the south,
Two girls in silk kimonos, both
Beautiful, one a gazelle.
But a raving autumn shears [5]
Blossom from the summer's wreath;
The older is condemned to death,
Pardoned, drags out lonely years
Conspiring among the ignorant.
I know not what the younger dreams – [10]
Some vague Utopia – and she seems,
When withered old and skeleton-gaunt,
An image of such politics.
Many a time I think to seek
One or the other out and speak [15]
Of that old Georgian mansion, mix
pictures of the mind, recall
That table and the talk of youth,
Two girls in silk kimonos, both
Beautiful, one a gazelle. [20]

Dear shadows, now you know it all,
All the folly of a fight
With a common wrong or right.
The innocent and the beautiful
Have no enemy but time; [25]
Arise and bid me strike a match
And strike another till time catch;
Should the conflagration climb,
Run till all the sages know.
We the great gazebo built, [30]
They convicted us of guilt;
Bid me strike a match and blow.

October 1927

Annotations
Eva Gore-Booth: (1870-1926), a writer who campaigned for women's suffrage and workers' rights.
Con Markievicz: Countess Constance Markiewicz, née Gore-Booth (1867-1927).
[1] ***Lissadell:*** A mansion in Co. Sligo where the Gore-Booth family lived.
[3] ***silk kimonos:*** a traditional Japanese dress
[4] ***gazelle:*** a small antelope known for its grace and elegance; Yeats is referring here to Eva
[7] ***The older:*** Constance
[7-8] ***condemned to death,/ Pardoned:*** Constance was sentenced to death for her part in the 1916 Rising. Her sentence was later commuted and she was released in 1917.
[8] ***lonely years:*** Constance's Polish husband returned to his homeland and she was separated from her children
[9] ***Conspiring among the ignorant:*** Yeats is critical of Constance's political activities in the years following the Rising
[11] ***Utopia:*** a place or state considered to be perfect or ideal
[16] ***Georgian:*** an architectural style current in the 1700s
[21] ***shadows:*** ghosts, spirits
[22] ***folly:*** foolishness, error
[28] ***conflagration:*** large, destructive fire
[29] ***sages:*** men revered for their profound wisdom
[30] ***gazebo:*** small, roofed structure used for outdoor entertaining
[31] ***They ... guilt:*** describes how the Protestant Ascendancy, to which Yeats and the Gore-Booths belonged, were mistreated and mistrusted by the Catholic majority after Irish independence

Tease It Out

1. Watch Video 20, which depicts Lissadell House in Co. Sligo, and answer the following questions:
   - What recent projects have been undertaken with regard to the house and its gardens?
   - What features of the house and its gardens strike you as appealing? Are there any features of the property that strike you as unappealing?
   - Is it a place where you personally would like to live or spend part of every year? Give a reason for your answer.
2. Where is the poet? Who is with him? What are these 'Two girls' wearing?
3. What time of day is it? What hints do we get that the weather is fine?
4. What does the adjective 'Great' suggest about Lissadell's windows? Could it suggest more than one thing?
5. The poet describes one of the girls as a 'gazelle'. What are gazelles known for? What does this comparison suggest about her appearance, especially about how she moves and carries herself?
6. What does the term 'raving' usually mean? What does it suggest about autumn's demeanour and appearance?
7. What impact does autumn have on the wreath of summer? What implement does autumn use to accomplish this?
8. Who do you think Constance was conspiring with later in her life? What was she hoping to achieve?
9. **Class Discussion:** The poet describes how Eva, the younger sister, dreamed of a 'Utopia'. What is a Utopia and what does this phrase suggest about Eva's political beliefs?
10. The aged Eva is presented as an 'image' of the political views she served throughout her life. What does this suggest about the poet's view of Eva's political work?
11. The poet often felt like seeking out the two sisters. Do you think he ever actually did this?
12. Consider the phrase 'mix/ pictures of the mind'. What activity does this wonderful metaphor describe?
13. **Class Discussion:** Lines 19 and 20 repeat lines 3 and 4. Would you agree that the lines have a different tone or significance this time around?
14. Why does the poet refer to the sisters as 'shadows' in line 21?
15. Describe in your own words what the sisters now 'know'.
16. The sisters, according to the poet, fought battles that were 'common'. What does the word 'common' mean in this context? Could it mean more than one thing?
17. Does the poet feel that the sisters were wise to engage in such struggles? Give a reason for your answer.
18. What, according to lines 24 and 25, is the only enemy of those who are beautiful and innocent?
19. In lines 26 to 27, the poet imagines himself lighting a series of matches. What would he like to set fire to?
20. If he's successful in this endeavour, what would he like the sisters to do? Where do you imagine this occurring?

Exam Prep

1. **Personal Response:** 'In this poem Yeats vividly and passionately recreates a perfect memory'. Write a paragraph in response to this statement. Then write a short text in which you describe a perfect memory of your own.
2. **Class Discussion:** 'The innocent and the beautiful/ Have no enemy but time'.
   - What does Yeats mean by innocence in this context?
   - What impact does time have on innocence and beauty?
   - What other 'enemies' might innocence and beauty have?
3. **Theme Talk:** 'This is a very sexist poem, arguing that women, especially women from affluent and cultured backgrounds, have no business getting involved in political campaigns. Instead they should focus on preserving their innocence and good looks'. Write a paragraph in response to this statement.
4. **Exam Prep:** 'Yeats emphasises the power of art to overcome old age, death and even time itself'. Write a response to this statement, making reference to 'In Memory' and at least two other poems on the course.

Language Lab

1. Can you identify two examples each of euphony and cacophony in this poem? How do they contribute to its atmosphere?
2. **Class Discussion:** What literary device does the poet use to describe the autumn?
3. 'This is a poem that makes great use of seasonal imagery, moving from summer to autumn to winter'. Write a few lines in response to this statement.

Swift's Epitaph

Swift has sailed into his rest;
Savage indignation there
Cannot lacerate his breast.
Imitate him if you dare,
World-besotted traveller; he   [5]
Served human liberty.

Annotations

Jonathan Swift: (1667-1745) was Dean of St Patrick's Cathedral, Dublin. He wrote poems, essays and political pamphlets that critised human greed and stupidity in all its forms. His works include Gulliver's Travels, A Modest Proposal and The Drapier's Letters. Yeats's poem is a translation, with some alterations, of the Latin epitaph on Swift's gravestone in St Patrick's Cathedral.

Epitaph: the inscription on a grave or tombstone

[2] ***Savage:*** fierce, violent

[2] ***indignation:*** anger aroused by injustice or unfairness

[3] ***lacerate:*** to tear, to wound, to cause emotional distress

[5] ***World-besotted:*** obsessed or infatuated with this world

Exam Prep

1. **Personal Response:** Google the term 'satire'; then watch Video 21. Who or what is being satirised in this extract? How is the satire being carried out? Is it easy to see why creators of satire, like Swift, might require moral courage?
2. **Class Discussion:** According to the poet, Swift served 'human liberty'. Suggest how Swift, as a writer, might be able to serve such a cause.
3. **Theme Talk:** 'Swift's emotions were 'Savage' but so were his writings'. Suggest one way in which a piece of writing might be said to exhibit a certain savagery.
4. **Exam Prep:** "Swift's Epitaph', like 'An Irish Airman Foresees his Death' and 'September 1913', features someone whose powerful, uncompromising principles causes him to jeopardise his own well-being'. Write two paragraphs comparing and contrasting these three poems.

Tease It Out

1. Have you ever heard or read the story of Gulliver's Travels? Write down everything you can remember about this tale. Then google its author, Jonathan Swift, and record five facts about his life, including the title of one other work he composed.
2. What is an epitaph, and where do we generally find them written?
3. **Class Discussion:** According to the poet, Swift has 'sailed' out of this life. What does this suggest about the manner of his passing?
4. To be indignant is to feel anger at something that seems unjust or unfair. What does Swift's tendency towards indignation suggest about his personality?
5. What word suggests that Swift's 'indignation' was especially intense and pronounced?
6. Based on your research into his life, suggest what might have provoked such strong emotions on Swift's part.
7. What phrase suggests that these extreme feelings had a deeply negative impact on his state of mind?
8. Why will Swift no longer be troubled by such emotions?
9. Suggest two different ways in which people of today might 'Imitate' Jonathan Swift.
10. '[I]f you dare'. The poet suggests that there might be negative consequences for those who choose to imitate Swift. What might these consequences be and how might they arise?
11. Is the 'traveller' referred to in line 5 a specific person? Or is the poet addressing every reader of his poem? Give a reason for your answer.
12. Would you agree that every one of us, in one way or another, is 'besotted' with this world? Write a few sentences in response to this question.

An Acre of Grass

Picture and book remain,
An acre of green grass
For air and exercise,
Now strength of body goes;
Midnight, an old house [5]
Where nothing stirs but a mouse.

My temptation is quiet.
Here at life's end
Neither loose imagination,
Nor the mill of the mind [10]
Consuming its rag and bone,
Can make the truth known.

Grant me an old man's frenzy,
Myself must I remake
Till I am Timon and Lear [15]
Or that William Blake
Who beat upon the wall
Till Truth obeyed his call;

A mind Michael Angelo knew
That can pierce the clouds, [20]
Or inspired by frenzy
Shake the dead in their shrouds;
Forgotten else by mankind,
An old man's eagle mind.Somebody loves us all.

Annotations

[1-5] *acre ... house:* reference to the farmhouse, Riversdale, in Rathfarnham, Co. Dublin that Yeats leased in 1932 for thirteen years

[10] *mill:* a machine or device for grinding or crushing

[11] *rag and bone:* unwanted items, odds and ends, bric-a-brac

[13] *frenzy:* mental agitation, wild excitement, mania

[15] *Timon:* Timon of Athens. In Shakespeare's play of the same name Timon becomes disillusioned with human society. He leaves the city of Athens and goes to live alone in a cave. As a result he acquires new insight and wisdom

[15] *Lear:* King Lear. In Shakespeare's play of the same name Lear exhibits great foolishness and arrogance. As a result he suffers greatly and goes insane. However, he emerges with greater wisdom and awareness

[16] *William Blake:* (1757-1827) poet and artist. Yeats views Blake as a visionary, who accesses truths beyond those associated with science, logic and reason

[19] *Michael Angelo:* Michaelangelo Buonarroti (1475-1564) Renaissance artist best remembered for painting the ceiling of the Sistine Chapel and for his statue of David

[22] *shrouds:* garments in which the dead were wrapped for burial

Tease It Out

1. What phrases suggest that the poet must focus on artistic intellectual pursuits?
2. Will the poet be neglecting his body entirely? Give a reason for your answer.
3. Only these few activities, we're told, 'remain' to the poet. Suggest other activities the poet might have once enjoyed. Why might these activities no longer be available to him?
4. What phrases indicate that the poet doesn't have much a social life anymore?
5. Consider the phrase 'Temptation is quiet'. Is the poet referring to a) sexual temptation or b) fun activities that might lure him away from the work of writing or c) something else entirely?
6. **Class Discussion:** Consider the term 'frenzy'.
   - Can you think of two or three examples of frenzied behaviour from fiction or real life?
   - **True or false:** The poet is terrified of occupying such a frenzied state of mind.
   - 'The phrase 'old man's frenzy' is surprising and contradictory'. Discuss this statement as a class. Do you agree?
   - Why does Yeats admire the Shakesperian characters King Lear and Timon of Athens?
7. What phrase indicates that William Blake achieved a great understanding of the universe?
8. The poet describes how Blake 'beat upon the wall'. Describe in your own words what you visualise when you read this line.
9. Which of Blake's activities does this beating represent?
10. **True or false:** Society, according to Yeats, has little interest in old men.
11. What image suggests that the mind of an old man can be powerful, perhaps even more powerful than that of a young man?
12. **True or false:** The great artist Michael Angelo had such a powerful mind when he was an old man.
13. What metaphor, in stanza 4, is used for the discovery of a great new truth?

Exam Prep

1. **Personal Response:** The poet mentions the possibility of remaking himself: 'Myself must I remake'. What do you think such remaking might involve? Can you think of anyone you know (or know of) who remade him or herself? What did this process involve?
2. **Class Discussion:** 'Art for Yeats is about more than entertainment or even beauty. It's about a search for fundamental truth'. Discuss this statement as a class. In what sense can films, music and novels reveal certain truths about our human existence? Do Yeats's poems, in the opinion of the class, touch on any such truths?
3. **Theme Talk:** 'Yeats is a poet who refuses to surrender to old age'. Discuss this statement in relation to 'An Acre of Grass', 'Politics' and 'Sailing to Byzantium'.
4. **Exam Prep:** 'The poetry of Yeats is both intellectually challenging and emotionally rewarding'. Write an essay in response to this statement.

Language Lab

1. The poet describes how he might shake the dead in their burial shrouds. What does he mean by this? Rank the following in order of plausibility:
   - He can bring the dead back to life.
   - The souls of the dead in the afterlife will be jealous of his achievements.
   - He will discovery new truths that disprove the conclusions of previous writers and thinkers.
2. **Class Discussion:** The poet considers the different ways that poets and writers might arrive at such 'truth'.
   - What image is used to describe regular, repetitive mental labour?
   - How might such labour differ from 'loose imagination'?
   - Can either process, according to the poet, lead him to the truth?
   - Do you think the poet found it easier to arrive at the truth when he was a younger man?

from Under Ben Bulben

V
Irish poets learn your trade,
Sing whatever is well made,
Scorn the sort now growing up
All out of shape from toe to top,
Their unremembering hearts and heads [5]
Base-born products of base beds.
Sing the peasantry, and then
Hard-riding country gentlemen,
The holiness of monks, and after
Porter-drinkers' randy laughter; [10]
Sing the lords and ladies gay
That were beaten into the clay
Through seven heroic centuries;
Cast your mind on other days
That we in coming days may be [15]
Still the indomitable Irishry.

VI
Under bare Ben Bulben's head
In Drumcliff churchyard Yeats is laid,
An ancestor was rector there
Long years ago; a church stands near, [20]
By the road an ancient Cross.
No marble, no conventional phrase;
On limestone quarried near the spot
By his command these words are cut:

Cast a cold eye [25]
On life, on death.
Horseman, pass by!

Annotations
Ben Bulben: mountain composed of layers of limestone that overlooks the town of Sligo
[3] *Scorn:* treat with contempt or disdain
[6] *Base-born products of base beds:* the current generation are lacking in moral worth and incapable of appreciating or understanding great art. They have been begotten by parents who are themselves 'base' and lacking in a similar manner
[7] *peasantry:* poor farmers that worked the land belonging to wealthy landowners
[8] *country gentlemen:* members of the landowning class
[11] *lords and ladies:* members of the aristocracy
[12] *That were beaten ... centuries:* describes how these lords and ladies often commanded armies in the fight against English rule from the 12th to the 20th century. Again and again, they were crushed or defeated by English oppression
[16] *indomitable:* impossible to defeat or overcome
[19] *ancestor:* John Yeats (1774-1848)
[22] *marble:* material typically used for creating gravestones
[22] *conventional:* following the usual or widely accepted way of doing things

Tease It Out

1. Yeats describes poetry as a trade:
   - Can you think of two or three well-known trades?
   - What does the writing of poetry have in common what these? In what ways is it different?
   - Do you find Yeats' description of poetry as a trade surprising? Give a reason for your answer.
2. Can you think of one or two ways in which poets might go about learning the 'trade' of poetry?
3. Poets, according to Yeats, should sing or write about 'whatever is well made'. Think about the idea of the 'well made' object. What are the first three examples that come to mind?
4. **True or false:** Yeats thinks poets should find inspiration in the younger generations of Irish people that are growing up around the country.
5. These younger generations, according to Yeats, are 'all out of shape'. What do you think he means by this? Rank the following in order of plausibility:
   - They have put on weight and need to spend more time at the gym.
   - They were born with poor character.
   - They are physically unattractive.
   - They are suffering from psychological stress or trauma.
6. **Class Discussion:** These younger generations, according to Yeats, are 'unremembering'. Working as a class, can you suggest a number of different things they might have forgotten?
7. The term 'base' has several different meanings. Which do you think is most relevant to line 6? Give a reason for your answer.
8. What two very different groups of people are mentioned in lines 7 to 8?
9. Another two groups are mentioned in lines 9 to 10? What does Yeats admire about each of these?
10. **True or false:** Yeats insists that Irish poets must be up with the times, must focus on contemporary society with all its changes and challenges.
11. Yeats refers to the 'indomitable' nature of the Irish people:
    - Is being indomitable the same as being victorious?
    - How, in the past, did the Irish people show their indomitable nature?
    - What, according to Yeats, will help them be indomitable in the future?
12. Where does the poet plan to be buried? What family connections does he have with this area?
13. What material is to be used for the headstone? Do you think this is a deliberate choice on the poet's part?

Exam Prep

1. **Personal Response:** 'This poem shows Yeats as a snob and an insufferable elitist. He looks down his nose at the ordinary people of contemporary Ireland, viewing them as base and unworthy'. Do you agree with this assessment? Write two or three paragraphs explaining your response.
2. **Class Discussion**: Working as a class, discuss the poet's mysterious epitaph:
   - What does it mean means to view something with a 'cold eye'? Consider the following definitions of cold and say which you think is most appropriate here: Objective; Unsympathetic; Disdainful; Unemotional
   - Why does it mean to cast such a 'cold eye' on life and death? What view of human existence is suggested by this phrase?
   - Who is the 'Horseman' in the poem's final line? Is Yeats addressing a specific person, the reader, a personification of death itself or something else?
3. **Exam Prep:** 'Yeats uses unforgettable language to explore the character of the Irish people'. Write an essay responding to this statement in which you mention this poem as well as 'September 1913', 'Easter 1916' and 'The Stare's Nest By My Window'

Language Lab

1. Consider Yeats's view of poetry as put forward in 'Under Ben Bulben':
   - Writing about something, according to Yeats, is the same as singing about it. What does this suggest about his view of poetry?
   - True poetry comes from craft and hard work as well as inspiration.
   - Poets can write about any subject they wish and still create great work.
   - List the various types of people that Yeats considers worthy subjects for poetry. What is about each one that he finds worthy of celebration?
   - For generations, according to Yeats, Ireland's 'lords and ladies' lead men into battle:
   - For how long did they fight? What was the object of their struggle?
   - What phrase indicates that they frequently met with defeat?
   - What attitude did they exhibit as they fought? Is this surprising?
   - Can you think of any historical figure that might be considered one of these lords or ladies?

Politics

'In our time the destiny of man presents its meanings in political terms.'
Thomas Mann

How can I, that girl standing there,
My attention fix
On Roman or on Russian
Or on Spanish politics?
Yet here's a travelled man that knows [5]
What he talks about,
And there's a politician
That has read and thought,
And maybe what they say is true
Of war and war's alarms, [10]
But O that I were young again
And held her in my arms.

Annotations

Thomas Mann: (1875-1955) a great German novelist and writer

[3-4] On Roman ... Spanish politics: the poem was written in 1938, a period of great political unrest in Europe. The Spanish, Russian and Italian (Roman) political systems all witnessed upheaval at this time

[10] war and war's alarms: in 1938 Hitler invaded Austria and Czechoslovakia, causing great alarm internationally and bringing a threat of war

Tease It Out

1. Watch Video 22, which contains newsreel footage from 1938, the year in which the poem was written. What significant political events were happening in Europe? How would you characterise the mood and atmosphere of the time, based on watching this footage?
2. The poet is having a conversation with two other men. How does he describe them?
3. **True or false:** The poet expects that these men are knowledgeable about the problems facing Europe.
4. What prevents the poet from listening attentively to these two men?
5. **True or false:** The poet wishes he could focus more attentively on what his two male companions are saying. Give a reason for your answer.
6. What do you imagine the poet's relationship with the girl to be? Do you think they know one another or do you think that this is the first time that he has seen her?
7. What is it that the poet wishes for in the last two lines of the poem? Why does he wish for this?

Exam Prep

1. **Personal Response:** This poem highlights how lust, even in old age, remains at the forefront of the male mind.
   - Would you agree that this is an accurate assessment of the poem?
   - How do you think the 'girl' feels about being the subject of the poet's attention?
   - Is it fair to describe 'Politics' as something of a sexist poem?
2. **Class Discussion:** 'Youth and age is one of Yeats' recurring themes'. Discuss this statement in relation to this poem, 'An Acre of Grass' and 'The Wild Swans at Coole'. In which poem is Yeats most accepting of the ageing process? In which poem is he least accepting?
3. **Theme Talk:** Does the poet believe it is his duty to deal with important political events? Or does he feel entitled to focus on private affairs of the heart? Explain your answer.
4. **Exam Prep:** Compare and contrast the manner in which 'The Second Coming' and 'Politics' deal with the prospect of social and political upheaval.

Language Lab

1. Do you think 'Politics' is a good title for this poem? Give a reason for your answer. What would you choose if you were asked to select an alternative title?
2. 'Why do you think that the poet uses the term 'Roman' instead of Italian?
3. Yeats placed 'Politics' at the very end of his *Selected Poems*. Can you suggest why he decided to round off his poetic career with this fairly short and simple poem? What does this choice suggest about his priorities as a poet and as a person?
4. Consider the syntax of the sentence that forms the first four lines of the poem. Why do you think the poet chose to structure it in this manner? How does Yeats's syntax enhance what is being described in the opening lines?

Elizabeth Bishop

Themes

An Observer of the Ordinary World

Again and again in her poetry, Bishop comes across as a keen observer of the ordinary world. In 'The Fish', for instance, she turns her attention to a creature that most people would find dull or even ugly; certainly not worthy of being 'stared and stared' at. She comes across as a highly observant person, noticing, for instance, the fish's lack of fight, how it 'grunts' when she holds it out of the water, and the barnacles and sea-lice that are resident upon its body. She notices, above all, the five hooks that have 'grown firmly' into the fish's mouth and the 'five old pieces of fish-line' that are still attached to them.

This tendency is also evident in 'The Bight', where Bishop exhibits a keen interest in the unattractive bay with its everyday goings on. She takes great care to describe the birds that soar above her head and dive into the sea, capturing their movements in vivid detail. She describes the deposits of grainy marl that form the surface of the bight. She describes the shark tails, hung from a length of 'chicken wire along the dock'. The poet, a keen observer of life around the bight, is aware that these are intended for the Chinese restaurant trade.

In 'At the Fishhouses', too, Bishop displays a keen interest in the ordinary world around her. This comes across in the poet's lovingly detailed depictions of the sea and the fir trees. But it's especially evident in her description of the seal, and in the 'relationship' she cultivates by singing to him each evening. There is something light-hearted, perhaps almost comical, about this depiction of the poet singing to an uncomprehending mammal, who looks at her with a strange mix of curiosity and indifference.

In 'Questions of Travel', meanwhile, her powers of observation take in everything from the vastness of the waterfalls to the 'fat brown bird' singing in the filling station. Her keen eye for detail is evident throughout the poem. She notices that one of the gasoline pumps in the filling station is broken. She notices that the station owner's clogs each produce a different sound. She notices that the design of the handmade cage show the influence of the Jesuit missionaries that came to Brazil centuries ago.

'Filling Station', 'The Armadillo' and 'In the Waiting Room' also display Bishop's keen powers of observation. In 'Filling Station', for instance, she notices the specific qualities of the grime that covers everything in the station. She notices how the comic books provide the 'only note of color' and how the Esso cans have been carefully arranged. She notices how 'marguerites' or flowers have been embroidered in the doily's surface and even recognises the type of stitchwork used: 'Embroidered in daisy stitch/ with marguerites, I think'.

In 'The Armadillo', meanwhile, she observes that the fire balloons appear on many nights, but not quite every night. She has tracked the balloons' flight paths and noted how they behave in different atmospheric conditions. Finally, 'In the Waiting Room' presents us with a young girl who seems to take an interest in everything around her, observing how the waiting room 'was full of of grown-up people,/ arctics and overcoats,/ lamps and magazines'. Even though she is too shy or uncomfortable to raise her eyes and look the grown-up people in the face, she carefully observes the 'shadowy gray knees,/ trousers and skirts and boots/ and different pairs of hands'.

Addiction

'The Prodigal' is a moving and honest portrayal of an addict. The prodigal suffers from severe alcohol addiction. He drinks even in the mornings, hiding bottles behind planks of wood. Like the character in the Bible story, the prodigal's vices have brought him to a terrible situation. He spends his days amid the filth and squalor of the pigsty. Even worse, he spends his nights there, too. He also suffers from terrible loneliness. Furthermore, we get the impression that his nights are racked by guilt and self-loathing.

The poem also emphasises how difficult it is for an addict to leave addiction behind, even when he realises the damage it is causing to his life. In the evenings, there are moments of 'shuddering insight' when the prodigal realises the full horror of his situation. However, in the mornings – as he drunkenly watches a sunrise – he feels 'reassured' that he can endure his miserable way of life for at least another year. In the end, it takes the prodigal 'a long time' to finally decide to give up his addictions and return to his father's house.

'The Armadillo' is another poem in which Bishop describes people who are caught up in what can only be described as compulsive behaviour. Of course, the local population are aware of the risks posed by the balloons that they release each June. They know that the fire balloons all too often destroy wildlife when they come crashing down to earth. Yet their devotion to their local saint compels them to continue observing this dangerous ritual.

Moments of Epiphany

Many of Bishop's poems are marked by moments of epiphany, moments when a person suddenly realises something profound and important about themselves and the world. In 'First Death in Nova Scotia', for instance, the narrator is a very young girl who has little or no understanding of death. No doubt, she has heard the words 'death' and 'dead' being mentioned by the adults around her, but she doesn't fully grasp what death is, or what it actually means for someone to die. Now, however, her young cousin Arthur has passed away and his body has been laid out in the parlour of the house. This compels the young poet, for the first time, to encounter death directly. She is forced into a terrible moment of awareness, one in which she must come to terms with this strange and unsettling concept.

Throughout the poem, however, the young poet attempts to shut out this uncomfortable new reality, to avoid thinking about death directly. In stanza 2, for instance, she focuses on the stuffed loon, rather than on her cousin's body. While in stanza 5, she tells herself that Arthur won't be around anymore, not because he is dead, but because he is heading off to the court of King George in London, where he will work as the 'smallest page'. But the poem concludes with the young poet on the cusp of awareness. She is about to realise that death is something permanent and scary and unalterable. Such knowledge will forever change how she views the world.

'Sestina' is similar in this regard. It is difficult not to read the poem in terms of Bishop's biography. We can't help but recall that Bishop's father died when she was only eight months old and that, when Bishop was five years old, her mother suffered a mental collapse and was institutionalised. The tragedy that has struck the family in the poem is 'known only to a grandmother'. The child is still too young to fully comprehend the terrible events that have occurred. Nevertheless, we get the impression that awareness of this tragedy is slowly dawning on her. She thinks of 'tears' running down the tea-kettle and filling the grandmother's cup. The drops from the kettle seem to dance 'like mad', an image that may well have been evoked by the poet's recollection of her mother's mental breakdown. Furthermore, she imagines the stove and the almanac talking about the tragedy: 'It was to be, says the Marvel Stove./ I know what I know, says the almanac'.

We get an impression that the child attempts to shield herself from sorrow by drawing houses. It's as if she tries to create in her imagination an ideal house, an alternative world where the tragedy that struck her never occurred. But this defence will only last for so long. The almanac seems to symbolise an unspoken awareness of the tragedy that is waiting to descend upon the child. It hovers above her in an ominous fashion and 'plants tears' in the child's drawing. We get the impression that tears have also been 'planted' in the child's life and will soon bear fruit when she becomes fully aware of the tragic events that have unfolded.

'In the Waiting Room' also features such a moment of epiphany. At the poem's conclusion, the poet realises that that she is just one more member of the vast human race that populates the planet – and that there is more that unites her with every other human being (especially the female members of the population) than sets her apart. At the start of the poem the young poet focused on what she believed made her unique, but she now realises that she has more in common with everyone else. It is as if she has undergone a procedure – something far more distressing than a filling or a root canal – that has altered her outlook and the way she thinks about herself. It is as if a door within her mind has been thrown open and can never be shut again.

When Bishop wrote 'At the Fishhouses', she was undergoing psychoanalysis in order to come to terms with her various childhood traumas. The poet uses an extraordinary simile to describe the waters off Great Village, depicting them as a vast and all-consuming sea of fire. But this is fire that's been 'transmuted' or transformed, so that it 'burns with a dark gray flame'. The poet describes it as a blaze so intense that it could burn through rock, consuming the 'blue-gray stones' of the seabed.

This bizarre depiction of the sea wonderfully suggests the treacherous nature of the unconscious mind. The sea is depicted as being filled with tormenting slate-grey flames, just as the unconscious mind is filled with potentially dangerous memories and emotions. To enter or even touch the sea is to risk physical pain. To confront the unconscious mind, similarly, is to risk psychological pain. But confront it, the poet must. For these burning waters represent not only the dangers and traumas that lurk within the unconscious but also the self-knowledge that can be found there: 'It's like what we imagine knowledge to be'. Like someone wading into a sea of flames, then, the poet must enter and explore her own unconscious mind. For it's only by doing so that she can gain the self-knowledge she so desperately craves.

In 'The Fish', the poet experiences a brighter and more hopeful insight. She realises that the old fish that she has snared is a survivor, a creature who has had to constantly fight to stay alive and has somehow managed to persevere. For a brief moment, the world around the poet seems beautiful and joyous, and the rainbow colours in the oily water suddenly seem to filter or flood into everything around her: 'everything/ was rainbow, rainbow, rainbow!' The poet is suddenly aware that the fish, like the poet herself, is a stubborn survivor and deserves to be set free: 'And I let the fish go'.

A Poet of Emotional Restraint

Bishop's poems tend to look outwards, focusing on and describing the external world in careful and minute detail. Rarely does the poet draw the reader's attention directly to herself by describing or discussing her own thoughts and feelings. Yet, despite this, the poet is very much present in her poems. We get a sense of her personality through her descriptions of her physical environment, and through her reactions to particular objects and events.

In 'The Bight', for instance, it's possible to see the bay, with all its messy activity, as a metaphor for the poet's own life on this particular birthday. Perhaps she feels that her-life is unfruitful or unproductive, that she's like the man-of-war birds that dive into the water but rarely come up with anything to show for their efforts. The 'torn-open, unanswered letters' might be a reference to the poet's own desk and her neglect of certain affairs, while the broken boats that have yet to be salvaged 'from the last bad storm' could also represent emotional or psychological damage from which the poet is still recovering.

'Filling Station' is another poem where the poet's observations of the external world reveal her inner life. Bishop was a rather fastidious person who appreciated neatness and order. No wonder, then, that the filling station that she comes across here appals and offends her – shocking her with its absolute filth.

'The Fish' features similarly oblique self-revelation. The poet doesn't directly reveal anything about her past predicaments or her present emotional state. And yet, through the poet's identification with the fish, we get a sense of the kind of person she must be. The five hooks lodged in the fish's lower lip tell us that it has faced great adversity and survived, that it has been hooked again and again, only to struggle and free itself each time.

The poet's bond with the fish, then, suggests that she too is someone who has displayed great resilience, who has struggled and survived. Bishop, after all, lost her father at a very young age and was separated from her mother when she was five. She also battled alcoholism and suffered from chronic illness most of her life. Survival, then, is the 'victory' that the poem celebrates in its thrilling, elated conclusion. Like the fish, the poet has suffered greatly and has survived against the odds.

Childhood

'First Death in Nova Scotia' is one of several poems in which Bishop wonderfully captures the mentality of childhood. The speaker's childlike innocence comes across when she compares Arthur's corpse to a doll 'that hadn't been painted yet' and his coffin to 'a little frosted cake'. The same innocence is evident in her readiness to believe, or almost believe, the story about Arthur bring summoned to serve as the 'smallest page at court'.

The young poet thinks of Jack Frost painting Arthur's corpse, which makes her think of him painting the maple leaves, which in turn makes her think of a song titled 'Maple Leaf (Forever)'. This popular song, written in 1867, served as one of Canada's unofficial national anthems. It has been suggested that in this phrase, the young poet exhibits a childlike logic, her mind flitting unpredictably from one topic to the next.

Throughout 'Sestina', too, there are moments when Bishop skilfully inhabits a child's point of view. The phrase 'clever almanac', for instance, has a distinctly childish ring to it. The child, presumably, is aware from observing the adults around her that the almanac contains predictions and folk wisdom. Therefore, in an amusingly babyish phrase, she refers to it as 'clever'. Similarly effective is the description of the stove as 'marvellous'. We can imagine that this is how the granddaughter might refer to the stove. To this innocent and childish girl, the stove is a wondrous and fascinating object. She therefore confuses the brand name 'Marvel' with the word 'marvellous'

The second half of the poem, in particular, is full of strange and bizarre occurrences. We get the impression, though, that these weird events are not 'real' but merely take place in the granddaughter's imagination. She imagines that the almanac hovers around the kitchen with a mind of its own and sends a rain of moons into her picture, that her grandmother's cup contains tears rather than tea and that the stove and the almanac have a brief conversation. With its extremely creative use of such images, the poem wonderfully captures how a child's imagination can run riot, viewing even simple household objects as living things and as a source of fear and wonder.

'In the Waiting Room' is another poem that artfully conveys a child's sense of the world. But it doesn't trivialise or romanticise childhood. On the contrary, it demonstrates that although childhood is a time of innocence, it can also involve trauma, stress and uncertainty.

Exile and Belonging

Bishop's father, we remind ourselves, died when she was only eight months old and her mother was institutionalised when she was five. In the years that followed, she was shunted from guardian to guardian in both Canada and the United States.

Because her childhood had been spent in so many different locations, Bishop felt that she didn't really come from anywhere. She didn't have a 'home' in the sense of a point of origin, a native place that she and her family hailed from and to which she could, return. This sense of what we might call 'homelessness' is indicated by the final enigmatic lines in 'Questions of Travel': 'Should we have stayed at home,/ wherever that may be?' Not only is she uncertain about where her 'home' might be, she's not even sure that she has one.

A similar sense of exile and homelessness is evident in 'At the Fishhouses'. In returning to Great Village, the fishing community that was the site of her earliest memories, the poet has found something resembling home. By reconnecting with her roots on her mother's side of the family, she has rediscovered a place that feels like her own point of origin, one that she feels she could return to again and again.

And yet we sense that this newly rediscovered 'home' is very much under threat. The fact that the poet sees only an old man on her evening walk suggests that this is an aging community. Indeed, the poet and the old man talk about how the population of Great Village is 'declining'. The young, no doubt, are keen to leave behind the hard life of this fishing community for the bright lights of the major cities. Consequently, as the elder generation die off, there is no one to take their place on the fishing boats. Great Village, it seems, is a community threatened with extinction.

Perhaps the old man's 'worn' shuttle and his old knife, which is 'almost worn away', serve as metaphors for a way of life that is in decline as fewer and fewer people enter the fishing industry. Even the fact that the poem is set at evening, just as darkness falls, reinforces our sense that Great Village might well be a community nearing its end.

The notions of exile and homelessness also feature prominently in 'The Prodigal'. The prodigal lives and works in absolutely miserable conditions. He could end his suffering simply by returning home. For a very long time he refuses to do so, however, deciding to 'endure' his self-imposed 'exile' instead of returning to his family. We get a sense, then, that the prodigal feels that he does not really have a home to go to anymore, that he is simply not welcome any longer in his father's house. The word 'home', it should be noted, is the only end-word in the poem that does not have a full rhyme, perhaps suggesting the difficulty that the 'concept' of home causes to the prodigal. As is so often the case in Bishop's poetry, the journey 'home' is not an easy one to make.

There are several poems in which Bishop presents herself as a detached, neutral observer of a community to which she doesn't belong and that she can't really understand. In 'Questions of Travel', for instance, the phrase 'as ages go here' suggests that she is a visitor rather than a native inhabitant of the environment that she is describing. She ponders what the clogs and cage might tell her about Brazilian history, but can do so only in a blurred and inconclusive manner.

'The Armadillo' is similar in this regard. The phrase 'in these parts', for instance, suggests that this is a community that the poet is still attempting to make sense of, rather than one in which she feels completely at home. Significantly, she takes no part in the ritual of the fire balloons that so engages the local population. Perhaps, as a visitor from a richer, more advanced country, she regards such rituals and beliefs as primitive and backward.

To the poet, then, the fire balloons are a strange local custom, one that is not only quaint and beautiful but also senseless and dangerous. She acknowledges the beauty that the fire balloons possess as they drift smoothly into the distance, but she also condemns the damage that they all-too-often cause when they fall earthwards.

Language

Attention to Detail

The poetry of Elizabeth Bishop is marked by its extraordinary attention to detail. This is especially evident in 'The Fish', where the poet paints a vivid picture not only of the fish's external appearance but also of its imagined inner organs. She focuses on every little detail, describing each one as clearly and as vividly as possible, until a very clear picture of the creature begins to form in the reader's mind.

The description of the fish's eye is particularly impressive. Bishop captures the off-silver colour that surrounds the iris, comparing it to 'tarnished tinfoil'. It is as if this tainted or dulled material has been packed in tightly around and behind the iris. The poet also describes how the eye's jelly-like lens, which the poet compares to 'isinglass', a layer of hardened gelatin, obscures the view of the iris. It is as if there is a layer of 'scratched isinglass' coating the fish's eye.

'The Bight' works in a similar fashion. The poet focuses on different aspects or features of the bight, describing each in great detail. The descriptions and details gradually acumulate until we have a complete picture of the landscape as it appears on this one particular day.

The description of the sponge boats returning to the harbour is particularly impressive. The poet compares them to 'obliging' retriever dogs bounding back to their master. She compares the rods that stick up out of the boats to 'jackstraws' that have been decorated with 'bobbles of sponges'. The description seems to perfectly capture not only the appearance of these vessels, but also something of the mood and atmosphere on this particular day in Key West.

'At the Fishhouses', yet another sea-themed poem, is arguably even more detailed. We see Bishop go into descriptive overdrive in her depiction of the five fish houses, with their angular roofs, for instance, and in her equally memorable depiction of the fir forest. In her depiction of the fish tubs and wheelbarrows Bishop appeals not only to our sense of vision, by describing how they are 'lined' or 'plastered' with scales that shimmer as they catch they light, but also to our sense of touch, by noting the 'creamy texture' of the accumulated scales. She even notes the flies that rest upon these objects, observing that they, like scales they crawl upon, are also iridescent.

This tendency is also evident in 'The Prodigal', where the poet describes the world that the prodigal inhabits in vivid and memorable detail, appealing to a number of our senses in the process. Interestingly, Bishop describes the pigsty's smell in visual terms, telling us that the odour is 'brown' and 'enormous'. She also appeals to our senses of hearing and of touch in depicting this stink, referring to the odour's 'breathing' and its 'thick hair'.

Here, Bishop uses a poetic technique known as synaesthesia, whereby an experience associated with one sense is described in terms of another. In her description of the dung on the pigsty's walls, Bishop skillfully appeals to the sense of touch, describing it as 'glass-smooth'. Another fine piece of description occurs in lines 22 to 23, which describes how the reflection of the farmer's lantern 'paces' alongside him as he returns to the farmhouse.

The poems set in Brazil, 'Questions of Travel' and 'The Armadillo', also feature exquisitely detailed descriptive passages. In 'The Armadillo', for instance, Bishop wonderfully captures the drifting fire balloons, focusing especially on the flaring candles within these delicate structures: 'the paper chambers flush and fill with light'.

In 'Questions of Travel', meanwhile, Bishop provides an equally vivid depiction of the mountainous landscape, with its streams, clouds and waterfalls. The crowded streams resemble 'slowmotion' waterfalls as they flow down the mountain: 'turning to waterfalls under our very eyes'. The poet imagines that over time these streams will turn into actual waterfalls through some unspecified geological process: 'For if those streaks … aren't waterfalls yet,/ in a quick age or so, as ages go here,/ they probably will be'.

Bishop is also known as a poet who typically zooms in on one specific detail that reveals the truth about an entire location or situation.

- We see this in 'Questions of Travel' when she focuses on the 'sad, two-noted, wooden tune' produced by the filling station owner as he walks around his premises, which wonderfully captures the air of desperation that clings to him and to his business. (The word 'disparate', so close to 'desperate', suggests this in a sly and brilliant fashion).
- In 'Filling Station', for instance, she focuses on the owner's ill-fitting overalls, describing them as 'a dirty,/ oil-soaked monkey suit/ that cuts him under the arms'. But these few short lines deftly captures the character and appearance of the filling station's owner. We can almost picture him in this filthy gear, his body hunched and rendered comical by the tightness of the overalls.

- The term 'monkey-suit' also makes us think of someone moving in an inelegant, ape-like manner.
- 'First Death in Nova Scotia', too, features several telling details that really bring the scene to life. Among these are the loon with its fake red eyes and the royal couples in the chronographs, with their feet snugly wrapped by the furred trains of the ladies' gowns.
- We also see this in 'The Armadillo' when the poet declares that the balloons resemble 'stars' as they drift across the sky: 'Once up against the sky it's hard/ to tell them from the stars'. However she corrects herself, declaring that the balloons in fact resemble not stars, but celestial bodies – Venus, Mars and the Moon – that are far closer than the stars and therefore seem far brighter and bigger in the night sky.

A similar focus on precision is evident in line 29 of the same poem, where the poet stresses that she didn't actually see the nest burn. She only assumed it was destroyed because she saw the owls flying away: 'The ancient owls' nest must have burned'.

Similar precision is evident in 'At the Fishhouses':

- She notes for instance, the 'steeply peaked roofs' of the fish houses and that the gangways that lad up them are 'cleated' to prevent the wheelbarrows slipping.
- She notes that the buildings near the waterfront have moss growing only on their 'shoreward walls'.
- She notes that the tree trunks on the boat ramps are laid at 'intervals of four or five feet'.
- Such precision is even evident when she discusses the hymns she sings to the seal each evening. She's careful to distinguish the Baptist hymns from 'A Mighty Fortress Is Our God', which is a hymn associated with the Lutheran tradition.

Detached and Neutral Tone

A somewhat detached and neutral tone dominates 'The Bight'. Bishop takes in the messy and chaotic scene before her in a casual, objective manner'. She never expresses or registers any intense emotion at what she sees on this occasion. There is a matter-of-factness about the descriptions she offers, no matter how odd or strange the scene before her might appear.

'Filling Station', too, is dominated by detached neutrality. The poem's opening ('Oh, but it is dirty!') betrays a sense of disgust. But this quickly gives way to a tone of neutral description and idle curiosity. Bishop wittily asks whether the plants have been oiled, and suggests that the plant on the porch resembles the filling station's workers: 'a big hirsute begonia'. She seems more interested in registering the smallest details than she is in expressing her inner life.

Both the 'The Fish' and 'The Armadillo' open with Bishop's signature detachment but evolve into a very different, more expressive tonality. 'The Fish' is neutral, almost emotionless, for most of its length, with the poet focusing on the myriad details of the fish's appearance, rather than on her own thoughts and feelings. (We might, however, detect a faint hint of pride and excitement when the poet declares that she caught a 'tremendous fish'). The tone changes towards the end of the poem when the poet realises just how much the fish has struggled throughout its long life. The poem closes with a sense of joy, one might almost say, elation.

'The Armadillo', too, sees Bishop's usual detached tone prevail for most of its length. For the first nine of its ten stanzas the poet functions as a kind of neutral observer While she describes the ritual of the fire-balloons, she does not directly reveal her feelings on the matter.

In sharp contrast, the final stanza is a direct outpouring of emotion. The poet's distress at the plight of the armadillo (as well as the sufferings of the baby rabbit and the owls) prompts an emotional outburst of anger and condemnation, an outburst that shatters the normally serene surface of her verse. The poet not only reveals her own anger but also, as we've seen, gives voice to the voiceless creatures that have seen their habitat destroyed.

It might be argued that 'In the Waiting Room' functions in a similar fashion. The beginning of the poem is characterised by almost banal observations, as the poet describes events in the waiting room in a flat, emotionless fashion : 'My aunt was inside/ what seemed like a long time'. By the conclusion of the poem, however, this flatness has disappeared, and Bishop skilfully changes the atmosphere from one of self-satisfied certainty to terrified disorientation. Bishop uses repetition and images of things spinning out of control to convey the child's sudden loss of equilibrium: 'I – we – were falling, falling'; 'the sensation of falling off/ the round, turning world'.

'Questions of Travel' is very much a poem of anxiety and unease, with the poet wondering where she should be and what, exactly, she should be doing with her life. As is so often the case with Bishop, however, the emotion is contained beneath the poem's rather serene surface. On the surface, the poet's tone throughout is relaxed, almost cheerful, as she probes the issues surrounding travel with a series of rhetorical questions (questions that require no answer). One might argue, however, that the poet's emotions are more directly expressed in the notebook entry with which the poem concludes.

'At the Fishhouses' is similar in this regard. This is a poem that deals with profoundly personal truths, with a poet's search to embrace and overcome long-buried trauma. The poem, however, features few expressions of direct emotion. And there is no direct reference to the painful childhood memories that the poet associates with Great Village.

It's only at the poem's conclusion, with its increasingly unrealistic depiction of the water, that we sense the painful and powerful emotions that lie beneath the seemingly serene surface of the verse. But even here Bishop operates indirectly, using the sea as a symbol of trauma and its uncovering, instead of tackling such concepts in a blunt and straightforward fashion.

Metaphor and Simile

'The Fish' features a number of striking similes. The fish's skin is compared to peeling wallpaper decorated with roses: the shapes on the fish's skin are 'like fullblown roses/ stained and lost through age'. The fish's flesh is 'packed in like feathers'. It has a 'pink swim-bladder/ like a peony'. The eyes move 'like the tipping/ of an object toward light.' The lines attached to the fish's jaw are 'Like medals with their ribbons/ frayed and wavering'. The fish's jaw is 'weaponlike'.

The poet also uses effective metaphors to describe the fish's appearance: the irises are 'backed and packed/ with tarnished tinfoil', and the lenses are 'old scratched isinglass'. The lines that hang from the fish's jaw resemble 'a five-haired beard of wisdom'.

Effective metaphors are also used in 'The Bight'. Bishop compares the marl protruding through the water to 'ribs'. The sponge boats are compared to 'obliging' dogs. The poet uses a striking simile when she compares the pilings to matches: 'the pilings dry as matches'. The pelicans are 'like pickaxes' when they dive 'unnecessarily hard' into the water. The man-of-war birds' tails are compared to scissors and wishbones. The shark tails shine like 'little plowshares' in the sun. The broken boats are 'like torn-open, unanswered letters'.

Bishop also uses persuasive similes and metaphors in 'Sestina'.
- In a fine metaphor, the drops of moisture on the kettle's side are compared to tears.
- In an equally fine simile, the buttons on the man in the child's drawing are compared to tears.
- In another effective simile, the moons falling from the almanac's pages are compared to tears, and we can imagine how the full, half and quarter moons depicted on the almanac's pages might resemble tears.
- In another striking simile, the almanac is compared to a bird: 'Birdlike, the almanac/ hovers half open above the child/ hovers above the old grandmother'. We can imagine the half-open pages acting like wings as the almanac flies around about the kitchen.

Personification occurs in lines 15 to 16, where both the rain falling on the roof and the droplets falling on the stove are depicted as dancing (Personification occurs when a non-human object is described as having human characteristics; in this instance, both the rain and the droplets are described as dancing, a very human activity.)

There are also several fine metaphors in 'The Prodigal'. The hay packed above the animals in the barn's hayloft is compared to 'clouds', and we can imagine it as cloudy golden puffs above the sleeping cows and horses. In line 11 the red light of sunrise is compared to a 'glaze' that is spread over the mud of the farmyard. The red glow of its reflection on the puddles is compared to fire: 'the burning puddles'.

In 'First Death in Nova Scotia', Bishop uses several convincing metaphors and similes in her description of the parlour in which the poem is set. In a memorable metaphor, the table on which the loon rests is compared to a frozen lake: 'He kept his own counsel/ on his white frozen lake,/ the marble-topped table'. In an equally fine simile, the young speaker compares Arthur's corpse to a little doll: 'He was all white, like a doll/ that hadn't been painted yet.' In another metaphor, Arthur's coffin is compared to a 'little frosted cake'.

The Fish

Fishing boats at Key West Florida, where Bishop often fished

LINE BY LINE

From her earliest childhood, Elizabeth Bishop had a keen interest in the sport of fishing. In 1937, when she was twenty-six years old, Bishop moved to Key West, a tropical island off the coast of Florida, which provides the setting for this poem. Over the ten years that she lived here, she fished on a regular basis.

The poem is based on an actual experience of fishing in Key West in 1938. In an interview, Bishop once said: 'I always tell the truth in my poems. With 'The Fish', that's exactly how it happened. It was in Key West, and I did catch it just as the poem says. That was 1938. Oh, but I did change one thing; the poem says he had five hooks hanging from his mouth, but actually he only had three. Sometimes a poem makes its own demands. But I always try to stick as much as possible to what really happened when I describe something in a poem'.

> The Atlantic goliath grouper, also known as the Caribbean jewfish, is a large saltwater fish common to the Florida Keys. It is found primarily in shallow tropical waters among coral reefs. These massive creatures can reach lengths of up to eight feet and can weigh more than 700 pounds.

The poem opens with the poet out on the water in a 'little rented boat'. The little boat that she sits in is old, worn and dirty. The boat's engine and bailer are rusty, and the 'thwarts', the crosspieces of timber used for seats, are cracked from being exposed to the sun. A pool of 'bilge', of engine oil and dirty water, has gathered on the floor of the boat.

The poet has just caught an enormous or 'tremendous' fish. The fish hangs from the hook that is lodged 'fast in a corner of his mouth'. We get a sense of the fish's size when the poet tells us that she holds him 'beside the boat/ half out of the water' so that she can observe him. This is not a fish that she can dangle on the line before her in order to get a better look at it – its sheer mass means that it remains not only outside the boat, but half submerged in the water.

The fish is obviously feeling threatened and produces a 'grunting' sound to signal its distress. The poet draws our attention to the fact that the fish is out of its element and far from comfortable. Its gills were designed to extract oxygen from the water, rather than inhale it from the air. To the fish, therefore, the air is repellent or 'terrible': 'his gills were breathing in/ the terrible oxygen'.

We might imagine that such an enormous fish would have put up a considerable struggle against the poet. But this fish 'didn't fight' and 'hadn't fought at all'. This, of course, surprises the poet. And it is, perhaps, for this very reason that she decides to hold the creature beside the boat and observe it rather than bring it into the boat and commence her journey back to land. She wishes to observe this anomaly – a creature of 'tremendous' size that did not put up any kind of fight whatsoever.

The fish's ugliness

The fish is far from a beautiful creature. The poet describes it as 'homely', which means plain or unattractive.

- It is 'battered' or damaged, its skin hanging from its body in places, like very old wallpaper peeling off a wall.
- Its skin is brown, and the patterns upon the skin a 'darker' shade of brown. The patterns form shapes on the skin that resemble roses: 'shapes like full-blown roses'. But these patterns are no longer as vivid as they once might have been, having faded and become 'stained' over the years. The colour and the shapes on the fish's skin again make the poet think of wallpaper.
- The fish is 'speckled with barnacles', small, shelled creatures that have attached themselves to its body. These barnacles form white, intricate, rose-shaped patterns: 'fine rosettes of lime'.
- The fish's skin is also 'infested with …. sea-lice'. Seaweed adheres to its body, and 'two or three' pieces hang from the underside of the fish. The seaweed is like some old, tattered, green coat that hangs off the fish in 'rags'.
- The poet also finds the fish's gills unsettling and 'frightening'. They are firm or 'fresh' and 'crisp with blood'. The poet knows how sharp these gills can be and how easily they 'can cut so badly'.
- The fish's face strikes the poet as gloomy, or 'sullen'. Its 'lower lip' is described as 'grim', which suggests that its mouth is frozen in an unpleasant and uninviting expression. Its jaws are described as threatening and 'weaponlike', a carefully structured 'mechanism' that could be used to inflict considerable damage.

The poet's imagination goes into overdrive as she pictures the interior of the fish's body. She thinks of the 'coarse white flesh' tightly packed and overlapping like a bird's 'feathers'. She thinks of the fish's 'big bones and the little bones'. She imagines the 'dramatic reds and blacks/ of his shiny' inner organs or entrails. She pictures the 'pink swim-bladder', the fish's internal gas-filled organ that helps it to control its buoyancy. The poet imagines this looking like a 'big peony', a vivid red flower.

The poet looks into the fish's eyes

The poet is especially fascinated by the fish's enormous eyes, which are described as being 'far larger' than her own.

- The fish, however, does not return her stare. Instead its eyes are drawn or tilt naturally 'toward the light'.
- The sclera or whites of the fish's eyes have a yellowish tint. Bishop uses a wonderful metaphor to describe this, declaring that stained and dirtied tinfoil has been packed in behind and around the irises: 'the irises backed and packed/ with tarnished tinfoil'.
- The lenses of the fish's eyes are described as opaque. Bishop uses a wonderful metaphor to describe this, declaring that the lenses are made from 'old scratched isinglass'. Isinglass is a jelly-like substance obtained from the bladders of certain fish, which can be hardened into thin, transparent sheets.
- The fish's eyes are described as shallow. This suggests the physical structure of its eyes, which are flatter and less inflated than those of human beings. But it also suggests something about the fish's mind, which is basic and unsophisticated compared to a human being.

The poet's respect for the fish

No sooner has the poet pulled the fish from the water than she begins to feel a sense of respect for this 'tremendous' creature. She refers to it as 'venerable', suggesting that it deserves respect because of its age and experience. The fish, as we've pointed out, is quite old and bears the marks of having survived for a long time in the waters off Key West.

The poet's respect for the fish increases when she notices the 'five big hooks' lodged firmly in its 'lower lip'. She realises that she is looking at something remarkable. For the fish has been snagged five times by the hooks of different fishermen. Each time, however, the fish fought and fought. Each time it thrashed and whipped its body in the water until it broke the fisherman's line. Each time it won its freedom.

Each hook has a piece of fishing line attached to it. These bear evidence of the fish's extraordinary efforts to break free from the various fishermen it bested over the years. One piece of line is described as being 'frayed ... where he broke it'. Another is 'crimped' or curled 'from the strain and the snap/when it broke and he got away'. The poet uses two wonderful metaphors to describe this array of hooks. Firstly, she compares them to military decorations. The hooks themselves are compared to 'medals' while the pieces of line are compared to the medals' decorative tassels. Secondly, she compares the hooks to a beard. We can imagine how the hooks and the ragged pieces of line might resemble whiskers jutting from the fish's lip. This beard suggests the fish's 'wisdom' and longevity.

The poet makes a decision

Noticing these hooks has a profound effect on the poet. She experiences a surge of emotion, a sense of elation and triumph. It's as if she is sharing in the fish's victories over the various fishermen that attempted to catch it.

Bishop uses a wonderful metaphor to describe this sudden rush of feeling, decaring that 'victory filled up/ the little rented boat'. Here, victory is presented as something almost physical and tangible. It's like a wave spilling into the boat, and filling it from the bottom to the top.

Firstly, this wave of 'victory' covers the bilge that has collected in the boat's floor. It continues to accumulate, submerging the 'rusted engine' and the equally rusted bailer. It rises further, covering the 'thwarts' or benches. Finally, the whole boat is filled with 'victory', as far as the 'gunnels', which mark the upper edges of the boat's sides.

This surge of emotion causes the poet to see the world in a different way. Everything in and around the boat suddenly seems intensely bright and colourful. The pool of bilge on the boat's floor had shimmered with a rainbow effect: 'the pool of bilge/ where oil had spread a rainbow'. But now this 'rainbow' effect expands to encompass everything the poet sees. The poet decides that the fish deserves to be set free and returned him to the water: 'And I let the fish go'.

THEMES

AN OBSERVER OF THE ORDINARY WORLD

This poem's most important line might be 'I stared and stared', for it highlights how Bishop is a keen observer of the ordinary world. In this poem, she turns her attention to an everyday sight, to a fish that is large but otherwise perfectly normal.

Most people would regard the fish as dull or even ugly, certainly not worthy of being 'stared and stared' at. But Bishop presents it as being fascinating or even magical:
- The fish's skin is compared to 'ancient wallpaper'.
- The patterns upon the skin are likened to 'full-blown roses'.
- Its jaw is compared to a perfectly designed mechanism.
- The 'coarse white flesh' beneath its skin is described as tightly packed feathers.
- Even the fish's half-blind eyes are depicted as hypnotic and fascinating.

The poet comes across as a highly observant person. She notices, for instance, the fish's lack of fight when she first caught it. She notices how it 'grunts' when she holds it out of the water. She notices the barnacles and sea-lice that are resident upon its body. She notices, above all, the five hooks that have 'grown firmly' into the fish's mouth and the 'five old pieces of fish-line' that are still attached to them.

MOMENTS OF EPIPHANY

In many of Bishop's poems, such careful focus and description leads to some important insight or revelation. 'The Fish' is no exception in this regard. The poet contemplates the fish and comes to a new understanding of this creature. She realises that the fish has lived for a long time and has fought and won many battles over the years. She experiences a moment of heightened emotion, of ecstasy and elation as she contemplates the fish's triumphs. This is unforgetably described by Bishop as a wave of 'victory' that washes over and fills the rented boat.

A POET OF EMOTIONAL RESTRAINT

Bishop, in this poem, experiences a range of emotions towards the fish:
- There is a sense of unease or disgust towards this creature with its 'sullen face' and its flaking skin.
- There is a growing sense of respect for this 'venerable' creature.
- There is a sense of pity for a creature who had fought so hard to resist its various captors but 'hadn't fought at all' on this occasion. The fish, it seems, is exhausted and doesn't have any fight left.
- There is also, no doubt, a sense of identity with the fish, for Bishop, like the fish, was a survivor. The fish had survived and been scarred by many battles over the years. Bishop, similarly, had survived and been scarred by numerous traumatic events from childhood on.

Bishop, however, is a poet of emotional restraint. She doesn't directly express her feelings about the fish. Instead, her reactions are conveyed through her detailed descriptions of the fish's physical features.

It is only at the end of the poem that the poet permits herself a moment of direct emotional expression. She describes how she is overcome with heightened feelings that seem to transform the world around her, making it seem for a moment that it is a blaze of colour.

THIS IS POETRY — ELIZABETH BISHOP
The Bight

LINE BY LINE

This poem was written in 1948. The poet was 37 at the time – in fact, the poem is set on her birthday – and she was living in Key West, a small U.S. island city that is part of the Florida Keys archipelago. A bend in the shoreline on the northwest side of the island creates the 'bight' that the poem describes, a wide bay and naturally protected harbour.

The Key West harbour was a busy fishing port when Bishop lived there. When the poem was written sponge harvesting was a major industry in Key West, and there would have been well over one hundred boats operating out of the bay.

The water

The poet is standing on the bight's dock or pier. She looks out at the water in the bay. It is low tide, so the water is not very deep. In fact, the water seems to be barely covering the seabed. The poet uses the word 'sheer' to describe the meagre presence of the water in the bay. The word 'sheer', which means transparently thin, is often used to describe fabric or clothing that is so fine that you can almost see through it. Here, it suggests that the water is barely concealing the seabed beneath. The still water, in the bright sunshine, has a light blue colour. The poet compares this colour to 'the gas flame' of a lantern or a stove 'turned as low as possible'.

Aspects of the seabed are exposed, emerging up through the thin layer of water in the bay. The poet describes how ridges of 'marl' or silt 'protrude' above the water's surface. They are like 'ribs' that poke through or are visible beneath the surface of the skin. These white mounds reflect the sun's intense light, dazzling the speaker: 'White, crumbling ribs of marl protrude and glare'. The word 'glare' can also mean to stare in an angry or fierce way. It is as if the marl is staring right back at the poet, returning her gaze.

The water in the bight doesn't seem to be behaving as water ought to behave: it 'doesn't wet anything'. The timber boats that float upon its surface are 'dry', as are the timber 'pilings', the long wooden poles driven into the seabed to support and secure the pier or dock. To the poet, the pale blue substance that coats the bay seems more like a strange form of gas ('peculiar gas') than a liquid. In fact, as she stands on the dock, she feels as if she 'can smell it turning to gas'. There is a hint of danger here. The combination of gas, matches and dry timber means that the whole bay can be seen as ready or set to ignite.

The birds

The poet describes the pelicans and the man-of-war birds that are present in the bay. Both are very large seabirds, and the poet is struck by their great size, describing them as 'outsize' or enormous.

The poet observes the pelicans diving into the sea to catch fish. They 'crash' into the water in a manner that she considers 'unnecessarily hard'. They behave like 'pickaxes' striking down on rock. Despite their intense efforts, they rarely emerge from the sea 'with anything to show'. The poet describes how they fly away in an amusing manner, jostling and shoving each other: 'going off with humorous elbowings'.

The man-of-war birds don't dive, but stay aloft, soaring on drafts of air that are not visible or evident to the poet on the ground. The poet describes how, as they fly, they use their long forked tails to steer. When they wish to swerve, they 'open their tails like scissors'. On other occasions, they 'tense' their tails, hardening them to create lift. When the tails are tensed in this manner they 'tremble' with the effort to hold hard against the drafts of air upon which they ride. Bishop likens the rigid tails to 'wishbones', the forked bone found between the neck and breast of a bird.

The boats

The poet observes the sponge boats returning to the harbour. She observes that these boats are continuously 'coming in'. To her, they seem like 'retrievers', dogs that are trained to go and retrieve game for hunters. The boats seem to have the 'obliging air' of these animals, a sort of good-natured willingness or eagerness to help or please.

The boats are untidy and scruffy. The numerous poles and hooks that the fishermen use to gather the sponge are standing up and sticking out of the boats at different angles. They resemble the small rods of wood that are used in the game 'jackstraw', a game in which players try to remove one slim rod or 'jackstraw' at a time without disturbing the others.

The poles sticking up out of the boats also resemble the bristles, or spiky hairs, on an animal's back, again calling to mind the image of dogs. The boats, the poet says, are 'bristling with jackstraw gaffs and hooks'. Hanging off the top of the poles and hooks are some of the sponges that the fishermen have harvested. The sponge is hung up to dry in the sun as the boats return to the harbour and the poet observes how they resemble 'bobbles', small balls of material, usually made of wool, used for decorating clothes.

Sea sponges are aquatic animals that cling to hard surfaces on the sea floor. Natural sea sponges are harvested from the bottom of the ocean by fishing boats that specialise in sponge fishing. Sea sponges are harvested by divers using specially designed cutting hooks or knives. When the sponges have been cut, the divers gently squeeze the entrails out of the sponges and take them back to the boats. The sponges are then pounded to clean them and covered with wet canvas sacks on the deck of the ship, where the heat from the sun releases a gas that rots the sponges' skins so that they can be more easily removed.

The poet observes the 'fence of chicken wire' – wire consisting of thin, flexible, steel wire with hexagonal gaps – that runs along the dock. The fence is used by the local fishermen to hang the severed tails of sharks up to dry. These shark tails will later be sold to Chinese restaurant owners and used to make soup. The poet describes the 'blue-gray' colour of the tails and the manner in which their smooth surfaces glisten in the sun. To the poet, these tails resemble the sharp, smooth, metallic blades of a plough: 'glinting like little ploughshares'.

At the end of the dock, a small yellow or reddish brown ('ocher') dredge is at work. A dredge is a machine, like a digger or excavator, used to remove material from a seabed or riverbed. The poet hears the constant clicking sound that the machine makes as it works. The rhythm of this clicking sound reminds her of the 'off-beat' rhythm of 'marimba' music. (The marimba is a percussion instrument consisting of a set of wooden bars that are struck with rubber mallets to produce musical tones.)

The storm

Key West is a place that experiences regular tropical storms. In fact, in the year that the poem was written, Key West experienced the most intense tropical cyclone that had been seen in the area in over a decade, the September 1948 Florida Hurricane. The poet observes that there are still a number of small boats 'piled up/against each other' or lying on their sides 'from the last bad storm'. Many of these boats have been badly damaged by the storm, their sides smashed or 'stove' in. Nobody has bothered to come and retrieve these boats, and the poet wonders if they will ever be 'salvaged'. These small white boats remind the poet of letters that have been torn open, tossed to one side and left unanswered on someone's desk.

The poet says that the bight is 'littered with old correspondences'. This is a place that the poet has visited often and has come to identify with. There is something very familiar about it – it is a place that she can readily relate to. It is as if she has been interacting with the harbour, communicating with it, even, for such a period of time that a whole pile of 'correspondence' has gathered and accumulated. We can imagine that the poet has come here on different occasions and in different moods and found some solace or comfort in it all. Here is a place that seems to correspond with her own messy and disorganised life.

As the poet listens to the mechanical dredge going about its business at the end of the pier, she reflects upon the happenings in the bight. There is much activity 'here', but it is an 'untidy' activity, and there is little order to the place. The sponge boats are 'frowsy', which means scruffy and unkempt, shark tails are hanging on the wire fence and the boats damaged by the recent storm have been left where the storm tossed them. Yet everyone goes about their business, and 'All the untidy activity continues'. There is something horrid and unpleasant about all of this. But there is something 'cheerful' about it all as well. As Bishop wrote to a friend shortly after: 'I wrote ['The Bight'] last year but I still think if I can just keep the last line in mind ('all the untidy activity continues, awful but cheerful'), everything may still turn out all right'.

THEMES

AN OBSERVER OF THE ORDINARY WORLD

This poem highlights Bishop's love and respect for the ordinary world. She exhibits a keen interest in this unattractive bay with all its everyday goings on. She observes all its aspects, from the birds swooping through the sky, to the marl that composes the seabed and the coastline, to the water itself, which resembles a thin, translucent fabric.

Bishop's poetry is also marked by its extraordinary attention to detail. Whenever she was fascinated by something, she would strive to describe it as accurately and clearly as possible.

- She notices, for instance, how the pelicans jostle each other in a manner that seems casual and lighthearted, as they emerge from the water.
- She notices the hooks, gaffs and other equipment stacked on the various spongeboats coming in and out of the harbour. She compares these to the jumble of sticks in the game of jackstraw.
- She notices the damaged 'white boats' that are piled up in one section of the harbour. These boats, she realises, are unlikely to ever be salvaged or restored. In a startling turn of phrase, she compares these boats to 'torn-open, unanswered letters'.
- She describes the shark tails, hung from a length of 'chicken wire along the dock'. The poet, a keen observer of life around the bight, is aware that these are intended for the Chinese restaurant trade.

A POET OF EMOTIONAL RESTRAINT

Bishop rarely expresses her emotions in a direct and unrestrained manner. Instead, her poems tend to look outwards, focusing on and describing the external world in careful and minute detail. Yet these descriptions can reveal a great deal about the poet and her inner state of mind.

The poem, we learn from the subtitle, was composed on the poet's birthday, an occasion when many people take stock of their lives. The bight, with all its messy activity, strikes the poet as a perfect metaphor for her own life at this moment in time.

The bight, we are told, is 'littered with old correspondences'. Correspondence, of course, can refer to an exchange of letters, but it also means a similarity or comparison. For everywhere the poet looks, she sees something that reminds her of her own life, or serves as a metaphor for her own situation.

The bight is depicted as a landscape of instability:
- The coastline is composed of 'marl', a loose, earthy deposit. These 'ribs of marl', we are told, are constantly 'crumbling', as they shift in shape and texture
- This instability is also evident in the 'pilings', the struts that hold up the various piers and boathouses around the bay. The pilings, we are told, are 'dry as matches', suggesting they could go up in flames at any moment.
- The tools on the sponge boats are stacked in an unstable manner, like the little sticks in a game of jackstraw.
- The bight is a place of storms that have left a number of boats with hulls that have been broken or 'stove-in'.

All this instability, of course, reflects the lack of certainty and security the poet feels in her own life and in her own consciousness. The storms that have blown through the bight symbolise the emotional turmoil that has blown through the poet's own life.

The bight is also depicted as a landscape of labour and industry.
- The sponge boats are constantly returning to shore to deposit their catch.
- Pelicans are constantly diving into the water as they hunt for fish.
- Fishermen have hung shark tails to dry on a fence of chicken wire along the pier.

Bishop describes all this activity as 'untidy', suggesting that it is chaotic and disorganised. In this regard, it mirrors the poet's own life, which is filled with the 'untidy' activity of attempting to forge a living as a freelance poet and writer.

The dredge is a particularly apt metaphor. It probes the seabed, bringing up 'dripping jawful(s) of marl'. Perhaps this represents how the poet must delve into his or her own unconscious mind to uncover hidden thoughts, emotions and associations.

The broken boats, as we have seen, are compared to envelopes that once covered unanswered letters. We sense here the poet's guilt for failing to reply or respond to certain letters she has received. Or perhaps this comparison suggests an even deeper guilt, about friendships she has found herself neglecting.

This grim, industrial bay is an 'awful' place in many ways. But it is also a 'cheerful' one, full of industry and activity. The poet's life too is 'awful' in many ways, as she grapples with alcoholism, childhood traumas and other problems. But her life, like the bight, is also filled with cheerfulness, suggesting that on this particular birthday in Key West, she feels that she has a lot to be thankful for.

At The Fishhouses

LINE BY LINE

This poem is set in Great Village, Nova Scotia, the Canadian fishing community where Bishop lived between the ages of three and six. Bishop always bore a great fondness for Nova Scotia and its landscape, and for her maternal grandparents, with whom she and her mother lived during this time. But Great Village was also associated with traumatic events in the poet's life. Elizabeth and her mother moved there shortly after her father's tragically early death. While Elizabeth was living in Great Village, her mother was committed to a mental hospital, and Elizabeth never saw her again. Eventually, at the age of six, Elizabeth was taken away to Massachusetts in the United States, to live with her dead father's parents. Elizabeth found this change especially jolting, referring to it, with only slight exaggeration, as a 'kidnapping'.

These events, then, were a source of terrible childhood trauma and of the emotional instability that haunted the poet as an adult. Many years after the events had taken place, Bishop's therapist suggested that she return to Great Village in an effort to come to terms with these terrible memories. For many years, then, Bishop made regular trips back to Great Village. These return visits were made not only out of love for the bleakly beautiful Nova Scotia landscape, but also in an effort to confront her childhood traumas and heal herself on a psychic and emotional level.

Setting the scene

The poet is taking an evening stroll along the Great Village coastline by Nova Scotia. She nears the village's fish houses. These are buildings where each day's catch of cod and herring is brought ashore. The area around the fish houses, unsurprisingly, stinks of fish, of cod especially. The smell, according to the poet, is strong enough to make 'one's nose run and one's eyes water'.

The fish houses have 'steeply peaked roofs' that allow for attic storage space, or 'storerooms in the gables'. These storerooms are accessed by means of wooden ramps or gangplanks. Having first been descaled and gutted, the filleted fish would be carried up these ramps in wheelbarrows. (The ramps are 'cleated', meaning they had strips of wood running across them to prevent the wheelbarrows rolling back down). Once in the storehouses, the precious fillets would be packed in salt or ice for preservation, until they could be transported to the markets of the towns and cities.

The poet notices an old man sitting by one of the fish houses. It is 'a cold evening' and, as we've seen, it's beginning to get dark. But the old man continues to sit there, nevertheless, busily repairing one of his fishing nets: 'an old man sits netting'. In the failing light, the poet can hardly make out the net itself: 'his net, in the gloaming almost invisible'. It strikes her as no more than a blob of colour, of 'dark purple-brown' in the fast descending -darkness.

The poet talks to the old man

The poet decides to go and talk to the old man. She strolls in his direction, passing the 'fish tubs' and wheel-barrows that sit outside the fish houses. As each fish was filleted, guts and scales would be cast into the 'huge' tubs. The wheel-barrows, meanwhile, would be used to cart the fillets of fish into the storage areas within the fish-houses themselves.

The poet approaches the old man and offers him a cigarette, which he accepts: 'The old man accepts a Lucky Strike'. The old man, it turns out, was a friend of the poet's grandfather, who has long since passed away. The poet and the old man make small talk in the dusk. Naturally, they discuss fish and the business of fishing. (Bishop, we remember, was herself very keen on fishing).

The poet is keenly aware that this is a hard-working man, one who has spent a life-time engaged in this difficult, unpleasant work. He has scraped, she realises, the scales off countless or 'unnumbered' fish. He has used the same old 'black old knife' for year after year of work at the fish houses, so much so that its blade is 'almost worn away'.

The old man is waiting 'for a herring boat to come in'. For now, he's happy to sit and chat, or to almost idly repair his netting. When the herring boat arrives, however, he will spring into action, gutting and descaling with his worn black knife until the 'huge tubs' are brimming with fish guts, until he's busy pushing wheelbarrows of freshly-gutted herring up the 'gangplanks' into the store rooms of the fish-houses.

The poet and the seal

The poet tells us about the seal that she encountered regularly during her evening walks: 'One seal particularly/ I have seen here evening after evening'. Eventually, the poet found herself attributing human emotions and motivations to this creature. She sensed that the seal 'was curious about [her]'. She also got the feeling that the seal 'was interested in music'. She indulged this apparent interest by singing to him.

The poet was raised in the Baptist tradition. To become a Baptist, you must be baptised by 'total immersion', by having your body completely covered with water. The poet wittily declares that the seal must also be a believer in total immersion. After all, doesn't it spend all day completely immersed in the water? But another, more serious, sense of total immersion will emerge as the poem goes on, with the poet determined to immerse herself in her own unconscious mind.

The poem's landscape also features a large forest. The poet uses hyperbole, or deliberate poetic exaggeration, to emphasise the forest's size, declaring that it consists of a million fir trees. The fir trees, of course, are green. But in the twilight they seem to have a 'Bluish' glow. These trees run right down to the water's edge, where poet sits chatting with the old man.

The sea

The poet contemplates the shallows, watching the waves ebb and flow above a bed of 'gray and blue-gray stones'. The stones have been eroded by the water's ceaseless passage, each one caressed by the waves into a 'rounded' shape. And beneath the stones there is 'the world', the layers of shingle, clay and rock leading down all the way to the earth's crust. The water, as the poet so memorably puts it, moves 'above the stones and then the world'.

The poet, in an inspired turn of phrase, describes how the waves go 'swinging above the stones', wonderfully capturing the regular, almost pendulum-like movement of each wave as it surges inward and drains away again.

The sea, the poet maintains, is always the same but always different. The poet, as we noted, takes a walk each evening around the harbour of Great Village and finds herself looking at the ocean. Each evening, the ocean seems to be the same mass of 'clear dark' water, 'swinging' inward and outward in the very same fashion: 'I have seen it over and over, the same sea'. Yet the poet also realises that each evening the waters off Great Village are only 'slightly' the same; each evening finds their depths subject to different flows and currents, their surfaces agitated by different winds.

The sea-bed's rocky springs, from which the burning water issues are compared to breasts and mouths, to the 'cold hard mouth of the world', to 'rocky breasts'. The burning water, then, is 'drawn' or 'derived' from these springs like milk issuing from the breast of a nursing mother.

Bishop tells us that this image had its origins in a dream she had about Ruth Foster, her psychoanalyst. The dream featured a 'wild & dark' storm in which Bishop imagined a 'baby size' version of herself feeding at Foster's breast. Bishop reassured herself that this must be 'a common dream about a woman analyst'.

Psychoanalysis emphasises early childhood trauma, especially trauma relating to one's parents. Perhaps the dream about 'breasts', therefore, mixes up trauma relating to Bishop's loss of her mother with the analyst who was helping her come to terms with that trauma.

The poet's description of the water moving 'Indifferently' over the rocks powerfully captures the unthinking nature of the sea. It reminds us that we're dealing with an inhuman force of nature, one that swings relentlessly inward and outward, utterly oblivious to the destruction it causes through storms, riptides and erosion.

To the poet, then, the icy water exhibits total freedom as it moves 'icily free above the stones'. The ocean, she says, 'seems suspended', as if this great body of water were not actually resting on the stones but was somehow hovering above them: 'The water seems suspended/ above the rounded gray and blue-gray stones'. It's as if the water were immune to the laws of physics and no longer constrained by currents and weather conditions, but could flow anywhere at any time.

ANALYSIS

THEMES

MOMENTS OF EPIPHANY

When Bishop wrote the poem, she was undergoing psychoanalysis in order to come to terms with her various childhood traumas. Indeed, as we noted above, it was her therapist who first suggested that she return to Great Village, a location associated with some of the events that scarred her childhood. Psychoanalysis involves exploring the unconscious mind and bringing to light various traumatic memories and emotions.

Throughout the poem, then, the sea serves as a symbol for the unconscious mind. The sea, according to the poet, is 'opaque', meaning that we cannot see down through the seawater. And the depths of the self, of the unconscious mind, are similarly obscure and are extremely difficult to experience or understand.

The sea, according to the poet, is 'swelling' or expanding and looks as if it is 'considering spilling over', as if it might come bursting across the jagged rocks, flooding the entire village. This reflects how unconscious trauma can spill over into our conscious lives, often resulting in poor decisions and erratic behaviour. Such trauma can threaten to overwhelm our lives ,just as the sea, during a flood, threatens to overwhelm the land.

Perhaps it's not too fanciful to imagine that the boat ramp also has a symbolic function: 'the long ramp leading into the water'. Perhaps the ramp represents the techniques of psychoanalysis. For just as the ramp allows us to move from the land to the ocean, so psychoanalysis allows us to move from the conscious to the unconscious mind.

The poet twice begins to contemplate the ocean, declaring that it is 'Cold dark deep and absolutely clear'. But she twice allows herself to be distracted. On the first occasion, she finds her focus switching from ocean to the seal that she encounters on her evening walks. On the second occasion, she finds her focus switching to the forest of fir trees behind her.

It's as if the poet can't bear to look at this 'dark deep' mass of water, this vast intimidating presence. And this, of course, reflects her unwillingness to engage with her own unconscious mind and to confront the various traumas that lurk within it.

Finally, the begins to confront the ocean directly. Its waters are presented as strange and highly dangerous:
- They are described as being 'bearable to no mortal', suggesting that no human being could stand to be immersed in them for very long.
- Even touching the water, according to the poet, would cause you great pain. Your wrist, she claims, would begin to 'ache immediately', the discomfort spreading inward until it penetrated your very bones.
- And 'your hand would burn' if you immersed it in the waves, as if you'd thrust it into a raging fire.
- Tasting the water, too, is highly dangerous. You'd experience bitterness, she claims, followed by an intense saltiness. And then your tongue would 'surely burn', as if you'd accidentally ingested acid.

The poet uses an extraordinary simile to describe the waters off Great Village, depicting them as a vast and all-consuming sea of fire. But this is fire that's been 'transmuted' or transformed, so that it 'burns with a dark gray flame'. The poet describes it as a blaze so intense that it could burn through rock, consuming the 'blue-gray stones' of the seabed

This bizarre depiction of the sea wonderfully suggests the treacherous nature of the unconscious mind. The sea is depicted as being filled with tormenting slate-grey flames, just as the unconscious mind is filled with potentially dangerous memories and emotions. To enter or even touch the sea is to risk tremendous physical pain. To confront the unconscious mind, similarly, is to risk tremendous psychological pain.

But the poet must confront it. For these burning waters represent not only the dangers and traumas that lurk within the unconscious, but also the self-knowledge that can be found there: 'It's like what we imagine knowledge to be'. Like someone wading into a sea of flames, then, the poet must enter and explore her own unconscious mind. For it's only by doing so that she can gain the self-knowledge she so desperately craves.

She imagines what such self-knowledge would feel like, were she to successfully acquire it. Such knowledge would be 'dark', like deep waters impenetrable to the sun. This image suggests the trauma's and horrors of the poet's childhood. Such knowledge would be clear, like water that is free from all pollutants and particulates, reflecting the new sense of clarity and self-awareness that the poet would gain. In another sense, self-knowledge would be 'salt', it would be difficult and abrasive to absorb but ultimately cleansing. Like waters that seem to swirl with a mind of their own, such knowledge would be 'free', reflecting the intense liberty that the poet will experience when she is finally unburdened of her past.

The poet imagines this strange burning water flowing out from springs within the rocks of the sea-bed. Once again, then, the burning water serves as a metaphor for self-understanding. Self-understanding must come from the very depths of the psyche, just as the watery fire comes from the very bedrock of the world. And it can only be 'drawn' or 'derived' from the depths of the unconscious with the greatest of mental efforts.

The burning water, the poet insists, is not only 'flowing' but also 'flown'. It flows or circulates like any normal liquid. But then it flies away, evaporating into the air.

- We can, if we're focused and determined, acquire the self-knowledge that the poet speaks about. This might be represented by cupping some of the seawater in our outstretched hands.
- By the time you come to an understanding of your psyche, your psyche will already have changed. For the subject of such knowledge is not stable, since it is a constantly shifting personality.
- Any self-knowledge we acquire, therefore, while valuable, will always be slightly out of date. This is represented by the water evaporating or flying away before our very eyes.

We can understand ourselves fully, therefore, for only the briefest moment, before our knowledge becomes 'historical', relating as it does at each point to a slightly earlier version of our constantly shifting personality.

AN OBSERVER OF THE ORDINARY WORLD

In 'At the Fishhouses' as in so many of her poems, we get a sense of Bishop as someone with a keen observer of the ordinary world. This comes across in Bishop's lovingly detailed depictions of the sea and of the fir trees. But it's especially evident in her description of the seal, and in the 'relationship' she cultivates by singing to him each evening.

The seal's response to her singing is oddly human-like; he stares at her and shakes his head as if he was wondering what on earth this strange, singing woman was up to. 'He stood up in the water and regarded me/ steadily, moving his head a little'.

The seal seemed to exhibit human-like indecision when he 'disappeared', only to quickly reappear again 'almost in the same spot'. He would shrug as if he were bored with this singing human but had nothing better to do than listen to her songs: 'then suddenly emerge with a sort of shrug/ as if it were against his better judgment'. The poet, then, captures how uncannily human seals can appear. Anyone who has observed these creatures at close quarters knows how oddly human their eyes and faces can appear, how they seem to mimic and exhibit human behaviours and emotions.

There is something light-hearted, perhaps almost comical, about this depiction of the poet singing to an uncomprehending mammal, who looks at her with a strange mix of curiosity and indifference.

EXILE AND BELONGING

Bishop, as we've already noted, had a traumatic childhood that involved her being moved between several different locations in Canada and the United States. As a result, she felt 'rootless', as if she didn't really come from anywhere.

In returning to Great Village, however, the poet has found something resembling home. She has reconnected with her roots on her mother's side of the family. Here she inhabits a community of which her extended family is very much a part. (The old man, for instance, 'was a friend of [her] grandfather'.) The poet, then, has rediscovered a place that feels like her own point of origin, one that she could return to again and again.

And yet we sense that this newly rediscovered 'home' is very much under threat. Indeed, the poet and the old man talk about how the population of Great Village is 'declining'. The young, no doubt, are keen to leave the hard life of this fishing community behind, and set off for the bright lights of the major cities. As the elder generation die off, therefore, there is no one to take their place on the fishing boats. Great Village, it seems, is a community threatened with extinction.

The fact that, when she is on her evening walk, the poet sees only an old man adds to our impression of an aging community. Perhaps the old man's 'worn' shuttle and his old knife, which is 'almost worn away', serve as metaphors for a way of life that is in decline as fewer and fewer people enter the fishing industry. Even the fact that the poem is set at evening, just as darkness falls, reinforces our sense that Great Village might well be a community nearing its end.

ANALYSIS

The Prodigal

LINE BY LINE

This poem can be read as an updating of the well-known parable from the Gospel of St Luke. Jesus tells us about a son who asks for his inheritance from his wealthy father and then heads off to a foreign country, where he squanders his money on drink, gambling and other vices. Eventually, his funds run out, and he ends up working in a pigsty. For a long time, he endures labouring in the muck and dung, as he is too ashamed to return home with his money spent and in such a lowly condition. Eventually, he can take no more, and he returns to his father, who forgives him and welcomes him with open arms.

There is a strong autobiographical element to this poem. Since her college days, Bishop had been a problem drinker. After leaving college, she spent a period attempting to break into New York's literary scene, during which she quickly developed into a full-blown alcoholic. According to her biographers, Bishop drank to combat feelings of low self-esteem and depression. As is so often the case, however, drinking only made these feelings worse. Her struggle with alcohol was lifelong, and was fought with varying degrees of success.

Stanza 1

Inspired by this parable, Bishop's poem describes an alcoholic farm labourer who not only works in but also sleeps in a pigsty. He is employed on a farm that is a long way from home. He is a voluntary 'exile', who would rather work in the pigsty than return to where he came from. The pigsty is described as unpleasant:

- The floor is 'rotten'.
- The walls are covered with dung: 'The sty was plastered halfway up with glass-smooth dung'.
- One female pig, we are told, consistently devours her own children: 'the sow that always ate her young'.

- There is something unpleasant or even slightly sinister about how the pigs' eyes follow the prodigal around the barn: 'the pigs' eyes followed him, a cheerful stare'.
- The foul stench of the place closes in around the prodigal in a way that is swamping and claustrophobic.

The odour has so overpowered the prodigal's sense of smell that he can no longer 'judge' it; he no longer notices its foulness: It 'was too close … for him to judge'. Unsurprisingly, the prodigal finds himself disgusted, or 'sickening', in this foul environment.

Like many alcoholics, the prodigal is secretive about his drinking, hiding pint bottles of whiskey, rum or other spirit behind the pigsty's planks of wood: 'he hid the pints behind a two-by-four'.

'On mornings after drinking bouts', the prodigal is struck by the beauty that the sunrise brings to the farmyard. The mud and puddles of the yard reflect the colour of the sunrise. The puddles seem to 'burn', and the mud is described as being 'glazed' with red. This beautiful sight seems to 'reassure' the prodigal, making him feel that his life in the barn is worth living: 'the burning puddles seemed to reassure'. In such moments, he feels he can continue to put up with the filth and squalor of the pigsty for at least another year instead of returning home: 'And then he thought he almost might endure/ his exile yet another year or more'. (Of course, this sense of 'reassurance' might also stem from the alcohol he has just consumed.)

Stanza 2

This stanza describes an evening in the farmyard. It is getting dark. The sun is 'going away', and the 'first star' has appeared in the sky. The prodigal completes what are presumably his last tasks of the day: 'Carrying a bucket along a slimy board'.

If the prodigal's mornings are sometimes filled with hope and reassurance, then his nights seem truly miserable. He views the 'first star' as a warning to him that night is on its way, which suggests that his nighttime hours are highly unpleasant. We can imagine his nights being filled with guilt and self-loathing caused by his addiction and by the fact that he has ended up living and working in such a squalid environment.

The prodigal's circumstances are contrasted with those of the farm animals. Each evening, the cows and horses are 'shut up' snugly in their barn, 'safe and companionable' like the animals in Noah's Ark. The pigs, meanwhile, snore contentedly: 'the pigs stuck out their little feet and snored'.

The prodigal's circumstances are also contrasted with those of the farmer for whom he works. His employer 'shuts the cows and horses in the barn' and returns to the comfort of his farmhouse by the light of a lantern. As he walks away, his lantern casts an 'aureole', or halo of light, on the farmyard's mud. This aureole seems to 'pace' along with him as he returns to the farmhouse: 'The lantern – like the sun, going going away –/ Laid on the mud a pacing aureole'.

The image of the farmer's lantern receding into the distance is almost unbearably sad; it powerfully emphasises the prodigal's isolation. These lines emphasise the intense loneliness of the prodigal's nights.

> The misery of the prodigal's sleeping arrangements is emphasised. While the farmer and his animals are comfortable, he must sleep amid the filth and discomfort of the pigsty. We also see the intense loneliness of his situation. The animals sleep in a 'companionable' togetherness, whereas the prodigal is completely alone. Our sense of his loneliness is reinforced when the farmer returns to his farmhouse for the night, leaving the prodigal behind in the pigsty.

'The Prodigal', then, is another poem where Bishop deals with moments of epiphany or understanding. For on evenings like this – as darkness is drawing in and he prepares for another night alone in the barn – the prodigal's mind is struck by moments of insight: 'He felt … shuddering insights, beyond his control,/ touching him'. He becomes aware of the full grimness of his situation, and shudders in horror at the awfulness of his life in the pigsty. These moments of horrified insight are 'beyond his control'. He may find these thoughts unwelcome or unpleasant but there is nothing he can do to avoid them. He cannot fend them off with drink, or with reassuring thoughts about the sunrise.

These 'shuddering insights' seem to relate to the prodigal's awareness of the bats that fly above the barn: 'he felt the bats' uncertain staggering flight'. It has been suggested that these bats flying blindly through the night serve as a metaphor for the prodigal's situation. Just as they stumble and fumble through the air, so the prodigal staggers and lurches through life, uncertain as to how he should live. Yet the bats, though blind, possess a 'homing instinct' that allows them to navigate safely. The prodigal, too – it is implied – possesses such a 'homing instinct', some inner drive or intuition that will eventually cause him to leave the pigsty and return to his father's house.

Surprisingly, however, these moments of 'shuddering insight' do not cause the prodigal to immediately change his life. Although he realises the misery of his situation, it is a long time before he can find it in himself to leave the pigsty behind and return home: 'But it took him a long time/ finally to make his mind up to go home'.

Representation of the Biblical parable of the Prodigal Son

THEMES

ADDICTION

'The Prodigal' is a moving and honest portrayal of an addict. The prodigal, as we have seen, suffers from severe alcohol addiction. He drinks even in the mornings, hiding his bottles of spirits behind planks of wood. Like the character in the Bible story, his vices have brought him to a terrible situation. He spends his days amid the filth and squalor of the pigsty. Even worse, he spends his nights there, too. He also suffers from terrible loneliness. Furthermore, we get the impression that his nights are racked by guilt and self-loathing.

The poem, then, paints an unflinching picture of the misery addiction brings. Yet it also highlights how addicts take comfort and solace in their own condition. Addiction may be a miserable way of life, but it is one they understand and are familiar with. This is presumably why the pigsty's foul odour no longer offends the prodigal. Even the 'glass-smooth' dung caked on the walls is presented as being somewhat attractive. The pigs, too, are depicted as having a certain curious attraction with their 'light-lashed' eyes and 'cheerful stare'. They offer the prodigal a strange kind of companionship, which is evident when he leans down to scratch the sow's head.

The poem also emphasises how difficult it is for an addict to leave addiction behind, even when he realises the damage it is causing to his life. The prodigal seems torn about changing his life. In the evenings, there are moments of 'shuddering insight' when he realises the full horror of his situation. His awareness of the bats flying through the sky reminds him that he could follow his instincts and return home, leaving his addiction and the pigsty behind. However, in the mornings – as he drunkenly watches a sunrise – the prodigal feels 'reassured' that he can endure his miserable way of life for at least another year. In the end, it takes the prodigal 'a long time' to finally decide to give up his addictions and return to his father's house.

EXILE AND BELONGING

Throughout her life, Bishop was something of a wanderer, dogged by feelings of restlessness and rootlessness. This notion of 'homelessness' is one that occurs several times in Bishop's poetry, including 'The Prodigal'. The prodigal lives and works in absolutely miserable conditions. He could end all this simply by returning home. Yet for a very long time, he refuses to do so, deciding to 'endure' his self-imposed 'exile' rather than return to his family. We get a sense, then, that the prodigal feels he does not really have a home to go to anymore, that he is simply not welcome any longer in his father's house. The word 'home' is the only end-word in the poem that does not have a full rhyme, which may suggest how difficult the 'concept' of home has become for the prodigal. As is so often the case in Bishop's poetry, the journey 'home' is not an easy one to make.

THIS IS POETRY
Questions of Travel
ELIZABETH BISHOP

LINE BY LINE

This poem describes events that occurred during a trip through Brazil the poet took in 1951, along with her companion Lota de Macedo Soares. The poem is set in the mountains near Petrópolis, the town near Rio de Janeiro where Bishop lived for a time with her lover Lota de Macedo Soares.

The poet looks out at this extraordinary vista of enormous peaks, with waterfalls running down their sides. Some of the mountains are so high that their summits breach the cloud cover, causing tendrils of cloud to drift down across their upper slopes. According to the poet, however, this landscape is unpleasantly cluttered. There are 'so many clouds', she declares, and 'too many waterfalls'. In fact there are so many waterfalls that their streams seem 'crowded' together as they rush down the slopes to the ocean below: 'There are too many waterfalls here; the crowded streams'.

Pressure, too, is a feature of this landscape. According to the poet, the weight of the cloud-mass forces it onto the peaks, pushing billows of cloud down the mountains' upper slopes: 'the pressure of so many clouds on the mountain tops/ makes them spill over the sides'. The cloud-mass, then, is pressed down upon the mountaintops like a lemon on a juicer.

The poet also associates this landscape with haste and hurry. The waterfalls, we're told, 'hurry too rapidly down to the sea'. Both the clouds and streams are described as always 'traveling, traveling' – the repetition emphasising the pace and relentlessness of their movement. Even time itself seems to be in a hurry. The age it takes for the cloud streams to become waterfalls will be a 'quick' one.

All in all, then, when the poet looks out at this seemingly spectacular landscape, she experiences stress rather than relaxation, anxiety rather than awe. The whole scene puts her in mind of pressure, haste and crowdedness. There is a note, too of weariness and indifference here, as if the poet has seen and experienced too much on her travels. We see this in the rather unpleasant images she uses. In a wonderful metaphor, the clouds spilling down the mountainside are described as 'streaks' and 'tearstains'. In an equally vivid simile, the mountains themselves are compared to the slimy hulls of capsized ships. We get the impression that Bishop is bored by sights like this one, that no mountain range, no matter how spectacular, can thrill her now.

Issues with travel

The poet, as she looks out over the mountains, meditates on the question of travel, highlighting several problems associated with travel and tourism. The first issue she raises is a very practical one, relating to the inconvenience of going abroad. 'Think of the long trip home', Bishop declares, suggesting that any experiences we might have in a foreign country aren't worth the sheer hassle of travelling there and back again.

The poet also raises the various ethical problems that surround tourism. She wonders where, from a moral point of view, 'should we be today?' Should be travelling, or should we stay at home? Tourism can contribute not only to global warming but also to economic and environmental problems in popular destinations. Perhaps, then, we really ought to cancel our travel plans and remain in our home countries?

The poet uses a wonderful metaphor to highlight one particular ethical issue, comparing the act of travelling abroad to that of going to the theatre. The foreign locations that we visit are compared to the theatre's stage, while the local people that we see on our travels are compared to its actors. We, the tourists who gaze at the locals as they go about their daily lives, are compared to the theatre's audience.

The poet wonders if it is right to watch these strangers in the hope that we will be entertained or will get an exotic photo for our Instagrams. Perhaps our touristic gaze is a kind of voyeurism, an invasion of the local people's privacy and an unwelcome intrusion into their lives.

Human beings, according to the poet, are always eager to see new things and sample new cultural attractions. Sometimes we're eager to see remarkable species of animal, such as 'the tiniest green hummingbird in the world'. Sometimes we're more interested in buildings and monuments and are keen to visit the 'old stonework' of a French cathedral or an ancient Brazilian temple.

We engage with such sights on only the shallowest level, however. They are, as the poet memorably puts it, 'instantly seen'. We spend only a second or two examining each one, perhaps posing for a photo to post on social media. Then we declare it to be 'delightful' (or cool or lovely or whatever) and move on to the next attraction: 'instantly seen and always, always delightful?'

Furthermore, many aspects of a foreign country, like the temple's old 'stonework', simply can't be understood by people from outside the culture that created them. To visitors, then, they will always remain 'inexplicable' and 'impenetrable', utterly impossible to understand. (To emphasise this point, Bishop repeats the word 'inexplicable'). Perhaps, therefore, the only way to know or understand a country is by actually living there.

The poet suggest that the impulse to travel and be a tourist, which so many of us experience, is a childish one. In her view, when we engage in tourism, we behave in a rather silly or hyperactive fashion, being 'determined to rush' from sight to sight, from attraction to attraction. And this childish impulse doesn't diminish with age. Instead, those who experience this impulse when young continue to do so until they very day they die: 'while there's a breath of life/ in our bodies'.

Bishop presents tourism as a form of gluttonous consumption. We fill our memories with mental images, or our Instagram accounts with digital ones, just as we might fill our bellies with treats from a food stall. In a wonderful metaphor, tourist's experiences are compared to 'folded' foodstuffs like crepes or tacos. From the poet's viewpoint, tourists mindlessly consume such experiences, just as they might consume such tasty treats: 'And have we room/ for one more folded sunset, still quite warm?'

The poet's final objection to travel is particularly unusual: she suggests that we're better off not visiting our dream destinations. Maybe she's suggesting that the reality of such destinations can never live up to the expectations we have for them, that it's better to stick with our imagined idea of a place, than to experience the disappointing reality.

The poet, it seems, has often dreamed of visiting this part of Brazil and has fantasised about the mountains that form such an impressive part of its lush landscape. Now that she's actually there, however, a part of her wishes that she'd stayed at home. To some extent, the poet now wishes that, instead of actually visiting this spectacular location, she had continued to see it only in her imagination: 'Should we have stayed at home and thought of here?' Each of us has dreams and ambitions. And we live in a society that emphasises the fulfilment of such goals. The poet, however, resists this pressure to make our every dream a reality: 'Oh, must we dream our dreams/ and have them, too?' This even applies to dream destinations, which the poet feels we might be better off imagining than visiting.

The journey to the waterfall

The poet thinks about the journey she made in order to reach this part of Brazil, recalling how she and her companion drove along one particular tree-lined road. Using a wonderful simile, she compares the trees to performers in a pantomime. Their blossom is compared to the performers' costumes, while the movement of their branches is compared to the gestures that the performers might make during a show.

'It would have been a pity', the poet says, to have missed out on this experience, 'not to have seen the trees along this road'. After all, the pink blossom lends the trees a great 'beauty'. There was something 'noble', she feels, something both imposing and uplifting about the sight of this tree lined highway.

But Bishop's experience of the trees wasn't entirely positive. She describes their appearance as 'really exaggerated' and compares them to performers in a pantomime, which suggests that there was something silly or over the top about their appearance.

While the poet and her companion were on their way to their destination in Brazil they 'had to stop for gas' at a filling station. This seems to have been in an extremely remote and poverty-stricken area. Its inhabitants were so poor that they even made their own shoes, carving crude wooden clogs from blocks of wood. While the poet and her companion were refuelling, a particularly heavy rain-storm arrived. They ended up staying in the filling station for several hours while the storm blew itself out.

The poet recalls the owner of the filling station. Because they were homemade, his two clogs were 'disparate' or unalike. Each was distinct in terms of weight and shape. Each made a different sound when it struck the filling-station floor, producing a 'two-noted wooden tune' as the owner walked around his premises. 'It would have been a pity', the poet feels, not to have experienced this 'clacking' sound. She notes that in another country, perhaps a more developed one, shoes would be mass-produced and 'tested' in a factory. Each individual shoe would be identical in terms of weight and shape, producing a similar 'pitch' or note when impacting the floor.

Perhaps the poet felt, therefore, that she was experiencing something fun and quirky. Or perhaps she felt as if she were experiencing the 'real Brazil', that she had, at least for a moment, left the commercialised modern world behind.

At the same time, however, the poet is forced to acknowledge that the filling station is a depressing environment. An air of desperation clings to its owner, as if he's been ground down by poverty. He takes little pride in his premises; the floor is 'grease-stained' and at least one of the pumps is 'broken'. He moves in a sloppy fashion, 'carelessly clacking' across the dirty floor.

The poet recalls the filling station owner's pet, a 'fat brown bird' that he kept in a cage above the broken petrol pump. It would have been a pity, she feels, not to have heard this brown bird's song. For the poet, the sound of its singing was more complicated, and no doubt more pleasant, than the clacking sound of the owner's clogs: 'A pity not to have heard/ the other, less primitive music of the fat brown bird'.

The poet is forced to acknowledge, however, that this memory also has a negative aspect. Although the bird might sing sweetly, it is still a prisoner, caged in this miserable filling station with its broken pump and its grease-stained floor. The bird's cage, like the clogs, was homemade. The poet was struck by the contrast between these two items. The clogs, being the 'crudest wooden footwear', were carved in a rough and ready fashion. The cage, on the other hand, was created in a fashion that was both 'careful' and 'finicky' or fussy. According to the poet, it was 'whittled' from bamboo, which suggests that it was carved in a slow, deliberate and repetitive fashion.

The clogs were created purely with function in mind, with no hint of style or decoration. The cage, on the other hand, was highly decorative. The fact that it's described as being 'of Jesuit baroque' suggests that it was a complex and elaborate structure. In fact, the poet describes it as a 'fantasy', suggesting that it was the product of real creativity and imagination.

As she sat in the filling station, the poet found herself wondering what possible 'connection' could exist between these two pieces of woodwork. Why, 'for centuries', have the people of rural Brazil produced elaborate cages for their birds, while continuing to make only the most basic footwear for themselves? What are we to make of such strange priorities?

The poet studied the birdcage, wondering what it might tell her about Brazilian history. The cage's elaborately woven bars, she felt, were a type of 'calligraphy' She studied those bamboo loops and squiggles just as one would study words and letters in a historical document. Ultimately, however, studying the birdcage told the poet little or nothing about Brazil's troubled past. The cage's patterns, therefore, are compared to 'weak calligraphy'. Perhaps the poet has in mind a document whose letters have faded over the years, or maybe one that was poorly written to begin with.

The poet recalls the rain that fell while she was in the filling station, waiting for the storm to pass by. She uses a wonderful simile to capture this dull, monotonous sound, comparing it to 'politicians' speeches'. The sound of the rain, she declares, was 'unrelenting'. For 'two hours' it never paused or altered or diminished in intensity.

The poet, therefore, took special pleasure in the silence that she experienced when the rain suddenly stopped. This, she says, was a 'sudden golden silence', which suggests her intense relief that the rain had passed and she no longer had to endure its monotonous drumming. As she sat in the suddenly silent filling station, the poet jotted a few lines in her notebook, and it's those notes – set apart by being printed in italics – that conclude the poem.

THEMES

AN OBSERVER OF THE ORDINARY WORLD

In 'Questions of Travel', as in so many of her poems, we get a sense of Bishop as someone with a keen observer of the ordinary world. Her powers of observation take in everything from the vastness of the waterfalls, to the pink-blossomed trees, to the 'fat brown bird' singing in the filling station.

Her keen eye for detail is evident throughout the poem. She notices that one of the gasoline pumps in the filling station is broken. She notices that the station owner's clogs each produce a different sound. She notices that the design of the handmade cage show the influence of the Jesuit missionaries that came to Brazil centuries ago.

A POET OF EMOTIONAL RESTRAINT

Bishop rarely expresses her emotions in a direct and unrestrained manner. Instead, her poems tend to look outwards, focusing on and describing the external world in careful and minute detail. This is certainly true of 'Questions of Travel', a poem of careful, detailed observation.

This emotional restraint, however, disappears in the poem's final lines. Here we see Bishop at her most raw and unrestrained, as she wonders about her place in the world. Tellingly, these final lines are set apart by being italicised. We feel like we are reading a personal notebook entry, rather than the careful, polished observations that usually characterise Bishop's poetry.

ANALYSIS

EXILE AND BELONGING
The nature of travel
The poem, it must be said, takes a rather dim view of the whole area of travel and tourism. Its opening shows how even the keenest travellers and tourists can become jaded from sightseeing. The poet responds to a spectacular landscape with weariness, almost with disgust, referring to the streams of cloud as 'streaks' and 'tearstains' and to the mountains as 'slime-hung'. She describes this vista in terms of pressure, haste and crowdedness, which suggests that the landscape brings her stress rather than happiness or relaxation.

The poem especially emphasises how difficult it is to really know or understand a foreign country. We see this in the filling station when the poet attempts to understand Brazil's past but can only do so only in the feeblest and most uncertain manner. The point is that, as tourists, we engage with foreign countries on only the most superficial level. What we witness will always be as artificial as a performance in a theatre. The 'old stonework' of monuments and other attractions will always remain 'inexplicable' and 'impenetrable'.

Such negativity is also present in her description of the journey to Petrópolis. The poet mentions six experiences she had while travelling there, declaring that 'surely it would have been a pity' to miss out on each one of them. As we have seen, however, the poet's description of each experience is highly qualified – each is depicted as having a negative as well as a positive aspect. Would the poet really have regretted missing out on these experiences? Or is she merely trying to convince herself that her journey to Petrópolis was worthwhile?

Bishop wonders, therefore, why we can't 'just stay at home?' She even refers to the 17th-century French theologian Blaise Pascal's famous suggestion that 'all the evil in the world comes from man's inability to sit quietly in his room'.

A sense of restlessness
The poem also highlights Bishop's acute sense of restlessness. During her adult years, Bishop regularly changed her place of residence. And when she did settle in one place, she experienced what we might describe as 'itchy feet', embarking on regular trips and excursions. She's one of those people who, until the day they die, will be 'determined to rush' about the place, visiting and revisiting various locales. She can't resist this impulse, even though she views it as one of 'childishness'.

The poet's restlessness makes her agitated and uneasy. This is suggested by the sense of haste and pressure in the poem's opening, with its streams and clouds that 'keep travelling, travelling', its waterfalls that 'hurry too rapidly'.

The poet seems to view her urge to travel as a failure of imagination. She sits at home and contemplates 'imagined places', places she's never been. She suggests that if her powers of imagination were greater, she'd be able to visualise such locations in extraordinary detail. Her mental image of these 'imagined places' would be so rich that she'd never actually feel the urge to visit them. She could simply 'stay at home?'

A sense of homelessness
Bishop's father, we remind ourselves, died when she was only eight months old and her mother was institutionalised when she was only four. In the years that followed, Bishop was shunted from guardian to guardian in both Canada and the United States.

Because her childhood was spent in so many different locations, Bishop felt that she didn't really come from anywhere. She didn't have a 'home' in the sense of a point of origin, a native place that her family came from and to which she could return. This sense of what we might call 'homelessness' is indicated by the poem's final enigmatic question: 'Should we have stayed at home,/ wherever that may be?' The poet is uncertain, therefore, as to where her 'home' might be, and whether she even has one.

For most of her adult life, Bishop had a modest independent income and no regular job. If she wished, therefore, she could live in or visit any 'Continent, city, country, society'. And yet she feels no sense of freedom: 'The choice is never wide and never free'.

Perhaps Bishop experiences no sense of 'choice' because her restlessness compels her to keep moving. Or perhaps she thinks that everywhere she visits is ultimately the same. For no matter where she goes, she's dogged by the same feelings of not belonging, the same sense of never truly being at home.

MOMENTS OF EPIPHANY
'Questions of Travel', like many of Bishop's poems, concludes with a moment of epiphany or understanding. For despite all these objections and criticisms, Bishop can't help wondering if travel might still be justifiable or even necessary. She can't help hoping that Pascal might have been wrong, or at least 'not entirely right' when he gave his famous advice about staying in one's room.

This understanding, however, is 'blurred' and 'inconclusive'. Should we be 'here, or there'? Should we be travelling, or should we have 'stayed at home'? Ultimately, Bishop refuses to answer. For it's a question that, given her own particular background and psychology, she feels unable to address in any definitive fashion.

THIS IS POETRY ELIZABETH BISHOP

The Armadillo

LINE BY LINE

'The Armadillo' is set in Petrópolis, Brazil, where Bishop lived with her partner Lota Soares for many years. Armadillos are medium-sized animals, about 150 centimetres long, that are native to Brazil and elsewhere in South America. They are distinguished by their long narrow snouts, their short legs and, especially by the leathery armour shell that covers their bodies. This protective covering is composed of overlapping plates that resemble the mail armour worn by medieval warriors. (This is why the armadillo's fist is described as 'mailed').

The feast day of Saint John, which falls on the 24th of June, was marked by a carnival in Rio and in other Brazilian cities. In the weeks leading up to this celebration, the local people would release fire balloons 'almost every night'. The community would gather and watch hundreds, maybe thousands, of these balloons drifting into the night sky: 'This is the time of year when … the frail, illegal fire balloons appear'.

Bishop describes these fire balloons as 'frail', suggesting their delicate design. Each balloon consisted of a thin paper shell, with an opening at the bottom. At the centre of the shell was placed a 'candle' made from paraffin wax. When the candle was ignited ,it heated the air inside the balloon, causing it to rise. Eventually, however, the candle would go out and the balloon would drift to earth again.

Like many fireworks, the balloons were declared 'illegal' by the authorities. This is because fire balloons tended to fall to earth with their candles still smouldering. Sometimes, on impact, the balloon's paper shell would go up in flames. This could lead to wildfires that consumed everything in the crashed balloon's vicinity: wooden houses, crops, cliffs or dried-out scrubland. Bishop even installed a sprinkler system on her own property as a precaution against the destruction that the fire balloons might cause.

But neither the risk of such environmental damage nor the threat of prosecution prevented the local population from indulging in this ritual celebration of Saint John. On most June nights, the fire balloons continued to fill the sky.

The beauty of the fire balloons
The poet clearly appreciates the balloons' mysterious beauty. From time to time, the paraffin in each 'paper chamber' flares, causing the flame to grow bigger and brighter. Then it dies down again. Bishop wonderfully captures this flickering effect, observing that each balloon seems to 'flush and fill with light/ that comes and goes'. We can imagine that such a vast flotilla of flickering spheres would indeed make a sight to remember. We can imagine hundreds, or even thousands of balloons drifting upwards, each one flickering on and off according to its own irregular rhythm.

The poet watches the balloons floating into the night sky:
- The balloons float upwards at an angle, their flight-path tracking the slope of the mountain: 'Climbing the mountain height'.
- A statue of Saint John, the saint that the fire balloons were designed to honour, sits on the mountain peak. The balloon float upwards toward his likeness: 'rising toward a saint/ still honored in these parts'.
- The balloons keep rising – higher than the statue, higher than the mountain peak – until they are 'up against the sky'.
- On a 'still' night, the balloons rise 'steadily', drifting upwards in an even fashion, untroubled by any winds. According to the poet, there is something 'solemn' about their movement. We can imagine how the sight of hundreds, or even thousands, of such balloons drifting slowly upwards might strike us not only as dignified and ceremonial but also as awe-inspiring and majestic.
- On such a windless night, the balloons rise so high that they seem to merge with the great mass of stars overhead. Bishop uses a wonderful metaphor to capture this optical effect, telling us that the balloons seem to 'steer between' the constellations.
- Finally, the balloons disappear from view altogether. They keep 'receding' or moving away. Their light keeps 'dwindling', becoming fainter and fainter as they rise so high that they are no longer visible.
- The poet tells us that observers on the ground feel forsaken by the fire balloons as they float out of sight. The observers feel dejected and abandoned now that they can no longer see the fire balloons' grace and beauty.

The danger of the fire balloons
On windy nights however, the movement of the balloons is not so graceful. Gusts of air cause them to stall or 'falter' in their gentle upward movement. They 'wobble' awkwardly in the breeze. Their movement becomes erratic and unpredictable, as they are tossed around by the wind. They 'flare and falter, wobble and toss'. Sometimes, the balloons are caught by a 'downdraft', a sudden current of air gusting down the mountain-side. Such gusts can carry the balloons dangerously close to people and to buildings: 'in the downdraft from a peak,/ suddenly turning dangerous'.

The previous night, a large fire balloon crashed into the ground behind the poet's property: 'Last night another big one fell'. The poet tells us that this balloon 'splattered like an egg of fire against the cliff behind the house'. And we can indeed visualise the spherical balloon as a kind of egg, but one that spills fire, rather than yolk and egg-white, on impact with the ground.

The poet observes how the crashed balloon set fire to the vegetation on the cliff side, causing great destruction. The flames consumed an 'ancient' nest where 'a pair of owls' had resided for years or even decades. The poet watched as these terrified birds fled the conflagration, flying 'up and up' into the night sky.

The owls, it seems, were on fire as they fled. The poet, in a brilliant descriptive touch, describes the flames as a pink stain on their 'black-and-white' feathers. She describes how they went 'whirling' through the sky: 'whirling black-and-white/ stained bright pink underneath'. We can imagine them wheeling about in confusion, but also, no doubt, striving to quench the flames that were consuming them. Finally, they disappeared from view, 'shrieking' in pain and terror as they did so.

The poet observes a rabbit leaping from the burning vegetation on the cliff-side: 'And then a baby rabbit jumped out'. It stared directly ahead in a 'fixed' fashion, as rabbits often do when in a panicked state. We can imagine that it was almost hypnotised by the inferno that suddenly surrounded it.

This 'baby' rabbit, it seems, was absolutely tiny, so small that it might fit in the palm of one's hand. The poet watched as it was consumed by the flames. She watched as it was reduced, before her very eyes, to a tiny a rabbit-shaped heap of ashes. This pile of ash is described as 'intangible', because if it was touched, it would crumble, losing its rabbit shape: 'So soft! – a handful of intangible ash'.

A single armadillo also attempted to flee the chaos. Its leathery armoured shell was 'rose-flecked' from the flames. It is unclear whether the armadillo is actually on fire or whether its shell is simply speckled with little pieces of burning material. Its head and tail are described as being 'down', as if it were cowering in fear in a desperate attempt to protect itself.

Giving voice to the armadillo
A notable feature of the poem is the fact that the final stanza is printed in italics. This is because the poet is speaking for the armadillo, attempting to articulate this poor animal's reaction to the human carelessness that has destroyed its home.
- She expresses the armadillo's feelings of terror and incomprehension as it flees this chaotic scene where flame has suddenly started 'falling' from the sky, a scene filled with panicking animals and their ear-splitting cries: 'O falling fire and piercing cry and panic'.
- She expresses the armadillo's anger at the destruction visited upon its habitat when she condemns the fire balloons for their 'Too pretty, dreamlike mimicry!'
- She observes how the armadillo raises its clenched fist against the sky, in a traditional gesture of anger and defiance. It's as if the armadillo is cursing or condemning the fire balloons and their creators.

The creature's rage is futile, however. It is too 'ignorant' to understand the destruction that has occurred and too weak to repair the damage or exact revenge.

THEMES

EXILE AND BELONGING

'The Armadillo', like 'Questions of Travel', tackles the theme of exile and belonging. The speaker presents herself as something of an outsider in the Brazilian community in which she lives. Her position as an immigrant, or a long-term visitor, rather than a native inhabitant, is one that really comes across throughout the poem.

The phrase 'in these parts', for instance, suggests that this is a community the poet is still attempting to make sense of, rather than one in which she feels completely at home. It is significant that she takes no part in the ritual of the fire balloons that so engages the local population. Perhaps, as a visitor from a richer, more advanced country, she regards such rituals and beliefs as primitive and backward.

To the poet, then, the fire balloons are a strange local custom, one that is not only quaint and beautiful but also senseless and dangerous. She acknowledges the beauty of the fire balloons as they drift smoothly into the distance, but condemns the damage they all too often cause when they fall earthwards.

AN OBSERVER OF THE ORDINARY WORLD

In 'The Armadillo', as in so many of her poems, we get a sense of Bishop as someone with a keen observer of the ordinary world. She notices, for instance, that the fire ballons appear on many nights, but not quite every night. She has observed the ballons' flight paths and noted how they behave in different atmospheric conditions. She's aware for instance that there's an 'ancient nest' at the back of her property where a 'pair of owls' have nested. She even notices, in the middle of the chaotic inferno caused by the crashed balloon, that the baby rabbit is of the 'short-eared' South American variety.

A POET OF EMOTIONAL RESTRAINT

Bishop is well-known as a poet of emotional restraint. Her poems tend to focus on careful description of the physical world rather than on the direct expression of emotion. This is true for most of 'The Armadillo'. The poet's tone is neutral, as she provides a careful description of the fireballoons soaring into the sky or splattering into the earth.

This emotional restraint vanishes, however, in the poem's final stanza. Here, as we've noted, she seeks to speak on behalf of the armadillo, and on behalf of the other creatures affected by the 'falling fire'. Here, Bishop seeks to expresses these creatures' feelings of anger and incomprehension, their reaction to the human carelessness and selfishness that have caused them so much harm. She gives voice to the armadillo's rage, condemning on its behalf the annual ritual that visits such destruction on the local wildlife: 'Too pretty, dreamlike mimicry!/ O falling fire and piercing cry/ and panic'.

'The Armadillo', then, can be read as an environmentalist poem, as a lament for mankind's careless indifference to nature. The poet's perspective contrasts strongly with that of the local people, who seem utterly indifferent to the 'falling fire and piercing cry/ and panic' that their tradition all too often produces. In one sense, then, the poem can be read as an attack on human selfishness and short sightedness, condemning our continuing engagement in unnecessary activities even when we know they damage the natural world.

ADDICTION

Despite all this destruction, however, the local people continue to celebrate their ritual. And 'almost every night', the fire balloons throng the sky. This is one of several poems, therefore, where Bishop describes people who are caught up in what can only be described as compulsive behaviour. The local population – of course – are aware of the risks posed by the balloons they release each June. They know that the fire balloons all too often destroy wildlife when they come crashing down to earth. They know that these balloons are 'illegal'.

Yet their devotion to their local saint makes them want to persist with this dangerous activity. They may also be motivated by the desire to uphold a tradition or by a strangely misguided sense of community spirit. Whatever the motivation, it is perhaps not too outlandish to regard this religious impulse as a form of addiction, a compulsion that people brought up in this tradition are powerless to resist or control. In this regard, the poem resembles 'The Prodigal', with its portrayal of a chronic alcoholic, and 'Questions of Travel', which touches on the notion of the compulsive traveller.

WAR

The Armadillo' was published in 1957, a year when Bishop, like the rest of the world, was concerned about the possibility of a catastrophic conflict between the United States and the Soviet Union. At the end of World War II, the United States had dropped atomic bombs on the Japanese cities of Hiroshima and Nagasaki. The Soviet Union had responded by testing its own atomic bomb in 1949. The 1950s, meanwhile, saw both sides developing vastly more destructive hydrogen bombs. Such weapons meant that any conflict between these two superpowers could spell the end of life on planet earth.

Anxiety about bombs, then, was much in the air when Bishop composed 'The Armadillo'. The balloons, as Bishop sees them, resemble such weapons in important respects. They are bomb-like because they are launched from a specific point on earth, only to come crashing down elsewhere, bringing great destruction. In their 'mimicry' of bombs, then, the balloons cause great destruction, bringing 'falling fire' wherever they descend.

In the face of such destructive forces, of course, the ordinary citizen can do little. We are as vulnerable as the immolated baby rabbit or the owls that wheel away, terrified, into the sky. We can, if we wish, protest against the proliferation and use of nuclear weapons. But our complaints will be as futile as those of the armadillo uselessly shaking his fist against the sky.

Sestina

LINE BY LINE

The poem is set in the kitchen of what might be a farmhouse. It is a rainy evening in September. The kitchen is occupied by a grandmother and her granddaughter. They sit by the stove on which a kettle is boiling, the grandmother reading jokes aloud from an almanac. Almanacs, once extremely popular in rural America, were like diaries in that they had a page for every day of the year. Each page contained jokes and folk sayings, as well as horoscopes, weather predictions and agricultural advice. Almanacs were often attached to a piece of string that would be looped around a hook on the farmhouse wall.

It seems that the family has been struck by some terrible sorrow. In line 6, we are told that, while the grandmother might laugh at the jokes in the almanac, she does so only 'to hide her tears'. This great sorrow is 'known only to a grandmother'. The child's mental capacity is not developed enough for her to fully grasp or comprehend the tragedy that has taken place. We get the impression that the grandmother 'hides her tears' in an attempt to shield the child from awareness of this terrible event.

The kettle makes a whistling noise as its water reaches boiling point: 'The iron kettle sings on the stove'. The grandmother declares that tea is ready, and she begins to slice some bread. The granddaughter, however, is distracted by the moisture running down the kettle's sides: 'but the child/ is watching the teakettle's small hard tears/ dance like mad on the hot black stove'. To the granddaughter, the moisture on the kettle resembles 'small hard tears'. Perhaps this indicates that on some level she is aware that a great sorrow has struck her family, though she may be too young to fully grasp the tragedy that has taken place.

The grandmother clears up after tea and returns the almanac to its hook. At this point, the poem becomes bizarre, dreamlike and sinister. The almanac begins to fly around the kitchen, like a kite on the end of its string: 'Birdlike, the almanac/ hovers half open above the child/ hovers above the old grandmother'. In line 22, we are presented with the strange and haunting image of the grandmother's teacup being 'full of dark brown tears' rather than tea. The stove and the almanac are depicted as having a conversation about the tragedy that has struck the family: 'It was to be, says the Marvel Stove./ I know what I know, says the almanac'.

Throughout the poem, the almanac is presented in a distinctly sinister light. The grandmother believes that the family tragedy was somehow 'foretold' by its horoscopes and predictions. There is something almost conceited about the almanac's declaration, 'I know what I know', as if it is proud of the fact that it predicted the family's loss. Furthermore, there is something ominous about the way it hovers above the child and her grandmother. Tellingly, at this point, the grandmother 'shivers'.

The granddaughter draws a house with her crayons. We can imagine this as a typically happy and simple, childish drawing, one composed of 'rigid' lines featuring a flower bed, a winding path and a man standing in the garden. The child shows this drawing 'proudly' to her grandmother.

Once again, however, the almanac is depicted in a sinister light. It hovers above the child's drawing. Little moons fall out of its pages, presumably from its star charts and horoscopes, and tumble into the child's picture. These little moons 'fall like tears', dropping into the flower bed that the child has drawn. The almanac declares that it is 'Time to plant tears'. There is something unsettling about the notion of these tears somehow taking root among the flower beds of the granddaughter's drawing.

The 'sestina' is a notoriously difficult poetic form, one that few English-language writers have been able to employ successfully. In this poem, however, Bishop displays consummate command of the form, perhaps using its intense difficulty and rigid structure to contain the difficult childhood emotions she feels compelled to explore. The sestina consists of six six-line stanzas and a three-line section called an envoi.

The sestina employs six 'end-words' instead of rhymes – in this case 'house', 'grandmother', 'child', 'stove', 'almanac' and 'tears'. The same six end-words must be used in each stanza. The position of each end-word shifts from stanza to stanza. 'Home', for example, concludes the first line of stanza 1, the second line of stanza 2, the fourth line of stanza 3, the fifth line of stanza 4, the third line of stanza 5 and the last line of stanza 6. The other end-words shift in a similar fashion. The envoi must contain all six end-words: three at the end of its lines and three in the middle.

CHILDHOOD

Like 'First Death in Nova Scotia' and 'In the Waiting Room', 'Sestina' wonderfully depicts the mentality of childhood. We see this in the description of the granddaughter staring at the kettle as it comes to boil and ignoring her grandmother's declaration that it is time for tea. We can imagine a young girl being mesmerised by the sight of 'tears' running down the kettle's side, and thinking how these drops resemble the rain on the farmhouse roof.

Childhood mentality is also artfully portrayed in the depiction of the granddaughter drawing a house with her crayons. She draws in the typically 'rigid', over-deliberate fashion of children everywhere. She approaches the task with an innocent and childish dedication, 'carefully' sketching a flower bed and showing the finished picture 'proudly' to the grandmother.

Throughout the poem, there are moments when Bishop skilfully inhabits a child's point of view. The phrase 'clever almanac', for instance, has a distinctly childish ring to it. The child, presumably, is aware from observing the adults around her that the almanac contains predictions and folk wisdom. Therefore, in an amusingly babyish phrase, she refers to it as 'clever'. Similarly effective is the description of the stove as 'marvellous'. We can imagine that this is how the granddaughter might refer to the stove. To this innocent and childish girl, the stove is a wondrous and fascinating object. No wonder, then, that at the end of the poem, the Little Marvel stove is explicitly said to be 'marvellous', just as its name promises.

As we have seen, the poem's second half is full of strange and bizarre occurrences. We get the impression, however, that these weird events are not 'real' and merely take place in the granddaughter's imagination. She imagines that the almanac hovers around the kitchen with a mind of its own and sends a rain of moons into her picture, that her grandmother's cup contains tears rather than tea, that the stove and the almanac have a brief conversation.

The grandmother notices none of these events. She goes about her business as if nothing strange is happening, reinforcing our sense that these bizarre occurrences take place only in the imagination of the child. This sense is further reinforced when the almanac 'secretly' plants moons in the child's drawing, somehow unnoticed by the grandmother as she 'busies herself about the stove'. The poem then wonderfully captures how a child's imagination can run riot, viewing even simple household objects as living things and as sources of fear and wonder.

MOMENTS OF EPIPHANY

Many of Bishop's poems are marked by moments of awareness or epiphany, moments when a person suddenly or gradually realises something profound and important about themselves or about the world.

It is difficult not to interpret 'Sestina' in terms of Bishop's biography. Bishop's father died when she was only eight months old, and when she was eight years old her mother suffered a mental collapse and was institutionalised. Following these tragic events, Bishop went to live with her maternal grandparents.

Turning back to 'Sestina' with these real-life tragedies in mind, the first thing we note is that the tragedy that has struck the family in the poem is 'known only to a grandmother'. The child is still too young to fully comprehend the terrible events that have occurred. Yet we get the impression that awareness of this tragedy is slowly dawning on her. She thinks of 'tears' running down the tea-kettle and filling the grandmother's cup. The drops from the kettle seem to dance 'like mad', perhaps suggesting the mental breakdown of the poet's mother. Furthermore, the poet imagines the stove and the almanac talking about the tragedy: 'It was to be, says the Marvel Stove./ I know what I know, says the almanac'.

We get an impression that the child attempts to shield herself from sorrow by drawing houses. It's as if she tries to create in her imagination an ideal house, an alternative world where the tragedy that struck her never occurred. The house she draws is described as 'rigid', which suggests that it is a tough and solid safe haven. The man in the drawing presumably represents the father that the young Bishop so tragically lost. Yet the fact that the man's buttons are like 'tears' suggests that, even in the idealised world of her drawing, the child cannot escape the dawning awareness of sorrow.

The child is protected from sorrow by her inability to understand. But this defence will only last for so long. The almanac seems to represent awareness of the tragedy that is waiting to descend upon the child. It hovers above her in an ominous fashion and 'plants tears' in the child's drawing. We get the impression that tears have also been 'planted' in the child's life and will soon bear fruit in the form of the terrible sorrow that will overcome her.

First Death in Nova Scotia

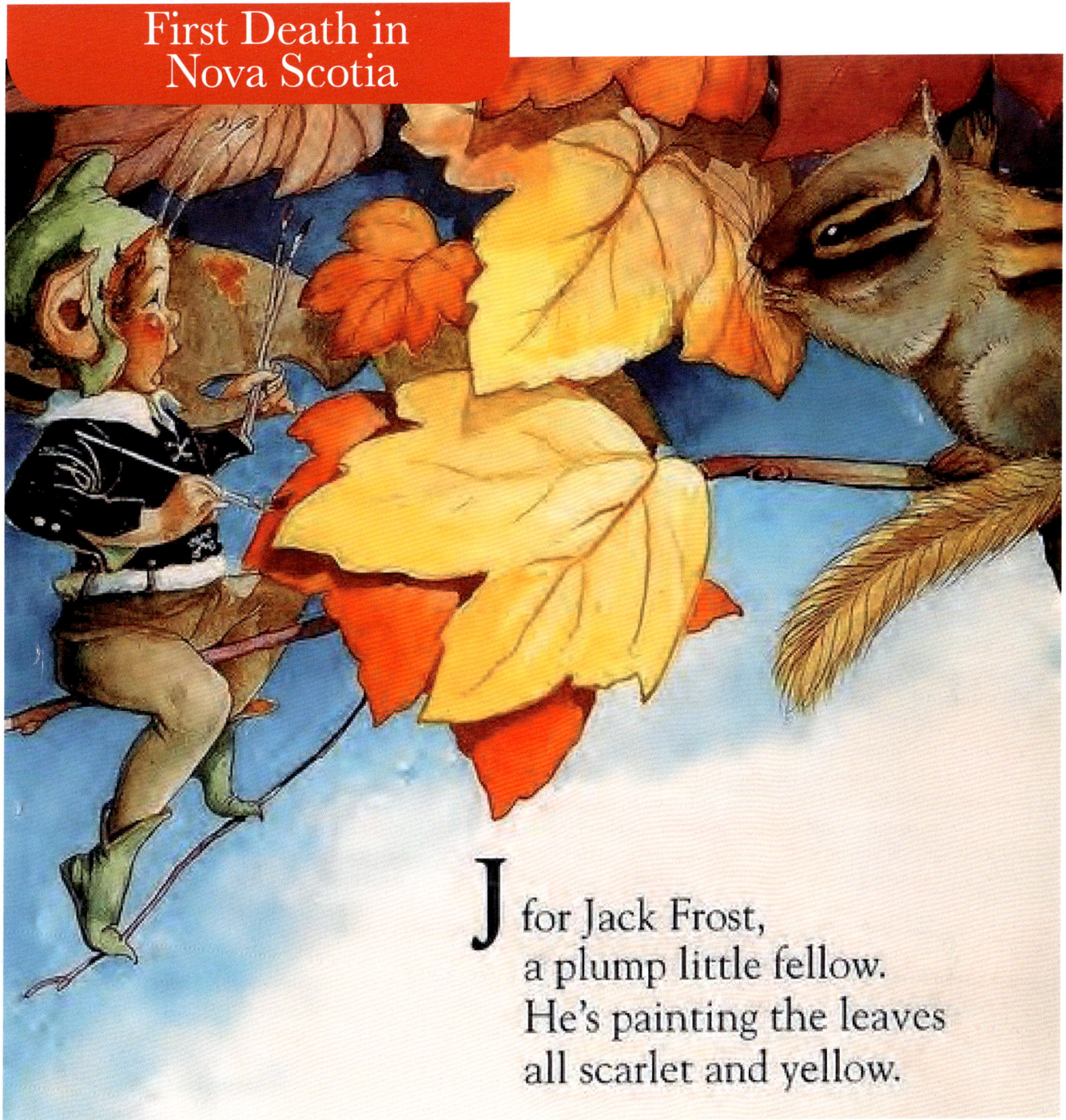

J for Jack Frost,
a plump little fellow.
He's painting the leaves
all scarlet and yellow.

LINE BY LINE

In 1915, when Elizabeth Bishop was four years old, her mother took her to live in Nova Scotia, a province in northwestern Canada. They moved in with her mother's parents in Great Village, a fishing community on the bleak but beautiful Nova Scotia coast.

The following year, Elizabeth's little cousin Arthur tragically passed. This was the young poet's 'first death', her first proper encounter with loss and dying. The poem powerfully describes her reaction to these strange, unsettling concepts and experiences.

The poet remembers how her mother 'laid out' Arthur's body, dressing the little boy's corpse and presenting it in a dignified fashion. Arthur's body is laid out in the house's 'parlour' or sitting room. We might think of this as the house's 'good room', one that sees little everyday use and is reserved for special occasions. We can imagine how this seldom-utilised space might be colder than the rest of the house during the Nova Scotia winter: 'In the cold, cold parlour, my mother laid out Arthur'.

The parlour features several ornaments. There are two chromographs which depicts King George V of England, who was then Canada's head of state, and other members of the royal family.

(Chromographs were an early type of colour photograph). One chromograph shows King George and Queen Mary. The other shows George's father, Edward VII, back when he was Prince of Wales. He is depicted alongside his wife, the then Princess Alexandra.

There is also a stuffed loon, which is a species of lake-dwelling bird distinguished by its white chest feathers and its black and white wings. This particular loon had been 'shot and stuffed' by the young poet's Uncle, who is the father of the dead little boy: 'by Uncle/ Arthur, Arthur's father'.

No doubt, friends and neighbours would be calling by to commiserate with the family following their loss. We can imagine how these visitors might first pay their respects to Arthur in the relatively formal environment of the parlour, before retiring to the kitchen for refreshments.

The stuffed loon
The four year old Elizabeth enters the parlour. But her attention, at first, is drawn to the stuffed loon, rather than to her cousin's body. She focuses especially on the plumage around the dead bird's breast, noting its intense whiteness. These feathers, she says, look 'deep', so fluffy that you could sink your hand into their yielding mass. They also look 'caressable'; they seem so soft that, when you see them, you want to reach out and touch them.

She notes the marble table on which the dead bird rests, comparing it to a frozen lake: 'his white frozen lake,/ the marble-topped table'. She describes how, as part of the taxidermy process, the bird's eyes have been replaced with pieces of red glass. To the young speaker, these pieces of glass resemble gems or precious stones: 'his eyes were red glass/ Much to be desired'.

The young poet's mother is also present in the parlour. She urges Elizabeth to bid her cousin a final farewell, lifting her up so that she is face to face with Arthur's body. She gives Eliazbeth a flower and instructs her to place it in the dead boy's hands: 'I was lifted up and given/ one lily of the valley/ to put in Arthur's hand'.

The young Elizabeth still doesn't directly contemplate her cousin's body, however. Instead, her attention is drawn to the coffin, which she compares to 'a little frosted cake'. We can imagine how the white coffin might strike the child as cake-like, how its puffy lining might resemble a cake's frosted topping. She also finds herself thinking, once more, about the stuffed loon, which seems to watch the coffin from the table on which it rests nearby.

Arthur's body
Only now does the young poet begin to focus on Arthur's body. She is taken aback by the intense whiteness of the corpse, which leads her to compare the body to an unpainted doll: 'He was all white/ like a doll/ that hadn't been painted yet'. How could Arthur be so white? The young poet explains this paleness to herself by referring to the legendary figure of Jack Frost:
- Jack Frost, she tells herself, had been given the task of painting Arthur's body, restoring it to its normal, colourful state: 'Jack Frost had started to paint him/ the way he always painted/ the Maple Leaf (Forever)'.
- Jack Frost, she tells herself, had set about his task. He had started by painting Arthur's hair: 'He had just begun on his hair, a few red strokes'.
- But then Jack Frost's work was interrupted, causing him to drop his paintbrush and run away.

As a result, Arthur's little body will never be restored to its normal, colourful state. It will remain forever deathly pale: 'Jack Frost had dropped the brush/ and left him white, forever'.

Jack Frost is a character from folk tales and popular culture. Often depicted as a mischievous little boy, he is a personification of winter, ice and snow. According to tradition, he paints windows with frosty, fern-like patterns during winter. He is also said to paint leaves and foliage red when autumn comes around. He is often, therefore, depicted with a brush and a paint-pot. The young poet, it seems, must have come across such an image in one of her picture books.

The chromographs
The young poet's attention is now drawn to the two 'gracious royal couples' depicted in the chromographs that hang on the parlour wall. The royal couples, she feels, look extremely cosy. They are dressed in the red often used by members of the British royal Family and wear 'warm' clothing that happens to be appropriate to the current winter weather.

The Queen and Princess wear dresses with 'ermine trains' that are designed to trail along behind them as they walk. ('Ermine' is in an expensive type of white fur that is derived from stoats). In the pictures, these trains are draped around the feet of the royal couples, making the royals seem even cosier: 'their feet were well wrapped up/ in the ladies' ermine trains'.

The young poet imagines that the royals have summoned Arthur to their court in London, where he will serve them as one of their pageboys: 'They invited Arthur to be/ the smallest page at court'. This could be a childish fantasy concocted by the speaker herself. However, it could also be the kind of gentle lie that an adult might tell a child to shield her from the truth about death. Perhaps Bishop's mother told her this fantastic story, wanting her to understand that Arthur will not be around anymore but also desiring to shield her from the harsh reality of death.

THEMES

MOMENTS OF EPIPHANY

Many of Bishop's poems are marked by moments of epiphany, moments when a person suddenly or gradually realises something profound and important about themselves and about the world.

In this poem, for instance, the narrator is a very young girl who has little or no understanding of death. No doubt, she has heard the words 'death' and 'dead' mentioned by the adults around her. But she doesn't fully grasp what death is, or what it actually means for someone to die.

We see this in her description of the stuffed loon. The poet describes how the loon has been silent since it was shot by her uncle: 'Since Uncle Arthur fired/ a bullet into him,/ he hadn't said a word'. The fact that this surprises the child, that she even considers it worth remarking on, indicates her lack of comprehension of the reality of death.

The loon, she declares, has 'kept its own counsel' where it sits on the marble-topped table. To keep one's own counsel means to keep one's thoughts to oneself. The young Elizabeth, then, seems to think that the stuffed loon could at any moment choose to break its silence, could burst into song or even speech. She seems to have no understanding, then, of what it means for something to die. She doesn't quite realise that the dead no longer go around talking and walking.

Now, however, her young cousin Arthur has passed away, and his body has been laid out in the parlour of the house. This forces the young poet, for the first time, to encounter death directly. She is forced into a terrible moment of awareness, one in which she must come to terms with this strange and unsettling concept.

Throughout the poem, however, the young poet attempts to shut out this uncomfortable new reality, to avoid thinking about death directly:

- In Stanza 2, for instance, she focuses on the stuffed loon, rather than on her cousin's body.
- Even when she is lifted up to place a flower in Arthur's hands, she tries to avoid contemplating his strange new state. She prefers to focus instead on the stuffed loon opposite him, or even on the coffin in which he lies.
- She notices the extreme whiteness of Arthur's corpse, but uses fantasy to explain away this pallor. She tells herself that Arthur is so white only because Jack Frost failed to paint him properly.
- In Stanza 5, she tells herself that Arthur won't be around anymore, not because he is dead, but because he is heading off to the court of King George in London, where he will work as the 'smallest page'.

Yet the young poet can't shut out death completely. For even as she considers the loon, Arthur seems to be at the back of her mind. For she describes the bird in terms more appropriate to her human cousin, telling us that he was 'caressable' and 'kept his own counsel'. It is also significant that the poet always refers to the dead bird as a 'he', rather than an 'it'.

We should also note how the word 'forever' is emphasised: by being bracketed off in line 33 and by being repeated in line 38. Despite the speaker's attempts to avoid thinking about death, she is becoming aware, on some level, that a final, irreversible change has taken place, that Arthur's eyes, 'shut up so tight', will never again be open.

At the poem's conclusion, however, the narrator seems to realise that this story just doesn't make sense: 'But how could Arthur go,/ clutching his tiny lily ... ?' Why was this obscure Canadian boy chosen for such an honour? And why is he required to undertake the journey to London alone, especially at this time of year when the roads are 'deep in snow'?

We get the impression that the fantastic stories she tells herself, about Jack Frost and about King George, aren't capable of shielding her from the truth. She seems to know, deep down, that the story about Arthur going off to be a page at court simply can't be true.

The poem concludes, then, with the young poet on the cusp of awareness. She is about to realise that death is something permanent and scary and unalterable. And such knowledge will change forever how she views the world.

CHILDHOOD

This is one of several poems where Bishop wonderfully captures the mentality of childhood.

- The speaker's childlike innocence comes across when she compares Arthur's corpse to a doll 'that hadn't been painted yet', and his coffin to 'a little frosted cake'.
- Her innocence comes across when she thinks of the loon's eyes as precious gemstones, 'much to be desired'. In reality, of course, they are only cheap pieces of glass that are used in taxidermy.
- The speaker's childhood innocence is also evident in how she believes, or almost believes, the story about Arthur bring summoned to serve as the 'smallest page at court'.
- We see the speaker's childlike imagination at work when she struggles to explain the whiteness of Arthur's corpse, and comes up with a vivid fantasy about Jack Frost and his paint brush.

The young poet thinks of Jack Frost painting Arthur's corpse, which makes her think of him painting the maple leaves, which in turn makes her think of a song entitled 'Maple Leaf (Forever)'. This popular song, written in 1867, served as one of Canada's unofficial national anthems. It has been suggested that in this phrase the young poet exhibits a childlike logic, her mind flitting unpredictably from one topic to the next.

THIS IS POETRY — ELIZABETH BISHOP

Filling Station

LINE BY LINE

The poet has been driving along some American highway. She has pulled in at some filling station on the roadside, no doubt to refuel and take a break from driving. This is a small, family-run station, a place where you can purchase fuel, top up on engine oil and perhaps get some basic repair work done.

The dirt
The poet is first struck by the filthy condition of the place, exclaiming 'Oh, but it is dirty!' The entire station is covered with a thin film of oil that is both black and 'translucent' or see-through. The poet finds this coating of oil 'disturbing', suggesting that it lends the station a depressing and unpleasant appearance.

Spillages probably account for some of this coating, and oil, no doubt, is transferred from workers' hands onto the various objects in the station. We can imagine that the air around the station is a mist of fumes and particulates that settles on everything. Over time then, oil has 'soaked' into every nook and cranny, has 'permeated' or seeped into every surface.

The filling station's owner has a grimy and unkempt appearance. He wears a pair of 'dirty' overalls that are a size too small for him and that catch him tight under the arms: 'cuts him under the arms'. The owner's sons, who 'assist' him in running the station, are also 'quite thoroughly dirty'. They are described as 'greasy', suggesting that they, like everything else in the station, are coated in grime and oil.

The station, then, seems hasn't been cleaned for years, if indeed it ever was.

The porch
The poet wonders if the owner and his family not only work but live here: 'Do they live in the station?' Beyond the station's petrol pumps there is a house with a 'cement porch' that seems to be their family home.

- A set of 'wickerwork' furniture has been arranged upon the porch. There is a 'wicker sofa' on which the family's dog rests in a 'comfy' fashion. There is also a 'taboret', which is a small portable cabinet.
- There is a 'doily' or decorative mat draped over the taboret. It is homemade, having been embroidered by hand rather than made in a factory.
- On the porch there is also a 'begonia', a garden plant with brightly coloured leaves. The poet describes this particular begonia as 'hirsute' or hairy, suggesting that it is a cheap and inelegant specimen.

The poet's description of the porch reinforces our sense of the station as a depressing and dreary environment. This furniture has also been badly damaged or 'crushed' over the years. Like everything else in the filling station, it has been saturated with oil: 'grease-impregnated'. The doily is described as 'dim', suggesting that it has a grubby, soiled appearance. Even the family dog is 'dirty'.

These lines also emphasise that there is a distinct lack of colour to the place. Every object in the station has been coated with oil and grime, making the objects' colours dull and uncertain.

The only truly colourful objects are some comic books, likely purchased by one of the owner's sons. These haven't been around long enough to acquire the coat of grime that covers everything else. They, therefore, stand out and 'provide/ the only note of color - / of certain color' in the filling station.

The Esso cans
The poet observes how the cans of oil to the front of the station have been lined up in a particular and deliberate manner. The word 'ESSO' is visible on the first, but the word is semi-obscured on the cans that follow, so that you can only see the '–SO'. As such, the text running along the row of cans reads 'ESSO-SO-SO-SO'.

These lines feature a playful use of personification, which presents cars or automobiles as being capable of human emotion. A human being might be left feeling 'high strung' after a long journey, experiencing physical tension and mental stress. A car, the poet playfully suggests, might also be left 'high strung' by such a journey, its engine strained and over-heated. A high strung human traveller might be soothed by the thought of a nice meal and a comfortable bed. A high strung automobile, the poet wittily suggests, might be soothed by the thought of an endless supply of engine oil that will ease and lubricate its overheated parts.

The contrast
The poet notices certain decorative touches, certain efforts to lend this dirty place a more pleasing appearance. She mentions the begonia, the doily, the wickerwork taboret and the deliberate arrangement of the Esso cans. The poet is baffled by these efforts at decoration. She uses the word 'why' no less than four times, indicating her confusion.

- These decorative touches strike her as 'extraneous' or utterly out of place in such a filthy environment.
- She is shocked that anyone would bother to make such an effort. For no amount of decoration could make this grim place seem any more attractive.
- All efforts at decoration, she suggests, are destined to be ruined. The doily is left soiled by the station's filthy air, the begonia is coated in oil, the wicker furniture is 'crushed', no doubt due to the neglectful and careless by the owner and his sons.

Yet, 'somebody' persists in making these futile efforts. Somebody continues to water the plant and carefully arrange the Esso cans. Somebody decided to place a taboret on the porch. Somebody used crochet and embroidery to create the doily, a detail that strikes the poet as being particularly out of place. Our assumption, of course, is that this 'somebody' is the station owner's wife. The wife, we assume, continues to do her best to make the station a more appealing place. The wife, it is worth noting, never appears in the poem. We assume that she remains in the house beyond the porch. But her presence is felt through the various decorative touches mentioned above.

THEMES

AN OBSERVER OF THE ORDINARY WORLD
In 'Filling Station', as in so many of her poems, we get a sense of Bishop as a keen observer of the ordinary world. She notices the specific qualities of the grime that covers everything in the station. She notices how the comic books provide the 'only note of color' and how the Esso cans have been carefully arranged. She notices how 'marguerites' or flowers have been embroidered in the doily's surface and even recognises the type of stitchwork used: 'Embroidered in daisy stitch/ with marguerites, I think'.

Bishop comes across as a relaxed and casual observer of the world around her. She addresses the reader in a conversational manner, as if we were travelling companions who had stopped with her at the station. We see this in the poem's opening line, when she exclaims about the filthy nature of the filling station and in line 14 when she wonders if the family actually live here. She even urges the reader to be 'careful with that match', as if we were about to light a cigarette and risk setting the entire oil-drenched place alight. This conversational tone is also evident when she jokes that the begonia must be oiled rather than watered, given its greasy, unpleasant appearance.

MOMENTS OF EPIPHANY
In many of Bishop's poems, such careful focus and description leads to some important insight or revelation. 'Filling Station' is no exception in this regard.

The poet, as we have seen, exhibits a rather snobbish attitude towards the filling station owner and his sons, painting an extremely unflattering portrait of these workers. They exhibit terrible personal hygiene, being 'all quite thoroughly dirty'. They are careless and neglectful, creating a filthy environment around themselves. They are depicted as crude, vulgar and uneducated. The term 'monkey-suit' even suggests that the poet views them as being a little animalistic.

Yet, even these unpleasant individuals have someone to love them. For the owner's wife, as we've seen, gives them care and attention, doing her best to make their working environment more pleasant.

The poet, then, is struck by a sudden moment of understanding. Everyone, she realises, has someone to nurture and take care of them. For if these lowly individuals can find somebody to love them, anyone can: 'Somebody loves us all'.

THIS IS POETRY — ELIZABETH BISHOP
In the Waiting Room

LINE BY LINE

The poem is set in Worcester, Massachusetts on the fifth of February, 1918. The young poet was six at the time and just three days away from her seventh birthday. America had joined the First World War in the previous year, and fighting would continue in Europe until the end of 1918. The winter of 1917 to 1918 was the coldest in Boston's weather history. According to weather records it stayed below 20 degrees from 29 December 1917 to 4 January 1918.

Bishop was living with her paternal grandparents in Worcester at the time when the poem is set. Although she was born in Worcester and spent the earliest years of her life there, she never felt at home in that city. She developed both asthma and eczema sores, which became so severe that she was confined to bed. 'In the Waiting Room' is set during this very unhappy and traumatic period in the young poet's life.

It is winter in Worcester, Massachusetts. The poet is aged six. She accompanies her Aunt Consuelo on a visit to the dentist. While her aunt is in with the dentist, the young poet sits quietly in the waiting room. The young poet is the only child in the room: the waiting room was 'full of grown-up people'. Everyone is wearing enormous winter coats, 'arctics and overcoats' to keep warm on this freezing cold winter evening. Lamps have been lit to brighten the room and magazines are stacked on a table to keep people amused or distracted while they wait.

The magazine

To the child, who must wait uncomfortably in a room full of 'grown-up people', the aunt seems to be in with the dentist for a very long time. In order to pass the time and feel less self-conscious the young poet takes a copy of National Geographic, and reads it. Bishop emphasises the fact that she 'could read' at this age. We get a sense of the child's pride at being able to do so. This poet also wishes us to know that when she says she 'read' the magazine, she means that she actually read all the words in the magazine.

National Geographic is a magazine that contains articles about science, geography, history and world culture. It features stunning pictures from places near and far, capturing the remarkable, beautiful and exotic features of the planet and the different peoples who inhabit it. Unsurprisingly, it's the photographs that really grab the young poet's attention and captures her imagination.

She describes some of the pictures featured in the magazine. There is a series of images of a volcano, at various stages of erupting. The first image shows the 'inside of a volcano' just as the eruption is commencing. Thick ash gathers inside the volcano as the pressure builds up in the magma chambers beneath. Bishop describes how the volcano is 'black and full of ashes' – we can imagine an aerial shot of the volcano, looking down into the dark vault at its centre. In the next image, the volcano is erupting; lava is spilling out over the top and running down the sides of the volcano in streams: 'then it was spilling over/ in rivulets of fire'.

There is a picture of 'Osa and Martin Johnson'. Martin Elmer Johnson and his wife Osa Helen Johnson were American adventurers and documentary filmmakers. In the first half of the 20th century, they captured the public's imagination through their films and books of adventure set in exotic lands. In the photograph that the young poet looks at, the couple are 'dressed in riding breeches,/ laced boots, and pith helmets'. We can imagine that they are on safari in Africa. The 'pith' helmet, also known as the 'safari' helmet, is a lightweight sun helmet made from the dried pith of a tropical plant.

The young poet is also exposed to shocking images of cannibals preparing a dead human body for consumption. The dead man is 'slung on a pole', ready to be suspended over a fire and cooked. A caption beneath the photograph refers to the dead man as 'Long Pig', a term used by a tribe in the Polynesian islands in the South Pacific for human flesh.

The young poet sees images of the Mangbetu people of the Democratic Republic of Congo. The babies in the photographs have 'pointed heads' that are 'wound round and round with string'. Members of the Mangbetu tribe considered the elongated skull to be a sign of higher intelligence and a status symbol among the ruling class. To ensure that their children developed the desired shape as they grew up, women in the community wrapped their babies' heads with tight cloths at birth.

The women in the Mangbetu tride also have wire wrapped around their necks, forcing their shoulders down and their heads up and giving the impression that their necks are considerably longer than normal. Stretching the neck in this manner was considered beautiful or desirable to the male members of the tribe. The young poet thinks how they resemble 'the necks of light bulbs'.

Although the stories and images she encounters are strange, frightening and disturbing, the young poet reads the magazine 'straight through'. She tells us that she is 'too shy to stop'. She is self-conscious, being the only child in a room full of adults. If she stops reading, she might have to engage with others in the room, they might talk to her out of politeness, but the young girl does not want this to happen. If she continues to read, just as we imagine all the other people in the room are doing, no one will bother with her. And so, even when she has read the magazine right through, the young poet studies 'the cover:/ the yellow margins, the date' – that will save her from looking at the other people around her.

A cry of pain

Suddenly she hears 'an oh! of pain' coming 'from inside'. It is her 'Aunt Consuelo's voice'. The cry of pain is brief and almost inaudible: 'not very long or loud'. The young poet is not 'at all surprised' that her aunt would make this noise. She says that, even at this young age, she knew that her aunt ' was/ a foolish, timid woman'.

But it was not the aunt who cried out in pain; it was the young poet, and this realisation startles the young girl: 'What took me/ completely by surprise/ was that it was me:/ my voice, in my mouth'. An involuntary cry has just erupted within her. The sound that has emerged which sounds exactly like her aunt's voice. This is why the girl immediately assumes that it is the aunt she has heard. But she quickly realises that it was her own voice that produced the sound, and is shocked to learn that her voice sounds just like her aunt's.

In order to understand why an involuntary cry of pain erupts within the young girl, we must remind ourselves of what she had recently endured.

She has had a traumatic childhood. Her father died before her first birthday, and her mother was committed to a mental hospital when she was five. She has been living with her grandparents in Worcester, but her health is rapidly deteriorating. She has developed asthma and severe eczema. There is a world war in progress, and the young girl, no doubt, is hearing reports about this each day. It is the worst winter on record. With all this going on, she finds herself alone in a room full of strange 'grown-ups'. And to top it all off, she has just been looking closely at some very disturbing and unsettling images. No wonder, it all gets to be too much for her. She has been trying desperately hard to hold it all in, to keep it all together, but it is too much for her body (or, indeed, her psyche, to take).

What surprises the young poet towards the end of the poem is that this cry of pain 'could have/ got loud and worse but hadn't'. With all that she has had to endure, and with the magnitude of the thoughts and questions that have been assaulting her mind, it would be understandable if the young girl had let out a loud scream and suffered some kind of breakdown or collapse.

The realisation

The fact that the sound of the young poet's voice resembles her aunt's triggers a number of unsettling thoughts and feelings. The young poet suddenly realises that she is not entirely unique. She shares a family voice with her aunt. In certain ways, therefore, she and her aunt are the same. This is the aunt that the young girl had just defined herself against. Her aunt is a 'foolish, timid' woman, whereas she is a bright, brave young girl. But now she has to identify with her aunt. It is as if they are both one, or that her sense of self has become fused with that of her aunt: 'Without thinking at all/ I was my foolish aunt'.

The poet is troubled by the notion that she is similar to her 'foolish' aunt and tries to focus on what it is that makes her unique. She is an 'I', an 'Elizabeth'. But she suddenly realises that everyone is an 'I', everyone has the individuality and the rich inner experience that she has. And the fact that she is an 'Elzabeth' offers little consolation, because of course there are many, many Elizabeths in the world.

The young poet realises that, if she is like her aunt, she is also similar to the other people in the waiting room, members of the wider community to which she belongs. She must also share traits, customs and characteristics with these people: 'you are one of them'. This thought frightens and perplexes the young girl. Why should she be just like them and not entirely unique and different? 'Why should you be one, too?' She does not even want to see what this entails or means: 'I scarcely dared to look/ to see what it was I was'. The young poet is tempted to raise her eyes and to look directly at or gaze upon that which she is destined to become – but she cannot bring herself to do so and instead casts a furtive 'sidelong glance'. Even then, she cannot lift her eyes higher than the knees of the people sitting close by.

The realisation that she is somehow similar to the strangers in the waiting room leads to the notion that she must also share somethings with the rest of humanity. It is as if the poet is suddenly seeing a web of connection that unites us all. Every person in the world is an 'I' and experiences the world just as the poet experiences it. Every person has similar needs and experiences the same emotions.

The young poet suddenly realises that she is in some ways the same as all the strange and alien people she saw in the magazine. This is especially true perhaps of the women with the 'awful hanging breasts'. The poet realises that she will grow up to become a woman. Her body will mature and change and she too will make efforts – albeit different ones from those made by the women in the magazine – to conform to the required standards of beauty. It turns out, then, that she has more in common with these women than she could ever than she could have ever imagined only a few short moments ago.

Great anxiety
The realisation that she shares traits with her 'foolish aunt' and with everyone else who inhabits the planet has a dramatic effect on the young poet. She is overwhelmed by the thoughts and questions that flood her mind, and things suddenly seem to be spinning out of control. She describes feeling as if she is suddenly 'falling off/ the round, turning world/ into cold, blue black space'. The 'turning world' represents the normal, everyday world that the young poet inhabits. In that world she is sure of the facts and knows what to do. But 'blue, black space' represents the vast unknown and the unknowable. This is where human understanding and reason falter and fail. The young poet feels as if she is about to fall from a place of certainty into this other, terrifying realm of uncertainty.

The young poet also describes what we might consider a panic attack. Suddenly, the light in the room seems too intense, and she begins to feel feverish, or 'too hot'. It is as if she is going to black out. Bishop describes the sensation of one enormous black wave after another crashing down upon the waiting room.

In order to arrest or control this – and perhaps to disguise the fact that she is experiencing such anxiety – the young poet keeps her eyes 'glued to the cover' of the magazine, focusing intently on the name and date. She also tries to steady herself by reminding herself that her birthday will be in three days. She latches on to this fact in an effort to 'stop/ the sensation of falling off/ the round, turning world'. But thoughts about her identity keep coming, and she tries desperately to make sense of it all.

The young poet realises that she will probably never have a stranger or more profound realisation than this in her life. She will never experience anything else that will so profoundly alter the way she thinks about herself and her place in the world: 'I knew that nothing stranger/ had ever happened, that nothing/ stranger could ever happen'.

The ordeal ends
And just as suddenly as the whole ordeal began, it ends. The poet somehow calms or steadies herself – or perhaps, the moment just passes naturally. It is as if her mind has refocused, has snapped out of one mode of thinking and resumed normal thought. The poet says that she was 'back in it'. She is back in the room, and the spinning and falling sensations have ceased. The poet re-orientates herself quickly. She remembers that the 'War is on'; that is is 'still the fifth/ of February, 1918'; that she is in 'Worcester, Massachusetts'; and that outside the warm and lamp-lit waiting room it is night and cold, and there is 'slush' on the ground.

The statement that 'The War was on' refers to the fact that World War I was still going on. But it can also be understood to mean that the young poet has now engaged with the world in a very different way. She has undergone a profound, life-changing experience and has been transformed by it. She leaves the waiting room a different person. She is no longer the innocent child who entered the room and and thought she was unique and special. She realises that she is one of billions of people inhabiting the planet and that she is no more unique or special than anyone else – in fact, she is essentially just the same as everyone else. She must now fight to differentiate herself, to not conform, perhaps. This is also a 'War' of sorts, and she now knows that she is very much 'in it'.

THEMES

CHILDHOOD
This is one of several poems where Bishop wonderfully captures the mentality of childhood.
- The young speaker exhibits a child-like shyness. She is unable to look the other waiting room occupants in the eye.
- There is a childish self-consciousness in the fact that she keeps reading the magazine, even though it makes her feel very uncomfortable. It is as if she feels she is being observed and judged by the other people in the room.
- Her childhood innocence is evident in her horrified reaction to the naked women in *National Geographic*.
- Such innocence is also evident when she uses certain childish phrases like 'The waiting room/ Was full of grown-up people'.
- We see it in her childishly proud declaration that she could read.

AN OBSERVER OF THE ORDINARY WORLD
'In the Waiting Room', just like so many of Bishop's poems, gives us a sense of the poet as a keen observer of the ordinary world. The young poet seems to take in everything around her, observing how the waiting room 'was full of of grown-up people,/ arctics and overcoats,/ lamps and magazines'. Even though she is too shy or uncomfortable to raise her eyes and look the 'grown-up people' in the face, she carefully observes their 'shadowy gray knees,/ trousers and skirts and boots/ and different pairs of hands'.

The young poet's keen eye for detail is perhaps particularly evident in her reading of the magazine, which she uses to avoid having to engage with any of the other people in the waiting room. She reads the magazine 'straight through' and studies each of the images carefully, noting the manner in which the explorers Osa and Martin Johnson are dressed ('riding breeches,/ laced boots, and pith helmets' and observing how the necks of the women resemble 'light bulbs'.

A POET OF EMOTIONAL RESTRAINT
Bishop is well known as a poet of emotional restraint. Her poetry tends to focus on observation and description rather than direct emotional expression. We see this at the beginning of 'In the Waiting Room', where, as we've seen, the young poet is preoccupied with the various details of the waiting room and its occupants.

As the poem goes on, however, the poet finds herself overcome by emotions that strike her as alien and inexplicable. Initially, she tries to keep these feelings in check, to keep her mind firmly focused on the external world of the waiting room. But the emotions triggered within her prove too strong. They threaten to overwhelm her, forcing her for a moment to lose her sense of self-control. A cry erupts within her and for a brief but terrifying moment the young girl fears that she is about to black out from the waves of a panic attack. But the young poet manages to regain control just before this happens. She is able to fix her attention again on the external world and focus on the fact that 'The War was on' and that outside 'were night and slush and cold,/ and it was still the fifth of February, 1918'.

MOMENTS OF EPIPHANY
When she enters the waiting room, the young girl has a rather simple and definite idea about who she is: she is six, she is young, she can read. She clearly defines herself against both her aunt and the other people in the waiting room. Her aunt is 'foolish' and 'timid', whereas the young poet is smart, self-composed and self-assured. The other people sitting close by in the waiting room are 'grown-up', whereas she is a child.

What the young poet does not realise is that her careful study of the magazine, with all its bizarre and unsettling images, is not just distracting her from the awkwardness of being in the waiting room; it is also slowly causing or building on some inner trauma or anguish that finally erupts in the involuntary emission of a cry.

The young poet is thrown into total consternation when she associates her voice with that of her aunt, and it begins to dawn on her that she and her aunt are not so different; in fact, they are in many ways the same. This leads to a disturbing realisation that she is not entirely unique, and that she shares traits and characteristics not only with her 'foolish, timid' aunt, but with the strangers in the waiting room and, indeed, the entire human race.

Essentially, the young poet is reaching an understanding that she is a member of the vast human race that populates the planet – and that there is more that unites her with every other human being (especially the female members of the population) than sets her apart. Whereas at the start of the poem the young poet focused on what she believed made her unique, she now realises that she has more in common with everyone else. It is as if she has undergone a procedure – something far more distressing than a filling or a root canal – that has altered her outlook and the way she thinks about herself. It is as if a door within her mind has been thrown open and can never be shut again.

Emily Dickinson

Themes

Nature

In poem after poem, Dickinson celebrates the beauty of the natural world. In 'A Bird, came down the Walk', for instance, the poet lovingly highlights the bird's bead-like eyes, the softness of the feathers on its 'Velvet Head', its unfurling wings and the exceptional grace and elegance with which it moves through the air.

'I could bring You Jewels', meanwhile, celebrates the beauty of a little flower the poet has noticed growing in a nearby meadow, the poet detailing the intensity of its 'Topaz' petals and bright green stem. 'I taste a liquor never brewed' finds the poet revelling in summer days when the meadows are fragrant with life and growth, when birds, bees and butterflies flutter about in the pleasant summer heat.

'A narrow Fellow in the Grass', too, reflects the poet's love of the natural world. Its farm-boy speaker clearly loves nature and spends much of his time outside. He proclaims his affection for the various creatures of the earth, referring to them as 'Nature's People'. This implies that he has a give-and-take friendship with many of the birds and animals in his locality: 'I know, and they know me'.

Dickinson, it must be noted, is often playful in her depiction of the natural world. 'A Bird, came down the Walk', for instance, is cute and almost comedic in its depiction of the little traffic jam that occurs on the garden path, the bird darting aside to let the beetle pass him by: 'And then hopped sidewise to the Wall/ To let a Beetle pass'. 'I taste a liquor never brewed' is similarly light-hearted, especially in its depiction of the humming-bird becoming so drunk on nectar, air and dew that it reels from flower to flower the way a drunk person might reel from bar to bar.

'I could bring You Jewels', too, is mischievous in its approach to nature, specifically in the poet's exaggeration of the flower's charms. This little bloom, she declares, would make a more fitting gift than even the most spectacular piece of jewellery, blazing as it does with the intensity of emerald and topaz.

Dickinson is a poet who persistently identifies the extraordinary in the everyday. 'A Bird, came down the Walk', 'I could bring You Jewels' and 'I taste a liquor never brewed' aren't inspired by conventionally magnificent spectacles. Instead, they suggest that even the most mundane sight, such as a bird walking down an ordinary garden path, devouring a worm and taking flight, can appear extraordinary.

'I taste a liquor never brewed', for instance, reminds us of the intoxicating beauty that can be found in an ordinary field in summertime. 'I could bring You Jewels' goes even further in its praise of the everyday, the poet claiming that a wildflower growing near her house is more special and exotic than berries from the Bahamas or the colours of Vera Cruz. Dickinson's poetry, then, reminds us again and again that beauty and mystery can be found in the ordinary world around us, if only we take the time to stop and look.

In her poetry, Dickinson comes across as someone intensely sensitive toward the natural world. This is especially evident in 'I taste a liquor never brewed'. We sense that the poet, like the hummingbird, was capable of getting 'high' on nature, that the sights, sounds and smells of the natural world induced in her a sense of ecstasy and intoxication.

A similarly manic enjoyment of nature is depicted in 'The Soul has Bandaged moments', where the poet portrays herself dancing 'like a Bomb' in a 'delirious' response to nature's beauty. Many readers feel that perhaps there is something a little unhealthy about this 'hyper' response to the natural world, as if it were the 'manic' flip side to the numb 'depression' that Dickinson describes in many of her poems.

'I could bring You Jewels' and 'A Bird, came down the Walk', also highlight this sensitivity. The conclusion of 'A Bird, came down the Walk', with its strange, dense web of imagery, captures the sense of awe experienced by the poet as she watches the bird take wing. In 'I could bring You Jewels', meanwhile, the poet is clearly deeply affected by her observation of the little flower, declaring that there's no better gift she could find for her beloved: 'Better—Could I bring?'

'There's a certain Slant of light' is one poem where Dickinson focuses on nature's bleaker and more depressing aspects. The poem highlights the fact that the natural world can sometimes have a negative impact on our state of mind, altering our psyches as it brings us the worst kind of 'internal difference'.

Both 'A Bird, came down the Walk' and 'A narrow Fellow in the Grass', emphasise the brutality and danger that exist in the natural world. In 'A Bird, came down the Walk', the bird savagely devours a worm and is itself in a fearful state, being permanently on the look-out for potential predators. The speaker in 'A narrow Fellow in the Grass', despite his love of animals, is not naive about the dangers of the natural world. He knows that certain species of grass-snake are dangerous and not to be trusted, as evidenced by the fear he experiences when he encounters one coiled up or sliding through the meadow.

The Workings of the Mind

Dickinson's great subject, according to several critics, is the human mind itself. We see this in 'I heard a Fly buzz', which movingly depicts a mind disintegrating at the point of death. There is something powerful about the repetition of 'and then' in these lines, as the speaker mechanically lists the stages of her mental collapse. The phrase is repeated three times, suggesting a relentless and unstoppable process of shutting down, one that, once it commences, cannot be stopped or delayed. As we read, we can almost feel the speaker's consciousness dwindling away.

Dickinson is a poet especially gifted when it comes to the portrayal of mental anguish. 'There's a certain Slant of light', for instance, depicts a mind 'oppressed' by a formidable mental burden, one that brings with it great inner 'Hurt' or psychological damage. This is a state of mind that involves being altered on the inside, in the depths of our psyche, 'where the meanings' reside.

'After great pain, a formal feeling comes', meanwhile, details the disturbingly numb mental state that occurs in the wake of great trauma. Although the 'Pain' of the poem's title has ended, its departure brings no relief or joy. Instead, there is almost a total lack of feeling and emotion. The speaker's body behaves as if it is living – but there is something stiff and mechanical about its actions and movements, as if it is just going through the motions without any thought or care: 'The Feet, mechanical, go round'.

The poem finishes on a rather disturbing note, suggesting that the speaker might not survive this post-traumatic period. There is a danger that the mind might never again spark with life, that the body will not be re-ignited with energy and vitality. There is a risk that the speaker will just descend further into 'stupor', that the numbness will utterly paralyse her body and her mind.

'The Soul has Bandaged moments' presents us with someone who experiences great highs and lows, who seems to swing, rapidly enough, from utter dejection to ecstatic joy. It suggests someone who is bi-polar, someone whose mood alternates between extreme euphoria and deep depression. The poem vividly captures such wild mood swings. Such mood swings are vividly brought to life by the images that Dickinson uses to portray the soul, first, as a prisoner confined in a terrifying dungeon, and then as someone dancing 'like a Bomb, abroad'.

It is surely in 'I felt a Funeral, in my Brain', however, that we find Dickinson's most unforgettable portrayal of mental suffering. Here the speaker finds herself confronting what can only be described as a nervous breakdown, imagining that a funeral is taking place inside her brain: 'I felt a Funeral in my brain'. The speaker, it seems, can't actually see the funeral. Instead, she feels and hears this terrible event, experiencing it through the sounds made by the mourners and through the vibrations that accompany each noise. It's as if she can hear, but not see, what's going on inside her own head.

Unlike 'After great pain' and "There's a certain Slant of light', "Hope' is the thing with feathers" has an uplifting message, describing as it does an inner resource of some kind that we can all draw on to help us get through such difficult times. Even at our lowest, the poem suggests, a sense of hope prevails, encouraging us to persevere.

Death

'I heard a Fly buzz', as we've seen, movingly portrays the process of death, showing how the speaker's sense of vision, and her sense of logic, blur as consciousness ebbs away. The poem is bleakly witty in its depiction of the indignity that surrounds the speaker's passing. The speaker has prepared for death, she has made her will and gathered her family around her. The moment of her demise is intended to be the solemn climax of a life well lived.

The last thing she hears, however, is not the soothing words of her family but the buzzing of a fly. The last thing she sees is not the faces of her loved ones but a fly floating in front of her. The speaker's last experience in this world is of a miserable and insignificant insect 'stumbling' as it buzzes around the room. Many readers feel that the fly's interruption makes the moment of the speaker's death seem a little ridiculous, robbing it of its intended grace and dignity.

'I heard a Fly buzz' doesn't specifically deny the existence of the afterlife. And yet, when the speaker's vision fades to black at the end of the poem, we are left with the distinct impression that the speaker now feels that this black oblivion is all there is, that no afterlife awaits her. The last thing the speaker 'witnesses' is not the glorious arrival of the 'King' but the uncertain buzzing of a stumbling fly.

'I taste a liquor never brewed' is much more positive in its depiction of life after death, as the bird is welcomed into Heaven by saints and angels. Heaven is memorably depicted as a joyful and carefree city of rest. The bird finds itself in the presence of the 'Sun', which, as we have seen, is generally taken to be Christ himself.

Heaven is depicted as a very real place, as a town whose inhabitants live in houses with windows, wear hats, and celebrate the arrival of each new soul. This positive and light-hearted depiction of the afterlife contrasts sharply with many of the other poems in which Dickinson addresses the themes of death and dying.

THIS IS POETRY   EMILY DICKINSON

'Hope' is the thing with feathers –

LINE BY LINE

Hope is the feeling that events will turn out for the best, that no matter how difficult or dire our circumstances, all will be good in the end. We often encourage those who are going through trying times not to lose hope. In this poem, Dickinson attempts to define what she understands hope to be and reflects on the role it plays in our lives.

Stanzas 2 and 3
The poet imagines life in terms of a voyage or a journey that we must each undertake. As we journey, we inevitably encounter challenges and hardships. The poet likens such hardships and trying times to adverse weather conditions, to strong winds and storms. Sometimes the hardships that we must endure are extreme. The poet uses remote and inhospitable landscapes to represent such times in life. She imagines being in the coldest place possible, some kind of freezing Arctic landscape: 'the chillest land'. She imagines being adrift on a sea that is as far from home as possible: 'on the strangest Sea'.

However, we are never alone as we journey through life. Every step of the way we are accompanied by a sense of hope. The poet imagines hope to be a bird that accompanies us through the good times and the bad. The bird is constantly singing to us, keeping our spirits up and up and encouraging us to go on. Its tune is most appreciated when times are especially tough: 'And sweetest – in the Gale – is heard'. It is then that we most need to hear its uplifting music, to feel encouraged to journey on.

Hope is a strong and resilient presence in our lives. It is capable of surviving and withstanding gales and storms. There is a sense in which hope is an indestructible force. No matter what the world throws at it, it survives. This little creature never stops singing 'at all'.

Yet, Dickinson does hint at the possibility of hope being damaged, saying that it would have to be a 'sore' storm to 'abash' this little bird. The term 'sore' suggests violence and severity, but it also suggests malice. It is as if such a storm would be intent on harming the bird, that it is 'sore' or smarting from something that causes it to act in this cruel and vengeful manner. To 'abash' is to destroy the self-confidence, poise, or self-possession of someone or something. So, the effect of such a storm on this bird would be to make it meek and silent.

Yet the phrase 'And sore must be the storm' suggests that no such storm can exist. It is much like the expression, 'It's an ill wind that blows no good', which we might take to mean that there is no situation so bad that somebody does not benefit from it.

In the poem's final lines, Dickinson describes hope as a selfless creature, something that gives us so much but asks for nothing in return. All the while that she was journeying, this 'little Bird' never asked her for a single thing. Even when things were at their worst, 'in Extremity', the bird did not look for 'a crumb' from the poet.

Stanza 1

The first four lines of the poem raise a number of interesting questions about hope and the poet's understanding of it. Why does the poet place the word 'Hope' in quote marks at the start of the poem? Hope is an abstract concept. It is not something we can easily identify or define. The poet, therefore, places the term 'Hope' in quote marks to convey the fact that it is not something of which we have a sure or ready grasp.

Why does the poet say initially that it is the 'thing with feathers', rather than simply a bird? Again, this stems from the fact that the poet is attempting to define a complex, abstract concept. She begins by thinking of the term in the broadest manner possible – It is a 'thing' – before getting more specific.

It is interesting that the first image the poet attaches to or associates with hope is 'feathers': ''Hope' is the thing with feathers'. We instantly, of course, think of a bird – What else has feathers? But the poet does not wish to simply say that hope is a bird. Rather, she wants tease out the manner in which hope operates and features in our lives.

The word 'feathers' introduces the notion of flight, of something that can take to the air and, conversely, descend from above. It also suggests that hope is not a part of who we essentially are; it is a separate entity.

Why does the poet say that hope 'perches in the soul'? As we have just suggested, the poet presents hope as something independent of us. It is a feathered 'thing' that somehow inhabits us. The manner in which it does this is interesting. The poet says that hope 'perches' within us. To perch is to alight or roost on an object, typically a branch or horizontal bar. This implies that hope is somehow separate from us but has come to rest or reside within us.

Dickinson's description of hope as a bird perching in the soul is also interesting because it connects or associates something physical with something that is non-physical or abstract. Our soul is the non-physical aspect of our selves; yet somehow this 'thing with feathers' comes to settle within it.

Why does hope sing a 'tune without the words'? Hope does not convey or deliver a specific message to us. It moves us, inspires or generates a feeling within us, much as music without any lyrics does. Hope does not, for example, tell us to get up and keep going; rather, it lifts our spirits, gives us a sense that things will work out for the best, without articulating how or why.

Why does the poet say that hope 'never stops' singing? This suggests that hope is a permanent force or presence in the world. It also suggests that, while hope resides within us, its message is constant. We may not always hear it it can, perhaps, be drowned out by fear and doubt – but it is always singing to us. Dickinson emphasises hope's permanence by telling us never stops 'at all'. This suggests that there is no imaginable force or circumstance in the world capable of overwhelming or silencing hope. No matter how bad things get, hope will continue to sing; we just need to attune ourselves to its song.

FOCUS ON STYLE

The poem consists of three four line stanzas with an ABAB rhyme scheme.

The poem is centred on the extended metaphor of life as a journey that we must each undertake. It is a journey that will take us to strange, uncomfortable and terrifying places. The freezing landscapes and unfamiliar seascapes represent such times and places in our lives. We also encounter many hardships and setbacks along the way. These are represented in the poem by storms and violent winds.

The journey that each of us must take through life is essentially a solitary one. But Dickinson says that we are never entirely alone in life. We each have a special form of companion with us on our difficult journey – our sense of hope. The poet imagines hope to be a bird that is housed within our souls, constantly singing to us and keeping our spirits up, even in the most trying times.

THEMES

THE WORKINGS OF THE MIND

The 'chillest land' and the 'strangest Sea'. Both settings suggest periods of great psychological anguish. We might imagine that dwelling in or journeying through the 'chillest land' represents moments when we are almost numb or frozen with horror, or perhaps just psychologically exhausted. This idea of being frozen or numb with the cold is also present in 'After great pain', where the poet likens the sort of stupor or mental numbness that follows periods of intense anguish and suffering to the experience of someone freezing in the snow.

The 'strangest Sea' might represent times in our life when we feel utterly isolated and alone, cut off from the rest of the world. We are reminded here, perhaps, of the description in 'I Felt a Funeral' of being 'Wrecked' and 'solitary' in some strange and alien environment. However, unlike 'After great Pain' and 'I Felt a Funeral', ''Hope' is the thing with feathers' has an uplifting message, describing as it does some inner resource that we can all draw on to help us get through such difficult times. Even at our lowest, the poem suggests, a sense of hope prevails, encouraging us to persevere.

THIS IS POETRY — EMILY DICKINSON

There's a certain Slant of light

LINE BY LINE

In this poem, Dickinson focuses on a particular variety of sunlight: 'There's a certain Slant of light'. Such light is typically evident on 'Winter Afternoons'. It has a cold, hard quality and is depressing rather than cheerful. The poet describes a 'Slant of light', and we can imagine this harsh glow angling out of the sky, breaking through the cloud cover in slanted shafts.

Damage

The light, we're told, 'oppresses' all those who witness it. Dickinson's use of the verb 'oppress' suggests that the light brings us misery and hardship. All those exposed to its glow find themselves suffering.

The damage caused by the light is psychological, rather than physical. It it brings a 'Hurt' that leaves no bodily wounds or injuries: 'We can find no scar'. Instead the light causes 'internal difference', changing us in a sinister fashion on the inside. It alters our very minds and souls, the place 'Where the Meanings are'.

Using a memorable turn of phrase, Dickinson refers to the light as the 'Seal Despair', suggesting how it robs us of all hope. All those exposed to its cruel glow find themselves sealed in their own anguish, trapped in utter hopelessness. They're unable to escape from, or even express, the negative emotions the light brings with it.

Oppressive

Dickinson's use of the verb 'oppress' also brings with it the idea of control and subjection, suggesting that the light dominates us in the same way that a tyrannical king might dominate his subjects. The light is presented as a cruel tyrant, from whose dominance no one can escape.

The winter light is, in many respects, worse than any human oppressor, like a corrupt president or abusive overlord. For such a human oppressor might be shown the error of their ways, might be taught to be a kinder and more compassionate ruler. The winter light, however, cannot be reasoned with in such a fashion. No one can 'teach' it anything: 'None may teach it- Any'. It is a merciless and implacable force of nature.

Dickinson uses an unexpected simile to capture the light's oppressive quality, comparing it to the hymns sung in a cathedral. Such 'Cathedral Tunes', she suggests, possess a great 'Heft' or weight, which suggests the sombre nature of their melodies. We imagine not uplifting gospel music, but gloomy and monotonous Latin psalms echoing through a cold cathedral. According to the poet, the winter light is similar to this liturgical music in that it 'oppresses' all exposed to it, dominating their minds and leading them into depression.

> We sense that Dickinson is punning on the word 'certain' in the poem's opening line. In one sense, of course, certain means specific or particular. The poet is referring to one specific type of light. But 'certain' also means definite and determined, suggesting the light's relentless and merciless quality.

Affliction
The winter light is presented as if it were some airborne plague or a form of lethal radiation. The poet describes it as an 'affliction/ Sent us of the Air', as though it were an illness or disease, floating down through the winter air to torment us. The 'Hurt' that it brings to us, therefore, can be described as 'Heavenly' because it originates in the sky over our heads, often referred to as the heavens.

In the presence of this affliction, the landscape becomes incredibly still and silent. Yet, this is more an eerie stillness than a moment of soothing tranquillity. For the poet says that the landscape seems to 'listen', and even the shadows seem to 'hold their breath'. The entire countryside seems filled with fear and trepidation, as if nature itself were cowering before the 'Hurt' that the light brings with it.

The poem concludes with a note of relief, as the speaker describes the departure of the light. We greet the disappearance of the light with an extraordinary sense of relief. We are as glad, the poet suggests, as someone who has survived a brush with death: 'When it goes, 'tis like the Distance/ On the look of Death'

FOCUS ON STYLE

Form
'There's a certain Slant of light', like most of Dickinson's poems, uses four-line stanzas with an ABCB rhyme scheme. The poem is marked by the concision common to Dickinson's poetry, in which words and phrases are regularly omitted. Such compression is especially evident in line 9: 'None may teach it   Any –'.

It's possible, as we've seen, to read this line as suggesting that light cannot be taught anything, cannot be reasoned with or be diverted away from its purpose.

The same line also suggests, however, that the effect of the light cannot be explained to anyone who has not experienced it. The light's misery cannot be explained to someone who has never experienced its glow. You have to see it for yourself.

Riddling and Paradoxical Language
'There's a certain Slant of light', like many of Dickinson's poems, is distinguished by riddling and paradoxical language. There are several instances where the poem subverts or unsettles our expectations.

Light, usually associated with hope and growth, is depicted here as a grim and oppressive force. Music – by definition airy and weightless – is presented as having 'Heft' or weight. The 'Cathedral Tunes', and by extension the winter light, is depicted as something solid and tactile; pressing down upon the speaker like a burden she is forced to carry.

The concept of 'Heavenly Hurt' is another startling reversal of our expectations. Heaven, which we usually think of as a place of bliss and calm, is presented as a source of misery and suffering. The phrase is an example of an oxymoron, an expression where the adjective appears to contradict the noun it describes. In this case, 'Heaven' is not a concept that we usually associate with 'Hurt'.

Metaphor, Simile, Figures of Speech
In this final stanza, Dickinson uses 'personification' to describe the atmosphere of nervous tension that fills the landscape when the light shines down. (Personification occurs when the poet gives human qualities to inanimate objects.) In this instance, the landscape 'listens' and the shadows 'hold their breath,' just as a human being would in the presence of a force as oppressive and menacing as the winter light.

It could be argued that in this stanza death itself is personified. Death seems to be represented as a person who approaches us when we are close to dying. As our life slips away, death's 'look' – or face – comes close to us. If we recover, however, his face recedes into the 'distance'.

Atmosphere
This is a poem that skilfully conjures an atmosphere of dread and trepidation, especially in the final stanza with its depiction of nature itself fearfully waiting for the oppressive light to vanish. We are presented with a dark and shadowy landscape, that holds its breath beneath the dreary and oppressive winter light. The presence of the 'Shadows' indicates how gloomy and dreary the landscape appears beneath the pallid sun.

THEMES

THE WORKINGS OF THE MIND
This poem powerfully depicts a state of mental anguish. The poet describes a state of mind that involves being 'oppressed' by a great mental burden, being affected by inner 'Hurt' or psychological damage and being sealed within 'Despair' and bereft of hope.

It's a state of mind that involves being altered on the inside, in the depths of our psyche, 'Where the Meanings' reside. The term meaning is being used in two different senses here. On one level, it refers to understanding, to our ability to make sense of the words, concepts and actions that surround us. The light, then, interferes with this capacity, making it difficult for us to make sense of our environments. But the idea of meaning as purpose or significance is also involved here, suggesting that those exposed to the light's harsh glow lose all sense of purpose; for them, life becomes a pointless and monotonous chore.

Is it realistic for Dickinson to declare that such a negative state of mind is caused by the malevolent sunlight pouring from the sky? Many of us, no doubt, find the watery winter sunlight a bit of a downer. But must it induce such crippling despair?

Perhaps Dickinson is describing, with surprising accuracy, what we would today call clinical depression, with its sense of oppressive hopelessness. Those who suffer from such a disorder are often highly sensitive to atmospheric conditions and find their condition worsening in winter, with its pale, weak sunlight.

RELIGION
It's tempting to view this poem as presenting an unusually bleak view of religion. There's a sense in which the winter light is presented as a punishment sent from God himself:
- The phrase 'Heavenly Hurt', on this reading, suggests that the light has been sent down from Heaven to do us harm: 'Heavenly Hurt, it gives us'.
- The description of the light as an 'affliction', meanwhile, reminds us of the plagues sent to punish the unfaithful in the Old Testament of the Bible.
- The description of the light as 'imperial' suggests that it originates with God himself, who might be regarded as the 'emperor' of the entire universe.
- The Book of Revelation describes how the opening of four sealed parchments releases four different forms of suffering - war, famine, plague and death - into the world. Now, it seems, another seal has been opened, unleashing the winter light and the 'Despair' that comes with it.
- It is perhaps not surprising, therefore, that the poet associates this grim winter light with hymns sung in a cathedral.

God, then, is presented as merciless and vindictive, rather than gentle and forgiving. He sends the winter light into the world, presumably as a punishment for humanity's failings. But this is a collective and indiscriminate retribution. The light oppresses all who are exposed to it, irrespective of whether or not they have tried to live a good life. Both the sinner and the good person will experience the 'Heavenly Hurt'. The God of this poem, then, is a cold and judgemental overlord rather than a loving father who cherishes each of his children individually.

NATURE
Many of Dickinson's poems depict nature as a source of joy and inspiration. 'There's a certain Slant of light', however, focuses on nature's bleaker and more depressing aspects. As we've seen, the poem suggests that the natural world can have a negative impact on our states of mind, altering our psyches as it brings us the worst kind of 'internal difference'. Once again we find Dickinson focusing on nature in its everyday aspects, finding terror not in an earthquake or tsunami but in a simple slant of light. The poem reinforces our sense of the poet as someone especially sensitive to the natural world, someone whose entire mood and mind-set can be altered by the quality of light outside her window.

I Felt a Funeral, in my Brain

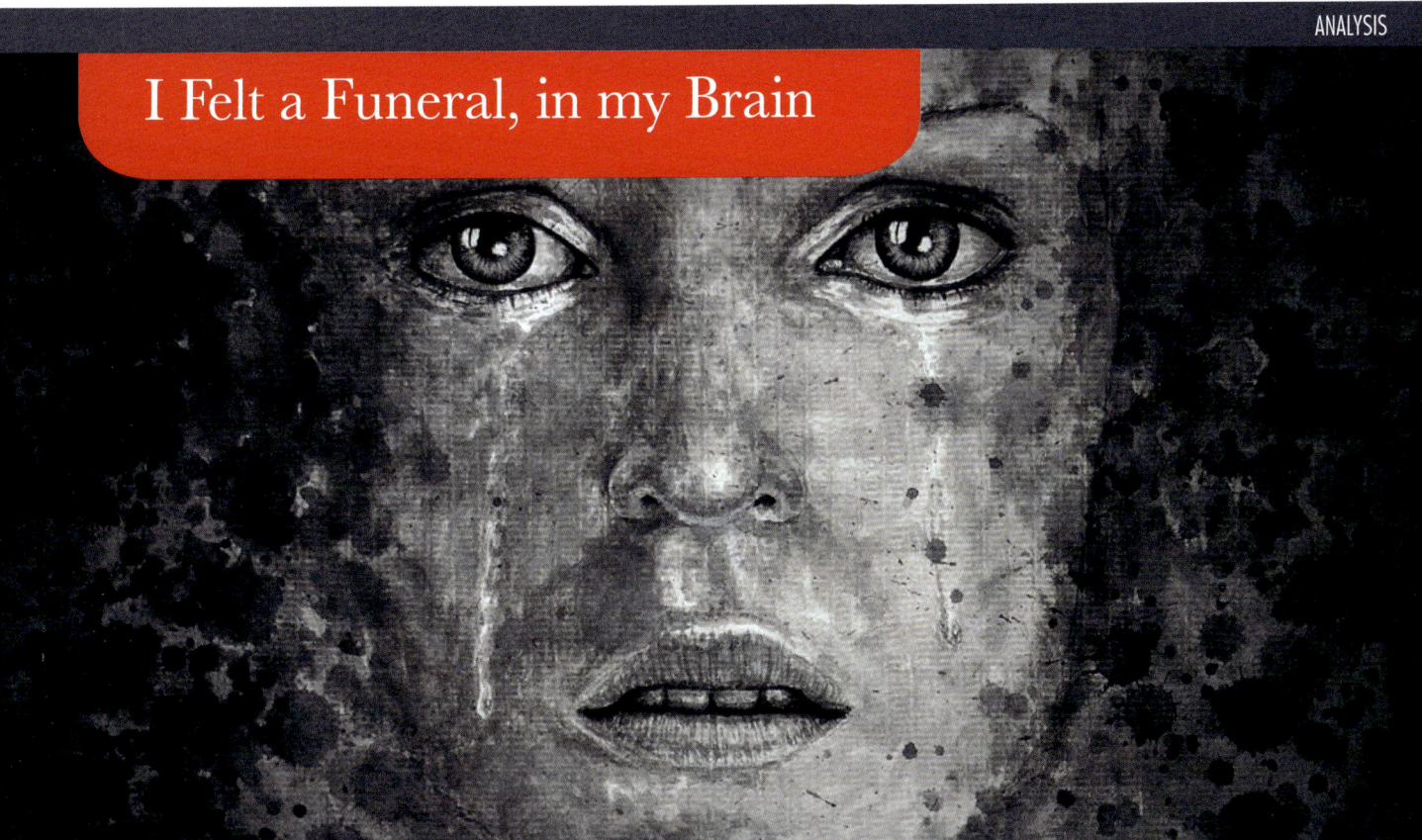

LINE BY LINE

Emily Dickinson is a poet who explores both the highs and lows of human experience. In this, one of her darkest poems, the speaker finds herself confronting what can only be described as a nervous breakdown. In the throes of this episode she experienced the sensation that a funeral was taking place inside her brain: 'I felt a Funeral, in my Brain'. The speaker, it seems, couldn't actually see this event taking place. For she provides no visual description of the mourners or the coffin. Instead, she feels and hears this terrible happening, experiencing it through the sounds made by the mourners and through the vibrations that accompany each noise. It's as if she can hear, but not see, what's going on inside her head.

Stanza 1

The speaker describes how she heard the mourners milling around before the funeral service proper began. According to the speaker, the mourners were 'treading' as they meandered 'to and fro', suggesting that they walked in a heavy and deliberate fashion. Furthermore, the mourners, we're told, 'Kept treading', which suggests that their pre-service mingling went on for a long time.

The speaker, then, felt these mourners stomping around inside her brain. She heard every heavy footstep echo inside her skull. She felt the impact of each footfall pressing into the grey matter of her brain. This is a startling image of invasion and violation, one that powerfully captures the pressure experienced by the speaker in this moment of psychological extremity. The speaker describes feeling that 'Sense was breaking through'.

This enigmatic declaration can be read in several ways. Perhaps 'Sense' refers to some meaning or message, some important lesson the speaker felt she was about to learn. She might have felt that something important was about to be made clear to her, like a ray of sunlight 'breaking through' the clouds.

Or maybe 'Sense' refers to the speaker's faculty of reason or understanding, which she fears is about to give way due to the psychological pressure she's experiencing. We might read the line as suggesting something like: 'It seemed that my sanity and mental health was about to be broken through, was about to be pierced and ultimately shattered by the mental strain under which I was operating'.

Stanza 2

Finally proceedings were called to order as the mourners took their seats and the funeral service itself began. But this development brought the speaker no respite. The thumping of the mourner's footsteps was now replaced by the equally abrasive sound of the funeral service itself. According to the speaker, the sound of the service resembled a drum beaten over and over again: 'And when they all were seated,/ A Service, like a Drum-/ Kept beating, beating'. We sense that there was something guttural and percussive about the preaching of the minister, something aggressively insistent about the prayers and responses of the congregation.

This percussive drone began to numb the speaker's mind: 'till I thought/ My mind was going numb'. The service's repetitive humming had an almost hypnotic effect on her, dulling her various mental faculties. Soon, she imagined, she would no longer be capable of any thought or feeling whatsoever.

Stanza 3

Eventually, the service reached its conclusion. Some of the mourners picked up the coffin and began to carry it off for burial: 'And then I heard them lift a Box'. The other mourners, we imagine, filed along behind the pallbearers. This funeral procession, we're told, made its way across the speaker's very soul. To the speaker, it felt and sounded as if the mourners were wearing footwear of the heaviest metal, 'Boots of Lead', as they marched. Each footfall produced not only a dull thudding sound but also tremors and reverberations, as it stomped down into her soul. These leaden boots made a creaking sound as they progressed, which suggests that under their weight the speaker's soul was beginning to buckle and give way.

This metaphor is extraordinary because it compares something immaterial and abstract (the speaker's soul) with something utterly physical and everyday (a wooden floor that's capable of creaking). This comparison masterfully captures the intense psychological pressure under which the speaker found herself, at a time when she felt as if her innermost self was being pummelled and was in danger of collapse.

Stanza 4

The speaker describes how, as the coffin was carried away, she heard the funeral bell begin to toll. She experienced a sound of overwhelming intensity, a ringing so loud that it seemed to emanate from outer 'Space' itself. It was if the very 'Heavens' above her were functioning as a kind of bell, as if the energy of every galaxy and nebula had been harnessed to produce chimes of such unbearable loudness: 'As all the Heavens were a Bell'.

The speaker, then, experienced a sound projected from every corner of the sky above her and from outer space beyond. She heard chimes so loud that they seemed to ring out through the entire planet. It was as if everything that existed in this world, every aspect of earthly 'Being', could do nothing but listen to this incessant ringing: 'And Being but an Ear'. We imagine here the sound of the funeral bell, slow, regular and mournful. But whereas a typical funeral bell rings for few minutes at most, the sound experienced by the speaker seems to go on and on, ringing out at regular intervals for hours or even days. The speaker, then, finds herself utter 'solitary', utterly alone in the throes of her mental breakdown. She experiences a sound that seems loud enough to fill the entire world but that only she can hear.

Small wonder, then, that the speaker refers to herself as 'Wrecked … here', as if she were a shipwrecked sailor who had washed up, dazed and disorientated, on the shores of some unknown land. Of course the other meaning of 'Wrecked', as in ruined or destroyed, also applies here, which suggests the speaker's devastated mental state.

The speaker, it seems, is someone who values serenity, who relishes peace and quiet above all else. This is wonderfully conveyed by the poet's personification of 'Silence'. Personification, we remember, occurs when an abstract concept is presented as if it were a human being. In this instance the concept of silence is presented as the speaker's relative and companion: the speaker and 'Silence' are depicted as members of the same 'Race', which suggests that they are members of the same family or tribe.

Silence, then, suffers with the speaker. Both are left 'Wrecked' and solitary, utterly isolated by the speaker's mental torment. Silence, like the speaker, is bombarded by the bell's incessant, terrible chimes. The suffering of Silence represents the speaker's loss of all hope, her fear that she may never again experience peace and quiet. For in a world where even Silence himself is bombarded by relentless noise, why would we expect to find serenity?

Stanza 5

The poem's final stanza powerfully depicts the collapse of reason itself, of the speaker's sanity or rationality: 'And then a Plank in Reason, broke'.

- The speaker's 'Reason' is compared to a wooden floor that is comprised of planks.
- The speaker depicts herself standing on this wooden floor. This suggests how we rely upon reason, how rationality and logic underpin for our lives and our understanding of the world around us.
- But a plank in the floor gives way, probably because it's been subjected to too much weight. This represents how the speaker's sanity collapses due to the psychological stress she has endured.
- The speaker falls through the gap created by the broken plank: 'And I dropped'. This represents her transition from sanity into what we must describe as insanity, into a state of mind no longer governed by 'Reason' as we know it.
- The speaker says that she 'dropped down, and down', which suggests that she fell for a long time down a narrow chute of some kind. This represents the vastness of the unconscious mind, illustrating how the speaker, after her sanity had collapsed, experienced a wide range of bizarre mental states.
- The speaker's fall was divided into a series of shorter plunges as she collided with the shaft's walls, causing her to bounce from one side to the other. This conveys the speaker's loss of control over her own mind. As she loses control, or falls, she finds herself shifting unpredictably from one mental state to the next.

Finally the speaker's fall was 'Finished', and she came crashing to the bottom of the shaft. This represents the end of the speaker's mental collapse. Her mind stops shifting manically from one state to another and comes to rest in a condition that we might even describe as 'normal', one that combines, no doubt, exhaustion and relief.

The poem's final line is open to several interpretations. Perhaps the speaker is suggesting that she 'Finished knowing' in the sense that her breakdown has concluded and that she's recovered her capacity for rational thought. Or maybe she's suggesting that, by enduring this traumatic episode, she has gained some important knowledge – about herself, perhaps, about suffering, or maybe about madness and sanity. Or maybe she's suggesting that she's no longer capable of knowing anything, that, post-breakdown, she will never again be confident in her own ability to analyse and understand the world.

FOCUS ON STYLE

'I felt a Funeral' uses a form common to most of Dickinson's poetry. It has five stanzas, each four lines long and with an ABCB rhyme scheme. For the most part, it uses lines of six syllables. The third line of each stanza has eight syllables. This poem features an atmosphere of slowly rising tension as the psychological stress experienced by the speaker increases to the point where her 'Reason' itself collapses.

The poem is typical of Dickinson's work in that it features several very inventive similes. In line 6, for instance, the prayers and responses of the funeral service are compared to a 'Drum', which suggests their percussive, repetitive qualities. The speaker uses an astonishing simile to describe the intensity of the ringing she experiences, declaring that it's as if these chimes were issuing from every corner of the 'Heavens', from outer space itself.

An interesting feature of this poem is the transition from 'Brain', in line 1, to 'mind', in line 8, to 'Soul', in line 10. Each term, we note, is increasingly more abstract. It's as if the speaker's discomfort begins as physical pain, as a throbbing in the physical organ known as the brain. Then it expands to a state of general mental distress, as suggested by the more abstract term 'mind'. Finally, as suggested by the term 'Soul', the speaker feels as if her entire being has been corrupted. As noted above, Dickinson's genius for imagery is evident in how she makes the 'Soul' and 'mind' seem concrete and tangible, presenting them as creaking floorboards, as a surface made from planks that are always on the verge of collapse.

This poem is often noted for its use of repetition, which captures both the ceaseless nature of the mourners' movement and the mounting psychological pressure endured by the speaker. We see this with the repetition of 'treading', 'beating' and 'Kept' in lines 3 and 7. Similarly, the words 'same' and 'again' in line 11 further emphasise the relentless nature of the pressure to which the speaker has been subjected.

THEMES

THE WORKINGS OF THE MIND

This poem is a powerful portrayal of a mind at the end of its tether, wonderfully evoking states of mind that are almost too extreme for words. The image of a funeral happening inside the brain is strange and startling, but it masterfully captures an extraordinary build-up of psychological pressure that was occurring inside the speaker's psyche.

Several techniques are used to register this build-up of psychological strain:
- The depiction of repetitive, percussive sounds: the 'treading' of the mourners as they mill about before the service, the 'beating' quality of the prayers and responses during the service itself, the thudding 'Boots of Lead' as the coffin is carried away
- The depiction of force and impact as the mourners' 'Boots of Lead' trudge across the speaker's very soul
- The driving rhythm of Dickinson's verse, too, contributes here, its repetitions powerfully registering the build-up of pressure inside the speaker's psyche.

This is a poem, then that highlights the fragility of our sanity and mental health. Our 'Reason', the speaker suggests, is like a wooden floor, comprised of planks, on which we stand with the greatest of uncertainty. At any moment, one of the planks might fracture and give way beneath us. This is a comparison that wonderfully captures the fragility of sanity and mental health. Just as a floorboard might shatter, if subjected to too much weight, so one's mental health might shatter if subjected to too much mental stress.

And just such a collapse is depicted in the poem's unforgettable final stanza as the speaker's 'Reason' finally gives way. She describes a sensation of plummeting 'down, and down', bouncing from one surface to another. This is a powerful image for the succession of strange, inexplicable mental states the speaker experiences now that she's moved beyond any conventional form of reason or sanity.

This plummet into unreason is no doubt frightening, the speaker colliding uncontrollably into one 'World', then another, experiencing any number of bizarre psychological conditions. But with this 'plunge' comes a sense of release, perhaps even of relief. We sense that the build-up of psychological pressure, having reached its climax with the collapse of the speaker's reason, is now over. Perhaps the speaker, having reached her lowest point, will now be able to rebuild her shattered psyche.

THIS IS POETRY | **EMILY DICKINSON**

A Bird, came down the Walk –

LINE BY LINE

This poem's opening lines are reminiscent of a wildlife documentary. Like the subject of a David Attenborough film, a bird walks down a garden path, oblivious to the fact that its activities are observed not only by the speaker but also, indirectly, by us, the readers of the poem: 'He did not know I saw'.

The speaker, therefore, functions like the narrator of just such a nature programme, directing our attention to specific aspects of the bird's behaviour:

- She describes how the bird strolls down the 'Walk' or garden path: 'A Bird, came down the Walk'.
- She describes how it pauses for a drink of water, sipping from the dew that has collected on a blade of grass: 'And then he drank a Dew/ From a convenient Grass'.
- She describes how it accommodates a beetle that is also using the pathway, moving toward the garden wall in order to let the insect crawl by: 'And then hopped sidewise to the Wall/ To let a Beetle pass'.
- She describes how the bird seized on a passing earthworm, biting it in half before devouring it.

We're told that the bird ate the worm 'raw', which seems rather redundant. After all, we hardly expect the bird to cook the worm before consuming it. The term 'raw', however, suggests the speed and ferocity with which the bird gobbled down its slithery treat.

Suddenly, the bird begins to move 'Like one in danger', as if it senses some nearby threat. The poet describes how the bird 'stirred' its head, and how its eyes began to move in a 'rapid' fashion. We can imagine its gaze quickly flickering this way and that, as it scans its surroundings: 'He glanced with rapid eyes/ That hurried all abroad'. Perhaps it senses the watching speaker. Or maybe it identifies some other potential peril.

The speaker offers the anxious bird a piece of bread. She does so in a cautious and tentative manner, not wanting to startle the bird and scare him away. However, the speaker is obviously not 'Cautious' enough. For no sooner does she approach the bird than it 'unrolls' or unfurls its wings and flies away.

The poem's final stanza is structured around one of Dickinson's most imaginative and vivid metaphors:

- Dickinson compares the air to a kind of ocean.
- The act of flying is compared to that of moving through water.
- The bird, for instance, is depicted as 'rowing' into the sky, his unfurled feathers functioning like oars that propel him upwards: 'And he unrolled his feathers/ And rowed him softer Home'.
- Butterflies, meanwhile, are depicted as 'swimming' through the air.
- When a flying creature takes wing it can disturb the air through which it moves. This is compared to the 'plashes' or splashes produced when we enter the water.

The poet imagines butterflies launching themselves from 'Banks of Noon', from ridges of plants and flowers on a sunny summer's day. They leap into the air, however, with extraordinary gentleness, causing no disturbances or splashes. As the speaker puts it, they swim 'plashlessly' through the air: 'Butterflies, off Banks of Noon/ Leap, plashless as they swim'.

Yet the bird's motion is even 'softer' than that of these imagined butterflies. According to the poet, it takes flight with more grace and elegance that any butterfly could muster: 'And rowed him softer home –/ Than ... Butterflies'. She can only watch in awe as the bird propels itself upward, into the sky which is its 'Home' or natural element:

The poet imagines a boat rowing across an ocean of silver-coloured water. Think of the greatest silver mine in the world, with the richest 'seam' of silver. Well, not even the product of such a seam could match the colour of this imagined ocean, so glittering and lustrous is its surface as the boat rows across it. She imagines that the boat's oars dip delicately in and out of the ocean as it travels. With each stroke they 'divide' its silver waters into two halves or sections, one on the boat's port side and one on its starboard side: 'Oars divide the Ocean'.

The bird's unfurled wings, as it takes flight, are compared to the oars of this smoothly-travelling rowboat. Just as the boat's oars propel it across the ocean, so the bird's wings propel it upwards. Yet the motion of the bird's feathers is smoother and more gentle ('softer') than that of any oars could be.

FOCUS ON STYLE

Tone
This poem features several shifts in tone. The tone of the first two stanzas is casual, playful and innocent. The worm, for instance, is described not as a slimy wriggling thing but as a 'fellow', suggesting that it's some kind of gentleman. Even the grass is described as 'convenient'.

The movement of the verse here is simple, almost reminiscent of a nursery rhyme, with its full rhymes between monosyllabic words: 'saw' and 'raw' in stanza 1, and 'Grass' and 'pass' in stanza 2. This simplicity is heightened by the fact that each line consists of one phrase, and that there are no run-on lines.

The atmosphere darkens in stanzas 3 and 4, as the bird becomes agitated and ultimately flies away. The verse's 'nursery rhyme' quality is abandoned, and the language used becomes more sophisticated. Full rhymes are replaced by the half-rhyme between 'Crumb' and 'home' in stanza 4, and with no rhyme at all in stanza 3 ('around' and 'Head).

The absence of the expected rhyme comes as a jolting surprise to the reader, suggesting how the bird is jerked into alertness by its awareness of a sudden potential threat. Furthermore, the run-on line between stanzas 3 and 4 can confuse our initial reading of the poem, perhaps suggesting the bird's confusion and agitation as it searches for potential threats: 'He stirred his Velvet Head// Like one in danger'.

In the final stanzas, the tone shifts to one of joyous exultation as the poet celebrates the majesty of the bird taking flight. The poem's syntax becomes much more intricate, with a single complex sentence stretching across ten lines and taking in several different and complex metaphors.

VERBAL MUSIC
In this poem, Dickinson makes liberal use of assonance and alliteration. In line 12, for instance, assonance occurs between 'Velvet' and 'Head', with their repeated 'e' sounds. We also see it in the phrase 'rowed him softer home', with its repeated 'o' sound. Alliteration occurs in lines 17, 18 and 19, with their repeated 'o', 's' and 'b' sounds: 'Oars divide the Ocean', 'Too silver for a seam', 'Butterflies, off Banks of noon'. This use of assonance and alliteration creates a pleasant or euphonious musical effect, reflecting the majesty and beauty of the bird, especially when it takes wing.

Vivid Imagery
The poem's opening stanzas, as we've seen, present us with images that are playful and almost cartoon-like with their depiction of the bird hopping to one side in order to let the beetle pass by. Similarly light-hearted is the depiction of the butterflies leaping from banks of vegetation in order to flit and hover through the air.

'A Bird, came down the Walk' also presents us with the hauntingly beautiful image of a single row boat making its way across a vast and glittering ocean. Even more majestic, however, is the image of the bird powering itself homeward on its unfurled wings.

Metaphor, Simile, Figures of Speech
As we've seen, 'A Bird, came down the Walk' features a conceit or extended metaphor that compares the air to an ocean, butterflies to swimmers and the bird's wings to oars. Dickinson uses an excellent simile to capture the fear apparent in the bird's eyes, comparing them to 'frightened Beads'.

THEMES

NATURE

Like many of Dickinson's poems, 'A Bird Came Down the Walk' celebrates the beauty of the natural world, specifically that of the bird encountered on the garden path. The poet lovingly highlights the bird's bead-like eyes, the softness of the feathers on its 'Velvet Head', its unfurling wings and the exceptional grace and elegance with which it manoeuvres itself skyward.

The poem, like many works by Dickinson, is playful in its depiction of nature, the opening stanzas presenting us with images that are cute and almost comedic. We see this homeliness in the depiction of the little traffic jam that occurs on the walk, where the bird hops aside to let the beetle pass him by: 'And then hopped sidewise to the Wall/ To let a Beetle pass'. Yet the poem also emphasises the brutality and fear that exist in the natural world. The bird savagely devours a worm and is itself in a fearful state, being on the look-out for potential predators.

Dickinson is a poet who persistently identifies the extraordinary in the everyday. 'A Bird Came down the Walk' isn't inspired by a conventionally magnificent scene. It doesn't describe swans gliding on a lake in winter, or cormorants soaring from a geological wonder like the Cliffs of Moher. Instead it suggests that even the most mundane sight, such as a bird walking down an ordinary garden path, devouring a worm and taking flight, can appear extraordinary. Like 'I could bring You Jewels' and 'I taste a liquor never brewed', this poem reminds us that beauty and mystery can be found all around us if only we take the time to stop and look.

> Several critics have suggested that it's possible to read 'A Bird, came down the Walk' as an allegory of a failed romantic relationship, with the male bird representing Dickinson's lost lover. We are reminded, perhaps, of the several intensely passionate correspondences that Dickinson conducted with various gentlemen over the course of her life, with Judge Otis Lord, for example, or the mysterious individual she referred to only as 'the Master'.

The poem, we imagine, is set in the garden of Homestead, the house where Dickinson lived and wrote from the age of 25. She speaks of 'the Wall' and 'the Walk', a very specific environment that she would have encountered every day of her adult life. It highlights, then, how to Dickinson this tiny farmstead served as an inexhaustible source of inspiration.

The poem also highlights Dickinson's intense sensitivity toward the natural world. The poet, we sense, is clearly someone deeply affected by her observations of nature, even in its most ordinary manifestations. The strange and dense web of imagery in the poem's final stanzas vividly conveys the awe felt by the speaker as she watches the bird take wing.

ANALYSIS

I heard a Fly buzz – when I died –

LINE BY LINE

In this poem the speaker addresses us from beyond the grave, telling us about the circumstances of her death. She describes lying on her deathbed, surrounded by various members of her family. We can imagine the speaker's mental and physical exhaustion, her body wracked, perhaps, by a combination of illness and old age. We can imagine that her family too are mentally and physically exhausted, having suffered the ordeal of watching a loved one drift towards death. We can imagine an atmosphere of great tension as they wait for the moment when the speaker will finally pass away.

A moment of calm
The speaker describes one oddly quiet moment that occurred as she lay upon her deathbed. The room had been noisy while the speaker was suffering on her deathbed. It would be noisy again as she experienced her final death throes. For a few moments, though, it was filled with quietness. The speaker compares this lull to the eerie stillness that can sometimes be experienced at the very centre of a storm system. 'The Stillness in the Room/ Was like the Stillness in the Air –/ Between the Heaves of Storm –'.

The loved ones
The speaker's loved ones had cried until they could cry no more: 'The Eyes around – had wrung them dry –'. We imagine an air of stress and expectancy, as the speaker's loved ones wait for the moment of death. We can imagine the unbearable tension they experienced as they waited for the 'last Onset' or attack of the speaker's illness, when she would finally pass away. According to the speaker, her loved ones were so tense that they found themselves almost unable to exhale. The air they breathed in remained held or gathered firmly in their lungs: 'And Breaths were gathering firm'.

The speaker describes how her loved ones expect that at the moment of death a 'King' will be present. No doubt, the 'King' they have in mind is Jesus, the Lord of Heaven, who will descend in order to ferry his loyal and faithful subject into Paradise. Perhaps the speaker shares her loved ones' religious beliefs, or perhaps she is more sceptical about religion and life after death.

Will and testament
Because the speaker knows that the end is near, she has prepared her last will and testament, 'assigning', or passing on, her various valuables to her loved ones. The items that she allocates to her loved ones are described as 'Keepsakes', suggesting personal effects, little tokens that will remind loved ones of her after she is gone.

The fact that the speaker wills only such keepsakes, rather than stocks and property, reinforces our sense that she is a woman: In Dickinson's time, women were seldom permitted to own and administer such assets.

There is one aspect, or 'portion', of the speaker that is not 'assignable', however, one that she cannot simply give to whoever she wants. This is her immortal soul, the ultimate destiny of which she cannot control.

The fly

During this final moment of quiet, as the speaker prepares for her illness's final onset, a fly has been buzzing in the room. The fly, we are told, is moving in an 'uncertain' and 'stumbling' fashion. This suggests the jerky, erratic motions of an insect that has been trapped too long in a room and is desperate to escape.

The speaker starts to lose consciousness. She describes how at this moment a fly 'interposed' or positioned itself between her and the available light: 'There interposed a Fly... Between the light- and me'. This image of a fly blocking out the light is a puzzling one. How could such a tiny creature place itself between the speaker and the available light source? This cryptic statement lends itself to several possible interpretations:

Perhaps the image of the fly blocking out the light represents the ebbing of consciousness, the diminishment of the speaker's vision as her system begins to finally shut down.

Perhaps, as the speaker passes away, her sight begins to fail and her vision narrows to a little tunnel. A fly floats into this reduced field of vision, making itself the last thing the speaker sees before she dies and darkness engulfs her completely. The image of the light-obstructing fly might also refer to the afterlife. Perhaps, as she lingers between life and death, the speaker imagines for a moment that she can see the light of Heaven, the glow of paradise into which she's being summoned.

But at the very second her brain shuts down, she realises that this glow is only a hallucination. It is replaced by onrushing blackness and the buzzing, stumbling fly. The speaker realises that oblivion, rather than eternal life, lies in wait for her.

The fly can also be read as an embodiment of Satan himself, arriving at the speaker's deathbed in order to claim her very soul. It is not surprising that the devil would appear in the form of a fly, because he is sometimes referred to as the 'Lord of the Flies'. Or perhaps the speaker just sees the Devil as a giant fly, mixing him up with the fly that she hears buzzing in the room.

The Devil, then, in this unsettling insect form, blocks out not only the light of this world, from which the speaker's spirit is being wrenched, but also the light of paradise, which she will never reach, because the speaker's soul, on this reading, is instead bound for eternal damnation!

> The gathered loved ones, presumably, don't think that Jesus will be physically visible at the loved one's deathbed. They probably think they'll 'witness' his presence by feeling his grace within their souls. Or maybe Jesus' presence will be evidenced by the serene and painless nature of the speaker's passing.

FOCUS ON STYLE

Form

'I heard a Fly buzz- when I died' uses a form common to most of Dickinson's poetry. It has four-line stanzas and an ABAB rhyme scheme. The poem has a regular rhythmic lilt, with four stresses in the first and third lines of each stanza, and three stresses in the second and fourth lines. The rhythm becomes jerky and irregular in the final stanza, suggesting the breakdown of the speaker's mental faculties at the moment of death.

Metaphor, Simile, Figures of Speech

Dickinson uses a fine simile to describe the momentary quietness in the room when the speaker is granted a brief respite from her suffering. The quietness, she says, is like that at the 'eye of a hurricane', the very centre of a storm. On either side of the storm's uneasily tranquil eye are great 'Heaves', a term that here refers not only to gusts or breaths, but also to the storm's force as it pushes and shoves against the landscape.

A similarly vivid metaphor is used to describe how the speaker's loved ones had exhausted their capacity for crying: 'The Eyes around – had wrung them dry –' Here, eye-balls are presented as being made from a spongy substance, a material that is squeezed in the act of crying so that moisture is forced out. According to the speaker, her loved ones' eyes had been 'wrung' in such a fashion until they had no moisture left to give, until they resembled a towel squeezed completely dry.

Tone and Atmosphere

'I heard a Fly buzz – when I died' wonderfully evokes an atmosphere of tension and expectation, as the speaker and her gathered loved ones prepare for the final onslaught of her illness. It joins other Dickinson poems in depicting a calm but uneasy interlude between bouts of suffering. In this regard, it is similar not only to 'The Soul has Bandaged moments', but also to 'After great pain, a formal feeling comes'.

THEMES

THE WORKINGS OF THE MIND

Dickinson's great subject, according to several critics, is the processes and performances of the human mind itself. In this light, 'I heard a Fly buzz' can be regarded as a triumph. For it provides, especially in its last six lines, a moving depiction of how a mind disintegrates or dissolves as life leaves it.

There is something powerful about the repetition of 'and then' in these lines, as the speaker mechanically lists the stages of her mental collapse. The phrase is repeated three times, suggesting a relentless and unstoppable process of shutting down, one that cannot be stopped or delayed, once it commences.

As we noted, the speaker's vision fails as she passes away. It is arguable that her sense of logic fails as well, and that she confuses the fly buzzing in the corner of the room with the blackness that floods her vision. We sense that in the speaker's befuddled mind these two events become mixed up, and she hallucinates that a giant fly is blocking out the light

A similar confusion is evident in the speaker's declaration that 'the Windows failed'. As the speaker died the room seemed to fill with darkness. To her it seemed that the windows 'failed' – that they were suddenly incapable of performing their function. They could no longer let light into the room.

This mental befuddlement also lies behind the speaker's description of the fly's behaviour. The speaker is aware of three different aspects of the fly's appearance and demeanour:

- The buzzing sound it produces as it flies.
- The 'stumbling' and 'uncertain' nature of its movements around the bedroom.
- The blue colour of its wings.

In her confused mental state, the speaker experiences a moment of synaesthesia. This occurs when we experience something associated with one sense in terms of something associated with another sense. In this instance, the speaker experiences the fly's buzzing not only in terms of sound but also in terms of colour and movement: 'With Blue – uncertain stumbling Buzz-'. We sense that this occurs because her failing brain can no longer adequately process or organise the sensory input it receives from the speaker's eyes and ears.

There's a sense, too, in which the speaker's consciousness resembles the fly buzzing haplessly against the window, as her mind stumbles from one thought or sensation to the next. The poem's final line, with its repetition of the verb 'see' reinforces our sense of her diminishing capacity.

The first instance of this verb refers to the ability to perceive, while the second refers to the ability to focus. The speaker, therefore, first finds herself unable to focus on the buzzing fly in the corner of the room and subsequently becomes incapable of perceiving anything. As we read, we can almost feel her consciousness dwindling away.

DEATH

The presence of the fly introduces an element of indignity into the speaker's passing. The speaker has prepared for death; she has made her will and gathered her family around her. The moment of her demise is intended to be the solemn climax of a life well lived.

The last thing she hears, however, is not the soothing words of her family but the buzzing of a fly. The last thing she sees is not the faces of her loved ones but a fly floating in front of her. The speaker's last experience in this world is of a miserable and insignificant insect 'stumbling' as it buzzes around the room.

Many readers feel that the fly's interruption makes the moment of the speaker's death seem a little ridiculous, robbing it of its intended grace and dignity. It's a bit like a bride falling over as she makes her way up the aisle to be married.

We like to think that we can control our lives, that we can live with a certain poise and grandeur. But the poem reminds us that circumstances often intervene, upsetting our plans in ways both big and small. This is especially true when it comes to dying, the manner of our deaths being all-too-often unexpected and outside of our control.

RELIGION

The speaker and her gathered loved ones strike us as religious people. The speaker, as we've seen, believes that one portion of her is 'unassignable', her immortal soul. Her loved ones, meanwhile, wait anxiously for 'the King' to be 'witnessed' in the room. They seem to believe that as the speaker dies, Jesus, the King of Heaven, will appear and carry his loyal subject's soul to paradise.

These expectations are not borne out, however. The poem doesn't explicitly state that there is no heaven. And yet, when the speaker's vision fades to black at the end of the poem, we are left with the distinct impression that the speaker realises that this black oblivion is all there is, that no afterlife awaits her.

This poem, then, presents a rather ironic and sceptical view of religion. There's a sense in which it pokes fun at the gathered family's religious expectations by means of a crushing anticlimax. The last thing the speaker 'witnesses' is not the glorious arrival of the 'King' but the uncertain buzzing of a stumbling fly.

THIS IS POETRY — EMILY DICKINSON
The Soul has Bandaged moments

LINE BY LINE

The poem's speaker is madly in love with someone. There are times when she is sure of her beloved's intentions, confident that he is faithful to her and loves her deeply. During these times, the speaker is deliriously happy. But there are occasions when the speaker is not sure of her beloved, when she becomes suspicious of his faithfulness to her. During these periods, the speaker is tortured and overwhelmed by jealous thoughts and suspicions.

The poem begins by describing an occasion where the speaker has been hurt by her lover's behaviour and is at the mercy of her suspicions and doubts. We don't know what – if anything – has triggered these suspicions. Perhaps her beloved has been behaving in a manner that is out of character. Perhaps the speaker has been made aware of her beloved's relationship with another. Someone may have told her this, or she might have seen him with someone else. Perhaps, however, the beloved has not done or said anything hurtful. Maybe it has been a while since she has heard from him, and she is assuming the worst.

Whatever has happened, some form of mental hurt has been inflicted upon the speaker. She has done her best to tend to this psychic hurt or wound. Her soul has been 'Bandaged'. The term 'Bandaged' suggests, perhaps, that the hurtful moment has passed, but the soul is still feeling weak and vulnerable. Perhaps the pain has not passed, however, and the bandages are merely disguising or concealing wounds that still smart.

In the wake of this trauma, the speaker is left feeling very weak and low. Her soul or psyche is so horrified by what it has experienced that it cannot move or 'stir'. It is as if the soul has been frozen with fear. The Soul's hair is described as 'freezing', which suggests that the Soul is both numb from the experience and unable now to react or respond to events.

In this weakened state, the soul is very vulnerable to jealous or suspicious thoughts. The poet personifies this jealousy, comparing it to a 'Goblin' that toys with the speaker's soul. The manner in which the Goblin behaves and interacts with the soul illustrates how suspicious or jealous thoughts take hold of the vulnerable mind, torturing and corrupting it.

The Goblin behaves in a seductive manner. He begins by greeting the soul rather formally, saluting her with 'long fingers', before tenderly rubbing or caressing the soul's hair. Finally the Goblin kisses the appalled soul. These actions suggest the manner in which suspicious thoughts can weasel their way into our minds, seducing us into believing them.

The Goblin's behaviour also hints at the forceful way in which suspicious thoughts take hold of us. There is something slightly violent or abusive about the manner in which the Goblin treats the soul. The verbs in stanza two progress rapidly from 'Salute' to 'Accost'. The Goblin lulls the soul with its formal salutation and the caressing of her hair, only to then 'Accost' or aggressively impose its will. All the while, the soul is frozen with fear, a passive victim to the Goblin's advances.

Such suspicious or jealous thoughts are contrasted with thoughts of love, which are personified by the 'Lover'. Whereas suspicious thoughts are rather brutal in their manner, boldly making their advances, thoughts of love are gentle and sweet. The 'Lover' does not even touch the soul, instead respectfully hovering over its lips.

Love is described as something 'fair' – something associated with honesty, beauty and truth. But suspicious thoughts are ultimately damaging to this positive emotion. Such thoughts, the speaker says, attack or 'Accost' the fair 'Theme' of love.

Moments of escape

There are occasions when the speaker is free of all such doubts and suspicions, when she is sure of her beloved's devotion. During such periods, the speaker's soul is filled with ecstatic joy and soars free. The speaker describes these occasions as 'moments of escape'. The soul is no longer confined by crippling doubt and suspicion. Free of doubt, the soul experiences a sense of liberation and freedom. Nothing can contain it or hold it back. It is energised and capable of 'bursting all the doors'.

The speaker compares the soul to a bee that has been confined to its hive all winter. The bee has a favourite flower, a 'Rose', that it visits during the summer. Over the long winter months the bee is unable to leave the hive and visit the flower that it loves; it is 'Long Dungeoned' from this rose. Suddenly summer rolls around, and the bee is free to leave the hive. It flies in an ecstatic manner to the rose. In fact, such is its joy at the prospect of once again seeing the rose that it seems to not even need its wings to stay aloft; it is 'delirious borne'.

When the bee eventually reaches the rose, it seems to become intoxicated with joy. It is as if the flower's nectar is an alcoholic beverage that the bee imbibes. (We are reminded here of the description of the bird in 'I taste a liquor'). The bee reaches a state of ecstasy where all negative thoughts and feelings are forgotten. Having sipped from the flower, the bee knows nothing but 'Noon, and Paradise'. To the bee, at this moment, it seems that it will always be noon on a summer's day and that the world will forever be a paradise for it to enjoy. The cold, isolated days spent in the hive are now a distant memory.

> The poet uses an interesting term to describe the manner in which the Goblin kisses the soul. It is said to 'Sip' from the soul's lips. To 'sip' is to take in or absorb, to drink from something constantly, a little at a time. The Goblin feeds off the vulnerable soul, seeming to gain or benefit from its vulnerability. The image of the Goblin sipping from the soul's lips also seems to anticipate the description of the bee in stanza 4.

We can imagine the speaker feeling the same as the bee, when she is again convinced that her beloved loves her. Her soul, which had been feeling wounded and weak, is suddenly lifted and re-energised. Whereas once the soul had been 'too appalled to stir', now it 'dances'. Whereas once the soul had felt bound in and confined, now it experiences great freedom and can travel far and wide or 'abroad'.

On these occasions, however, the soul seems incapable of measured joy and happiness. It loses all self-control and behaves in a reckless manner. It doesn't just quietly leave the space where it had been feeling weak and vulnerable, where it was trapped by fear, as a prisoner who has been released might walk slowly out of the prison. Instead, the soul bursts through the doors. Also, the manner in which it dances seems reckless and dangerous. Dickinson compares the soul's dancing to a 'Bomb', suggesting that the soul could explode at any moment, causing harm not only to itself but also to others. The behaviour is suggestive of a manic state of mind, of someone who goes from one emotional extreme to the other.

> The American Civil War was fought in the United States from 1861 to 1865. The years of the Civil War corresponded with Dickinson's most intense period of productivity as a poet, during which she is thought to have written roughly half of her total number of poems. Although Dickinson never wrote specifically about the Civil War, some of the imagery she uses - such as 'She dances like a Bomb' - seems to reflect the bloody turmoil that raged across the country during these years.

The soul is also said to swing 'opon the Hours'. We might think of the 'Hours' as representing the clock and the routine of the day. The soul, in its state of delirious happiness, pays no heed to this clock; it is as unconstrained by time just as it is by space. In fact, the soul seems to have fun with the whole notion of routine, swinging upon the 'Hours'.

Retaken moments

But it seems that these moments of ecstatic joy, times when the soul is entirely free of doubt and suspicion, are relatively short-lived. It doesn't take long - and it doesn't take much - for the soul to once again be overwhelmed by doubt. When such doubts and suspicions return, it is as if the soul has again been apprehended and incarcerated. It is as if the authorities have finally caught up with the escaped soul and are leading it back to its cell or dungeon. The soul is like a criminal or 'Felon' who escaped from jail only to be re-captured or 'retaken'.

The manner in which the soul is retaken is rough and brutal. Metal bands connected by a chain are placed around the soul's feet. Dickinson describes the soul's feet as 'plumed', suggesting that they have feathered wings that enable the soul to soar and fly. However, the shackles make it impossible for the soul to now take flight.

The apprehended soul is also prevented from singing. In a particularly disturbing image, the poet describes how 'staples' have been driven into the 'song' to silence the soul. The poet presents the 'song', the soul's expression of joy, as something corporeal rather than abstract. It is as if the 'song' is the soul's companion, someone that accompanies it during its moments of delirious happiness. However, when these moments come to an end, the 'song' is swiftly silenced. It is as if those who have shackled the soul have also brutally dealt with the 'song'. We can imagine how the metal staples have been used to bind its lips.

It is as if the soul has had some piece of twisted metal attached to its mouth that prevents it from expressing itself. When the apprehended soul eventually arrives at its prison cell, the Goblin or 'Horror' is there to welcome her once 'again'. Such moments, the poet says, are not spoken of. These are private humiliations, to be suffered and endured alone. Dickinson says that these moments are 'not brayed of Tongue'. To bray is cry or shout in a loud and harsh manner, like a donkey. Perhaps the soul, when it is feeling ecstatic, is able to shout in such a manner. However, when the soul has been wounded and tortured by suspicion, it suffers alone and in silence.

FOCUS ON STYLE

Conceits and Extended Metaphors

The poem uses the notion of prison and the soul as prisoner to describe the feelings of dejection and ecstasy that the speaker experiences. Whenever the speaker feels uncertain about her beloved's faithfulness to her, it is as if her soul has been incarcerated in some terrible dungeon where a horrible Goblin awaits her. Whenever these doubts are allayed or disappear, and the speaker is reassured of her beloved's love for her, it is as if her soul has been set free.

Vivid Imagery

The poem features a lot of what we might term 'gothic' imagery. There is the gloomy setting of the dungeon where the soul is confined during its periods of doubt and suspicion. There is the grotesque appearance of the Goblin, a hideous creature that toys with the soul, torturing and humiliating it. There is also the terribly violent images of the apprehended soul, with shackles upon its feet and, perhaps most brutally, the 'staples' in the 'song'.

Atmosphere

The atmosphere at the beginning and the end of the poem is dark and unsettling, full of menace and fear. This gloomy, nightmarish atmosphere lifts and changes in the middle of the poem, where for a brief spell the soul is free of doubt and experiences an ecstatic joy and sense of freedom.

THEMES

LOVE

The poem presents the idea of love as something beautiful and good; it is a 'Theme – so – fair'. Love is associated with such virtues as gentleness and respect, presented as something pure. The 'Lover', who personifies this notion of love in the poem, is so gentle and considerate when it comes to the soul that he merely hovers above its lips rather than boldly kissing them.

However, love can be undermined or threatened by suspicions and doubts. Such suspicions make us question whether the love we believed existed was ever so pure and true. The Goblin represents such suspicions in the poem. He takes advantage of the soul's vulnerable state to disabuse it of the notion that such pure love exists.

The poem illustrates how being in love can make us ecstatically happy. The speaker's soul seems to soar and fly when she is sure of her beloved's fidelity. It is said to dance and to feel no bounds or restrictions. Being in love fills us with positive thoughts and feelings. However, being in love can also cause us to feel absolutely miserable. The poem begins and ends with descriptions of the speaker overwhelmed and horrified by thought that her beloved is not faithful to her. Such doubts torture the soul, leaving us feeling trapped, weak and alone.

THE WORKINGS OF THE MIND

The poem presents us with someone who experiences great highs and lows, who seems to swing, rapidly enough, from utter dejection to ecstatic joy. It suggests someone who is bi-polar, someone whose mood alternates between extreme euphoria and deep depression. The poem vividly captures what it feels like to feel so low and so high, using memorable images of the soul being confined in a terrifying dungeon, on the one hand, or dancing 'like a Bomb, abroad' and swinging upon 'the Hours', on the other. Such images bring the inner workings of the mind vividly to life.

I could bring You Jewels – had I a mind to

LINE BY LINE

The speaker wants to give her beloved a gift. She considers several different possibilities. If she wished, she says, she could present her lover with a selection of precious stones: 'I could bring You Jewels – had I a mind to'. We imagine a fistful of glittering gems: diamonds, pearls and rubies.

Alternatively, she could present her lover with a selection of aromas or 'Odors'. These would come from the city of Santo Domingo, the capitol of the Dominican Republic and one of the most beautiful cities in the Caribbean: 'I could bring You Odors from St. Domingo–'. We might imagine here not only the scent of the surf but also of the myriad exotic fruits and meats to be found in the city's bustling quayside markets.

She could also present her lover with a selection of 'Colors'. These would come from the city of Vera Cruz, a great port on the Gulf of Mexico: 'I could bring You … Colors –from Vera Cruz'. We imagine here the whitenss of the unspoilt beaches, the vivid green of the palm trees, the sparkling blueness of the Caribbean sea.

Finally, the speaker could give her beloved berries that come all the way from the Bahamas, a chain of islands in the Caribbean Sea: 'Berries of the Bahamas—have I—'. We imagine here succulent figs and cherries, and other still more exotic types of fruit that would have been all but unknown in Amherst where Dickinson was born and raised.

The flower

The speaker, however, rejects each of these possible gifts, instead deciding to offer her beloved a flower that she has seen growing nearby. Such a modest token of affection strikes her as more suitable or appropriate than the expensive items mentioned above: 'Suits Me- more than those'.

Dickinson uses a wonderful metaphor to describe this flower's brightness, comparing it to a tiny flame. It is, she says, a 'little Blaze' that can be seen 'Flickering ... in the Meadow'. We can imagine it resembling a tiny camp-fire burning brightly in the meadow next to Homestead, the house in which Dickinson spent practically her entire adult life.

Dickinson provides a detailed description of this flower. Its petals are Topaz in colour, suggesting a vivid, iridescent blue. No human artist or decorator, she says, has ever managed to equal the intensity of this naturally-occurring shade: 'Never a Fellow matched this Topaz'. The flower's 'Swing' or stem, meanwhile, is described as 'Emerald', suggesting a lustrous green.

The flower is not merely the same colour as certain precious stones, such as topaz or emerald; like them, it is also an incredibly precious item. Indeed this little bloom, in the poet's view, is more valuable than any gem.

A 'dower' or dowry was the sum of money a woman's family gave to her husband when he married her. If a potential husband was unimpressed by the dowry on offer, a marriage had little chance of going ahead.

In the 16th Century, Francisco Bobadilo was the governor of the West Indies and was widely considered to be one of the richest men who had ever lived. This wealthiest of individuals, therefore, would expect any potential wife to be accompanied by an enormous dowry. The poet, however, says that this little flower, all by itself, would make a worthy dowry for such an incredibly wealthy gentleman: 'Dower itself- For Bobadilo'. The poet, then, presents this little flower as an item of incredible value.

Perhaps Dickinson was thinking of her own mother, Emily Norcross, whose dowry had to be transported for three days by horse-drawn carriage when she married Edward Dickinson in 1828, road and rail links being still very primitive in the Massachusetts of that time.

FOCUS ON STYLE

Form
Like the vast majority of Dickinson's poems, 'I could bring You Jewels' deploys an ABCB rhyme scheme. There are several instances of half rhyme, for example between 'those' and 'Cruz' in the first stanza and between 'Blaze' and 'those' in the second stanza. The poem is marked by the concision common to Dickinson's poetry, where words and phrases are regularly omitted. Such compression is especially evident in the poem's final line. Instead of 'What better gift could I bring you?' we get the much more concise phrase: 'Better—Could I bring?'

Verbal Music
Like many of Dickinson's poems, 'I could bring You Jewels' is rich in assonance and alliteration. Assonance occurs in line 4, with its repeated 'c' sound ('Colors' and 'Cruz') and in line 5, with its repeated 'b' sound ('Berries' and 'Bahamas'). Assonance also occurs in line 3, with its repeated 'o' sound, in line 9, with its repeated 'e' sound ('Never' and 'Fellow'), and in line 11, which also has a repeated 'o' sound ('Dower' and 'Bobadilo').

This combination of assonance and alliteration lends the poem a pleasant musical quality, reflecting both the exotic splendours of the Caribbean and the more homely beauty of the flower in the meadow.

Vivid Imagery
In this poem, Dickinson uses several Caribbean or exotic images, referring to berries from the Bahamas, smells from Santo Domingo and colours from Vera Cruz. Dickinson, though she never travelled, was prone to using imagery from such exotic locales, journeying in her imagination where she never ventured in real life.

Metaphor, Simile, Figures of Speech
The speaker uses a wonderful metaphor to describe the little flower, comparing it to a tiny flicker of flame: a 'little Blaze/ Flickering to itself – in the Meadow'. The presentation of the flower as a 'Blaze/ Flickering' captures the brightness and warmth of its colours. In a further metaphorical flourish, the stem is described as the flower's 'Swing', and we can imagine the 'head' of the flower swinging back and forth as the stem bends in the breeze.

Tone
'I could bring You Jewels' is generally considered to be playful and light-hearted in tone. This owes something to Dickinson's use of hyperbole, or poetic exaggeration. No one, the speaker declares, has ever found a sapphire that could match the 'Topaz' of the flower's petals. Furthermore, she maintains that the 'Emerald' of its stem would be a sufficient dowry for Bobadilo. She puts forward these deliberately outrageous exaggerations in order to stress the beauty of the humble flower.

It has also been suggested that the poem's tone is one of confidence and swagger. The speaker advertises her poetic gifts and her literary skills. She could, if she desired, conjure up the jewels for us, or the colours of Vera Cruz, through her descriptive powers. The poem, then, can be read as a celebration of poetry's power to bring colours, sounds and smells – anything the poet might imagine – floating into our minds.

The poem's lighthearted tone also owes something to its 'riddle-like' qualities. We are never actually told that the 'little Blaze/ Flickering' with its 'Emerald Swing' is a flower. The reader has to work it out him or herself from the clues provided in the poem. In this respect, it is similar to 'I taste a liquor never brewed'.

THEMES

NATURE
Like many of Dickinson's poems, "I could bring You Jewels" celebrates the beauty of the natural world, specifically that of the little flower the poet has noticed growing in a nearby meadow. The poet lovingly describes the flower's blossom and stem, highlighting the intensity of its blue and green.

The poem, like many works by Dickinson, is playful in its depiction of nature, specifically in the poet's exaggeration of the flower's charms. She considers jewels as a potential gift but ultimately opts for the flower instead, declaring that this little bloom, in it's own way, is a spectacular piece of jewellery, blazing as it does with the intensity of emerald and topaz.

Dickinson is a poet who persistently identifies the extraordinary in the everyday. 'I could bring You Jewels' isn't inspired by what we'd ordinarily consider an example of nature's majesty, like a sunset or a mountain vista. Instead, the poem focuses on something most of us would regard as commonplace and unremarkable: a flower growing in a field.

The speaker claims that this little plant is more special and exotic than berries from the Bahamas or the colours of Vera Cruz. The poem, then, reminds us that beauty and mystery can be found all around us if only we take the time to stop and look. If we do so, we might find that things in our own backyards are as special as the exotic sights and smells of Caribbean islands or other exotic locations.

The poem also highlights Dickinson's intense sensitivity to the natural world. The poet, we sense, is someone who responds deeply to nature, even in its most ordinary aspects. She is clearly deeply affected by her observation of the little flower. There is a moving simplicity and sincerity about the poem's final line, in which the poet declares that there's nothing better she could give her lover: 'Better—Could I bring?'

LOVE
This little poem occupies a place within an ancient poetic tradition: the idea of the poem as a gift. It is easy to imagine Dickinson enclosing this poem with a letter to one of her close correspondents – a practice, in fact, that she often engaged in. 'I could bring You Jewels', therefore, functions as a token of the poet's esteem and admiration for someone she holds dear.

But who is the poem addressed to? Most readers are inclined to view it as a love poem, and are left with the impression that Dickinson is addressing a potential lover rather than a close friend.

Perhaps Dickinson is thinking of Judge Otis Philip Lord, a friend of her father's, with whom she enjoyed an intense and passionate correspondence. Or perhaps she's thinking of the gentleman she refers to as 'Master' in three extraordinarily passionate letters of 1858-61. The precise identity of this gentleman has never been established.

A CELEBRATION OF POETRY
It's unlikely that the speaker has a selection of precious stones lying around that she can simply hand over to her lover. And it's equally implausible that she owns a package of berries shipped thousands of miles from the Bahamas. And how could she present her lover with abstract, intangible things like colours and odours?

In a sense, though, the poet can 'give' her friend these extraordinary gifts by describing them in her poetry. She can present her lover with jewels and berries, with colours and odours, by writing a poem that summons up these things in the lover's imagination.

Perhaps above all else, then, this poem celebrates the power of poetry and the imagination. It can be read as a confident statement of the speaker's descriptive abilities. It asserts that poetry and literature have the ability to bring entire worlds to life in our imaginations.

THE WORKINGS OF THE MIND
There's an amusing moment of personification in line 6, where the flower is presented as if it were a person, capable of independent actions, choices and decisions. The flower, we're told, chooses to flicker 'to itself'. It enjoys its beauty for its own sake. It doesn't show off or care what anyone else thinks of it. This suggests that the flower's beauty is of the humble and everyday kind, rather than the spectacular and remarkable kind.

The speaker chooses the flower to be her gift, then, because it serves as a metaphor for her own psyche. She sees herself, like the flower, as modest rather than showy, as confident and independent rather than a follower of the crowd.

In this sense, the flower 'suits' her better than any other potential gift. In offering the flower, then, she presents her lover with something that is not only beautiful but also representative of her own personality.

THIS IS POETRY — EMILY DICKINSON

A narrow Fellow in the Grass

LINE BY LINE

The first thing to note about this poem is that it's spoken by a man. This becomes clear in line 11 when the speaker refers to his boyhood: 'But when a Boy'. The speaker might be a farmer or farm labourer, someone who grew up in the countryside and is familiar with the meadows and wildlife of 19th-century New England, where snakes were fairly common. Perhaps Dickinson is imagining herself as her brother Austin, or as one of the farmhands who worked on the family farm.

Lines 1 to 4

The speaker describes a grass snake he's seen in the locality where he lives and works. He describes it in a fairly friendly and amiable manner: 'A narrow Fellow'. He notes that this creature can be glimpsed 'Occasionally' as it crawls through the grassy pastures. It's not an everyday sight, but it's common enough that one must remain alert for its presence.

The speaker describes the snake's movement as graceful and light, saying that it 'rides' or skims along the grass. He also describes how the snake moves quickly in and out of visibility, as suggested in line 3: 'You may have met Him – did you not'. The speaker highlights the suddenness with which the snake can appear at your feet: 'His notice sudden is'.

Lines 5 to 10

In stanza 2, the speaker further describes the unique movement of the snake. As the snake propels itself forward, it disturbs the grass through which it crawls. The speaker uses a simile to describe the snake parting the grass in much the same way as a comb parts hair: 'The Grass divides as with a Comb'. Here, you can visualise walking through the meadow when all at once you feel the grass parting under you and catch the briefest glimpse of the snake's crawling body: 'A spotted Shaft is seen'. But before you even have a chance to react, the grass 'closes' or returns to normal. You might then notice how the grass 'opens further on', parting a few metres away, as the snake continues its journey through the field.

The speaker tells us that the snake has a preference for cool, moist surroundings. He notes how it likes 'a Boggy Acre', poor land that is unsuitable for growing crops: 'A Floor too cool for Corn'.

Lines 10 to 16

The speaker then recalls the younger days he spent running 'Barefoot' through the meadows. He can remember coming across a snake 'more than once' during his childhood. Initially, he would mistake it for a discarded whip, unravelling on the ground: 'Have passed, I thought, a Whip lash,/ Unbraiding in the Sun'. The word 'Unbraiding' conveys a wonderful sense of the snake's sinuous movements.

When the boy bent down to retrieve the 'Whip', however, he quickly realised it was in a fact a snake. The whip 'wrinkled', or twitched, and disappeared: 'It wrinkled And was gone'.

Lines 17 to 24

The speaker then shifts into describing his love of nature, how close he feels to the natural world from working outside all day. He claims to be on friendly terms with many forms of wildlife: 'Several of Nature's People/ I know, and they know me'. He has a strong feeling of affection for and even friendship towards the animals, birds and insects he sees around him: 'I feel for them a transport/ Of Cordiality'.

The snake, however, is another story. While the speaker has attempted to portray the snake in as friendly a manner as possible throughout the poem, referring to it as 'Him' and a 'Fellow', there is no hiding the fact that the speaker fears the snake. It makes no difference whether he encounters the snake 'alone' or when 'Attended' by a companion: he still fears it.

In the poem's closing lines, the speaker gives us a vivid description of the physiological reactions that fear brings with it. Seeing the snake causes shortness of breath and a bone-chilling sensation: 'Without a tighter Breathing/ And Zero at the Bone'. Ultimately, the speaker cannot fully accept the snake as one of 'Nature's People'.

FOCUS ON STYLE

Tone and Atmosphere

The tone changes drastically over the course of the poem. It begins in a conversational manner, with the speaker appearing to ask the reader questions: 'You may have met Him? – did you not'. There is also something genial and playful about how the speaker refers to the snake as a 'narrow Fellow' who 'Occasionally rides', as if the snake is a gentleman whom the speaker sometimes encounters in the street.

By the end of the poem, however, the tone has changed drastically, as the speaker recounts his bone-chilling feelings of fear upon seeing the snake: 'a tighter Breathing/ And Zero at the Bone'. This brilliantly describes how our nerves prickle when we feel scared. Although he wants to be genial towards the snake and accept it as one of 'Nature's People', the speaker can't quite shake off that spine-tingling feeling.

Vivid Imagery

Interestingly, Dickinson never uses the word 'snake' in the poem. However, the way she describes the creature's movement leaves us in no doubt as to what it is. One effective thread of imagery throughout the poem is the association of the snake with hair. We see this in stanza 2, when she describes the snake combing the grass: 'The Grass divides as with a Comb'. In stanza 4, she again likens the snake to hair when she describes it as 'Unbraiding' or unravelling on the ground. These associations of the snake with hair give us a sense of its long, winding, smooth movement.

The speaker personifies the snake, as well as other creatures, throughout the poem. We see this in the way he refers to the snake as 'Him' and 'Fellow', and refers to the animal kingdom as 'Nature's People'. This demonstrates how close he feels to nature. Furthermore, in line 4, he compares the snake to a guest who does not give much notice before coming for a visit: 'His notice sudden is'. In stanza 3, he describes the snake as a discerning person with likes and dislikes: 'He likes a Boggy Acre'. We get the sense that the speaker is trying to overcome his fear of the snake by relating to it as if it were a person.

THEMES

NATURE

The speaker of the poem clearly loves nature and spends much of his time outside. He is knowledgeable about the snake's appearance, movements, and preferred habitat: 'He likes a Boggy Acre,/ A Floor too cool for Corn'. He has encountered the snake often enough to be able to describe its behaviour in detail: 'His notice sudden is'.

He proclaims his affection for wildlife, referring to the creatures as 'Nature's People'. This implies that he has a give-and-take friendship with many of the creatures in his locality: 'I know, and they know me'. Despite his love of animals, however, the speaker is not naive about nature. He knows that the snake is dangerous and not to be trusted, as evidenced by his feelings of fear: 'a tighter Breathing/ And Zero at the Bone'.

DEATH

The speaker is keenly aware of the danger and the possibility of death when he sees the snake. Though many snakes of New England are harmless, there are two venomous varieties: rattlesnakes and copperheads. Even when the speaker sees a harmless snake, he must wonder for an instant if it's one of the poisonous types. In the closing lines, the poet brilliantly describes the fight-or-flight response, the physical sensations we feel when we perceive danger: 'a tighter Breathing/ And Zero at the Bone'.

RELIGION

There are Biblical overtones to the poet's description of the snake. In the Book of Genesis, the serpent tricks Eve into eating fruit from the forbidden Tree of Knowledge, an act which results in Adam and Eve being thrown out of Paradise. The snake in the poem is also described as something of a trickster, one that appears in a 'sudden' manner, passing by your feet before you even have time to react. It is also portrayed as a deceitful creature that fools the boy into believing it's a 'Whip lash'.

THIS IS POETRY — EMILY DICKINSON
I taste a liquor never brewed –

LINE BY LINE

'I taste a liquor never brewed' is one of Dickinson's happiest and most playful nature poems. The poem makes most sense if we imagine it being spoken from the point of view of a bird that goes 'reeling' through the meadows on a summer's day, sipping nectar from various flowers. The hummingbird was a creature that had a special significance for Dickinson, so much so that she referred to herself as 'the hummingbird' in several of her letters.

Stanzas 1 and 2

The bird describes how it travels through the fields on 'endless summer days'. We imagine here the long and lazy days in June and July, days so bright and sunny it seems they will never end.

As the bird journeys across the meadows, it becomes extremely drunk. Three different substances contribute to the bird's sense of intoxication: the nectar it sips from various wild flowers, the dew it drinks from grasses and the fresh summer air itself.

The bird describes itself as a 'Debauchee', a person given to excessive indulgence. The bird, however, over-indulges in dew rather than in alcohol. It also describes itself as an 'Inebriate' or drunkard. But it gets drunk on the fresh summer air rather than on any alcoholic beverage.

The bird thinks of these summer substances as alcoholic beverages. But they are a liquor that was 'never brewed'; they are the product of no industrial process or human intervention, instead occurring naturally in the fields and meadows.

The bird compares theses summer substances to the beer from the Rhineland, an area in Germany famous for the quality of its brewing. The 'Vats' of the Rhineland's many breweries are filled with a bewildering variety of beers and ales. According to the bird, however, none can match the potency of the nectar it sips from the flowers of the meadow. No product of the Rhineland could be as intoxicating as the dew and the fresh summer air: 'Not all the Vats upon the Rhine/ Yield such an Alcohol!'

These substances leave the bird so intoxicated that it goes spinning and whirling through the meadows: 'Reeling- thro endless summer days'. The verb 'to reel' suggests movement that is wild, erratic and out of control, the type of motion one might associate with an extremely drunk person.

The bird, then, goes 'Reeling' between the blue flowers of the meadow, travelling from one to the other in search of nectar. Using a witty metaphor, the bird compares these flowers to pubs or 'inns'. Each flower is filled with intoxicating nectar, just as inns are filled with alcoholic beverages.

> Line 2 mentions tankards that have been 'scooped' or shaped out of pearl. It's possible that this refers to white 'pearly' clouds, suggestng how intoxicating dew spills from the clouds the way beer might pour from a tankard.
> It's more likely, however, that this line refers to white flowers. Just as 'Tankards' contain beer, so the flowers contain nectar. They are portrayed as being made from 'pearl' in order to reflect their intense, virginal whiteness.

Stanza 3

The bird focuses on a purple 'Foxglove' plant, which, like the blue flowers mentioned above, is compared to a pub or inn: A bee enters the foxglove and nestles within its petals, just as a patron might enter a public house and make himself comfortable at the bar. The bee becomes 'drunken' on the foxglove's nectar, just as a pub's patron might become drunk on beer and spirits. Eventually, closing time will arrive and the pub's owner will ask the customer to leave. Similarly, the foxglove's petals will eventually tighten and close up, ejecting the bee from its comfortable drinking place: 'When 'Landlords' turn the drunken Bee/ Out of the Foxglove's door'.

The bird also describes how butterflies will 'renounce' or give up nectar the way an alcoholic might swear off alcohol. They are said to have vowed to never again consume a 'dram' or measure of this intoxicating substance. The bird, however, is determined to never stop drinking nectar. Unlike the bee, it will never permit itself to be ejected from the source of this substance it loves so much. Unlike the butterfly, it will never take a vow of abstinence. Indeed, the bird vows to consume even more nectar in the future: 'I shall but drink the more!' It's as if the bird will take advantage of the fact that the bee and the butterfly have stopped drinking, savouring the nectar they would otherwise have consumed.

Stanza 4

Unlike the ejected bee or the abstaining butterfly, then, the bird will continue with its drunken ways until the day it dies. On its death it will be welcomed into heaven by saints and angels. Heaven is depicted as a town or city where the saints run to the windows of their houses to see a bird entering paradise. The angels ('Seraphs') will 'swing their snowy Hats', throwing them into the air to celebrate the arrival of this 'little Tippler'. (The 'little Tippler' is the intoxicated bird, 'tippler' being a slang word for drinker).

Dickinson uses a final, memorable metaphor to describe the bird's arrival in heaven. The bird, she says, will be 'Leaning against the – Sun –'. The image of the bird being in physical contact with the sun suggests the intense, perhaps almost unbearable, brightness of Christ's presence, a presence that the bird will experience in paradise. The fact that the bird is 'leaning' suggests that it is tired after its busy life and welcomes the rest the afterlife will provide. It 'leans' in a way that recalls how a farmer might lean against a fence after a long day's work.

> Many critics believe that this poem was influenced by the philosopher Ralph Waldo Emerson, who Dickinson greatly admired. Poets, Emerson believed, should be so attuned to nature that the sight, sound and taste of water alone are enough to intoxicate them. As Emerson himself puts it: 'The poet's habit of living should be set on a key so low that the common influences should delight him. His cheerfulness should be the gift of the sunlight, the air should suffice for his inspiration, and he should be tipsy with water.'

FOCUS ON STYLE

Form

'A Bird, came down the Walk' uses a form common to most of Dickinson's poetry. It has four-line stanzas and an ABAB rhyme scheme. It is written in 'ballad metre', which means there are four stresses in the first and third lines of each stanza, and three stresses in the second and fourth lines. Fittingly, for a poem that celebrates intoxicated states, the verse is fast-paced, 'reeling' from one line to the next.

Verbal Music

Like many of Dickinson's poems, 'I taste a liquor never brewed' makes wide use of assonance and alliteration. Assonance, in particular, is responsible for creating a pleasant, euphonious musical effect suited to a poem of celebration. The repeated 'e' sound in 'endless summer', and the repeated 'o' sounds in 'Out of the Foxgloves Door', for instance, generate a soothing music.

Metaphor, Simile, Figures of Speech

Much of the poem is structured around a 'conceit' or extended metaphor, one that compares the enjoyment of nature (especially nectar) to the enjoyment of alcohol. The bird, as we've seen, gets high on nature the way a drinker might get high on alcohol. This is why the bird describes itself as a 'Tippler' and 'Inebriate' and a 'Debauchee'. In stanza 1, as we have seen, white flowers are described as 'Tankards', or drinking glasses. In stanza 2, blue flowers are compared to 'inns', or pubs. This comparison is reinforced in stanza 3, where the speaker depicts a bee, drunk on nectar, being ejected from a Foxglove, just as a drinker might be ejected from a bar by its owner.

Vivid Imagery

The poem is distinguished by several playful and exaggerated images. A prime example is the image of heaven as a city, as a place where the saints run to the windows of their houses and where angels go 'swinging' their hats in what we can only take to be celebration. The image of a drunken bee being given his marching orders is also quite amusing.

Riddling and Paradoxical Language

The poem's riddling qualities also contribute to its playful and light-hearted tone. For instance, we are not actually told that the phrases 'Tankards scooped in Pearl' and 'inns of molten Blue' refer to flowers. Readers must figure these things out for themselves. The title phrase, 'I taste a liquor never brewed' has a similar riddling quality. We pause as we consider what the poet might be talking about. After all, what kind of liquor was never 'brewed' by human hand?

THEMES

NATURE

This poem, as is so often the case with Dickinson, celebrates the splendours of the natural world, specifically the pleasures of long, hot summer days. It depicts meadows fragrant with life and growth, flowers of such an intense blueness that they seem 'molten' or on fire; birds, bees and butterflies flitting hither and thither.

Like 'A Bird, came down the Walk', this poem is playful in its depiction of the natural world. There is something cute and almost comedic about the image of the bird becoming so drunk on nectar, air and dew that it reels from flower to flower, just as a drunk person might reel from bar to bar. Similarly playful are the depictions of the butterflies swearing abstinence and of the bee entering, and subsequently being ejected from, the foxglove's 'inn'.

The poem also reminds us of Dickinson's intense sensitivity to the natural world. We sense that the poet, like the hummingbird, is capable of getting 'high' on nature, that the sights, sounds and smells of the natural world induce in her a sense of ecstasy and intoxication.

The poem can also be read as a celebration of the everyday, suggesting the extraordinary beauty that can be found within an ordinary sight like that of a field in summer. Maybe Dickinson thinks that, like the hummingbird, we should be left blissful and ecstatic by the nature that surrounds us. We should be so open to the beauty of the natural world that it intoxicates us in the same way that liquor does.

This poem portrays an enjoyment of nature that is wild, manic and intoxicated. This is suggested in particular by the image of the bird reeling through the meadow. A similarly manic enjoyment of nature is depicted in 'The Soul has Bandaged moments', where the poet depicts herself dancing 'like a Bomb' in a 'delirious' response to nature's beauty. Many readers feel that perhaps there is something a little unhealthy about this 'hyper-sensitive' response to the natural world, as if it was the 'manic', flip side to the numb 'depression' that Dickinson describes in many of her poems.

DEATH

The poem's conclusion provides a memorable depiction of the afterlife, as the bird is welcomed into Heaven by saints and angels. Heaven is depicted as a joyful and carefree city of rest. The bird finds itself in the presence of the 'Sun', which, as we have seen, is generally taken to be Christ himself.

Heaven is depicted as a very real place, as a town whose inhabitants live in houses with windows, wear hats and who celebrate the arrival of each new soul. This positive and light-hearted depiction of the afterlife contrasts sharply with many of Dickinson's other poems that deal the themes of death and dying.

RELIGION

'I taste a liquor never brewed', then, presents a positive view of religion, suggesting that God will reward his faithful subjects, keeping a place for them in heaven's sunlit city.

This contrasts sharply with the view of religion expressed in 'There's a certain Slant of light', which depicts God tormenting us by sending down from Heaven a strange light that does us psychological harm. It also contrasts with the view of religion expressed in 'I heard a Fly buzz – when I died', which seems to mock religious hope.

We sense that God welcomes those who tirelessly appreciated nature during their lives, who relished the earth He created. The bird, then, is welcomed into heaven because of the drunkenness, gluttony, and excess it exhibited during its life. This is deeply ironic, of course, because such excessive behaviour is typically condemned by religion!

After great pain, a formal feeling comes –

LINE BY LINE

The speaker has recently experienced a bout of 'great pain', of extraordinary mental anguish. The pain has passed, but it has left a strange numbness and lethargy in its wake. The poet describes this state of mind as a 'formal feeling'. Several different meanings of the term 'formal' can be applied here:
- The feeling is marked by formality or ceremony. There is nothing spontaneous about it. It adheres to strict convention and ritual.
- It has the form or appearance of feeling but lacks any spirit.
- It is perfunctory, something that occurs in a mundane way, without care or thought.

Nerves
The speaker describes how different aspects of her body and her psyche are feeling and behaving in the wake of the pain she has recently endured. She first describes the condition of her 'Nerves'. As it is used here, the term 'Nerves' can refer to the body's nervous system, to the physical fibres that transmit signals around the body. Each nerve is also an aspect of the speaker's mental state, however. For instance, we might say of someone suffering from anxiety that his or her nerves are bad.

The speaker's nerves were recently in a highly elevated state. She experienced a state of anxiety and extreme tension, one that manifested itself both physically and mentally. But now this state of tension has passed. Where once her nerves were agitated, they now 'sit' still.

The speaker uses two literary devices to convey the state of her nerves and to describe the eerie calm that has come over her:
- First, she uses personification, depicting the nerves as people attending a ceremony. Perhaps we might imagine a crowd seated silently in a church, possibly attending a funeral service.
- She then uses a simile, comparing the nerves to 'Tombs'.

The images of people seated in a formal or ceremonious manner and of 'Tombs' convey a sense of rigidity and vitality and of a lack of emotion and spontaneity.

Heart
The speaker then describes how her inner self or psyche is holding up in the the aftermath of the pain that she has recently experienced. She uses the term 'Heart' to refer to this inner self. The 'Heart', we're told, has recently been forced to bear or carry a great weight: 'The stiff Heart ... that bore'. This suggests the intense strain to which her psyche was subjected during her recent bout of mental anguish. The 'Heart', we are told, is 'stiff', which suggests that, in the wake of this assault, her psyche is numb and unfeeling.

The speaker says that the 'Heart' cannot remember much, if anything, of the burden it was forced to carry. Did it carry this weight recently, or in the distant past? Did such an ordeal actually happen to it at all? Indeed, the 'Heart' is not itself sure how long it has existed for. Has it been around for centuries, or just for a normal human life-span?

The poem's reference to the heart's questioning conveys the intense disorientation that has gripped the speaker's psyche. In this moment of eerie calm, she finds herself confused and befuddled. She can't quite make sense of who or where she is. The terrible mental anguish that she has just experienced seems distant and unreal.

Feet

In this state of eerie calm and numbness, the speaker finds herself walking aimlessly in circles. There is something 'mechanical' and 'Wooden' about the manner in which she goes round and round, suggesting the unthinking or unconscious nature of her movement. In a sense, the speaker might be said to resemble a robot, mindlessly executing a pre-programmed set of instructions. She is no longer operating in a conscious manner; it is as if she has been hypnotised and is no longer controlling her own feet.

The speaker feels obsessively compelled to walk in this pattern. She simply must repeat this action over and over again. In this condition, she would walk through 'Ought' or anything placed along the path before her. If snakes or scorching hot coals were present on the path, the speaker would walk through or over them. If the path before her melted away, leaving only 'Air', she would continue walking anyway, presumably falling over the freshly created precipice.

The speaker, then, describes how her feet have grown 'Regardless', suggesting that they have become indifferent and uncaring. They are compelled to keep walking, irrespective of the surface on which they are walking.

Perhaps surprisingly, the speaker describes this state as one of 'contentment', suggesting that she experiences a measure of ease and satisfaction as she circles robotically. She compares what she feels to 'Quartz' or 'stone', suggesting an utterly rigid and unfeeling mental state. This contentment, then, is one of numbness and emptiness; after all, if you don't feel anything, you can't feel bad.

The speaker describes this period as the 'Hour of Lead'. Lead is an element with several vivid associations:

- It is a heavy metal and is proverbially associated with slowness and lethargy. For example, an unfit footballer might be said to have lead in his boots.
- Lead is also a poison, and prolonged exposure to it can cause serious illness or death.
- Lead is also characterised as a base metal, a crude or ugly substance for which people have little value.

The 'Hour of Lead' therefore suggests an especially grim mental interval, one characterised not only by lethargy and inertia but by feelings of worthlessness. Perhaps the speaker also feels that her mind is slowly becoming toxic and poison-filled, as this period of eerie calm continues.

The speaker imagines how she will look back on this period of eerie calm, if she manages to outlive or survive this experience. She will recall this ordeal, as someone rescued from an Arctic snow-drift might recall the experience of nearly freezing to death: 'As Freezing persons, recollect the Snow'.

She mentions three stages that an Arctic survivor might experience. The first stage is the 'Chill' that sets in as cold overcomes the body. 'Stupor' follows as the mind's processes begin to shut down. Finally, a sense of 'letting go' leads to an acceptance of one's fate. The speaker, in her state of eerie calm, feels that she is undergoing a similar process. Unlike the Arctic survivor, though, who, presumably, was rescued at the last minute, it is unclear whether she will survive her ordeal.

FOCUS ON STYLE

Metaphor, Simile, Figures of Speech

The poet personifies the 'Nerves', describing them being seated in a 'ceremonious' fashion. The poet also personifies the inner self or 'Heart', presenting it as someone who has been traumatised and left feeling confused and discombobulated.

In the poem's final stanza, the poet compares this period she must now endure to what those trapped in snow might experience. If she does survive this period in her life, she might remember it with the same intensity as someone trapped in Arctic conditions and rescued at the last minute might remember the freezing conditions: 'As Freezing persons, recollect the Snow'.

Vivid Imagery

The 'Hour of Lead' is an especially powerful image. We can imagine someone being exposed to this poisonous substance in some horrific manner, perhaps being forced to inhale a cloud of lead-filled fumes, or having this metal injected into his or her system. Of course, the speaker in the poem has not experienced such torture, but such images convey her poisoned and lethargic state of mind.

Verbal music

Dickinson's use of repeated 'o' sounds in the poem serves to create a sense of weariness and exhaustion. The long 'o' sounds in 'grown', 'stone', 'bore' and 'before' create a sombre music that compliments the grim experience that the poet is describing.

THEMES

THE WORKINGS OF THE MIND

Dickinson is a great poet of the inner self. Her poems are finely attuned to the workings of the human mind and to the vast range of human emotions and feelings. In 'The Soul has Bandaged moments', for example, the poet vividly captures the emotional swings that sometimes accompany being in love, describing how we can go from delirious highs to debilitating lows in no time at all. In 'I taste a liquor', she wonderfully describes what it is like to be full of joy and free of care. In contrast, 'There is a certain Slant of light' masterfully captures feelings of great despair and depression.

In 'After great pain', Dickinson describes the rather strange and disturbing psychological state that someone might experience after enduring some great mental trauma. Although the pain has ended, it is not followed by any sense of relief or joy. Instead, there is an almost complete absence of feeling and emotion. It is as if the speaker of the poem has been utterly drained of vitality and spontaneity.

Dickinson suggests this lack of spontaneity by describing the speaker's feeling as 'formal'. The body behaves as if it is living, but there is something stiff and mechanical about its actions and movements, as if it were just going through the motions, without any thought or care: 'The Feet, mechanical, go round'. The poet describes this lack of feeling as a form of 'contentment'. But this state of mind is brings no satisfaction; it is a stone's contentment, devoid of any feelings whatsoever.

The poem finishes on a rather disturbing note, by suggesting that the speaker might not survive this post-traumatic period. There is a danger that the mind might never again spark with life, that the body will not be re-ignited with energy and vitality. There is a risk that the speaker will just descend further into 'stupor', that the numbness will eventually paralyse the body and that all conscious thought will cease. At this point, the will to live will be lost and the speaker will let go, just as one who is trapped in snow might eventually lose their fight to survive.

John Donne Themes

Sex and Seduction

Donne's early poems, written while he was as a law student at Lincoln's Inn in London and a well-known 'visitor of ladies', present a cynical, we might say misogynistic, view of sex and seduction. 'Song: Go and catch a falling star', for instance, suggests that women can never be 'true' when it comes to matters of love and sexuality. Women who are in relationships will always cheat. Women who are single will always sleep around in an inappropriate manner. This is especially true, the poet suggests, of 'fair' or beautiful women. In fact, finding a woman who is both 'true' and 'fair' is no more possible than catching a falling star or working out why the Devil has cleft feet.

The poet even imagines undertaking a 'pilgrimage' to see such a woman as if she were one of the wonders of the world. But such a pilgrimage, he concludes, would be futile. For even the truest of beautiful women will not remain true for very long and will have slept with two or three men before his pilgrimage is concluded.

The poem, then, can be read as an extremely cynical piece of relationship advice from the poet to his male readers: avoid getting emotionally involved with women, he seems to suggest, because they cannot be trusted and will only hurt and betray you. Women, presumably, should instead be viewed only as objects of physical attraction.

Both 'The Flea' and 'The Dream' present a similarly cynical view of sex and seduction. In both poems, the poet's focus is entirely on the achievement of sexual satisfaction. In 'The Flea' we sense the poet's desperation to sleep with the object of his affection. He is willing to use any argument, no matter how outlandish, in order to overcome the lady's objections and lure her to his bedchamber. In 'The Dream', too, the poet is willing to deploy any argument he can to convince his beloved to sleep with him. As such, his characterisation of love as being something 'pure' and above the concerns of society is merely a cynical ploy, one designed to lure the object of his affections into bed.

Honour and Reputation

Both 'The Flea' and 'The Dream' are concerned with the theme of sexual virtue, with the idea that women become dishonourable or immoral if they engage in sex outside marriage. In 'The Flea', for instance, the lady is determined not to yield to the poet's advances, and she is conscious of how her honour will 'waste' away if she does so. To sleep with this man outside of wedlock would be a great 'sin' and 'shame'. In 'The Dream', too, the object of the poet's affections is concerned about her 'honour' and is fearful of the damage that sleeping with the poet might have on her reputation.

In both poems, the poet attempts to overcome the lady's objections. In 'The Flea', for instance, the poet asks the lady to 'mark', or consider, how a flea has sucked blood from the poet himself and now it's sucking blood from the lady: 'It sucked me first and now sucks thee'. Their blood has, therefore, been mixed together inside the flea's body, their bodily fluids being 'mingled' just as they would be in sexual intercourse. And yet no shameful act or sin has been committed: 'Thou knows't this cannot be said/ A sin, nor shame, nor loss of maidenhead'.

In 'The Dream', meanwhile, Donne argues that love can only be 'pure' if it is untarnished by doubts and fears. To love in a 'pure' manner, he says, is to be 'brave', for it means not caring what others might think. But if people allow thoughts of shame and honour to enter their minds, it weakens and spoils this love: 'That love is weak where fear's as strong as he'.

In both poems, it should also be noted, the poet displays scant regard for the woman's honour, and for the lasting damage their night of pleasure would cause to the lady's reputation. There is an ironic contrast, therefore, between 'The Flea' and 'The Dream', on the one hand, and 'Song: Go and Catch a Falling Star' on the other. In 'Song: Go and Catch a Falling Star', the poet laments that there are no women who possess both beauty and sexual virtue. In 'The Flea', meanwhile, he has finally encountered such a woman. And he responds by doing everything in his power to seduce her, thereby compromising her sexual virtue forever.

Love and Marriage

In an early poem like 'The Flea', Donne exhibits what might be called a casual disregard for marriage and commitment, envying the flea's ability to enjoy itself 'before it woo' and comparing its bloated body to a marriage bed. 'The Flea' can be contrasted, therefore, with Donne's later poetry, which presents a more spiritual or romantic view of love and marriage.

In 'The Sun Rising', for instance, Donne emphasises that his relationship with his wife is the only thing of value, the only thing that matters to him. His beloved, he declares, is 'everything'. Being with her makes him feel like a king, like the wealthiest man in the world. The room in which they lie together is the only place that matters, the only place that really exists.

'The Anniversary', written on the first anniversary of Donne's meeting with his future wife, also highlights the centrality of love and marriage to the poet's life. He and his beloved are so important to each other that they 'rule' each other's lives. The poet is his lover's 'king' because he rules her, but he is also her 'subject' because she rules him.

'A Valediction: Forbidden Mourning' is also a testament to the depth of the poet's feelings for his wife. The poem, like many by Donne, approaches the subject of love in a rather intellectual and argumentative manner. But there are also moments of genuine emotion, especially related to the image of the mathematical compass at the poem's conclusion.

The poem highlights how lovers remain in one another's minds even when they are physically distanced. The poet, as we've seen, stresses that Anne will remain at the centre of his thoughts while he travels. Thoughts of Anne will ensure that he behaves appropriately while abroad and that he returns home to England when his journey is concluded.

The Mystical Nature of Love

Several poems by Donne present love as something spiritual and transcendent. Both 'The Sun Rising' and 'The Anniversary', for instance, suggest that love is immune to the passage of time. True love, according to the 'The Sun Rising', is 'all alike', is utterly unchanging. It doesn't 'know' or care about the seasons that come and go. It is unaffected by the passing 'hours, days, months'. 'The Anniversary' also depicts love as somehow magically outside the normal course of time. The poet imagines that the relationship between himself and his beloved is the only thing in the world not subject to ageing and decay (By the end of the poem, however, he has adopted a humbler and more realistic vision of love, accepting that love must triumph over time, not by being timeless and unchanging, but evolving as the years go by).

Both 'Song: Sweetest Love, I do not go' and 'A Valediction: Forbidding Mourning' suggest that the poet and his wife are joined by an almost mystical bond. In 'Sweetest Love', for instance, the poet suggests that his wife's sighs and tears 'waste' not only her own life but the poet's life, too. Each is like the 'life force' of the other. Therefore, on a spiritual or psychological level they can never be apart.

'A Valediction: Forbidden Mourning' makes a similar point, arguing that the poet and his wife are 'Inter-assured of the mind' enjoying an intense mental connection that they don't fully understand themselves. Their souls, he maintains, 'are one' and can never be breached or separated. He even suggests that their relationship has secret, sacred aspects and is associated with the celestial spheres rather than with this earthly domain.

Sin and Redemption

A recurring feature of Donne's 'Holy Sonnets' is the manner in which they emphasises Donne's extraordinary sinfulness. In 'Thou hast made me', for instance, Donne describes his heart as having turned to 'iron', wonderfully capturing how sin has corrupted his life and his mind. He claims to be such a terrible sinner that he cannot 'sustain' himself for even an hour without giving into the Devil's temptations.

'Batter my heart' makes a similar point. The poet is so corrupted by sin that he compares himself to a defective pot or vase, one that the sculptor has no choice but to cast aside. Sin has taken over his life, the way a usurper might seize a town not rightfully his. He even compares himself to sin's fiancé, emphasising the intense and intimate nature of his relationship with sin. In 'At the round earth's imagined corners', Donne goes even further, implying that he's more sinful than anyone else who has ever lived or died. His sins would, therefore, require an 'abundance' of forgiveness on God's part.

But the Holy Sonnets also highlight Donne's eagerness for redemption. In 'Thou hast made me' he is desperate to be cleansed of sin, for God to 'repair' his corrupt soul. In 'Batter my heart', meanwhile, he calls on God to forcibly 'untie' or 'break' his relationship with sin. He wants God to 'Batter [his] heart', to enter his life in a forceful, almost violent manner. He wants to be broken by God's love so that he can be made anew. 'At the round earth's imagined corners', too, highlights Donne's eagerness to atone for his sins and make himself right with God.

A striking feature of the Holy Sonnets is Donne's demand for what might be described as 'special treatment' from God. In 'Batter my heart', for instance, the poet is convinced that he is beyond any ordinary means of redemption. He is so sinful that he must be utterly demolished and remade. God, he insists, must 'bend' or apply all of His extraordinary 'force' in order to make this happen.

We also see this in 'Thou hast made me' when the poet calls on God to 'repair [him] now'. The poet doesn't want to bother with the usual business of redemption, with prayer, the sacraments and good deeds. Instead, he wants God to take immediate and decisive action, cleansing him instantly of sin. 'At the round earth's imagined corners' is similarly demanding. The poet insists that he, unlike ordinary Christians, cannot be guided to redemption by prayer and the sacraments. Instead, he needs Christ to enter his life directly in some special manner so he can be taught how to repent.

THIS IS POETRY | **JOHN DONNE**

Song: Go and catch a falling star

LINE BY LINE

'Go and catch a falling star' was likely written in the 1590s, when Donne was a law student at Lincoln's Inn in London. Like other poems written during Donne's student days, it was not published in any book or periodical. Instead, it was copied out and circulated around London's literary scene. Donne's audience consisted of fellow students and literary gentlemen, many who would have been known to him personally. His goal, therefore, was to impress this almost exclusively male readership.

Stanza 1

The poem's opening stanza presents the reader with seven tasks or challenges. Donne first instructs his reader to 'Go and catch a falling star'. He is referring to the streaks of light that can be seen in the night sky and that resemble 'falling' or dropping from the skies. One could imagine, from a distance, that it might be possible to hold out a hand and catch one of these falling objects. But doing so, of course, is impossible (These streaks of light in the night sky are actually caused by meteoroids falling into the Earth's atmosphere and burning up).

Donne then instructs his reader to impregnate or 'Get with child' a 'mandrake root'. The mandrake is a Mediterranean plant whose roots can have an uncannily human appearance. Women who wanted to become pregnant would sleep with mandrake roots beneath their pillows, believing that it aided conception. But there is no magic ritual, of course, that might allow us to make a mandrake root pregnant.

Donne asks his reader to figure out the nature of time itself: 'Tell me where all past years are'. We could imagine a scholar in Donne's time asking such a question. Is time actually substance of some kind? And what happens to time that is 'used up' after we have experienced it? But such a question, of course, is impossible to answer.

Donne then asks his reader to solve an arguably even more difficult riddle, wanting to know 'who cleft the devil's foot'. The Devil is traditionally depicted as having hoof-like feet that are 'cleft' or split into two toes. Donne wants his reader to figure out who is responsible for this aspect of the Devil's appearance. Did God grant him these goat-like feet? Or did the Devil himself choose such an appearance? Or did the Devil lose a bet with some quick-witted human being and end up with 'cleft' feet forever'?

Donne asks his reader to teach him how to hear the singing of mermaids, who were known for their enchanting voices. The reader, presumably, would have to locate a colony of mermaids somewhere off the English coast. He also have to determine the time of the day when the mermaids are most likely to burst into song. He would then have to 'teach' this information to the poet. This task, of course, is just as impossible as those mentioned above.

Donne also wants to be taught how to avoid the emotion of envy. Donne brilliantly refers to 'envy's stinging', capturing how we experience envy as an almost physical pricking. Donne's reader would have to develop a series of techniques that 'keep off' or fend off this toxic emotion. He would then have to teach these tricks to the poet himself. But coming up with such techniques, given what we know of human nature, would be all but impossible.

Finally, Donne asks his reader to find the circumstance that would allow an honest person to get ahead in life. He uses a nautical metaphor to convey this. A person with an 'honest mind' is compared to a ship. Advantageous circumstances, meanwhile, are compared to a wind that will fill the ship's sails allowing it to 'advance'. But such a wind, Donne implies, is impossible to locate. The poem, then, puts forward a very cynical view of human existence, suggesting that dishonest people prosper while honest people fall behind.

Stanza 2
Donne is convinced that women can be true or fair but not both. Indeed, Donne is convinced that his reader could travel around the world and never find a woman who possesses both of these qualities:

- His reader could travel for 'ten thousand days and nights', which equates to about 27 years.
- His reader could travel until he was an old man: 'Till age snow white hairs on thee'.
- His reader could even have supernatural abilities, such as the gift of second sight, and be capable of perceiving things that are invisible to ordinary men: 'If thou be'st born to strange sights,/ Things invisible to see'.
- His reader would return with tales of the 'strange wonders' he experienced while on his travels. Donne imagines sitting down with his returning reader to hear tales of strange people and faraway lands: 'Thou, when thou return'st,/ wilt tell me,/ All strange wonders that befell thee'.

But his reader will 'swear' that nowhere, even during such an epic journey, did he encounter a woman who is both true and fair.

Stanza 3
Donne concedes that it just might be possible for his reader to encounter such a woman in the course of such an epic journey. If his reader were to encounter such a woman he must write to Donne immediately, telling him where she can he found: 'If thou find'st one, let me know'. Donne says that he would happily travel a great distance to see such a woman: 'Such a pilgrimage were sweet'.

But Donne quickly changes his mind and declares that he would not undertake a 'pilgrimage' in order to meet a woman his reader had deemed both true and fair. In fact, he wouldn't even go to meet her even if she lived next door: 'I would not go,/ Though at next door we might meet'.

This is because no beautiful woman can remain true for very long:

- Donne's reader might come across a beautiful woman who is true at the time of their meeting: 'Though she were true, when you met her'.
- She might even remain true while the reader writes to Donne informing him of this discovery: 'And last, till you write your letter'.
- But before Donne arrives ('ere I come') she will have slept with two or three other men: 'she/ Will be/ false…to two, or three'.

Science and Superstition
Donne was living during a time of great scientific learning and discovery. But it was still also a very superstitious time, with people believing a great number of things that we might find strange or surprising today:

People believed that the sight of a shooting' or 'falling' star brought good luck or served as a portent or signal that good fortune was on its way.

Mandrake plants were believed to have magical powers and were much in demand throughout Europe at the time. Men would sometimes carry the plant in their pocket, believing that it would help them attract their desired lover. It was also believed that these plants emitted a terrifying scream when they were uprooted!

The first stanza also hints at the idea of witches, which people of Donne's time believed to be very real. The mentioning of the mandrake root calls to mind the strange plants and herbs that witches would use to make their magic potions. Witches were also commonly believed to be responsible for the envious thoughts that troubled people's minds.

DONNE'S METAPHYSICAL STYLE

Outrageous Claims and Demands
'Go and catch a falling star', like many of Donne's poems, features outrageous claims and demands. The opening stanza, as we've seen, sets the reader a series of bizarre and impossible tasks. The second stanza make the outrageous – not to say misogynistic – claim that nowhere on earth can be there be found a woman who is both true and fair.

The poem's most extreme claim, however, comes in the third stanza, where the poet imagines hearing that a 'true' and 'fair' woman is living next door to him. The poet declares that by the time he had put on his coat and made his way next door she would no longer be true. In fact, she would have slept with two or three other men! Here, of course, Donne is using hyperbole, or deliberate poetic exaggeration, in order to emphasise the falseness of the 'fairer sex'.

Inventive Metaphors and Similes
Stanza two features an inventive simile where white hairs are compared to snow. Donne personifies 'age', presenting it as someone who sprinkles white hair on us, whitening the surface of our heads just as snow whitens the surface of the earth when it falls.

Paradox and Contradiction
Donne is well known as a poet of paradox and contradiction. We see this in stanza 3. Pilgrimages are usually thought of as difficult and arduous journeys. But Donne's pilgrimage in this instance would be 'sweet'. The poet would take joy in this long journey, despite its difficulties, delighted at the prospect of the 'true' and 'fair' woman to whom he is travelling.

Form
The fact that the poem is titled 'Song' tells us that this lyric was intended to be chanted or sung, possibly with musical accompanied. The poem's short lines and regular rhyme scheme lend it to such a performance.

THEMES

SEX AND SEDUCTION
This poem presents a cynical, we might say misogynistic, view of women. Women, the poet suggests, can never be 'true' when it comes to matters of love and sexuality. Women who are in relationships will always cheat. Women who are single will always sleep around in an inappropriate manner.

This is especially true, the poet suggests, of 'fair' or beautiful women. In fact, finding a woman who is both 'true' and 'fair' is no more possible than catching a falling star or working out why the Devil has cleft feet.

The poem's second stanza is wittily misogynistic. We can imagine Donne's male audience chuckling at his depiction of his reader travelling the whole world, encountering all kinds of 'strange wonders' but meeting no woman who is both true and fair.

This misogynistic attitude is most evident in the poem's final stanza. The poet, as we've seen, imagines undertaking a 'pilgrimage' to see such a woman as if she were one of the wonders of the world. But such a pilgrimage, he concludes, would be futile, for even the truest of beautiful women will not remain true for very long and will have slept with two or three men before his pilgrimage is concluded.

The poem, then, can be read as an extremely cynical piece of relationship advice from the poet to his male readers: he seems to suggest that they should avoid becoming emotionally involved with women because they cannot be trusted and will only hurt and betray you. Women, presumably, should instead be viewed only as objects of physical attraction.

This poem takes an extremely bitter and cynical view of love. Women, the poet argues, are by their very nature inclined to be unfaithful. In fact, women are so untrustworthy in matters of the heart that it's impossible to find a woman who is both beautiful and faithful. And even if you do find such a woman, it's only a matter of time until her true treacherous nature is revealed: 'Though she were true, when you meet her … Yet she/ Will be/ False'.

The Flea

LINE BY LINE

In 'The Flea', the poet addresses a lady who he is trying to get into bed. The lady, however, is reluctant, feeling that her honour will be lost if she surrenders to his advances. This is especially true because she still retains her 'maidenhead', or virginity.

Donne, we must remember, was writing at a time when women were all too often branded dishonourable or immoral if they slept with a man outside marriage. The lady, then, resists the poet's advances in order to preserve her honour, denying him the pleasures of a sexual encounter. The poet tries to overcome her reluctance through a series of witty, outlandish arguments, all of which are based around the idea of the flea.

Their blood is already 'mingled'

The poet attempts to convince her how harmless or unimportant ('How little') sleeping together would be. He does so by asking her to 'mark', or consider, a flea hopping around the room:

- The flea has sucked blood from the poet himself. Now it's sucking blood from the woman: 'It sucked me first and now sucks thee'.
- Their blood has, therefore, been mixed together inside the flea's body: 'And in this flea our two bloods mingled be'. The flea is now filled with 'one blood made of two'.
- Their bodily fluids have been 'mingled' just as they would be in sexual intercourse.
- And yet no shameful act or sin has been committed. The woman's honour is still intact: 'Thou knows't this cannot be said/ A sin, nor shame, nor loss of maidenhead'.

The woman, therefore, has no reason to resist the poet's advances. Sleeping with the poet will prove no more sinful than being bitten by the flea. Indeed, because their blood has been combined, it's as if they've already slept together anyway.

The flea delights in its own physicality, pampering itself by feasting on blood until it's bloated and swollen: 'And pampered swells with one blood made of two'. It indulges in physical pleasure without 'wooing' or seeking any long-term commitment like that of marriage: 'Yet this enjoys before it woo'. The poet wishes that he and this woman could be more like the flea, that they too could enjoy the pleasures of the flesh before they are married: 'And this, alas, is more than we would do'.

A special kind of 'marriage'

The poet claims that the mingling of their bloods in the flea's body is a special kind of marriage, one 'more' meaningful and profound than any conentional union: 'Where we almost, nay more than married are'.

- He inisists, then, they have been 'met' or been joined together in wedlock despite the disapproval of their parents, and even the objections of the lady herself: 'Though parents grudge, and you, we are met'.
- The flea's body is presented as the temple where their marriage has been celebrated: 'this/ Our … marriage temple is.' It has become, therefore, a holy place.
- The flea also serves as their 'marriage bed'. Again Donne is referring to the mingling of their blood inside the insect's body. Their essences, he claims, have combined there just as a married couple's essences combine on the first night of marriage.

The poet argues, therefore, that because they are already 'married', she can have no objection to sleeping with him!

Killing the flea would be sinful

The lady, it seems, is so unimpressed by the poet's argumnets that she threatens to kill the flea. The poet, however, asks her to 'stay' or restrain herself, saying that if she does so she will spare three lives: 'three lives in one flea spare'. For by swatting the insect she will kill not only the flea itself but also a part of the poet and a part of herself. The flea, having sucked their blood, contains a little piece of each of them: 'This flea is you and I'.

The poet argues that by killing the flea the woman will commit three sins:

- She will murder the poet, or at least that part of him that is inside the flea.
- She will commit the sin of suicide or 'self-murder' because part of her is also inside the flea: 'Let not to this, self-murder added be'.
- She will commit the sin of sacrilege, the destruction of a sacred place. This is because, as we have seen, the flea has become the holy temple of their marriage.

The lady triumphs?

The lady ignores the poet's plea for mercy and acts in a 'Cruel and sudden' manner. She kills this innocent flea whose only crime was taking a single drop of her blood: 'In what could this flea guilty be,/ Except in that drop which it sucked from thee?' She swats the creature and her nail is 'Purpled' with its blood.

The lady laughs in triumph. She has disproved the poet's argument in favour of sparing the flea's life. She has killed the flea and yet no harm has come to herself or to the poet. Contrary to his warning, she has been guilty of neither murder nor suicide: 'Yet thou triumph'st and says't that thou/ Find'st not thyself, nor me the weaker now'. The poet, however, attempts to turn her triumph against her. ''Tis true', he agrees, that in killing the flea she has not damaged herself. But this merely proves that her fears about sleeping with him are false: 'then learn how false fears be'. Killing the flea caused little or nothing of her life force to waste away. Similarly, yielding to his advances will cause little or nothing of her 'honour' to waste away: 'Just so much honour, when thou yields't to me/ Will waste, as this flea's death took life from thee'.

DONNE'S METAPHYSICAL STYLE

Weird and Wonderful Arguments
This is another poem where Donne's Metaphysical style is in evidence, in particular his tendency to deploy zany and fantastical arguments:
- He argues that two people being bitten by the same flea amounts to a kind of sexual intercourse.
- He argues that two people being bitten by the same flea amounts to a kind of marriage.
- He argues that in killing the flea the lady will take 'three lives' and commit three very different sins.
- 'He argues that she will lose no more honour in yielding to him than she lost life force in killing the flea.

Donne offers an argument in favour of each of these outrageous and outlandish points. Yet he does not aim to convince us that they are actually true. He sets out rather to impress us with the inventiveness and ingenuity of his debating style.

Outrageous Claims and Demands
Another aspect of Donne's Metaphysical style is his tendency to make outrageous claims. We see this when he declares that the lady is literally killing him by denying him the pleasures of her body: 'Though use make you apt to kill me'. Indeed, he suggests that through 'use', or practice, the lady has become 'apt', or skilled, at killing him.

Inventive Metaphors and Similes
Another aspect of Donne's Metaphysical style is his tendency to use metaphors that compare two seemingly very different things. We see this in stanza 2, where the flea is compared to a temple in which the poet and the lady have been married. The flea, he declares, is a church with 'living' and 'jet' black walls where he and his lady have been 'cloistered' or sheltered (Donne's use of the word 'cloistered' reinforces the impression that the flea's body has become a holy place. To cloister someone is to confine him or her to the holy and peaceful seclusion of a monastery).

'The Flea' was written in the 1590s, when Donne was a law student at Lincoln's Inn in London. The poem would have been copied out and circulated among London's literary set.

In Donne's time, believe it or not, there was a tradition of love poems that mentioned fleas. Donne's goal is to push this concept further than any of his rivals or contemporaries. He wants to come up with arguments and metaphors that impress his exclusively male audience with his wit and ingenuity.

'The Flea', then, is more a display of dazzling argumentative skill than it is a genuine attempt at seduction. After all, we may wonder whether such a bizarre discussion about a flea would be sufficient to seduce any reasonable woman!

THEMES

SEX AND SEDUCTION
In this famous poem of seduction, we sense the poet's desperation to sleep with the object of his affection. He seems happy to resort to almost any tactic to lure this lady to his bedchamber. He is willing to use any argument, no matter how outlandish, to overcome her objections.

'The Flea' is a highly playful poem. There is something teasing, almost flirtatious, about the way the poet and the lady clash wits. The poet's arguments and comparisons are meant to dazzle and amuse rather than be taken seriously.

LOVE AND MARRIAGE
'The Flea', it might be argued, presents a cynical view of love and marriage, the poet's focus being entirely on the achievement of sexual satisfaction. The poet, in fact, seems to have a casual disregard for marriage and commitment, envying the flea's ability to enjoy itself 'before it woo' and comparing its body to a marriage bed. 'The Flea' can be contrasted, therefore, with 'The Anniversary' and 'A Valediction: Forbidding Mourning', which present a more spiritual or romantic view of marriage.

HONOUR AND REPUTATION
'The Flea', as we have seen, is concerned with the theme of sexual virtue, with the idea that women become dishonourable or immoral if they engage in sex outside marriage. We see this in how the woman is determined not to yield to the poet's advances and she is conscious of how her honour will 'waste' away if she does so. To sleep with this man outside of wedlock would be a great 'sin' and 'shame'.

There is an ironic contrast between 'The Flea' and 'Song: Go and Catch a Falling Star'. In 'Song: Go and Catch a Falling Star', the poet laments that there are no women who possess both beauty and sexual virtue. In 'The Flea', meanwhile, he has finally encountered such a lady. And he responds by doing everything in his power to seduce her, thereby compromising her sexual virtue forever.

The poem, therefore, highlights a double standard that prevailed in Donne's time and that to lesser extent still exists today. It's okay, the poem suggests, for a young man like Donne to be a 'visitor of ladies'. But women, on the other hand, are harshly judged if they sleep around. The poet, it should also be noted, displays scant regard for the woman's honour, and for the lasting damage their night of pleasure would cause to the lady's reputation.

The Dream

LINE BY LINE

Stanza 1

The poet is obsessed with a particular lady. However, he has been unable to lure her into bed. While sleeping in his chamber, he dreams that he and the lady are making love. His dream is interrupted when that very lady comes into his room and wakes him up.

We might ask how the lady managed to enter the poet's chamber. It's likely that both the poet and the lady are 'at court' and are resident in some great palace or manor where they would have had easy access to one another's accomodation.

Ordinarily, the poet would have been annoyed have such a 'happy dream' broken, to be awakened from such an erotic reverie. But because it's the lady herself who woke him, he can't be too irritated:

- He addresses the lady with soft, endearing words, calling her 'Dear love'.
- It was wise, he declares, for the lady to wake him. The subject or 'theme' of his dream, the poet's desire idea of making love to this woman, is so powerful and 'strong' that it needs to be acted upon. It is a 'theme' more suited to the 'reason' or rationality of the waking world, than to the 'phantasy' of dreams.
- Anyway, his dream, in a sense, wasn't broken at all. He was dreaming about the lady and now the lady is really here. So his dream has been continued: 'My dream thou brok'st not, but continued'st it'.
- His dream of lovemaking was interrupted before it could reach its conclusion. But maybe he and the lady could 'act' or complete this lovemaking in the real world: 'let's act the rest'.

The poet, therefore, urges the lady to 'Enter [his] arms' and succumb, finally, to his advances.

Stanza 2

Donne flatters the lady, declaring that her eyes are brilliantly bright and radiant. It was the brightness of her eyes, he claims, rather than any noise she made, that roused him from his slumbers. Her eyes he declares, are so bright that they woke him like a torch shining in his face.

The lady, he declares, is so beautiful that she has an angelic appearance. Indeed, when he first woke up he thought it was an angel rather than a human being standing in his room: 'Yet I thought thee…an angel, at first sight'.

Donne also claims that the lady is capable of seeing into his heart and reading his mind, of knowing his deepest thoughts and desires. When she entered the room and he was sleeping she knew exactly what he was dreaming: 'thou knew'st what I dreamt'. Not only this, but she knew that he was close to reaching the climax of his dream: 'thou knew'st when/ Excess of joy would wake me'.

But angels, the poet knows, are not capable of reading the thoughts of humans. It is 'beyond an angel's art' to do so. And so, the poet declares, the lady must be some kind of a goddess or divine being if she can read his mind and know his deepest thoughts and desires. To consider her a mere angel would, therefore, be disrespectful, irreverent or 'profane': 'it could not choose but be/ Profane, to think thee any thing but thee'.

The Lady is 'so true'

Throughout the poem Donne makes references to 'truth' and to what is 'true'. In the opening stanza, he tells the lady that she is 'so true' that simply thinking about her is sufficient to make dreams reality and fantastical tales or imaginings real lived experiences that are recorded in the annals of history: 'Thou art so true that thoughts of thee suffice/ To make dreams truths, and fables histories'.

The term 'true' has a number of relevant meanings here:

- Donne is suggesting that the woman is very real and authentic, as opposed to some figment of his imagination.
- But he is also implying that the lady is sincere and honest. There is nothing disingenuous or duplicitous about her behaviour.
- She is also 'true' in the sense of being loyal and faithful to him. Her entering his room, he suggests, is a clear sign that she is committed to him and wishes to make love to him.

Making love would, therefore, not only make his fantasy a reality but it would somehow demonstrate the sincerity of her love and feelings for the poet.

Stanza 3

We can imagine the lady has been sitting on the poet's bed, listening to his flattering words. Perhaps he has been holding her hand and gazing into her eyes as he speaks. But his words fail to convince her to get into bed with him, and eventually she stands up and starts to leave the room.

As the lady makes her way towards the door, the poet expresses his disappointment and frustration. He tells her that when she entered the room and all the while she remained there, she was acting in accordance with her true impulses and desires.

She entered his room, he suggests, because she wanted to demonstrate how 'true' her feelings are for him. As such, her presence in the room revealed her true feelings and character, not only to the poet but to herself: 'Coming and staying show'd thee, thee'.

But when she gets up and leaves the room the poet doubts that she is acting in accordance with her true desires and impulses. She is allowing fears of how society will judge her to determine her behaviour. As such, she is no longer being true to herself: 'now/ Thou art not thou'.

The poet associates love that is unaffected by earthly concerns and matters with the 'spirit'. Such love, he says, is 'pure', untarnished by doubt and fear. To love in such a manner is to be 'brave', for it means not caring what others might think about the manner in which we behave and act. But if people allow thoughts of shame and honour to enter their minds, it weakens and spoils this love: 'That love is weak where fear's as strong as he'.

Donne tells the lady that she is being guided by her fears and thoughts of shame and the need to preserve her 'honour', rather than her natural desires. As such, her love for the poet is not 'all spirit, pure and brave'. It is mixed up with thoughts of 'fear, shame' and 'honour'.

One last hope

As the lady leaves his room, the poet holds out one last hope. He imagines that she came to rouse his passions and is now leaving with the intention of returning to excite even greater passion.

In this regard, the poet says, she is treating him like a candle. New candles can sometimes be difficult to light because their wicks are soft. However, a candle that has been lit and extinguished is much easier to reignite. As such, it was customary to light and extinguish new candles in order to prepare the wicks and ensure that they would light quickly when required.

Donne suggests that when the woman entered the room she roused his passion. Her leaving the room now dampens or extinguishes this passion. However, just like the new candle that has been lit and extinguished, the poet's passion can be quickly reignited or aroused: 'Perchance as torches, which must ready be,/ Men light and put out, so thou deal'st with me'.

The poet says he will hold this happy thought and 'dream' or imagine that the lady will soon return to his room: 'then I/ Will dream that hope again'. Without such hope he would rather 'die'. The final line can be read as a dramatic threat, a last effort to make the woman return. The poet will literally die if she does not make love to him and restore his faith in their relationship. However, the word 'die' also has sexual connotations and can mean to orgasm. Donne, of course, intends such a pun. If the woman does not return to satisfy him he will have to take matters into his own hands.

THEMES

THE MYSTICAL NATURE OF LOVE

Like 'Sweetest Love' and 'A Valediction: Forbidding Mourning', this poem presents love as something spiritual and transcendent. Donne talks of love being 'all spirit' and 'pure', suggesting that when people are truly in love their relationship transcends the physical and the earthly.

Donne argues that true love ought to be unaffected by any earthly concerns. Lovers, he suggests, should not care what others in society think about their actions and behaviour. Thoughts of 'shame' or 'honour' only weaken love's bond. If someone is truly in love, the poet claims, he or she should be true to their feelings and not allow fear to dictate or determine what they do. Love that is devoid of fear and doubt is 'pure', something spiritual that transcends all earthly fears and concerns.

HONOUR AND REPUTATION

However, unlike 'Sweetest Love' and 'A Valediction', this poem is not addressed to the poet's wife, but to an unmarried lady that the poet is looking to seduce. The fears that the poet alludes to are, for the lady in question, very real. Women who engaged in sex outside marriage were judged harshly by society and were classed as being dishonourable and immoral for their behaviour.

Donne, of course, is very conscious of this. He, therefore, uses the idea of 'pure' love to convince the lady to overcome her fears of society's opinions and values. If she is afraid and ashamed to make love to him then her love is not pure: 'That love is weak where fear's as strong as he;/ 'Tis not all spirit, pure and brave'. Rather than being strong for resisting the poet's seductive efforts and protecting her character and reputation, the lady is being 'weak' and cowardly for allowing such concerns to guide her judgement and determine her actions.

In this regard, 'The Dream' can be compared to 'The Flea', another poem where the poet displays scant regard for the woman's honour, and for the lasting damage their moment of pleasure would cause to the lady's reputation.

SEX AND SEDUCTION

Ultimately, of course, 'The Dream' is a clever poem of seduction. Donne is willing to deploy any argument he can to convince his beloved to sleep with him. As such, his characterisation of love as being something 'pure' and above the concerns of society is merely a cynical ploy, something constructed to help him achieve his desired objective. It is he, and not the lady, who is ultimately being false and disingenuous.

DONNE'S METAPHYSICAL STYLE

Outrageous Claims and Demands

This is another poem where Donne's Metaphysical style is in evidence, in particular his tendency to make outrageous claims:
- He claims that it was the power and intensity of the lady's eyes that woke him from his slumbers, that they shine as brilliantly as a torch or a flash of lightning.
- He claims that the lady is so 'true' that just thinking about her is enough to make dreams reality: 'Thou art so true that thoughts of thee suffice/ To make dreams truths'.
- He claims that the lady is capable of reading his mind and knowing his deepest desires, dreams and thoughts: 'thou sawest my heart,/ And knew'st my thoughts'.

Inventive Metaphors and Similes

Another aspect of Donne's Metaphysical style is his tendency to use metaphors that compare two seemingly very different things. In the final stanza, he compares the sexual arousal of men to the lighting and extinguishing of candles, suggesting that just as candles which have been recently lit and extinguished can easily be lit again, so can men be easily re-aroused: 'Perchance as torches, which must ready be,/ Men light and put out'.

Weird and Wonderful Arguments

This is another poem where Donne deploys highly imaginative and fantastical arguments to achieve a desired goal or objective. Here he argues that his beloved woke him from his slumbers because she knew he was dreaming that he was making love to her. He claims that such erotic dreams are 'too strong' for fantasy and that they need to be acted out in reality. His beloved, he argues, should agree with him on this, because she is a lover of truth and, therefore, should wish to 'make dreams truths'.

Tone

The tone of the first two stanzas is bright and positive as the poet seeks to charm the lady who has entered his room. He is at times complimentary ('thou wak'd'st' me wisely', 'Thou art so true', 'I thought thee … an angel') and seductive ('Enter these arms, for since thou thought'st it best,/ Not to dream all my dream, let's act the rest'). However, the tone of the last stanza is different. Here the poet comes across as wounded, cynical and rather bitter, accusing the lady in question of not being 'brave' and 'true'.

THIS IS POETRY — JOHN DONNE
The Sun Rising

LINE BY LINE

The sun is an interfering 'old fool'

The poet has spent the night in bed with his beloved. The morning has arrived and the sun's rays come pouring in through the window. The poet is anything but happy with this. The sun's bright beams are a clear reminder that the day has begun and it is now time to get back to their day-to-day lives. They must now leave the chamber – and each other – and go about the business of the day.

The poet personifies the sun, imagining that it has arrived at their particular house and is now peering in through the curtains, calling upon them to get out of bed and go about their duties.

- The sun, he declares is an 'old fool'. It is like an elderly person whose mental faculties are beginning to decline.
- The sun, as a result, has become 'unruly', has started to behave in a disorderly or disruptive manner.
- It has also become 'saucy', suggesting that it's given to rude and inappropriate behaviour.
- The sun, however, is still as 'pedantic' as it ever was, meaning that it is finicky and overly fussy. It is especially pedantic, of course, when it comes to timekeeping.
- The sun is also described as 'busy' or meddlesome. It goes around interfering in the affairs of others, reminding them that their hours of play or rest are at an end.

The sun, then, is personified in an extremely unflattering fashion. It is both an interfering busybody and a rather confused elderly person capable of all kinds of rude and rowdy behaviour.

The poet is irritated and asks the sun why it is bothering him: 'Why dost thou thus?' He asks the sun to leave him and his lover alone, to go away and bother other people instead:

- The sun, he suggests, should 'chide' or scold schoolboys who have slept in and are late for their lessons.
- It should also chide apprentices who are 'sour' or unhappy at having to spend yet another day at work. These apprentices, we imagine, are lingering in bed, rather than rushing to the workshops of their masters.
- It should wake the king's 'court-huntsmen' who need to rise and ready themselves for a day in the saddle: 'Go tell court huntsmen that the king will ride'
- It should 'call' peasants, the poor agricultural labourers, to the duties or 'offices' of the harvest: 'Call country ants to harvest offices'.

Time, Donne suggests, is 'run' or regulated by the sun because we use the sun's 'motions', its journey around the sky, to determine hours and days, months and years.

Donne, in the poem's opening stanza, uses the term 'season' in the older sense of an appropriate period of time. For lovers, then, there is a season or appropriate time for lovemaking. There is also a season or appropriate time for taking a long walk on the beach. There is also a season or appropriate time for enjoying a romantic meal together.

Donne wishes that these seasons weren't regulated by the sun's motions: 'Must to thy motions lovers' seasons run?' He wishes that the seasons of lovers behaved differently to ordinary time, that a walk on the beach could last months or a night of passion for a hundred years.

The sun is weak, the lovers powerful

The sun's beams are usually considered to be extremely 'strong'. They are also 'reverend', or worthy of great respect. Many religions and religious practices, after all, are based around the sun and its light.

The poet, however, disputes this view of the sun's intrusive light. The sun, he suggests, has no reason to believe that its beams are 'so reverend and strong'. The poet, after all, can simply 'eclipse' or block them out simply by closing his eyes: 'I could eclipse and cloud them with a wink'. But the poet says that he will not 'eclipse' or 'cloud' the sun in this manner, because it would mean losing sight of his beloved: 'But that I would not lose her sight so long'.

The poet compares the sun's beams to the eyes of his beloved. His lover's eyes, he suggests, are far brighter and more radiant. They are so dazzling that the sun itself could be blinded by looking into them: 'If her eyes have not blinded thine'.

The wealthiest king

The poet makes the extraordinary declaration that he's ruler of the entire Earth. His lover, he declares, is 'all states', is every country and kingdom in the world. And he, as the man in his beloved's life, is the 'prince' or ruler of all these lands: 'She's all states, and all princes, I'.

The sun, he declares, as it embarks on its daily journey around the world, will notice that things have changed. It will notice that the kings it saw yesterday are no longer in their palaces. They might now be employed as huntsmen or as lowly peasants in the fields. If the sun asks about these fallen kings it will be told that their powers and titles have been transferred to the poet himself: 'thou shalt hear, All here in one bed lay'. The poet and his beloved, then, are the only true princes in the world. Any other princes the sun might encounter, as it journeys around the world, are merely players or actors. These false princes play at being the poet and his beloved: 'Princes do but play us'. They pretend to exercise power that really belongs to the poet himself.

The poet declares that all the world's honours – all noble titles, all stately offices – belong to him now. Any other honours the sun might witness, as it journeys around the world, are only 'mimic'. They are mere imitations of the true honours that have been awarded to the poet.

The poet also declares that the all the world's wealth now belongs to him. Any other apparent wealth the sun might witness, as it journeys around the world, is merely 'alchemy'. It is counterfeit and ultimately worthless, as all genuine riches are rightfully the poet's now.

The poet urges the sun to look for the islands of the East Indies, famous for their spices, and the islands of the West Indies, famous for their gold mines. These islands, according to the poet, will not be where the sun 'left' them or last saw them. Instead, they will 'lie' with the poet in his bedroom.

These lines are famously open to interpretation. Perhaps the poet is suggesting that the ownership of these islands has been transferred to him, and that the deeds and relevant paperwork are with him in his bedroom. Or perhaps he's making the rather surreal suggestion that the islands have magically been shrunk down and transported to his bedroom, where he studies them as if they were a unique and extraordinary ornament.

Contracting

The poet then pushes things even further declaring that beyond their bedroom, nothing really exists: 'Nothing else is'. Everything in the world has been 'contracted' or compressed into these four walls.

The sun, he suggests, should be happy that the world had been 'contracted' in such a fashion. The sun's duty, he reminds it, is to 'warm the world'. But the sun is old now – having been around for billions of years – and like an old pensioner needs to slow down and take it easy: 'Thine age asks ease'. Thankfully, the sun now only needs to 'warm' a single chamber, the poet's bedroom, for these four walls contain everything that exists: 'Shine here to us, and thou art everywhere'.

Each day it need only circle their bed to perform its duty. The bed is the centre around which it will revolve and the walls of the bedroom will define its circular orbit: 'This bed thy centre is, these walls thy sphere'.

Science and Superstition

John Donne lived through an exciting period of scientific discovery and many of his poems exhibit a keen interest in this new learning. However, at the time of this poem's composition, it was still widely believed that the Sun revolved around the Earth. Although Copernicus had detailed his theory of the Earth and the other planets rotating around the Sun in 1543, it took more than a century for this to become widely accepted. As such, 'The Sun Rising' describes a geocentric understanding of the universe, in which the Sun revolves around the Earth.

The mentioning of 'alchemy' in the third stanza reminds us that, despite the great advances in science in the 17th century, ancient beliefs and superstitions still prevailed. Alchemists believed it was possible to turn base metals like iron and lead into gold. They based their theories on the assumption that the world and everything in it are composed of four basic elements (air, earth, fire and water). It was thought that by changing the proportions of these constituent elements, base metals could be transformed into gold.

DONNE'S METAPHYSICAL STYLE

Outrageous Claims and Demands

Donne, like the other Metaphysical poets of his generation, was fond of making outlandish claims and statements that meant to provoke the reader. This is nowhere more apparent than in 'The Sun Rising':

- He declares that his beloved's eyes are so radiant that they are capable of blinding the sun itself.
- He declares that he's the ruler of the world, the wealthiest man in the world and the true holder of all the world's honours.
- He even declares that the entire world has been 'contracted' into his bedchamber, that nothing else exists.

Inventive Metaphors and Similes

The poet uses a metaphor to describe the workers in the fields, calling them 'country ants'. The comparison suggests both their great number and their industriousness. An equally vivid metaphor is used to describe the passage of time. The future is compared to a roll of fabric or material. As time progresses, pieces of cloth are torn from this roll, used and then discarded. The past, therefore, is compared to a pile of rags, all the 'hours, days and months' that have been used up by time's relentless progress.

The poem, as we've seen, is very playful in its personification of the sun, presenting it as an elderly and raucous busybody. Donne playfully depicts the sun looking down on the Earth's surface as it makes its daily journey around the world, noticing various kings, continents and islands. The sun, Donne suggests, has a rather high opinion of itself, regarding its beams as both powerful and worthy of respect. The final stanza, as we've seen, emphasises the sun's great age, depicting it as an elderly worker who needs to start thinking about retirement.

Form

'The Sun Rising' is a lyric poem consisting of three ten-line stanzas following a ABBACDCDEE rhyme scheme. The poem is a variation on the 'aubade' form, a morning love song usually about lovers separating at dawn. Donne, as usual, comes up with us own inventive twist. Instead of pleading with his lover to linger a little longer, he berates the sun for waking them and for signalling that their night together is at an end.

'The Sun Rising' is also a famous example of apostrophe, which occurs when a poet addressed an inanimate object. Donne, in this light-hearted poem, addresses the sun in a variety of tones, conveying everything from irritation, to triumph to sympathy.

THEMES

LOVE AND MARRIAGE

The poet emphasises the strength of his feelings for his beloved. He longs to spend more time with her and is irritated that the sun has risen, signalling that their night together is at an end.

The poet praises his beloved's beauty, declaring that he is unwilling to close his eyes in order to shut out the sun's intrusive light. He doesn't want to lose sight of her beauty for even a second. He uses hyperbole to emphasise the radiance of her eyes, declaring that they are capable of blinding the sun itself.

The poem was likely written around 1604, not long after Donne and Anne were married. They were living in Surrey, not far from London, in a small house belonging to a cousin of Anne's. Donne was 32 at the time and had just been released from prison, having served a short sentence for marrying Anne without her father's approval. Despite these difficult circumstances, it seems that this was a happy time in the poet's life, as 'The Sun Rising' seems to illustrate.

In the second half of the poem, Donne emphasises that the love they share is the only thing of value, the only thing that matters to him. His beloved, he declares, is 'everything'. Being with her makes him feel like a king, like the wealthiest man in the world. The room in which they lie together is the only place that matters, the only place that really exists.

These sentiments of course are common in love poems and love songs from the middle ages to the present day. But Donne, typically, puts his own twist on these common sentiments and pushes them to an extreme. We are not, of course, meant to take these statements literally. They are deliberately hyperbolic or exaggerated in order to emphasise the intensity of the poet's feelings for his beloved and the extraordinary richness she brings to his life.

THE MYSTICAL NATURE OF LOVE

This poem, like 'The Anniversary', emphasises the mystical nature of love. 'True love', Donne suggests, is 'all alike'. These feelings never change, remaining constant as the years go by. The passage of time, therefore, is irrelevant to true love. True love doesn't 'know' or care about the seasons that come and go, each with its particular 'clime' or set of weather conditions. The passing 'hours, days, months' change much about the world. But they have no effect on true love.

The Anniversary

A John Donne Manuscript discovered in 2015

LINE BY LINE

In the poem, Donne celebrates the love he felt for Anne More, the woman who was to become his wife. Donne first met Anne around 1597, when he started working for her uncle, Sir Thomas Egerton, and they quickly fell in love. This poem was written on the anniversary of their first meeting.

Powerful and admirable things

The poet mentions a number of prestigious people, concepts and entities:

- He mentions 'kings' and their 'favourites'. These 'favourites' were courtiers who enjoyed an especially close relationship with the king. They frequently gained power and prestige as a result.
- He mentions 'beauties' and 'wits'. The term 'beauties' refers to those known throughout the land for their extraordinary good looks. The 'wits', on the other hand, are famous for their intelligence, for their original and inquiring minds.
- Donne also mentions the 'glory of honours'. This refers to noble titles and grants of land that might be bestowed by the crown on its loyal servants. It also refers to powerful and lucrative positions within the government, some of which were held for life (Donne's boss, Sir Thomas Egerton, for instance, was made 'Lord Keeper of the Great Seal').
- Finally, Donne refers to 'the sun itself', which 'makes' or regulates time. For we count hours, months and years according to the Earth's annual journey around the Sun.

Each of these, the poet notes, is subject to ageing and decay. Each is 'elder by a year, now' than it was on the day he first saw his beloved. Each draws closer to its destruction with every passing year: 'All other things to their destruction draw'.

The kings and favourites will age and pass away. Mental prowess and physical beauty, too, will be destroyed by the passage of time. Political power and prestige, too, will inevitably prove fleeting; the 'glory of honours', after all, can be lost as well as won. Even, the 'sun itself', which exhibits a fire and fury beyond human comprehension. will eventually fizzle out and expire.

The poet's relationship with Anne

Only the poet's relationship with Anne is immune to such aging and destruction because the love they feel for one another will never decay, will never diminish in intensity: 'Only our love hath no decay'. Their love, unlike the kings and courtiers, unlike the sun itself, will exist forever.

Their love, then, is presented as being outside the ordinary course of time. The whole idea of 'yesterday' or 'tomorrow' doesn't apply to the love that they share. Instead their emotions exist in an unchanging and eternal present: 'But truly keeps his first, last, everlasting day'.

A love continued in heaven
Yet the poet quickly realises there is a problem with this argument. His and Anne's love may be ageless but their bodies are not. Death, then, will come for them just as it will come for the nobles or princes mentioned in Stanza 1. Eventually their physical bodies will be no more: 'Alas, as well as other Princes, we ... Must leave at last in death, these eyes, and ears'. The poet and his beloved, like everybody else, will be laid in the grave: 'Two graves must hide thine and my corse'.

Why must the poet and his beloved be buried in two separate graves?
The poem, as we have seen, was written on the anniversary of Donne's first meeting with Anne Moore, the niece of his employer Sir Thomas Egerton. Donne's relationship with Anne was largely conducted in secret, as the couple knew that Anne's family would be bitterly opposed to any relationship between them.

The couple realise, therefore, that it will be extremely difficult for them to marry. And because they are not married they will be buried separately, each with his or her own family. The poet laments that they must be separated at death in this manner: 'If one might, death were no divorce'.

The couple's relationship, therefore, has a bittersweet quality, represented by the 'sweet salt tears'. It is sweet because it is characterised by the passion and excitement of new love. But it is bitter because they realise that it will be extremely difficult for them to marry or openly be together.

Yet their souls will continue to exist. Their souls will 'remove' themselves from their buried bodies and journey to heaven, existing forever 'above' this earthly world: 'When bodies to their graves, souls from their graves remove'. Their souls, therefore, will be able to 'prove' or sustain their relationship after death: 'But souls ... then shall prove/ This'. It's possible, perhaps, that their love will even increase in the heavenly afterlife: 'or a love increased there above'.

The poet, however, isn't entirely satisfied with the idea of continuing the relationship in Heaven. Here on Earth they enjoy a unique and private relationship. The poet fears that such an exclusive, unique relationship won't be possible in the afterlife. In Paradise, the poet and his beloved might 'be thoroughly blessed' but they'll be no different from the rest of God's faithful souls: 'But we no more, than all the rest'.

The poet chooses life
The poem concludes, therefore, with the poet focusing on this life rather than on the next. He and his beloved must 'live' and love each other 'nobly', in a true and honest fashion. They must make the most of the years together as they pass: 'Let us ... live, and add again,/ years and years unto years'.

They must 'refrain' or control the 'true and false fears' that affect every relationship. 'False' fears relate to things that will never happen; for example, he and his lover hurting or betraying each other. 'True' fears, on the other hand, are directed towards difficulties that inevitably arise in life, things like sickness and old age.

The poet seems confident he and his beloved will attain the milestone of having been together for sixty or 'threescore' years. He declares that they will 'write' something on each anniversary of their first meeting, perhaps imagining an exchange of cards or letters. But their relationship will remain fresh, passionate and exciting. Each anniversary will be like their first anniversary, each new year will stretch before them as if it were only the second year of their relationship: 'till we attain/ To write threescore, this is the second of our reign'.

DONNE'S METAPHYSICAL STYLE

Weird and Wonderful Arguments
This is another poem where Donne's Metaphysical style is in evidence. We see his tendency to deploy outlandish and fantastical arguments. In Stanza 1, for instance, he argues that the affection between him and his beloved is the only unchanging thing in the world. In Stanza 2, meanwhile, he argues that relationships between human beings can be continued and even improved on in Heaven.

Inventive Metaphors and Similes
Donne, like the other Metaphysical poets of his generation, was especially fond of using conceits or extended metaphors in his work. This poem is structured around a conceit or extended metaphor that compares lovers to kings:
- This notion is introduced at the very beginning with the phrase 'All Kings'.
- In lines 23 to 24, the poet describes how he is both his lover's king and subject.
- A similar point is made in lines 13 to 14, where he declares that they are princes of each other: 'as well as other Princes, we/ (who prince enough in one another be)'.
- At the poem's conclusion, therefore, their relationship is described as 'reign', or a period of rule.

Another aspect of Donne's Metaphysical style is his tendency to use metaphors that compare two seemingly very different things. We see this in line 18 where thoughts are described as 'inmates' or prisoners of the soul. According to the poet, love is the soul's only natural and constant emotion: 'souls where nothing dwells but love'. All 'other thoughts' (for example those associated with hatred, fear and jealousy) are merely the soul's 'inmates'. They are imprisoned in the soul during this life but they are released from it at the moment of death and do not travel with it to Heaven.

THEMES

THE MYSTICAL NATURE OF LOVE

'The Anniversary' is another poem where Donne presents love as an almost mystical bond. The first stanza depicts love as somehow magically outside the normal course of time. The poet imagines that the relationship between himself and his beloved is the only thing in the world not subject to ageing and decay.

By the end of the poem, however, he has adopted a humbler and more realistic vision of love. The poet, in stanza 3, no longer craves a changeless, timeless relationship. He concludes by suggesting that the only way love can triumph over time is not by being timeless and unchanging but by altering and adapting with the lovers as the years go by.

LOVE AND MARRIAGE

The poet is highly conscious that every relationship has its lows as well as highs. The poet's relationship is characterised by 'true oaths' exchanged between him and his beloved, promises that they will always love one another and will always remain faithful.

But it is also characterised by worry, difficulty and conflict. They experience 'false fears', moments when one lover worries about being betrayed by the other. They also experience 'true fears' when they worry about the conflicts and difficulties that inevitably arise in any relationship.

The poem concludes, then, with the poet stressing that he and his beloved must 'love nobly', in a true and faithful fashion. They must overcome the worries, difficulties and conflicts that affect every relationship. By working together they can ensure that their relationship retains its freshness and excitement for sixty years or even more.

He and his lover are so important to each other that they 'rule' each other's lives. The speaker is his lover's 'king' because he rules her, but he is also her 'subject' because she rules him.

All kings are scared of treason, of being betrayed by one of their subjects. Yet the poet and his lover are 'safer' than other kings because they each have only one subject, a subject extremely unlikely to betray them: 'Who is safe as we? where none can do/ Treason to us, except one us two?'

DEATH

Donne is a poet keenly aware of the passage of time and its effects. This awareness is evident in 'The Anniversary', as he notes how every person and object in the universe, no matter how powerful or prestigious, is inevitably drawn towards its destruction. The bodies of the poet and his beloved, too, will age, die and be laid in the grave.

The poem, like several others by Donne, touches on the idea of the afterlife. The poet seems confident that the souls of both he and his beloved will make it to Heaven, where they will continue their relationship. Indeed, so assured is he of his place in Paradise that he almost complains about it, lamenting the fact that 'there above' their love affair will lack some of the uniqueness it enjoys here on Earth.

This poem, then, contrasts forcefully with the three 'holy sonnets' on the course, especially with 'Thou hast made me'. In the sonnets, Donne expresses a deep and profound concern with sin, with the possibility that only hell awaits him after death. In this poem, however, he seems convinced that Heaven is his ultimate destination.

THIS IS POETRY | **JOHN DONNE**

Song: Sweetest Love, I do not go

LINE BY LINE

This poem, many scholars believe, was written in 1611, when Donne left England to go on a trip to Europe with a nobleman named Robert Drury. Donne's wife Anne was not in the best of health at the time, and was greatly distressed by Donne's departure. Donne, in the poem, attempts to console his wife, using a wide range of arguments to ease her anguish.

Stanza 1

He begins by reassuring his wife that he still loves her more than anybody else. She is still his 'Sweetest love'. He is not leaving because he is bored or weary of their relationship: 'I do not go/ For weariness of thee'. On his travels he will not be looking for someone new or better to take her place: 'Nor in the hope the world can show/ A fitter love for me'.

The poet accepts that is wife is terribly distressed at his departure. But her grief, he insists, might actually do her good, helping to prepare her for his own inevitable death. The poet, after all, must eventually die someday: 'But since that I/ Must die at last'. His wife can prepare for this inevitability by experiencing grief as he leaves her now. His departure will be a 'feigned' or pretend death, a death that is 'in jest'. Yet it will prepare for the real thing: ''tis best,/To use myself in jest/ Thus by feign'd deaths to die'.

Stanza 2

The poet comapares his journey to Europe to the sun's daily journey around the earth:

- The sun's journey is an incredibly quick one, circling the entire world in a single day. The previous evening the sun disappeared into the western horizon: 'Yesternight the sun went thence'. Yet this morning it rose in the east once more: 'And yet is here today'.
- The poet claims that his journey to Europe and back will be even quicker : 'But believe that I shall make/ Speedier journeys'.
- After all, he has much less distance to travel than the sun: 'Nor half so short a way'. The sun must travel all around the earth while he is travelling only to Europe and back.
- His motivation to travel quickly is much greater than the sun's. The sun is an emotionless object which travels unthinkingly, while he is filled with desire to return to his wife as quickly as possible.
- He will outpace the sun itself because he travels on the wings of love. His feelings for his wife will provide the

'spurs' that drive him on: 'since I take/ More wings and spurs than he'.

Of course, the poet doesn't mean he will literally be moving faster than the sun. He is using hyperbole, or deliberate poetic exaggeration. He simply wants his wife to know he's going to come back to her as soon as possible. So to make this point, he reaches for a comparison with the fastest moving object he can think of, the sun, which travels all around the world in a single day.

Stanza 3

The poet now attempts to comfort his wife in a more abstract and philosophical fashion. The poet laments the weakness of mankind, especially in relation to the good and bad circumstances that come our way: 'O how feeble is man's power'.

The poet laments the fact that happy times always seem to pass us by. We lack the ability to hold on to happiness, to extend these episodes of joy: 'That if good fortune fall,/ Cannot add another hour'. And once a particular time of happiness has vanished from our lives we cannot bring it back: 'Nor a lost hour recall!'

The poet also laments how we respond to the setbacks and difficulties that affect us. All too often, he suggests, we respond by moaning and weeping, and adopting a miserable and self-pitying attitude. By doing so, we make the misfortune greater: 'But come bad chance/ And we join to'it our strength'. Our poor attitude extends the life of such misfortunes: 'we teach it … length'. Our poor attitude permits or even encourages such misfortunes to completely overwhelm us: 'Itself o'er us to'advance'.

The poet is implying, of course, that his wife should stop moaning and weeping about his departure because doing so only makes things worse. Instead, she should face this this 'bad chance' with a stoic and accepting attitude.

Stanza 4

In Stanza 4, the poet uses emotional blackmail in an attempt to get his wife to stop crying:

- The poet's wife claims to love him. But this can't be true if she's moaning and weeping at his departure: 'It cannot be/ That thou lov'st me as thou say'st'.
- For her grief hurts him terribly. When he sees her crying, he feels his health decline: 'When thou weep'st, unkindly kind,/My life's blood doth decay'. Every time she sighs a piece of his soul disappears: 'thou … sigh'st my soul away'.
- The poet's wife, then, is not the only one wasting away with grief. Her sorrow is causing the poet himself to waste away as well.

Therefore, if she loves him like she says she does, she will cease her moaning and weeping. She will stop wasting both their lives in this fashion: 'It cannot be/ That thou lov'st me as thou say'st,/ If in thine my life thou waste'.

Stanza 5

The poet concludes by urging his wife not to imagine any of the bad things or 'ills' that might happen to him on his journey: 'Let not thy divining heart/ Forethink me any ill'. 'Forethink', in this instance, means to imagine or predict.

This is one of several poems where Donne suggests the level of superstition common in the seventeenth century when Donne was writing. The poet refers to his wife's 'divining heart', suggesting that she has the gift of prophecy or 'divination', that she can somehow sense or predict the future.

To worry or 'forethink' in this way, he suggests, is a dangerous activity, as it might cause the 'ill' she worries about to come true. This is a superstition many of us are guilty of from time to time. We tend to avoid considering the bad things that might happen to us or those we love, as if thinking about these negative possibilities might make them come to pass.

DONNE'S METAPHYSICAL STYLE

Weird and Wonderful Arguments

Donne, like the other Metaphysical poets of his generation, was fond of making weird and wonderful arguments in his poetry. In this poem, he makes several statements that seems outlandish, bizarre or completely wrong.

- In stanza 2, he argues that his journey to Europe and back will take less time than the sun's daily journey around the earth.
- In stanza 3, he argues that his wife's tears and sighs are not a sign of her love for him. In fact, they show that she does not love him at all.
- In stanza 5, he argues that he and his wife can never actually be apart at all.

In every instance, however, he manages to offer a seemingly sensible argument in support of his outlandish claim. Donne, it's important to note, does not aim to convince us that his claims are actually true. He sets out rather to impress us with the inventiveness and ingenuity of his debating style. He aims to show us that he can make anything sound reasonable, that his command of language and ideas is so great and that he can produce an argument in favour of any notion whatsoever, no matter how bizarre or incorrect it might be.

Paradox and Contradiction

Paradox, another hallmark of the Metaphysical style, features in line 27. The poet describes how his wife's grief is both kind and unkind ('unkindly, kind'). It's a kindness because it shows how much she loves him. But it's an unkindness because seeing her in tears causes him so much pain.

Inventive Metaphors and Similes

The Metaphysical style was also known for its inventive metaphors. Donne deploys a typically inventive metaphor in line 16, where the poet's feelings for his wife are compared to 'wings' and 'spurs' that will enable or encourage him to travel extremely quickly on his journey. Metaphorical language also features in stanza 4. According to the poet, his wife's distress is causing him to waste away. With her every sigh part of his soul disappears, with her every tear his life's blood drains from his body.

Form

'Sweetest Love', like a number of Metaphysical poems, is described by its author as a 'song'. We can imagine the poem, with its short, snappy lines and regular rhyme scheme, being set to music and sung by a minstrel in the court.

THEMES

LOVE AND MARRIAGE

'Sweetest Love', like 'The Anniversary', highlights the stresses and difficulties that can arise in any long-term relationship – in particular, the distress felt by one member of the couple when the other departs on a long trip.

Donne's response to this distress is a complex one. Lines like 'That art the best of me' and 'Sweetest Love, I do not go' strike us as genuinely emotional. We can imagine them spoken in the genuine tones of a loving husband, as the poet attempts to reassure and console his wife in her distress.

There are moments, however, when the poet's response to his wife's distress seems cold and even clinical. We see this when he urges his wife to think of his departure as a preparation for his death. We also see it when he muses on man's relationship to the ills and sorrows that befall us.

The poet, no doubt, must have felt sorrow and guilt as he left his wife behind. And his discomfort, no doubt, was made worse by the fact that she was moaning and weeping as he left. There is a sense, therefore, in which the poet seems more concerned about his own feelings than he is about those of his wife. He wants his wife to stop crying to ease his own distress. We see this in Stanza 3, when he urges her to adopt a more stoic and accepting attitude. We also see it in Stanza 4, where he suggests that her weeping drains away his very life force.

THE MYSTICAL NATURE OF LOVE

Like 'The Anniversary' and 'A Valediction: Forbidding Mourning', this poem presents love as something spiritual and transcendent. The poet suggests that he and his wife are joined by an almost mystical bond. He seems to imply that they share a single soul or life force – that they exist in one another and can therefore never be truly apart.

This is evident in the poem's conclusion, where the poet suggests that the bond between them is so powerful that they keep one another alive. We also see it in the suggestion that the wife's sighs and tears 'waste' not only her own life but the poet's life, too. Each is like the 'life force' of the other. Therefore, on a spiritual or psychological level they can never be apart. Even when he's hundreds of miles away they will still, in an important sense, be one: 'They who one another keep/ Alive, ne'er parted be'.

The poet suggests that love's power will allow him to travel faster than the sun as it makes its journey around the earth. He urges his wife to imagine that they will part only for the length of a night's sleep: 'But think that we/ Are but turned aside to sleep'. While these lines are not to be taken too literally, they suggest the mystical bond between the lovers, a link of such intensity it defies the normal laws of space and time.

A Valediction: Forbidding Mourning

LINE BY LINE

Donne wrote this poem for his wife, Anne, in 1611, just before embarking on a trip to Continental Europe. Anne was heavily pregnant at the time and since the poet's trip was set to last a number of months, it must have been difficult for them to part. The poem, therefore, is an attempt to reassure Anne that everything will be fine, that their love will remain intact and that the poet will return safely in good time.

Melting away

Donne tells his wife that they ought to part in a calm and peaceful manner, without any grief or struggle. There should be no struggle, no attempts made to hold him back and prevent him from leaving. She should have no fear when it comes to his departure. In fact, the poet suggests, Anne ought to be encourage him to go.

The poet suggests that they should 'melt' away from one another: 'So let us melt, and make no noise'. Water transitions from one state to another, from solid to liquid, in a gentle and almost imperceptible manner. The poet and his wife should transition from togetherness to separation, in a manner that is equally gentle and imperceptible. There should be no shedding of tears or deep, mournful sighs as they separate, no 'tear-floods' and 'sigh-tempests'. In fact, there should be no outward displays of emotion at all.

Virtuous men

Virtuous men, Donne suggests, face death in an almost relaxed manner. They are completely at ease on their deathbeds. This is because they know they've lived a good life and that their souls are destined for heaven. They can pass 'mildly away', without any outward signs of physical struggle or emotional turmoil. They can softly tell their souls 'to go', knowing that everything will be all right. They pass away imperceptibly, their breathing gradually growing weaker and weaker. This process is so gentle that those gathered around their deathbeds can't be sure when they've breathed their last: 'As virtuous men pass mildly away,/ And whisper to their souls to go'.

The poet and his wife should leave each other like a virtuous man leaves this world. They should have a gentle almost imperceptible leave-taking, one marked by no signs of emotional distress.

The sacred and profane

Donne refers to the idea of the sacred and profane that exists in certain religions. The sacred refers to the secret, hidden aspects of a religion. The profane, on the other hand, refers to the stuff of everyday life.

- The sacred aspects of a religion are known only to the religion's priests. Similarly, the most important aspects of the poet's marriage are known only to the poet and his wife.
- It is forbidden for priests to share their secret knowledge with the 'laity', with ordinary people. To do so is a form of 'profanation', a dragging of the sacred down to the level of the everyday.
- Similarly, it is inappropriate for the poet and his wife to reveal the most emotional and private aspects of their relationship. Exposing their relationship in such a fashion would also be a form of 'profanation', making their love less scared and more ordinary.

The poet and his wife, therefore, should take their leave quietly, ensuring that their emotions are hidden from their neighbours.

Ordinary lovers

The poet describes ordinary lovers, whose love is purely earthly or 'sublunary'. These lovers share a connection that is grounded or 'elemented' in the physical. They are connected only through the ordinary physical senses of sight, sound and touch: 'whose soul is sense'. Their relationships, because they are based on such a physical connection, cannot 'admit' or cope with physical separation.

Donne and his wife, in contrast, experience a form of love that is somehow mystical or unearthly. Indeed, their bond is so mysterious that they don't fully understand it themselves: 'That our selves know not what it is'. Donne describes how they are 'Inter-assured' of mind, enjoying a psychological and spiritual connection. The poet and his wife, therefore, are less bothered by physical separation, by being unable to hold hands, kiss or look into each other's eyes: '[We] Care less, eyes, lips, and hands to miss'.

Donne uses a metaphor from metallurgy, the study and manipulation of metals, to emphasise just how special his relationship is. Ordinary relationships are described as 'Dull', suggesting that are base, lumpen and valueless. Donne's relationship, on the other hand, is described as 'refined', suggesting metal that has all its impurities removed, leaving a perfect priceless substance.

Donne draws a contrast between the earth, on the one hand, and the 'spheres' or heavens on the other (Ancient thinkers, from Plato to Copernicus, believed that space was divided into perfect spheres rather than being an endless empty expanse). Donne associates ordinary relationships with the earth. His own relationship, meanwhile, is associated with the heavens.

- Disturbances of the earth – earthquakes, landslides and so forth – are keenly felt by the population at large.
- Disturbances in ordinary relationships, similarly, are noticed by the broader community. We notice the troubled couple arguing or giving one another the silent treatment.
- Disturbances of the heavenly spheres, however, are hardly noticed by the population at large.
- This disturbance in Donne's relationship, similarly, should be unnoticed by the broader community. He and his wife shouldn't cry or weep or moan. They should give no indication at all that anything is amiss.

A union of their souls

Donne declares their two souls are so intimately bound together that they are essentially 'one'. When he travels further and further away, their mingled soul will stretch, growing thinner and thinner. But it will never break or sever. Their mingled soul will experience an 'exposition' but never a 'breach'. Donne uses a wonderful simile to illustrate this, comparing their mingled soul to a gold bar that is beaten by a gold smith. The gold, he imagines, will thin and expand as it is beaten until it's as thin as the air itself: 'Like gold to airy thinness beat'. But it will never break.

The compass metaphor

Donne uses a striking metaphor to illustrate the connection he shares with his wife, comparing their two souls to the 'feet' or legs of a mathematical compass. Their souls are bound together by love, just as the compass's legs are fastened by a hinge.

- When no circle is being drawn, the two feet of the compass are united. This represents the time Donne and Anne have spent together at home.
- When a circle is being drawn the two feet are separated. This represents the period of Donne's travels, when he and Anne must be apart.
- Donne compares Anne to the 'fixed foot' of the compass, to the foot that remains stationary while the compass is in use. This represents how she must remain at home while the poet travels.
- Donne, himself, meanwhile is compared to the 'other' foot of the compass, to the foot that holds the pencil and traces the circle's rounded or oblique shape. This represents how Donne must soon depart on his travels: '[I] must,/ Like th' other foot, obliquely run'.
- The 'other foot' travels around the 'fixed foot'. Donne, metaphorically, will travel around Anne. She will remain at the centre of his thoughts no matter where he goes.
- The fixed foot ensures that the other foot traces a 'just' or proper circle. The thought of Anne, similarly, will ensure that Donne behaves in a 'just' fashion as he travels. The thought of his wife will ensure that he doesn't sleep with any other women or behave otherwise inappropriately.

The fixed foot ensures that the other foot's tracing of a circle begins and ends at the same point. This represents how thoughts of Anne will ensure that the poet returns home. He won't remain on the continent, abandoning his wife and starting a new life in Florence or Madrid. Anne, he insists, will make his journey end at home, right where it begun.

Science and Superstition

Donne, we remember, was writing during a period that saw not only the beginnings of modern science but also the persistence of ancient superstition. We see this when he describes how people would 'reckon' or consider earthquakes and similar happenings. People, he says, would wonder what the earthquake 'did', attempting to understand its causes and consequences in a rational fashion. But they also looked for meaning in such phenomena, regarding them as mystical omens or signs of God's displeasure. A similar fusion of science and superstition is evident in the metaphor of the mathematical compass. Here Donne reveals an awareness of geometry, of the technique required to make a just circle. But these lines, arguably, are also marked by the idea – common among mathematicians at the time – that the circle was a special, spiritual shape, one that embodied God's perfection.

Science and superstition also feature in the notion that outer space can be neatly divided into perfect spheres that rotate around one another. Sometimes, it was believed, the interaction of the spheres produced beautiful music. But sometimes the spheres clashed, producing a 'trepidation' or disturbance that echoed throughout the universe, being 'greater far' than that produced by any earthquake. The concept of celestial spheres, of course, strikes us as ridiculous today. But it was developed and believed in by great mathematicians and astronomers and can be regarded as a stepping stone towards our modern understanding of the universe.

DONNE'S METAPHYSICAL STYLE

Outrageous Claims and Demands

This is another poem where Donne's Metaphysical style is in evidence. Throughout the poem, he makes a number of outrageous claims in an effort to comfort his wife and prevent her from mourning his departure:

- He claims that their love is something scared, something that only they can know and fathom, and that it would be a 'profanation' if the general public were to witness them grieving.
- He claims that their love is based on a spiritual bond and that, therefore, they will not miss being able to touch, hold and see each other when Donne is away: 'But we … Care less eyes, lips, and hands to miss'.
- He claims that because their love transcends this earthly realm, their separation will not have any physical or emotional effects.

Perhaps the most outrageous claim that the poet makes is that he and his wife can never be truly separated because they share the one soul: 'Our two souls, therefore, which are one … endure not yet/ A breach, but an expansion'.

Inventive Metaphors and Similes

Another aspect of Donne's Metaphysical style is his tendency to use metaphors that compare two seemingly very different things.

- We see this in the opening stanza when the poet compares their parting to a 'virtuous' man's death.
- He compares the impact that separation has on ordinary lovers' relationships to the effects of earthquakes. Turmoil in the relationship he shares with his wife, in contrast, is compared to disruptions amongst the heavenly spheres.
- The poet compares the manner in which their single soul will expand as he travels to the expansion of hammered gold.

Donne, like the other Metaphysical poets of his generation, was especially fond of using conceits or extended metaphors in his work. 'A Valediction', as we have seen, ends Donne using the extended analogy of a mathematical compass to illustrate the manner in which his soul is connected to his wife's. The comparison also illustrates just how central Anne is to the relationship.

Paradox and Contradiction

The poem centres around a paradox or contradiction which the poet makes every effort to overcome. On the one hand, Donne wishes to argue that he and his wife share a love that is deeper, richer and more profound than any other. On the other hand, he wishes to convince his wife that they should feel no grief or pain when they separate. In order to overcome this contradiction the poet ends up having to resort to a further paradox. Their separation, he claims, will actually be a form of an expansion of their shared 'soul'.

THEMES

LOVE AND MARRIAGE

'A Valediction: Forbidding Mourning' is a testament to the depth of the poet's feelings for his wife. The poem, like many poems by Donne, approaches the subject of love in a rather intellectual and argumentative manner. But there are also moments of genuine emotion, especially related to the compass metaphor at the poem's conclusion.

There is a sense, as in 'Sweetest Love, I do not go', that the poet is desperate to avoid a scene and any 'tear-floods' or 'sigh-tempests' that might accentuate his guilt at leaving Anne behind. But the poet, we sense, is also making a heartfelt effort to console his wife. And perhaps also console himself.

The poem highlights how lovers remain in one another's minds even when they are physically distanced. The poet, as we've seen, stresses that Anne will remain at the centre of his thoughts while he travels. Thoughts of Anne will ensure that he behaves appropriately while abroad and that he returns home to England when his journey is concluded.

THE MYSTICAL NATURE OF LOVE

The poet emphasises the mystical nature of his relationship.

- The relationship has certain secret and sacred aspects, something that must not be shared with ordinary people.
- Their relationship is associated with the celestial spheres rather than with this earthly domain.
- They are 'Inter-assured of the mind' enjoying an intense mental connection that they don't fully understand themselves.
- They also enjoy an extraordinary spiritual bond. Their mingled souls 'are one' and can never be breached or separated.

The poet's marriage, therefore, is presented as being far superior to ordinary relationships. Ordinary couples are associated with the profane rather than the scared and with the sublunary earth rather than the heavens. Ordinary couples are grounded in a purely physical connection, lacking the intense mental and spiritual bonds enjoyed by the poet and his wife. Ordinary couples cannot bear to be apart because they need to see and touch one another to maintain their relationship. For the poet and Anne, however, given their mystical union, such physical separation will be easy to endure.

THIS IS POETRY | **JOHN DONNE**

Batter My Heart

LINE BY LINE

In 'Batter my heart', as in the other Holy Sonnets, Donne presents himself as an extraordinary sinner:
- God has attempted to redeem the poet from sin. God, as the poet puts it, has attempted to 'mend' him as if he were a defective object: 'you… seek to mend'. We might 'knock' or tap such a defective object, for instance, in an effort to remove its dents. Or we might attempt to cover up its imperfections by breathing on it and rubbing it to make it shine: 'breathe, shine'
- But the poet, like an object too defective to be repaired, is so sinful that he is beyond any conventional redemption.
- Such an utterly defective object, of course, needs to be scrapped and rebuilt from scratch. The poet, similarly, needs to be destroyed and then remade.

The poet, therefore, calls on God to 'Batter [his] heart', to forcefully strike his heart over and over again. The 'heart', of course, represents our most intimate thoughts and feelings. The poet therefore is calling on God to assault, and ultimately demolish, his mindset, his lifestyle, his very personality.

The poet, then, describes how he wants God to 'break, blow [and] burn' him. It's as if the poet wants his limbs to be snapped. It's as if he wants to be lashed by howling gales. It's as if he wants to be consumed by roaring flames. These powerful, violent metaphors wonderfully convey how the poet wants God to forcefully end his current sinful existence.

Once this process of destruction or demolition is complete, the poet wants God to 'make [him] new,' to reshape his lifestyle and personality. We might say that he wants to be born again, to begin an entirely new life that would be lived in service to his God.

The poet, therefore, needs to be 'overthrown'. He needs to be utterly destroyed, reduced to nothing. He will then 'rise' and 'stand' once more, being rebuilt or reconstituted as a new, more virtuous version of himself. This process of destruction and recreation, the poet suggests, will require a great effort from God. God, he insists, must 'bend' or apply all of His extraordinary 'force'.

Lines 5 to 8

In these lines, the poet uses a famous conceit, comparing himself to a town that has been 'usurped' or taken over by a foreign power:

- The townsfolk know that their loyalty is 'due' to their rightful king, who is currently absent from the town, rather than to the usurper who currently occupies the town. The poet, similarly, knows that his true loyalty lies with God, who is absent from his life, rather than with sin, which currently occupies his life.
- The town's citizens 'labour' to cast out the usurper and 'admit' their rightful ruler back into the town. The poet, similarly, struggles to turn away from sin and let God back into his life.
- The citizens' efforts, however, are in vain or 'to no end'. They cannot expel the usurper from their town. The poet, similarly, finds it impossible to live a life that is not dominated by sin.

The rightful king has appointed a viceroy or govener to the town. God, similarly, has given the poet the gift of reason, the faculty of rationality and logic.

The viceroy's role is to govern the town properly while the rightful king is away. Reason's role, similarly, is to govern the poet's life, ensuring that he lives in dignity and decency.

The viceroy, however, has proved to be a 'weak' governor and has allowed the town to be taken over by the enemy. Reason, similarly, has turned out to be weak when it comes to governing the poet's life and has allowed him to be taken over by sin. Rationality and logic, after all, are all too often useless in the face of temptations towards lust, gluttony or anger.

The viceroy, we're told, has also turned out to be 'untrue' or untrustworthy, suggesting that he has actively collaborated with the enemy. Reason, similarly, has turned out to be untrustworthy. Reason, after all, can be seduced by all kinds of fancy arguments that seem to justify sinful behaviour, that lead us away from the path of righteousness.

The viceroy, then, has effectively allowed himself to taken prisoner by the enemy. The poet's faculty of reason, similarly, has been 'captived' by sin. Only a direct and forceful intervention by God himself, one that reshapes his soul and personality, will be enough to cast sin out of his life.

Lines 9 to 14

The poet, in these lines, addresses God the way one might address a lover.

- He tells God how much he loves Him and how he would gladly ('fain') be loved in return: 'Yet dearly I love you and would be loved fain'.
- The poet, however, is trapped an intense relationship with sin, which is God's eternal enemy. The poet emphasises the intensity of this relationship by memorably declaring that he and sin are engaged to be married. 'But [I] am Betrothed unto your enemy'. The poet calls on God to 'divorce' him from this degrading relationship. He wants God to forcibly 'untie' or 'break' the knots of his addiction to the pleasures of this world.
- Donne, memorably, declares that he wants to be imprisoned by God: 'Take me to you, imprison me'. He wants God to take full control of his life and personality. Otherwise, he will just drift back to a sinful existence.

The poem concludes with Donne calling on God to 'enthral' and 'ravish' him. The term 'enthral' has two different meanings. It can mean to enslave, reinforcing our sense that Donne wants to submit utterly to God's will. It can also mean to captivate, suggesting how Donne wants God to utterly occupy his attention. His mind must be filled with thoughts of God's goodness; otherwise, he will start to experience temptation again, and sinning will seem like an alluring prospect.

The term 'ravish', similarly, has two very different meanings. It can mean to delight, suggesting how Donne wants to be thrilled and overjoyed by God's presence in his life. It can also mean to sexually violate, suggesting how Donne wants God to forcefully enter his life and his mind.

The poem's final lines are based around two paradoxes or contradictory statements.
The first paradox occurs when the poet says that he can only be free if he is enthralled or enslaved. He can only be released from the grip of sin if he allows God's love to completely take over his life.

The second paradox relates to the idea of ravishing. Normally, in Donne's time, sexual activity was considered to leave one less pure or 'chaste'. Donne, however, states that being ravished is actually the only route to purity and chastity. It's only through God forcefully entering his life and mind that can he become a pure and virtuous person.

THIS IS POETRY — JOHN DONNE

THEMES

SIN AND REDEMPTION

A recurring feature of Donne's poetry is the strange joy he takes in presenting himself as a terrible person. His sins, he seems to suggest, are far greater than those of the average man or woman. His whole life and personality, he suggests, have been taken over by sin:

- He is so corrupted by sin that he compares himself to a defective pot or vase, one that the sculptor has no choice but to cast aside.
- Sin has taken over his life, the way a usurper might seize a town not rightfully his.
- He even compares himself to sin's fiancé, emphasising the intense and intimate nature of his relationship with sin.

But the poem also highlights Donne's desperation for redemption. He wants God to forcibly 'untie' or 'break' his relationship with sin. He wants God to 'Batter [his] heart', to enter his life in a forceful, almost violent manner. He wants to be broken by God's love so that he can be made anew.

In 'Batter my heart', as in the other Holy Sonnets, Donne demands what might be described as 'special treatment' from God. God, we imagine, has reached out to the poet through prayer and the sacraments, offering him redemption from his sinful ways. The poet, however, is convinced that he is beyond such ordinary means of redemption. He is so sinful that he must be utterly demolished and remade.

A striking feature of 'Batter My Heart' is the demanding or challenging tone the poet takes with God. God has already taken action to cleanse the poet of sin. But the poet feels that God 'As yet' has not done enough. The poet, therefore, will require a greater effort from God from now on. God, he insists, must 'bend' or apply all of His extraordinary 'force'.

The poem's closing lines, however, are arguably more humble in tone. The poet accepts that he must surrender to God's love, and that he must allow God to enter his life and dominate his existence. It is only by doing so that he be can free from sin and live a 'chaste' or righteous life.

DONNE'S METAPHYSICAL STYLE

Outrageous Claims and Demands

Donne is known for his tendency to make outrageous demands and this is nowhere more evident that in 'Batter my heart'.
- He demands that God batter or assault his very psyche.
- He calls on God to break him and burn him.
- He wants God to imprison, enthral and even ravish him.

Indeed, many readers have been disturbed by the violence that characterises these demands, which strike us as far more extreme than the requests one might find in conventional prayers.

Inventive Metaphors and Similes

Donne, like the other Metaphysical poets of his generation, was especially fond of using conceits or extended metaphors in his work. And it's often been suggested that 'Batter my heart' is organised around three such comparisons:
- In lines 1 to 4, as we have seen, the poet compares himself to a defective object of some kind. Critics have suggested that Donne is referring to a vase or piece of pottery. We can see how some, though maybe not all, of the verbs in these lines might relate to the potter's craft.
- In lines 5 to 8, as we've seen, the poet compares himself to a captured or usurped town.
- In lines 9 to 14, meanwhile, the poet compares himself to a person trapped in a degrading relationship.

The scholar Raymond-Jean Fontain has argued that Donne derives these conceits from the Bible. In the Old Testament, when the people of Israel disobeyed God, the prophets compared them to an imperfect pot, a captured city or a woman betrothed to her true love's enemy. In 'Batter my heart', Donne adapts these biblical images to describe his own predicament as a sinner desperate for redemption.

Form

'Batter my heart', like the other 'holy sonnets' on the course, is a variation on the Shakespearian sonnet, being divided into three quatrains and a final rhyming couplet. The poem is a kind of prayer to the Holy Trinity, or 'three-personed God', and the idea of the Trinity determines its structure. Just as the Christian God is divided into three distinct persons, so the poem is divided into three distinct parts: lines 1 to 4, lines 5 to 8 and lines 9 to 14. The poet also uses verbs in sets of three. For example, 'knock, breathe, shine' and 'break, blow, burn'.

Thou hast made me

LINE BY LINE

This poem, like the other 'Holy Sonnets', was written sometime between 1611 and 1615. This was a difficult time in Donne's life. It was a time of financial difficulty. Hor his once promising diplomatic career was a thing of the past, and he had spent a decade scraping a living doing bits and pieces of legal work. It was also a time of great responsibility, as he had a wife and ten children to support. He also had to contend with a series of illnesses that affected both himself and the other members of his family.

Donne feels that the end of his life is fast approaching: 'for now mine end doth haste'. He is not an old man, being only in his early forties. But he is so mentally and physically drained that death seems a real possibility. He uses a wonderful metaphor to describe what he views as his approaching demise: 'I run to death and death meets me as fast'. We can imagine death and the poet running to meet each other like lovers across a field in an old romantic movie.

Wasting away

The poet is highly conscious that he is a sinful person. Sin, he suggests, corrupts not only his immortal soul but his physical body. Sin resides within his body like some disease. It causes his body to 'decay' and his 'flesh' to shrivel up and 'waste' away: 'my feebled flesh doth waste/ By sin in it'.

Sin, the poet laments, has taken quite a toll on his body. He has grown 'feeble'. His eyesight has begun to fail to the point that all his perceptions are 'dim'. Donne, then, presents himself as having prematurely aged, by years of hard work, childcare and financial worry.

The poet laments that for him life's pleasures are a thing of the past: 'And all my pleasures seem like yesterday'. Perhaps he is suggesting that he no longer has the time or money to engage in pleasurable activities. Perhaps he misses being part of the glittering social and cultural life of London. Or perhaps he's so depressed that he can no longer take joy in life's simple pleasures, like the sunset or the singing of a bird.

The poet wonders why God went to the trouble of creating him if He's only going to let him rot away: 'Thou hast made me, and shall thy work decay?' The poet wants God to 'Repair' him. He wants God to take away his sins. Doing so will not only cleanse his soul; it will also restore his body. Sin, as we've seen, is presented as the cause of the bodily decay that has affected the poet.

Spatial metaphor

The poem is structured around the conceit of the speaker being unable to look in various directions: 'I dare not move my dim eyes any way':

- He's afraid to look in front of him. This represents how he is terrified to contemplate the future, for he knows he only has a short while to live before death comes: 'death before doth cast/ Such terror'.
- He's reluctant to look behind him. This represents his unwillingness to contemplate the past. Doing so fills him with 'Despair', reminding him of all the pleasures he can no longer enjoy.
- He is terrified to cast his eyes downward. This represents his terror of hell. He feels that sin weighs him down, threatening to drag him downwards into eternal damnation: 'to towards hell doth weigh.'

There are times, however, when the speaker can look 'upwards', when he can pray to or commune with God: 'Only thou art above'. At such moments the poet feels himself 'rise again'. He feels the burden of sin lessen and senses himself grow closer to God. Perhaps, too, he feels relief from the feelings of terror and despair that have so gripped him. The poet accepts, however, it is only with God's 'leave' or permission that such moments can occur: 'and when towards thee/ By thy leave I can look'.

God and the Devil

The poem's final lines focus on the Devil, who is presented as the common foe to both God and man. The Devil is very 'old', having been around in one form or another since the creation of the universe, and has mastered the 'art' of temptation. He can be extremely 'subtle' in his temptations, preying on each individual's weaknesses and insecurities. He can make sinful acts appear harmless or even justified.

Donne, therefore, finds it almost impossible to resist the Devil's wiles and stratagems. He is incapable of passing even sixty minutes without a sinful deed or thought: 'That not one hour I can myself sustain.' No matter how hard he tries, he cannot maintain or sustain a righteous way of life.

The poet knows it's only with God's help that he can resist temptation. He must rely on God's 'grace', on His favour and assiatnce. It only through such grace that the poet order to 'prevent' or overcome the Devil's 'art'. Donne uses a vivid metaphor to depict this. God's grace is comapared to a winged bird that will carry him along, safely above the traps and snares placed by the Devil.

Donne also uses the metaphor of the magnet to describe his relationship with God. He imagines God functioning 'like adamant' or a magnet, pulling his 'heart' upwards: 'thou like adamant draw mine iron heart'. This wonderfully suggests how God will help the poet to focus on what might be described as higher things, on faith, hope and charity rather than on sinful thoughts and ideas.

DONNE'S METAPHYSICAL STYLE

Outrageous Claims and Demands

'Thou hast made me' like many of Donne's poems features outrageous claims and demands. We see this when he demands that God immediately 'repair' his sin-damaged soul. An outrageous claim, meanwhile, features in line 12 where the poet suggests that he can't go a single hour without sinning.

Inventive Metaphors and Similes

Donne's Metaphysical style is once again in evidence in this poem, in particular his tendency to use metaphors that compare two seemingly very different things. We see this in line 14, where God is compared to a magnet that will draw the poet's 'iron heart' upwards towards contemplation of the divine. God has been compared to many things over the centuries but a magnet is surely one of the more unusual. Lines 5 to 10, as we have seen, are structured around the conceit of the speaker being terrified to look in various directions: 'I dare not move my dim eyes any way'.

Form

Like 'Batter my heart', and 'At the round earth's imagined corners', this is one of Donne's 'holy sonnets'. It is a 'Shakespearian' sonnet, divided into three quatrains and a couplet, each with a different focus.

The first quatrain focuses on the terrible reality of growing older, the second on the poet's inability to look in any direction and the third on the Devil's subtle 'art'. The closing couplet, meanwhile, attempts to resolve the various questions raised throughout the poem.

Tone

The poem opens with a commanding or challenging tone. The poet wonders why God went to the trouble of creating him only to let his body and soul be corrupted by sin: 'Thou hast made me, and shall thy work decay?' The poet seems almost irritated with God's inaction. It's as if he believes he can convince God to do things his way, to take action where and when Donne requires: 'Repair me now'.

The poem's closing lines, however, are much more humble in tone. He accepts that it is only with God's 'leave', or permission, that he can pray or contemplate goodness: 'and when towards thee/ By thy leave I can look'. The poet emphasises that he is powerless in the face of sin and temptation. It is only with God's help that he has any chance of turning away from sin and focusing on higher things.

THEMES

SIN AND REDEMPTION

In 'Thou hast made me', like the other Holy Sonnets, Donne emphasises his own extraordinary sinfulness. He describes his heart as having turned to 'iron', wonderfully capturing how sin has corrupted his life and his mind. He claims to be such a terrible sinner that he cannot 'sustain' himself for even an hour without giving into the Devil's temptations.

But the poem also highlights Donne's eagerness for redemption. He is desperate to be cleansed of sin, for God to 'repair' his corrupt soul. In 'Thou hast made me', as in the other Holy Sonnets, Donne demands what might be described as 'special treatment' from God. We see this when he calls on God to 'repair [him] now'. The poet doesn't want to bother with the usual business of redemption, with prayer, the sacraments and good deeds. Instead, he wants God to take immediate and decisive action, cleansing him instantly of sin.

For the poet, it's important to note, hell is no metaphor or abstraction – it's something very real and very scary. He is keenly aware that his sins will condemn him to damnation. He thinks of them as a dead weight dragging him downwards into eternal torment. This is especially the case because the poet is getting older and feels that he could die at any minute.

This poem is unusual in that it suggests sin causes not only the soul but also the body to decay. As the poet puts it, 'my feeble flesh doth waste/ By sin in it'. The poet, then, seems to suggest that sin is responsible for the weakness of his flesh and the dimness of his eyes. In healing his soul, therefore, God will also restore his body.

The poem opens with a commanding or challenging tone. The poet wonders why God went to the trouble of creating him only to let his body and soul be corrupted by sin: 'Thou hast made me, and shall thy work decay?' The poet seems almost irritated with God's inaction. It's as if he believes he can convince God to do things his way, to take action where and when Donne requires: 'Repair me now'.

The poem's closing lines, however, are much more humble in tone. He accepts that it is only with God's 'leave', or permission, that he can pray or contemplate goodness: 'and when towards thee/ By thy leave I can look'. The poet emphasises that he is powerless in the face of sin and temptation. It is only with God's help that he has any chance of turning away from sin and focusing on higher things.

DEATH

'Thou hast made me', lke other poems by Donne, emphasises the poet's keen awareness of death. Death, he stresses, is not only inevitable, but could also happen at any time. This comes across in the striking personification of death as a kind of lover the poet rushes to embrace. There is a real urgency, therefore, to Donne's appeal for redemption.

Donne is a poet keenly aware of transience, of how everything fades with the passage of time. This poem, in particular, focuses on how the passage of time affects the body. It powerfully captures the frailty and indignity of ageing, which each of us must endure as death approaches. The poet presents his final years as a time of physical suffering, of 'dim eyes' and 'feeble flesh', a time when all life's pleasures are in the past.

The afterlife is another theme that recurs throughout Donne's poetry. In this poem, as we've seen, the poet regards death as a terrifying prospect and senses the real possibility that Hell rather than Heaven awaits him after death. It is only through God's help and intervention that he will be able to enter the heavenly kingdom.

This poem, then, can be contrasted with 'The Anniversary'. In 'The Anniversary', the poet regards death as essentially no big deal and seems certain that he and his beloved will be free to continue their relationship in Paradise.

THIS IS POETRY — JOHN DONNE

At the round earth's imagined corners

LINE BY LINE

The poem's opening lines refer to the Book of Revelation, chapters 8 to 11. These chapters describe how the end of the world will be signalled by the sound of seven trumpet blasts blown by angels. Donne longs for the end of the world to come. He longs to hear these trumpets ringing out: 'At the round earth's imagin'd corners, blow/ Your trumpets, angels'.

Donne imagines what the end of the world would be like:
- The souls of every single person who has lived and died will 'arise' from death
- This would be an extraordinary number of souls: 'numberless infinities'
- Each soul would reunite with its body.
- These remains, of course, are 'scattered' all over the world, some buried in graveyards, others lost at sea.

Donne lists some of the different ways in which people have died since the world began. He first mentions the victims of 'the flood', which is associated with the story of Noah and his Ark: 'All whom the flood did … o'erthrow'. He then mentions those who will be consumed by flames as the end of the world approaches. The Book of Revelation describes how the end of the world will be preceded by infernos, asteroid strikes and other catastrophic events.

The poet also mentions other more mundane causes of death:
- Those who died because of 'war'.
- Those who died due to a 'dearth' or scarcity of food.
- Those who died naturally of 'age'.
- Those who died from disease or 'ague'
- Those who were the victims of 'tyrannies', of wicked rulers or regimes.
- Those who took their own lives out of 'Despair.'
- Those who were put to death in accordance with the 'law'
- Those who were killed by 'accident' or chance.

There are also, of course, those who are still living when the end of the world arrives. These people will have suffered through the various crises and catastrophes that precede the end of the world. They will hear the angels' trumpets sounded at the earth's four 'corners'. Then they will see or 'behold' God Himself as He enters His creation. These survivors will have made it to the end of the world without dying, and now they will never 'taste death's woe'. They will never endure the terror and uncertainty of death. Their souls will never depart from their bodies and their bodies will never rot in the ground. Instead, they will ascend, body and soul, into heaven.

This, of course, is why Donne is so eager for the end of the world to occur during his lifetime. He wants to be one of the few who never has to die, who avoids 'death's woe' and makes it directly to paradise.

A change of heart

But the poet suddenly has a change of heart, deciding that he is no longer so eager for the world to end. He addresses Christ, asking Him to let the souls of the dead 'sleep' a little longer.

The poet believes himself to be a very sinful man. In fact, he fears that he might be the most sinful man to have ever lived: 'above all these my sins abound'. The poet, therefore, needs to ask for Christ's 'grace', for His favour or forgiveness. Because he is such a terrible sinner, he would require an 'abundance' of this 'grace', an extraordinary level of forgiveness. It would be too late, he feels, to ask for such forgiveness when the end of the world has come: "Tis late … When we are there'.

The poet, therefore, wants the end of the world to be delayed. This will allow him the time he needs to get himself right with God. He wishes to remain on the earth's 'lowly ground' and atone for his sins.

The poet is desperate to 'repent'. He wants to not only express remorse for the things he has done, but he also wants to renounce sin and lead a better life. But he feels that he is incapable of doing so. He is too prone to sinning, too susceptible to temptation. He needs Christ to come directly into his life and teach him how to be a better human being.

THEMES

SIN AND REDEMPTION

Throughout his poetry Donne seems to get a perverse pleasure in presenting himself as a terrible person. His sins, he seems to suggest, are far greater than those of ordinary people. In this poem, he even implies that he's more sinful than anyone else who has ever lived or died. His sins would, therefore, require an 'abundance' of forgiveness on God's part.

The poem also highlights Donne's eagerness for repentance and redemption. He is desperate to atone for his sins and make himself right with God. Donne, however, feels that his redemption can only be achieved with special treatment. He cannot, like other Christians, be guided to redemption by prayer and the sacraments. Instead, he needs Christ to enter his life directly in some special manner so he can be taught how to repent.

The fear of hell and damnation is another recurring feature of Donne's poetry. To Donne, we remind ourselves, the prospect of hell was something very real and something to be greatly feared. We see this when he asks for the end of the world because the end of the world brings with it the final judgement, when God assesses the souls of all who have lived. The poet fears that, due to his sinful nature, he will fail this judgement, and will be cast into damnation rather than ascending directly into heaven.

DEATH

This sonnet is a powerful meditation on mortality. The first eight lines (the octet) forcibly remind us that death lies in store for each of us. Every one of the 'numberless infinities' of people who have lived throughout then ages are now dead. They may have met their ends through a myriad of different ways but they all have the grave in common.

The poem, too, highlights Donne's own terror of dying. Indeed, he calls on God to end reality itself so he won't have to face dying. He would prefer to still be alive when the world ends so he can be transported directly to heaven without ever having to die. Indeed, it is only concern about his soul's sinful state that causes him to think better of the world ending immediately.

DONNE'S METAPHYSICAL STYLE

Outrageous Claims and Demands

Like the other Metaphysical poets of his day Donne enjoyed making outrageous claims, statements and comparisons. In this instance he demands no less than the end of the world itself. Equally outrageous is his claim that he is the most sinful person who has ever lived or died.

Inventive Metaphors and Similes

The poet, as we have seen, wants Christ to enter his life and teach him how to repent. Receiving Christ into his life is compared to receiving a letter of 'pardon'. Envelopes containing official documents were sealed with wax to ensure privacy. Donne, however, imagines an envelope that has been sealed, not with wax but Christ's own 'blood'. A pardon sealed in blood seems more serious than one sealed with wax. The mention of blood of course also brings to mind Christ's crucifixion, where he suffered for the sins of all mankind.

Paradox and Contradiction

There is something paradoxical about the poem's opening line, which describes how the earth is round but also has corners. The 'four corners of the earth' is an everyday phrase, and one that also occurs in the seventh chapter of the Book of Revelation: 'I saw four angels standing on the four corners of the earth'.

Form

'At the round earth's imagined corners' is a Petrarchan, or Italian sonnet. In the octet, or the first eight lines, the poet calls on God to end the world immediately. While in the sestet, or the last six lines, he calls on God to delay. The poem's 'volta' or turn occurs with the word 'But' in line 9, where the poet changes his mind about wanting the world to end.

Tone

The poem opens with a commanding tone, with the poet adopting an almost God-like role, calling on the world to end and issuing instructions to the angels and the souls of the dead. The poem's closing lines, however, are much more humble in tone, with Donne presenting himself as a human being upon the earth's 'lowly ground', someone deeply flawed and desperately in need of God's mercy and grace

Science and Superstition

John Donne lived through an exciting period of scientific discovery and many of his poems exhibit a keen interest in this new learning. He uses the term 'imagined' to describe these corners because he knew very well that the Earth is round. The 'corners' that he has in mind are the corners of a map of the world (English maps from the Renaissance often featured illustrations of angels blowing trumpets in the four directions: North, South, East and West.) Donne, therefore, calls on the angels to take up position at four equivalent points around the world.

Patrick Kavanagh Themes

Poetry and the Role of the Poet

In 'A Christmas Childhood', a notable moment occurs when the six-year-old Kavanagh pauses to trace the letters on the inscription on Christmas morning. Here we see that Kavanagh, even though he was still learning to read and write, had a fascination for the written world. Kavanagh claims that although he was only six years old, he was still a poet: 'My child poet picked out the letters'. Of course, he had yet to write or compose anything, but he possessed the sensitivity to language essential to all true poets.

As Kavanagh got older he began to conceive of the poet as a loner, someone who avoids all participation in communal sports and pastimes. In 'Inniskeen Road: July Evening' he expresses his conviction that the poet must place himself outside of society. He must, like Alexander Selkirk, become a voluntary outcast. He must regard parties and get-togethers as frivolous distractions and focus instead on the contemplation of higher things.

This sense of himself as an outsider stemmed in part, no doubt, from the attitude of the local community towards artists and poets. In 'Shancoduff', Kavanagh describes how the local cattle-drovers view him as an impractical dreamer. A more practical person might, they suggest, be able to make this unpromising farmland turn a profit. But a poet, with his head in the clouds, has no chance of making any money from these bleak, rushy fields: 'A poet? Then by heavens he must be poor'.

Kavanagh's response to the cattle-drovers' remarks ('I hear and is my heart not badly shaken?') can be read two ways. Perhaps the poet is greatly upset, shaken both emotionally and psychologically. Or perhaps he acknowledges deep-down that the drovers are correct: his poetic mindset makes him an impractical and ineffective person. But we can also read this line as a defiant rejection of the stereotype. The poet's heart may not be 'shaken' at all by the drover's comments. Or perhaps he feels it is perfectly possible to combine a poetic outlook with a practical way of life.

'Inniskeen Road' captures Kavanagh's conflicted feelings about the poetic life. As a poet, he feels he shouldn't go to the dance, but as a young man in his twenties he can't ignore it entirely. He leaves the family farm in Mucker, walking nearly a mile along a country lane until he reaches the Inniskeen Road. He then stands there until the very last bicycle has gone by. This conflict is also present in the poem's final couplet. The poet presents himself as a 'king', declaring that this 'mile' of the Inniskeen Road is his 'kingdom'. Kavanagh feels so alone that he fancies the whole world has been permanently deserted, that he's within his rights to claim this stretch of public road as his own personal 'kingdom'. In one sense, his new 'kingdom' is a magical place. It is filled with nature's beauty, with 'banks', 'stones' and a wide variety of wildflowers. But in another sense, this 'kingdom' is a place of loneliness and sorrow, for crucially the poet himself is the kingdom's only inhabitant.

'Epic', too, has the poet anxiously pondering what the poet's role ought to be. In this poem he worries that he's been writing about the wrong kind of thing. He worries that's been focused on a 'local row' between the Duffys and the McCabes when he should be engaging with global conflicts like those discussed at the Munich conference. Kavanagh feels liberated, however, by Homer's example. He realises that he can write about local matters and still produce good work. He realises that he can stay true to his own inspiration, writing about the goings in Ballyrush and Gortin, and still become a poet of substance. If the 'local' was good enough for Homer, then it's good enough for Patrick Kavanagh.

In 'On Raglan Road', Kavanagh exhibits a certain confidence and self-assurance, at least when it comes to his abilities as a poet. In this poem we see Kavanagh's high regard for poetry and artistic creation. He is proud of the poems he writes for his beloved, which vividly capture her 'dark hair'. True artists, like himself, the poem suggests, are rare and possess special abilities, knowledge and understanding that are unknown to ordinary people.

Yet his notion that poets need solitude and ought to avoid distraction if they are to write great poems remains. True artists, Kavanagh suggests, must avoid getting caught up in matters of love and sexuality. They must resemble angels. Their minds must remain on higher things, on 'gifts of the mind', on communing with the 'true gods' of inspiration. Surrendering to love and sexuality, the poem implies, can seriously impair an artist's creative abilities. In the poem's last line, Kavanagh suggests that he has been stripped of his poetic capabilities, just like an angel that has lost its wings.

A close brush with death in his fifties reinforced Kavanagh's belief that anything – no matter how everyday or banal – could be the subject matter for a poem. Poetry, he believed, did not have to be about great events or beautiful sunsets. Anything that the poet loves can enter his poetry, even a drab and 'functional' hospital ward. As he so memorably puts it in 'The Hospital', 'nothing whatever is by love debarred'. The poet ought to write as honestly and as plainly as possible about the things that move and inspire them, no matter how ordinary these things might be. We should, Kavanagh says, 'record love's mystery without claptrap'. 'The Hospital' also suggests that poetry has the power to preserve that which is fleeting and transitory. When the poet writes about or describes something he loves, he 'snatches' that thing or that moment 'out of time'. If it is not noted or recorded, it vanishes.

This notion that poetry ought to record the beauty of the ordinary world without 'claptrap' is also evident in 'Canal Bank Walk'. Kavanagh describes his longing to express his love for the splendour of the natural world. He wants to 'ad-lib' his poems, to compose spontaneously rather than planning his writing in advance. He wants to use over-flowing speech that comes directly from the emotions. He wants to write in an instinctive and unselfconscious manner, to avoid rationally analysing the words that flow from him.

'Lines Written on a Seat on the Grand Canal' concludes with Kavanagh meditating on how he might be commemorated after his death. Rather than a fancy monument or elaborate tomb, he wants a simple bench to be erected in his memory on the banks of the Grand Canal. Such a bench, he feels, would be a beautiful commemoration of his life: 'Commemorate me thus beautifully'. It would represent the person he truly was, reflecting his love of nature in general, and of these canal banks in particular. It would allow others to sit and relish the sights and sounds of the canal, just as he did when he was alive. Perhaps those who sit there might even spare a thought for the poor dead poet, remembering his great love for this little corner of Dublin town.

Rural Life

Kavanagh's poetry depicts rural Ireland in a brutally realistic fashion, avoiding all nostalgia and sentimentality. 'Shancoduff', for instance, provides a vivid portrait of rural life in the early part of the 20th century. The life of the farmer, as Kavanagh presents it, is one of toil and hardship. The image of the poet struggling uphill with a sheaf of hay gives us a sense of how difficult farming must have been in the 1920s, before tractors and other farm machinery became commonplace. The poet, we sense, must make this climb every day, no matter what the weather, hauling feed, tools and instruments up the seven hills. We are reminded, too, that many farms around Ireland consisted of poor land, of 'hungry hills' where poor farmers struggled to eke out a living. The image of the drovers reinforces our sense of rural hardship. Here are men who spend their lives leading cattle on foot across the countryside, taking shelter where they can from the elements.

'The Great Hunger' is another poem which presents a brutal, uncompromising view of rural Ireland, highlighting how life on small farms was one of back-breaking toil. But this poem also describes the tragic predicament that many farmers of the time found themselves in. These men would devote themselves to work on the farm, postponing marriage until it was too late. They would end up living frustrated solitary, lonely lives, often regretting the fact that they never started a family of their own.

'The Great Hunger' highlights how men like Maguire were denied personal and intellectual development. As a result they were dehumanised, turned into little more than apes. It highlights how impossible it was for men like Maguire to escape their plight. They were incapable of even imagining another existence. The poem's key irony, then, is that the land thrives at the expense of those who work on it. In an attempt to ensure their fields' survival, to stave off a repeat of the Great Famine of the 1840s, the farmers have allowed another 'Great Hunger' to emerge, a terrible starvation of the emotions and the spirit.

'A Christmas Childhood' also provides an unflinching view of rural Ireland in the early twentieth century. This is a world of unrelenting hard work, of potato pits and paling posts, of cows being milked in the freezing dawn. This is a world marked by poverty, one where a pen-knife is an extraordinary Christmas gift. But, in contrast with 'Shancoduff' and 'The Great Hunger', there is also a real sense of community and friendship in this poem. We see this as the neighbouring families make their way across the bog. We see it in the kind of banter exchanged between the passing old man and the poet's father. We can imagine a cheerful gathering of the community both before and after Christmas mass.

A Celebration of the Everyday

'Shancoduff', like many of Kavanagh's poems, is a celebration of the everyday. The poet's farm is a perfectly ordinary place, perhaps even an unlovely one. But to the poet it is one of extraordinary beauty. The farm's seven hills, in the poet's eyes, are as striking and spectacular as a great mountain range like the Alps: 'These are my Alps'. The poet finds beauty in the ice and snow that lingers for months in the farm's various nooks and crannies. These frozen patches, in a memorable metaphor, are compared to sparkling coins: 'the bright shillings of March'. And when he struggles up the highest of those hills he experiences a sense of exhilaration and accomplishment comparable to that of a mountaineer who has scaled the Matterhorn itself.

'A Christmas Childhood' emphasises the beauty and strangeness that exist in common, everyday things. Usually, we are too busy and too preoccupied to notice the beauty in the mundane things that surround us. Yet the poem gives many examples of mundane things that can appear beautiful and special if we look at them the right way: a simple green stone, for instance, or the tracks made by cattle as they wander to a watering hole.

In 'The Hospital', Kavanagh celebrates an ugly, functional building that might be described as 'an art lover's woe'. As we noted above, such a building would likely evoke negative emotions and feelings. To the speaker, however, it seems extraordinary. Even its gravel yard is a source of 'inexhaustible adventure'. As such, the poet demonstrates, everything can be considered wonderful, if looked at the right way.

'Canal Bank Walk' reminds us that even the most 'banal' sights can appear beautiful and mysterious. Even the most 'banal' sights imaginable – a bird gathering materials, a patch of grass, a stick 'trapped' in mud – can fill us with awe and inspiration, if only we take the time to slow down and appreciate their hidden beauty.

'Lines Written on a Seat', meanwhile, compares the canal banks to Mount Parnassus, the lock to Niagara Falls and a bargeman's tales to the great myths of old. For these humble sights and sounds, the poem suggests, will strike us as epic and extraordinary, if only we take the time to slow down, to look and listen properly. The poem also makes an interesting point about mindfulness, about being present in the world. It invites us to pause for a moment amid the hustle of daily routines. It invites us to rest upon a park bench, say, and take in the world around us. It invites us to look and listen closely to everyday sights and sounds. In doing so, it will allow us to perceive the wonder hidden in the everyday. Silences will seem 'tremendous' and light 'fantastic'. Ordinary sights – such as a barge or a swan or a reflected bridge – will take on an extraordinary beauty.

Although Kavanagh questions the wisdom of writing poems about local events at the beginning of 'Epic', by the end of the poem Kavanagh's faith in the local has been restored. The poet, we sense, truly believes once more in the greatness and importance of his homeplace. He defiantly celebrates the local, unspectacular feud between the Duffys and McCabes, declaring it a more than fitting source of poetic inspiration.

Innocence and Experience

Kavanagh considered childhood innocence to be a most precious thing. His poems celebrate the manner in which children were able to see the everyday world around them as magical and full of wonder. The poet mourned the fact that such innocence must in time be lost. As we experience more of the world our sense of innocence fades away, along with the wonder that comes with it.

Kavanagh imagined that it might just be possible to restore our sense of innocence through a process of deliberate self-denial and sensory deprivation. When we emerge from such a period, we will look at the world as if we were children once again. Everything will seem new and wonderful. We will have undergone a profound spiritual and psychological transformation.

'A Christmas Childhood' is all about such a fall from innocence into experience. Kavanagh associates his entire childhood with the Christmas season. Christmas, of course, has many different associations, both secular and religious. But Kavanagh has in mind, no doubt, the mystery and awe experienced by children around the festivities, as well as the concepts of sinlessness and salvation associated with the infant Jesus.

The poet, having been tempted by the world of adult sophisticated experience, has lost his sense of childlike wonder. 'Now and then' he can remember particular moments from his childhood when he was filled with wonder and delight. Most vivid of all, it seems, is his memory of the Christmas when he was six years old. But he will never enjoy such wonder in his adult life. The poet has been cast out of childhood's 'gay/ Garden' and there can be no going back.

In 'Advent' Kavanagh describes how he wants us to coax or 'charm' something of childhood back into our lives. The mentioning of 'dry black bread and sugarless tea' symbolises a shift in mindset. We must learn to narrow our focus. We must take the time to really contemplate a particular sight or sound, like a 'dreeping hedge' or a 'slanting hill', rather than being constantly wrapped up in the bigger picture. By concentrating in such a fashion, by narrowing the 'chink' through which we view the world, we might start to see the 'heartbreaking strangeness' that exists in such seemingly ordinary sights.

'Canal Bank Walk' is all about the poet's effort to adopt a new mindset, which Kavanagh compares to a new dress for his soul. But this 'new' mindset isn't actually all that new – it's a reversion to the mentality of childhood. The poet wants to cast off what we might describe as 'experience', the tired, monotonous mindset of adulthood. The poet wants to be redeemed or saved from 'experience', just as a religious person might be redeemed or saved from sin. The canal and its surroundings, as we have seen, offer the poet the possibility of such redemption. These slow-flowing waters, therefore, bring to mind the water used in baptism and other religious rituals. They would cleanse the poet's psyche of experience, enabling him to start afresh. But attaining redemption and gaining this new mindset isn't easy. The poet must become extremely mindful. He must train himself to slow down and find the wonder in every 'habitual' sight he comes across.

Inniskeen Road: July Evening

LINE BY LINE

This poem was written when Kavanagh was in his twenties. It is set on a fine summer's evening in his native Co. Monaghan. A dance is being held in the barn of a local farmer named Billy Brennan. People from all over the locality are making their way to the festivities.

At the time, we must remember, dance halls were a rarity in remote areas like Inniskeen. Dances, therefore, would be held in various barns, huts and haylofts. The music was provided by live musicians playing melodeons, accordions and fiddles. The price of admittance ranged between two and four pence.

The poet, however, has chosen not to attend this particular dance. Instead, he stands on the roadside watching the people of the parish as they make their way to Brennan's barn. The dance-goers travel on bicycles and in small groups – cars, we remember, being exceptionally rare in the Ireland of the 1920s: 'The bicycles go by in twos and threes'.

The poet focuses on the younger dance-goers, those who, like him, were in their twenties. These youngsters communicate using a 'wink-and-elbow language' as they cycle along the road. We can imagine a young man winking at a girl he fancies as he overtakes her on his bicycle. We can imagine two young people who fancy each other exchanging significant glances. We can imagine one friend nudging another, alerting her to the fact that the boy she fancies is cycling by.

This banter and flirtation takes place in a kind of 'half-talk'. Little is stated directly, but meanings are understood. A young man might joke with a girl he fancies, instead of directly telling her he fancies her. Acquaintances might discuss their romantic possibilities in a roundabout way, never directly stating who it is they would like to leave the dance hall with that evening.

Much of their almost wordless communication, therefore, focuses on the 'mysteries' of attraction, love and sexuality. Their 'language', according to the poet, is one of 'delight'. They exhibit great excitement and anticipation as they make their way to Brennan's barn, each hoping that they might leave the dance in the arms of that special someone.

The deserted road

It's now 'Half-past eight' in the evening and the poet is still loitering on the Inniskeen road. He looks up and down the road, gazing about half a mile in either direction. There's 'not a spot' to be seen, he declares, using a colloquial expression which means there is not a person in sight. The sun is sinking in the evening sky, and it has begun to cast or throw shadows of the trees and houses on the ground. However, it doesn't cast a shadow of a single human being: 'no shadow thrown/ That might turn out a man or a woman'. For the dance is in full-swing by now and everyone has gathered in Brennan's.

These lines convey the poet's sense of solitude or isolation. He's standing on an utterly empty road that only an hour ago was filled with the bustle of the dance-goers passing by. He must be keenly aware that nearly everyone else in the parish has gathered for an evening of togetherness and fun. We can imagine him standing alone thinking of the energy, music and laughter that must be filling Brennan's barn right now.

The poet refers to an old superstition that stone paths kept the secrets of those who walked on them. These secrets, the story went, could be magically released if the stones were tapped on in a certain fashion. At half-past eight on this particular evening, however, there is no danger of any such secrets being released as not a single footstep strikes the roadway.

This reference to 'tapping' feet also highlights Kavanagh's loneliness and sense of missing out. It is as if he can't stop thinking about the feet-tapping in Brennan's barn as the melodeons play.

The poet's plight
Poets, according to Kavanagh, require solitude for the purposes of 'contemplation'. It allows them to think deeply about life and to compose meaningful verses. But 'every poet', he suggests, 'hates' this need for solitude because it leaves them feeling lonely and isolated.

Poets tend to speak about solitude in a 'solemn' manner, as if it were something magnificent or awe-inspiring. But we should not take this 'talk' too seriously because even as they outwardly praise solitude they are inwardly cursing it.

To be a poet, then, is to stand outside the community around you. It is, in a sense, to be a community of one. Kavanagh uses a witty metaphor to describe this, comparing the life of a poet to a country with a single inhabitant, who must function not only as the king and governor but also as the nation's only subject. A poet's 'plight', therefore, can be compared to that of Alexander Selkirk. Selkirk was a Scottish sailor who spent four years marooned on a small island in the South Pacific.

FOCUS ON STYLE

Form
'Inniskeen Road: July Evening' has many features of a Petrarchan sonnet. It is divided into an octet rhyming ABABCDCD and a sestet rhyming EFEFGG. There is a 'volta' or turn between the octet and the sestet. The octet describes the scene on Inniskeen Road on that particular evening. The sestet, meanwhile, meditates on the 'plight' of being a poet.

Imagery
The poem is structured around the contrast between two very different images. On the one hand, we have the bustle of the dance-goers making their way to Billy Brennan's barn. On the other hand, we have the poet standing alone in his 'mile' of lonely 'kingdom'.

THEMES

POETRY AND THE ROLE OF THE POET
Antoinette Quinn, in her biography of the poet, says that Kavanagh 'conceived of the poet as a loner, avoiding all participation in communal sports and pastimes, a monk or ascetic repressing his sexuality for a higher spiritual good'. The poet, then, must place himself outside society. He must, like Alexander Selkirk, become a voluntary outcast. He must regard parties and get-togethers as frivolous distractions and focus instead on the contemplation of higher things.

But poets, as we've pointed out above, hate this need for solitude and long to socialise like any other member of society. We see this in the desolate loneliness of lines 5 to 8, where the poet stands on the road alone as the sun sinks behind him, thinking, no doubt, of the fun and flirtation that must be going on in Billy Brennan's barn.

The poem, then, captures Kavanagh's conflicted feelings about the poetic life. As a poet, he feels he shouldn't go to the dance, but as a young man in his twenties he can't ignore it entirely. He leaves the family farm in Mucker, walking nearly a mile along a country lane until he reaches the Inniskeen Road. He then stands there until the very last bicycle has gone by.

This conflict is also present in the poem's final couplet. The poet presents himself as a 'king', declaring that this 'mile' of the Inniskeen Road is his 'kingdom'. Kavanagh, as we've seen, feels so alone that he fancies the whole world has been permanently deserted, that he's within his rights to claim this stretch of public road as his own personal 'kingdom'.

In one sense, his new 'kingdom' is a magical place. It is filled with nature's beauty, with 'banks', 'stones' and a wide variety of wildflowers. But in another sense this 'kingdom' is a place of loneliness and sorrow, for crucially the poet himself is the kingdom's only inhabitant.

This sense of conflict is reinforced by the pun 'every blooming thing' in the poem's final line. In one sense, of course, 'blooming thing' refers to the flowers Kavanagh can see as he looks along the Inniskeen Road. But 'blooming', in another sense, is a very mild swear word, one that suggests Kavanagh's irritation and frustration with the poet's solitary life.

In real life, however, Kavanagh often succumbed to temptation and attended dances that were taking place in the locality. According to Antoinette Quinn, Kavanagh 'was a poor dancer, lumbering, uncoordinated and graceless. He generally joined a group of male wallflowers, middle-aged spectators who passed the time commenting on the merits and demerits of the dancing couples'. We get a sense of the social awkwardness at the opening of the poem as Kavanagh watches the bicycles go by. We sense that the flirtation exhibited by the courting couples doesn't come naturally to him, that he can't quite master the 'half-talk code' in which his peers speak about sexuality and romance.

Shancoduff

Patrick Kavanagh saving the hay with his sister Josie and brother Peter

LINE BY LINE

This poem is set on a farm purchased by the Kavanagh family in 1925 when the poet was 20 years old. The farm stretched across seven hilly fields in the townland of Shancoduff a few miles from the family's home in Mucker. Kavanagh's father passed away in 1929, and the young poet found himself responsible for the day to day running of the farm as well as a great deal of manual labour.

Incurious Hills

'Shancoduff' opens with a notable use of personification, which occurs when an inanimate object is presented as if it had human characteristics. Here, the farm's seven hillsides are presented as a row of human beings staring constantly in one direction. They look north in the direction of Armagh, studying the Monaghan landscape which lies before them, including the little town land of Glassdrummond.

The hilly fields are fascinated by this vista. They exhibit no curiosity about anything that might be going on behind them. They have never looked east to witness the sun rise: 'My black hills have never seen the sun rising'. They just keep staring fixedly ahead.

The hillsides are depicted as taking pleasure from the landscape they study so intently. They are described as being 'happy', for instance, when they see rays of early morning light strike the whitewashed chapel of Glassdrummond: 'are happy/ When dawn whitens Glassdrummond chapel.'

Kavanagh refers to the story of Lot's wife, which appears in the Bible's Book of Genesis. Lot's wife, whose name is never mentioned, was instructed by God not to turn around as she fled the burning city of Sodom. But curiosity got the better of her and she couldn't resist turning around for one quick peak. God punished her by turning her into a pillar of salt.

The hills of Shancoduff, as Kavanagh presents them, are very different to Lot's wife. They exhibit no curiosity whatsoever about what is going on behind them: 'Lot's wife would not be salt if she had been/ Incurious as my black hills that are happy'.

Life on Shancoduff

The poet provides us with a memorable portrait of the farmland on which he labours. The fields are filled with rushes rather than lush green grass. Their surface is rough and uneven, with many gullies and hollows that sunlight never reaches. One of the hills on which the farm is situated, known as 'Rocksavage', features a 'Big Forth' or mountain stream.

Conditions on this hill farm can be bleak, especially in winter. Snow collects in the various gullies and crevices and remains un-melted there for months, long into the spring. The exposed hillsides are subject to cold 'sleety winds'.

The harshness of this environment is especially evident when the poet describes new-born calves 'perishing' in one of his fields. We can imagine these fragile creatures shaking and shivering in the harsh conditions that prevail upon the hillside. The farm's rushy pasture produces no grass for the calves to graze on. The poet, therefore, must scale the 'black hills' with a 'sheaf' or bundle of hay to keep these poor animals alive.

In her biography of Kavanagh, Antoinette Quinn outlines what a typical working day consisted of during this period for the young poet:

Rise at 6 to 7 a.m. on weekdays, feed the hens, milk the cows, tend the fire, prepare the breakfast, work all day on the farm ... home at noon for dinner (cabbage or turnips, potatoes or colcannon and sometimes bacon), finish work at sunset in time for tea (soda bread, a couple of boiled eggs and mugs of tea) ... At night time, when his mother and the younger children had gone to bed, he enjoyed a quiet hour or so alone reading by the fire, sipping a mug of milk or cocoa.

The Cattle-Drovers

The poem's closing lines focus on a group of cattle-drovers, men charged with herding cattle across the countryside. The drovers have paused at the edge of Kavanagh's hilly farm. They shelter in the bushes from the cruel March winds. The poet is passing by and overhears them discussing the condition of his farmstead.

The cattle-drovers note the poor quality of the land, declaring that it consists of 'hungry hills'. This phrase is yet another example in the poem of personification. The hills are depicted as being capable of hunger, just as a human being might be. The poor quality soil longs for nutrients, minerals and fertiliser, just as a hungry human being might long for a good meal. They note that the farm is so barren that even the 'water-hen and snipe', birds known for their ability to survive in hostile environments, have 'forsaken' its hillsides.

FOCUS ON STYLE

Metaphor, Simile and Figures of Speech

The poem is also rich in personification. Kavanagh, as we've seen, playfully personifies the hills on which his farm is situated. The hills are presented as being capable of curiosity and happiness. They are presented as individuals who are content with their own native environment and have no desire to experience anything else.

Stanza 2 features a conceit or extended metaphor:
- The lingering patches of ice are compared to 'bright' silver coins.
- The hill farm is compared to the owner of these shillings and is said to 'hoard' them jealously.
- The nooks where the ice lingers are compared to the owner's pockets.
- The sun is compared to a would-be thief who 'searches in every pocket' for these shillings.

Another conceit features in stanza 3. The rushes that grow on the hillside are compared to facial hair, while the wind is compared to a hand stroking that rushy growth: 'The sleety winds fondle the rushy beards of Shancoduff'.

Verbal Music

Euphony features in the opening stanza where the repeated broad vowel sounds combine to create a pleasant verbal music. We see this in phrases like 'Eternally they look northward to Armagh' and 'When dawn whitens Glassdrummond chapel', where the profusion of 'o' and 'a' sounds creates a memorable effect. Cacophony, meanwhile, features in lines 9 to 10 where the clashing consonants create a jarring verbal music, one suited to the image of the 'perishing calves' and the poet's difficult uphill climb.

Imagery

'Shancoduff', like many of Kavanagh's poems, is rich in imagery of rural life. Especially vivid is the image of the three newborn calves 'perishing' on the exposed hillside. Equally memorable is the image of the sunbeams probing the hillside's various nooks and crannies. Also notable, of course, is the image of the wind ruffling the rushy growth that covers the seven hills.

THEMES

POETRY AND THE ROLE OF THE POET

The cattle-drovers evoke the stereotype of the poet as an impractical dreamer. A more practical person might be able to make this unpromising farmland turn a profit. But a poet, with his head in the clouds, has no chance of making any money from these bleak, rushy fields: 'A poet? Then by heavens he must be poor'.

Kavanagh overhears these remarks and responds with a rhetorical question: 'I hear, and is my heart not badly shaken?' We can read this two ways. Perhaps the poet is greatly upset, shaken both emotionally and psychologically. Perhaps he acknowledges deep-down that the drovers are correct: his poetic mindset makes him an impractical and ineffective person.

But we can also read this line as a defiant rejection of the stereotype. Perhaps the poet's heart isn't 'shaken' at all by the drovers' comments. He might well feel it is perfectly possible to combine a poetic outlook with a practical way of life.

Perhaps we sense Kavanagh's guilt about the double-life he was living at the time. It is possible he felt that in dividing his attention between poetry and farming, he was doing justice to neither.

Antoinette Quinn describes how Kavanagh attempted to combine these two professions: 'He had developed a habit of walking about with cuttings of poems from journals or handwritten copies stuffed in his pockets, and he hid some of these in the hedges of the farm so that he could consult them at odd moments during the day. When an idea or a phrase for a poem struck him out in the fields, he srcibbled it on the inside of his cigarette packet. So his literary interests spilled over into his farming activities and the days were less dichotomised between manual work and writing'.

Poets, Kavanagh often claimed, are inevitably outsiders in the societies they inhabit. We get a sense of this in 'Shancoduff' where the drovers' comments suggest that in 1920s Monaghan poets were regarded as peculiar and impractical. The drovers, and perhaps society at large, view the poet as a somewhat ridiculous figure, worthy of pity or of scorn.

RURAL LIFE

'Shancoduff' provides a vivid portrait of rural life in the early part of the 20th century:

- The life of the farmer, as Kavanagh presents it, is one of toil and hardship. The image of the poet struggling uphill with a sheaf of hay gives us a sense of how difficult farming must have been in the 1920s, before tractors and other farm machinery became commonplace. The poet, we sense, must make this climb every day, no matter what the weather, hauling feed, tools and instruments up the seven hills.
- We are reminded, too, that many farms around Ireland consisted of poor land, of 'hungry hills' where poor farmers struggled to eke out a living.
- The image of the drovers reinforces our sense of rural hardship. Here are men who spend their lives leading cattle on foot across the countryside, taking shelter where they can from the elements.

Kavanagh, then, depicts rural Ireland in a brutally realistic fashion, avoiding all nostalgia and sentimentality.

A CELEBRATION OF THE EVERYDAY

'Shancoduff', like many of Kavanagh's poems, is a celebration of the everyday. The poet's farm is a perfectly ordinary place, perhaps even an unlovely one. But to the poet it is one of extraordinary beauty:

- The farm's seven hills, in the poet's eyes, are as striking and spectacular as a great mountain range like the Alps: 'These are my Alps'.
- And when he struggles up the highest of those hills he experiences a sense of exhilaration and accomplishment comparable to that of a mountaineer who has scaled the Matterhorn itself (The Matterhorn, we remember, is the highest Alpine peak).
- The poet even finds beauty in the ice and snow that lingers for months in the farm's various nooks and crannies. These frozen patches, in a memorable metaphor, are compared to sparkling coins: 'the bright shillings of March'.

Many of Kavanagh's poems – like 'The Hospital' or 'Canal Bank Walk' – involve shutting out the world at large in order to focus on a particular landscape or location. Often, it is only through such focus that the world's wonder and beauty can be revealed. 'Shancoduff' is no exception in this regard. The poet, as we've seen, is utterly focused on his little hill farm, which he regards as his own personal Alps. The hills themselves are depicted as exhibiting a similar focus. They stare 'eternally' northwards, focusing forever on a single ordinary landscape.

This focus on the local is evident in the many place names Kavanagh chooses to include. He mentions 'Armagh', 'Glassdrummond chapel', 'the Big Forth of Racksavage', 'the Featherna Bush' and 'Shancoduff'. The inclusion of so many place names indicates the poet's great love for the area and his determination to celebrate this seemingly ordinary locality.

Epic

THIS IS POETRY — PATRICK KAVANAGH

LINE BY LINE

It is 1938. Two County Monaghan families, the Duffys and the McCabes, are engaged in a dispute over a plot of land. The plot in question seems to lie on the border between their respective properties. The plot is fairly small, measuring only 'half-a rood', or quarter of an acre. Its soil is of poor quality, being little more than 'rock'. It seems that the dispute over this humble piece of ground has dragged on for a long time. We can imagine how it might have given rise to bad blood between the families. We can imagine arguments and fistfights breaking out in the local pub.

The Duffys and McCabes have now gathered by this piece of contested territory, in order to determine once and for all which family is its rightful owner. There is a chance that the issue might still be resolved by argument and negotiation. But there is also a chance that it will be resolved by violence; both families have come armed with pitchforks and are ready to fight. The plot in question, according to the poet, has been 'surrounded' by the two families and their respective supporters: we imagine that the Duffys are gathered on one side of the plot, while the McCabes are gathered on the other. The plot itself, then, is like a 'no-man's land', the area in the middle of a battlefield between two massed opposing armies.

The Duffys, from their side of this 'no-man's land', hurl curses at their opponents: 'I heard the Duffys shouting "Damn your soul!"' Then the leader of the McCabes advances, stepping into the disputed plot of ground. He is stripped to the waist like a boxer ready to do battle: 'Old McCabe stripped to the waist, seen/ Step the plot'. He continues striding forward, ignoring or 'defying' the 'steel' of the Duffys' pitchforks.

Old McCabe gestures to the line of stones that, in his opinion, marks the 'march' or boundary between the Duffy farm and the McCabe farm. This boundary he suggests, of course, will leave the disputed quarter-acre in the possession of his own family: 'Here is the march along these iron stones'.

Lines 8 to 11

The poet notes that this dispute in County Monagahn took place in 1938, the same year as the Munich peace conference: 'That was the year of the Munich bother'. We are invited, then, to compare events in Munich to those in Monaghan:

- The Munich conference concerned the ownership of the Sudetenland, a large territory in Czechoslovakia. The dispute in County Monaghan, as we've seen, concerns only the ownership of a little slice of rocky ground.
- The Munich conference involved four great European powers: France, Germany, Britain and Italy. The dispute in County Monaghan involved only two local families.
- In Munich, the failure of negotiations would lead to a terrible Europe-wide conflict, one sure to cost millions of lives. In Monaghan, the failure of negotiations would lead only to a brawl between gangs of 'pitchfork-armed' farmers.

The poet wonders which of these events was 'most important'. The obvious answer, of course, is the Munich peace conference. That coming together of European leaders, one that temporarily averted World War Two, is surely far more significant than two families arguing over half a rood of rocky ground.

Kavanagh has always had 'faith' in his native Monaghan as a source of inspiration. Its townlands, like 'Ballyrush and Gortin', were ordinary places full of ordinary people doing ordinary things. But he was convinced that writing about these ordinary events would allow him to create great work. Now, however, Kavanagh feels 'inclined' to doubt the townlands of Monaghan as a source of inspiration: 'I inclined/ To lose my faith in Ballyrush and Gortin'. Perhaps it isn't possible, after all, to write great poetry about such places with their ordinary happenings. Perhaps great poetry can only be written about major historical incidents, like the Munich conference, and the storm of war that was waiting to break over Europe.

Homer's ghost

Kavanagh, however, finds himself thinking of the Greek poet Homer, who lived about 2,700 years ago. Homer's most famous work is the *Iliad*, an epic poem almost 16,000 lines long. It is set during the mythic Trojan War, which saw a coalition of Greek kingdoms lay siege to the ancient city of Troy. The poem features epic battles and heroic warriors like Hector and Achilles.

Kavanagh, as we've seen, worries that he's been writing about a petty dispute when he should be engaging with matters of global importance. But then he realises that Homer, too, was writing about 'such/ A local row' when he composed the *Iliad*. For the conflict between the Greeks and Trojans, like that between the Duffys and McCabes, was insignificant by the standards of modern warfare. The Siege of Troy, after all, involved only a few thousand men fighting over a few square miles of territory.

But Homer took this 'local row', this clash of clans in an obscure corner of Bronze Age Europe, and 'made' it into an extraordinary epic poem, one that for centuries has stood at the heart of western culture. Perhaps Kavanagh, too, can make something from his own 'local row'. Perhaps he can be inspired by this County Monaghan feud to produce a poem of lasting significance.

THEMES

POETRY AND THE ROLE OF THE POET

This poem is very much about artistic anxiety and self-doubt. Kavanagh, as we've seen, is worried that he's been writing about the wrong kinds of thing. He worries that he has been focused on a 'local row' between the Duffys and the McCabes when he should be engaging with global conflicts like those discussed at the Munich conference.

Kavanagh feels liberated, however, by Homer's example. He realises that he can write about local matters and still produce good work. He realises that he can stay true to his own inspiration, writing about the goings-on in Ballyrush and Gortin, and still become a poet of substance. If the 'local' was good enough for Homer, then it's good enough for Patrick Kavanagh.

Homer is one of the immortal 'Gods' of poetry, those whose work will live on forever. These Gods, according to Kavanagh, create 'their own importance'. They make even minor events seem important by writing about them so brilliantly that they are remembered for centuries. Perhaps Kavanagh, too, can make his 'own importance'. Perhaps he can confer significance on the minor events of County Monaghan by writing about them with such flair that they will be remembered by future generations.

A CELEBRATION OF THE EVERYDAY

'Epic' presents a highly localised view of the world. The townlands of County Monaghan are 'important places' where 'great events', like the clash between the Duffys and McCabes, are constantly unfolding. The Munich conference, on the other hand, is little more than a 'bother'. The conference and other global events are not to be taken too seriously. What really matters is the latest news from Ballyrush.

It's possible to read sarcasm and irony in these opening lines, as if Kavanagh is mocking this localised worldview. By sarcastically describing the townlands of County Monaghan as 'important places' that are home to 'great events' he actually makes the opposite point, suggesting that these are insignificant places where nothing of consequence ever occurs.

But by the end of the poem, as we've seen, Kavanagh's faith in the local has been restored. The poet, we sense, truly believes once more in the greatness and importance of his homeplace. He defiantly celebrates the local, unspectacular feud between the Duffys and McCabes, declaring it a more than fitting source of poetic inspiration.

RURAL LIFE

Kavanagh, it must be pointed out, doesn't paint an 'idealised' or 'perfect' portrait of life in County Monaghan. Instead, he attempts to shows the difficulty and poverty of rural life as it really was. The Duffys and McCabes are so poor that they are reduced to fighting over a tiny piece of hard, poor quality soil through which 'iron stones' come bursting. 'Epic', then, echoes 'The Great Hunger', with its powerful and moving depiction of rural hardship. It also brings to mind 'Shancoduff', where the poet-farmer takes great pride of ownership in his black hills with their poor-quality soil.

FOCUS ON STYLE

Form

An epic is a long poem that narrates the deeds and adventures of legendary heroes. Kavanagh's poem, however, is quite short and deals with the Duffys and McCabes rather than legendary heroes of the past. The title, therefore, reflects Kavanagh's uncertainty about his subject matter:

- In one sense the title is ironic: by titling his poem about the Duffys and McCabes 'Epic', he emphasises just how petty and insignificant their quarrel actually is in the greater scheme of things.
- Perhaps Kavanagh feels that the Duffys and McCabes deserve only a 'mini-epic', one that's only fourteen lines long, rather than the thousands of lines that Homer devoted to the heroes of the Trojan War.
- But there's also a sense in which Kavanagh's choice of title is defiant. For Kavanagh, as we've seen, genuinely believes that the events of Ballyrush and Gortin are 'great' in their own way and deserve to be celebrated in poetry.

The poem is a sonnet with an ABBA CDDC EFG FEG rhyme scheme. However, all the rhymes are half-rhymes: 'stones' rhymes with 'soul', 'claims' rhymes with 'times', 'seen' rhymes with 'steel' and 'Gortin' rhymes with 'importance'. It has been suggested that Kavanagh uses these imperfect rhymes because the subject he writes about is not usually considered perfect or appropriate material for poetry.

Verbal Music

There is an interesting use of cacophony in lines 3 and 4, where the harsh clashing vowel sounds in 'half a rood of rock, a no-man's land' suggests the harsh unforgiving soil these two families are fighting over. A similar harsh musical effect is created in line 8 by the phrase, 'Here is the march along these iron stones'. Cacophony also features in lines 6 to 7, where the harsh sound of the words suggests the rage of the two factions as they prepare to engage in battle.

THIS IS POETRY — PATRICK KAVANAGH

from The Great Hunger

Poster for the Abbey's 2020 production of a stage version of 'The Great Hunger'

LINE BY LINE

This is the first part of 'The Great Hunger', a long poem often considered to be Kavanagh's masterpiece. It is an outpouring of bitter social criticism in which Kavanagh casts a cold eye on the social conditions that pertained in the rural Ireland of the twenties, thirties and forties.

The poem describes the life of Patrick Maguire, a farmer who has worked the stony grey soil of Co. Monaghan all his life. When we meet Maguire he is sixty-three years old and filled with bitterness and regret that he has never married. We get the impression, in fact, that he has never experienced romantic or sexual intimacy.

Work

The poem is set on an October evening. Maguire, with the aid of some workmen, is gathering potatoes on his farm. This is exceptionally difficult and unpleasant work, especially on a wet October evening in the time before mechanised potato pickers:

- Maguire and his men must reach deep into the earth for each potato that they pick. '[W]eedy clods' of soil must be turned over. The clumps of soil are compared to the knotted 'skeins' of fabric that must be teased apart to reveal the precious potatoes: 'Turn over the weedy clods and tease out the tangled skeins'.
- The freshly picked potatoes are placed in a basket that has been balanced precariously in a hollow.
- They are then carried by horse-drawn cart down the 'ruckety pass' towards Maguire's barn.

Maguire is anxious that not a single potato is lost during transport back to the barn: 'see that no potato falls/ Over the tail-board'. The farm, we sense, requires constant care and maintenance. Maguire, for instance, is conscious that the uneven or 'ruckety pass' needs to be resurfaced: 'that's a job we'll have to do in December,/ Gravel it and build a kerb on the bog-side'.

We get the impression that Maguire is rather grumpy and irritable. He gruffly dispenses orders to his men: 'Pull down the shafts of that cart, Joe'. He is irritated by the intrusion onto his land by a neighbour's donkey: 'Is that Cassidy's ass/ Out in my clover?' He complains that his dog is not where it should be: 'Curse o' God/ where is that dog?/ Never where he's wanted'.

Postponing Marriage

Maguire, as we noted above, has never pursued marriage. His mother encouraged him to postpone doing so until she was dead and the farm had passed to his name. His mother, we are told, 'praised the man who made a field his bride', encouraging him to focus on farm work rather than on romantic pursuits.

Maguire and men like him were victims of a dynamic known as 'familism'.
- Male farmers tended to marry late in life – they could be in their fifties or even their sixties. They would usually marry women much younger, who were still of a child-bearing age.
- After a few years the male farmer would pass away, leaving his wife to endure a long widowhood.
- These widows would then discourage their eldest sons from marrying. They didn't want to see another younger woman become the mistress of the house. They didn't want to be reduced to the status of a guest in their own home. They were even afraid they might be ejected from their own homes to make way for their son's new family.
- Widows had several tactics to deter their sons from marriage. They would refuse to sign over the family farm, making it difficult for their sons to find a bride. They would threaten their sons with disinheritance. They would condition their sons to believe that devoting themselves to the land was more important than starting a family.

As a result of this, many men like Maguire did not marry at all. And those who did marry did so late in life, perpetuating the cycle into the next generation.

Maguire, as we noted above, is sixty-three years old. He has spent years living with his widowed mother, waiting for her to die so he could begin to court one of the local women. But his mother, we learn elsewhere in the poem, lived on until she was ninety-one. By the time she died, Maguire was nearly an old man himself and it was too late for him to pursue love.

Maguire's plight was extremely common in the Ireland of the time. Indeed, the narrator implies that most of the local farmers and farmhands are in a similar situation. Some of Maguire's men promised themselves that this would be the year that they would finally defy their parents and seek out a wife: 'Who was it promised marriage to himself'. This would be done, they told themselves, in time for Halloween and its traditional games. But the year has gone by and no marriage has been arranged.

For Maguire, whole years have rapidly slipped by. The narrator uses a wonderful metaphor to describe this. Maguire's wasted years are compared to birds he frightens away: 'he flung a stone in the air/ And hallooed the birds away that were the birds of the years'. The years, like the birds, have departed at Maguire's own urging, leaving nothing behind.

Wisdom

Maguire thought he was wise to avoid marriage and children: 'And he thought himself wiser than any man in the townland'. Maguire, we're told, 'laughed' and 'shook a knowing head' as he discussed such matters over 'over pints of porter' in the local pub. We imagine him laughing at the foolishness of married men, shaking his head as he struggled to understand why in God's name they made such a crazy decision.

For children, he maintained, had no business on a farm:
- They would be a 'tedious' nuisance, for instance, during the busy sowing season ('hurrying fields of April'). He imagines how children would get in the way of the farmhands who take big 'spanning' steps across the 'wide furrows', sowing the new crop.
- Farmers must also remain alert for crows. The noise of children playing, however, would make it harder to hear the crows cawing. This would allow the birds to descend and devour freshly planted seeds: 'crows could bring/ The seed of an acre away'.
- But we sense that deep down Maguire always wanted children. He only 'pretended' to himself that children would be an unwelcome presence in his life.

Maguire, then, convinced himself that his mother was right when she urged him to avoid starting a family and instead focus on the land. On this windy October evening, however, he starts to experience doubts about the wisdom of her advice: 'His dream changes like the cloud-swung wind/ And he is not so sure now if his mother was right'. Indeed, he realises deep-down that his mother had an ulterior motive when she urged him to postpone seeking a bride: 'he knows that his own heart is calling his mother a liar'.

Maguire looks at his house and 'haggard' or hay-yard. He wishes, no doubt, that a wife and children would be there to greet him at the end of his day's work. He can no longer keep up the pretence that he no longer wants children. He can no longer convince himself that his life-choices were wise ones: 'O God, if I had been wiser'. There is something terribly sad about Maguire's desperate, disappointed sigh as he realises the error of his ways.

Soil

Maguire, therefore, has an intense relationship with the land on which he works. He is 'lost in the passion that never needs a wife', devoting himself to the soil in the way other men devote themselves to wives and families. According to the narrator, Maguire 'lives that his little fields may stay fertile'. His whole life is dedicated to ensuring that crops flourish and the soil is maintained in good order. It is even implied that Maguire will be buried in one of his fields rather than in the local churchyard: 'When his own body/ Is spread in the bottom of a ditch'.

The irony, of course, is that Maguire's own 'fertility' is sacrificed for that of his fields. Maguire might be described as 'infertile' in two senses. First, he gives up his desire to father children. Second, he lives a barren lifestyle, devoid of spiritual and emotional development. These sacrifices, of course, are made just so the land will continue to bear potatoes.

Maguire's relationship with the soil is an intensely intimate one. He doesn't just stand there directing his farmhands. Instead he works in a literally hands-on fashion. The narrator describes how his fingers 'probe' into the earth as he searches for potatoes. His moustache is caked or 'wattled' with clay. Mud covers his hands as if it were a pair of gloves. The poem's opening line highlights how central the soil was to Maguire and men like him: 'Clay is the word and clay is the flesh'. Their 'flesh', their bodily strength, is used in service of the clay and their bodies are covered in clay at the end of each working day. Even their language and conversation is confined to the soil they work on: 'Clay is the word'.

Maguire, we sense, was always awkward and self-conscious when it came to the opposite sex. Flirtation, it seems, never came easily to him. In fact, he would become aggravated and uncomfortable when he was in mixed company and the females started to laugh or screech in a flirtatious manner. Maguire knew that the women, like him, were experiencing sexual desire: 'when they screamed he knew that meant/ The cry of fillies in season'. But he was also repulsed by this flirtatious behaviour, reacting to it like a 'rat' that refuses to eat 'strange bread'.

According to the narrator, Maguire's 'destiny' was to have relationships with women, to marry and to start to have a family. Something, however, prevented him from walking this 'easy road'. This was partly, no doubt, because Maguire, like the young Kavanagh himself was shy and awkward around the opposite sex. But it was also due to the influence of the Catholic Church, which regarded sexuality as something shameful and grotesque.

Dehumanised

The narrator emphasises the destructive nature of the culture that prevailed in rural Ireland. Using a wonderful metaphor, he describes rural Irish culture as a 'monster hand' that shapes and twists the children born into it so they grow up to be almost subhuman: 'No monster hand lifted up children and put down apes/ As here'. No other society, according to the narrator, is as bad 'As here' in producing men who resemble 'apes', who are intellectually and emotionally stunted.

The small farms of rural Ireland are also personified as a monstrous presence. These 'irregular fields' hold farmers like Maguire in a deadly 'grip' from which there can be no escape: 'O the grip, O the grip of irregular fields! No man escapes'.

Maguire and his men, then, have been denied any form of spiritual, cultural or intellectual development. They move, we're told, like 'mechanised scarecrows'. Their lives of deprivation and hard labour have made them more like robots or straw-stuffed dummies than flesh-and-blood human beings with authentic emotions.

Kavanagh himself, we remember, was a farmer much like Maguire. Kavanagh, of course, escarped the hardships of 1920s rural Ireland and moved to the city to pursue a literary career. For Maguire, however, escape is not only impossible but unimaginable. Maguire, the narrator suggests, simply couldn't envisage leaving the farm behind and becoming a teacher or a salesman, for instance. He couldn't even envisage working on a better farm, where the soil is more fertile and the ditches run straight: 'It could not be that back of the hills love was free/ And ditches straight'.

FOCUS ON STYLE

Form

An important feature of the poem is that it is related by an impersonal narrator. The narrator and the reader are presented as invisible witnesses to Maguire's life, as if we were standing there on the hillside watching Maguire and his men go about their work: 'why do we stand here shivering?'

The narrator addresses the reader directly. He wonders if watching these men at work can teach us anything about the human condition: 'If we watch them an hour is there anything we can prove'. The narrator calls on a personification of the power of imagination to assist him: 'Come with me, Imagination'. With the aid of 'Imagination', the narrator will make the 'years run back'. The remaining sections of 'The Great Hunger' are a kind of flashback, describing Maguire's life from his youth to the poem's 'present day', and revealing how he ended up in his present miserable condition.

The poem concludes with the narrator addressing the month of October as a farmer might address a horse. He urges October to be quiet, calling on the hens not to cackle, the horses not to neigh, the trees to make no sound as the wind blows through them and the ducks not to quack. This silence, presumably, is required so that the narrator can concentrate on the work of imagination, allowing Maguire's life story to be told.

THEMES

RURAL LIFE

'The Great Hunger' presents a brutal, uncompromising view of rural Ireland.

- It highlights how life on small farms was one of back-breaking toil.
- It highlights how men like Maguire were bamboozled into postponing marriage until it was too late.
- It highlights how men like Maguire were consumed by their relationship to the soil.
- It highlights how men like Maguire were denied personal and intellectual development. As a result they were dehumanised, turned into little more than apes.
- It highlights how impossible it was for men like Maguire to escape their plight. They were incapable of even imagining another existence.

The poem's key irony, then, is that the land thrives at the expense of those who work on it. In an attempt to ensure their fields' survival, to stave off a repeat of the Great Famine of the 1840s, the farmers have allowed another 'Great Hunger' to emerge, a terrible starvation of the emotions and the spirit.

'The Great Hunger' was quite controversial when it was first published in 1947. For decades, Irish poets and playwrights had depicted an idealised, tourist-friendly image of rural Ireland. But Kavanagh, unlike most Irish writers, had spent decades living and working on an Irish farmstead. Here he explodes the myth of the idyllic countryside.

The poem was first published in Horizon, an English magazine. It was considered indecent by the Irish authorities because of its frank discussion of sexuality and its unflattering depiction of rural Irish life. As a result, all copies of Horizon destined for Irish bookshops were seized by the guards. Kavanagh, by all accounts, was delighted that his poem had caused such a stir.

RELIGION

In poems like 'Canal bank Walk' and 'A Christmas Childhood' religion is presented in a positive light. 'The Great Hunger', however, is highly critical of religion, especially of the Church's attitude towards sexuality.

The poem, we must remember, is set in a time when the Catholic Church was a dominant force in Irish society. Religion plays a central role in the lives of Maguire and men like him. Maguire, as we've seen, created a 'June altar' on his land. When he dies his grave will be marked by two 'coulters' or plough blades 'crossed in Christ's name'.

The influence of the Church meant that sexuality was regarded as foul, grotesque and shameful. Lovers, the Church maintained, produced 'grotesque shapes' as they succumbed to the 'foulest fire' of passion and desire. Kavanagh takes issue with this view. Sexuality, he believes, is a true and honest aspect of the life that God has given us: 'God's truth is life'. It is in no way grotesque or shameful.

As we've seen, the dynamic known as 'familism' prevented Maguire from marrying. The influence of the Catholic Church, meanwhile, meant he couldn't pursue romantic and sexual fulfilment outside of marriage. This is represented by the image of the horse and the clover:

- The clover represents 'late passion', the possibility that in his later years Maguire might experience sexual fulfilment.
- The horse 'cranes' its head over the wall, desperate to reach the clover. He manages to brush it with his lips but cannot get quite close enough to eat it. Maguire, similarly, longs for sexual fulfilment that he cannot find.
- The horse is kept from the clover by bushes and boulders. Maguire is kept from sexual fulfilment by the false morality of the Catholic Church: 'In the gap there's a bush weighted with boulders like morality'.

The narrator maintains that these boulders of morality represent a formidable obstacle. To cross them is to go against the mores and values of an entire society. In a small rural community like Maguire's, to flout the rules of morality was to risk drawing the anger of the local priest and becoming some kind of social outcast: 'The fools of life bleed if they climb over'.

The opening line, then, is a parody of two key Christian pronouncements, reflecting the narrator's bitterness towards the Catholicism that dominated the Ireland of the time. It echoes not only the first sentence of the Bible ('In the beginning was the word') but also a refrain from the Angelus, which at the time was said nightly in many Irish households: 'The word was made flesh and dwelt amongst us'. The narrator believes that the devotion displayed by Maguire and his men to their religion has not brought them happiness or salvation. Instead, it has helped to keep them unfulfilled and undeveloped, imprisoned in their world of 'irregular fields'.

The reference to the soil as 'the Book of Death' over which the men bend also has religious connotations. The Bible, of course, is often referred to as a 'book of life'. Irish Catholicism, the narrator implies, is for these men a religion of clay and death rather than of hope and life. It is a creed that keeps these 'broken-backed' men tied to the soil.

The 'queen/ Too long virgin' calls to mind the Virgin Mary, Queen of Heaven. We can read the line, therefore, as an attack on the farmers' devotion to the Church, which, as we have seen, played a key role in their sexual frustration. They have spent their lives worshipping the Virgin, when they should, the narrator believes, have been in pursuit of real women.

A Christmas Childhood

THIS IS POETRY — PATRICK KAVANAGH

LINE BY LINE

The 'gay/ Garden' of childhood

Children, because they are so innocent, find wonder in the most ordinary things. Kavanagh thinks back to his own childhood, remembering some of the everyday sights and sounds that filled him with astonishment.

He found wonder, for instance, in the sight of frost forming on the outdoor pits that were used for storing potatoes. There was also something 'magical', he recalls, about the sound of metal fence-posts vibrating in the wind. Equally thrilling was the evening light in a field full or 'ricks' or haystacks. The poet was awestruck, too, by an apple tree in December. The tree, he remembers, retained a few pieces of fruit which were covered in frost and glinted in the winter light.

But this childhood innocence could not last. For Kavanagh, like all young children, was 'tempted' by the world, by which he means the 'world' of sophisticated adult experience.
Kavanagh, like all young children, was eager for the 'knowledge' that this adult world seemed to offer. He wanted adult experiences, adult understanding and adult consciousness.

The knowledge offered by the world, however, came with a terrible price. For gaining this knowledge meant losing his childhood innocence. He was no longer capable of finding wonder in the everyday sights and sounds that surrounded him. Kavanagh emphasises this point when he declares that this knowledge emerged from 'clay', which in his writing is always a negative term, suggesting death, deceit and disappointment.

Kavanagh compares the loss of his childhood innocence to the story of the Garden of Eden:

- Adam, in that famous Bible story, inhabited a miraculous and blissful garden. For children, too, the entire world is a 'gay/ Garden', a place of wonder and delight. This is because every single aspect of the world strikes them as being marvellous.
- Adam, in the story, was tempted by Eve. The poet, as we've seen, was tempted by 'the world': 'O you, Eve, were the world that tempted me'.
- Adam succumbed to temptation and ate the fruit. The poet, similarly, succumbed to temptation and consumed the knowledge offered by the world.
- The price of Adam's new knowledge was exile from the Garden of Eden. The price of the poet's new knowledge was expulsion from the 'gay/ Garden' of childlike wonder.

There are moments, Kavanagh declares, when he can remember what it was like to view the entire world as such a garden of delight: 'Now and then/ I can remember something of the gay/ Garden that was childhood's'. He recalls what it was like to be thrilled by the most everyday sights and sounds. He recalls how 'any common sight' resembled a beautiful face that had been 'transfigured', that had been made astonishingly radiant and glorious.

But the poet, like every other adult, has swapped innocence for knowledge. He can remember and relive certain moments of childlike wonder. But he will never have new experiences of this type. He can never recapture that childhood mentality. Never again will such 'common' or mundane sights fill him with astonishment and awe.

The knowledge offered by the world is associated with sexuality. The poet presents the world of sophisticated adult experience as a female temptress: 'O you, Eve, were the world'. We get a sense then that the poet associates the loss of innocence with the beginnings of sexuality.

The knowledge offered by the world is also tainted with death. Death, Kavanagh declares, exists within this knowledge like a seed within an apple: 'the knowledge that grew in clay/ And death the germ within it'. For children, as they grow older, develop an awareness of mortality, slowly realising that they and everyone around them must eventually pass away.

Remembering Christmas
In the poem's second section, the poet remembers a Christmas morning from his childhood. He was only six years old, or 'six Christmases of age'. Like many children on Christmas morning, the young poet woke up early. It was still 'dawn', so early that when he looked out his window stars were visible in the winter sky: 'There were stars in the morning east'. He saw that the morning was a cold one, that the whole landscape was covered in a 'silver' layer of frost.

The poet quickly got dressed as if he was eager to be outside: 'I pulled on my trousers in a hurry'. However, he paused briefly while leaving the house and with his finger traced an inscription that has been carved into 'grey stone': 'My child poet picked out the letters/ On the grey stone'. Kavanagh doesn't specify what these letters actually were. But they are likely the name of some mason or manufacturer, who erected the cottage's stone walls or laid its paving stones many years ago.

The young poet made his way to the front door of the house:
- His father was playing the melodeon, a type of button accordion, at the front gate. The sound of his playing drifted across the 'wild bogs' around the poet's house.
- His mother was busy in the 'cow-house'. Because it was still quite dark she was milking the cows by lamplight.
- People from the locality were making their way to early mass, their footsteps crunching the ice as they trudged along the country road: 'Mass-going feet/ Crunched the wafer-ice on the pot-holes'.
- A passing mass-goer praised the quality of his father's playing: "Can't he make it talk –/The melodeon".
- The young poet, exhibiting the shyness we often associate with six-year-olds, remained hidden in the doorway until this neighbour had gone by: 'I hid in the doorway'. Perhaps his self-consciousness is evident in his body language, specifically the manner in which he tightens his coat around him.

The young poet, it seems, had been given a new penknife for Christmas. We get a sense that this present, with its 'big blade' and its 'little one for cutting tobacco', made him feel grown up. He used the knife's big blade to carve six notches in the door frame, one for each year of his life so far.

Wonder
Many aspects of this Christmas morning struck the young poet as being beautiful or wonderful. He found wonder, for instance, in the 'silver' layer of frost that covered the landscape: 'In silver the wonder of a Christmas townland'.

His father's melodeon-playing, too, seemed magical. He imagined that the stars in the early morning sky were twinkling in time to the father's playing: 'There were stars in the morning east/ And they danced to his music'. The young poet imagined that the people of the locality, the Lennon and Callan families for instance, have been summoned by the father's playing: 'Across the wild bogs his melodeon called/ To Lennons and Callans'. In reality, of course, these local people were simply heading to mass.

Even the sound of cows being milked beguiled the young poet. The cows, of course, were being milked by hand by his mother. We can imagine the young poet lingering outside the cow-house listening to the sound of fresh milk spilling into the metallic bucket: 'Outside in the cow-house my mother/ Made the music of milking'.

Bethlehem in Mucker
The six-year-old poet, we can imagine, had been learning about Jesus' birth and the story of the nativity was fresh in his mind. On that morning, then, his imagination ran away with him and he fancied that Jesus's birth was happening this very morning in the parish outside his window.

From the moment he woke, he had the sense that some incredible event was taking place: 'I knew some strange thing had happened'. And when he looked out from the farmhouse door, the landscape of his native Monaghan seemed to merge with the landscape of Bethlehem all those centuries ago:
- The frost that covered the landscape around the poet's house seemed to merge with the 'frost of Bethlehem' that might have been present all those centuries ago on the morning of Christ's birth.
- The cowshed for a moment seemed like the stable where Jesus was born.
- A stable-lamp had been hung at the stable door. The young poet imagined that this was the star that hovered above the stable where Christ was born: 'the light of her stable-lamp was a star'.
- The poet noticed three whin bushes blowing in the wind. To the young poet, they seemed to be moving across the landscape, as if they were the Three Wise Kings approaching on their camels: 'three whin bushes rode across/ The horizon – the Three Wise Kings'.

THIS IS POETRY — PATRICK KAVANAGH

THEMES

INNOCENCE AND EXPERIENCE
This poem, as we have seen, is all about the fall from innocence into experience. The poet, having been tempted by the world of adult sophisticated experience, has lost his sense of childlike wonder. 'Now and then' he can remember particular moments from his childhood when he was filled with wonder and delight. Most vivid of all, it seems, is his memory of the Christmas when he was six years old. But he will never enjoy such wonder in his adult life. The poet has been cast out of childhood's 'gay/ Garden' and there can be no going back.

Kavanagh, it's important to note, titles the poem 'A Christmas Childhood' rather than, as we might expect, 'A Childhood Christmas'. Kavanagh, therefore, associates his entire childhood with the Christmas season. Christmas, of course, has many different associations, both secular and religious. But Kavanagh has in mind, no doubt, the mystery and awe experienced by children around the festivities, as well as the concepts of sinlessness and salvation associated with the infant Jesus.

The poet tellingly remembers a Christmas when he was six years old. Seven, traditionally, is held to be the age of reason, when children start to gain the knowledge and experience that Kavanagh calls 'the world'.

A CELEBRATION OF THE EVERYDAY
Like many of Kavanagh's poems, 'A Christmas Childhood' emphasises the beauty and strangeness that exist in common, everyday things. Usually, we are too busy and too preoccupied to notice the beauty in the mundane things that surround us. Yet the poem gives many examples of mundane things that can appear beautiful and special if we look at them the right way: a simple green stone, for instance, or the tracks made by cattle as they wander to a watering hole.

RURAL LIFE
'A Christmas Childhood', like many of Kavanagh's poems, provides an unflinching view of rural Ireland in the early twentieth century. This is a world of unrelenting hard work, of potato pits and paling posts, of cows being milked in the freezing dawn. This is a world marked by poverty, one where a pen-knife is an extraordinary Christmas gift.

But there is also a real sense of community and friendship. We see this as the neighbouring families make their way across the bog. We see it in the kind of banter exchanged between the passing old man and the poet's father. We can imagine a cheerful gathering of the community both before and after Christmas mass.

POETRY AND THE ROLE OF THE POET
A notable moment occurs when the six-year-old Kavanagh pauses to trace the letters on the inscription on Christmas morning. Here we see that Kavanagh, even though he was still learning to read and write, had a fascination for the written world. Kavanagh claims that although he was only six years old, he was still a poet: 'My child poet picked out the letters'. Of course he had yet to write or compose anything, but he possessed the sensitivity to language essential to all true poets.

FOCUS ON STYLE

Form
An interesting aspect of this poem is that it combines two poems that were composed separately: the first in 1940 and the second in 1943. The first section is more abstract and philosophical, while the second section provides a powerful illustration of the first section's theme, emphasising that a childhood mentality can be remembered but never recaptured.

Metaphor, Simile and Figures of Speech
The poet uses a wonderful metaphor to capture the evening light at harvest time. The 'ricks' or stacks of hay have been arranged in a wall, that is described as the 'gable' or wall of 'heaven itself'. The light that filters through the gaps between the ricks is said to emanate from paradise. An equally vivid simile is used to describe the young poet's prayer, which is compared to a white rose, specifically one that might have been pinned to the Virgin Mary's blouse. The poet, then, associates his youthful prayer with stainless whiteness, with innocence and virginity. It stands in sharp contrast to the world of sophisticated adult experience which he will soon discover.

Imagery
This poem is rich in vivid imagery. Especially memorable is the depiction of the sparkling frost-covered landscape, with its 'winking glitter' in the early morning light. Equally vivid is the depiction of the father playing the melodeon at the farmhouse gate while the stars vibrate in the east and the people of the parish crunch across the boggy countryside.

Verbal Music
There is an onomatopoeic quality to the phrase 'Mass-going feet/ Crunched the wafer ice' in which we can almost hear the ice being broken by the trudging feet of the poet's neighbours. Onomatopoeia is also present in line 32, with describes the sound of the bellows being twisted to stoke the fire on this freezing Christmas morning. The clashing 't' an 'w' sounds mimic the shrill whistle of the bellows wheel being turned: 'Somebody wistfully twisted the bellows wheel'.

The poem is also rich in assonance and alliteration, in phrases such as 'winking glitter', with its repeated 'i' sounds, and 'Cassiopeia was over/ Cassidy's hanging hill', with its repeated 'c' and broad vowel sounds.

Advent

'bring/ You and me to the yard gate to watch the whins ...'

LINE BY LINE

Advent, like many of Kavanagh's poems, deals with the innocence of childhood. Children, because they are so innocent, view the world as an extraordinary place. To them, the entire world is filled with 'newness'. Even the most ordinary sights and sounds seem wonderful.

The poem is addressed to Kavanagh's 'lover'. It is possible, of course, that the poet is referring to an actual lover here, to a woman he was involved with or was pursuing around the time of the poem's composition. But it's also possible that he is referring to an aspect of his own self. Perhaps he is referring to the poetic, creative facet of his personality. Or perhaps he is referring to his soul.

Kavanagh recalls experiencing such wonder during his own childhood. He remembers a 'black slanting Ulster hill'. This was a perfectly ordinary sight, one most adults would pass without a second glance. But it filled the young poet with an amazement that was profoundly affective : 'spirit-shocking/ Wonder'.

He also recalls listening to an 'old fool', who wandered the roads around Inniskeen. We picture an old man, perhaps not fully of sound mind, droning on and on about whatever comes into his head. Adults, no doubt, found this individual a nuisance and would go out of their way to avoid his 'tedious talking'. But the young poet was filled with 'astonishment' by his ramblings. He viewed the 'old fool' as a 'prophetic' figure, as if like the prophets of old he was revealing great secrets about the universe and the future.

Experience

But gradually children start to experience more and more of the world. Kavanagh outlines his understanding of experience:

- Experience is associated with 'knowledge', for children, as they grow older, acquire new skills, ideas and information.
- Experience is associated with consciousness, for children, as they grow older, become more aware of themselves, others and the world around them.
- Experience is also associated with 'reason', for children, as they grow older, become more rational and logical.
- Finally, experience is associated with 'pleasure', by which Kavanagh probably means pleasure of a sexual nature. As children become teenagers their sexuality inevitably starts to develop.

Experience – with all its knowledge, consciousness, reason and pleasure – seems to offer us great benefits. Kavanagh compares it an employer offering a purse of coins in return for our service. But the benefits of experience turn out to be illusory. We realise too late that our 'wages' have been minted not from valuable metals but from worthless 'clay'.

Lines 7 to 8 feature an interesting use of personification, one that's reminiscent of Greek mythology . Here the concept of 'Doom' is presented as if it were a human-like figure, some dark tyrannical king or a vengeful god. Knowledge, Kavanagh suggests, is the rightful property of Doom. We steal it from him, only to find we have no use for it, that it does not benefit us in any way. If anything, it corrupts us, allowing Doom's baleful influence to enter our lives: 'The knowledge we stole but could not use'.

Experience, according to Kavanagh, robs us of our child-like innocence and the sense of wonder that comes with it. Kavanagh uses the metaphor of looking through a crack or 'chink' to describe this:
- When we are children we have a limited set of experiences. Kavanagh compares this to gazing through a narrow opening.
- As we grow older we have a broader and more varied set of experiences. Kavanagh compares this to gazing through a wider opening.
- The more we experience, the more we 'test' and 'taste', the more innocence fades away. The wider the 'chink' we look through, the less wonder there is in our lives.

Recovering Innocence

Kavanagh, then, sets out to cast off the false benefits of experience and return to the innocence of childhood. He sets out to deliberately narrow the 'chink' through which he views the world. For a number of weeks he will drastically limit the sights, sounds and tastes he experiences.

He will remain at home, in a kind of self-imposed house-arrest. He will keep his rooms 'darkened, increasing the sensory deprivation. He will only consume what is necessary to stay healthy. And what little he does eat will be deliberately tasteless and un-enjoyable: 'dry black bread and the sugarless tea'. Here Kavanagh seems inspired by the old tradition of the 'advent' or nativity fast, when Christians, for forty days in the run up to Christmas, would enter a period of fasting and self-denial.

When Kavanagh goes back out into the world again, everything will seem fresh and new. He will be like an innocent child seeing things for the first time. Through this process of self-denial, then, he will have reclaimed the 'luxury of a child's soul'. The wonder and astonishment he once perceived in ordinary things will 'awake for [him] once more'. Things that now seem 'stale' will seem filled with 'newness' once again.

Innocence Recovered

Through such a process we will be able to rid ourselves of experience, casting its worthless 'wages' into the 'dustbin'.
- We will turn away from pleasure and consciousness.
- The knowledge that we 'stole' from 'Doom' will be returned to its rightful owner.
- We will no longer seek the benefits of logic and reason. We will cease to analyse or question the beauty that surrounds us, instead accepting it for what it is: 'we shall not ask for reason's payment/ The why of heart-breaking strangeness in dreeping hedges'.

This process of sensory deprivation, then, will lead to a great 'difference' in mindset, one that makes everyday noises 'burn' with mystery and meaning: 'we will have no need to go searching/ For the difference that sets an old phrase burning'. Ordinary sounds – the swish of butter being churned, the banter of 'village boys', the talk of 'decent men' busy in their gardens – will strike us like exquisite, captivating music.

It will lead to a kind of rebirth or renewal, one that is symbolised when Kavanagh imagines himself walking out to the 'yard gate' of his old homestead in Mucker, County Monaghan. He imagines standing there utterly captivated by the most ordinary sights imaginable: by 'whins' or furze bushes, by 'bog holes' and by 'cart tracks'.

Such renewal, Kavanagh suggests, will bring extraordinary richness to our lives: 'Won't we be rich, my love and I'. He is not, of course, referring to financial riches. Instead he's referring to a kind of spiritual or psychological wealth, one that allows us to take joy in the 'ordinary plenty' of this life.

Advent as a Christian Poem

'Advent' is also a deeply Christian poem, one that reflects Kavanagh's very personal religious beliefs. God, the poet maintains, is present all around us, in the beauty of the natural world and even in the speech of human beings. Kavanagh, however, insists that God's presence can't be subjected to logical analysis: 'Nor analyse God's breath in common statement'. We experience it instead in an instinctual and emotional fashion.

Kavanagh's Christian outlook also influences his understanding of innocence and experience:
- Experience is associated with the Christian concept of sin.
- The sensory deprivation that casts off experience, meanwhile, is associated with Advent, a period of prayer, penance and fasting in the weeks leading up to Christmas.
- The regaining of innocence is associated with Christmas itself. We see this when the poet contemplates 'old stables' in his native Monaghan, reflecting the fact that Christ was born in a very similar building two thousand years ago. For a moment, as in 'A Christmas Childhood', Monaghan and Palestine are fused in the poet's imagination.
- The enjoyment of this newfound innocence is associated with the period after Christmas: 'O after Christmas we'll have no need to go searching'.

This will be a period when 'Time begins' once again for the poet, when he embarks on a whole new phase of his existence. It is associated with January, therefore, the month of new beginnings. Innocence will be present in his life just as Christ at that time of year is present in a special way for Christians: 'And Christ comes with a January flower'.

THEMES

INNOCENCE AND EXPERIENCE

Let's briefly summarise Kavanagh's argument in this poem:
- When we are innocent children, everything seems filled with wonder.
- Gradually, as we experience more of the world our sense of innocence fades away, along with the wonder that comes with it.
- We can restore our sense of innocence through a process of deliberate self-denial and sensory deprivation.
- When we emerge from such a period, we will look at the world as if we were children once again. Everything will seem new and wonderful.
- We will have undergone a profound spiritual and psychological transformation.

We might ask ourselves, however, if Kavanagh is right to utterly reject knowledge, consciousness and pleasure. Most of us, after all, feel that the benefits of these faculties are genuine, rather than false and 'clay-minted'.

But Kavanagh, we must point out, doesn't literally want us to become children once again. He knows that we can't unlearn the knowledge and reason we have acquired through growing up. Instead, he wants us to coax or 'charm' something of childhood back into our lives.

The 'dry black bread and sugarless tea', then, symbolise an ongoing shift in mindset. We must learn to narrow our focus. We must take the time to really contemplate a particular sight or sound, like a 'dreeping hedge' or a 'slanting ... hill', rather than being constantly wrapped up in the bigger picture. By concentrating in such a fashion, by narrowing the 'chink' through which we view the world, we might start to see the 'heart-breaking strangeness' that exists in such seemingly ordinary sights.

FOCUS ON STYLE

Form

'Advent' takes the form of two sonnets, each with a semi-regular rhyme scheme. The first is addressed to the poet's 'lover', the second to the poem's reader.

Metaphor, Simile and Figures of Speech

Kavanagh uses a wonderful metaphor to describe the swishing sound of butter being churned, comparing it to a 'whispered argument'. Another metaphor, as we've seen, compares the benefits of experience to worthless coins that have been minted out of clay. It's worth noting that clay in Kavanagh's poetry is associated with deceit, death and disappointment.

Imagery

'Advent', like many of Kavanagh's poems, is rich with imagery of rural life. We are presented with the the poet standing amazed before a 'slanting Ulster Hill, 'bog-holes' and 'cart-tracks'. There is a neat contrast between the 'lurching' boys, up to no good as they wander around the village, and the 'decent men' busy shifting wheelbarrows full of dung.

Kavanagh comes with a neologism, an entirely new word, to describe the appearance of hedges after rain. The hedges, he declares, are 'dreeping', both dripping and weeping, as raindrops collect and fall from their branches and their leaves.

THIS IS POETRY | PATRICK KAVANAGH

On Raglan Road

LINE BY LINE

This poem was written in the autumn of 1944, when Kavanagh was living in a boarding house on Raglan Road. It was inspired by Hilda Moriarty, a 22-year-old medical student at University College, Dublin. Hilda, at the time, was considered one of the most beautiful women in the city.

Stanza 1
The poet first met his beloved while walking along Raglan Road 'on an Autumn day'. He fell in love with her immediately. He was especially captivated by her long 'dark hair'. He seemed to sense that falling for this woman would bring him suffering and misery. He 'saw the danger' that loving her would bring.

In a startling metaphor the poet imagines this woman's hair weaving itself into a 'snare'. A snare, of course, is a trap made of rope that tightens around those unfortunate enough to step into it. The poet senses, therefore, that he is likely to become obsessed with this beautiful woman. He will be unable to stop thinking of her. He will be unable to stop desiring her, despite all the misery she brings him.

The poet realises that he will 'rue' or regret falling under this woman's spell. But he can't help pursuing the relationship anyway. He seems to view the grief that is coming his way as something natural and inevitable, like leaves falling from the trees of October: 'I said let grief be a fallen leaf'.

Stanza 2
A few weeks has passed and the relationship between the poet and this dark-haired woman is in full swing. The poet describes himself and his lover walking happily down Grafton Street. They 'trip lightly' along together; sauntering in a casual, carefree manner.

In a metaphorical sense, however, they are walking along the edge of a 'deep ravine', a steep gorge or chasm. The 'ravine', of course, represents the deep despair the poet will experience at the end of the relationship. The poet depicts himself walking along the 'ledge' of this 'ravine', representing how he could be cast into such despair at any moment. The fact that he 'trips lightly' represents his efforts to remain cheerful, to keep thoughts of the relationship's inevitable conclusion out of his mind.

Women, the poet suggests, 'pledge' or promise all kinds of things, especially during moments of passion or romance. But their pledges are not to be trusted. In fact, they are worthless and entirely unreliable. All they do is lead innocent lovers like the poet into the chasm of despair: 'A deep ravine where can be seen the worth of passion's pledge'.

Stanza 3
The poet describes how he gave his lover 'gifts of the mind'. This suggests that he introduced her to a wide range of books and idea relating to history, philosophy, literature and so on. The poet also composed many poems for his beloved, working on them without any 'stint' or rest. These poems feature her name and celebrate her dark, lustrous hair, which Kavanagh, using a marvellous simile, compares to 'clouds over fields of May'.

The poet personifies inspiration, presenting this force as a family of 'true gods', not unlike the Muses of Greek mythology. Real artists, the poet suggests, invoke these gods by means of a 'secret sign', by means of a ritual involving mystical symbols, words or gestures. By doing so, they summon the power of the 'true gods' into their minds and bodies, enabling them to create great music ('sound'), sculpture ('stone'), literature ('word') and paintings ('tint'). Kavanagh, as one of these real artists, is privy to the 'secret sign' used within these rituals of inspiration and he has given his beloved an incredible gift by sharing with her this sacred knowledge.

Kavanagh, of course, doesn't believe that artists enage in bizarre cult-like rituals. The 'secret sign' functions as a metaphor for the intensely mysterious processes that occur when a great artist goes to work. These lines suggest, therefore, that the poet has told his beloved about aspects of his creative practice, details he would share with nobody else.

Stanza 4
This final stanza describes the end of the couple's affair. The speaker watches his lover walk quickly away from him: 'I see her walking now/ Away from me so hurriedly'. She leaves him behind on a street haunted by ghosts, which probably represent the speaker's memories of their relationship: 'On a quiet street where old ghosts meet'.

FOCUS ON STYLE

Form
An important feature of 'On Raglan Road' is that it was written to be sung. The poem, then, has several features common to many Irish ballads. It has an AABB rhyming scheme. It also has many internal rhymes; for example 'hair' and 'snare' in line 2, and 'leaf' and 'grief' in line 4.

'On Raglan Road' has been sung and recorded countless times and in 2019 was voted Ireland's favourite song. Kavanagh borrowed the tune and the recurring phrase 'dawning of the day' from an old Irish air.

THEMES

A NEGATIVE VIEW OF WOMEN AND LOVE
Kavanagh uses an interesting metaphor to describe the process of falling in love, comparing it to travelling along 'the enchanted way' This suggests, of course, the magic and mystery of a loving relationship. Yet it also has the slightly sinister implication that by falling in love with the woman, the speaker will find himself in her power. He will be 'enchanted' by her, held in her thrall as if he was hypnotised or under a spell.

The poet seems to regard love as a waste of time. There are better things to do, he feels, than focus on a love affair: 'The Queen of Hearts still making tarts and I not making hay'. The poet thinks his time would be better spent on some useful occupation – 'making hay' – rather than hanging around with this beautiful young woman. The speaker's disregard for love is also shown by his reference to the 'Queen of Hearts'. He associates romance with a character from a nursery rhyme, making it seem silly and childish.

The poet accuses himself of loving 'too much', of letting his feelings for this beautiful, black-haired woman run away with him. He failed to control his emotions and as a result threw away his 'happiness'.

The poet, it must be said, depicts his lover in a rather negative light. Her beauty, he says, is a trap or 'snare'. Her 'pledges', as we've seen, are not to be trusted. He depicts her as an enchantress who will enslave him with the magic spell of her beauty, and lure him 'along the enchanted way' to his doom in the 'deep ravine'. He describes her most damningly of all as a 'creature made of clay', which in Kavanagh's poetry is always associated with deception and depair.

Many readers feel that this is an unfair and stereotypical portrayal of a woman as an evil temptress, a stereotype that goes back to the Bible when Eve tempted Adam with the apple in the Garden of Eden. Others detect a note of misogyny in the poem, suggesting that Kavanagh attributes these untrustworthy characteristics not only to this woman but to women in general.

POETRY AND THE ROLE OF THE POET
The poet comes across as someone who has a very high regard for poetry and artistic creation. He seems proud of the poems he writes for his beloved, which vividly capture her 'dark hair'. True artists, like himself, the poem suggests, are rare and possess special abilities, knowledge and understanding that are unknown to ordinary people.

True artists, Kavanagh believed, must avoid getting caught up in matters of love and sexuality.
- True artists, he suggests, must resemble angels. Their minds must remain on higher things, on 'gifts of the mind', on communing with the 'true gods' of inspiration.
- The poet, however, has succumbed to temptation. He has allowed himself to be drawn into love and sexuality - he has 'wooed not as [he] should'.
- He has been dallying with this beautiful woman when he should have been busy 'making hay', developing his poetic practice.

Surrendering to love and sexuality, the poem suggests, can seriously impair an artist's creative abilities. Kavanagh, in the poem's last line, suggests that he has been stripped of his poetic capabilties, just like an angel that has lost his wings.

THIS IS POETRY   PATRICK KAVANAGH

The Hospital

'nothing whatever is by love debarred ...'

LINE BY LINE

On 31 March 1955 Kavanagh underwent surgery for lung cancer in St James' Hospital (formerly the Rialto Hospital) in Dublin. It was discovered that his left lung was in bad condition and needed to be entirely removed, along with one of his ribs. Kavanagh ended up spending two months in hospital recovering from the procedure.

According to Antoinette Quinn, Kavanagh would later 'look back on the two months spent in the Rialto Hospital as the happiest in his life. It was the happiness of feeling safe and secure. Once he had adapted to the hospital regimen, he liked the fixed routines. He was protected from all his financial anxieties that had harassed him in recent years ... He was delighted to find himself a star performer, the centre of attention'. Kavanagh wrote 'The Hospital' the following year, recalling his stay with great fondness.

The ward
The poet recalls the ward in which he stayed. It was a long, narrow room. The beds were lined up in a row on one side of the room. Each bed had a curtain that could be drawn around it to create a private cubicle or space: 'square cubicles in a row'. The proximity of the beds, of course, meant that you could hear the sounds of your neighbour. Kavanagh humorously recalls having to listen the sounds of the man 'in the next bed snoring'.

The Rialto hospital, at the time, was one of a number of 'chest' hospitals in the country, dealing with chronic and advanced stages of tuberculosis, an infectious disease affecting the lungs. The poet describes the ward in which he stayed as 'functional', highlighting how the room was designed to be a practical and useful space. On the wall opposite the beds was a row of washbasins. The walls are made of concrete and are unadorned and unpainted. It is, Kavanagh acknowledges, 'an art lover's woe', a place that someone who has an eye for beauty, design and detail would despair of.

Exploring the hospital
As Kavanagh spent two months in the hospital, he came to know it very well. As soon as he was well enough, he would take walks from his ward through the hospital and, when the weather was fine, around the hospital grounds. We get the impression that the poet loved to explore and that he became acquainted with every detail of the hospital.
- He describes how one of the hospital's corridors 'led to a stairwell' that brought you out into a 'gravelled yard'.
- He recalls the Rialto Bridge, the bridge at the back of St James's Hospital where the South Circular Road crossed a disused railway line.
- He mentions the fact that the gate at the main entrance to the hospital had been 'bent by a heavy lorry'.
- He mentions how he discovered a 'seat at the back of a shed' that was positioned in the perfect spot to catch the sun at a particular time of day.

What 'love' does

Over the course of his stay in the hospital, Kavanagh became very fond of the place. In fact, such was his affection for the hospital that he says he 'fell in love' with it while he was there. We can imagine someone saying how they fell in love with a beautiful city or landscape, enthralled and captivated by its beauty. But a 'functional' chest hospital is not a place we might normally associate with the stirring of such passion. Yet, Kavanagh argues, everything, no matter how ordinary or banal, is capable of being loved. Nothing whatsoever is excluded or 'debarred' from such an emotional response: 'Nothing whatever is by love debarred'.

The poet describes love as a transformative energy or 'heat' that radiates out from those who experience it. The object of our affections is then transformed by our love. It ceases to be an ordinary object and takes on a whole new significance and meaning.

Kavanagh offers the example of the hospital's 'gravelled yard'. To most people, we can imagine, this space might have appeared dull or ugly. But to the poet the yard became an 'inexhaustible adventure'. We can imagine how the poet might have walked around the hospital yard each day, seeing or discovering something new, some little detail that he had not spotted previously. Perhaps it might have been the manner in which the sun struck the walls or the particular sound that the gravel made underfoot as he walked. These small details would fill the poet with great delight and pleasure.

THEMES

POETRY AND THE ROLE OF THE POET

'The Hospital' conveys Kavanagh's belief that anything – no matter how everyday or banal – could be the subject matter for a poem. Poetry, he believed, did not have to be about great events or beautiful sunsets. Anything that the poet loves can enter his poetry, even a drab and 'functional' hospital ward. As he so memorably puts it, 'nothing whatever is by love debarred'.

When a poet names or includes someone or something in a poem, it is often a demonstration of their great love or affection for that person or thing. It is what Kavanagh terms a 'love-act'. It is also a form of commitment or 'pledge', a record of the love that the poet feels.

Love is a mysterious thing. It is hard to know why certain things inspire such intense emotions in us. Yet, despite the intensity and mystery of love, poetry should seek to describe it as honestly and plainly as possible. We should, Kavanagh says, 'record love's mystery without claptrap'.

'The Hospital' also suggests that poetry has the power to preserve that which is fleeting and transitory. When the poet writes about or describes something he loves, he 'snatches' that thing or that moment 'out of time'. If it is not noted or recorded, it vanishes. It is as if the poet is lying on the bank of a stream watching the water rushing by. He sees a leaf upon the water and reaches in to snatch it before it has drifted by.

A CELEBRATION OF THE EVERYDAY

In 'The Hospital', Kavanagh celebrates an ugly, functional building that might be described as 'an art lover's woe'. As we noted above, such a building would likely evoke negative emotions and feelings. To the speaker, however, it seems extraordinary. Even its gravel yard is a source of 'inexhaustible adventure'. As such, the poet demonstrates, everything can be considered wonderful, if looked at the right way.

FOCUS ON STYLE

Form

The poem is a sonnet, consisting of 14 lines. The first eight lines (the sonnet's octet) describe the hospital and reveal the poet's love for this place. In the poem's final six lines (the sonnet's sestet), Kavanagh reflects on the nature of love and the role of the poet when it comes to explaining 'love's mystery'. The first eight lines feature an ABBAABBA rhyme scheme, while the final six lines feature a ABCACB rhyme scheme.

Verbal Music

Kavanagh uses assonance and alliteration to great effect in the poem. In line 8 he repeatedly uses vowel sounds to capture the manner in which the gravelled yard opened up a whole world of adventure for him: 'the inexhaustible adventure of a gravelled yard'. Broad 'a' sounds are also a feature of the poem's final line: 'Snatch out of time the passionate transitory'. The poet uses repeated soft 's' sounds in the eleventh line: 'The seat at the back of a shed was a suntrap'. The sibilant sounds convey the soothing and relaxing qualities of this space.

THIS IS POETRY — PATRICK KAVANAGH
Canal Bank Walk

LINE BY LINE

In March of 1955, Kavanagh underwent surgery for lung cancer. He had one of his lungs removed and ended up spending two months in hospital following the procedure. He spent the summer of 1955 convalescing. He would spend hours each day lying on the grass along the banks of the Grand Canal in Dublin. As Antoinette Quinn writes: 'He could be idle for hours on end without any sense of guilt, and this he thought hastened his cure. The canal bank, with its dry wiry grass, was like 'a little sample' of the fields of Drumnagrella or Shancoduff'.

Kavanagh described this period as one of the happiest in his life. Following his lengthy stay in hospital, the outside world seemed utterly fresh and thrilling. Like many people who survive a brush with death, he was determined not to take the little things in life for granted. He relished the fact that he was under doctor's orders to do as little as possible, feeling that it gave him the excuse to finally slow down and spend hour after hour watching the world go by.

Lines 1 to 4
The poet is walking along the Grand Canal and notes that the trees, weeds and wildflowers that grow along the banks are in full bloom. Kavanagh uses a wonderful compound adjective 'leafy-with-love' to describe the abundance of leaves that are visible. This phrase suggests not only the poet's love for nature, but also what might be described as nature's 'love' for the poet and for humanity in general. For nature, of course, cherishes and nourishes us in all kinds of ways.

The waters of the canal offer him 'redemption'. Redemption can be described as the action of regaining possession of something. The poet in this instance wants to regain his childhood innocence. Redemption can also be also defined as the action of being saved from sin or error. The poet, in this instance, wants to be saved from the world of sophisticated adult experience. He wants to look at the world around him as a child would, perceiving wonder in every ordinary thing.

But such 'redemption' must be earned. The poet must become extremely mindful. He must learn to appreciate sights and sounds that are 'habitual' or everyday. He must even learn to appreciate sights and sounds that are 'banal' or boring. Kavanagh must 'grow with nature', slowly developing a mindset that is in tune with the natural world. There was a time, he suggests, when he 'grew' with nature in such a fashion. But that was 'before', back in his childhood days, when he had yet to sample the world of sophisticated adult experience. Now he must 'grow' with nature 'again'.

Kavanagh's use of 'wallow' is superb. The verb, in its strictest sense, means to roll around in mud or water. The verb, then, suggests several different things about the mindset the poet wishes to adapt:

- It suggests slowing down. The poet must learn to pause and really notice what's going on around him.
- It suggests immersion. The poet must immerse himself in the ordinary beauty, blocking out other more complicated thoughts, such as those relating to politics and finance.
- It suggests luxuriating. The poet must learn to take a self-indulgent delight in these 'habitual' and 'banal' phenomena.

This wallowing, Kavanagh suggests, is the 'will of God'. God, as the poet sees it, wants human beings to relish every aspect of His creation, even those aspects that might seem everyday and boring. Such mindfulness, then, is not only a form of self-improvement. It is also a moral duty.

Lines 5 to 8

The poet mentions some of the ordinary sights he is now determined to appreciate. He starts with what is surely one of the most 'banal' sights imaginable, a stick that has become 'trapped' or lodged in the canal's muddy banks. But the poet manages to find beauty in this most ordinary sight, describing how the stick's smooth wet surface is shimmering 'bright' in the afternoon sun.

He must learn to appreciate the sight of the wind as it ruffles the hair and clothing of two young lovers. This couple are 'kissing on an old seat' on the canal-side. Kavanagh playfully personifies the wind, depicting it as a 'third party' eager to insert itself into their amorous moment. He must learn to relish, too, the sight of a bird gathering material for its nest. Kavanagh introduces a reasonably witty pun when he declares that the bird is utterly focused on its 'beat'. The term 'beat' suggests the bird's regular rounds, the route it wanders again and again as it searches for nest material. But it also, of course, brings to mind the beating of the bird's wings as it flits from place to place.

The bird, Kavanagh declares, is 'delirious' as it works, which suggests a state of wild excitement or ecstasy. It has 'abandoned' itself to this extreme state, which suggests that it no longer seeks to control or inhibit its emotions.

The Gospel of John refers to Jesus Christ as 'the Word'. The bird, we are told, is preparing a 'nest for the Word'. The suggestion, then, is that Christ will come into the world, that He will be hatched in an egg on the bank of the canal. This image of Jesus as a hatchling, as a new born bird, is striking. But we needn't take it too literally. By identifying Christ with nature, Kavanagh makes several points:
- He emphasises that to appreciate the natural world is to do the 'will of God'. Therefore, by relishing the sights and sounds of the canal, he will bring Christ into his life.
- Christ, in Kavanagh's poetry, is often associated with childhood innocence. The coming of 'the Word', therefore, will coincide with the poet's 'redemption', when his own childhood innocence will be restored.

Lines 9 to 14

The poet, then, must let himself be 'enraptured' and 'encaptured' by the ordinary world. He must permit himself to be enthralled and captivated by sticks and birds and breezes. He must realise that even such familiar sights are actually 'unworn', that they possess an extraordinary freshness when we look at them in the right way.

He mentions two more ordinary sights and sounds that might accomplish such 'encapturing':
- The first is the grass growing on the canal banks. Kavanagh uses the adjective 'fabulous', emphasising how extraordinary he finds this banal feature.
- The second is the sound of the wind blowing through the branches of a beech tree.

For decades, ever since he lost his childhood innocence, Kavanagh has failed to appreciate such ordinary sights and sounds. But he realised that something was missing, that there was a huge or 'gaping' psychological 'need' in his life. Now he is determined to address this need by appreciating the ordinary sights and sounds that surround him. His senses will no longer be starved of their beauty.

Kavanagh use apostrophe to make this point. Apostrophe occurs when a poet addresses an inanimate object. Kavanagh, in this instance, addresses the canal banks and by extension the natural world as a whole.

He begs nature to place him under its spell, to 'encapture' and 'enrapture' him. He asks nature to nourish his soul or psyche with sights and sounds of extraordinary beauty: 'Feed the gaping need of my senses'.

He asks nature to give him 'ad lib', to inspire him so that he can speak in a manner that is spontaneous and improvised. An 'ad lib' occurs when an actor or performer speaks off the cuff, rather than relying on a pre-prepared script.

The poet declares his determination to pray in a particular manner.
- The poet wants to 'ad lib' his prayers, which means that he wants to pray using phrases and sentences that are spontaneous and improvised.
- He wants to pray using 'overflowing speech'. This suggests a long continuous stream of words. It also suggests that his prayers will express emotions that have been pent up inside him for a long time, but that come pouring out as he prays.
- He wants to pray 'unselfconsciously'. He doesn't want to filter or analyse what he's saying as he prays. He wants his prayers to be a raw and direct expression of his emotions.

The poet, of course, is using prayer in the normal sense, meaning the uttering of words that are directed towards God. But for the poet, we sense, prayer also means the act of writing poetry. He wants every poem he writes – even those that have no specific religious content – to honour God and his creation. The poet longs to adopt a new outlook. It would be based around a simple love of 'green and blue things', of grass and leaves and water. It would also be based around 'arguments that cannot be proven'. He wants to believe in things that cannot be shown to be true by logic, science and rational deduction. He might want to believe, for instance, that God exists or that human beings are fundamentally decent and kind.

The poem concludes with a startling metaphor:
- The poet compares his soul to a female lover (A similar point is made in 'Advent', where he refers to his soul as 'Lover').
- His belief system, meanwhile, is compared to a 'dress'.
- Our belief systems affect our souls, deeply influencing how we think and act. Wearing a particular dress, similarly, can affect a woman, changing how she perceives herself and even the world around her.
- The poet feels that his soul deserves a new belief system, one that is positive and loving, just as a female lover might deserve the gift of a new dress.
- By adopting such a belief system, he will 'honour' his soul, giving it the respect it deserves, just as he might honour a female lover by giving her the gift of a new dress.

THEMES

INNOCENCE AND EXPERIENCE

This poem is all about the poet's effort to adopt a new mindset, which Kavanagh compares to a new dress for his soul. But this 'new' mindset isn't actually all that new – it's a reversion to the mentality of childhood.

The poet wants to cast off what we might describe as 'experience', the tired, monotonous mindset of adulthood. The poet wants to be redeemed or saved from 'experience', just as a religious person might be redeemed or saved from sin. The canal and its surroundings, as we have seen, offer the poet the possibility of such redemption. These slow-flowing waters, therefore, bring to mind the water used in baptism and other religious rituals. They would cleanse the poet's psyche of experience, enabling him to start afresh.

But attaining redemption and gaining this new mindset isn't easy. The poet must become extremely mindful. He must train himself to slow down and find the wonder in every 'habitual' sight he comes across.

A CELEBRATION OF THE EVERYDAY

'Canal Bank Walk', like many of Kavanagh's poems, celebrates the everyday, reminding us that even the most 'banal' sights can appear beautiful and mysterious. Even the most 'banal' sights imaginable – a bird gathering materials, a patch of grass, a stick 'trapped' in mud – can fill us with awe and inspiration, if only we take the time to slow down and appreciate their hidden beauty.

POETRY AND THE ROLE OF THE POET

Kavanagh, as we have seen, declares his determination to 'pray' in a certain manner. But he also, we sense, wants to write in this manner. He wants to 'ad-lib' his poems, to compose spontaneously rather than planning his writing in advance. He wants to use over-flowing speech that comes directly from the emotions. He wants to write in an instinctive and unself-conscious manner, to avoid rationally analysing the words that flow from him.

FOCUS ON STYLE

Form

'Canal Bank Walk' is a sonnet featuring a regular rhyme scheme. As with many sonnets, there is a 'volta' or turn between the octet and the sestet. The octet (or first eight lines) describes the scenes along the canal banks, while the sestet (or final six lines) is an 'apostrophe', that sees Kavanagh address nature directly.

Verbal Music

The poem consists of only three sentences, each with numerous clauses that flow from one to the next. This rush of words captures the poet's exuberant state of mind as he walks along the canal bank praising God. It also, of course, suggests the ever-flowing waters of the canal itself.

Metaphor, Simile and Figures of Speech

'Canal Bank Walk', like many of Kavanagh's poems, is rich in figurative language. We see hyperbole, or deliberative poetic exaggeration, when the poet describes a patch of grass as being 'fabulous'. Neologism, meanwhile, features in line 9, where Kavanagh uses the term 'encaptured', a new word of his own invention.

There is an interesting use of metaphor, when the 'fabulous grass' is compared to a 'web'. We can imagine the grass, like a spider web, having a sticky, adhesive surface that holds the poet in place, forcing him to contemplate the beauty of the canal.

Metaphor features when the poet compares the wind to a 'third/ Party', presenting it as an extra, would-be lover, that attempts to muscle in on the courting couple.

Metaphor also features when the poet describes the sound of the wind blowing through the beech tree. The rustling sound of its leaves is compared to a chorus of 'voices' that will recur eternally, coming back summer after summer.

Lines Written on a Seat on the Grand Canal

Statue of Patrick Kavanagh sitting on a bench by the Grand Canal

LINE BY LINE

This poem was written in 1958, when Kavanagh was recovering from a battle with cancer that had seen one of his lungs removed. The poet, in the wake of this brush with mortality, finds himself thinking about his own inevitable demise. He reflects on how he would like to be remembered after his passing.

The poet is visiting Dublin's Grand Canal, one of his favourite urban beauty spots, on a beautiful day in 'mid-July'. He finds himself sitting on a bench that has been 'erected to the memory' of a Mrs O'Brien (He was aware, no doubt, that other benches had been placed along the Canal as memorials to lovers of the area).

The poet is inspired by this gesture and decides that he too would like to be remembered in such a fashion. He declares that any memorial erected in his memory should be located near water: 'O commemorate me where there is water'. And ideally it should be located by the waters of the canal he loved so much: 'Canal water preferably'.

A loving description of the canal

This stretch of the canal, according to Kavanagh, is exceptionally peaceful. Its banks are devoid of noise and bustle, being filled with a 'tremendous silence'. Its waters are described as 'stilly' and 'greeny', suggesting that on this summer's day their deep greenness is unruffled by even the slightest puff of wind.

From where Kavanagh is sitting, he can see one of the canal's locks (A lock is a short stretch of canal with a gate at either end that allow barges to move from low ground to high ground). Water has gathered in this particular lock. The poet listens intently as the build up of water is released and gushes downwards.

Kavanagh uses 'hyperbole', or deliberate exaggeration, to describe this effect. He declares that water cascades from the lock with the force of an immense waterfall, producing a great 'roar' as it thunders downwards. Indeed, he compares this humble downpour to the great Niagara Falls themselves: 'Where by a lock niagarously roars/ The fall'.

Hyperbole also occurs when Kavanagh compares the canal banks to Parnassus, a mountain that in Greek mythology was home to the Muses, the goddesses of inspiration. Legend had it that any poet or artist who visited Parnassus was sure to be inspired. The canal banks, according to Kavanagh, will have a similar effect on their visitors. Those who 'find [their] way' to this little corner of Dublin will find themselves speaking in poetry rather than prose. Everything they say will be poetic, will be coloured by rhyme, metaphor and beautiful turns of phrase.

Kavanagh watches as a swan glides along the canal, its head resting on the surface of the water. Kavanagh playfully personifies the swan, suggesting that its head is 'low' because it's feeling sheepish or apologetic: 'A swan goes by head low with many apologies'. Personification, we remember, occurs when a non-human creature is presented as if it had human characteristics.

Kavanagh lovingly describes the arched bridges that span the canal. Each arch, on this still summer's day, is reflected perfectly in the water. Each arch and its reflection combine to form an oval shape. Kavanagh uses a wonderful metaphor to describe this effect, comparing these oval shapes to human eyes. The poet playfully suggests that light moves through these 'eyes' just as it moves through the retina of a human being: 'Fantastic light looks through the eyes of bridges'.

The Grand Canal, we remember, stretched all the way to Laois and Offaly, where it joined the River Shannon. In the late 1950s barges still worked its length, bringing goods to and from Dublin. The poet watches one such barge come by, making its way towards the city centre. The barge, he imagines, has had a long journey to Dublin, visiting Athy and 'other far-flung towns' along the way.

Kavanagh declares that the barge carries not just any cargo but 'mythologies'. He is referring, no doubt, to the news and gossip picked up by the bargemen as they travelled through various 'far-flung towns' en route to the capitol. These ordinary tales, Kavanagh suggests, are as deep and meaningful as the 'mythologies' of Greece, Rome and Egypt.

THEMES

POETRY AND THE ROLE OF THE POET

Kavanagh had for years written in almost obscurity. Then he'd been saddled with notoriety as one of Dublin's drunken characters. Now in his later years he finally knew something resembling genuine fame, his work gaining the esteem and affection of his literary peers and the general reading public.

The poem concludes, then, with Kavanagh meditating once more on how he might be commemorated after his death. He's aware that he's something of a public figure now. But he wants no fancy monument. He doesn't want a tomb that's 'hero-courageous', that would befit some famous military leader. He's thinking, no doubt, of a tomb that's been carved out of marble and decorated with lions, horses and winged figures representing victory.

Instead, he wants a simple bench to be erected in his memory on the banks of the Grand Canal. Such a bench, he feels, would be a beautiful commemoration of his life: 'Commemorate me thus beautifully'. It would represent the person he truly was, reflecting his love of nature in general, and of these canal banks in particular. It would allow others to sit and relish the sights and sounds of the canal, just as he did when he was alive. Perhaps those who sit there might even spare a thought for the poor dead poet, remembering his great love for this little corner of Dublin town.

A CELEBRATION OF THE EVERYDAY

This poem also makes an interesting point about mindfulness, about being present in the world. It invites us to pause for a moment amid the hustle of daily routines. It invites us to rest upon a park bench, say, and take in the world around us. It invites us to look and listen closely to everyday sights and sounds.

In doing so, it will allow us to perceive the wonder hidden in the everyday. Silences will seem 'tremendous' and light 'fantastic'. Ordinary sights – such as a barge or a swan or a reflected bridge – will take on an extraordinary beauty.

There is, as we've seen, a humorous element to Kavanagh's hyperbolic description of the Canal. But maybe the poet is only half-joking when he compares the canal banks to Mount Parnassus and the lock to Niagara Falls or a bargeman's tales to the great myths of old. For these humble sights and sounds, the poem suggests, will strike us as epic and extraordinary, if only we take the time to slow down, to look and listen properly.

FOCUS ON STYLE

Form

This is a sonnet with a regular rhyme scheme. But Kavanagh's extensive use of half-rhyme, too, contributes to the poem's playful and casual atmosphere. We see this in the rhyming of 'Brother' with 'water', of 'stilly' with 'beautifully', of 'silence' with 'islands' and of 'bridges' with 'courageous'.

This is a playful, light-hearted poem, one in which the poet addresses the reader in a casual fashion throughout. We see this in line 3 when he refers to the reader as 'brother', suggesting a friendly familiarity between author and audience. We also see this in line 11 when he urges the reader to 'look', as if we were sitting on the bench beside him.

Verbal Music

Kavanagh uses consonance, assonance and alliteration to capture the lazy, laid-back atmosphere of the canal on a fine summer's day. Alliteration, for instance, adds a pleasant verbal music to line 1, with its repeated 'w' sound: 'where there is water'. It also occurs in line 11, with its repeated 'b' sound: 'a barge comes bringing'

Consonance appears in the opening lines, which feature a number of words ending in 'y' or 'ly': 'preferably', 'stilly', 'greeny' and 'beautifully'. The repetition of these 'y' and 'ly' sounds creates a pleasant, euphonious music. It also produces an onomatopoeic effect, mimicking the gentle, lulling sound of water lapping the canal banks.

Assonance, meanwhile, features in lines 2 to 4, with their repeated broad vowel sounds: 'canal water', 'greeny at the heart of summer', 'thus beautifully'. It also occurs in lines 13 to 14, with their repeated 'o' sounds: 'O commemorate me with no hero-courageous/ Tomb'. This profusion of broad vowels not only creates a pleasant verbal music but also slows the pace of the verse, conjuring a laid-back summer atmosphere.

There is an interesting contrast between this poem and 'Canal Bank Walk'. This poem, as the title suggests, is very much a sitting poem, whereas 'Canal Bank Walk', of course, is very much a walking poem. This poem, as we have seen, conjures an atmosphere of intense stillness. 'Canal Bank Walk', on the other hand, has a propulsive forward momentum generated by its endless rush of statements and clauses.

Metaphor, Simile and Figures of Speech

This is a poem where Kavanagh indulges his flair for neologisms, or newly coined expressions. We see 'stilly' and 'greeny', for instance, in lines 2 and 3. 'Niagarously', meaning similar to the Niagara Falls, features in line 5, while 'Parnassian', meaning similar to Mount Parnassus, features in line 8. The adjective 'hero-courageous', meaning worthy of a courageous military hero, features in line 13.

The poem is also notable for its use of 'hyperbole', or deliberate exaggeration, as Kavanagh presents the canal as a truly special location:

- The silence is 'tremendous' and the light is 'fantastic'. Nothing on these banks, it seems, is anything less extraordinary.
- Even the canal's most industrial sights are presented as extraordinary, with the poet urging us to 'look!' at the working barge bringing cargo from the midlands to Dublin city.
- The canal's lock, as we've seen, is compared to the Niagara Falls, while its banks are compared to Mount Parnassus.

This humorous use of neologism and hyperbole contributes to the poem's playful, light-hearted atmosphere.

Derek Mahon Themes

Community and Isolation

Many of Mahon's poems deal with states of extreme or hellish isolation. Captain Oates, during his final walk as depicted in 'Antarctica', endures the unimaginable isolation of the Antarctic tundra: the tent receding behind him, the nearest civilisation hundreds of miles away, the icy landscape stretching out in every direction around him.

In 'After the Titanic', the disgraced Bruce Ismay endures isolation of a different kind. He lives out a life of seclusion, utterly cut off from the rest of society: 'Now I hide/ In a lonely house behind the sea'. He suffers intense feelings of despair and psychological isolation, best captured by the powerful image of his 'soul' screaming out 'in the starlight'.

'Day Trip to Donegal' hauntingly transitions from community to isolation. There is a real sense of community in the opening of the poem, where the speaker and his companions are cooped up in the car together. They visit friends while in Donegal and leave one another with the promise that they will soon be in touch again. By the end of the poem, however, this sense of community has been replaced by one of utter isolation. It's hard to imagine an image of greater isolation than that of the poet drifting alone on the water in the midst of a raging storm with no one to offer him help, advice or rescue.

A number of Mahon's poems describe how being part of a community brings certain moral demands. In 'After the Titanic', for instance, Bruce Ismay is part of the community on board the ship. It is expected that he, being a gentleman, will sacrifice his life for the women and children on board. Ismay initially meets this demand – assisting in escorting women and children to the few lifeboats on the *Titanic*. At the last moment, however, he rejects the demands of the community and puts his own life first, taking a seat on the final lifeboat. For doing so, Ismay pays a heavy price. He is humiliated and vilified for his behaviour and ends up living the lonely life of an outcast. At the end of the poem, he makes a heartfelt plea that he be included in our 'lamentations', that we consider him when we mourn those who perished in the tragedy.

'Antarctica' is another poem that focuses on the obligations that come with being a member of a community, in this case, the doomed community of Scott's expedition. Mahon wonders if there was something criminal about Oates's self-sacrifice: 'Need we consider it some sort of crime[?]' Did Oates commit some sort of crime by walking suicidally into the snow-storm? Did his companions commit some sort of crime by letting him go?

Mahon, however, rejects the idea that their behaviour was criminal or immoral, simply declaring 'No'. Both Oates and his companions were responding to the demands placed on them by their small community. Everyone in the tent knew the severity of the situation. Everyone knew that Oates was the 'weakest' and a liability to the team as a whole. Everyone knew that his 'numb self-sacrifice' was necessary in order to give the others a greater chance at survival.

'Ecclesiastes', too, highlights the moral demands communities can place on its members. The poet feels that he could and, perhaps, should embrace the role of a joyless, hectoring prophet. The repetition of 'God' and 'you could' reinforce our sense of his horror at this realisation. But the poet, we sense, is unlikely to surrender to this impulse. He is unlikely to abandon his current carefree lifestyle. We see this at the poem's conclusion where his comment 'you could do it, God/ help you' indicates that he has nothing but pity and contempt for anyone who would assume the role of such a religious leader.

Such demands also loom large in 'As it Should Be', where the speaker feels morally obliged to organise and carry out a murder on behalf of his community. The speaker insists, of course, that he didn't act out of cruelty, or to satisfy some personal grudge. Instead, he was concerned about the welfare of the community's children, who he refers to tenderly as 'kiddies'. The speaker is convinced that the children will appreciate what he has done, the lengths to which he has gone to protect them. They will thank him, and those who helped him in the killing, for providing them with an orderly and harmonious environment where everyone follows the proper 'method' of living.

The stifling nature of community

Mahon's poetry reminds us that communities can become stifling and controlling. In 'Ecclesiastes' for instance, the world of Protestant Belfast is presented as one with little tolerance for dissent and diversity. It is a community where the swings are tied up and everyone goes to church. You live your life in a 'God-fearing' manner and you are eventually buried in the 'heaped/ graves of your fathers'.

'As It Should Be' makes a similar point about the conformist nature of communities. Communities, the poem suggests, tend to be based around 'method' on long-established norms, habits and procedures. They tend to insist that every member behave in a similar fashion, following this 'method'. There is often little tolerance for those, like the 'mad bastard', who depart from the community's norms.

Those who don't fit in can find themselves mocked and shunned. They can find themselves blamed for all sorts of the community's woes, such as unseasonable weather or the disturbed sleep of children. They can find themselves expelled from the community altogether, or even, in extreme cases like this one, 'hunted' and 'gunned down'.

Remembering History's Victims

Mahon, in much of his work, attempts to speak out on behalf of history's forgotten victims. In 'A Disused Shed in Co. Wexford', for instance, the speaker associates the mushrooms with the 'Lost people of Treblinka and Pompeii'. Treblinka was a concentration camp in Poland where the Nazis murdered thousands of Jews. Pompeii was an ancient Roman city where thousands died when Mount Vesuvius erupted in AD 79. The poem, therefore, sympathises with all those who have suffered and died through natural disasters or through man's inhumanity to man.

The victims of such tragedies, of course, are long dead. They are voiceless and 'wordless' and cannot speak for themselves. Mahon, however, imagines them as beseeching the people of the present to tell their stories: 'They are begging us you see, in their wordless way'. The poem, then, presents us with a powerful challenge, asking us to remember these 'Lost people' and 'speak on their behalf'. If we do so their agonies and their 'naïve labours' will not have been for nothing.

'Rathlin' is another poem that reveals Mahon's deep compassion for history's forgotten victims. The poet is keenly aware of the 'unspeakable violence' that was visited upon Somhairle's people in 1575. He remembers the terror of the last victim, whose scream was brutally cut short. He also registers the rage and horror that must have afflicted Somhairle as he listened to the women and children of his tribe being slaughtered.

In 'Antarctica', Mahon takes a somewhat different tack, speaking on behalf of someone who has been re-evaluated rather than forgotten. For decades Oates was regarded as a heroic figure. Then he came to be regarded as a somewhat 'ridiculous' one. Mahon's poem, however, invites us to focus once more on the 'sublime' nature of Oates's self-sacrifice.

'After the *Titanic*', meanwhile, centres on an individual usually considered to be a villain rather than a victim. The poem, however, does not judge Ismay, instead focusing on the terrible anguish he must have suffered in the aftermath of the *Titanic*'s sinking. In one sense Ismay 'got away in a boat'. But on another level he never escaped the tragedy.

Mahon and Ireland

There are several poems in wiche Mahon touches on Ireland's troubled history. 'Rathlin', for instance, presents Irish history as a seemingly endless series of struggles between England and Ireland, between Protestant and Catholic, one in which the 'unspeakable violence' of 1575 leads to the 'bombs [that] doze in the housing estates' of the 1970s and 1980s.

'The Chinese Restaurant in Portrush' also gestures towards this history of conflict and division that has defined Irish history. Tellingly, the poem names two separate locations: Portrush, which is in Northern Ireland, and Donegal, which is in the Republic of Ireland. It reminds us, therefore, that Ireland is a divided place. The poet refers to the 'invasion' of tourists that will soon overrun Portrush. But this somewhat humorous description reminds us of the various actual invasions that Ireland has witnessed over the centuries.

There are moments, however, when Mahon permits himself to be optimistic about Ireland's future. 'The Chinese Restaurant in Portrush', for instance, describes a beautiful, peaceful moment. It seems to the poet that the conflicts of Irish history could be set aside. The wolfhound, representing Ireland and Irish history, is 'old' and dozing 'in the sun', suggesting that the island is entering a less aggressive and agitated phase. The town of Portrush is 'as it might have been', had the Troubles never occurred, gentle and pleasant in the first spring sunshine. Mahon, on this afternoon when the world seems 'young', senses the possibility that the conflicts and narrow-mindedness of the past might finally be set aside in favour of a new beginning.

In 'Rathlin', the poet's optimism is perhaps more cautious. The island is presented not only as a bird 'sanctuary' but also as a sanctuary from history itself. It is a place of 'singular peace', one where the conflict and violence of Irish history no longer occurs. The poet's return journey to the mainland, therefore, takes on a metaphorical aspect. The boat's occupants – blinded by spray, tossed around on 'pitching surfaces' – are 'unsure' which direction they are facing. The Irish people, similarly, are uncertain about what kind of future we are heading for. Will it be a future of 'singular peace' represented by Rathlin? Or will it be a future of hatred and conflict represented by the mainland?

'Kinsale' is another poem in which Mahon dares to hope for a better future. The 'dark' rain that has been falling is associated with Ireland's troubled past, with religious oppression, economic decline and with the seemingly endless conflict between Ireland and England, Catholic and Protestant, that has caused so much suffering over decades and centuries. But Mahon, in the moment after the rain stops falling, permits himself to be optimistic. He imagines a future in which the problems mentioned above are resolved or become less severe. He imagines a future in which no Irish person will be forbidden from flourishing and realising their potential.

THIS IS POETRY | DEREK MAHON

Grandfather

Belfast shipyards

LINE BY LINE

In this poem, Mahon remembers his paternal grandfather. The grandfather, like generations of Mahon's relatives, spent his life working in Belfast's thriving shipbuilding industry. He was a boilermaker by trade and spent countless hours in the boilerrooms of various ships that were under construction, installing the machinery that enabled these huge ships to make their way across the oceans.

The grandfather continued working until he was quite old. Finally, however, he fell foul of a workplace accident. Mahon is vague on the precise details of this incident. However, it seems that the grandfather was 'Wounded' by some tool or piece of equipment in the shipyard.

The grandfather's injuries were severe enough to end his career in the shipyard. It also meant that he was no longer able to live alone. Since his wife had passed away some years before, he went to live with the young poet and his family in their house.

Mahon, we remember, was an only child. He describes himself as having being a quiet, thoughtful boy: 'a strange child with a taste for verse'. We can imagine, therefore, how fascinated he must have been by this new addition to the household. He vividly remembers his grandfather arriving in an ambulance and being stretchered into the house: 'They brought him in on a stretcher from the world'.

The grandfather's daily life

Thankfully, the grandfather 'soon recovered' and was up and about again. The poet provides a memorable portrayal of the grandfather's daily life in his new home:

- The grandfather was an early riser: 'Even on cold/ Mornings he is up at six'. We get the impression that he would be the first to get up each morning and would busy himself around the house while the others were still in bed.
- The grandfather, it seems, would be absent from the house for most of the day. He was 'Never there when

you call'. We get the impression that the young poet and his parents didn't really know what the grandfather was doing during these lengthy absences.

- Only 'after dark' would the grandfather return to the house. We get the impression that he rarely greeted the other members of the household on his return. They would hear him taking off his 'great boots' in the hallway and then heading up to his room and shutting his door.

The grandfather also engaged in carpentry or DIY, working with 'a block of wood' and a 'box of nails'. We can imagine him erecting shelves, perhaps, or making cupboards. According to the poet, he did so 'discreetly' or secretively. This suggests that he worked when there was no one else around and didn't discuss what he was building with the other members of the household. The poet amusingly describes how the grandfather was 'up to no good' when he undertook such projects. We can imagine the young poet's parents complaining about dust and noise and half-finished contraptions that were left lying around the place.

A sketch of the grandfather

The grandfather, even in old age, remained physically strong and powerful. We see this in how he recovered quickly from his injuries. The phrase 'great boots', too, suggests his imposing stature. The terms 'thumping' and 'banging', meanwhile, reinforce our sense of his imposing physical presence. There was nothing dainty, then, about the grandfather. He was a big, burly boilermaker, who made his presence felt wherever he went.

The grandfather also comes across as someone who was resilient and uncomplaining. This was someone who didn't mind getting up early in the morning, no matter how cold it was! The phrase 'Wounded but humorous' suggests that he didn't complain about the injuries caused by his accident. Instead, he made light of the accident and the considerable suffering it must have caused him.

The poet also emphasises the grandfather's mental sharpness, even in old age. The grandfather, according to the poet, was 'as cute as they come', was as quick-witted and intelligent as anyone could hope to be. The phrase 'Nothing escapes him' emphasises that the grandfather was a highly observant person, one whose 'shrewd eyes' had the ability to assess and evaluate all he saw.

The grandfather's second childhood

The grandfather's life changed the moment he was stretchered into the young poet's house. He was no longer burdened with the responsibilities of work, of managing his finances or of running his own household. In an important sense, he was no longer part of the world of work and adult responsibility. As a young man, he had ventured out into this world, gaining employment in the shipyards. Now, as an old man, he was leaving it again: 'They brought him in on a stretcher from the world'

For years, the grandfather had been too pre-occupied with work to think much about the past. Now, in retirement, he has the time to dwell on his long-ago childhood. He has the space to 'recapture' aspects of his own personal history, incidents and details that no one else living can recall: 'a childhood/ Only he can recapture'.

There is a sense of the grandfather enjoying something of a 'second childhood' while residing in the young poet's house. As we noted above, the grandfather no longer has any real responsibilities. He is free to come and go as he pleases, and to tinker about with various projects and activities that may or may not be finished.

There is something childlike, too, about how the grandfather went 'banging round the house' We get the impression that he made quite a bit of noise as he moved from room to room and wasn't terribly bothered about who he disturbed. There were moments, it seems, when the poet's exasperated parents felt like they had taken in a 'four-year-old' child rather than an elderly man.

The grandfather and the future

The grandfather, it seems, has an old-fashioned, mechanical clock in his room. Such clocks had to be wound each evening to ensure they kept accurate time. They would be synchronised or 'set against' the radio, often against the chimes of Big Ben which were broadcast at 10pm each evening.

Mahon, however, declares that his grandfather sets his clock not against the radio but 'Against the future'. This is an example of the poetical device known as 'metonymy', which occurs when a thing or concept is referred to by the name of something closely associated with that thing or concept. Mahon, in this instance, refers to the radio as the 'future'. It is as if the wireless radio, this new-fangled device, represents a future that will be increasingly defined by technology, connectivity and communication.

The grandfather, according to the poet, took a dim view of this technological future. He was someone from an earlier age, who didn't appreciate or even understand the modern world that was dawning in the Belfast of the 1950s and 1960s. The grandfather, we sense, attempted to avoid thinking about these societal changes as much as possible. Metonymy is once again used to illustrate this mindset. We are told that the grandfather would 'bolt the door' not against any physical intruders, but against the future itself. To the grandfather, then, the future is something invasive and intrusive, something to be repelled as much as possible.

FOCUS ON STYLE

Metaphor, Simile and Figures of Speech

Mahon uses a wonderful metaphor to describe this process of remembering. The grandfather's childhood memories are compared to a landscape of sorts. The stresses and strains of working life are compared to 'rows' of industrial equipment that obscure this landscape. The grandfather's newfound mindfulness is compared to these 'gantries' and 'Boiler-rooms' rolling away to reveal the hidden vista they have so long obscured.

Polished Forms

Mahon's gift for polished forms is evident in this perfectly turned sonnet. The sonnet's octet, or first eight lines, is jaunty and humorous in tone. The sestet, meanwhile, is somewhat darker and more serious, as it highlights the grandfather's intense privacy and a disquiet regarding a future that is fast approaching. Each line in the sonnet rhymes with one other line. As is often the case in Mahon's poetry, half-rhymes are prevalent. For example, he rhymes 'dark' with 'clock', 'night' with 'out' and 'recovered' with 'childhood'.

THEMES

THE NATURE OF POETRY

Mahon, throughout his life, had a very idealised view of the way an artist should live. He sees something of this in the lifestyle adopted by his grandfather after retirement:

- The artist, like the grandfather, should be free to keep his or her own hours.
- The artist, like the grandfather, should be somewhat detached from the 'world' of everyday work and responsibility.
- The artist, like the grandfather, should be 'shrewd' and observant.
- The artist should be free to engage with various projects as he or she sees fit, just as the grandfather picks up and puts down various bits of DIY around the house.

Mahon's writings, including the poems dedicated to his children, suggest a writer who struggled with domestic life over the years. We get the impression that Mahon, like the grandfather in this poem, was someone who often felt somewhat apart from the various households of which he was a member.

It is also worth noting that Mahon, like the grandfather, has little time for many of the societal, technological shifts that define our present and our future.

COMMUNITY AND ISOLATION

The grandfather, on the one hand, is clearly a member of the household; he sleeps under the same roof as the poet and his parents, he shares their food and he interacts with them from time to time. But he is also an intensely solitary individual. The grandfather, we're told, 'escapes us all'. His daily routine seems designed to minimise interaction with the other members of the household. His communication, too, is minimal; he remains discreet not only about his DIY projects, but also about his movements during the day. Our sense of the grandfather as a private, secretive person is reinforced by the fact that he bolts the door of his bedroom each evening.

Daytrip to Donegal

'That night the slow sea washed against my head ...'

LINE BY LINE

The poet and some friends have travelled from Belfast to a seaside village in Donegal. They arrive in the afternoon, their legs stiff from the car journey, and set about performing the errands that brought them there: 'there were things to be done,/ Clothes to be picked up, friends to be seen'.

The poet provides a memorable depiction of the Donegal landscape. The hills, he declares, are a vivid and intense green in colour. He uses hyperbole to emphasise their extraordinary greenness, suggesting that nowhere on earth could you find a 'deeper' shade of green.

The sea, however, is less attractive. The sea off the coast of Ireland, according to the poet, tends to have a 'grave/ Grey' colour. But the waters around the coast of Donegal, he maintains, look particularly bleak and oppressive: 'the sea the grimmer in that enclave'.

The poet describes Donegal as an 'enclave'. An enclave is a piece of territory surrounded by a larger territory that is culturally or ethnically distinct. This captures how Co. Donegal is a part of the Republic of Ireland largely surrounded by Northern Ireland. It also suggests how Donegal is a predominantly Catholic county surrounded by counties that are predominantly Protestant.

The Fish

The poet walks down to the pier and watches the fishing boats give 'up their catch'. The fishermen, we can imagine, haul large crates of fish from their trawlers and place them on the quayside. Each crate contains a huge number of freshly-caught fish, many of which are still alive.

The phrase 'A writhing glimmer of fish' wonderfully coveys how each crate contains a vast silvery mass. The phrase is arresting both visually and musically. We can almost visualise the fish squirming and wriggling in the crates. The repeated 'i' sound, meanwhile, reinforces the power of the image, generating a sinewy, sensuous music.

The crates, it seems, are placed in trucks for transport to Belfast and other cities. The price of fish, as the poet knows, is 'Ten times' greater in the city than it is here in the fishing village. In the city, away from the fishing grounds, fish are in less plentiful supply and can therefore fetch higher prices.

The poet is taken aback at the vast quantity of fish extracted from the ocean. He seems almost surprised that the herring and mackerel return 'year after year' to the fishing grounds. Perhaps someday, due to overfishing, these species will die out and the supply of fish will be exhausted.

The poet watches a few fish that have fallen onto the deck of one of the trawlers. He focuses on their 'attitudes', the positioning and movement of their bodies. These 'attitudes' indicate the 'agony' the fish must be enduring as they struggle to breathe out of water. These attitudes also indicate 'heartbreak', as if the fish are experiencing despair and sorrow at the premature ending of their lives.

The Return to Belfast Suburbs

After a few hours, the speaker and his friends return to Belfast: 'We left at eight, drove back the way we came'. They travel down 'muddy' lanes that take them away from the fishing village, the sea 'receding' or fading into the distance behind them: 'The sea receding down each muddy lane'. Eventually, they reach the suburbs of Belfast where the speaker lives. The poet is dropped off at his house and bids his friends goodnight, promising to phone them soon: 'Give me a ring, goodnight, and so to bed'.

The poet presents the suburbs as rather boring and mundane. The phrase 'changed-down into suburbs' refers to the driver putting the car into a lower gear as they near their destination. However, it also suggests that suburban life represents a 'change down', or lowering in excitement and intensity. The suburbs are not a place for revelry and nightlife. It is only midnight but everyone, it seems, is sunk in a sleep, suggesting that they have been in bed for hours.

The suburbs are also presented as a place of comfort and safety. They are tucked inland, far from the dangers and the destructive forces of the sea. The suburbs will be disturbed by 'no gale force wind'. Storms that form off the coastline seldom travel this far inland and when they do their force is greatly diminished.

The suburbs, however, aren't completely impervious to the elements, for winter, according to the poet, has 'left its mark' on the neighbourhood. The pavements are coated in frost that glistens in the streetlights: 'The time of year had left its mark/ On frosty pavements glistening in the dark'.

The poet's night time experience

That night the poet has a terrifying vision. Perhaps he experiences an intensely realistic nightmare or a vivid flight of fancy as he lies on the edge of sleep. Or perhaps he has been drinking heavily for several days and experiences some kind of hallucination brought on by alcohol withdrawal. But this experience, whatever its precise nature, feels intensely real to the poet.

He seems to think that he's been transported somehow back to the coast and is lying immobile on some beach or cove while the tide comes in around him. Or maybe he thinks that seawater has flooded the entire country and is pouring into his bedroom, rising to the level of the bed in which he lies.

The poet describes how water comes washing 'against [his] head'. Water, he declares, comes 'Spilling into [his] skull', penetrating his ears, mouth and nose. There is a 'harbour wall' nearby and the poet can hear waves caressing the huge boulders that lie at its foundation.

The poet seems to feel his body fusing with the coastline he visited that day. The waves, we're told, are 'performing their… erosions' against his head just as they erode the coastline. He imagines that water is 'Spilling' into his skull just as it might come spilling into a cave along the coastline. The term 'spine', meanwhile, suggests that the water is simultaneously washing against the harbour wall and the poet's body.

The vision, it seems, continues all night long, with 'slow wave' after 'slow wave' washing against the poet. Then, 'At dawn' it enters a terrifying new phase:

- The poet has been carried 'far out' to sea, either floating in the water or aboard some kind of craft or vessel.
- He is surrounded by a raging storm, lashed at by the wind and rain.
- He is utterly alone. There is no one to rescue him, no one to teach him how to survive this ordeal: 'nobody/ To show me how, no promise of rescue'.
- The poet is utterly unprepared for this situation. He has no relevant skills, no 'reassurance' or confidence that he will be able to survive.

The poet has always known that he might find himself in a situation like this one. However, he constantly failed to plan or prepare for such an eventuality, never giving it much 'Forethought' or consideration. As he floats desperately on the water, therefore, he curses his lack of preparedness: 'Cursing my constant failure to take due/ Forethought of this'.

The poet describes how he makes desperate 'Overtures' to the elements. Overtures, in this instance, are efforts to open negotiations with an opposing party. The poet's pleas, of course, are in 'vain' or futile. The weather does not negotiate.

At the beginning of the poem, it is the fish that struggle hopelessly to survive on land. At the end, it is the human speaker who makes vain attempts to survive on the vastness of the ocean. His desperate pleadings to the wind and rain can be compared to the futile writhing of the fish in stanza 2. Like them, he is out of his natural element. Both the fish on the pier and the speaker on the vast ocean make vain attempts to survive in unspeakably alien and hostile environments.

FOCUS ON STYLE

Word Choice
Mahon's choice of the verb 'flopping' is typically incisive; it suggests how awkwardly the fish move when taken out of their natural element, but also their agony and desperation as they slowly run out of oxygen. The verb 'contrive' is equally well chosen. It suggests that the poet's 'overtures' are carefully constructed in a deliberate effort to gain sympathy from the elements. But it also suggests that the overtures are a little insincere.

Imagery
'Day Trip To Donegal', like many of Mahon's poems, is rich in coastal imagery. The poet mentions the extraordinary green of the Donegal hills, the menacing 'grave grey' of the sea and harbour walls that are slowly marbled by countless immeasurable weaves.

Verbal Music
'Day Trip to Donegal', like much of Mahon's poetry, makes extremely skilful use of sound effects:

- The alliterative repetition of the harsh 'gr' sound in 'grave', 'grey' and 'grimmer' generates a cacophonous musical effect, emphasising the ocean's bleakness and severity.
- The repeated sibilant 's' sound in the phrases 'slow sea', 'spilling into the skull' and 'stones that spine' mimics the sound of the sea washing against the coast.
- Assonance creates a sweet, euphonious effect through the repeated 'e' sounds in 'deeper green', suggesting the beauty of the hills.
- Onomatopoeia occurs in lines 11 to 12. The verse here has an uneasy, jumpy quality, in which we can almost hear the dying fish 'flopping about the deck'.

THEMES

NATURE
Mahon always was a poet with a deep concern for the environment. His compassion for the dying fish is highlighted by how he refers to their suffering in very human terms, describing their 'attitudes of agony and heartbreak'. But this compassion, we sense, is mixed with guilt because the poet, no doubt, is one of the city-dwellers whose demand for fish drives this exploitation. Perhaps this guilt and pity stays with the poet throughout the day, causing him to be reminded of the dying fish when he sees the frost 'glistening' frost on the suburb pavement. Perhaps it also causes his terrifying nighttime vision in which nature, it might be said, avenges its exploitation at human hands.

The poem, then, highlights how human exploit the resources of the natural world. This is represented by the fishermen on the pier in Donegal who plunder the ocean, taking vast quantities of fish from its depths. This, of course, is driven by commercialism and consumer demand.

The poem also highlights how nature will eventually punish us for this exploitation of its resources. This is represented by the poet's nighttime vision. It's difficult for a contemporary audience to not think of rising sea levels and global temperatures when we read these lines. But they also bring to mind deforestation, desertification, air pollution and other terrible consequences due to our disregard for the world that surrounds us.

The poem also highlights the wilful ignorance humans exhibit towards the environment. This is represented by how the poet curses himself as he drifts upon the water. He has long known that something is wrong and needs his attention but he has failed to act and now it is too late. This wonderfully reflects how we as the human race often only change our behaviours when it is already too late, when the sea and air are polluted and the climate is forever altered.

'Day Trip to Donegal' is one of the poems where Mahon highlights nature's destructive side, specifically the destructive power of the sea. The effect of each individual wave is 'immeasurable', too small to be measured or even noticed. But over time countless such waves occur, and taken together they have an enormous impact on the coastline. It marbles, then wears away, the harbour wall and threatens to consume entire villages as it slowly cuts away the earth on which they stand: 'Muttering its threats to villages of landfall'. It also spawns terrible storms that eventually make 'landfall', reaching the coastline and spreading inland.

COMMUNITY AND ISOLATION
'Day Trip to Donegal' hauntingly transitions from community to isolation. There is a real sense of community in the opening of the poem, where the speaker and his companions are cooped up in the car together. They visit friends while in Donegal and leave one another with the promise that they will soon be in touch again. By the end of the poem, however, this sense of community has been replaced by one of utter isolation. It's hard to imagine an image of greater isolation than that of the poet drifting alone on the water in the midst of a raging storm with no one to offer him help, advice or rescue.

THIS IS POETRY | **DEREK MAHON**

After the *Titanic*

LINE BY LINE

The speaker of the poem is Bruce Ismay, the manager of the White Star Line for which the *Titanic* sailed. Ismay came to international attention as the highest-ranking White Star official and one of the few men to survive the sinking on 14 April 1912. The *Titanic* had an estimated 2,224 people on board when she struck an iceberg that fateful night. The ship, however, only had a total of 20 lifeboats, with a capacity to carry about half of those on board.

When it was clear that the ship was sinking, an order was put out that the seats aboard these life vessels be given to women and children. Many of the men aboard the ship, including Ismay, set about escorting the women and children to the lifeboats and ensuring that they were safely lowered to the sea. These men – later characterised as heroes for their behaviour – committed to remaining on board and going down with the ship. Ismay assisted in this process but at the last minute he made the decision to board the final lifeboat.

Ismay remembers sitting in the lifeboat, 'shivering' with the cold and floating 'on the dark water' only a short distance from the colossal ship that was rapidly sinking and breaking apart.

Unable to bear the terrible sight, Ismay says that he turned his head away, towards the iceberg which had caused the ship to sink. But he could not block out the appalling sounds as the vessel and everything aboard crumbled and sank:

- He mentions the children's 'prams' that would have been flung about as the ship heaved upwards and split in two.
- He mentions the 'pianos' which would have gone skidding across the floors of the entertainment rooms, smashing to bits against the walls.
- He mentions the sideboards full of plates and glasses in the ship's dining rooms that would have crashed and shattered as the ship reeled.
- He makes reference to the band that kept on playing as the ship sank, describing how their 'ragtime' music was eventually cut short or 'shredded' as the ship plummeted to its depths.
- He mentions the sounds of the ship's enormous boilers exploding or 'bursting' and the great metal fittings – such as the winches used for hauling the ropes in – being ripped from the ship's decks.

The 'heroes' who remained on board the ship sank to the bottom of the ocean with the vessel. But Ismay says that he 'sank as far that night as any/ Hero'. There are a number of ways that we can interpret this statement:

- Ismay is describing how the kind of illustrious life he had been accustomed to living ended when the ship sank.

- Ismay is describing how he changed that night, how a part of him died when the ship went down. His ambition, his goals and dreams, his ability to take pleasure in the joys of life all ended or 'sank' with the ship.
- Ismay is describing how he sank into a deep state of depression, from which he never re-emerged.

Ismay describes his life as 'costly'. This might be a reference to the privileged and luxurious lifestyle Ismay had enjoyed as the manager of a prestigious company. But the term 'costly' might also be a reference to Ismay's decision to board the final lifeboat. It could be argued that in doing so he cost the life of someone else on board, a woman or child, perhaps, who could otherwise have been saved.

The inquiry

Ismay was savaged by both the American and the British press for deserting the ship while women and children were still on board. Some papers called him the 'Coward of the *Titanic*' or 'J. Brute Ismay', and suggested that the White Star flag be changed to a yellow liver, a symbol of cowardice.

The inquiry into the tragedy did not have any sympathy for Ismay and what he had to endure that night. They labelled him a coward and said he 'got away in a boat', suggesting that he was only interested in preserving his own life and did not care about the lives of the other passengers who remained aboard the ship.

Ismay says that the inquiry 'humbled' him. The term 'humbled' suggests a number of things:
- The inquiry humiliated him, making him feel ashamed and embarrassed for his behaviour.
- They treated him with contempt and disrespect.
- They made him feel pathetic and inadequate. Whereas once he was the respected head of a prestigious firm, now he was made to feel like a low-life and scoundrel.

Ismay's life after the tragedy

The tragedy sent Ismay into a state of deep depression from which he never truly emerged. He kept a low profile afterwards, living part of the year in a large cottage in Connemara. His illustrious career over and his reputation in tatters, Ismay looked to escape from the world. Ismay describes how he now lives in a 'lonely' house close to or 'behind' the sea. The term 'lonely' suggests the remoteness of the house. But it also suggests the loneliness that Ismay now endures, as he leads a solitary life, cut off from society.

The fact that Ismay, after such a traumatic maritime experience, chooses to live so close to the sea might strike us as ironic or strange. The sea is a constant reminder of the tragedy and the role that he played in it. In choosing to live next to the sea, it is as if Ismay is torturing himself. We get the impression, perhaps, that there is an element of self-hatred involved in this decision, that he deserves to suffer what he has done.

Especially painful for Ismay are thoughts of the women and children who perished in the icy depths that night. The sounds of the sea washing against the shore serve as a constant reminder of these victims. Mahon uses a wonderful image to capture the manner in which Ismay's mind is tormented by the sea. Thoughts and memories of these women and children are compared to 'broken toys and hatboxes'. It is as if the sea regularly carries these in upon the tide and deposits them at the door of Ismay's house.

Such is Ismay's depression and anguish that he can no longer take any pleasure from life. The beauty of the natural world, the splendour of the changing seasons 'mean nothing' to him now: 'The showers of/ April, flowers of May ... nor the/ Late light of June'.

Ismay's suffering is particularly acute on 'seaward' mornings when the wind blows in from the sea. On such occasions Ismay stays in bed and takes his 'cocaine', which would have been prescribed to alleviate his depression and anxiety.

The bouts of depression that Ismay must endure on these occasions are truly horrific. He describes the sensation of drowning, of plummeting to the icy-cold, black depths of some ocean. Whereas the heroes who sank with the ship drowned once, Ismay describes how he drowns 'again and again'. And as he sinks into this black and terrible depression, Ismay's mind is filled with the faces of those who perished that fateful night.

Ismay describes these faces as 'dim', suggesting that he cannot now recall them vividly. He also says that these were people he 'never understood'. Perhaps Ismay is referring to the ordinary workers on the ship, the many men who worked for him but with whom – because of class differences – he could never identify. But it might also be the very wealthy passengers aboard the *Titanic* that Ismay is alluding to. Perhaps he never felt any connection with these members of the British aristocracy who did not have to work, as Ismay did, for a living.

It might also be that Ismay was never much of a social person and did not easily establish close relationships with his peers. Certainly, following the tragedy, Ismay lives a very solitary life. When he is suffering from one of his bouts of depression he 'will see no one'. It is his gardener who is tasked with communicating with the 'strangers' who pass by the house, curious, no doubt, to hear about the notorious survivor of the *Titanic*.

FOCUS ON STYLE

Verbal Music

Mahon uses a repetition of hard consonant sounds to reflect the unpleasant sound of the ship breaking apart: 'a pandemonium of/ Prams, pianos, sideboards, winches,/ Boilers bursting'. Lines 18 to 19, meanwhile, feature repeated soft 's' and long vowel sounds, capturing Ismay's anguish and suffering: 'my poor soul/ Screams out in the starlight'.

Metaphor, Simile and Figures of Speech

Mahon uses an interesting metaphor to convey the suffering that Ismay endures. He describes how Ismay's 'heart/ Breaks loose and rolls down like a stone'. The metaphor suggests the heaviness of Ismay's heart. It also reminds us of the great weight of the ship sinking to the depths of the ocean. The 'term' stone also suggests a certain numbness or deadness, a sense that Ismay is no longer properly alive.

Word Choice

Mahon's choice of the term 'pandemonium' to describe the turmoil aboard the ship is a perfect example of the poet's craft and precision. Pandemonium refers to a situation in which a crowd of people act in a wild, uncontrolled or violent way because they are afraid or confused. But the word is also another term for hell (It was coined by Milton to designate the capital of hell in Paradise Lost). As such, it captures the inner turmoil that Ismay must endure as he witnesses the *Titanic* crumble and the hellish depression into which he is cast.

THEMES

REMEMBERING HISTORY'S VICTIMS

This is another poem that gives a voice to one of history's victims. In this case, it is Bruce Ismay, someone that history has labelled a villain and a coward. The poet does not judge Ismay or say whether his actions were right or wrong. Instead, he seeks to explore the terrible anguish that the man must have suffered in the aftermath of the tragedy. Although the inquiry said that Ismay 'got away' the night the *Titanic* sank, Mahon's poem suggests that Ismay never escaped. By giving Ismay a voice, Mahon allows us to feel compassion and sympathy for a man the world would prefer to label a villain and to forget.

COMMUNITY AND ISOLATION

A number of Mahon's poems describe how being part of a community brings certain moral demands. In order to be a considered a member of any given community, there are things we are expected to do. In 'After the Titanic', Ismay is part of the community on board the ship. It is expected that he, being a gentleman, will sacrifice his life for the lives of the women and children on board.

Ismay initially meets this demand – assisting in escorting women and children to the few lifeboats on the *Titanic*. But at the last second he fails. He rejects the demands of the community and puts his own life first, taking a seat on the last lifeboat. In doing so, Ismay pays a heavy price. He is humiliated and vilified for his behaviour and ends up living the lonely life of an outcast. At the end of the poem, he makes a heartfelt plea that he be included in our 'lamentations', that we consider him when we mourn those who perished in the tragedy.

Many of Mahon's poems deal with states of extreme or hellish isolation. In 'After the Titanic' we are presented with the harrowing image of Bruce Ismay 'shivering on the dark water' in a small lifeboat. In the years following the disaster, the disgraced Ismay lived a life of seclusion: 'Now I hide/ In a lonely house behind the sea'. He suffered intense feelings of despair and psychological isolation, best captured by the powerful image of his 'soul' screaming out 'in the starlight'.

NATURE

The poem reminds us of the natural world's indifference to man and all his grand schemes and dreams. 'After the Titanic' reminds us how the supposedly unsinkable ship was sent 'thundering down' by its collision with the iceberg. Its mention of stormy weather in lines 15 to 16 also brings to mind nature's dangerous and menacing side. In 'After the Titanic', the image of Ismay sitting alone upon the 'dark water' suggests the vastness and the indifference of the ocean.

But the poem also highlights the beauty of the natural world. Mahon wonderfully captures the splendour of the changing seasons: 'The showers of April, flowers of May ... the/ Late light of June'.

Ecclesiastes

LINE BY LINE

Mahon left Northern Ireland when he went to attend Trinity College, Dublin. When he did so, he abandoned not only Belfast, but also the Protestant faith in which he had been raised.

The poem is named after a book of the Old Testament, which is known not only for its wisdom and poetic beauty but also for its bleak view of human existence. The poem can be read as a kind of 'interior dialogue', in which Mahon is actually speaking to himself. He attempts to work out his thoughts and feelings on the city and culture in which he was raised.

Mahon flirts with the possibility of returning to live in Belfast indefinitely. He imagines that he might re-embrace the Protestant faith in which he was raised. In fact, he considers doing so to an extreme extent, becoming a prophet or spiritual leader of Protestant Belfast.

Belfast Sundays

This Protestant culture in which the poet was raised took the concept of the Sabbath very seriously. On Sundays, all forms of work and recreation were forbidden. Instead, people were encouraged to focus on prayer and the contemplation of God.
- On Sundays, the shipyards would be silent because no work was permitted to take place.
- The swings in the public parks would be 'tied-up' so that children couldn't use them.
- The shops would be closed and the streets 'empty'
- The only busy places were the churches, which he describes as 'dank' or unpleasantly damp and chilly.

The poet, however, tells himself that he could 'grow to love' these rather dismal Sundays in Protestant Belfast.

Ireland can be a pretty bleak place in January, especially when it rains. But Belfast, the poem suggests, is especially grim on such occasions.

The poet, however, feels that he could 'grow to love' these 'January rains' that fall on the 'dark doors' of the city. He must learn to love the grim Antrim landscape: the dark hard January rains, the dark doors of Belfast city, the bleak hills and the boggy meadows filled with the graves of his ancestors.

A prophet's lifestyle

The poet imagines the self-punishing lifestyle he would adopt if he were to become a spiritual leader of his people.
- He must wear only black clothing.
- He would drink nothing but water.
- His diet would be one of extreme self-denial as he permitted himself only 'locusts and wild honey'.

Such a lifestyle, he suggests, would 'nourish' or strengthen his religious commitment, making him a true spiritual leader. The poet's use of the term 'fierce zeal' is interesting here. 'Zeal' suggests a passionate enthusiasm. But 'fierce zeal' suggests something more intense and ungovernable, a single-minded conviction that the poet and his chosen religion are in the right while everyone else has gone astray.

The poet, of course, doesn't really think that he would survive on 'locusts and wild honey', both of which are in short supply in modern-day Belfast. This was the self-punishing diet of the Biblical prophet John the Baptist. The phrase, then, is a symbolic one, representing how the poet will eat only small quantities of the simplest foods. He won't eat for comfort or enjoyment. He won't let himself be distracted by the pleasures of the flesh.

Mentality

The poet, if he wants to become a spiritual leader of his people, must adopt a particular mentality.

- He must let his heart grow 'cold'. He must leave behind all feelings of sympathy and empathy.
- He must avoid anything that is fun, frivolous or light-hearted. These aspects of life are regarded as a dangerous 'heat' that might thaw his cold heart: 'shelter your cold heart from the heat/ of the world'.
- He must be especially careful to minimise his contact with women and children.
- He must learn to ignore the arguments, excuses and objections of others. He must 'not/ feel called upon to understand and forgive'.
- He must learn to speak with 'afflatus', with inspiration and authority that comes – or seems to come – directly from the heavens. Such afflatus would, however, be 'bleak', suggesting that it relates to judgement and condemnation.

This is a disturbing list, but especially unsettling is the mentioning of women and children. The 'bright' adorable eyes of children might cause a prophet to feel tenderness and kindness. Children, therefore, must be avoided. Women, meanwhile, are depicted as a form of 'inquisition', which means a prolonged and intensive questioning. Being around women, it is implied, will cause the prophet to question his vocation. They must, therefore, also be avoided.

The poet's current lifestyle

We get a sense that the poet currently enjoys a laid-back, somewhat carefree existence devoted to travel and art. The banjo suggests his love of music, literature and art. The bandana and stick, meanwhile, suggest his love of travel.

In the 19th century, travellers would use a bandana and stick as a rough form of rucksack. Possessions could be wrapped in a bandana, which would then be tied to the end of a stick and carried over the traveller's shoulder.

The speaker urges himself to 'Bury that red/ bandana and stick, that banjo'. This symbolises abandoning his current carefree way of life in order to become a spiritual leader of his people.

Prophet as king

The poet, by embracing this prophetic role, could make himself a 'king' of Protestant Belfast. He imagines that the Protestants of Belfast are waiting for him, eager for him to assume the role of their spiritual leader: 'this is your country … your people await you'. They will greet him not with flags or palm branches but with laundry dangling on washing lines: 'their heavy washing/ flaps for you in the council estates'.

The poet refers to an old proverb coined by Erasmus: 'In the land of the blind, the one-eyed man is king'.

- At the moment, the poet is mentally 'fully sighted'; he is an intelligent, intellectually aware and open-minded young man.
- In order to become a prophet, he must give up some of this open-mindedness. He must 'Close one eye'.
- Yet he will never be as blinkered as the Protestant people of Northern Ireland. These people, it is implied, are completely intellectually blind.

Metaphorically speaking, then, the poet will be a 'one-eyed man' among the blind. But in a land of blind people, being able to see out of one eye leaves you in a privileged, powerful position.

The poet imagines himself working as a prophet, preaching on a street corner to the people of Protestant Belfast. He imagines himself engaged in 'rhetoric', the art of public speaking. Rhetoric also implies deceit and insincerity, suggesting that this brand of religion is fake and not to be trusted.

The poem's last line adapts a famous quotation from *The Book of Ecclesiastes*. The phrase in question, 'There is nothing new under the sun' suggests that everything has happened before, that even seemingly novel situations have already been discovered and dealt with by humanity.

The poet would offer his people 'nothing under the sun'. This phrase implies that he will offer his people not the brightness and happiness we associate with the sun but only darkness and misery. It implies that he would promise his people nothing, and that all his promises are false.

The poet imagines himself being 'stiff/ with rhetoric'. This suggests the straight-backed, imposing posture he will adopt as he preaches to his people. The term 'stiff' also suggests the severe and inflexible mindset you need to possess as a spiritual leader.

FOCUS ON STYLE

Verbal music

The poem generates a powerful and consistent verbal music. It consists of four sentences that rush down the page, spilling from clause to clause, from commandment to commandment. This creates a powerful sense of urgency and raw emotion, suggesting how the poet is both fascinated and repulsed by the culture in which he was raised.

Word Choice

Mahon's precision when it comes to word choice is evident in 'purist', which refers to someone who insists on tradtional rules and structures. This term, of course, suggests Mahon's precise and deliberate approach to poetry, but it also hints how he has been influenced, despite himself, by his Protestant upbringing, with its rigid and traditional approach to life.

Sensual Imagery

Mahon's gift for imagery is evident in his depiction of Belfast 'January rains'. These rains, we are told, darken the city, suggesting that the rain restricts visibility, making everything murky and dismal. Mahon describes how they 'sink hard' into the surrounding landscape. This suggests that the rains come pelting down, saturating the bogs and meadows and sinking deep into the soil.

THEMES

COMMUNITY AND ISOLATION

This poem reminds us how communities can become stifling and controling. The world of Protestant Belfast, as Mahon portrays it, is not one that tolerates dissent and diversity. It is a world where the swings are tied up and everyone goes to church. You live your life in a God-fearing manner and you are eventually buried in the 'heaped/ graves of your fathers'.

The poem also highlights the moral demands such a community can place on its members. The poet, as we've seen, feels that he could and, perhaps, should embrace the role of a joyless, hectoring prophet. The repetition of 'God' and 'you could' reinforce our sense of his horror at this realisation.

But the poet, we sense, is unlikely to surrender to this impulse. He is unlikely to abandon his current carefree lifestyle. We see this at the poem's conclusion where his comment 'you could do it, God/ help you' indicates that he has nothing but pity and contempt for anyone who would assume the role of such a religious leader.

MAHON AND IRELAND

The poet presents a very negative portrait of the Protestant religion in which he was raised:
- This type of religion is described as 'puritan', meaning it regards nearly all pleasure and luxury as sinful.
- Its adherents are described as 'God-fearing', suggesting that they view God as a terrifying, vengeful force rather than as a being of love.
- Its adherents are described as 'God-chosen': they believe that they alone are chosen by God to be saved, that they alone know what it is to be righteous.

The poet left this religion behind a long time ago. But the bleak faith of his childhood still influences his personality. The poet attempts to conceal this influence. He uses various 'wiles' or ruses to conceal this influence. He 'smiles' to convince the world he is light-hearted and liberated rather than God-fearing. But deep-down he knows that he can never escape and that the influence of his childhood religion will always be with him.

The poem, as we've seen, presents a far from flattering picture of Belfast. But the poet realises that the city, whatever its faults, will always be a part of his mind and personality. On one level, he is the dank churches and the empty streets of Belfast: 'you are (the/ dank churches, the empty streets'). This is the place, after all, where generations of his ancestors are buried: 'the heaped graves of your grandfathers'. Because he grew up in Belfast, no matter how far he travels that city will be a part of his psychological make-up.

We might question, however, whether Mahon doesn't go too far in his criticism of Protestant Belfast. We might question his depiction of its people as intellectually blind and 'credulous' or gullible. We might also question the extent to which he depicts their faith as bleak, rigid and uncompromising.

The poem can be viewed as a spewing of raw, exaggerated emotion, triggered by Mahon's return to his homeplace after many years away, rather than a sober and balanced appraisal of the Protestant community.

THIS IS POETRY | **DEREK MAHON**

As it Should Be

LINE BY LINE

An isolated community

This poem takes place in and around an unnamed coastal village. It's tempting, because of Mahon's background, to assume an Irish setting. But no country is actually specified. And events like those described in the poem did (and do) take place all over the world. This village, then, could be anywhere from Tennessee to Afghanistan.

The village, it seems, is too remote to be properly policed by the state authorities. It is possible, therefore, to murder someone and get rid of the body without the authorities really noticing. This is especially true if the local community is on your side. No one is going to kick up a fuss and draw the state's attention to the disappearance.

The speaker is a leading member of the village's community. Perhaps his prominence comes from wealth and power. Maybe he has the biggest farm in the area or runs the village store. Or perhaps his prominence comes from his charisma and force of personality. In any event, the speaker has great power in the community and can persuade others to follow his lead.

The speaker refers to another resident of the village, whom he refers to as 'the mad bastard'. Mahon provides us with little concrete information about the 'mad bastard'. But he seems to be something of an oddball, someone who doesn't quite fit into village life. Maybe he dresses in an outlandish fashion or exhibits unusual habits and behaviours. Maybe he is someone who refuses to participate in community events and gatherings. Maybe he has ideas and opinions that differ from those held by the community at large.

Method and madness

The speaker has been deeply troubled by the presence of the 'mad bastard' in his village. The village, he believes, has always been governed by 'method'. It is a community that does things according to a long-established set of procedures that have been handed down by custom and tradition. And the speaker wants things to stay that way.

The 'mad bastard', therefore, presents a problem. For society to function properly, everyone must follow the 'method', but the 'mad bastard' refuses to do so. His presence, therefore, is having a very negative effect on village life. He has caused ripples of unease to spread throughout the community, making everyone tense and agitated.

This unease has even spread to the children of the village, who have become subdued and despondent. They no longer play in their usual noisy, jovial fashion. Many of them have been experiencing nightmares. Even the weather conditions, according to the speaker, have been affected by the 'mad bastard's' presence, becoming unseasonably harsh.

We can sense that the problem of the 'mad bastard' is a relatively new one. Perhaps he is an outsider who has only recently taken up residence. Or perhaps he's a native who has returned to the village having spent some time away. Or perhaps he is a long-time resident who has recently taken up new ideas and behaviours.

It is as if the speaker views the village community like a human body. He views the 'mad bastard', meanwhile, as an infection or a disease. Even a mild infection is enough to throw off the workings of the entire body. Similarly, the 'mad bastard', though only one person, is upsetting the workings of the entire village.

The hunt by night

The speaker, we sense, has been discussing the 'mad bastard' with other male members of the community:
- He has convinced them that the 'mad bastard's' presence poses a threat to the community.
- He has persuaded them that this problem needs to be permanently eliminated.
- He has persuaded them that it is their duty to come together with their rifles and kill the 'mad bastard', ending his malign influence once and for all.

We imagine that the speaker and his companions went to the 'mad bastard's' place of residence and attempted to shoot him dead. The 'mad bastard', however, managed to flee the scene and made off across the countryside.

The speaker and his companions were determined, almost desperate, to see this man dead. We see this when they track him relentlessly through all kinds of difficult terrain, never giving up the chase: 'We hunted the mad bastard/ Through bog, moorland, rock'. We also see it in how they show no mercy when they finally caught up with him in a 'blind yard', a yard with only a single entrance and exit, from which the 'mad bastard' could not possibly escape.

The speaker and his companions could have used this opportunity to give their victim a stark warning, telling him on pain of death never to come back to town. They might have even reinforced this point by wounding him or beating him up. Instead, however, they simply 'gunned him down'.

They got rid of the body by means of a 'tide burial', casting the 'mad bastard's' remains into the sea and letting the tide carry it away. This burial, according to the speaker, took place 'during school hours'; we get the impression that the speaker and his companions shot their victim around dawn and disposed of his body around mid-morning.

Harmony restored

Since the 'mad bastard's' death, according to the speaker, things in the village have greatly improved:
- The mood of the local children is much better. They happily play like they used to, chasing one another and gallivanting along the coastline. The speaker describes how their 'cries echo lightly', suggesting the carefree shouts and laughter of children at play.
- The children no longer experience nightmares: 'Since his tide burial … Our kiddies have known no bad dreams'.
- Even the weather, according to the speaker, has improved. The air, he declares, 'blows softer', suggesting a warm, summery breeze. The harsh conditions associated with the 'mad bastard's' presence are no more.

We get the impression that harmony has been restored to village life.

What is meant by the 'moon in the Yellow River'?

Li Po was a Chinese poet who lived between 701 AD and 762 AD. According to tradition, he drowned while being ferried by night across the Yellow River. He thought that the moon's reflection in the river's waters was the moon itself that had somehow fallen from the sky. He attempted to embrace this fallen object and fell overboard. Li Po, it must be noted, was extremely drunk at the time of this incident.

The story of Li Po, to the speaker, represents fantasy, playfulness and imagination. These qualities are okay among children, but they are not to be trusted among adults. The 'mad bastard', the speaker implies, exhibited such characteristics. He was prone to 'idle talk', to foolish and irrelevant chatter that revealed his playful and fantastical notions.

With the murder of the 'mad bastard', such 'idle talk' has been eliminated, at least for now. And the speaker is determined that no such talk will never return to the village.

FOCUS ON STYLE

Polished Forms
'As It Should Be' can be considered a loosely crafted sonnet. Some of its rhymes, like that between 'bastard' and 'yard', are full rhymes. Some, like that between 'river' and 'departure', are half rhymes. Other lines have no rhyme at all. The sonnet form, it should be noted, has traditionally been associated with the themes of love and romance. Perhaps Mahon felt that this rougher, looser version of the form was appropriate for the themes of hatred and murder.

Word Choice
Mahon is well known for his precision when it comes to choosing individual words and phrases. We see this with 'tide burial', a phrase that describes how the speaker disposed of the 'mad bastard's' body by casting it into the sea and letting the tide carry it away.

Verbal Music
Cacophony features in lines 3 to 45, where the various hard consonants combine to create a grating verbal music, one well suited to this description of the 'mad bastard's' grisly death. Euphony, meanwhile, features in line 11, where the repeated broad vowel sounds create a pleasant verbal music appropriate to this description of the 'kiddies' at their games along the coastline.

Sensual Imagery
'As It Should Be', like many of Mahon's poems, features several vivid images. Especially memorable is the image of the speaker and his companions pursuing the 'mad bastard' across the countryside through all kinds of difficult terrain. Equally vivid is the depiction of the depot or delivery yard where the 'mad bastard' met his end. This 'blind yard' with its 'electric generator' seems to have been a rather bleak and industrial location. The speaker memorably personifies the lorries that were parked there, declaring that were 'sleeping' as they waited to be dispatched on another day's deliveries.

The phrase 'star-lit west' conjures up an image of the dawn; the eastern half of the sky already bright while stars are still visible in its western half. It suggests that the speaker and his companions hunted their victim all night long, before catching and shooting him around dawn. They disposed of the body, we're told, 'during school hours', which suggests the mid-morning.

THEMES

COMMUNITY AND ISOLATION
Communities, the poem reminds us, can often be stiflingly conformist. They tend to be based around 'method' on long-established norms, habits and procedures. They tend to insist that every member behave in a similar fashion, following this 'method'. There is often little tolerance for those, like the 'mad bastard', who depart from the community's norms.

Those who don't fit in can find themselves mocked and shunned. They can find themselves blamed for all sorts of the community's woes, such as unseasonable weather or the disturbed sleep of children. They can find themselves expelled from the community altogether, or even, in extreme cases like this one, 'hunted' and 'gunned down'.

The mad bastard's fate might strike us as extreme. But it's not too hard to think of real life instances where an entire community turns on a member who is judged to have stepped out of line. Such vengeance can be wreaked not only in isolated coastal villages, but also in communities that are virtual and online.

The poem's speaker is someone who identifies completely with the community in which he lives. This sense of belonging is emphasised by his use of the pronoun 'We' rather than 'I'. This is someone, we sense, who always puts his community before himself, who is deeply concerned with the village's overall welfare. But he also feels that he represents the community and is entitled to speak on its behalf.

He is especially anxious, as we've seen, about the welfare of the community's children, who he refers to tenderly as 'kiddies'. He was concerned by their disturbed sleep and strange demeanour. He takes satisfaction from seeing that they are back to normal, declaring that this is how it 'should be'.

The poem, then, is one of several by Mahon where communities place moral demands on individuals. The speaker feels morally obliged to organise and carry out the murder. The speaker insists, therefore, that he didn't act out of cruelty, or to satisfy some personal grudge. Instead, he did what he had to do for the welfare of the community and its children. The speaker is convinced that the children will appreciate what he has done, the lengths to which he has gone to protect them. They will thank him, and those who helped him in the killing, for providing them with an orderly and harmonious environment where everyone follows the proper 'method' of living.

A Disused Shed in Co. Wexford

LINE BY LINE

This poem deals with a colony of mushrooms that were cultivated in the 1920s by the owner of a large estate in Co. Wexford. The owner was an amateur mycologist, someone who specialises in growing mushrooms and other fungi. He picked a particular shed 'Deep in the grounds' of his estate as a suitable place in which to grow his specimens. We can imagine how the coolness and darkness would have made it a hospitable environment for fungi.

The mycologist, however, was forced to leave his estate behind, abandoning the mushrooms in their shed. The mushrooms heard him walk down the gravel path outside their shed for the last time. His departure is described as endless, or 'interminable', suggesting he left very slowly and reluctantly. After that, he never returned to tend them: 'He never came back'.

It is important to note that the mushrooms are depicted as having what can only be described as human characteristics. They are capable of seeing and hearing, of being patient, of hoping and of desiring. They suffer very human torments like nightmares and insomnia. They are depicted as speaking and even screaming. They even seem to have throats.

The mushrooms have been in the shed for about fifty years: from 'the civil war days' of the 1920s until the poet discovers them in the 1970s. Much has happened over those decades. The big house at the centre of the estate was converted into a hotel, which subsequently burned down, presumably as the result of an accident. But in all that time, not a single person has opened the door of the mushroom shed, meaning that they have spent a 'half century, without visitors, in the dark'.

The poet discovers the mushrooms when he is exploring the hotel grounds with some friends. The poet, it seems, is holidaying in this part of Ireland. He is carrying a camera and a light meter, a piece of photographic equipment. His travels follow a relaxed schedule or 'itinerary'.

The poet notices the disused shed and almost randomly decides to open its door. The shed's lock is so rusted that it cracks under the poet's hand, allowing him to easily open the shed's door. The rusty hinges creak as the door swings open: 'the cracking lock/ And creak of hinges'.

The shed contains a great deal of bric-a-brac, bits and pieces that were stashed there by the mycologist over fifty years ago. The poet mentions 'bathtubs' and 'washbasins', for instance. He notices spider webs and a great deal of 'mildew', a mould, he imagines, that has been formed from the corpses of dead flies: 'flies dusted to mildew'.

THIS IS POETRY **DEREK MAHON**

The poem's opening stanza
The poem does not focus on the mushrooms immediately. Instead, its opening stanza presents a list of abandoned, forgotten places. We begin with a mine in Peru that has been 'worked out' or stripped of all its precious metals. The mine is almost entirely silent now, having been 'abandoned' by the miners that once worked there. But there are some quiet, almost imperceptible activities:

- The poet imagines an echo trapped forever, a sound wave endlessly bouncing back and forth between the tunnels of the mine.
- He imagines 'wildflowers' fluttering as the breeze moves through the lift-shaft.
- He imagines condensation forming on the ceiling of one of the tunnels. Droplets of condensation regularly drip on to the tunnel floor. The poet wonderfully captures the ticking sound this produces, comparing the condensation to 'a slow clock'.

The poet also imagines a compound in India. This, like the mine, seems to have been abandoned. The only activity is that of the wind 'dancing' through the compound. The only sound is that of a door that continually bangs.

The poet now imagines a 'place' even more obscure and insignificant, focusing on a 'crevice' that has formed in the wall of a limestone house.
- A barrel for collecting rain water rests against the house (No doubt, a pipe running from the gutters, funnels rain water into the barrel).
- The barrel fills to the brim, its surface 'rippling'.
- Then water spills over the side of the barrel, running down the wall of the house.
- This erodes the limestone wall, creating the crevice that the poet has in mind.

The next set of 'places' imagined by the poet is equally obscure. He thinks of the various 'corners' of fields and gardens where dogs go to bury their bones. These corners tend to be overgrown and out-of-the-way, where the hidden bones are unlikely to be discovered.

Each of these places is abandoned, insignificant and forgotten. Yet, according to the speaker, they are places where 'a thought might grow'. These silent forgotten places could serve as the starting point for thought or meditation. Despite their apparent insignificance, these abandoned locales might inspire us to think seriously about the world we live in.

But the poet's attention is seized by the colony of mushrooms. He estimates there are about 'A thousand' mushrooms altogether. They still occupy the trays of soil in which the mycologist planted them all those years ago.

Becasue the shed is windowless, the mushrooms' only source of light is the keyhole in its door: 'light since then/ Is a keyhole rusting gently after rain'. The mushrooms, according to the speaker, 'crowd to the keyhole'. We can imagine how the mushrooms' stems are bent in its direction, desperate for the little light that it provides.

What has life been like for the mushrooms?
The mushrooms for decades have longed to be released from the shed's grim confines: 'What could they do there but desire?' But there was nothing practical the mushrooms could do to help themselves. They could only wait for someone to come along and open the shed door: 'They have been waiting ... since civil war days'. Patience, therefore, has become second nature to them over the decades: 'they have learnt patience'.

Silence
The mushrooms, we are told, have 'learnt' silence over the years. This suggests that they have come to understand silence as if it were a language. They have come to recognise different types of silence, each with its own qualities and textures. This is because they exist in an almost total silence that is only occasionally interrupted by a noise from outside the shed: 'once a day, perhaps, they have heard something'.

The poet imagines that they might have heard 'masonry' loosening and trickling downward as the shed walls slowly decay around them, or a 'shout from the blue', a roar or exclamation from the blue-skied world outside. They might have heard a 'lorry changing gear', or rooks cawing in the trees of the estate. These sounds are all unremarkable or unpleasant. The mushrooms endure such silence that they treasure and celebrate these rough, ordinary noises, whenever they are lucky enough to hear them.

Atmospheric conditions
The shed's atmospheric conditions are pretty hellish. It is unventilated, meaning that the air is 'stale'. There is little moisture, meaning the mushrooms endure a 'drought'. And the few droplets that form are described as 'rank' or foul.

The mushrooms, according to the poet, have been sweating for decades as they sit there in the shed. Their 'vegetable sweat' produces a 'foetor', a strong, foul smell. This image of the mushrooms trapped in their own stench for decade after decade is both powerful and disturbing.

Unsurprisingly, given these terrible atmospheric conditions, many mushrooms have died over the years. The poet masterfully describes how their 'pale flesh' crumbles into flakes, which are absorbed back into the very soil they grew out of: 'There have been deaths, the pale flesh flaking/ Into the earth that nourished it'.

Normal sleep is impossible in this bleak environment. Insomnia is common, and when the mushrooms do sleep they suffer terrible nightmares. Some nightmares are prompted by the terrible atmospheric conditions that prevail in the shed. Others are prompted by witnessing the death and decay of fellow mushrooms: 'And nightmares, born of these and the grim/ Dominion of stale air and rank moisture'.

Strong and weak
The poet focuses on the mushrooms that are 'nearest the door'. Becauase these mushrooms are closest to the keyhole, they get the most light. As a result, they 'grow strong', becoming bigger and bigger over the years.

But as these mushrooms 'nearest the door' increase in size, they block out more and more of the light. This means less and less light reaches the mushrooms further back in the shed's interior. Mahon uses a memorable metaphor to describe this process, suggesting that the mushrooms 'nearest the door' are jostling or hustling the weaker ones out of the way: 'Elbow room! Elbow Room!'

The poet focuses on the weaker mushrooms that are deeper in the shed's interior. Because they are further away from the keyhole, they know only a permanent 'twilight': 'dim in a twilight of crumbling/ Utensils and broken pitchers'. For decades these weaker mushrooms have been 'Expectant': they have imagined that sooner or later their circumstances would change. The poet imagines them 'groaning/ For their deliverance', crying out in an anguished voice to be saved. But they have been waiting for 'so long' that all hope has been abandoned. Now, only the 'posture' or appearance of expectancy remains.

The mushrooms' desperation
The mushrooms have 'Grown beyond nature now'. It seems that the years of surviving in the darkness have left the mushrooms warped, mutated and unnatural-looking:
- The description of them as 'magi', as sorcerers or wizards, suggests there is something bizarre or otherworldly about their appearance.
- They are compared to 'moonmen', suggesting how their pale, bulbous caps might be said to resemble the moon. But the term also suggests that the mushrooms have developed an otherworldly appearance, as if they were an alien lunar species.
- The mushrooms seem to have long, mutated stalks that remind the poet of the triffids, plant-like, alien invaders from a famous 1950s science-fiction novel and film.

The mushrooms have also been left in an incredibly weakened state by their ordeal, their fragility captured by the terms 'soft', 'frail' and 'Powdery'. They are so weak that the only sign of life from them is the 'ghost of a scream', a scream so inaudible that it is hardly a scream at all. The mushrooms, the speaker says, are 'soft food for worms'. They are at the point of death, ready to collapse back into the earth and be devoured by worms.

Decades of almost total darkness have left the mushrooms unable to handle light. They are highly uncomfortable, therefore, when the lock finally cracks and daylight rushes in: 'A half-century, without visitors, in the dark –/ Poor preparation for the creaking lock'. The poet's camera flash strikes them with the ferocity of 'a firing squad'.

The mushrooms beg the poet and his companions to help them: 'They are begging us, you see, in their wordless way'. Somehow, despite their feverish weakness, they lift their 'frail heads' towards him. It is as if they are using the last of their energy to ask for his assistance, beseeching him for help in 'gravity and good faith', in a serious and honest fashion.

The mushrooms ask the speaker to do three things:
- Ideally, they want the poet to save their lives; they beg him to 'do something', and to 'Save us, save us'.
- If this is not possible, they want the poet to record their suffering, to tell their story for them: 'to speak on their behalf'.
- If the poet refuses to do either of these things, if he simply walks away, then they want him to at least leave the shed door open as he does so, rather than confine them once more to the darkness: 'Or at least not to close the door again'.

To the mushrooms, after fifty years of almost complete darkness, the poet seems to be a kind of god. He has total power over them. He can help them in some fashion or he can simply walk away and leave them in darkness once more. They beg this 'god' not to abandon them. If he does so, their years of naïve labour, of enduring the shed's grim horrors in the foolish hope of rescue, will all have been for nothing: 'Let not our naive labours have been in vain!'

It seems that the poet has turned up too late to save the mushrooms' lives. We get the impression that the mushrooms are beyond saving. 'A half century, without visitors, in the dark' is 'Poor preparation' for rescue. There is still a chance, however, that even if the poet cannot save the mushrooms' lives he will speak out on their behalf and tell their story for them.

THIS IS POETRY — DEREK MAHON

THEMES

REMEMBERING HISTORY'S VICTIMS
'A Disused Shed' calls on us to remember all those who have suffered throughout human history. The speaker associates the mushrooms with the 'Lost people of Treblinka and Pompeii'. Treblinka was a concentration camp in Poland where the Nazis murdered thousands of Jews. Pompeii was an ancient Roman city where thousands died when it was buried by lava after Mount Vesuvius erupted in AD 79. The poem, therefore, sympathises with all those who have suffered and died through natural disasters or through man's inhumanity to man.

The victims of these tragedies are long dead. They cannot speak for themselves. They are voiceless and 'wordless'. Yet they long to be remembered in some fashion, for the story of their suffering to be told. They are imagined as beseeching the people of the present to tell their stories for them: 'They are begging us you see, in their wordless way'.

The poem's epigraph is a desperate appeal to be remembered. 'Let them not forget us' goes the plea, and this might be the motto not only of the mushrooms but also of all history's victims, who long for their lives to be remembered even if they themselves must die. The poem, then, presents us with a powerful challenge. We get the impression that is too late to save the mushrooms, just as it is obviously too late to save the people of all the historical disasters such as Treblinka and Pompeii. As the mushrooms remind the speaker, 'We too had our lives to live'. If we 'speak on their behalf' and remember these 'Lost people', then their agonies, their 'naïve labours', will not have been for nothing.

MAHON AND IRELAND
This is another poem in which Mahon touches upon Ireland's troubled history. The mention of the Irish Civil War brings to mind not only that bloody conflict but the conflicts that have bedevilled Ireland over the subsequent century.

We get the impression that the mycologist was a member of the wealthy protestant Anglo-Irish class, who owned most of the 'Big Houses' in the country at that time. When Ireland was under British rule, this Anglo-Irish class had enjoyed great power. However, they were finally swept aside when Ireland gained independence in the 1920s. Many members of this class found little welcome in the newly independent state. Some had their big houses burned down by Republican forces. Others, like the mycologist, had their lands 'expropriated' or confiscated. The fate of these grounds, therefore, serves as an image for Anglo-Irish decline. The once-proud estate became a hotel and then a derelict site with a burnt-out mansion and a disused shed.

FOCUS ON STYLE

Polished Forms
The poem has six stanzas of ten lines each. Each line rhymes with another line in the same stanza. However, there is no repeated pattern between the stanzas. Furthermore, many of these rhymes could be described as half-rhymes or even quarter-rhymes. For instance, 'dances' rhymes with 'confidence', 'barrels' rhymes with 'burials', and 'cloud' rhymes with 'wood'.

Verbal Music
There are several memorable instances of onomatopoeia in this poem. In line 3, the phrase 'slow clock of condensation' summons up the noise of condensation dripping in the empty mine. Similarly, in the wonderful phrase 'gravel-crunching interminable departure/ Of the expropriated mycologist' we can almost hear the sound of the landowner walking away down the gravel path.

We also see onomatopoeia in lines 42–3: 'the cracking lock/ And creak of hinges'. The repetition of the hard 'ck' sound in 'cracking lock' suggests the noise of the lock on the shed door breaking. The onomatopoeic 'creak', meanwhile, conjures up the sound it makes as it swings open on its rusty hinges. It could also be argued that onomatopoeia is present in line 47 where the phrase 'flash-bulb firing-squad' conjures the noise made by the flash of an old-style camera.

Word Choice
Mahon is well known for his precise and deliberate choice of individual words. We see this in his choice of 'firmament', meaning night sky to describe the shed's interior wall and ceiling. The keyhole, meanwhile, is compared to the night sky's one and only 'star'. This wonderfully captures the shed's almost total darkness, and how it is illuminated only by a single beam of light creeping through the keyhole.

Equally impressive is his choice of 'querulous' to describe the singing of the rooks in the 'high wood' around the shed. This term, which means complaining, wonderfully captures the abrasive nature of their song.

The phrase 'Powdery prisoners of the old regime', meanwhile, perfectly captures the mushrooms' condition. The mushrooms are prisoners, confined to the shed for decades. The description of them as 'Powdery' captures their brittle, fragile flesh. The phrase 'old regime', meanwhile, reminds us that they were cultivated by an Anglo-Irish landowner, the 'regime' that once dominated Ireland.

The Chinese Restaurant in Portrush

'A framed photograph of Hong Kong'

LINE BY LINE

The people of Portrush have endured a harsh winter. The air has been 'sharp' or biting along the Antrim coastline. Cold winds have been blowing from the north and freezing mist has drifted inland from the sea: 'the north wind and the sea mist'.

The poet, however, finds himself in Portrush on one of the first fine days of springtime. The sunlight, he declares, is so brilliant and beautiful that it resembles the light of heaven itself. The change of seasons, according to the poet, has softened the air around the town, making everything warmer and more pleasant: 'spring/ softening the sharp air of the coast'.

The poet describes how front doors are open all along the main street. These doors, of course, have been 'shut all winter', in an effort to keep out the wind, rain and freezing fog. We can imagine, however, that on this fine day the owners of shops and houses might leave their front doors open, eager to let light and air into their premises.

Portrush, the poet reminds us, is a resort town, one that's popular with tourists during the summer months. But it is still early in the springtime and the year's first 'visitors' have yet to arrive: 'Before the first visitor comes the spring'. In a few weeks, however, the tourist season will commence and an 'invasion' of holiday-makers will come flooding into the town.

The poet is relaxing with his paper and a casual lunch of 'prawn chow mein' in the local Chinese restaurant. He notes how the spring sunshine lends Portrush a pleasant atmosphere. It seems that every person and creature in the town exhibits a relaxed and carefree manner.

- The girl who passes the restaurant is described as 'light-footed', suggesting that she walks in a carefree manner.
- An old dog is dozing contentedly in the warmth of the spring sunshine: 'And an old wolfhound dozes in the sun'.
- The poet humorously describes the gulls as 'window-shopping', suggesting that they flit from window to window, fluttering unhurriedly about the street.
- The Restaurant's owner, too, seems to be in an easy-going state of mind. He stands at the doorway of his establishment, whistling a 'little tune'.

The proprietor is looking out across the bay at the distant 'hills of Donegal'. Mahon uses hyperbole to capture the exquisite quality of the light that falls on these distant hills, declaring that it emenates from heaven itself.

The yachts in the bay have been moored all winter, but now one 'hoist a sail' and starts to move across the water. To the proprietor this 'first yacht' of the sailing season resembles an 'ideogram', a character from the Chinese system of writing. Mahon's skill for metaphor is on display here: we can imagine how the vessel's body, sail and mast might resemble different strokes that combine to create a single Chinese character.

The proprietor, we are told, stands 'at the door as if the world were young'. Mahon, in this memorable phrase, wonderfully captures how the spring sunshine lends the world a sense of beauty, possibility and newness. The proprietor seems fascinated by the landscape that lies before him, as if it and he had just come into being and he was perusing it for the very first time.

MAHON AND IRELAND

The poem hints at the conflict and division that has defined Irish history over the centuries:

- Tellingly, the poem names two separate locations: Portrush, which is in Northern Ireland, and Donegal, which is in the Republic of Ireland. It reminds us, therefore, that Ireland is a divided place.
- The mention of the Northern Counties Hotel also hints at this division, reminding us that the Northern counties belong to a separate state.
- The poet refers to the 'invasion' of tourists that will soon overrun Portrush. But this somewhat humorous description reminds us of the various actual invasions that Ireland has witnessed over the centuries.
- The mention of the 'wolfhound' too brings to mind Ireland's problematic history, as this particular animal has long been used as a symbol of Irish nationhood in art and literature.

The poem was written during the Troubles in Northern Ireland, a particularly brutal episode in Ireland's troubled history. The poet is keenly aware of the impact the Troubles have had on towns like Portrush. Portrush, he says, could have been 'Gentle', it could have been 'almost hospitable'. But the Troubles have made it a harsher, less welcoming place.

But in this beautiful, peaceful moment it seems to the poet that the conflicts of Irish history could be set aside. The wolfhound is 'old' and dozing 'in the sun', suggesting that Irish history is entering a less agressive and agitated phase. The town of Portrush is 'as it might have been' had the Troubles never occurred, gentle and pleasant in the first spring sunshine.

Mahon, on this afternoon when the world seems 'young', senses the possibility that the conflicts and narrow-mindedness of the past might finally be set aside in favour of a new beginning.

COMMUNITY AND ISOLATION

The poet presents himself as someone who both is and isn't a member of the Portrush community. Mahon left Co. Antrim in 1960, when he was 19 years old, and has returned on this occasion for only a brief visit. Does Mahon, therefore, think of himself as just another tourist? Or does his status as a returning native set him apart from those who will invade the town during the summer months?

The poet comes across as a detached observer, someone who is present in Portrush but not part of the community. We can imagine him enjoying his chow mein as he casts an amused, interested eye over the happenings in the street. Tellingly, he eats Chinese food and sits beneath a photograph of Hong Kong. It's as if even during this return visit, the poet is one foot in Northern Ireland and one foot somewhere else.

The restaurant proprietor, too, is presented as someone who both is and isn't a member of the local community. We sense that the proprietor as a business owner is very much a part of local life. But we also sense that as an immigrant, he doesn't quite fully belong (The photo on the restaurant wall suggests that he was born in Hong Kong and then moved to Northern Ireland, where he started this business).

This comes across in Mahon's depiction of him standing in the doorway of his restaurant, gazing out across the bay, whistling a 'little tune' from his homeland. The proprietor, Mahon imagines, experiences a moment of homesickness as he gazes out over the bay. The yacht, for a moment, reminds him of an 'ideogram', a character from the Chinese system of writing. He finds himself 'dreaming of home', thinking wistfully of Hong Kong, where he was raised. Both Mahon and the proprietor are people apart. In one regard, Co. Antrim can be considered their home. But in another important sense, both are very much outsiders.

FOCUS ON STYLE

Polished Forms

Mahon's flair for polished forms is again evident in this poem. The poem resembles a sonnet, in that it is divided into two distinct sections. The first section, which is twelve lines in length, describes the main street in Portrush. The second section, meanwhile, which is eight lines in length, focuses on the Chinese restaurant and its proprietor.

The poem doesn't have a formal rhyme scheme, but it is held together by a complex web of half-rhymes and internal rhymes. We see a half-rhyme, for example, between lines 14 and 16, where 'Hong King' rhymes with 'young'. We also see it between lines 17 and 19, where 'sail' rhymes with 'Donegal'. Internal rhyme, meanwhile, features in lines 11 and 12, where the phrases 'gulls go' and 'old wolfhound' echo one another.

Metaphor, Simile and Figures of Speech

For centuries, Ireland has been personified as a female figure in literature and poetry, often as an old lady in need of assistance, or as a young maid in need of rescue. It could be argued that Mahon engages in such personification here, presenting the girl who walks past the hotel as his vision of what Ireland is, or could become.

- The girl walks lightly, suggesting that Ireland, if it wished, could become a carefree place, unburdened by the conflicts of the past.
- She 'Strides' confidently along the street, suggesting the potential for Ireland, both North and South, to become a confident, outward-looking community.
- Tellingly, she carries a 'book-bag', suggesting the role education must play in resolving the conflicts of the past and creating a better future.

Rathlin

LINE BY LINE

The poet is on his way to visit Rathlin Island, travelling with some friends on a little boat powered by an 'outboard motor'. Rathlin is an island off the coast of County Antrim that is renowned for its rugged beauty. It is a bird sanctuary with a large population of puffins, shearwater, razorbills and other species. The island has about 150 permanent inhabitants and is visited by many tourists over the summer months.

As the poet journeys towards the island, he thinks about a terrible massacre that took place there in 1575, when over six hundred people – mostly women and children – were slaughtered in cold blood.

The victims of the massacre were the people of Somhairle Bui Mac Ghonnaill, a Gaelic chieftain who resisted English rule in Ireland. To protect the families of his warriors, he placed them in a fortified castle on the island, while he went off on a military campaign. However, English forces under the Earl of Essex stormed the island and laid siege to the castle. When the castle surrendered, Essex had all its inhabitants put to death.

The poet imagines the last victim of the massacre, most likely a woman or a child. He imagines how she cried out in terror as she was approached by a soldier. He imagines how her throat was cut before she could even finish screaming: 'A long time since the last scream cut short'.

Mahon imagines that the massacre was followed by an eerie, 'unnatural silence'; as if all the living things on the island were stunned into quietness by the terrible slaughter. He imagines that this unnatural silence was eventually replaced by a 'natural' one, in which the creatures of Rathlin could be heard again: 'the shearwater, by the sporadic/ Conversation of crickets'.

The poet imagines that the wind blowing around Rathlin served as 'a bleak reminder' of the atrocity, echoing the screams of those murdered by Essex's men. There's an element of personification in this description, with the wind portrayed as a ghostly or 'metaphysical' presence that has haunted the island for decade after decade.

The poet reaches the island

Mahon imagines that the island is uninhabited and has been so since the terrible events of 1575. He imagines that for 'Ages' since the massacre the only sounds on the island have been natural ones. He imagines that Rathlin has been lost in a kind of 'dream-time', a concept from Aboriginal Australia that suggests a period of time suspended outside the flow of normal history.

The poet imagines, then, that he and his friends are the first people to set foot on Rathlin since the massacre: 'As if we were the first visitors here'. He imagines that centuries of stillness have been broken by the 'report' or blast of their boat's outboard motor as they dock at the island's pier. The birds, he suggests, are 'amazed' at the sight of these visitors, as if they have never seen a human before. But the arrival of the poet and his friends signals that this 'dream-time' is at an end.

The poet on the island

The poet provides a memorable depiction of Rathlin's unique environment. The island's landscape is a rugged, mountainous one. Some of its peaks are so high that they are capped with ice. Its famous cliffs have sheer faces and high rocky summits: 'rock-face and cliff-top'. Spirals of 'sea-smoke', a type of mist created by cool, sea air, drift upward towards these icy peaks.

The poet clearly appreciates how the 'whole island' is a 'sanctuary' for birdlife. The verbs 'whistle and chatter' wonderfully capture the din of the island's bird population. The term 'Evacuating', meanwhile, suggests how whole flocks of gulls and gannets take flight as one from the surface upon which they have been perching.

The poet notices the lighthouse that sits on the west side of the island. The island's people are the 'custodians' or keepers of this important structure. The lighthouse emits a single beam, a 'lone light' that is cast out upon the seas below. It is a 'simple' but effective means of communication, one that sends a clear 'statement' of warning to passing ships.

As the poet looks towards the mainland, he can't help thinking about the Northern Irish Troubles, which were then in one of their bloodiest phases. He finds himself thinking about the 'Bombs' that have been planted in the housing estates of Belfast and other towns and cities: 'bombs doze in the housing estates'.

Leaving the island

Soon it is time for the poet and his friends to leave the island. The poet notes once more the island's tranquillity, declaring it to be a place of 'singular' or exceptional 'peace'. This extraordinary stillness, he says, is disturbed only by the sound of the birds and by the 'roar' of the boat's motor as he and his friend's set off from the pier.

As they depart, the poet finds himself thinking once again about the 'unspeakable violence' that took place on Rathlin in 1575. He remembers how Somhairle Bui, the rebellious chieftain, found himself trapped on the Antrim coast during the massacre amd was 'powerless' to intervene while the women and children of his tribe were put to the sword. Because Rathlin is only a few miles from the mainland, Somhairle Bui could clearly hear the terrified 'screams' of the victims as they were carried across the waters 'upon the wind'.

The trip back to the mainland takes place across 'turbulent sea'. The surfaces of the water are described as 'pitching', suggesting that they tilt and lurch. The poet finds himself 'Spray-blind' as foam from the ocean's surface flies into his eyes. The poet and his friends find themselves disorientated, 'Unsure' of which direction their boat is headed.

THEMES

NATURE

This is one of many poems where Mahon reveals his keen eye for the natural world. He appreciates Rathlin as a place of 'singular' serenity and beauty. He relishes its rugged landscape, its rare and exotic birdlife and the stunning views across the ocean, with their hazy blend of sea and sky. Mahon also captures the great variety of noises made by the island's wildlife: the chirping of the crickets, the 'cry' of the shearwater, the 'whistle and chatter' of the other species of bird that inhabit it.

Yet the poem's final lines suggest nature's darker side. There is a sense of threat and uncertainty as the poet and his friends leave the island, blinded by spray and tossed about on the 'pitching surfaces' of the 'turbulent sea'. We are reminded that nature is not only beautiful but can also be a deadly and menacing force. In this sense, Rathlin recalls 'Day Trip to Donegal', 'After the Titanic' and 'Antarctica'.

REMEMBERING HISTORY'S VICTIMS

This is one of the many poems where Mahon reveals a deep compassion with those who have suffered throughout history. The poet is keenly aware of the 'unspeakable violence' that was visited upon Somhairle's people in 1575. He remembers the terror of the last victim, whose scream was brutally cut short. He also registers the rage and horror that must have afflicted Somhairle as he listened to the women and children of his tribe being slaughtered.

FOCUS ON STYLE

Polished Forms
Rathlin again highlights Mahon's careful crafting of polished forms. In 'Rathlin', each line rhymes with another line in the same stanza. Mahon makes extensive use of half-rhyme throughout the poem: 'chatter' with 'freighter', 'shearwater' with 'motor', 'cap' with 'top', and 'mainland' with 'wind'.

The parallels between the first and third stanzas lend the poem a certain symmetry. Both stanzas begin with the phrase 'A long time since'. Both refer to the screaming that occurred during the massacre of 1575. Both describe the sounds of the shearwater, of the wind and of the boat's motor disturbing the peace of the island's tranquillity.

Sensual Imagery
Mahon's gift for sensual imagery, especially imagery associated with seas and coastlines, is evident in his depiction of Rathlin as a mystical, dream-time island. The fact that everything is blurred by 'sea smoke' and 'oceanic haze' lends the place a dream-like atmosphere. Even the occasional passing freighters, he says, are drowsy, or 'somnolent'.

Verbal Music
Mahon uses assonance and alliteration to reinforce the island's dream-like atmosphere. The repeated 's' sound in phrases like 'Cerulean distance', 'oceanic haze' and 'seasmoke' generate a pleasant, lulling music. Assonance creates a similar effect: the repeated broad vowel sounds in lines 13 to 16 slows the pace of the verse, contributing to this laidback, lazy mood.

There are also several instances of onomatopoeia in this poem. In the phrase 'whistle and chatter', we can almost hear the shrill noise of the birds as they take flight from the rocks and cliffs where they have been perching. In the phrase 'sporadic/ Conversation of crickets', with its repeated hard consonants, we can almost hear the sound of the crickets chirping.

Word Choice
Mahon is well known for his precise and deliberate choice of individual words. We see this when he describes the birds on Rathlin as 'Oneiric', which means dream-like. This suggests the exotic nature of certain species that inhabit the island: they are so startling in appearance that they might have stepped out of a dream. But it also reinforces our sense of Rathlin as a 'dream-time' island, a place that somehow exists outside of normal space and time.

Such care is also evident in his choice of the beautiful adjective 'cerulean' – meaning a deep or azure blue – which applies to both the ocean and the sky, the two blending together in a haze on the faraway horizon: 'cerulean distance, an oceanic haze'.

Mahon's precision is also evident when he uses the verb 'doze' to describe the bombs that were at that time a feature of Irish life: 'bombs doze in the housing estates'. An inactive bomb might be thought of as being asleep. A bomb that is set to explode might be thought of as half-asleep or dozing. But it will awake for the briefest of moments, reeking carnage and

MAHON AND IRELAND
'Rathlin' presents Irish history as a seemingly endless series of struggles between England and Ireland, between Protestant and Catholic, one in which the 'unspeakable violence' of 1575 leads to the 'bombs [that] doze in the housing estates' of the 1970s and 1980s.

The poet, however, suggests that Rathlin is 'through with history'. He views it as a place where nothing ever changes, where history has stopped. The island, as the poet imagines it, is lost in a 'dream-time', a mystical period somehow outside the normal flow of time.

The island, then, is presented not only as a bird 'sanctuary' but also as a sanctuary from history itself. It is a place of 'singular peace', one where the conflict and violence of Irish history no longer occur.

The poem, therefore, sets up a contrast between two very different realities. On the one hand, we have the mainland, which represents hatred and conflict. On the other hand, we have the island, which represents peace and tranquillity.

The poet's return journey, therefore, takes on a metaphorical aspect. The boat's occupants are left blinded and disorientated by the 'turbulent sea' over which they travel. The Irish people, similarly, are left befuddled by the competing narratives of history.

The boat's occupants – blinded by spray, tossed around on 'pitching surfaces' – are 'unsure' which direction they are facing. The Irish people, similarly, are uncertain about what kind of future the are heading for. Will it be a future of 'singular peace' represented by Rathlin? Or will it be a future of hatred and conflict represented by the mainland?

THIS IS POETRY — DEREK MAHON

Antarctica

Scott and his party at the South Pole. Captain Oates is on the far left.

LINE BY LINE

In late 1912, the British Naval Officer Robert Falcon Scott led an expedition that aimed to be the first ever to reach the South Pole. Scott and his party, including Captain Laurence Oates, reached the Pole on 18 January 1913, only to discover that the Norwegian explorer Roald Amundsen had beaten them to their destination.

Scott and his men suffered a horrendous journey back across the frozen wasteland. The conditions were much worse than they had anticipated and they found themselves hindered by blizzards, bad luck, starvation and ill-health.

On the 16 of March, Oates, who was suffering from severe frostbite, walked out of his tent and into a snowstorm, sacrificing himself so that his companions might have a better chance of survival. Oates's efforts proved in vain, however, as Scott and the remaining members of the team perished a few days later. Oates's final words, 'I am just going outside and may be some time', were recorded in Scott's diary, which was late recovered from the Antarctic.

Oates's Self-Sacrifice

The poem opens with Oates and his companions reading in their tent as a storm rages outside. Oates delivers his famous last words and prepares to walk out into certain death: 'I am just going outside and may be some time'. His companions simply 'nod' and keep on reading, as if nothing untoward were taking place, as if Oates is only stepping out momentarily and will be back in no time at all. Mahon, in a wonderful phrase, describes how the others pretend 'not to know' what is going on. They are fully aware of the sacrifice Oates is about to make. But they do not acknowledge it, to Oates, to each other or even to themselves.

Mahon masterfully describes Oates's terrible final walk:

- Oates experiences a terrible combination of heavy snowfall and a violent wind. We can imagine how the wind hurls falling snow against his face and body, 'howling' terribly as it does so.
- Oates, we're told, is 'goading' or driving himself forward and upward. We sense that he is fighting the urge to turn back. We sense that he is eager to reach the point of no return, where turning back will cease to be a realistic option.
- Mahon uses a typically wonderful metaphor, comparing Oates to a 'ghost'. This suggests how the expedition's hardships have left him emaciated and mentally drained. He is at the point of death, practically a ghost already.
- He 'begins to climb' up some Antarctic ridge or hill, knowing that the higher he goes the less oxygen there will be and the quicker death will come.
- Gradually, the sanctuary of the tent 'recedes', becoming more and more distant.
- Then the numbness of hypothermia begins to take hold and Oates can no longer feel anything, not even the agony of his frostbitten feet.
- He experiences 'vertigo', a sense of spinning and dizziness. Then he lapses into unconsciousness.

The Ridiculous and the Sublime

For decades, the story of Oates's sacrifice was taught to generations of British schoolboys. Mahon, no doubt, would have heard the tale at 'Inst', the famous secondary school in Belfast that he attended. Scott and his team were presented as intrepid but tragic explorers, bravely venturing where no other human being had ever thread. Oates, in particular, was presented as the last word in heroism.

Over time, however, people began to question the legend of Captain Oates. They began to see something 'ridiculous', something macho and egotistical, about the race to the South Pole. Why would anyone, after all, risk their lives to plant their country's flag in a desolate corner of the earth that had no strategic or scientific value? They began to see something 'ridiculous', too, in the failure of the expedition, regarding Scott and his team as arrogant bunglers, whose failure to prepare and communicate properly led to their demise.

Mahon accepts that there is something ridiculous about the race to the Antarctic and the failure of Scott's expedition. Oates's sacrifice, however, represents something 'sublime' at the heart of this ridiculous situation. It is 'sublime' in the sense that it involves a gesture of extraordinary beauty, one that defies easy description.

The explorers' grim situation is compared to a pitch-black night in which no stars 'glimmer'. Oates's sublime self-sacrifice is compared to a 'glow', a faint but unmistakable light within this darkness.

Indeed, Mahon suggests that Oates, through his 'numb self-sacrifice', transforms this situation entirely. Just as in chemistry, an enzyme transforms one substance into another, so Oates's sacrifice transforms Scott's 'ridiculous' failure into a narrative of selfless generosity, a potential source of inspiration for us all.

Mahon is especially impressed by the silent and stoic manner with which Oates goes about leaving the tent. He knows it is 'time to go', that he has become a liability, and he 'takes [his] leave ... Quietly'. He doesn't make any demands or accusations. He doesn't make any speeches advertising his own heroism. Instead, he slips away with as little fuss as possible.

Oates's death fits with Mahon's philosophy of life. Human beings, according to Mahon, shouldn't take life too seriously, as human existence is an earthly 'pantomime', a somewhat 'ridiculous' performance in which each of us participates. We must recognise when it is time to go, when our lives have come to their natural end. And when that hour arrives, we must take our 'leave' casually, almost light-heartedly, realising that human

THEMES

REMEMBERING HISTORY'S VICTIMS

In much of his work, Mahon attempts to speak out on behalf of history's forgotten victims. In 'Antarctica', however, he speaks on behalf of someone who who has been re-evaluated rather than forgotten. For decades, as we've seen, Oates was regarded as a heroic figure. Then he came to be regarded as a somewhat 'ridiculous' one. Mahon's poem, however, invites us to focus once more on the 'sublime' nature of Oates's self-sacrifice.

COMMUNITY AND ISOLATION

'Antarctica', like many of Mahon's poems, focuses on the obligations that come with being a member of a community, in this case, the doomed community of Scott's expedition. Mahon wonders if there was something criminal about Oates's self-sacrifice: 'Need we consider it some sort of crime[?]' Did Oates' commit some sort of crime by walking suicidally into the snowstorm? Did his companions commit some sort of crime by letting him go?

Mahon, however, rejects the idea that their behaviour was criminal or immoral, simply declaring 'No'. Both Oates and his companions were responding to the demands placed on them by their small community. Everyone in the tent knew the severity of the situation. Everyone knew that Oates was the 'weakest' and a liability to the team as a whole. Everyone knew that his 'numb self-sacrifice' was necessary in order to give the others a greater chance at survival.

Many of Mahon's poems depict individuals in an extreme state of isolation. But Oates, during his final walk, is surely the most isolated of them all: the tent receding behind him, the nearest civilisation hundreds of miles away, the icy landscape stretching out in every direction around him.

FOCUS ON STYLE

Mahon's skilful use of form is on display in 'Antarctica'. He uses a form called 'villanelle', which revolves around two repeating lines. The repetition might suggest the poet's own efforts to come to terms with Oates's sacrifice, the questions about his death going round and round his head. This repetition also suggests Oates's swirling, repetitive thoughts during his final journey. It also, perhaps, suggests the repetitive sounds of the howling winds.

The poem features a powerful instance of onomatopoeia in line 5: 'Goading his ghost into the howling snow'. We can almost hear in the repeated 'o' sounds the ferocious blowing of the storm.

THIS IS POETRY | DEREK MAHON

Kinsale

LINE BY LINE

Mahon is in the harbour town of Kinsale, Co. Cork, a place where he would later live for many years. It has been raining constantly for days, maybe even weeks. He describes how rain has been falling on the spires of the churches in and around Kinsale and on the bogs in the town's hinterland that stretches in the direction of the Bandon river.

- Mahon describes the rain as 'dark', which suggests rainfall so dense and unrelenting that it obscures the landscape.
- He describes the rain as 'deep-delving'. It has been raining so heavily that rainwater has soaked the surface of the earth and seeped deep beneath the soil.
- Mahon personifies the rain, describing it as 'deliberate'. We get the impression that the rain has been intentionally oppressing the people of Kinsale and the surrounding areas and is doing so in a planned and careful manner.
- The term 'browsing' adds to this personification. There is something vaguely sinister about the manner in which the rain caressed the landscape, as if it were searching for something or someone.

Now the rain has finally stopped and the sun has come out. A fresh, sea-breeze blows through the town. The poet walks around the town and takes in the suddenly altered landscape:

- Rainwater is evaporating from the roof-slates of the various buildings around the town, rising in the form of steam: 'our ... slates are steaming in the sun'.
- The wet slates reflect the clear skies above, giving them a 'sky-blue' appearance.
- He passes the yachts moored in the harbour, noting how the breeze causes them to sway and bob.
- The yachts produce a pleasant bell-like sound, as the breeze causes the ropes to clatter against their masks.

The poet notes how the town's windows shine as they reflect the sunlight: 'We contemplate at last/ shining windows'. The word 'contemplate' gives us a sense that the poet pauses and relishes the sight of these 'shining windows'. The phrase 'at last' suggests his relief to see and feel the sun again after such an extended period of rainfall.

FOCUS ON STYLE

Verbal music

In lines 1 to 3, assonance and alliteration are used to create a sombre and melancholy effect. Alliteration occurs through the repetition of the 'd' sound in 'deep-delving, dark, deliberate'. This slows down our reading of the line, creating a solemn effect. The repeated long broad-vowel sounds in these three lines slows the pace of the verse, creating a sad musicality.

A happier and more upbeat musical effect is created in lines 4 to 6. Alliteration is again used in line 4, the repeated sibilant 's' sound creating a pleasant musical effect. It also quickens the pace of the line, allowing our tongues to slip from one word to the next.

We see assonance in line 5 where the repeated broad-vowel sounds create a pleasant or euphonious musical effect: 'our yachts tinkling and dancing in the bay/ like racehorses'. The assonance in the phrase 'shining windows' also contributes to the overall musical effect with its repeated 'i' sound.

Metaphor, Simile and Figures of Speech

The simile in line 6, which compares the yachts to dancing racehorses, may seem outlandish, but is strangely fitting. Yachts and racehorses are generally associated with speed, freedom and travel. The fact the yachts are depicted as 'dancing' further suggests their grace and power.

Yachts and racehorses are, of course, high-class, luxury items. By mentioning them, Mahon's signals the newfound wealth Ireland was just beginning to experience after decades of poverty. But they also hint at problems of privilege and inequality that come with such wealth.

Sensual Imagery

The poem wonderfully captures the glittering freshness that the Irish landscape can exhibit after a long spell of rain. We get a sense of the poet's exhileration at being outdoors after a long period of being cooped up inside. He dares to think, as many of us do in such moments, that such heavy, oppressive rain is a thing of the past, that this newfound brightness will be with us for a long time to come.

THEMES

MAHON AND IRELAND

Mahon associates the 'dark' rain that has been falling with Ireland's troubled recent past:

- Mahon, no doubt, has in mind the oppressive role religion played in restricting people's liberty.
- He has in mind the economic problems that beleagured Ireland for many decades.
- He also has in mind the seemingly endless conflict between Ireland and England, Catholic and Protestant, that caused so much suffering over decades and centuries. In 1601, we remember, the town of Kinsale was the site of a major battle in that ongoing conflict.

The 'shining windows', meanwhile, are associated with the better, brighter future Mahon imagines for the country. Mahon, in this moment after the rain stops falling, permits himself to be optimistic. He imagines a future in which the problems mentioned above are resolved or become less severe. He imagines a future in which no Irish person will be forbidden from flourishing and realising their potential.

Paula Meehan Themes

The Strength and Power of Women

Many of Meehan's poems feature strong female characters, women who, though their lives are hard, find the strength to persevere and endure. Her poems offer us a vivid insight into what life was like for many women living in Dublin's inner city in the 50s and 60s.

The poet's own mother had to work hard all her life to maintain the household and look after the family. Meehan describes her mother's life in 'The Pattern'. Nearly all the poet's memories of her mother involve work of some kind. Meehan describes how on one occasion her mother 'must have stayed up half the night' to finish mending a dress for her to wear to school the next day. Even her leisure activity, knitting, is work of a kind: we can imagine her knitting hats, gloves and other useful items. In 'Hearth Lessons', the mother is presented as quite a formidable woman. Each week she must manage the little money that the father earns and ensure that the family survives.

The women in the poet's childhood neighbourhood were often the primary breadwinners in their respective households, bringing home a wage that kept utter poverty and despair at bay. Their jobs often involved doing difficult, repetitive work. In 'The Exact Moment I Became a Poet', Meehan describes a local sewing factory where many of her classmates' mothers, aunts and sisters worked. She recalls how one of her primary school teachers warned the class to behave themselves or they might 'end up' working in such a sewing factory.

The young poet was deeply upset by how her teacher presented the sewing factory as a worthless and undesirable place of employment. Meehan appreciated the drudgery of such work, but even at a young age she recognised that the women working in the sewing factory retained a certain dignity and pride despite their circumstances. She realised that the women of the factory took great pride in what they did, in producing garments that were well made and hard-wearing. Miss Shannon's words, she realised, 'robbed' the women of this 'dignity', making their 'labour' seem utterly menial and pointless.

This ability to take pride in the work that had to be done was also evident in the poet's mother. In 'The Pattern', Meehan describes how her mother would polish the floor of the family flat in a methodical manner, ensuring that it gleamed and shone when she was done. In 'Buying Winkles', meanwhile, we see how the lady selling the winkles takes great pride in what she is selling, telling the young poet to tell her mother that she 'picked them fresh this morning'. She also remains good-humoured, patiently telling the young poet how to remove the winkle from the shell, despite the fact that she would have told the young girl how to do this on numerous other occasions. This woman, we must remember, would have been up early in the morning to collect the winkles that she now sells on the streets in the cold of the evening.

'Cora, Auntie' is another poem that offers us a portrait of a woman who possessed great strength and spirit. The poet's aunt Cora is presented as a flamboyant and fearless individual, someone who lived life on her own terms. The opening lines of the poem present us a with memorable image of the aunt facing death down like a gunslinger in a Western movie. But instead of being armed with pistols, the aunt faces death with 'a bottle of morphine in one hand/ and a bottle of Jameson in the other'. The startling addition of the red sequins to the wedding dress tells us something about the aunt's personality. We get a sense of someone who liked to do things differently, to bring her own unique style to situations and occasions. The fact that the poet kept these sequins over the years tells us just how powerful a presence this glamorous woman was in her life.

Poverty and Hardship

Meehan's poems give us an insight into the poverty and hardship that were common in Ireland when the poet was a child. 'Buying Winkles' suggests that money was very tight in the poet's family. The mother would 'spare' the poet sixpence, suggesting that each week they were just getting by, living hand to mouth. The condition of the tenement block in which the young poet lived also hints at this hardship. We get the impression that the building was not well maintained and that the bulb on the stairs had been blown for a considerable amount of time. The description of the men 'heading out for the night' suggests, perhaps, how many of the men in the locality would regularly go and drink in bars as a means of escape from the hardship that they had to endure.

'The Pattern' highlights the fact that there were few options available to people to improve their lot in life. This was especially true when it came to women. The poet's mother was born into the Ireland of the 1930s. The country was extremely poor. It was also a narrow and closed-minded place. There were extremely limited opportunities for education and advancement. This was especially so for the working class into which the mother was born.

'Hearth Lesson', meanwhile, highlights the toxic effects that poverty can have on a relationship. For the poet, even as a child, understood that poverty caused the constant strife between her parents: 'Even then I can tell it was money/ the lack of it day after day,/ at the root of the bitter words'. The constant lack of money made both of her parents tense, irritable and frustrated. It led to unceasing tensions between them, to blazing rows and 'brooding' periods of silence. The father's wages, it is made clear, were never quite enough to cover the family's expenses. The mother, we sense, had to scrimp and save as she managed the household budget. There was always the pressure of unpaid bills, of upcoming expenses that needed to be covered from the household's meagre resources.

Family

'The Pattern' is a moving exploration of the relationships between mothers and their eldest daughters. Such relationships, Meehan suggests, all too often turn sour: 'Some say that's the fate of the eldest daughter'. We get the impression that much of the tension between Meehan and her mother arose because of the great differences between them. The poet, we sense, is someone given to introspection, to reflecting on her own life, to contemplating her own thoughts and emotions. She is prone to looking into the mirror, searching for a 'glimmer of her true self'. The mother, on the other hand, is not given to such introspection. She spent little time, the poet imagines, contemplating her own face when she saw it reflected in the floor's polished surface. She simply shrugged and moved on with her work.

'My Father Perceived as a Vision of St. Francis', meanwhile, emphasises how even close family members can sometimes be a mystery to us. Sometimes, family members keep things hidden from one another. We see this when the poet declares that the box room contained 'secrets'. There were items hidden about the room, she sensed, that her brother didn't want her to discover. Sometimes, family members simply stay quiet about aspects of their lives. The poet's father, for instance, had never told her that he feeds the birds each morning. Sometimes, we don't notice certain things about family members, even ones that we see regularly. The poet, for instance, had never noticed how age was catching up with her father: 'He was older than I had reckoned'. It was only on this particular morning that she noticed 'for the first time' how his shoulder was stooped and that his leg was stiff.

And yet, 'The Pattern' suggests, we are often more alike our parents than we might like to admit or acknowledge. In this poem, we can detect some of the mother's meticulousness in how the young poet explores the city, getting to know it section by section. The mother, meanwhile, exhibits something of the daughter's introspection when she's photographed in the Phoenix Park. The poet wishes that she had a chance to explore these similarities. She wishes her mother had lived on until the poet herself had matured: 'I wish now she'd lasted until after/ I'd grown up'. They would have been two independent women, neither reliant on the other. They would have been unburdened of family commitments: 'without tags like mother, wife,/ sister, daughter'. They could have got to know each other afresh, first as acquaintances and then, perhaps, as friends: 'We might have made a new start'. The poem's great tragedy, then, is that the mother passed away before such a new start could be made.

'Prayer for the Children of Longing' highlights the suffering and agony that families endure when they lose a child. The poet mentions the terrible moment when the police come to knock on the door to inform the parents that their child has died. Such loss is felt most acutely at Christmas time. The description of the spirits of the dead children singing reminds us of the innocence of the child and how at this time of year the young should be singing carols and enjoying the magic of Christmas.

Meehan's poetry also captures the joy, love and support that families provide. In 'Cora, Auntie', for example, the poet remembers the women that played important roles in her childhood – her mother, grandmother and aunts. Meehan compares these women to 'stars' whose light is only now reaching her. It is as if only now as an adult she can fully appreciate their strength and character: 'Cora, Marie, Jacinta, my aunties,/ Helena, my mother, Mary, my grandmother-/ the light of those stars// only reaching me now'. The poem also highlights how powerful the love between family members can be. Meehan describes how it was 'love unconditional' that kept her aunt Cora alive towards the end.

Nature and Spirituality

In Meehan's poetry, the natural world is presented almost as a single organism, as if all its animal and plant life combine to form a unitary life-force or intelligence. Meehan developed this understanding of the natural world when she lived in California during the 1960s. She was influenced by Buddhism and Eastern philosophy, by the hippie movement and by American poets such as Gary Snyder who combined mysticism and environmentalism.

There are moments when Meehan suggests that the natural world is worthy of veneration, that we might pray to nature just as religious people pray to God. In 'Prayer for the Children of Longing', Meehan appeals directly to the great fir tree that has been erected in the middle of Dublin city. She imagines the landscape of the tree's native land. The poet associates this natural landscape with 'clarity', tranquillity and 'silence'. She prays that the tree might somehow bring these conditions to bear on these urban streets, to grant the people of Dublin's north inner city a chance to heal.

In 'The Statue of the Virgin', the statue adopts a very spiritual view of nature, regarding the earth as a divine being. The earth, however, is very different from the God of the Catholic faith. First, it is female rather than male. Second, it wants people to express rather than repress their sexual desire. The earth, according to the statue, calls on human beings to be fertile too, to engage in 'coupling' or sexual activity: 'when the earth herself calls out for coupling'.

The sun, too, is presented as a kind of goddess, one that the statue venerates or worships. The sun is described as our 'centre', reflecting the fact that our whole lives, in a sense, are spent orbiting the sun. The earth, meanwhile, is compared to a dancer that traces a circle, over and over again, around the sun's central point. The sun is described as our 'molten mother'. The term 'molten', of course, reinforces our sense of the sun's incomprehensible heat, causing us to envision a sphere of churning lava. The description of the sun as our 'mother' also reminds us that we depend on the sun's heat and light for our very survival.

There are also moments, Meehan suggests, when it is possible for human beings to commune with nature, to attain an almost mystical oneness with the natural world. Such communion in Meehan's poetry is presented as a source of healing and renewal. In 'Death of a Field', the poet laments the fact that a local field is set to be destroyed in order that a housing estate can be built. The poet highlights the great loss of flora and wildlife that will result. She suggests that we undervalue and under-appreciate the importance of the field and the rich life it contains. At the poem's conclusion, she imagines walking out into the field at night in order to connect with the field. The poet describes how she longs to establish an intimate, spiritual connection with the field, imagining how it might wrap or coat her in its silky dew.

This is how he appeared to her for a single sunlit moment in an ordinary 'Finglas garden'. This vision, no doubt, was partly caused by the fact the poet had just woken up and had been jerked out of a dream by the sound of the horse next door. But Meehan's visionary spiritual experience, in this instance, is prompted, not by conventional religion but by nature itself. The poet, we sense, was overwhelmed by the beauty of the scene in the yard before her, by the sight of the father suddenly struck by sunlight as he was surrounded by a 'pandemonium' of birds. The poem, then, is typical of Meehan's work, in that spirituality and nature are closely linked.

Social Justice

Meehan is a poet with an acute sense of social justice. Even as a primary school student, she was keenly aware of social inequality. In 'The Exact Moment I Became a Poet', she describes how she realised early on that people in her part of inner city Dublin were denied the opportunities granted to those from more privileged parts of the city. And this lack of opportunity, of course, was passed down from one generation to the next. In this poem, society is compared to a nightmarish factory where generation after generation of 'mothers, aunts and neighbours' from inner city Dublin are processed. The image of these women being 'trussed up' suggests how they were constrained by lack of opportunity. The image of them being mutilated by a giant sewing machine suggests how their underprivileged lives left them mentally and physically damaged.

'Prayer for the Children of Longing', meanwhile, outlines what any healthy, functioning society should offer and provide to its young. It should provide security, sheltering them from drugs and violence. It should provide them with a secure and healthy space in which to grow and develop. It should inspire them and nurture and develop their dreams and aspirations. Society should be blowing the young people's minds with exciting possibilities. The streets of Dublin's north inner city should have been able to promise them all these things and then deliver on these promises. But society has failed these children.

'The Statue of the Virgin' is yet another poem that highlights Meehan's acute sense of social justice. We see her once again giving voice to the voiceless. In this instance, she invites, or we might say forces, the reader to remember the story of Ann Lovett in all its grim sorrow. The poem draws a stark contrast between and Ann and the society of which she was a part. The rest of the town was 'tucked up' safe and warm, while Ann, alone in the cold of a January night, suffered the agony of childbirth. The image of the towns being 'tucked up' in scandals, bargains, prayers and promises is a powerful one. It suggests that such concerns envelop their minds just as sheets and blankets envelop their bodies when they go to bed at night.

These lines remind us that the people of the town failed Ann as her pregnancy wore on. No one noticed that things weren't quite right with her. There was no one Ann felt she could turn to, no older member of society with whom she could share her 'secret'. The people of the town were too wrapped up in their own affairs – in 'bargains' and business dealings, in their hopes and 'prayers', 'promises' they had to keep or get out of.

In 'Them Ducks Died for Ireland', Meehan urges us to 'salute' not only the great heroes but also those in the background of history's great events. She reminds us that those ordinary workers also made great sacrifices and displayed great courage. Such a 'salute', of course, could take many forms. It could be an exhibition or a school project, or a poem of remembrance like this one.

Buying Winkles

Gardiner Street in winter

LINE BY LINE

This poem relates to a period when the young poet and her family lived in a flat on Gardiner Street in Dublin city centre. On certain, special occasions the poet's mother would give her a 'tanner' or sixpence coin to go and buy a bag of winkles. The poet says that her mother would 'spare' her this sum of money, suggesting that it was something she could barely afford to give. The young poet would then dash excitedly out of the flat. As she would leave, her mother would warn her to be careful and not to talk to any strange men along the way.

The poet would descend the stairs of the apartment complex. She recalls how the light bulb in the stairwell had 'blown' and never been fixed. The young poet found this dark space scary, and would imagine that it was haunted. She would descend the stairs as quickly as she could to avoid the ghosts she imagined lurking here: 'I'd dash from the ghosts/ on the stairs where the bulb had blown'. When she finally emerged from the dark stairwell onto Gardiner Street, she would feel great 'relief' to be out in the open.

Winkles, also known as periwinkles, are small, edible shellfish. They are common to Irish shores and can often be found attached to rocks at low tide. They are easy to gather by hand and were commonly sold in paper bags or in newspaper wrapping.

The young poet would be happy if it was a clear evening. On such occasions she would be able to gaze up at the 'strip of sky' visible between the rows of 'tall houses' that lined the street. When the sky was clear she might be able to see some stars. On some rare occasions the moon would be visible in this strip of the sky. When this happened it made the occasion all the more special: 'A bonus if the moon was in the strip of sky'.

But even if the weather was not good and it was raining, the poet was still 'happy'. She loved the way the winkles would look when they were wet from rain. The shells would take on a rich, dark blue colour and 'glisten'. To the poet these shells were 'like little/ night skies themselves'.

The Winkle Seller

The young poet would buy the winkles from a woman outside the Rosebowl bar. This woman would have gone out early in the morning to gather winkles from rocks at low tide along the shores of Dublin Bay. She would then bring the winkles into the city and set herself up in this familiar spot where locals and passersby could purchase these delicious delicacies.

- The poet vividly recalls the manner in which this woman would be set up:
- She would be sitting on an 'orange crate', a timber box used for transporting fruit.
- She would have buckets or 'pails' full of winkles that she had picked from the rocks that morning.
- These pails were kept inside a pram, which was a convenient way to transport and hold the heavy load.
- She would use newspaper to wrap the winkles. She would twist the paper at the end to create a cone shape that would securely hold a large quantity of winkles.

As the young poet waited to buy the winkles she would glimpse into the Rosebowl Bar every time the door swung open. She seems to have been intrigued by the place:

- She recalls the way the light was reflected in the 'golden mirrors' that adorned the walls.
- She recalls the distinctive odours that would emanate from the bar, wafting out to where she stood on the street. The poet recalls the particular musk of the men gathered inside mixed with the odour of alcohol.
- Meehan also recalls the warmth of the place. We can imagine how snug and cosy this place seemed on a cold winter's evening.

The poet describes how she 'envied each soul in the hot interior'. We can imagine how the activity and the atmosphere might have appealed to the young poet. Here was a space where people could relax and be at ease, enjoying jokes and banter. Perhaps, considering the tensions that sometimes existed at home, this place struck the poet as an ideal escape from strife that sometimes defined family life.

As she was purchasing the winkles, the young poet would ask the woman to demonstrate the exact way to extract the winkle from its shell. The woman would happily go through the steps with the young girl:

- She would take a long pin which was used to fasten her shawl.
- She would then use this pin to remove the small disc covering the entrance to the shell, which protected the winkle inside. This disc is compared to an 'eyelid', something the winkle can close to seal itself off from the world outside.
- When this barrier was removed, the woman would gently press the pin into the winkle, causing it to tighten and 'grip' the pin.
- This would enable the woman to 'slither' or extract the winkle from the shell.

The young poet would request this demonstration each time she purchased winkles. We get the impression that she knew very well how to do this, but she would ask the woman to show her again because she knew that if she did, she would get to eat the extracted winkle. And it was this 'extra winkle', the poet says, that always tasted the 'sweetest'. Tasting the winkle was like tasting or experiencing the sea: 'The sweetest extra winkle/ that brought the sea to me'.

Heading back home

When the demonstration was finished, the woman would wrap the winkles in sheets of newspaper. She would place a quantity of winkles onto a sheet of paper and then twist the paper at both ends, creating a secure pouch or package that the customer could carry home. When these packages were ready, the young poet would race home proudly.

The poet uses a memorable metaphor to describe the bulging packages of winkles she would carry home, comparing them to 'torches'. We can imagine how the newspaper was twisted in such a way that when it was filled or loaded with winkles, it took on the appearance of a torch. The glistening winkles would be like the flame that would burn at the head of the torch.

The comparison conveys how, to the young poet, these winkles possessed some special, magical quality. It was like as if the packages of winkles were torches that would aid the young girl on her journey back home through the dark and perilous streets. The comparison also suggests the immense pride that the young poet experienced as she made her way home bearing these very special packages.

FOCUS ON STYLE

Metaphor, Simile and Figures of Speech

The poet uses a wonderful simile to describe the manner in which the winkles' dark shells would take on a deep blue colour when wet, comparing them to 'little/ night skies'. She also uses a memorable simile to describe the appearance of the packages of winkles that she would carry home, comparing them to 'torches'.

Playful Language

'Buying Winkles' wonderfully captures the young poet's excitement at being given this very special task. Meehan captures the thrill that she felt as she raced out of the flat, down the dark stairs and out on to the street where she weaved a 'glad path' through the men heading out to the pub that evening.

Vivid Imagery

The poem offers us a wonderful snapshot of life in inner city Dublin in the 1950s. The poet mentions specific places such as Gardiner Street, where her flat was located, and the Rosebowl Bar. We get a sense of life in this part of the city during the evening, with the women in the poet's neighbourhood relaxing at the doors to their buildings and leaning out of upstairs windows.

The men would be heading out to the local bars. The image of the woman selling the winkles is especially memorable. We can picture the cart upon which she sat and the pram that was used to transport and hold the buckets of winkles. Meehan also captures something of the dialogue of inner city Dublin, remembering how the woman would give her a message for her mother: 'Tell yer Ma I picked them fresh this morning'.

THEMES

THE STRENGTH AND POWER OF WOMEN

In many of Meehan's poems we encounter strong female characters, women who, though their lives are hard, find the strength to persevere and endure. The woman selling the winkles on the streets of Dublin is someone who has been up early in the morning gathering the winkles along the shore. It is now evening – and a cold evening at that – and she sits on the footpath in the city, selling the winkles she has gathered.

Although her life is very difficult, she takes pride in what she is selling, telling the young poet to tell her mother that she 'picked them fresh this morning'. She also remains good-humoured, patiently telling the young poet how to remove the winkle from the shell, despite the fact that she would have told the young girl how to do this on numerous other occasions.

The poem also gives us the impression that there is strong community of women in the area that support each other and look out for one another. As the young poet passes along the streets on her way to buy the winkles she waves 'up to women at sills or those/ lingering in doorways'.

CHILDHOOD

The poem wonderfully captures the simple pleasures of childhood. We get a sense of how magical something as simple as a bag of winkles can be to a young child. Such simple pleasures are also evident in the delight the young poet takes in seeing the moon or stars visible between the rows of houses.

The poem also illustrates just how exciting the world can appear to children. The young poet races down the stairs of her tenement building, imagining that ghosts dwell in the dark stairwell. She seems to relish being out at this late hour, waving to the women standing in doorways or leaning out the windows of their flats. As the young poet makes her way down the street, she jumps 'every crack in the pavement', superstitiously believing that threading on these cracks will bring her bad luck. The young poet's return journey home is particularly magical. She proudly carries the packages of winkles home as if they contained the most wonderful riches.

POVERTY AND HARDSHIP

The poem gives us an insight into the lives of hardship and poverty that were common in Ireland when the poet was a child. The poem's opening line suggests that money was very tight in the poet's family. The mother would 'spare' the poet sixpence, suggesting that each week they were just getting by, living hand to mouth.

The condition of the tenement block in which the young poet lived also hints at this hardship. We get the impression that the building was not well maintained and that the bulb on the stairs had been blown for a considerable amount of time. The fact that the poet mentions how she would envy 'each soul in the hot interior' of the bar also suggests that she was not dressed well for the cold and, perhaps, also that her own flat might not have been that warm.

The description of the men 'heading out for the night' suggests, perhaps, how many of the men in the locality would regularly go and drink in bars as a means of escape from the hardship that they had to endure. As we mentioned above, the young poet seems to have been intrigued by the glimpses of these men drinking in the bar, envying the cosy scene she witnessed.

THIS IS POETRY — PAULA MEEHAN
The Pattern

LINE BY LINE

This poem describes the poet's complicated relationship with her mother, Helena, who was born in Dublin in 1933. In 1968, the Meehan family moved to Finglas from Dublin's inner city. There Meehan attended St Michael's Girls' Secondary School. During these years Meehan's relationship with her mother became very difficult. Though they lived in the same house, they grew 'bitter and apart'. They seldom spoke to one another. When they did speak, their conversations turned into rows so explosive the poet describes them as 'wars'.

The poet remembers one shocking incident when her mother struck her across the face. This clearly affected the poet deeply – she can still recall the stinging sensation she experienced: 'the sting of her hand/ across my face in one of our wars'. We are not told what caused the mother to lash out in this way. Perhaps this incident occurred when the poet was expelled from St. Michael's Holy Faith Convent for organising a student protest. Or perhaps the mother didn't approve of the hippy-influenced music scene the poet was drawn to when she was about fifteen years old.

The two grew even further apart when the poet went to study English, History and Classical Civilisation at Trinity College. By the time the mother died at the tragically young age of forty-two, they had grown utterly estranged. The poet's complicated feelings towards her mother continued even after the mother's death. Many years have passed, but the poet has never gone back to visit her grave.

Polishing the floor
The poet thinks back to her childhood, when she would have been seven or eight years old. At that time her family lived in a flat on Séan MacDermott Street in Dublin city centre. The poet remembers how her mother would scrub and polish the floor of the flat's living-room.

- We get a sense that the mother was methodical in her work. She would start 'at the door', covering an area within an 'armreach' of where she kneeled. Only when that area was completed would she move on to the next.
- The mother was also clearly disciplined in her work. She would scrub and polish until 'her knees grew sore', only then stopping for a cup of tea.
- She was also someone who took pride in her work and was determined to do a good job. We see this in how she buffed the wax polish until it exhibited 'a high shine'

The poet, along with her brothers and sisters, were instructed to remain in the bedroom while their mother scrubbed and polished. The poet describes how the lavender scent of the polish would filter or 'percolate' through the air of the apartment: 'The smell/ would percolate back through the flat to us'. Finally, when the mother was finished, she would call the children into the living-room so they could amuse themselves by skating in their socks on the freshly polished floor.

Altering the dress

The poet now focuses on a different memory, recalling an evening in late summer when was twelve or thirteen years old. The following day would see the young poet start secondary school and her mother was altering a 'crimson' dress for her to wear.

The young poet stayed up quite late, long after her younger siblings had gone to bed, keeping her mother company while she worked at these alterations. The young poet and her mother, we sense, enjoyed a moment of friendly intimacy as they sat together by the fire. We can imagine the two of them chatting while the mother cut and sewed.

The mother, while they sat by the fireside, recounted a story from her own teenage years. The dress being altered once belonged to the mother herself and she wore it during her own teenage years. Once she was wearing it when her father caught her out on a date with a boy. Her father responded by flying into a terrible rage.
- He insulted the mother's boyfriend, using terms such as 'lout' and 'cornerboy'.
- He insulted the mother, it is implied, by using terms such as 'slut' and 'prostitute'. We can imagine the shock and shame the mother must have felt being addressed in this manner by her own father. Even years later she still can't bring herself to repeat these slurs: 'I needn't tell you/ what he called me'.
- We can imagine the mother's humiliation as she was dragged 'in by the hair … in front of the whole street'.
- He brutally removed the makeup she had been wearing for her date in what can only be described as a form of assault. There is a real violence to how he holds her head 'under the kitchen tap'. We can imagine the mother's agony as he went at her with the scrubbing brush and carbolic soap that were usually used for scrubbing clothes.

This was clearly a traumatic incident for the mother, one that has lingered vividly in her memory.

Eventually, the teenage poet had to go to bed herself. She woke up the next morning to find the alteration complete and the dress ready for her first day at her new school. Her mother had also provided her with 'three new copybooks' and a new tip or 'nib' for her fountain pen. Also waiting for her was a St Christopher medal, a small silver pendant 'strung on a silver wire' so it can be worn around the neck. These were traditionally worn by travellers as charms to keep them safe on 'perilous' journeys through 'unchartered realms'.

The poet, however, was put off by the fact the dress was second-hand. To her this previously owned item was a 'stigma', a mark of disgrace. It 'spelt poverty', showing clearly to her friends and neighbours that her family was struggling to get by. Wearing the dress made her feel embarrassed and ashamed.

The poet, then, exhibited little 'grace' or gratitude for the mother's efforts in altering the dress. We can imagine her grumbling as she puts it on and leaving it crumpled on the ground when she takes it off. We can even imagine her wearing it in a deliberately ungraceful fashion, failing to adjust it so it fits her figure properly. She was relieved when she grew too big to wear the dress and did not have to wear it anymore: I grew enough to pass// it on by Christmas to the next in line'.

The poet recalls how in her early teenage years she developed a new sense of curiosity and independence. Each day after school she would wander the streets of Dublin, roaming further and further from the family home on Séan MacDermott Street: 'I was sizing/ up the world beyond our flat'.

There was something deliberate and meticulous about the way the poet explored the city:
- The phrase 'sizing up' suggests that she was carefully considering and forming opinions about the world at large.
- She would explore the city 'patch by patch', getting to know one area before moving on to the next.
- Gradually she developed a sense of the city's geography, of how its streets, squares and diamonds fitted together.
- She was especially fascinated by the river, and would stand there for hours watching it pulse by.
- She would also watch ships 'coming and going' in Dublin Port.

The young poet was certain that one day she would board such a ship and let the river carry her out beyond the harbour to the open sea. She would make her way to some exotic, far-off destination, such as Zanzibar, off the coast of East Africa, or the great Indian city of Bombay, or the ancient civilisation of Ethiopia.

The mother in the Phoenix Park

The poet now focuses on a photo of her mother which was taken many years ago in the Phoenix Park. The mother was heavily pregnant at the time. There is something graceful or regal about the mother's bearing. She looks like she could be a member of an aristocratic family, those who are 'born to' or inherit great estates with their 'formal gardens'. She looks like she could be the owner of the rose garden in which she sits, rather than a woman from a flat on Séan MacDermott Street who is visiting a public park.

But the poet also gets the impression that her mother was experiencing great sorrow. The mother seems utterly wrapped up in these sorrowful thoughts. She is so distracted that she only half realises she is being photographed: 'She stares out as if unaware/ that any human hand held the camera'. She seems utterly disconnected from what's going on around her: 'wrapped/ entirely in her own shadow'.

Knitting and skeins

The poem concludes with another two memories related to the mother's knitting. First, the poet recalls her mother knitting by the fire. She remembers how her mother would be silent, lost in concentration and focusing on her knitting pattern. She would give a 'sporadic' or occasional 'mutter' when she came to 'a hard place in the pattern'. Like many people she would attempt to make sense of the instructions by reading them aloud.

Second, she would remember helping her mother create neat balls of wool. She would have to kneel before her mother holding a 'skein', a large, knotted clump of wool. She was required to hold the skein stretched taut between her hands. This would allow her mother to draw out a continuous thread of wool, which she would roll into neat balls.

The poet would frequently become distracted and loosen her grip upon the skein. She'd find herself fascinated by the shadows the fire cast on the ceiling. She would imagine that the shadows were clouds and that she herself was a kite swimming among them: 'If I swam like a kite too high/ amongst the shadows on the ceiling'. She would be equally fascinated by the light the fire cast on the floor. She would imagine that these were flickering pools and she was a fish travelling through their depths: 'or flew like a fish in the pools/ of pulsing light'.

The mother, it seems, would be frustrated by her daughter's lapses in concentration. She would snap the daughter out of her daydreams by yanking on the skein. This would remind the daughter to focus on the skein and hold it at the appropriate tightness. The poet uses a wonderful metaphor to describe this, declaring that her mother was reeling her back to reality like a fish being reeled onto land: 'she'd reel me firmly/ home, she'd land me at her knees'.

The mother, it seems, has been teaching the daughter how to knit. She has urged the daughter to properly follow the various knitting patterns they have been using. But the daughter, it seems, is unwilling or unable to do so: 'One of these days I must/ teach you to follow a pattern'. We can imagine how the daughter might let her imagination run away with her, departing from the pattern's plan, as she knits rows and stitches of her own devising.

THEMES

FAMILY

This poem is a moving exploration of the relationships between mothers and their eldest daughters. Such relationships, Meehan suggests, all too often turn sour: 'Some say that's the fate of the eldest daughter'. We get the impression that much of the tension between Meehan and her mother arose because of the great differences between them.

The poet, then, views herself as very different to the mother. The phrase 'Little has come down to me of hers' refers to physical heirlooms the poet has inherited from her mother. But it also reflects the poet's belief that she has inherited few of her mother's traits and characteristics.

The poet, we sense, is someone given to introspection, to reflecting on her own life, to contemplating her own thoughts and emotions. She is prone to looking into the mirror, searching for a 'glimmer of her true self'. The mother, on the other hand, is not given to such introspection. She spent little time, the poet imagines, contemplating her own face when she saw it reflected in the floor's polished surface. She simply shrugged and moved on with her work.

The poet, as we highlight below, comes across as highly imaginative. The mother's relative lack of imagination comes across in her 'sensible' colour choices when she knits. The poet is rather dreamy and prone to lapses in concentration. We see this when she repeatedly loses focus and and lets the skein of wool go slack. The mother, on the other hand, values focus and concentration in all she does, whether it is knitting, sewing, polishing the floor or unravelling a skein of wool. The mother – focused but unimaginative – always follows the 'pattern' when she knits. The daughter, prone to letting her imagination run away with her, never does.

Perhaps, however, the poet and her mother are not so different after all. There is something about the mother's meticulousness, for instance, in how the daughter explores the city, getting to know it section by section. The mother, meanwhile, exhibits something of the daughter's introspection when she's photographed in the Phoenix Park. As we've seen, she seems so distracted, so lost in her own thoughts that she is unaware of what's going on around her.

The poet wishes that she had a chance to explore these similarities. She wishes her mother had lived on until the poet herself had matured: 'I wish now she'd lasted until after/ I'd grown up'. They would have been two independent women, neither reliant on the other. They would have been unburdened of family commitments: 'without tags like mother, wife,/ sister, daughter'. They could have got to know each other afresh, first as acquaintances and then, perhaps, as friends: 'We might have made a new start'. The poem's great tragedy, then, is that the mother passed away before such a new start could be made.

THEMES

BECOMING A POET

'The Pattern' shows us how, even as a child, Meehan was a highly imaginative person. She can spend hours watching the river flowing by lost in fantasies of faraway lands or studying the fireplace's patterns of light and shadow. An interesting feature of this passage is how the poet imagines kites swimming and fish flying. This suggests pure imaginative freedom. The poet conjures a world where the rules of physics don't apply and in which anything can happen. In the poet's imagination, the ocean can be composed of air, while the sky can behave like water.

The poet's burgeoning imagination is evidenced when she imagines a robe that has been dyed in a colour of extraordinary purity, a shade so intense it couldn't possibly exist in the real world. The robe, in the poet's imagination, morphs and twists, transforming into a 'word' or a piece of text. Here we sense not only the poet's active imagination, but also her growing fascination with the written word. She is beginning to realise that through writing she can capture these visions and convey them to other people.

POVERTY AND HARDSHIP

The mother was born into the Ireland of the 1930s. The country was extremely poor. It was also a narrow and closed-minded place. There were extremely limited opportunities for education and advancement. This was especially so for the working class into which the mother was born.

The mother had a very limited and constrained life. She had little education and no career outside the home. The poem suggests that she married the first man she ever dated and had her first child the following year. From a relatively young age, therefore, she was expected to devote herself to a life of housework and childcare.

If the mother had been born in a different time, during a different phase of Irish history, she could have flourished like her daughter and achieved a fulfilling life. History, then, has brought the mother 'to her knees', robbing her of such fulfilment. The photograph taken in the Phoenix Park shows her wrapped/ entirely in her own shadow', lost in melancholy thoughts of what her life might have been

Perhaps the mother, like the poet, once dreamed of faraway places like Zanzibar. But she realises now that she will never make such journeys. Her life is confined to her flat and a few square miles of Dublin city: 'the world beyond her/ already a dream, already lost'.

THE STRENGTH AND POWER OF WOMEN

The mother, however, didn't succumb to these difficulties – instead, she stayed strong for the sake of her family.
- The mother is presented as extremely hard-working. Nearly all the poet's memories of her, in fact, involve work of some kind. Even her leisure activity, knitting, is work of a kind: we can imagine her knitting hats, gloves and other useful items.
- We get the sense that the mother had to be extremely resourceful and resilient in order to steer the family through a lifetime of hardship and poverty. We see this when she re-purposes a dress declaring that there is 'Plenty of wear in it yet'.
- The mother is highly protective of her 'brood' and will do anything, we sense, to protect her six children: 'It'll be over my dead body anyone harms a hair of your head'.
- But the mother is also capable of great tenderness towards her daughter. We see this when she 'must have stayed up half the night/ to finish the dress', determined that her daughter will look good on her first day back. Tenderness is also suggested when she gives her daughter the copy books, the nib and the St. Christopher's medal.

The poem, then, highlights the central role that mothers play in the lives of their children. We see this when the poet describes how she and her siblings would skate around their mother on the freshly polished floor. She uses a beautiful simile to describe this, declaring that the children orbited the mother just as planets orbit the sun.

Meehan, at the poem's conclusion, sees 'Tongues of flame' in her mother's eyes. Perhaps this is simply an optical effect, the mother's dark eyes reflecting the glow of the fireplace. Or perhaps the young poet is thinking of the tongues of flame that in the Bible descended on the apostles, granting them extraordinary powers and abilities. Perhaps the poet senses that her mother, too, is capable of extraordinary things. But the mother, alas, was never granted the opportunity to fulfil this potential.

Continuity

This poem is very much about the patterns of inheritance, how traits or characteristics repeat across the generations, like stitches in a knitted garment.

The grandfather's ferocious temper, evident when he drags the mother 'in by the hair', is passed down to the mother, and comes across when she strikes her daughter in the face.
The grandfather's meticulousness is evident when he scrubs 'every spick of lipstick and mascara' from the mother's face. The mother is similarly meticulous when she polishes the floor of the apartment. The poet herself, in turn, is meticulous in her explorations of Dublin town.

Sometimes, of course, we don't like the idea of inheriting our parents' characteristics. The mother, for instance, describes the grandfather as a 'tyrant', perhaps not realising that she has inherited some of his tyrannical ways. The poet makes a similar point, declaring that 'Little has come down' to her from her mother. But the poem, as we've seen, suggests that they have more in common than she might think.

THIS IS POETRY — PAULA MEEHAN

The Statue of the Virgin at Granard Speaks

LINE BY LINE

This poem is centred on the poetic device known as personification. Personification, we remember, occurs when an inanimate object is depicted as if it had human characteristics. Meehan, in this instance, personifies a statue of the Virgin Mary. The statue in question can be seen in a grotto on the outskirts of the town of Granard, County Longford. The statue is presented as being capable of speech. It is presented as being capable of experiencing physical sensations like cold and discomfort. It is presented as being capable of emotional states like puzzlement and sexual desire.

The grotto in which the statue stands came to national attention due to the tragic death of Ann Lovett, a 15-year-old schoolgirl from the town. Ann had become pregnant but had managed to keep the pregnancy secret from her family and friends. On 31 January 1984, knowing her baby was coming, she went to the grotto alone to give birth. By the time Ann was discovered, her baby was already dead. Ann herself passed away some hours later. The story became a national scandal and greatly influenced the debate on women, sexuality and pregnancy in Irish life.

1

It is All Souls' Night, the Night of 2 November. It is extremely cold: 'It can be bitter here at times like this'. It is extremely windy, with a gale 'sweeping' through Northern Ireland, 'across the border' and down into County Longford. The wind, according to the statue, carries 'seeds' or pellets of ice that are capable of cutting 'to the quick', which suggests that they can penetrate the skin to damage vital and sensitive organs.

The people of Granard, unsurprisingly, are all 'tucked up safe' in bed. Indeed, not even 'wild things', such as badgers and foxes, are forced to endure these icy conditions. These creatures are normally active during the nighttime. But this particular night is so bitter that they have 'gone to earth', finding shelter in burrows, hedges and the hollows of trees.

The statue complains, therefore, that she alone is exposed to the elements on this brutal All Souls' Night. The statue, of course, is utterly immobile and must remain in its grotto, despite the terrible weather: 'and I/ stuck up here in this grotto'. It must continue with its 'vigil' all night long (A vigil, we remember, is a period of watching and waking that takes place during the hours usually devoted to sleep).

The statue, therefore, must endure the utter darkness of this overcast November night. There isn't a single star or planet glinting in the sky that might cheer it up as it maintains its vigil. It must also endure the wind's cacophony: 'The howling won't let up'. The sound of the wind, it seems, resembles a series of long mournful cries that just go on and on. The statue must also endure the wind's unpleasant odour. The statue describes how it can 'taste' this unpleasant mixture of turf-smoke and stagnant water, suggesting that the wind is blowing directly into its mouth.

> The statue refers to the Northern Ireland Troubles, which were on going when the poem was written. The statue imagines the sinister activities that are taking place in 'garrison towns' such as Newry, or 'walled cities' such as Derry, or in the 'ghetto lanes' of East and West Belfast.
>
> 'Garrison towns' were towns in which the British Army were permanently stationed. Such towns tended to grow and prosper because of the British presence. The term 'ghetto' meanwhile refers to a city district reserved for people of a particular faith. Parts of Belfast were sometimes referred to as ghettos because they were predominantly inhabited by either Catholics or Protestants.
>
> Men, in these towns, cities and ghettos, engage in 'death tactics'. They plan and carry out assassinations, bombings and shootings. They 'hunt each other' and engage in 'night manoeuvres', heading out each night to murder and maim under cover of darkness.
>
> There's an element of fantasy or 'poetic licence' as the statue suggests that the wind informs it about these grisly nighttime killings. It's as if the wind, as it sweeps through Northern Ireland, picks up and carries the whispering of the conspirators as the plan their 'night manoeuvres', the sound of the gunshots, the screams of the dying.

2

The statue describes how the people of the locality come to the grotto. They address the statue as if it were Mary, the mother of Jesus: 'They call me Mary'. They speak to it as if it were a divine being, referring to it as 'Blessed' or 'Holy'. They even 'kneel before' the statue and pray to it.

Visitors to the grotto also associate the statue with the concept of the virgin birth, which states that Mary was 'mated' or had sex with 'no mortal man'. Instead, she was still a virgin when she gave birth to Jesus, who was conceived through a miraculous intervention on the part of the Holy Spirit.

The statue, however, seems surprised that the local people address it in this way: 'They call me Mary'. It seems perturbed that people come and kneel before it offering up their prayers. The statue, then, seems clear in its mind that it is not actually the Virgin Mary. It is no divine or semi-divine being. It didn't experience any miraculous virgin birth and didn't witness the crucifixion in Palestine two thousand years ago. It's just a sculpted piece of marble that has spent decades perched within its grotto.

The statue, using a wonderful simile, compares the prayers of the local people to sparks that drift upward from a bonfire then 'wink out'. The statue views their prayers, like such sparks, as being beautiful but fleeting. The prayers express noble sentiments and feature beautiful turns of phrase. But they serve no lasting purpose. The statue can't imagine that they are heard or answered by any spiritual being. It seems puzzled by all this praying, by what it regards as an utterly futile activity.

3

The statue emphasises that the weather isn't always terrible in Granard: 'It can be lovely here at times'. Each season, according to the statue, bangs its own particular beauty to the fields beside the grotto.

The statue thinks of spring and early summer when boys and girls who have made their first communion come to the grotto. At that time of year wildflowers such as 'cow parsley' and 'haw blossom' bloom in the surrounding area. The statue describes how these wildflowers are a 'riot' in the hedgerows, suggesting their abundant unstoppable growth. They exhibit a pristine whiteness, one far more striking than that of the 'frocks' worn by the communion girls.

In midsummer, meanwhile, the grotto is frequently visited by newly-married couples: 'Or the grace of a midsummer wedding'. Midsummer, of course, is a time of extraordinary fertility. We can imagine lavish, luscious growth in the surrounding area, as plants, trees and flower all flourish.

At such moments the statue is filled with sexual desire:
- It longs to be 'incarnate' or made flesh. It longs to exchange its immobile plaster form for one made of flesh of blood, so it can touch and be touched.
- The statue uses a wonderful metaphor to describe this impulse, declaring that it wants to 'break loose of [its] stony robes'.
- The statue, then, wants to lie with a human man. It wants to be 'tousled' or caressed in a bed that is 'honeyed' or sweetened with physical 'intimacy'.

Tellingly, the statue tends to experience these moments of desire when a newly-married couple has come to visit it. It's as if the statue envies the couple's passion and affection. These moments of desire also occur in summertime, reflecting the widespread assumption that sexual desire and activity are more prevalent during the summer months.

The statue associates the season of autumn with 'burial[s]' and we can imagine how funeral parties might stop at the grotto as they make their way from church to cemetery. In autumn, according to the statue, the landscape engages in 'pageantry', in an elaborate beautiful display. The wind is sweetened with the scent of fallen pears as it causes clouds to 'scud' or career eastward across the sky. Berries grow so abundantly in the surrounding area that they are a heavy 'burden' to the hedgerows on which they flourish. 'Windfalls', fallen apples and pears, lied hidden in the 'orchard grasses'.

4

On this November night, however, the weather is absolutely terrible. The fierce winds sound like 'keening', which suggests human beings wailing over the body of a deceased loved one. The gale blows relentlessly and the statue must endure its howling night long, without a single break or 'respite': 'But on this All Souls' Night there is/ no respite from the keening of the wind'.

The sound of the wind, the statue suggests, is so loud that it could wake the corpses in the nearby graveyard: 'I would not be amazed if every corpse came risen/ from the graveyard' (This of course is an instance of hyperbole or deliberate poetic exaggeration).

In what sense are the dead the 'conscience of the town'? When the people of the town make moral judgments they invoke the dead. The say things like 'My grandfather would be so ashamed of me if he saw me doing this' or 'What would your Aunt Josephine say if she could see you in such a state?' The dead are imagined to be morally flawless and provide an impossible standard against which the living must measure their behaviour.

The statue imagines that the awakened corpses would howl in 'exaltation' or delight as they wandered around the cemetery. They would be elated, she imagines, to be active and animate again after years or centuries in the grave. They would produce an unpleasant or cacophonous sound, 'a cacophony of bone', that mingles with the roaring of the gale.

- When the dead were still alive, their lives were governed by the town's Catholic morality.
- But even in death they are still involved in this morality. For they remain, according to the statue, the 'conscience of the town'.
- The dead's only 'release' from this moral system can come through the destruction of the town itself.

- It imagines their revived corpses shouting at the sky, begging or 'imploring' God to trigger the day of 'judgment' and the end of the world.

For this would mean the end of the town and their 'release', finally, from its system of morality.

5
On stormy nights such as this one, the statue finds itself thinking of Ann Lovett and her tragic passing: 'On a night like this I remember the child'.
- She recalls how Ann was only fifteen years old on that terrible day: 'She…who came with fifteen summers to her name'.
- She recalls how Ann took refuge in the grotto: 'and she lay down alone at my feet'.
- She recalls how Ann, in the throes of childbirth, was utterly alone, lacking any moral or medical support: 'without midwife or doctor or friend to hold her hand'.
- The statue recalls how Ann, as she gave birth alone, was 'in extremis', was in an extreme state of mental and physical distress.

Ann, like many people, responded to a terrible situation by praying for help from God. To Ann, the statue represented the Blessed Virgin. Ann wanted the statue to 'intercede with heaven', to act as an advocate or intermediary. Ann hoped that the statue would reach out to God on her behalf, that the statue would ask God to alleviate her plight.

The statue, however, did nothing practical to help Ann: 'I did not move,/ I didn't lift a finger to help her'. Nor did the statue respond to Ann's request to 'intercede with heaven'. It didn't reach out to God on Ann's behalf. It didn't 'whisper the charmed word' that might have moved God to act and help Ann in her hour of greatest need.

THEMES

NATURE AND SPIRITUALITY
The statue adopts a very spiritual view of nature, regarding the earth as divine beings of a kind. The earth, however, is very different from the God of the Catholic faith. First, it is female rather than male. Second, it wants people to express rather than repress their sexual desire. In summer time, as we've seen, the earth is maximally fertile. And the earth, according to the statue, calls on human beings to be fertile too, to engage in 'coupling' or sexual activity: 'when the earth herself calls out for coupling'.

The sun, too, is presented as a kind of goddess, one that the statue venerates or worships. The statue longs for the winter solstice, which falls on 21 December each year. That date represents a 'turn back to the light'. The days slowly start to get longer and the sun's presence is felt more in the world.

The statue, at the end of the poem, prays to the sun directly: 'O sun'. The statue's prayer, like many prayers, involves a list or 'litany' of names for the deity being prayed to:
- The sun is described as our 'centre', reflecting the fact that our whole lives, in a sense, are spent orbiting the sun. The earth, meanwhile, is compared to a dancer that traces a circle, over and over again, around the sun's central point.
- The sun is described as a 'burning heart', suggesting the extraordinary potency of its flames.
- The sun is described as our 'molten mother'. The term 'molten', of course, reinforces our sense of the sun's incomprehensible heat, causing us to envision a sphere of churning lava. The description of the sun as our 'mother', meanwhile, reminds us that we depend on the sun's heat and light for our very survival.

The statue calls on the sun to 'have pity' on us poor human beings. It's as if the statue wants the sun to intervene in human affairs and somehow make the world a better place. We sense, however, that the statue's prayers, like those of Ann on the day she died, are likely to remain unanswered. The earth's dance, we fear, is destined to remain a 'foolish' one, as we human beings will almost certainly remain thoughtless, selfish and judgemental. We will continue to produce societies where innocent people like Ann are victimised and destroyed.

SOCIAL JUSTIC
The poem draws a stark contrast between and Ann and the society of which she was a part. The rest of the town was 'tucked up' safe and warm, while Ann, alone in the cold of a January night, suffered the agony of childbirth. The image of the towns being 'tucked up' in scandals, bargains, prayers and promises is a powerful one. It suggests that such concerns envelop their minds just as sheets and blankets envelop their bodies when they go to bed at night.

These lines remind us that the people of the town failed Ann as her pregnancy wore on. No one noticed that things weren't quite right with her. There was no one Ann felt she could turn to, no older member of society with whom she could share her 'secret'. The people of the town were too wrapped up in their own affairs – in 'bargains' and business dealings, in their hopes and 'prayers', 'promises' they had to keep or get out of.

These lines also suggest that that the town was characterised by the judgemental sexual morality associated with the church. 'Prayers', of course, were central to life. We get the impression that the townsfolk were quick to judge those involved in 'little scandals' that occurred around the parish. But some townsfolk, of course, despite their prayers and judgement, were likely to behave in scandalous behaviour themselves.

THEMES

RELIGION

Sectarianism
The poem, it must be said, presents a very negative view of Christianity. The mention of the Northern Ireland Troubles, for instance, reminds us that Christianity, over the centuries, has given rise to a wide variety of violent conflicts. These conflicts tend to be sectarian in nature, involving a clash between different sects or branches of the Christian faith.

The Troubles, we remember, were in part such a sectarian conflict, a struggle between a Catholic community on one side, and a Protestant community on the other. The statue refers to the 'various names of God', suggesting how both sides in the conflict have a different understanding of God and use different prayers and phrases to address the divine. But each side believes that God is with them. They believe that by killing they are doing God's will and 'invoke' or seek his blessing as they engage in their 'death tactics'.

A faith of Misery and suffering
The poem focuses on the Catholic version of Christianity in particular, presenting it as a faith obsessed with misery and suffering. We see this when the local people refer to the statue as 'Mother of all this grief'. There is an element of metonymy here, which occurs when we refer to something by the names of something with which it is closely associated. Jesus, in this instance, in referred to as 'all this grief' because he is so closely associated with suffering and sorrow.

But the term 'Mother of all this grief' also brings to the mind the Catholic religion as a whole. Mary, after all, is frequently referred to as the mother of the church. The phrase suggests that the Catholic faith is centred on grief and suffering, that it celebrates and elevates misery and suffering. This is evident in the way visitors to the grotto dwell on the crucifixion and associate the statue with that grisly event: 'They fit me to a myth of a man crucified'. The statue, in their minds, is linked to the various tortures Jesus suffered: being whipped or scourged, falling several times as he carried the cross through Jerusalem, having a 'thorny crown' placed mockingly on his head, enduring the 'hammer blow of iron' as his wrists and ankles were nailed to the cross.

The statue's own hardships arguably reinforce our sense of Catholicism as a religion of suffering. The statue, as we have seen, must maintain its vigil all night long no matter what the weather, enduring 'seeds of ice' and the incessant howling of the wind. This calls to mind the tendency in Catholicism to make the body suffer in order that it be cleansed of sin.

Sexuality
The poem also reminds us of how the Catholic faith represses and mistrusts sexuality. This is suggested by the fact that a virgin, a woman 'mated to no mortal man', plays such a central role in the religion. The faithful utter phrases like 'Blessed, Holy, Virgin', suggesting that for them Mary's holiness is wrapped up in her asexual nature.

In the Catholic faith, then, sexual activity is regarded, metaphorically speaking, as a stain or tarnish. Mary, being a virgin, is regarded as 'immaculate' or unstained. The statue, on the other hand, longs to be 'maculate' or stained. It longs to take on a human form and engage in sexual activity. The mention of a 'midsummer wedding', meanwhile, brings to mind the Church's disapproval of sexual relations outside of marriage. Midsummer is a time of maximum fertility, when, as the statue puts it, 'the earth herself calls out for coupling'. But good Catholics must refrain from such 'coupling' unless they've been married in the eyes of God.

The statue's description of how it's trapped in 'stony robes' serves as a powerful metaphor for this sexual repression. The statue, in these lines, presents itself as a sensual human being held prisoner within a hard outer casing that prevents it from expressing its sexuality. The people of Catholic Ireland, similarly, are held prisoner within the church's rules and regulations, strictures that prevent them from expressing their sexuality.

Guilt and Shame
This repressive morality, unsurprisingly, gives rise to great deal of shame and guilt when it comes to sexual matters. This is heartbreakingly evident in the case of Ann Lovett, who, as we have seen, felt obliged to keep her pregnancy a secret. This is emphasised by a famous instance of metonymy: 'and she pushed her secret out into the night'. Metonymy, as we noted above, occurs when we refer to something by the name of something with which it is closely associated. Ann's baby, in this instance, in referred to as 'her secret' because he was so closely associated with secrecy and shame.

The failure of Catholicism
It was this shame, of course, that caused Ann to give birth alone 'without midwife or doctor or friend to hold her hand'. It was this shame that led to her tragic and all too avoidable death. There is a bitter irony, then, in the fact that Ann sought refuge in the grotto and called out to the Virgin Mary for help, as it was the faith represented by the grotto and its Virgin that had led to her predicament in the first place.

The statue, as we've seen, describes how it 'didn't lift a finger to help' Ann in her hour of need. In one sense, of course, this shouldn't surprise us. For the statue, as we pointed out above, is only an immobile piece of plaster. It is no divine or semi-divine being. It could neither help Ann in any practical way nor intercede on her behalf with God.

But the statue's failure to act can also be read on a symbolic level. The statue can be seen as a symbol for the church. The statue's inability to help, meanwhile, can be seen as a symbol of the Church's failure. The church failed not only Ann but entire generations of Irish people by offering them judgement rather than kindness, by making them ashamed of their sexuality and their very selves.

THIS IS POETRY — PAULA MEEHAN

Cora, Auntie

LINE BY LINE

The poem is a tribute to the poet's aunt, Cora. Cora was the poet's mother's sister. She lived in Dublin until 1961, when she emigrated to England. Meehan was six at the time. Cora remained in London for the rest of her life.

Cora's last year

The poet recalls how Cora looked shortly before she died. She was sick with cancer and had been receiving chemotherapy. The treatment and the long illness left her aunt frail and weak. Her body had 'withered'. Her skin looked 'Old' and she very frail and thin. Meehan describes her emaciated body looked like a 'bag of bones'.

Meehan describes how close to death her aunt was at this point. She personifies 'Death', imagining it as some sinister figure that was always lurking close to Cora at this time. But Cora remained unperturbed by death, treating it with defiance and good humour.

- Meehan recalls how her aunt would fearlessly confront the fact that she was going to die. She describes Cora as a gunslinger and 'Death' as a foe or enemy she had to face. The strong pain medication the aunt was taking and the whiskey that she would drink are compared to pistols that Cora would use in a face-off with Death.
- She recalls how her aunt would never treat her pending death in a sombre or serious manner. Instead, Cora is described as 'laughing at Death', as though he were some ridiculous, comical figure.
- Cora would use humour to ward off any negative thoughts of death, making light of the fact that she was going to die. Meehan compares her aunt to a medieval knight taking part in a jousting contest. Humour is compared to the 'lance' that her aunt carries. As she charges towards her adversary, Death, she tilts or lowers this lance in order to knock her opponent from his horse: 'humour a lance// she tilted at Death'.

Although the aunt was in a lot of pain, she did not behave like someone defeated or tortured by her condition. The poet recalls her aunt tolerating or 'bearing the pain'. Nor did she speak like someone who felt persecuted. There was, Meehan says, no 'crucifixion' in her voice. Instead, when Cora spoke, the poet heard tones of exaltation, great happiness and 'glory' in her voice.

Rather than become morose and withdrawn, it seems Cora became even more of a force in her final year. We get the impression that Cora was always flamboyant and exuberant and that she remained this way until the very end. The poem, after all, opens with the memorable image of her holding a bottle of morphine in one hand and a bottle of whiskey in the other.

This aspect of Cora's character further reinforces Meehan's description of what it was like to head out onto the London streets with Cora. At this stage, due to her weakened condition, Cora had to use a 'motorised invalid scooter' to get around. Meehan recalls how her aunt would career recklessly down the street out in front of the trams. She was, as Meehan says, the bane of the tram drivers operating in the area: 'Scourge of Croydon tram drivers'. If she was not on the street she would be driving recklessly along the footpaths, forcing anyone who was walking at a leisurely pace to jump out of her way. Meehan characterises such pedestrians as 'High Street dossers', a term we can imagine her aunt might have used for anyone who got in her way. A dosser is a slang term for someone who is idle or lazy.

Despite the fact that her illness and treatment had left her looking old and haggard, Cora remained in many ways youthful. The aunt's hair, which had fallen out when she was receiving chemotherapy, 'grew back'. The poet recalls how the hair was 'thick and curly as when she was a girl'. And her eyes, though they grew 'darker and stranger' as her conditioned worsened, always held a youthful twinkle: 'always a girl in her glance'.

The aunt's name, the poet points out, has associations with youth. Cora comes from the Greek Kore, which means 'the girl' or 'the maiden'. In Greek mythology, Kore was another name for Persephone, the goddess of fertility and vegetation who was associated with the blossoming of the flowers and plants in spring and summer: 'promising blossom, summer, the scent of thyme'.

The wedding dress

The poet switches to a different memory of her aunt. She recalls a time when her aunt was a young woman preparing for her wedding. It was nineteen sixty-one and Cora was 'nearly twenty-one'. The poet vividly remembers her aunt standing up on the kitchen table in her 'white satin dress'. Around the table stood the poet's mother, her other aunts and her maternal grandmother. They are sewing red sequins to the bottom of the dress. As the women standing around the table attach the sequins, Cora 'moves slowly round and round'.

Meehan was a young child at the time. She recalls how she was barely tall enough to 'see over' the table. As the women attended to Cora's dress, she walked around them, orbiting the table. She also remembers being under the table 'singing'. But it is the sequins that were being sewn to the hem of the dress that the poet remembers most vividly. They were of the most intense red colour: 'red as berries'.

Cora was set to emigrate to England shortly after the wedding. Meehan tells us that she was 'weeks from taking the boat to England', which is euphemism for the fact that her aunt had to leave Ireland in order that she and her husband could find stable employment and survive. Meehan recalls how the cards that the aunt received before she departed remained standing on the mantelpiece for weeks after Cora left. These were cards from her family and friends, wishing her luck as she embarked on newly married life abroad. The poet remembers how the cards had the traditional images or 'emblems of luck' that often feature on wedding cards.

Meehan also remembers how the cards had images of large keys, which the poet describes as 'emblems … of access'. These keys were meant to symbolise how her marriage was unlocking a whole new life for her. But the term 'access' suggests that in moving to England, Cora was accessing opportunities that were just not available to her in Ireland at the time.

Finding the sequins

The bright red sequins that Cora had sewn into the hem of her wedding dress really captured the young poet's imagination. After her aunt left for England, she spent a year searching the house for sequins that had fallen from the dress and got scattered around the house. Meehan remembers how she would find them everywhere, 'in the pillowcase,/ under the stairs,/ in a hole in the lino'. These small items would be discovered in the most unlikely of spots, 'in cracks and crannies' all over the house.

In her search for the sequins, the young poet discovered a variety of other items, bits of jewellery that had broken, fallen and got lost: 'odd beads and single earrings,/ a broken charm bracelet, a glittering pin'. The young poet treasured each item she found, gathering them all 'into a tin box'.

The poet has kept this tin and she opens it now 'in memory' of her aunt. The items inside the tin are described as 'coinage', suggesting the sequins and other bits of jewellery are like valuable old coins. But the term coinage can also refer to anything made, invented or fabricated. As such, the word calls to mind the aunt's creative spirit, her ability to turn situations, no matter how difficult or grim, into occasions of fun and excitement.

Opening the tin reveals once again the aunt's 'glamour', her singular enchanting style. Meehan describes her aunt as an 'emigrant soul', calling to mind the fact that the aunt had to leave Ireland and move to England. But the term also conveys the fact that the aunt is now dead and her soul has moved on to another realm.

THEMES

THE STRENGTH AND POWER OF WOMEN

The poem offers us a wonderful portrait of someone with great character and spirit. Cora is presented as a flamboyant and fearless individual, someone who lived life on her own terms. The opening lines of the poem present us with a memorable image of the aunt facing death down like a gunslinger in a Western movie. But instead of being armed with pistols, the aunt faces death with 'a bottle of morphine in one hand/ and a bottle of Jameson in the other'.

The startling addition of the red sequins to the wedding dress tells us something about the aunt's personality. We get a sense of someone who liked to do things differently, to bring her own unique style to situations and occasions. The fact that the poet kept these sequins over the years tells us just how powerful a presence this glamorous woman was in her life.

FAMILY

The poet also remembers the other women that played important roles in her childhood. Meehan compares them to 'stars' whose light is only now reaching her. It is as if only now as an adult she can fully appreciate their strength and character: 'Cora, Marie, Jacinta, my aunties,/ Helena, my mother, Mary, my grandmother-/ the light of those stars// only reaching me now'. The poem also highlights how powerful the love between family members can be. Meehan describes how it was 'love unconditional' that kept the aunt alive towards the end.

BECOMING A POET

We get the sense that Cora offered the young girl a different way of seeing things, opening her eyes to the possibility of transcending the circumstances of her life. Cora represented 'glamour' and individuality. She showed the young poet the possibility of striking out on your own, of being true to yourself. Meehan seems to have been quite taken with the aunt from an early age, imagining her to be like one of the charaters in the books she read as a young child. She compares the vivid redness of the sequins to the colour of maidens' lips and the red of the 'blood on the snow' in 'Child's old ballads'.

We get the impression that Cora might have been something of an influence on Meehan becoming a poet. Meehan compares the red of the sequins to the pen she uses to compose the poem, saying the sequins are 'as red as this pen/ on this white paper'. The description of the poet snatching a moment out of the 'chaos' of her life to write these lines at her own kitchen table might also be a reflection of the wonderful mayhem of Cora's life.

THIS IS POETRY — PAULA MEEHAN

The Exact Moment I Became a Poet

LINE BY LINE

This poem is set in 1963 when Meehan was 8-year-old pupil in Central Model Girls' School, Gardiner Street. The poet remembers an occasion when she and the rest of her classmates had become distracted from their lessons and were chatting and laughing. She recalls how Miss Shannon, her teacher at the time, attempted to silence the classroom.

Miss Shannon, in an effort to gain the class's attention, rapped her duster against the easel that was holding up her blackboard. A 'cloud' of chalk dust flew upward from the duster, leaving her 'half obscured' for a moment. She urged her pupils to be quiet, issuing them a stark warning. If they didn't 'Attend' or pay attention at school they would never find a good job later in life. They will only be able to secure employment in the local 'sewing factory': 'or mark my words you'll end up/ in the sewing factory'

The poet is upset
The young poet was deeply upset by Miss Shannon's words, by how her teacher presented the sewing factory as a worthless and undesirable place of employment. After all, some of her classmates had mothers who worked there. These classmates, no doubt, would be embarrassed to hear their mothers' workplace referred to in such a fashion. Indeed, the young poet herself also experienced such embarrassment; her own aunt worked in that very factory, as did a number of her neighbours.

The young poet was particularly upset by Miss Shannon's use of the phrase 'end up'. This phrase, she realised, suggested a negative or undesirable outcome. It implied that those who worked in the sewing factory had failed in life. It implied that they were stuck in lowly, meaningless jobs no one would ever willingly sign up for.

The young poet felt that the 'labour' in the sewing factory had its own particular 'dignity'. She must have realised that this work, while not fancy or highly-paid, was important in its own way. She must have realised, too, that the women of the factory took great pride in what they did, in producing garments that were well made and hard-wearing. Miss Shannon's words, she realised, 'robbed' the women of this 'dignity', making their 'labour' seem utterly menial and pointless.

The poet acknowledges that she's engaging in 'back construction', that she's altering or reconstructing a memory. We see this when she depicts her eight-year-old self using terms like 'dignity' and 'labour'. The poet accepts that she didn't actually know these terms when she was eight years old. However, she did have some grasp of the feelings and concepts to which these terms relate: 'Not that I knew it then, / not in those words'.

A vision formed by words
Miss Shannon's words triggered the young poet's imagination, leading to a strange and disturbing flight of fancy:
- She found herself imagining the sewing factory with its crew of 'mothers, aunts and neighbours'.
- She imagined that these women had been 'trussed', which suggests that their legs and arms were tied together, and placed on a 'conveyor belt'.
- She imagined that the women were being 'sewn up' like chickens being readied for the oven: 'the way my granny/ sewed the sage and onion stuffing/ in the birds'.

We imagine a procession of women, tied-up and helpless, being shunted along the conveyor belt until one by one they come to some monstrous sewing machine that mutilates their bodies.

FOCUS ON STYLE

Metaphor, Simile and Figures of Speech
The poem concludes with a most memorable metaphor:
- Human beings are compared to chickens.
- Our self-esteem is compared to the 'lovely shiny feathers' that cover a chicken's body.
- Hurtful words are compared to hands that pluck the chicken's figures.

Plucking hands will leave a chicken 'naked', utterly stripped of its feathers. Hurtful words, similarly, can leave a human being emotionally naked, stripped of our dignity and self-esteem. Meehan, then, captures the power of hurtful words, such as those spoken by Miss Shannon in that long-ago classroom, to leave us diminished, belittled and humiliated.

Verbal Music
'The Exact Moment I Became a Poet', like many of Meehan's poems, is rich in imagery. The poet wonderfully captures an everyday classroom scene (the teacher banging her duster amid a loud of chalk dust) as well as the surreal and nightmarish image of the 'trussed' women on the conveyor belt.

THEMES

BECOMING A POET
Meehan, in this poem, describes a crucial moment in her childhood, one when she first realised the power of words. She suddenly understood that words could have a powerful effect on the imagination. Her teacher's comments triggered a flight of fancy image that was not only distressing but also exceptionally vivid: 'I saw them'. For a moment, in her mind's eye, she could see the 'trussed' women on the conveyor belt with a strange and disturbing clarity.

She suddenly understood, too, that words could powerfully affect the emotions. Miss Shannon's remarks about the factory, she realised, had the power to hurt not only the factory workers themselves, but also hurt the workers' daughters nieces and neighbours who sat beside her in the classroom, so that they felt weak, vulnerable and exposed: 'words could pluck you,/ leave you naked'.

The eight-year-old Meehan, then, at that precise moment 'became a poet'. She didn't, of course, immediately start writing poems and getting them published. But she knew that she would spend her life devoted to language. She would begin to learn, starting right now, how to make language work for her. She would harness the power of words to shape images in people's minds. She would use language, just like Miss Shannon had done in the classroom, to affect the emotions of those who heard and read her.

Miss Shannon, on this occasion, used language in a negative fashion. Her words, as we've seen, were wounding and diminishing. The eight-year-old Meehan, we sense, is determined to use language in a much more positive fashion. She will interrogate the powerful in society while providing a voice for the voiceless, weak and vulnerable.

SOCIAL JUSTICE
We sense that the poet, even as a primary school student, was keenly aware of social inequality. She realised that people in her part of inner city Dublin were denied the opportunities granted to those from more privileged parts of the city. And this lack of opportunity, of course, was passed down from one generation to the next.

The poet's daydream vividly conveys this social inequality. Society is compared to a nightmarish factory where generation after generation of 'mothers, aunts and neighbours' from inner city Dublin are processed. The image of these women being 'trussed up' suggests how they were constrained by lack of opportunity. The image of them being mutilated by a giant sewing machine suggests how their underprivileged lives left them mentally and physically damaged.

CHILDHOOD
'The Exact Moment I Became a Poet' wonderfully captures the mentality of childhood. The poem Meehan reminds us that eight-year-old children can understand ideas such as 'labour' and 'dignity', even if they lack the words to express such concepts. It also reminds us that children tend to have exceptionally vivid imaginations that sometimes lead them to strange and disturbing flights of fancy.

STRENGTH AND POWER OF WOMEN
The poem also touches on the strength and power of women, another of Meehan's recurring themes. She reminds us that in the inner city Dublin of the 50s and 60s it was working women like these – often doing difficult, repetitive work – who were the primary breadwinners in their respective households, bringing home a wage that kept utter poverty and despair at bay.

The poet, looking back, realises that Miss Shannon, in one way, was correct in her assessment of the sewing factory: 'allowing also/ the teacher was right'. Meehan's own experiences of life have taught her that such factories are exhausting and dehumanising places in which to make a living: 'and no one knows it like I do myself'. Meehan herself, then, wouldn't want to spend her life working in such a place of employment. But Meehan, even as she accepts the truth of Miss Shannon's comments, insists that the 'mothers, aunts and neighbours' who worked there retained a certain 'dignity'. She insists that their labour, while far from glamorous, had value and meaning.

THIS IS POETRY — PAULA MEEHAN

My Father Perceived as a Vision of St. Francis

LINE BY LINE

This poem is set in the house in Finglas where Meehan spent her teenage years. She had returned to stay in the house for a few days. She was visiting her father who still lived there, her mother having passed away some years before.

The poet recalls how she was woken by a 'piebald horse' that was kept in the garden next door. The horse whinnied loudly, causing her to wake 'out of a dream' with a start. It was still dawn when the poet was so rudely awakened. Everyone else in the house was still asleep: 'The rest of the house slept'.

The poet lay in bed and listened to the sounds of the early morning. She heard the clinking sound of glass bottles as the milkman left his delivery 'on the doorstep'. She heard 'the first bus' of the day pull up at the bus stop on the road outside. Then the poet heard her father start moving about downstairs. She heard him 'rake' the previous night's ashes from the fireplace. She heard him 'plug in the kettle' as he prepared to make a cup of tea. Finally, she heard him as he 'unlocked' the back door and 'stepped out' into the garden.

The poet went to the window. It was so early that the sun had not yet fully risen; the eastern half of the sky was bright, while the western half was still dark and speckled with stars. She notes how autumn is transitioning into winter: 'Autumn was nearly done'. It is a cold morning, the first on which frost is visible on the roof slates of the housing estate.

The poet watches her father in the garden below. She suddenly realises that her father is becoming an old man: 'He was older than I had reckoned'. She notices for the first time that he is showing the effects of age: his hair is silver, his shoulder is stooped and his leg is stiff. She wonders what he is doing in the garden at this early hour: 'What's he at? / So early'.

Suddenly, an enormous flock of birds descended upon the garden: 'They came then: birds'. The flock, it seems, consists of hundreds of birds and a wide variety of species are represented: 'birds / of every size, shape, colour'.

Birds must have come from all over the housing estate: from the 'hedges and shrubs' of neighbouring gardens, from the eaves of houses, from the roofs of garden sheds. They must have come from further afield as well, from the nearby industrial estate and from 'outlying fields'. The poet even imagines that birds have come from Dubber Cross, a green area several miles away, and from the ditches of the North Road, which leads from Finglas to Dublin Airport.

We realise that the father, unbeknownst to the poet, had been feeding the birds on a daily basis. The birds of the surrounding area had got used to receiving a dawn snack from him. They would gather expectantly in his garden every morning. Suddenly, the father 'threw his hands up' and cast 'fistfuls' of breadcrumbs into the air. The garden, at that moment, became a 'pandemonium', a scene of extraordinary disorder. We can imagine the chaos that ensued as with birds flapping and squawking as they scrambled for the crumbs.

Until that point, the chimney of a nearby house had prevented the sun's rays from directly reaching the garden. But then the sun climbed a little higher in the sky, clearing this obstruction: 'The sun // cleared O'Reilly's chimney'. Direct sunlight suddenly struck the garden and the poet's father was illuminated.

The poet, for a moment or two, saw her father very differently:
- The father seemed 'radiant', which suggests that bright light was being emitted from his body.
- The father seemed 'whole' as if his various physical infirmities had miraculously been healed.
- The father seemed 'young again', as if the aging process had been miraculously reversed.
- The father seemed transfigured into Saint Francis of Assisi.

The poet emphasises that he was a 'perfect vision' of Francis as he stood there surrounded by birds. It's as if the great saint's mighty spirit had descended upon the father, transforming him utterly.

The transfiguration described by the poet, then, is a truly remarkable one. She sees an ordinary Dubliner transformed into a saint and miracle worker, one of Europe's greatest cultural and spiritual figures.

Birdlife, of course, are the connection between these two seemingly very different men. Saint Francis is known for his kindness towards birds of all kinds. The poet, as sunlight hits the garden, realises that her father has in his own way been displaying such kindness, as he feeds the birds of the locality each morning.

FOCUS ON STYLE

Vivid Imagery

Especially memorable is the depiction of the father surrounded by birds while the sun 'cleared O'Reilly's chimney'. There is something cinematic, meanwhile, about the poet's description of how birds have come from all over the surrounding area. We are taken from the garden of the housing estate to the outlying fields of Finglas, the poet's descriptions functioning like a camera that pans slowly across a landscape.

Equally vivid is the depiction of the frost that had 'whitened' the roof slates of the housing estate. This indicates that 'Autumn was nearly done', that winter was coming. It brilliantly reflects how the father was entering what might be described as the winter of his life as old age takes hold.

THEMES

NATURE AND SPIRITUALITY

A vision occurs when someone sees something that isn't really there, or that no one else can see. Visions are usually considered different to hallucinations. People who are hallucinating think that false perceptions are reality. Someone experiencing a vision, on the other hand, doesn't think their perceptions are real in any ordinary sense. They realise that they are seeing an alternative or mystical version of reality.

The key word in the poem's title, then, is 'perceived'. The poet doesn't believe that her father has been de-aged, healed and transformed into a 13th century Italian saint. Rather, this is how she 'perceived' him. This is how he appeared to her for a single sunlit moment in an ordinary 'Finglas garden'.

This vision, no doubt, was partly caused by the fact the poet had just woken up, had been jerked out of a dream by the sound of the horse next door. Human beings, of course, are more susceptible to such visionary moments when we're not quite fully awake. The vision might also have been caused in part by the poet's heightened emotional state. She must have experienced a sense of shock as she suddenly noticed how old age was beginning to affect her father, coupled, no doubt, with the sorrowful realisation that he wouldn't be around forever. She must have experienced feelings of tenderness towards her father as she learned for the first time about his daily kindness towards the birds of the locality.

Visions are thought of as spiritual experiences prompted by religion. But Meehan's visionary spiritual experience, in this instance, is prompted, not by conventional religion but by nature itself. The poet, we sense, was overwhelmed by the beauty of the scene in the yard before her, by the sight of the father suddenly struck by sunlight as he was surrounded by a 'pandemonium' of birds. The poem, then, is typical of Meehan's work, in that spirituality and nature are closely linked.

FAMILY

The poem emphasises how even close family members can sometimes be a mystery to us. Sometimes, family members keep things hidden from one another. We see this when the poet declares that the box room contained 'secrets'. There were items hidden about the room, she sensed, that her brother didn't want her to discover. Often family members simply stay quiet about aspects of their lives. The poet's father, for instance, had never told her that he feeds the birds each morning. Sometimes, we don't notice certain things about family members, even ones that we see regularly. The poet, for instance, had never noticed how age was catching up with her father: 'He was older than I had reckoned'. It was only on this particular morning that she noticed 'for the first time' how his shoulder was stooped and that his leg was stiff.

THIS IS POETRY — PAULA MEEHAN
Hearth Lesson

Portrayal of Zeus and Hera

LINE BY LINE

In this poem, Meehan remembers her childhood, specifically the years when she and her family lived on Séan MacDermott Street in Dublin city centre. During this period the relationship between her parents was quite turbulent. They would regularly fight and argue. The poet remembers how she would crouch 'by the fire' while these arguments raged around her.

The poet wittily compares her parents to Zeus and Hera, who in Greek mythology were king and queen of the gods. Zeus and Hera, according to legend, were husband and wife but endured a famously fractious marriage. The poet compares her father's insults to the thunderbolts Zeus would hurl at his enemies. Her mother, meanwhile, looked at the father with such contempt that she is reminded of Hera's 'killing glance' (Hera, according to legend, could cause those who displeased her to drop dead merely by looking at them).

Seeing and raising

The poet mentions some of the accusations that were traded between the parents during these rows. The father, for instance, would accuse the mother of having a 'fancyman', of being too friendly and flirtatious with another man. He would also accuse her of putting on 'airs and graces', of pretending that she is posher and more important than she really is. He would even accuse 'every last one' of her siblings of being mentally unwell.

The mother, meanwhile, would accuse the father of spending too much time at the local snooker club. She would also accuse him of being too obsessed with horse-racing, suggesting that he spends all his time thinking about jockeys and horses, ignoring his wife completely. She would wittily suggest that the only way for her to get his attention would be to 'neigh' like a horse herself.

The poet compares her parents to two poker players gambling on which has the better hand of cards. The first player opens the betting by placing a certain value of chips in the centre of the table. The second player 'sees' or matches this amount and 'raises' the stakes by adding more chips of his own. Then the first player 'sees' or matches this greater amount, before raising the stakes even further.

Her parents, according to the poet, behaved in a similar fashion. Her father would open their brutal game with a particular criticism of her mother. Her mother would 'see' or match this, by saying something just as critical about the father. She would then 'raise' or escalate the row by saying something even more negative. Her father would not only 'see' or match this insult, but also escalate the row even further, saying things that are even more hurtful.

Umpire, net and court

The poet compares her parents' rows and arguments to the sport of tennis. In a rally, tennis players trade shots. Her parents, similarly, trade insults and accusations. The poet compares herself to the net in these peculiar tennis matches. Tennis players, of course, attempt to hit the ball over the net. Her parents, similarly, attempted to speak over the young poet's head. This suggests that they didn't want her know the precise nature of their disagreements and phrased their arguments in words she was unlikely to understand.

The poet also compares herself to the matches' umpires or referees. This suggests that at times she was called upon to adjudicate in her parent's arguments. We can imagine, for instance, the father urging the young poet to agree with him that the mother's siblings are crazy, or the mother asking for her opinion on the father's obsession with horse-racing.

Finally, the poet compares herself to the court on which these matches were contested. This suggests that some of the insults and accusations involved her. Maybe we can imagine the mother accusing the father of ignoring her or the father accusing the mother of not providing her with a proper diet.

The last, astonishing word

The poet views her parents' various rows and arguments as a single on-going competition, the objective of which was to have the 'last word'. Both parents, she suggests, were attempting to come up with an argument or insult to which there could be no reply, which stunned the other into silence. This cruel game, we sense, dragged on for months or even years, with neither participant able to silence the other in such a definitive fashion.

Suddenly, however, their grim competition came to an end. And it did so in a manner no one in the household was 'prepared' for or expected:

- The poet's father at the time worked as a bookmaker's clerk. Every payday he 'handed up his wages' to the mother. She would then use the money to manage the household, purchase the groceries and pay various bills.
- The poet remembers one particular 'teatime' when the father handed over his wages as usual. The mother 'straightened' the notes he'd given her, as if she were preparing to count them and start budgeting for the week to come.
- 'Suddenly', according to the poet, the mother exhibited a great weariness. We can imagine her shoulders slumping and an exhausted expression flashing across her face.
- Then, without warning, she cast the entire week's wages into the fire.
- The mother accompanied this extraordinary gesture with a single, simple phrase: "'It's not enough', she stated simply'.

But this simple phrase, accompanied by the gesture of burning the banknotes, is 'the last, the astonishing word' in their long-running competition. The father, we imagine, stood there in a shocked and astonished silence while the money burned. For once, he had no comeback, insult or argument of his own with which to respond. The mother had finally and definitively won.

Meehan describes how the flames, as they consumed the banknotes, emitted a multi-coloured glow: 'blue and pink and green'. The poet also describes how the flames 'sheered' or swerved from the cinders at the bottom of the fireplace to the chimney breast at its top, causing shadows to jump and flicker across the room.

There was something 'alchemical', almost mystical, she says, about this colour. Alchemy, we remember, was a forerunner to chemistry that involved using fire, metal and other materials in a variety of processes that were both magical and scientific

We might wonder, of course, if the burning money really caused the flames to jump in such a fashion and exhibit such a weird 'alchemical' glow. Perhaps this 'marvellous sight' is a trick of memory. Perhaps the poet, as she looks back on this long ago experience, recalls the flames as being more dramatic than they really were.

THEMES

THE STRENGTH AND POWER OF WOMEN

'Hearth Lesson' is also typical of Meehan's poetry in that it highlights the strength and power of women. The poet's mother comes across as quite a formidable woman.
- She ensured that her husband 'handed up his wages' each week.
- She steers her family as best she can through a period of poverty and hardship.
- She is more than able to stand up to her husband during their many rows, matching his arguments and insults.
- It is the mother, as we have seen, who has the 'last word' in the long-running competition with her husband.

We get a sense that the mother was a woman of extraordinary potential, someone who could have achieved great things in life. This potential, however, remained unfulfilled due to the poverty and hardship in which she found herself. The phrase 'It isn't enough', then, may refer not only to the father's wages, but also to the mother's circumstances. She wanted more from life and was desperate for opportunities and possibilities that never could be hers.

We might question however, if the mother hasn't gone too far in this regard. We sense that the father, like many men, was largely defined by his work, by his ability to provide for his wife and family. For a long time, however, his wages were inadequate to do so. Everyone in the household knew this: 'And we all knew it wasn't [enough]'. But it has never, we sense, been spoken aloud.

The mother not only gives voice to this unpleasant truth, but she also casually burns the wages he worked hard to bring home. By doing so, she undermines her husband's very identity, highlighting his inadequacy as a breadwinner. The father, we imagine, must have been left feeling worthless and humiliated by his wife's 'astonishing word'.

FOCUS ON STYLE

Metaphor, Simile and Figures of Speech
The poet uses a number of imaginative comparisons to describe the arguments between her parents. She compares her parents to the gods Zeus and Hera, to poker players and to tennis players. She uses an equally simile to capture the flames' brightness and vibrancy, comparing them to 'trapped exotic birds'.

Vivid Imagery
Meehan's gift for vivid imagery is on display when she describes the behaviour of the flames as they consumed the banknotes, capturing how they emitted a bizarre multi-coloured glow and skittered in the fireplace.

Playful Language
'Hearth Lesson', though it is a serious poem, provides us with a hint of Meehan's trademark playfulness. We see this when she compares her parents, two ordinary working-class Dubliners, to the Greek gods Zeus and Hera. Such light-heartedness is also evident in her depiction of the parents' insults; in the father's accusation that the mother's family are all crazy, for instance, or in the mother's claim that only by neighing like a horse could she get her husband's attention.

THEMES

POVERTY AND HARDSHIP
The poem highlights the toxic effects that poverty can have on a relationship. The poet, even as a child, understood that poverty caused the constant strife between her parents: 'Even then I can tell it was money/ the lack of it day after day,/ at the root of the bitter words'. The constant lack of money made both of her parents tense, irritable and frustrated. It led to unceasing tensions between them, blazing rows and 'brooding' periods of silence.

The father's wages, it is made clear, were never quite enough to cover the family's expenses. The mother, we sense, had to scrimp and save as she managed the household budget. There was always the pressure of unpaid bills and of upcoming expenses that needed to be covered from the household's meagre resources.

This hardship, the poet emphasises, dragged on 'day after day', year after year, leaving the mother psychologically worn down. We see this when the poet describes how the mother was overcome by an extraordinary weariness as she contemplated the 'rumpled' notes.

The burning of the wages, while astonishing and theatrical, is also self-destructive and wasteful. There is the obvious question of how the family are going to manage for the rest of the week. There are several ways of looking at this gesture:
- We can view it as a gesture of exhaustion. Perhaps the mother simply couldn't take another week struggling to make ends meet. Burning the notes, in a strange sense, simplified her situation. Having no money meant there was no need for careful budgeting.
- We can view it as a gesture of defeat and resignation. The mother wants her family to enjoy a reasonably high standard of living. But she realises that her husband's wages are 'not enough' to achieve this and never will be.
- We can also view it, of course, as an attempt to win the long-running and bitter competition with her husband.

CHILDHOOD
'Hearth Lesson' provides a brutal and unflinching portrayal of childhood. The young poet's crouched position by the fireplace suggests the trauma she endured as she listened to her parents 'battle it out'. It also suggests her desire not to be drawn into these disagreements, to somehow escape this toxic environment. We can picture her staring into the fire, making herself as small as possible, wishing she was somewhere else.

There is something witty about the poet's comparison of her parents to Zeus and Hera. But it also suggests the trauma she endured. To the young poet, the arguments of these fully grown adults were epic and explosive, like the clash of two vengeful gods. Her parents, as we have seen, attempted to shield her from the content of their argument, using language that she as a young girl is unlikely to understand. But not all of the balls 'are lobbed over her head'. She still understands enough. Even more traumatic for the poet were those times when her parents gave one another the silent treatment. There were lengthy periods, it seems, when the mother and father would refuse to speak to one another. And if they absolutely had to communicate, they would use the young poet as a go-between rather than address one another directly.

Their silence, according to the poet, was accompanied by a great deal of 'brooding' or moodiness. We can imagine the young poet walking on eggshells amid a tense and toxic atmosphere. Small wonder, then, that she describes these periods as a 'particular hell'. Indeed, she actually preferred her parents' arguments to these days of unbearable, silent tension: 'Even then I can judge it's better/ than brooding and silence'. This trauma, we sense, has remained with the poet into adulthood. Simply hearing the expression 'money to burn' or 'burning a hole in his pocket' causes her to relive this ordeal. The poet's use of the present tense highlights the immediacy of these recollections: 'I am crouched…I'm net, umpire…Even then I can tell'. It's as if she's back on Seán MacDermott Street, enduring the anguish of her parents' disagreements.

Prayer for the Children of Longing

LINE BY LINE

This poem was commissioned by the community of Dublin's north inner city to remember their children who died from drug use. Meehan read the poem on the occasion of the lighting of the Christmas tree on Buckingham Street. Gathered around the tree on this occasion were the families of those who had lost children to drug use.

Where has the tree come from?

It is coming up to Christmas. The lights on a large Christmas tree in Buckingham Street in the heart of the north inner city are being turned on. This magnificent or 'Great' tree has come from a forest in the 'far northern' hemisphere. We might imagine a forest in Norway, perhaps, where many large fir trees are grown. The tree has only recently been cut down and transported to Dublin. The poet observes how it is still coated with sap, the watery fluid that circulates through plants and trees: 'Still rich with the sap of the forest'.

The poet imagines how this 'far northern forest' must look at this time of year. She pictures a place of ice and snow. We can imagine the landscape covered in a blanket of snow, its rivers and lakes frozen. Snow covers the trees and shards of glittering ice hang from the branches.

The poet imagines the 'silence' and the stillness of this northern winter landscape. We can imagine a still winter's day, the sky clear and blue overhead. We can imagine the snow that covers the landscape adds to the silence, blanketing the forest floor and branches of the trees, silencing any rustling sounds: 'The snow's breathless silence'.

The streets of Dublin's north inner city

Dublin witnessed epidemic levels of heroin addiction in the 1980s. This epidemic was concentrated in small pockets of Dublin's inner city, particularly in areas with a history of poverty and disadvantage. A report commissioned at the time found that in north central Dublin, for example, 10% of 15 to 24 year-olds had used heroin in the previous year.

Meehan focuses on the manner in which drug use has devastated the north inner city, blighting and destroying the lives of the young. She personifies the 'streets' in order to convey the manner in which this area has affected the lives of the young people who must live and socialise here. These streets should represent a safe place, a space where the young can grow, develop and mature. However, the streets in this area are hostile and dangerous, blighted by drugs and violence.

Meehan thinks about the manner in which these streets have destroyed many young lives. She thinks of how some children have been seduced or coaxed into taking drugs. We can imagine how dealers might encourage the young to accompany them to some secluded place where they offer them a chance to try something that will '[blow] their minds'.

The poet refers to the young people who have tragically lost their lives to drugs as the 'children of longing'. The phrase suggests how these children's lives remained unfulfilled. They were 'longing' for something better than they got, for a way out of the cycle of poverty and drug addiction that characterised the lives of so many people living in Dublin's north inner city in the 80s and 90s.

It is possible that Meehan's choice of this phrase was influenced by the book Children of Longing, which was published in 1970. This book was contains accounts of the firsthand experiences and aspirations of black teens and young adults. It was edited by Rosa Guy, an American writer who drew on her own experiences to create fiction for young adults that usually concerned individual choice, family conflicts, poverty, and the realities of life in urban America and the West Indies.

The poet describes how those who take drugs are immediately bewitched or 'spellbound' by them. It is as if they have been placed under an evil spell from which they can never escape. And once they are hooked on drugs, they are caught in a vicious cycle of addiction that will ultimate destroy them. Meehan describes how the 'streets' have 'defeated' so many young people. She describes the burden and the toll that living with addiction brings, crippling lives that were once full of hope and potential. The poet describes how many of the young have been 'brought them to their knees', left felling powerless and without hope.

She describes how the streets have stolen the young away from the care and protection of their families: 'out of reach of our saving'. She describes how the streets have claimed the lives of some of the young people. The poet imagines the 'scream' of the victim, the sound of the police or ambulance siren and the 'knock on the door' when the police come to inform the parents of what has happened.

What does the poet wish for?

The poet appeals to the tree, asking it to grant this area of Dublin a moment of stillness and silence, a brief respite from the pain and suffering which the heroin epidemic has wrought. The poet longs for the freezing temperatures of the forest where the tree grew to somehow 'freeze' the streets of Dublin's north inner city. For a brief spell, Meehan imagines, the city streets would stand frozen, as still and silent as a northern winter forest.

For this brief moment, all the pain, violence and suffering of the streets would be suspended:

- The poet imagines a young person using a needle to inject drugs into their veins. She imagines the needle being frozen 'in its tracks', not reaching the arm of the user (The term 'track' might also refer to the scar created by continuously injecting a needle into the same point in the body over and over again. The needle, therefore, has punctured the track mark but it is frozen before the drug is injected).
- The poet imagines someone raising a knife to stab another person in the back. She imagines the knife being frozen just before it reaches its victim.
- The poet imagines that freezing conditions will for a moment stop the killing on the streets. It will freeze the 'scream' of the victim, the 'siren' of the police or ambulance, and the 'knock on the door' when the police call to the victim's house to inform his or her parents of the tragedy.

But this moment wouldn't just freeze the activities in the streets. It would also allow those who have gathered around the tree a moment of respite from their mental anguish and pain.

In this frozen moment there would be a suspension of all human emotion. The poet imagines a state of mind which she associates with the frozen northern landscape:

- For this brief moment their minds will not be burdened or preoccupied with any painful thoughts or memories. They will become as clear as 'ice'.
- For a brief moment they will not feel any anguish, pain or regret. There would be an absence of feeling, a numbness, which the poet associates with the 'comfort of snow'.
- For this brief moment they will forget the tragic events that have scarred their lives. Meehan associates this with the 'cool memory of trees'.

There is something cold and inhuman about the state of mind that the poet describes, but she knows it will offer those who are suffering a moment of relief from their anguish and pain.

For a brief moment they will feel nothing at all.

The poet imagines that in this frozen moment the spirits of these lost children will return. She imagines that in the absolute silence and stillness it will be possible to hear the 'breath of the children'. Meehan also imagines that these children are singing. In the frozen silence it will be possible to hear the 'song of the children'.

As those gathered around the tree speak the names of those loved ones they have lost to drugs, Meehan prays that their spoken names might somehow merge with the wind that blows 'through the branches' of the tree and that they become one with the soothing sounds of the river that flows through the city: 'Let their names be the song of the river'. These lines conjure up powerful images of freedom and release. The poet's final wish that 'their names be the holiest prayers' captures her wish that these children should never be forgotten.

FOCUS ON STYLE

Metaphor, Simile and Figures of Speech

The poet uses personification throughout the poem. She appeals to the tree that has been placed on Buckingham Street, calling on it to somehow act in a manner that might bring peace and solace to an area in Dublin that had been blighted by drugs and violence. The poet also personifies the 'streets'. It is as if the 'streets' have behaved in a sinister manner, seducing the children and wrecking their lives. It is the 'streets' that promise the children a bright future, only to betray them and stab them in the back. The 'streets', of course, represent the greater society.

Vivid Imagery

Meehan wonderfully captures the beauty and atmosphere of the 'far northern forest' where the tree grew. She describes the pristine snow that coats the landscape and the utter stillness that is to be found in such places.

THEMES

SOCIAL JUSTICE

The poem outlines what any healthy, functioning society should offer and provide to its young. It should provide security, sheltering them from drugs and violence. It should provide them with a secure and healthy space in which to grow and develop. It should inspire them and nurture and develop their dreams and visions. Society should be blowing the young people's minds with exciting possibilities.

The streets of Dublin's north inner city should have been able to promise them all these things and then deliver on these promises. But society failed these children. It has, Meehan suggests, betrayed them. The phrase 'knife in the back' might be read as a description of such a betrayal. Rather than raise them to the heights to which they aspired, the streets 'brought them to their knees', broke their dreams and crippled them with addiction.

NATURE AND SPIRITUALITY

In Meehan's poetry, the natural world is presented almost as a single organism, as if all its animal and plant life combine to form a unitary life-force or intelligence. Meehan developed this understanding of the natural world when she lived in California during the 1960s. She was influenced by Buddhism and Eastern philosophy, by the hippie movement and by American poets such as Gary Snyder who combined mysticism and environmentalism.

There are moments when Meehan suggests that the natural world is worthy of veneration, that we might pray to nature just as religious people pray to God. There are also moments, Meehan suggests, when it is possible for human beings to commune with nature, to attain an almost mystical oneness with the natural world. Such communion in Meehan's poetry is presented as a source of healing and renewal.

In this poem, Meehan appeals directly to the great fir tree that has been erected in the middle of Dublin city. She imagines the landscape of the tree's native land. The poet associates this natural landscape with 'clarity', tranquillity and 'silence'. She prays that the tree might somehow bring these conditions to bear on these urban streets, to grant the people of Dublin's north inner city a chance to heal.

FAMILY

The poem highlights the suffering and agony that families endure when they lose a child. The poet mentions the terrible moment when the police come to knock on the door to inform the parents that their child has died. Such loss is felt most acutely at Christmas time. The description of the spirits of the dead children singing reminds us of the innocence of the child and how at this time of year the young should be singing carols and enjoying the magic of Christmas.

THIS IS POETRY | PAULA MEEHAN

Death of a Field

LINE BY LINE

Planning permission has been granted for the construction of forty-four houses in a field close to where the poet is living. A site notice or 'Notice' has been placed at the entrance to the field. Such notices give a description of the nature and extent of the development and state to which planning authority the planning application is being made. Such a notice must be placed on site for five weeks from the date of receipt of the planning application.

In this case, the planning authority is Fingal County Council and planning permission is being sought for the construction of forty-four houses. Although no construction has yet taken place, the field, according to the poet, is 'lost' at this very moment. It is as if the site notice is a form of death warrant, an irreversible sentence that canot be overturned. The houses will be built and the field site will eventually be destroyed.

The poet thinks of the field as an intricate organism. She imagines that all the plant life in the field combines to form a unitary intelligence. The field's 'flora' or plant life – its grasses, flowers and herbs – function like some form of collective memory. These flowers and plants have been growing here for many years. It is as if they carry within them a shared memory or understanding of the field.

There is a sense in which the field's mix of different flowers, grasses and herbs is its identity. The moment these plants are lost, the field ceases to have an identity. It is as if its mind has been cleansed of all memories: 'the memory of the field disappears with its flora'.

The poet describes the impact that the field's loss will have on the wildlife in the area. Much of the hedging around the field will be destroyed, leaving many birds without a place to build their nest. The birds that do remain – 'the woodpigeons in the willow' and the 'finches in what's left of the hawthorn hedge' – will struggle to find the food they need to survive. These birds would have lived off the worms and grubs in the field's soil. Meehan imagines how these birds will continue to sing in the summer, but that their song will now be a 'hungry' one.

The field's plant life will also suffer. Meehan personifies some of the plants and flowers that grow in the field. She mentions 'yarrow', a wildflower with feathery leaves and heads of small white or pale pink aromatic flowers, which has long been used in herbal medicine. She describes how this plant will be left 'yearning' and will be left with an intense longing for the field in which it has long blossomed. She describes the scarlet pimpernel's 'plight' or predicament. It is as if this flower is going to be left destitute, without a home.

The poet thinks of how the field served as a discreet space for the young people in the area to get up to mischief. The field, with its long grass and hedges, would have provided the ideal place for the local kids and teenagers to smoke their first cigarette or take their 'first tokes' or inhalations of marijuana. The field was also where many teenagers would experience their earliest, and somewhat awkward, sexual experiences: 'first gropes'.

The houses
When the field has been destroyed, the construction of the houses in the estate will commence: 'The end of the field as we know it is the start of the estate'. Meehan imagines how these houses will eventually become family homes. The poet thinks of the many joyful moments and events that will take place in these homes. Each house, she says, will become a 'cargo of joy'. It is as if each house is a form of container that will eventually be filled with times of happiness and cheer. The house functions, she suggests, as a form of vessel that holds and contains these happy moments, its 'cargo of joy', carrying them through the years.

But these houses will also be places of 'sorrow'. Meehan thinks of the troubles that many families experience – the tragedies, setbacks and disappointments, the arguments, the bitter words and the brooding silences. For some, these houses will become places where negative feelings foster and flourish. They will be, for some, a 'nest of sorrow'.

The poet also thinks of the myriad cleaning products that these houses will contain. Each house, she says, will be a 'nest of chemical'. Detergents, surface cleaners, dishwashing tablets and air fresheners will quickly fill the cupboards and shelves. Meehan mentions a number of common 'chemical' cleaning products, such as 'Pledge', which is used when dusting, and 'Brasso', which is used to polish metal.

Meehan laments the fact that so many natural herbs will be destoyed in order that the houses be built.
- She mentions dock leaves which are used to soothe nettle stings. The cooling properties of their leaves are also used to soothe insect bites and stings, as well as scalds, blisters and sprains.
- The teasel herb is used to make certain medicines. People traditionally take teasel to treat skin conditions such as psoriasis. It is also put on the skin to treat arthritis.
- She mentions 'herb robert', which has traditionally been used to improve the functioning of the liver and gallbladder.

The fact that she juxtaposes herbs with a variety of 'chemical' products suggests that nature's potent and powerful remedies are being sacrificed and replaced with commercial products that are, in many cases, bad for the environment.

A walk at night
Soon the field will be gone. And the only record of its existence will be a map of the area as it was prior to the estate's construction. Meehan imagines this map file saved on 'some architect's screen'. In time, she says, the field will become 'solely map memory'.

The poet decides to take a last walk out into the field at night. This will enable her to experience the field alone, without the disturbing presence of architects, engineers and construction workers. In the stillness and silence of the night, she will be able to experience the field in an intimate way, sensitive to its every sound and movement.

Meehan describes how she will be 'Barefoot' so that she can 'know the field/ Through the soles of [her] feet'. She will be able to feel the texture of the grass and the dew that will be forming its blades in the cool of the night. In the silence of the night, she imagines how she will be able to hear the the gentle rustling of the trees' many leaves. She thinks how each green leaf is like an individual being, each producing its own distinctive sound, which she likens to song: 'hear/ The myriad leaf lives green and singing'.

The poet wishes that she could somehow come to 'possess' the field, that she could somehow seize or take control all the beauty, vitality and life that it contains. The poet longs to preserve this rich natrual treasure. The poet also imagines the field somehow coming to 'possess' her. She imagines being coated in the field's dew. She imagines how this 'slick' and shiny substance would coat or cover her like a 'caul' or membrane. She would be held within this silky covering, which would be rendered white in the moon's pale light: 'it possess me/ Through its night dew, its moon white caul/ Its slick and shine

THEMES

NATURE AND SPIRITUALITY

In Meehan's poetry, the natural world is presented almost as a single organism, as if all its animal and plant life combine to form a unitary life-force or intelligence. Meehan developed this understanding of the natural world when she lived in California during the 1960s. She was influenced by Buddhism and Eastern philosophy, by the hippie movement and by American poets such as Gary Snyder who combined mysticism and environmentalism.

In 'Death of a Field', the poet presents the field as a living organism. It has its own distinct 'memory', which is held within the flowers and herbs that grow there. Each element in the field, every blade of grass and every leaf that grows upon the branches of the trees is considered a living being that possesses its own distinctive identity.

The field, the poet suggests, comprises of a mind-boggling variety of life – and, also extraordinary potential for future life. She mentions the 'seeding head' of the plants, the dry cluster of seeds that sit atop the different plants in the field. Each seed is capable of becoming a new plant. There is the potential for so much future life in these clusters of seeds that the poet says it would be impossible to calculate the loss when the field is gone: 'Who amongst us is able ... To number the losses of each seeding head?'

Meehan also mentions the vast number of insects that can be discovered in the field. Some of these insects are responsible for spreading the seeds that gather at the tops of the flowers and for carrying pollen from plant to plant: 'The million million cycles of being in a wing'. There is a sense here of life constantly renewing itself, of endless fertility. Meehan describes the 'profligacy' of the natural world, the abundance of life that is evident in 'every beat of time'. She suggests that we have no idea of the magnitude of loss that occurs when a field like this is destroyed: 'Who amongst us is able to number the end of grasses/ To number the losses of each seeding head?'

Meehan also believes that it is possible for human beings to commune with nature, to attain an almost mystical oneness with the natural world. Such communion in Meehan's poetry is often presented as a source of healing and renewal. We see this in the poem's final lines, where Meehan describes walking out into the field at night in her bare feet. She is sensitive to its every sound and movement and describes a longing to 'possess' the field or to have the field 'possess' her.

FAMILY

The description of the houses as 'Nest[s] of sorrow' and 'cargo[es] of joy' suggests that in an estate of forty-four houses there are inevitably going to be families that enjoy a relatively happy and peaceful life and those who are going to be afflicted with troubles and difficulties. Meehan, of course, knew all too well, as many of her poems testify, that family life is not always easy.

SOCIAL JUSTICE

Many of Meehan's poems highlight the plight of individuals that society has neglected, forgotten or ignored. Here she highlights the 'plight' of a field that is going to be destroyed in order that a housing estate can be built. The poem suggests that when it comes to such trade-offs, we do not appreciate what is being sacrificed and lost.

FOCUS ON STYLE

Playful language

Meehan uses wonderfully playful language to capture the manner in which the field has served as a location for the town's teenagers to escape and hide. She describes the corners of the field and the secluded spots in the long grass and amongst the trees as 'hidey holes'. Here, she says, teenagers have traditionally experienced their 'first smokes, first tokes' and 'first gropes'.

Metaphor, Simile and Figures of Speech

Meehan describes how the magpies in the field sound 'like flying castanets'. Castanets are small wooden rattles, made in the shape of two bowls or cups, fitted together, tied by a string and then fastened to the thumbs. The comparison captures the rhythmic clicking sound that the magpies make.

Meehan compares the houses to nests, suggesting how these are places of sanctuary where children can be born and raised. But, as we mentioned above, the poet highlights how these structures might protect the inhabitants from external threats and dangers, but it does not safeguard against the sorrows that can afflict families within their homes.

In the poem's final lines, Meehan compares the coating of night dew to a membrane or 'caul'. The comparison brings to mind a kind of cocoon, the silky case spun by the larvae of many insects for protection. The poet imagines being coated and wrapped in this dewy substance. Perhaps she hopes that this 'caul' will preserve, insulate or protect her from the hardships that she is experiencing.

Them Ducks Died for Ireland

Statue of Countess Markiviecz

LINE BY LINE

'Them Ducks Died for Ireland' comes from a sequence titled 'Six Sycamores', which explores the beauty of Georgian Dublin whilst also exploring its complicated history. As Meehan put it: 'Because I grew up in a Georgian house, albeit a tenement slum, I know how they work ... I love those buildings; the intricacies of the craftwork, and the imagination ... and yet what they stand for ... I have real problems with that'. The sequence was commissioned by the Office of Public Works, whose headquarters are on St Stephen's Green in Dublin.

Light in the OPW
The poet is in the OPW building on St Stephen's Green working on her commission. This Georgian mansion has floorsboards made of oak and old-style 'sash' windows. Meehan is thinking about history, about time and the passage of time. In an extraordinary metaphor, she compares time to the evening light that is pouring through the sash window and spilling onto the 'oaken boards'. She presents time as a tangible presence in the room, a liquid substance that flows down the window panes and gathers in puddles on the floor.

The Green as lung
The Green, in a memorable metaphor, is compared to a 'great lung'. This reminds us of how plants, through the process known as photosynthesis, take in carbon dioxide and emit oxygen.

The poet thinks of nature's 24-hour cycles. Each evening the sun sets, the moon rises and the stars appear. Each morning the opposite happens: the moon sets, the sun rises and the stars disappear once more.

She also thinks of nature's yearly cycles, the constant 'seasons turn' from spring to winter and back again. These natural rhythms, she suggests, constantly alter the Green's plants, trees and grasses, shifting the nature of the gasses they 'exhale'.

The poet is standing close to the 'sash window' of the OPW, looking out at the Green below. Her breath, as she exhales, forms a mist on the 'pane' of the window before her. In a vivid simile, the oxygen emitted by the Green is compared to the breath exhaled by the poet: 'The Green...exhaling like breath on the pane'.

Memories of 1916
Meehan remembers that St Stephen's Green was seized by rebel forces during the 1916 Rising. The rebels dug trenches around the Green and erected barricades. They were attacked by British artillery and many buildings around the Green went up in flames.

The poet wonderfully compares the pond at the centre of the Green to a 'mirror'. She imagines that it must have reflected the flames that consumed the buildings around the Green. She also imagines that it must have reflected the dark palls of 'smoke' that drifted overhead.

The poet remembers the Irish patriot Countess Markievicz, who along with Michael Malin, commanded the rebel forces on the Green. The poet imagines the Countess striding confidently across the green. We can picture her dressed in full military uniform, issuing orders and encouraging her men to resist the British bombardment.

The rebels had declared a republic free of British rule. And, as Markievicz walked across the Green, the destiny of that fledging republic walked with her. Her actions and decisions as a commander would help determine if the Republic survived or was quickly extinguished: 'a Republic's destiny in a Countess' stride'.

Patriots like Markievicz were utterly dedicated to their cause and were willing to pay 'the bloodprice' for Irish freedom. They were prepared to kill British soldiers. They were also prepared to kill Irish people they felt were collaborating with the British state and to give their own lives for the cause they served. The Countess's colleague, Michael Malin, for instance, was among the 16 leaders executed after the surrender of the rebels. Markievicz, too, was condemned to death, only to have her sentence commuted because the British authorities were reluctant to execute a woman.

The sight of this 'bloodprice', of the rebels killing and being killed, had a complicated effect on the Irish people. For some, it was a 'summons' to national 'pride'. They wanted to fight on, to follow the rebels' example and finally end British rule in Ireland. But for others, it was a cure or 'antidote' to national pride. They were horrified by the bloodshed and destruction of the Rising and became wary of nationalism in all its forms, realising the violence it could lead to.

Those who pick up the pieces

Meehan, however, wants to focus on the ordinary people who are forgotten by history. She doesn't want to write about famous commanders like the Countess. She doesn't even want to write about the rank and file soldiers who fought and died around the Green. Instead, she wants to write about those who worked in the background of the conflict.

- She mentions 'stretcher bearer[s]' who carry wounded soldiers to safety. Meehan no doubt remembers that St Stephen's Green served as a field hospital during the Rising. But such stretcher bearers can be seen in many conflicts around the globe.
- She mentions 'nurse[s] in white' who tend to the wounded and the dying. Meehan, of course, has in mind not only the nurses who attended the wounded in 1916 but also those nurses who have served in countless other conflicts before and since.
- She mentions the ones who 'pick up the pieces'. This brings to mind the workers who cleared away the rubble in the wake of the Rising, who set about repairing Dublin's damaged streets and buildings. But such repair work, of course, is necessary after every conflict.

Commanders like Countess Markievicz are at the centre of historical events. The nurses, stretcher bearers and construction workers, on the other hand, 'live at the edge' of these events. They can be glimpsed working away at the periphery of the action, or they appear once the action is concluded in order to 'pick up the pieces'.

Meehan points out how these ordinary workers all too often die while working 'at the edge' of these great historical moments. A construction worker might be killed by falling rubble, for instance, or a nurse might be struck by a stray bullet.

Meehan emphasises what these ordinary workers 'endure'. This suggests their physical and mental strength and their ability to keep going, even in adverse circumstances. It also suggests the courage they exhibit as they undertake tasks that are often dangerous or even life-threatening. These are people who are determined to get the job done no matter what. Meehan, therefore, stresses the importance of remembering and honouring these ordinary workers. We must 'salute' these unknown heroes just as we salute the major personalities like Countess Markievicz.

Each conflict leaves behind psychological wounds, a legacy of bitterness and division. Eventually these wounds are healed. The bitterness and division prompted by the conflict is resolved or, at least, forgotten. Remembering these ordinary workers, Meehan suggests, is much easier once such healing has occurred: 'When we've licked the wounds of history, wounds of war// we'll salute the stretcher bearer'. A nation, the poet suggests, must come to terms with the big issues of a conflict before it can 'salute' those who lived and died at the conflict's 'edge'.

These ordinary heroes are never the subjects of biographies or documentaries. They hardly feature in the history books. They do, sometimes, leave a vague trace in the historical record. Their names might be mentioned in passing in a newspaper report. We might glimpse them in the corner of a photograph. Or their actions might be recorded in reports that have been filed, archived and forgotten.

Meehan has come across one such report while conducting research for her 'Six Sycamores' sequence. The report in question was written by the Park Superintendent of Stephen's Green in 1916. The report describes the damage caused to the Green by the events of the Rising, recounting how birds were shot, 'garden seats broken' and 'shrubs destroyed'.

Meehan sits by the sash windows in the OPW and reads this 'archival footnote' in the 'fading light' of evening. She realises that this Park Superintendent was one of the ordinary heroes mentioned above. It was his job to pick up the pieces once the great events of the Rising had concluded. He had to repair the park benches, replant the shrubberies and replace the birds that had been shot.

We erect statues to our great heroes, making the 'gesture/ of commemorating them ... in bronze and stone'. But we erect no statues to the ordinary workers like the Park Superintendent. We make no 'gesture' of commemoration towards them. They survive only as an 'archival footnote'.

The poet exhales as she stands before the window of the OPW and her breath forms a mist upon the glass. This 'breathmark', she realises, will exist only for a moment before vanishing.

Both the statues and the archival footnotes, the poet realises, are as 'fragile' as this 'breathmark'. They too will exist only briefly before vanishing. The statues may exist for hundreds of years before they weather away. The archival footnote too may last for a long time before it is disposed of or disintegrates. But the lifespan of these objects in the grand scheme of human existence covers only the briefest of moments.

THEMES

SOCIAL JUSTICE

In 'Them Ducks Died for Ireland', as in many of her poems, Meehan sets out to speak on behalf of those who have been forgotten. She urges us, as we have seen, to 'salute' not only the great heroes but also those in the background of history's great events. She reminds us that those ordinary workers also made great sacrifices and displayed great courage. Such a 'salute', of course, could take many forms. It could be an exhibition or a school project, or a poem of remembrance like this one.

The poet also makes the point that no form of commemoration will last forever. She is highly conscious of time's passage, presenting it as an almost palpable, liquid presence in the drawing room of the OPW. And time, she emphasises, will erode all forms of memory, from archival records to statues made of bronze or stone.

FOCUS ON STYLE

Form
The poem, somewhat unusually for Meehan, has a regular form. It is a Petrarchan sonnet, rhyming ABBA BCCB DEFDEF.

Playful use of language
In the 'Six Sycamores' sequence, Meehan combined two very different tones. She used sonnets written in hightened poetic language. She also included snatches of ordinary Dublin speech.

We see this in 'Them Ducks Died for Ireland', which combines a sonnet written in such complex, metaphorical verse with a title that is a snippet of Dublin street talk. We can imagine an ordinary Dubliner hearing about the wildfowl that were shot in St Stephen's Green and remarking that 'Them ducks died for Ireland', wittily comparing these unfortunate birds to those who martyred themselves for Irish freedom.

The sonnet form represents, for Meehan, the beauty of the Georgian mansions she was writing about, while the snippets of everyday speech reflect the ordinary lives that are lived in and around these beautiful buildings. As Meehan put it in an interview:

I wanted to put them together, to say this is a sonnet, but this is an actual human voice, unornamented in plain speech with its own vignette out of life. Just as the ordinary life goes on in these beautiful structures, these edifices. So I wanted to get a conversation between the casual throw-away vernacular of the little pieces and the more tightly wrapped language and ritualised energy of the sonnets.

Adrienne Rich

Themes

Love and Relationships

'Trying to Talk With a Man' and 'From a Survivor' movingly recount the story of a marriage. 'From a Survivor' begins with those early, heady days when the couple were convinced of their own specialness, when they believed their relationship would prove invulnerable to life's challenges. 'Trying to Talk With a Man', too, recounts those happy times filled with music and cookies, with movies and 'afternoons on the riverbank'. This was a period when even the couple's struggles, as symbolised by 'suicide notes' mentioned in 'Trying to Talk with a Man', brought them closer together.

Such togetherness, however, did not last. Over time the couple's relationship came to be characterised by an emotional distance, by a terrible 'silence' at the heart of their marriage. As 'From a Survivor' makes clear, they came to realise that their early optimism had been desperately naive. They realised that, like everybody else, they were destined to 'share' in the failings of the human race.

In 'Trying to Talk With a Man', then, the couple have come to the desert not only to protest against nuclear weapons, but also to confront the toxic silence that's eating away at their relationship. For it's not only the military that will be 'testing bombs' in this desert landscape. The couple, in a metaphorical sense, are braced for a detonation of their own. Their conversation will be emotionally explosive as they have a full and frank discussion about the state of their marriage, finally confronting the silence at the heart of their relationship.

The drive into the desert was a final 'test' of themselves and of their relationship: 'as if we were testing anything else'. The poet hoped that in the space and silence of the desert they might have found a way to discuss their difficulties. This hope, however, has proved a false one, because their difficulties, it seems, are too embedded to be overcome. The exit sign reflected in her husband's eyes points the only way forward.

'From a Survivor', then, details the ultimate failure of the couple's marriage and its grim aftermath, which saw the poet's husband tragically take his own life. But the poem movingly reminds us how affection can survive even the most traumatic break-up. The poet still retains a great deal of affection for her former husband, recalling, with perfect clarity, what his body looked like: 'Your body is as vivid to me / as it ever was'. She wishes that he, like her, had been capable of survival, of taking the great 'leap' into a new and better kind of existence.

Suffering and Survival

Many of Rich's poems deal with the twin topics of suffering and survival. 'From a Survivor', for instance, highlights the suffering experienced by the poet and her husband as they contended with the 'failures of the race', with the stress such failures placed upon their marriage and, ultimately, with the breakdown of the marriage itself.

The poet celebrates the fact that she has outlived such suffering, has came through this terrible ordeal with her life and sanity intact. The poet, we sense, grimly rejoices in her own resilience, in her own hard-won status as a survivor. She is confident in her own endurance, knowing that, no matter what life throws at her, she will survive.

'The Roofwalker', too, presents psychological suffering. It focuses on a speaker who for many years has denied her own identity, living a life that was chosen for her rather than one she sought out for herself. We get a sense of suffocating claustrophobia as the speaker describes how she found herself trapped beneath a 'roof [she] can't live under'. The speaker has effectively assembled her own prison, working extremely hard to fashion an inappropriate and suffocating existence for herself. The speaker, however, did not succumb to this suffering, instead finding the courage to change her life and start anew.

In 'Living in Sin', we sense that life in the little studio has brought the young woman little but suffering. The reality of life there has not lived up to her expectations. She assumed, that there would be 'no dust upon the furniture of love', but the studio has turned out to be far grottier and dingier than she expected. Furthermore, her relationship with her boyfriend is not at all what she imagined it would be.

Her feelings of foolishness and failure are memorably described as the jeering of 'the minor demons'. It's easy to imagine such self-criticism as the insidious whisper of a demon, its jeers and mockery echoing through our minds as it reiterates over and over what a mess she's made of things.

There can be little doubt, however, that the young woman will survive this ordeal. Each evening finds her a little less in love with her boyfriend and their life together: 'By evening she was back in love again,/ though not so wholly'. Eventually, no doubt, she will fall out of love completely and leave the studio behind, emerging all the stronger for having come through such trials.

'The Roofwalker', 'Living in Sin' and 'From a Survivor', then, depict speakers who suffer and survive. They depict women who suffer life's blows but emerge physically and mentally intact. Their ordeals may leave them scarred, but they never surrender their physical well-being or their sense of self.

The subject of 'Aunt Jennifer's Tigers', alas, cannot be considered a survivor in this sense. Aunt Jennifer, the speaker fears, will be 'mastered' by the various ordeals that afflict her. On a physical level, her already trembling body will become even weaker and more debilitated. On a psychological level, her remaining self-belief and self-assurance will drain away, so that she scarcely has a will of her own anymore. By the time of her death, which is some years in the future, she will be broken in both body and mind: 'When Aunt is dead, her terrified hands will lie/ Still ringed with ordeals she was mastered by'.

We sense, however, that one aspect of Aunt Jennifer's personality will survive her various ordeals; namely her artistic sensibility. It is only through her knitting, then, that Aunt Jennifer can resist, in a metaphorical sense, the ordeals to which she's been subjected. For even when Aunt Jennifer is lying in her grave, the tigers she created will 'go on prancing', their grandeur still visible to all who see the panel she so artfully constructed

Forging Yourself

Many of Rich's poems feature women who forge their own existences, who leave behind their old lives to create whole new lifestyles – even new identities – in an often scary process of reinvention.

'From a Survivor', for instance, shows how in the years since her husband's death the poet has gone on to make such a leap, to change her life in a fundamental fashion. Her new approach to living involves seeing life as a 'series' of moments, as a matter of existing in the present rather than being constantly preoccupied with the future and the past. It involves seeing the extraordinary in the ordinary, seeing each moment as a wonderful gift, as something not only 'brief' but also 'amazing'.

'Living in Sin' depicts a less successful effort at self-renewal. The young woman in the poem has attempted to forge a new identity for herself, leaving behind her family and starting a new bohemian life with her boyfriend. This attempt at self-forging, however, has backfired. The studio turns out to be miserable and her relationship dysfunctional. As a result, the young woman must now leave the studio behind and make another attempt to discover who she really is, to become who she needs to be.

In the conclusion of 'The Roofwalker' the speaker compares herself to a 'naked man' running across the rooftops of the city. There is something bizarre and perhaps even a little amusing about such an image. But it's also a conclusion that evokes a haunting sense of vulnerability and sorrow. For the repetition of the word 'naked' emphasises the man's exposure and vulner-ability. We feel the speaker's sense of helplessness as she finds herself between lives, having abandoned her old identity while still being in the process of forging a new one.

Aunt Jennifer in 'Aunt Jennifer's Tigers', unfortunately, seems destined never to manage such an escape. Indeed, the speaker points out that the ring symbolising her misfortunes will remain on her finger even when after she's died, suggesting that even in death Aunt Jennifer will find no release from the forces that have oppressed her.

In it is only in the realm of artistic expression that Aunt Jennifer manages to forge her own identity. The tigers she so carefully fashions can be viewed as a strange kind of self-portrait, as representing the confident, even fierce, person that Aunt Jennifer might have come had her life worked out differently. Her only escape from the ordeals that have come to define her is an imaginative one, into the forest landscape she so carefully creates.

The Subjugation of Women

The Power of Men over Women

'Our Whole Life', like many of Rich's poems, touches on the subjugation of women. The poem presents a male-dominated language that has arisen from a male-dominated civilisation. This is a world where women are oppressed and kept in their place, much as the colonising French kept the conquered Algerians in check for over a hundred years. The poem, then, presents a grim view of white Western males, depicting how they oppress not only women in their home countries but also African and Asian peoples abroad, as they pursue their imperial and post-imperial projects of domination.

Such subjugation is also evident in 'From a Survivor'. During the years of their marriage, the poet thought of her husband as an all-powerful, almost divine figure, regarding his body as the 'body of a god'. In the 1950s and 1960s, we remind ourselves, marriage was a very unequal institution; a woman was expected to respect and obey her husband and be guided by him in all things. The poet, it seems, internalised these values, coming to see her husband almost as her lord and master, granting him a great deal of 'power over [her] life'.

'Trying to Talk With a Man' is another poem that deals with the power men have traditionally wielded over women. When the poet stands next to her husband in the observation post, she can feel heat radiating from his body. The poet, in a startling turn of phrase, compares this heat to 'power'. Similarly, the poet compares her husband's eyes to stars of extraordinary brightness: 'your eyes are stars of a different magnitude'. Her husband's eyes remind her of how each star is a raging furnace, powered by endless nuclear reactions that take place deep within their cores.

Her husband, then, with his dry heat and blazing eyes, reminds her of the nuclear explosion that's shortly due to take place.

The poet might be reminded of how the masculine drive to dominate others led to the creation of nuclear weapons (as well as all other weapons of mass destruction) in the first place. She is reminded, too, it seems, of how men use their privilege and power to oppress not only women in America but also less privileged populations overseas

Unequal Relationships
Both 'The Roofwalker' and 'Aunt Jennifer's Tigers' presents an extremely negative view of marriage, viewing it as an unequal institution that kept women in the power of the men they married. (These poems, we must remember, were written at a time when women were expected to love, honour and obey their husbands).

In 'The Roofwalker', the poet laments how peer pressure and family expectation forced her into a marriage – and a lifestyle – she never really wanted. Now she has left married life behind like someone slipping out of a house in which she's been held prisoner. Aunt Jennifer's marriage, meanwhile, is presented as an 'ordeal' through which she is controlled and 'mastered', one symbolised by the 'massive weight' of the wedding band that sits upon her finger.

'The Uncle Speaks in the Drawing Room' also deals with the subjugation of women. The uncle strikes us as an old-fashioned, conservative type of a man. We can imagine him droning on and on, his comments addressed at the other men gathered in the drawing room. Perhaps he is trying to impress these other men with his pompous waffle, in an effort to reinforce his own sense of authority. We can imagine him talking over the heads of any of the women gathered and simply ignoring these women if they dare to offer an opinion on the subject.

'Living in Sin' also highlights the inequality that existed (and that all-too-often persists) between the sexes. It is the young woman, unsurprisingly; who attempts to keep the apartment in some kind of decent condition while the man spends his time playing the piano and wandering the streets in search of cigarettes.

The young woman's artistic and rebellious boyfriend seems a world away from the privileged and conservative uncle in 'The Uncle Speaks in The Drawing Room'. But they are similar in their disregard for the women in their lives. The uncle drones on and on, inviting no input or comment from the women in the drawing room. Similarly, the young woman's boyfriend seems utterly uninterested in what she has to day, utterly oblivious to the misery she's suffering through. He just yawns, shrugs and walks out the door.

The poem, then, highlights how even supposedly sensitive and enlightened men can reinforce this traditional inequality. It demonstrates how, even today, women can be victims in a 'man's world'. Indeed, the inequality that dominates their relationship is the real 'sin' with which the young couple are living.

Women Empowering Themselves
Yet Rich's poetry also demonstrates how women can overcome make domination and learn to empower themselves. In 'From a Survivor', the poet describes how, since her marriage came to an end, her confidence and self-belief have developed greatly. She has also developed a new, more feminist consciousness, one that emphasises equality and amity between the genders. Society, too, has changed over the intervening years; women are no longer expected to worship and obey the men in their lives. The 'pact/ of men and women in those days' isn't quite the same as it is today.

As a result of all these changes, the poet has a clearer understanding of who her husband was: 'my feeling for it [her husband's body] is clearer'. She no longer thinks of him as an all-powerful figure with 'the body of a god'. Instead, she understands that he was just an everyday human being, with normal abilities and limitations: 'I know what it could and could not do'. She no longer feels capable of being dominated by him, or by any other man.

'Power, too, depicts a woman who empowered herself, showing how Marie Curie gained not only professional power, becoming one of the most influential and authoritative figures in her field, but also political and economic power, because her discoveries had a profound impact on many different aspects of society. She also commanded power in a literal, physical sense, handling elements that were capable of emitting terrifying levels of energy.

The power wielded by Curie, then, massively outclasses the power enjoyed by the quack doctor. He was merely a con-artist who temporarily seduced and charmed his unwitting customers, but Marie Curie changed the world forever. Rich, therefore, shows how Marie Curie empowered herself, overcoming the restrictions that are often placed on women. But her power came at a terrible price, her physical health destroyed by the toxic materials with which she worked. In this regard, Curie's career exemplifies the scarifices required by women as they empower themselves. She shows how hard women must struggle to succeed in what is still very much a 'man's world'.

Gender

'Diving Into the Wreck' provides a fascinating take on gender, suggesting that at the moment of birth each human being is essentially ungendered. As we grow, however, society teaches and conditions us to speak, walk, play, behave and dress in a particular manner. In doing so, a part of who we are, or who we potentially can be, is suppressed and ignored.

However, the poet imagines that somewhere deep inside our unconscious minds we possess a memory of what it was like to exist in this gender-neutral way. In the poem, she imagines journeying deep into her unconscious to discover and explore this memory. She presents this journey or exploration as a deep-sea dive.

The memory that the poet is seeking to find in the depths of unconscious is like the wreck of a ship that lies far below the surface of the sea. The poet wishes to access her unconscious mind and explore this memory of our lives before they were defined by the social construction of gender.

The poet believes that our lives could be a whole lot richer if we allowed our complete or full personalities to develop and flourish, that there are possibilities of being we are neglecting. The poet imagines that the memory of her ungendered self might contain a wealth of 'treasures', ways of understanding that could open up whole new ways of being and experiencing life and the world.

'Our Whole Life' also touches on the notion of gender, presenting language itself as a male-dominated system, one designed for and by men. The poem movingly depicts the frustration felt by women as they attempt to communicate in a system not calibrated for their experiences, not designed to capture how they see and experience the world.

Women's descriptions of their experience, therefore, are necessarily fuzzy and inaccurate, like a document translated from one language to another: 'Our whole life a translation'. For women, language obscures as much as it expresses, like a layer of paint slathered on a wooden surface. For Rich, this inability to communicate evokes feelings of dread and claustrophobia, feelings she articulates through images of confinement, pain and suffering.

But Rich also describes how the 'meanings' of male-created language might be eliminated or 'burnt-off', allowing women's experience to be expressed in a truthful and natural fashion. She hopes that the 'knot of lies' that presently binds women might someday be 'undone'. Indeed, she suggests that this knot is 'eating at itself', as if it is unstable and destined to unravel, thereby liberating the women it currently constrains.

Privilege and Oppression

'The Uncle Speaks in the Drawing Room' is spoken by a member of a very wealthy and privileged family. He has not had to work for this wealth and privilege – it is something that he inherited and takes for granted. He thinks that wealthy, powerful families such as his are superior to other elements in society, particularly the working classes. He speaks of 'our kind' as though he and his family were a superior form of the human race. The protestors, in contrast, are described as angry brutes and are characterised as a 'mob' of 'missile-throwers'.

The uncle's privileged life is, of course, predicated or based on the suppression of the ordinary workers. As long as they are powerless to change society, the uncle and his family can maintain their privileged position. But we get the sense that things are beginning to change and that the workers are not going to just let this go and allow things to go on as before. However, the uncle is incapable of seeing this, blinded and assured by the family's long history of wealth and dominance.

'Trying to Talk with a Man' also depicts people who live a privileged life. The poet and her husband enjoy a comfortable, well-to-do existence, one characterised by a reasonable level of luxury and leisure. Increasingly, however, they have begun to sacrifice more and more of their free time to campaig against oppression in its various forms. Their hobbies and intellectual pursuits have begun to take a back seat to activism. The fight against their government's oppressive policies have begun to take over their lives: 'What we had to give up to get here'.

The contrast between the poet and her husband, on one hand, and the uncle, on the other, couldn't be clearer. While the uncle is determined to enjoy his luxurious lifestyle, the speaker and her husband actively sacrifice theirs. The uncle is contemptuous of the protestors, whereas the poet and her husband actively join the protest movement. The uncle resists and fears change, whereas the poet and her husband actively embrace it.

'The Roofwalker' also touches upon this issue. We sense that the speaker's previous life-style was one of privilege and comfort, represented by the image of a relaxing, lamp-lit room with 'cream wallpaper'. It was an existence engineered by careful 'measurings' and 'closing of gaps', one designed to shut out the outside world, with all its threats and tribulations.

We might imagine, therefore, that the speaker seldom looked beyond her cosy existence, seldom thought about those less privileged than herself, whose difficulties, in a real sense, made possible her own relatively luxurious lifestyle. We also note, however, that the speaker of the poem has now abandoned this privileged existence and has set out to reinvent herself, to forge a new life in which she will, no doubt, be more conscious of those less fortunate than herself.

THIS IS POETRY — **ADRIENNE RICH**

Aunt Jennifer's Tigers

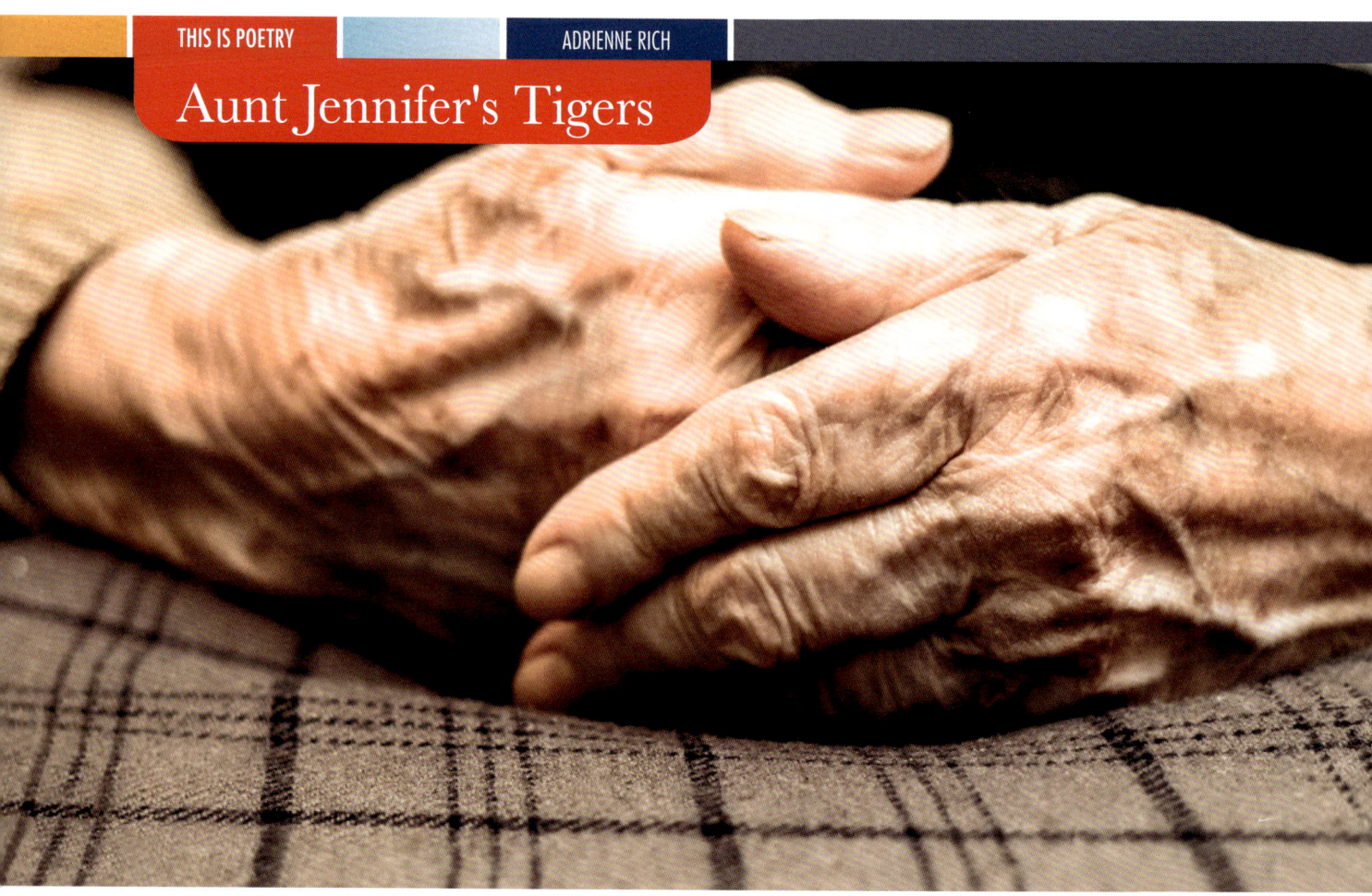

LINE BY LINE

Aunt Jennifer

In this poem, the speaker describes her Aunt Jennifer knitting a decorative screen. The screen is adorned by an image of tigers moving through a jungle. The poem focuses on the contrast between the knitted tigers (who seem powerful, fearless and full of energy) and Aunt Jennifer herself, who, we're told, has suffered a number of 'ordeals' throughout her life.

Aunt Jennifer seems to have endured the trauma of physical illness, which has left her body weak and permanently shaking. Her fingers are 'fluttering' as she knits, and she is so feeble that she can scarcely manipulate her knitting needles: 'Aunt Jennifer's finger fluttering through her wool/ Find even the ivory needle hard to pull'.

Aunt Jennifer's 'fluttering' fingers also indicate that she has suffered ordeals of a psychological nature. Such mental trauma has left her extremely timid and inhibited, the reference to her 'terrified hands' indicating the extent of the damage she has suffered.

Aunt Jennifer has also suffered the ordeal of marriage. Her wedding ring is described as a 'massive weight' that 'sits heavily' upon her hand, functioning as a powerful symbol for the great mental burden that marriage placed upon her.

The tigers

The speaker describes the knitted screen that her aunt so carefully produced, which features several brightly coloured tigers. The tigers are described as 'denizens' or inhabitants of a 'world of green', which suggests that the panel depicts a forest environment. It also depicts a number of men, who are shown gathered beneath one of the forest's trees.

The tigers are described as 'Bright topaz' in colour, which tells us that they are a rich and luminescent yellow. Their bodies are described as 'sleek', which suggests both the silken nature of their fur and the trim, elegant nature of their physiques.

There are moments when the tigers go 'prancing' through their jungle environment, moving with exuberant, springing steps. There are also moments when the tigers 'pace' through the undergrowth, moving in a slower and more deliberate fashion as they stalk their prey.

Rich uses the term 'chivalric' to describe the tigers' movement, a quality pertaining to medieval knights and knighthood. This suggests that the tigers exhibit the strength and ferocity of a medieval warhorse. But it also brings to mind the arrogance and entitlement of a mediaeval lord, parading on horseback as he surveys his domains.

The tigers, then, move with 'certainty', which suggests that they are utterly fearless and self-confident. They are completely unconcerned by the human beings that Aunt Jennifer has included in the image: 'They do not fear the men beneath the tree'. The men pose no threat to these ferocious beasts. On the contrary, we sense that it's the men who ought to be afraid

Aunt Jennifer and the tigers

The contrast between Aunt Jennifer and the tigers she created could not be starker:

- Aunt Jennifer, as we've seen, is physically weak. The tigers, in contrast, exhibit great physical strength, their 'sleek' bodies moving in a powerful fashion as they pace or prance.
- Aunt Jennifer is depicted as a most timid and uncertain person. The tigers, in contrast, exhibit great 'certainty' as they move with an emphatic confidence through the forest.
- Aunt Jennifer is depicted as a 'terrified', timid and easily intimidated person. But the tigers are utterly 'unafraid'. They will be cowed or intimidated by no man: 'they do not fear the men beneath the tree'.
- Aunt Jennifer, according to the speaker, has been 'mastered' by her marriage and by the other 'ordeals' that she has suffered through. The tigers, in contrast, are 'proud' creatures whose confidence and physical strength prevents them from being mastered by anyone or anything.

FOCUS ON STYLE

Form

'Aunt Jennifer's Tigers', like many of Rich's early poems, is written in strict and regular form. The poem consists of three four-line stanzas, each with an AABB rhyme. As Rich's career progressed, her style would evolve to become much looser, deploying free verse rather strict rhyme schemes, and featuring jagged collage-like passages.

Metaphor, Simile, Figures of Speech

The poem features an interesting use of synecdoche, whereby a part of an object or person represents the whole. In this instance, Aunt Jennifer's hands represent her personality as a whole. Her hands, we're told, are 'terrified', suggesting her cowed and intimidated nature. The fact that they flutter and struggle to manipulate the needle suggests her physical weakness, as well, perhaps, as he psychological diminishment. Of course the 'wedding' that sits 'so heavily' upon her hand is highly symbolic, representing the great burden marriage has place upon Aunt Jennifer's life.

Imagery

This poem is based around the rich image of Aunt Jennifer's screen: the dazzling yellow topaz of the tigers, the forest's trees creating a vivid world of green, the tigers' sleek fur almost tangible. Aunt Jennifer's needlework is of such a high quality that the creatures she's created seem to move with a will of their own. The poem, then, celebrates the ability of the artist or craftsman to create something powerful and glorious out of even the most dismal of circumstances.

THEMES

THE SUBJUGATION OF WOMEN

Like many of Rich's poems, 'Aunt Jennifer's Tigers' presents an extremely negative view of marriage. Aunt Jennifer's marriage is presented as an 'ordeal' through which she is controlled and 'mastered', an ordeal symbolised by the 'massive weight' of the wedding band that sits upon her finger.

Perhaps Aunt Jennifer didn't get on with her husband and as a result endured a bad marriage full of resentment and recriminations. However, Aunt Jennifer's cowed and timid state of mind also suggests that her husband was overbearing and domineering, a bully who controlled Aunt Jennifer by diminishing her sense of self and chipping away at her self-confidence.

But it's also the institution of marriage itself, as opposed to any one particular marriage, that is presented as an 'ordeal'. Marriage, the poem suggests, is an instrument by which a male-dominated society controls and dominates women. And in those days, we must remind ourselves, marriage was a terribly unequal arrangement: wives were expected to obediently serve their husbands and to always put their husband's needs before their own.

An interesting contrast can drawn between Aunt Jennifer, in the present poem, and the uncle in 'The Uncle Speaks in the Drawing Room'. The uncle, filled with an inflated sense of his own wisdom, with an unearned self-confidence, presumes to speak not only for himself but also for his whole family. In contrast, we sense that Aunt Jennifer is such a timid person that she lacks the confidence to speak at all. The ordeals she's suffered have rendered her voiceless, her only mode of self-expression being the panels that she knits.

FORGING YOURSELF

Many of Rich's poems feature women who forge their own existences, who leave behind their old lives to create whole new lifestyles – even new identities – in an often scary process of reinvention.

Aunt Jennifer, unfortunately, seems destined never to manage such an escape. The speaker suggests that she has been completely 'mastered' by her various ordeals and will remain so until her death. Indeed, the speaker points out that the ring symbolising her misfortunes will remain on her finger even after her death. This suggests that even in death Aunt Jennifer will find no release from the forces that have oppressed her. Even when she's lying in her grave, people will think of her in terms of the ordeals that defined her life: 'When Aunt is dead, her terrified hands will lie/ Still ringed with ordeals she was mastered by'.

In it is only in the realm of artistic expression that Aunt Jennifer manages to forge her own identity. The tigers she so carefully fashions can be viewed as a strange kind of self-portrait, an image of the confident, even fierce, person that Aunt Jennifer might have become if her life had turned out differently. We sense that she imagines herself as such a poised and pacing beast, inhabiting a world where, instead of being 'terrified', she is the one who does the terrifying. Her only escape from the ordeals that have come to define her is an imaginative one, into the forest landscape that she so carefully creates.

SUFFERING AND SURVIVAL

Several of Rich's poems ('The Roofwalker' or 'From a Survivor', for example) portray speakers who suffer and survive. The speaker's aunt, alas, cannot be considered a survivor in this sense. Aunt Jennifer, the speaker fears, will be 'mastered' by the various ordeals that afflict her. On a physical level, her already trembling body will become even weaker and more debilitated. On a psychological level, her remaining self-belief and self-assurance will drain away, so that she scarcely has a will of her own anymore. By the time of her death, which is some years in the future, she will be broken in both body and mind.

We sense, however, that one aspect of Aunt Jennifer's personality will survive her various ordeals; her artistic sensibility. She may be oppressed until her confidence is shattered and her sense-of-self is utterly diminished, but her talent and artistic vision will continue. She still manages to create a screen that's brimming with colour, confidence and energy, bedecked with jewel-coloured tigers stalking arrogantly through the forest. It is only through her knitting, then, that Aunt Jennifer can survive, in a metaphorical sense, the ordeals to which she has been subjected.

Furthermore, the tigers she knitted will survive long after she herself is dead, their grandeur still visible to all who see the panel she so artfully constructed. Even when Aunt Jennifer is lying in her grave, the tigers she created will 'go on prancing'. The poem, then, celebrates how works of art can outlive their creators. For as long as the tigers continue to prance and pace, a part of Aunt Jennifer will always be alive.

The Uncle Speaks in the Drawing Room

LINE BY LINE

The poem is set in the drawing room of a wealthy, privileged family. The house that they occupy is located on a square, perhaps in a large town or city. A drawing room is a room in a large, private house in which guests are often received and entertained. It's not a room where the homeowners would normally spend their free time but one in which guests are hosted before and after dinner. The drawing room is typically situated near the entrance and close to the front door, so guests can go directly inside without having to pass through other rooms.

We get the impression that this is a very grand house; there is mention of a balcony and a gate that separates the property from the square. The reader senses that this is an 'old money' family, a family that has been rich for generations. Those of the current generation have not had to work to become rich; they have simply inherited the family estate. The poem's speaker mentions certain expensive items that have been passed down through the generations – crystal vases and chandeliers and a particularly valuable 'antique ruby bowl'. These 'treasures' have been 'handed down' and are 'in the keeping' of the family.

It is a time of social unrest. The poorer elements of society are on the march. We can imagine that they are unhappy with how their lives are shaped and constrained by inequalities of wealth and social class.

A large crowd of people has now gathered in the square just outside the gates of the house. They are obviously very angry, speaking in 'bitter tones' and, in some cases, even holding 'stones', which they seem intent on throwing at the house. We are told that they are staring angrily at the property: 'Gazing with a sullen stare/ At window, balcony, and gate'.

Certain members of the family have gathered in the drawing room to listen to the uncle, possibly the most senior (male) member of the family, as he speaks about the situation. We can imagine that this is an informal gathering, perhaps after dinner. The family have retired to the drawing room to relax and unwind before going to bed.

Perhaps the uncle is holding a glass of brandy and smoking a cigar, standing by the fire-place or strolling around the room. We might picture the aunt sitting demurely in her chair, perhaps working on her tapestry, like the aunt whose knitting is the subject of Rich's poem 'Aunt Jennifer's Tigers'. Other members of the family might be reading or playing cards. Perhaps no one is really listening to the uncle, but he waffles on regardless.

The uncle describes the crowd as a 'mob', a derogatory term that suggests that the crowd is disorderly and intent on causing trouble. The term 'mob' also implies that the crowd is comprised of the lower or working classes. The uncle says that the people in the square are ill-tempered or 'sullen'. They are speaking in what he regards as 'bitter tones'. Some of those gathered in the square are holding stones, handling them as though preparing to cast them at the house. It seems that this is not the first time that such a crowd of people has gathered to demonstrate frustration and anger. The uncle says he has seen them 'of late', implying that they have been around for a while and that he has encountered them on a number of occasions.

The uncle, however, dismisses the threat and significance of the crowd. He considers their actions to be foolish and feels certain that their anger and frustration will soon blow over, and things will go on as normal: 'These are follies that subside'. He also does not believe that any of the crowd will throw stones: 'Not that missiles will be cast'. No one has yet dared to throw a stone at the house, and the uncle assumes that the crowd are afraid to do so: 'None as yet dare lift an arm'.

But the uncle does not rule out entirely the possibility that things could get a little ugly or out of hand. He reminds the family that this is not the first time that they have had to deal with the threat of violent social unrest. The uncle recalls a time, perhaps from his childhood, when some particularly violent upheaval threatened the property.

The uncle does not say what exactly this upheaval was, referring to it only as a 'storm'. But it was most likely a war or battle – The uncle describes how the house was shaken by 'a thunder-roll' – which suggests the exploding of weapons and bombs. This was back when the uncle's grandfather was still alive. As the war raged not too far from the property, the grandfather's primary concern was for the valuable glass ornaments in the house, in particular an 'antique ruby bowl'. The uncle recalls how their grandfather was greatly disturbed when the explosions caused this bowl to vibrate or shake: 'our grandsire stood aghast/ To see his antique ruby bowl/ Shivered in a thunder-roll'.

Now that the family are once again caught up in some form of social unrest, the uncle advises that their focus should again be on the preservation of all fragile glass items that have been 'handed down'. The uncle presents himself and the family in a somewhat heroic light, suggesting that it is their duty to protect such finely crafted glass bowls from the savages beyond the gates. He tells those gathered in the drawing room that the family members are all that now 'stand between' the craftsmen who made these beautiful objects and the 'missile-throwers' who wish to destroy them.

The uncle makes reference to some 'calmer age', to some time in the past when the underprivileged accepted their lot in life and did not agitate for change. It is likely that the uncle is hearkening back to some pre-industrial period, when those labouring on the land of the wealthy had no access to education and there was little or no social mobility.

However, the uncle and his family live in a very different time, a time when the underprivileged are making noises and demands, agitating for greater equality and social justice. But the uncle cannot imagine that the people over whom his family have ruled for generations can bring about any meaningful change and disrupt the status quo. The worst scenario he can imagine is that stones will be thrown and glass will be broken.

FOCUS ON STYLE

Tone, Mood and Atmosphere
The poem is spoken entirely by the uncle. As we mentioned above, this is a man full of his own importance. He speaks in a pompous and superior tone, fully assured that what he says is true and right. We can imagine that we are joining him mid-speech, that he has been waffling on for a while about various subjects, barely registering or caring about anyone else's opinion.

The uncle's superior tone is nowhere more evident than when he describes the people who have gathered in the square. He belittles this crowd and the significance of their gathering, describing their demeanour as 'sullen', their actions as 'follies' and their talk as nothing more than 'mumurings'.

Symbols
The valuable glass ornaments in the poem symbolise or represent the wealth and privilege of the uncle and his family. The stones that the crowd carry represent the power they possess to bring about change. It seems that they don't have much, but they nevertheless pose a real threat to the fragile glass items that symbolise social privilege. There is a suggestion here that the uncle's world is more fragile than he would like to imagine or believe.

THEMES

PRIVILEGE AND OPPRESSION

The uncle is a member of a very wealthy and privileged family. He has not had to work for this wealth and privilege; it is something that he inherited. It is all he has ever known and he takes his good fortune for granted.

The uncle believes that he and his family are entitled to their wealth and privilege, merely because of who they are. He thinks that wealthy, powerful families such as his are superior to other elements in society, particularly the working classes. He speaks of 'our kind' as though he and his family were a superior form of the human race. The protestors, in contrast, are described as angry brutes, as a 'mob' of 'missile-throwers'.

It is, of course, in the uncle's interests to think of himself in this way. His only goal is to shore up and protect the privileged life to which he has become accustomed. The uncle presents this desire in a somewhat noble and heroic light, suggesting that he and his family have been tasked with the duty of preserving the beautiful pieces of glass that were crafted by long-deceased 'glass-blowers'.

The uncle's privileged life is, of course, predicated or based on the suppression of the ordinary workers. As long as the workers are powerless to change society, the uncle and his family can maintain their privileged position. But we get the sense that things are beginning to change, and that the workers are not going to just let this go and allow things to go on as before. However, the uncle is incapable of seeing this, blinded and reassured by his family's long history of wealth and dominance.

THE SUBJUGATION OF WOMEN

Of course, this poem, like many poems by Rich, can be read as a comment on how women are subjugated in society. The uncle strikes us an old-fashioned, conservative type of a man. We can imagine him droning on and on, his comments addressed to the other men gathered in the drawing room. Perhaps he is trying to impress these other men with his pompous speeches, in an effort to reinforce his own sense of authority. We can imagine him talking over the heads of any of the women gathered and simply ignoring these women if they dare to offer an opinion on the subject.

This poem can be contrasted with 'Aunt Jennifer's Tigers' in which the aunt does not speak. She expresses herself through her embroidery, but she does not possess a real voice in the family. As we mentioned above, it is easy to imagine the aunt sitting in the very room in which the uncle speaks, silently embroidering her tapestry while he drones on.

THIS IS POETRY — ADRIENNE RICH

Storm Warnings

LINE BY LINE

The poet is sitting at home in the afternoon reading a book. There is a barometer or weatherglass, an instrument for measuring air pressure, in the room. The poet has been observing how the 'glass has been falling all afternoon', indicating that a low-pressure system is moving in and that a storm might be on the way.

The poet puts the book she has been reading down on 'a pillowed chair' and walks around the house, going from 'window to closed window' to observe what is happening outside. She observes how the strengthening winds are causing the branches on the trees to bend: 'watching/ Boughs strain against the sky'. She notes the darkening, turbulent clouds that are filling the sky, describing the sky above her as a 'zone/ Of gray unrest'.

The poet thinks about what is happening in the atmosphere around her. She realises that cold air is pushing in from colder, polar regions. She refers to the area in which she is living as 'this polar realm'.

The cold air blowing in from these polar regions displaces the warmer air. This creates something of a vacuum and causes the surface air pressure to drop. The poet refers to this vacuum as 'a silent core of waiting', a space that will eventually be filled when further cold air rushes in to fill the void: 'the air/ Moves inward toward a silent core of waiting'. Of course, we cannot see any of this – the 'currents' of air that are moving in and are 'undiscerned', not perceived by the eye.

The description of the area or 'realm' in which the poet lives as 'polar' suggests a number of things. It might be a reference to the cold air systems that blow in from the polar regions and cause storms. Perhaps, however, we should understand the term 'polar' metaphorically. The poet feels that she is living in an emotionally cold environment, a place without love and affection. The term 'polar' can mean opposite in character or nature, as in 'polar opposites'. Understood in this way, the term suggests the emotional swings of someone who is bipolar, the movement from euphoria to despair.

The poet considers certain 'elements' that have a major impact on our daily lives and over which we have basically no control, including time and the weather. We can record and measure these 'elements', but we cannot 'avert' the changes that they bring. If we could foresee and avert all the undesirable consequences of these elements, we could be said to have mastered them: 'Between foreseeing and averting change/ Lies the mastery of all elements'.

But we cannot do so. We can measure aspects of the weather – wind speed, air pressure, air temperature – but we cannot fully control them. Similarly, we can measure time, but this does not mean we have any 'mastery' over time. The fact that we can use a watch and tell the time doesn't mean that we can control the time.

Breaking or destroying the instruments that measure aspects of the weather has no effect or impact on the weather itself. The 'shattered fragments of an instrument' are not any 'proof against the wind'. Essentially, we are at the mercy of these elements and can do relatively little to protect ourselves against them. Even if we can predict what the weather is going to be like, we cannot control it; the weather comes on 'Regardless of prediction'.

The poet is accustomed to such storms. She lives in a region that is 'troubled' by such events. There are things, therefore, that she has 'learned to do' when these storms arise:

- As the winds pick up and the clouds gather, the poet draws the curtains so that she does not have to see the darkening skies.
- She lights a candle to alter the darkness that results from the cloud cover.
- Although the doors and windows are all shut, a draught of wind still enters the house through the keyhole. The candles are 'sheathed in glass' to shield the delicate flames from this 'keyhole draught'.

These are relatively insignificant things, and the poet is well aware that they do nothing to avert or alter the storm. It seems that these rituals can provide the poet with some comfort, however, or at least enable her to endure another storm.

FOCUS ON STYLE

Personification

The poet personifies the weather, creating a sense of menace and uncertainty. The winds are described as 'walking overhead'. The 'silent core', the area of low pressure, is said to be 'waiting'. The poet also describes the sound of the wind coming through the keyhole as an 'insistent whine'.

The description of the winds 'walking overhead' calls to mind certain myths or stories that some ancient civilisations told to explain the weather. The ancient Greeks, like other ancient civilisations, often attributed weather changes and natural phenomena to the gods. For example, lightning was a way for Zeus, the sky god, to show his anger. Aeolus was the god of the winds. He was appointed by Zeus to guard the storm winds which he kept locked away inside the floating island of Aeolia, releasing them whenever the gods wanted to use them to wreak havoc.

Tone, Mood and Atmosphere

There is an atmosphere of mounting tension in the poem, as the storm gathers. The poet has been sitting comfortably, reading a book. But her eye is being drawn to the barometer and its falling mercury. She senses that a storm is on its way, that there are winds 'walking overhead' that will soon reach her door. As the poet walks from window to window she sees how the wind is causing the branches of the trees to 'strain against the sky'. Clouds are gathering and moving overhead. In the first stanza, the sky is a zone/ Of gray unrest', but in the final stanza it 'goes black'. The poet seems to be isolated, helpless and vulnerable. Her curtains and candles seem such paltry defences against the storm gathering around her.

THEMES

SUFFERING AND SURVIVAL

Just as we cannot control the external atmospheric conditions, so we cannot control our internal moods and feelings, the emotional 'weather in the heart'. We can attempt to predict how we are going to feel and to alter the way we feel, but we are ultimately powerless when it comes to our psychological states. This is especially true of bouts of depression, which 'come on/ Regardless of prediction'.

There are things that people prone to depression have learned to do to diminish the impact of the depression when it comes (just as those living in areas prone to storms have learned to do certain things when storms are approaching). But these are relatively small things and do little to avert or alter the depression.

PRIVILEGE AND OPPRESSION

The storm that is gathering might, therefore, be understood as a symbol of the troubles and turmoil in the world. We might think of political upheavals in other countries, of wars and famine, of economic collapse. The poet is conscious of these things, but she has learned to live with their existence and to essentially block them out. She knows that she is powerless to control or avert such catastrophes and turmoil. She lives with the knowledge that these things are happening, but she can only hope and pray that they will not touch or affect her.

THIS IS POETRY — ADRIENNE RICH

Living in Sin

LINE BY LINE

This poem is set in an American city in the 1950s. It describes a young woman who has moved in with her boyfriend, who seems to be some kind of composer or musician. The couple have moved into a little 'studio' apartment, which combines fairly basic living quarters and an artist's workspace.

The young woman, it seems, has joined her boyfriend in the 'bohemian' society of the day. These bohemians were determined that their days would be devoted to making paintings, music or literature; and their nights to socialising with like-minded individuals. They avoided conventional employment and, to save money, typically lived in squalid, low-rent accommodation.

They rejected their society's moral standards, especially when it came to alcohol, drugs and sex. The couple in the poem, for instance, are 'Living in Sin', living together without being married, a state of affairs that would have been greatly looked down on by 'normal' society in 1950s America. They also rebelled against many other social conventions, rejecting everything from material success to the necessity of dressing neatly and keeping a clean house.

When persuading the young woman to move in with him, the boyfriend had described, in ideal terms, what their shared studio apartment would look like. A perfect image of their living quarters had 'risen at his urging' in the woman's mind. She imagined an attractive and comfortable space featuring a 'plate of pears' and a 'piano with a Persian shawl' draped over it. She realised that they were moving into an old and rundown building where there would likely be mice. But she imagined that these would be 'amusing' and 'picturesque' creatures, more like toys for cats than filthy and disgusting vermin.

Prior to moving in with her boyfriend, then, the woman had a somewhat idealised view of what their life together would be like. She imagined, no doubt, that she and her partner would be poor but happy, living a free and easy lifestyle among the city's artistic community. The reality, however, has proved very disappointing.

1

When the young woman imagined living with her partner she never thought of housework, of dusting or cleaning or other boring activities of this kind. She imagined that their apartment 'would keep itself', that somehow, as if by magic, it would always be clean and tidy. She imagined that their furniture, somehow, would be immune to dust: 'no dust upon the furniture of love'.

The young woman, of course, isn't a fool. She knew on some level that their apartment, like any other, would require scrubbing and dusting. But she didn't think about such mundane activities when she envisaged their life together. Instead she imagined a passionate and idyllic existence filled with music, art and stimulating intellectual conversation.

2

The young woman, as we noted, didn't think she was moving into a luxury apartment. But she wasn't quite prepared, we sense, for the filth, squalor and disrepair that she encountered in her new studio accommodation. The windows, for instance, are covered with a thick layer of dirt or 'grime'. The taps are described as 'vocal', which alludes to the low, humming noise that is emitted by trapped air whenever the taps are turned on. This is, no doubt, because the building is an old one, with ancient and defective plumbing. Worst of all, the apartment seems to be infested with beetles, which have their nest within the 'moldings', strips of decorative wood attached to walls and furniture. Rich uses a clever metaphor to describe this beetle infestation, comparing the nest to a 'village' that sends out lone insects as 'envoys', or messengers, to explore the wider world.

The studio, then, is far grimmer and grimier than anything the young woman could have expected. The young woman, however, regards these wishes as a form of 'heresy': 'half heresy to wish the taps less vocal/ the panes relieved of grime'. Heresy can be thought of as a sinful or inappropriate belief, one that goes against the established teachings of a religion. The young woman, then, feels that it's somehow wrong to complain, even inwardly, about life in the apartment. After all hasn't she got the kind of existence she always dreamed of, an apartment of her own and a free-and-easy artistic lifestyle with the man she loves?

Heresy is also an opinion profoundly at odds with what is generally accepted. The young woman has entered a bohemian world where cleanliness is treated with suspicion and regarded as a boring middle-class virtue. The true artist, it was believed, was too busy focusing on art and ideas to keep a clean house. Yet the young woman can't repress her desire for cleanliness. And, once her boyfriend has gone out to buy cigarettes, she makes a half-hearted effort to tidy up, making the bed and dusting some of the furniture: 'she…pulled back the sheets and made the bed and found / a towel to dust the tabletop'. (Tellingly, she's forced to use a towel in order to do the dusting, suggesting that bohemian households, like the one she now occupies, are disinclined to use, or even purchase, cleaning products).

3

The young woman's expectations have also been thwarted when it comes to her relationship with her musician boyfriend. She imagined, no doubt, that her boyfriend, because he doesn't have a conventional job, would devote himself to his music. In reality, however, he seems to spend little time playing or composing. Indeed, he plays just 'a dozen notes' on the piano before declaring that it is too 'out of tune' for him to do any artistic work. (We get a sense, however, that this may be just an excuse he uses to avoid knuckling down to the business of playing and composing).

Instead of getting on with this creative work, the woman's boyfriend seems to just mooch around the apartment, yawning and looking at himself in the mirror: 'he shrugged at the mirror / rubbed at his beard'. Eventually, he wanders 'out for cigarettes'. We get the impression, however, that he will spend the day drifting in and out of bars and coffee shops, chatting with his artistic friends.

The young woman, no doubt, imagined that when she and her boyfriend moved in they would enjoy a genuine partnership. In reality, however, their relationship seems a very distant one. The boyfriend comes across as uncaring and self-absorbed, utterly wrapped up in himself and his half-hearted musical ambitions. He scarcely acknowledges the young woman as he plays his dozen notes and gazes at himself in the mirror. His 'shrug' seems to indicate his indifference toward both the studio and the young woman herself. Then, he heads out 'for cigarettes', abandoning her for the rest of the day.

FOCUS ON STYLE

Metaphor, Simile, Figures of Speech

Rich uses personification several times throughout the poem when describing different aspects of the studio. This emphasises the role of the studio as a main 'character' in the poem:

- She wishes that the taps were 'less vocal', which almost makes the taps sound like an irritating, noisy neighbour.
- The stairs outside the studio are so creaky that they 'writhe' under the milkman's tread, as if in agony.
- The beetle that she sees in the cupboard is described as an 'envoy from some village in the moldings', as if the beetle has come to her with a specific message.

In the final lines, the poet uses a simile to describe daybreak, referring back to the 'milkman's tramp' in line 9: 'she woke sometimes to feel the daylight coming/ like a relentless milkman up the stairs.' The fact that the woman compares the coming of morning to the noisy milkman suggests the annoyance and dread with which she faces each new day.

Imagery

In this small, domestic scene, Rich finds several surprising and vivid images. Perhaps the most striking is that of the 'three sepulchral bottles' in line 11. When full, these bottles of wine promised an evening of merriment and enjoyment. When the bottles are empty, however, they become 'sepulchral' – gloomy and tomb-like.

A striking aspect of this poem is the way it portrays night and day. Often in poetry, daytime is a hopeful, cheerful time, whereas night is dark and depressing. Here, however, it's the opposite. Daytime is oppressive and unforgiving, highlighting the couple's miserable life. Night, however, is a romantic and dreamy time that allows her to reconnect with her partner: 'By evening she was back in love again'.

THEMES

SUFFERING AND SURVIVAL

Small wonder, then, that the young woman suffers from loneliness, frustration and depression. The reality of life in the studio apartment has not lived up to her expectations. She assumed, quite wrongly, as we've seen, that young lovers would somehow be spared the need for housework, that there would be 'no dust upon the furniture of love'. Furthermore, the studio itself has turned out to be far grottier and dingier than she expected. Finally, and most importantly, her relationship with her boyfriend is not at all what she imagined it would be.

The young woman's suffering is evident throughout the poem:
- We sense it when she lets the 'coffee pot boil over on the stove'. We sense that she's so distracted, so wrapped up in her own negative thoughts and emotions, that she sets the pot to boil but then forgets about it completely.
- We sense it when she imagines that the beetle's eyes are staring at her: 'on the kitchen shelf among the saucers / a pair of beetle-eyes would fix her own'. We sense that the young woman feels that the insect is gazing at her in a mocking or questioning fashion.
- We sense it when she describes how the stairs 'would writhe' under the milkman's footsteps, twisting as if in pain. Here the young woman is surely projecting her own psychological discomfort onto the stairway.

However, the most haunting image associated with her suffering is surely that of 'the minor demons'. Sometimes, when we make a bad decision in life, we criticise ourselves. We may experience this self-criticism as a voice inside our heads. The poem provides a wonderful metaphor for this phenomenon, describing how the young woman was 'jeered by the minor demons' as she sat alone in the studio apartment. It's easy to imagine such self-criticism as the insidious whisper of a demon, its jeers and mockery echoing through our minds as it reiterates over and over what a mess we've made of things.

The young woman's sufferings are at their most intense when dawn comes. For the daylight itself strikes her as cold, rather than warming or cheerful. The empty wine bottles it reveals, or 'delineates,' strike her as 'sepulchral', suggesting that they resemble tombs or gravestones: 'that morning light so coldly would delineate the scraps/ of last night's cheese and three sepulchral bottles'. Both comparisons, of course, suggest the young woman's intensely negative state of mind.

Like many depressed people, the young woman suffers from a form of insomnia and wakes several times during the night: 'throughout the night/ she woke sometimes'. As she lies there, she finds herself dreading the approaching dawn. We sense that lying in the dark the young woman can forget about her suffering. But the 'the daylight coming' will not only coldly illuminate the squalor of the studio; it will also make it more difficult for her to ignore the faults in her relationship.

Living in the studio, then, has brought the young woman little but suffering. But she will find it difficult, we sense, to leave this life behind. During the day she falls out of love, both with her boyfriend and with the lifestyle they share together. By the time evening comes, however, she finds herself 'back in love again'. We sense that, by this time, she has convinced herself that life in the studio is worth persevering with and that her relationship still has something to offer. After all, her decision to move in with her boyfriend was a momentous one, and she must be reluctant to reverse it.

There can be little doubt, however, that young woman will survive this ordeal. Each evening finds her a little less in love with her boyfriend and their life together: 'By evening she was back in love again,/ though not so wholly'. Eventually, no doubt, she will fall out of love completely and leave the studio behind. She will be all the stronger for having come through such trials.

FORGING YOURSELF

The young woman has attempted to forge a new identity for herself, leaving her family behind and starting a new bohemian life with her boyfriend. This attempt at self-forging may have backfired. For the studio is miserable, and her relationship is dysfunctional. The poem emphasises, then, that forging yourself is an ongoing task. For the young woman must now leave the studio behind and make another attempt to discover who she really is, and become who she needs to be.

THE SUBJUGATION OF WOMEN

The poem also highlights the inequality that often still persists between the sexes. It is the woman, unsurprisingly, who attempts to keep the apartment in some kind of decent condition, while the man spends his time playing the piano and wandering the streets in search of cigarettes.

The young woman's artistic and rebellious boyfriend seems a world away from the privileged and conservative uncle in 'The Uncle Speaks in The Drawing Room'. But they are similar in their disregard for the women in their lives. The uncle drones on and on, inviting no input or comment from the women in the drawing room. The young woman's boyfriend seems utterly uninterested in what she has to day, utterly oblivious to the misery she's suffering through. He just yawns, shrugs and walks out the door.

The poem, then, highlights how even supposedly sensitive and enlightened men can reinforce this traditional inequality and demonstrates how, even today, women can be victims in a 'man's world'. For the inequality that dominates their relationship is the real 'sin' with which the young couple are living.

One of the most important themes in 'Living in Sin' is the sharp contrast between fantasy and reality. The young woman imagined that her existence in the studio would be perfect, an exciting life lived with a sensitive young artist in a beautiful apartment. As we have seen, however, the reality has turned out to be very disappointing.

The Roofwalker

LINE BY LINE

We imagine the speaker sitting in her bedroom or her study, looking out across the city landscape. Nearby is a row of houses, still under construction. Dusk is falling: 'Over the half-finished houses / night comes'.

All day long, builders have been working on the roofs of these unfinished houses. But twilight has brought their day's labours to an end. The pulleys they use to hoist materials on to the roof are no longer tight with strain but are 'slack' and loose.

The speaker, we imagine, has put up with the noise of construction all day long: the hammering of nails, the humming of power-tools. The sudden absence of such a racket makes the evening seem especially silent: 'It is/ quiet after the hammers.

A few of the workmen, however, linger on one of the roofs: 'The builders / Stand on the roof'. Perhaps they're simply enjoying a cigarette and a chat at the end of their day-long exertions. Or perhaps they're examining the site and planning the next stages of construction.

As the sun goes down, its red glow frames these builders, so that they seem enlarged. The speaker says that they resemble 'Giants' standing on the buildings, that their 'figures' seem to 'pass magnified' as they walk backwards and forwards across the half-finished roofs.

The speaker uses a startling metaphor to describe the sight of the builders on the roof:

- The roof on which the workers stand is compared to the deck of a ship: 'the roofwalkers, / on a listing deck'. The speaker imagines a deck that's 'listing', or tilting to one side, because the roof is unfinished and uneven. Because the roof looks red in the glow of the evening, she imagines that it is a burning deck.
- The evening sky above the workers is compared to the ship's sail: 'The sky / is a torn sail'. (We can imagine how the square of evening sky visible through the speaker's window might resemble a sail's rectangular cloth).
- The fast-approaching night, meanwhile, is compared to a vast and dangerous wave. Darkness will fall on the unfinished roof like a wave crashing violently over a ship, soaking its occupants and flooding its surface: 'the wave / of darkness about to break / on their heads'.

This is a powerfully desolate image. The speaker compares these builders – 'these roofwalkers' – to sailors in an absolutely terrible predicament: adrift on the open sea, their ship listing and aflame, a great black wave about to crash over their heads. It's an image that captures the danger and difficulty of being a roofer, with all the risk of accidents and exposure to the elements that such work involves.

1

The speaker has recently made great changes in her life. She has traded in her old lifestyle for a new one that's radically different. She has completely altered her identity, changing how she sees herself and how she presents herself to the world.

The speaker reflects on the old life that she recently left behind, comparing her previous existence to a roof that she painstakingly constructed. Just as a roof offers us shelter from the elements, so this old lifestyle had provided her with financial and psychological security.

The builders on the unfinished house expend a great effort as they lay the roof. Similarly, the creation of her old lifestyle involved great effort by the speaker, a level of effort she describes as 'infinite exertion'. The builders' work is careful and painstaking, the laying of each roof-tile involving any number of 'calculations'. The speaker was equally painstaking in the assembly of her old life; she carefully created around herself a lifestyle that was stable, secure and comfortable, one that many of her peers, no doubt, would have regarded as little less than perfect.

The builders are guided by an architect's blue prints as they go about their work. Similarly, the speaker was guided by definite plans as she struggled to establish her old lifestyle. She envisaged a future of professional success, financial comfort and marital happiness.

2

Gradually, however, the speaker realised that she never wanted this kind of life in the first place: 'A life I didn't choose / chose me'. In constructing this perfect existence, she was responding to peer pressure, to the expectations of others and society at large, rather than to her own deepest desires. The life she'd so carefully constructed, therefore, was as much a prison as it was a sanctuary.

The speaker realised that she could no longer exist in such a fashion. Eventually, she made the difficult choice to leave her old life behind. She regrets having wasted so much effort, having put so much time into fashioning a life she was ultimately forced to abandon: 'Was it worthwhile to lay…a roof I can't live under?'

3

The speaker, then, dismantled her old life like someone destroying the ceiling and roof of the house in which they live. Without the structures and routines of her old life, she is emotionally vulnerable. She's like someone on top of a half-finished and roofless building in bad weather: exposed, defenceless and afraid.

She compares her situation to that of the builders on the rooftop: 'I feel like them up there'. Just as the builders on the roof are 'exposed' to rain and wind, so the speaker is exposed to emotional turmoil as she sets out on her new life.

When they are working on roofs, builders are constantly at risk of falling and seriously injuring themselves. The speaker, too, is likely to suffer trauma. Like the builders, she is 'due to break [her] neck'. Any neck-break the speaker suffers would of course be metaphorical rather than literal. Perhaps she fears that she'll suffer a complete mental breakdown, brought on by the strain of leaving her old life behind.

Now the speaker is faced with the prospect of starting completely afresh, of creating a brand new life from scratch. But she doesn't feel capable of accomplishing such a task. She compares herself to a roofer equipped with the wrong tools for the task he's been assigned: 'even / my tools are the wrong ones/ for what I have to do'. Perhaps she existed in her old way of life for so long that she simply can't imagine how a new one might be constructed.

The builders, as we've seen, are presented as huge figures, as 'Giants' framed against the evening sky. The speaker, too, thinks of herself as a kind of giant, as being 'larger than life'. The speaker, we sense, experiences a feeling of exhilaration as she sets out on her new life. She feels elated, and that she is as unstoppable as any giant. But the phrase 'larger than life' also conveys a sense of visibility and vulnerability. Perhaps the speaker feels that she stands out more, now that she's changed her life. Perhaps she feels that the people around here are more likely to notice her and talk about her.

ANALYSIS

THEMES

SUFFERING AND SURVIVAL

Like many of Rich's poems, 'The Roofwalker' deals with the twin themes of suffering and survival. The speaker has suffered the agony of living a lie, of pretending to be someone she wasn't. We get a sense of suffocating claustrophobia as the speaker describes how she found herself trapped beneath a 'roof [she] can't live under'. For too long she denied her own identity, living a life that was chosen for her rather than one she sought out for herself. The speaker effectively assembled her own prison, working extremely hard to fashion an inappropriate and suffocating existence for herself.

The speaker did not succumb to this suffering, however. She did not lose her mind or attempt to take her own life. Neither did she simply take the easy option by resigning herself to a life that was not giving her what she wanted. Instead she found the courage to change. The poem, then, celebrates the bravery and tenacity of life's survivors, of those who withstand and overcome the challenges that confront them.

The poem essentially shows us what Rich meant when she offered her famous definition of personal responsibility: '[Responsibility] means, therefore, the courage to be 'different'. ... There is an immense difference between a life that is actively lived and one that consists merely of passive drifting. Once we begin to feel committed to our lives, or responsible to ourselves, we can never again be satisfied with the old, passive way'.

However, 'The Roofwalker' also makes it clear that the speaker's sufferings are far from over. Although she has shown that she has the courage she needed to escape from her old life, she is going to need even more courage in the future. Now, she must face the challenge of creating an entirely new life from scratch.

FORGING YOURSELF

In 'The Roofwalker', as we've seen, the speaker uses images associated with roofs and roofing to describe her situation as she transitions from one lifestyle to another. The poem's conclusion takes this conceit in a startling and unexpected direction, as the speaker compares herself to a 'naked man' running across the rooftops of the city. There is something bizarre and perhaps even a little amusing about such an image. But it's also a conclusion that evokes a haunting sense of vulnerability and sorrow.

For the repetition of the word 'naked' emphasises the man's exposure and vulnerability. We feel the speaker's sense of helplessness and exposure as she finds herself between lives, having abandoned her old identity while still being in the process of forging a new one.

The fact that she imagines herself as a man who is not only naked but also 'fleeing', suggests the speaker's desperation to leave her old life behind. But it also highlights her fear that this old existence will not so easily be consigned to the past. The description of the man as 'ignorant' suggests the speaker's uncertainty regarding what she should do next, her uncertainty regarding what kind of life she should create for herself and how this might be done.

The speaker notes that her life could so easily have been different. Just one moment of decision has set her on this new path. Only a 'shade of difference' separates her from her old existence. If she had chosen differently, she would still be enjoying her previous, comfortable lifestyle rather than her disorientating new one. Instead of resembling a naked man desperately scrambling across the rooftops, she could have been more like someone relaxing in a cosy bedroom: 'who could with a shade of difference /be sitting in the lamplight / against the cream wallpaper'.

> It's also worth noting that when Rich wrote 'The Roofwalker', which appeared in her 1963 collection *Snapshots of a Daughter-in-Law*, she herself was still — on the surface at least — a happily married woman. She was still enjoying a comfortable lifestyle with her husband and her three sons; the family were dividing their time between Manhattan and Vermont. It was only in 1970 that she would take the great step of leaving the marriage behind and embarking on the next phase of her life. Rich herself, then, unlike the speaker in the poem, had yet to leave behind the roof she couldn't live under.

It's notable that when the speaker imagines her old life she thinks of herself 'reading... about a naked man / fleeing across the roofs'. She imagines herself reading about a naked roofwalker 'not with indifference' but with great interest and concern. This image suggests that for a long time the speaker has been preoccupied with the idea of change. And even as she lived her old, comfortable lifestyle, she knew that such change was necessary. It's as if she couldn't keep the idea of escape, with all the vulnerability and danger it entails, out of her head.

THE SUBJUGATION OF WOMEN

'The Roofwalker', like many of Rich's poems, touches on the subjugation of women. The poem was written at a difficult time in Rich's life, a period when her marriage was collapsing. Rich had become disillusioned with marriage, coming to view it as an unequal institution that kept women in the power of the men they married. (The poem, we must remember, was written at a time when women were expected to love, honour and obey their husbands).

Rich, too, became increasingly disillusioned with the 'perfect' and 'successful' lifestyle that she and her husband had constructed over the years of their union. It was peer pressure and family expectation, it seems, that forced her into a marriage – and a lifestyle – she never really wanted. Now, like someone who has slipped away form a house in which they were being held prisoner, she has left her married life behind.

THIS IS POETRY — ADRIENNE RICH

Our Whole Life

LINE BY LINE

'Our Whole Life' is a powerful meditation on the nature of language itself. The poem strikingly presents language as gendered and male-dominated. We're inclined to think of language as a neutral tool for communication. According to Rich, however, language is anything but neutral. Instead, it's extremely gender-biased.

Every language (whether it be English or Chinese, Mongolian or Spanish) was created by a male-dominated society, evolving over time to suit the needs of men rather than women. When women speak or write, therefore, they are forced to use 'the oppressor's language'. They must use words created by the very men who keep them down.

Women must use vocabulary and grammar designed to communicate a male, rather than a female, perspective on reality. This means that it's extremely difficult for women to communicate the truth about their lives.

Certain aspects of female experience are simply impossible to express in these male-created languages. Other aspects can be expressed only in a blurred and distorted fashion. Rich refers bitterly to the 'permissible fibs', brilliantly capturing how male-created languages allow women to communicate only certain aspects of their beings, and then only falsely and imprecisely. The remaining aspects of women's experiences can't really be conveyed at all by means of male-dominated languages.

Women and language

Rich uses several inventive comparisons to describe to describe the horror of women being forced to use an alien and inappropriate language. Women, she memorably declares, are bound in 'a knot of lies'. Constrained by the binds of an alien language, there is little they can express. And what little they can say will be in an important sense untrue.

Women's experiences are compared to a surface that's been painted over. The bare, unpainted surface might be thought of as women's real, lived experience. The paint might be thought of as the alien or inappropriate language in which that experience must be expressed. The words women use, then, tend to obscure, rather than reveal, the reality of their experiences, just as a layer of paint obscures the surface to which it is applied.

Rich also imagines a child attempting to communicate with a doctor, endeavouring to explain the symptoms and sensations associated with his illness: 'Trying to tell the doctor where it hurts'. We can imagine a child struggling to describe, for instance, a 'recurring, shooting pain in the area around my solar plexus' or a 'persistent, throbbing headache'. Just as the child lacks the vocabulary to explain the nature of such discomfort, so women lack the linguistic tools to adequately express their experiences.

Rich also uses the metaphor of 'dead letters', which are pieces of mail that have gone astray within the postal service:
- A woman sets out to communicate her experience through language, just as a letter-writer sets out to correspond with his intended recipient.
- However, the woman's true meaning is lost in the alien language she must use to express herself, just as the letter is lost in the postal system.
- The truth of women's experience, therefore, can never be properly communicated, just as dead letters are destined to never reach their intended destination.

Man on fire

The poem's most striking comparison, however, is surely that of the Algerian man 'who walked from his village, burning'. Here Rich is probably referring to an image from a warzone that she saw in a newspaper or on television. 'Our Whole Life' was written during the Algerian War (1954–62), which was fought between France and the Algerian National Liberation Front. In this most bitter and bloody conflict, Algeria, which had been under French rule since 1830, finally gained its independence.

The image depicts a man on fire, his 'whole body' ablaze. Behind him is his village, which has just been firebombed by the French colonial army. Tellingly, the man walks rather than runs from his ruined home. It's as if he knows there's no hope of escape and therefore no point in running. It's as if he's been so ground down by years of conflict that he no longer has the physical strength or mental will to even attempt to run away.

This is a circumstance to which language cannot do justice. There are no words in English, French, Arabic or any other tongue that can adequately express such horror. Only the image of the burning man himself, rather than any verbal description, can adequately convey his plight: 'and there are no words for this// except himself'.

The experiences of women, according to the poet, are like the image of the burning man. Neither can be adequately expressed through language. The image of the burning man cannot be adequately explained because its very horror strains the capacity of language. The experiences of women, meanwhile, cannot be adequately described or explained because women are constrained by the shackles of an alien language system.

FOCUS ON STYLE

Form

'Our Whole Life' is written in the very loose style associated with Rich's later work, a far cry from the tight, formal stanzas of an early poem like 'Aunt Jennifer's Tigers'. There is an a element of what we might describe as 'collage' about the poem, as it combines different strips of language to make an exhilarating if disorientating whole. For instance, we move without explanation from the image of the blowtorch to the image of the dead letters, and from the image of the child at the doctor's office to the image of the burning Algerian.

There's an important sense in which the poem's form enacts its meaning. The poem, with all its chopping and changing, resists and pushes beyond ordinary meaning, just as Rich seeks to resist and push beyond the male-dominated languages that surround her.

Metaphor, Simile, Figures of Speech

The poem uses several memorable metaphors and similes to describe women's difficulties in communication. In a powerful simile, as we've seen, Rich compares the situation of women to that of the burning Algerian: 'like the Algerian…' Another simile compares women's plight to the painted-over surface that just might be stripped clean by a blowtorch: 'meanings burnt-off like paint…'.

Metaphors come into play when Rich compares women's efforts at communication to 'dead letters' and when she says that they are bound within a 'knot of lies'. This latter image is particularly bizarre and surreal. Lies are presented almost as living creatures — snake-like or worm-like entities — that have been woven together into a breathing, seething rope. The rope is described as 'eating at itself', as if the various lies that make it up can't resist biting and tearing at each other: 'Words bitten thru words'. And while such an image is difficult to visualise precisely, it powerfully conveys the constrictions that prevent women from expressing themselves.

Another literary device, metonymy, features in line 13. Metonymy occurs when a word associated with a thing is substituted for the thing itself. In this instance, Rich writes 'a cloud of pain' instead of, as we might expect, 'a cloud of flame'. here pain, something we associate with fire, is substituted for fore itself, wonderfully capturing the burning Algerian's agony as he walks away from his ruined village.

The poem is dominated by imagery of pain and violence: the blowtorch, the knotted rope devouring itself, the child struggling to communicate with the doctor, the burning Algerian man. In one sense, this reflects the great harm that male-created language inflicts on women's psyches. But it also reflects the almost violent desperation of Rich's efforts to escape this and create a new, more equitable language of the future, one in which all genders will be able to express themselves.

THEMES

GENDER AND COMMUNICATION

The poem movingly depicts the frustration felt by women as they attempt to communicate in a system not calibrated for their experiences, not designed to capture how they see and experience the world. Women's descriptions of their experience are necessarily fuzzy and inaccurate, like a document translated from one language to another: 'Our whole life a translation'.

For Rich this inability to communicate evokes feelings of dread and claustrophobia. She associates it with images of confinement, pain and suffering. She describes a person confined, almost choked perhaps, by a knot of lies. She imagines the efforts of a child in pain to communicate with his physician. She also pictures a man, his whole body aflame, fleeing the wreckage of his village.

For women, as we've seen, language conceals as much as it reveals, like a layer of paint slathered on a wooden surface. But Rich is also conscious of how the 'meanings' of male-created language might be eliminated or 'burnt-off', allowing women's experience to be expressed in a truthful and natural fashion. It's as if a blow-torch were directed at this painted surface, stripping the paint away and revealing the unvarnished surface underneath: 'meanings like burnt-off paint/ under the blowtorch'.

Rich also describes how the 'knot of lies' that presently constrains women might someday be 'undone'. Indeed, she suggests that this knot is 'eating at itself', as if it were unstable and destined to unravel, thereby liberating the women it currently constrains. What lies behind this hint of optimism? Why is Rich convinced that the ties of male-created language must eventually undo themselves, like a knot slowly fraying as its loops rub against each other? Perhaps Rich hopes that the existing male-created languages will adapt to better accommodate female experience. Perhaps she feels that such a change is more likely to occur as more and more women come to occupy positions of power in business, science, media, education and so on. Or perhaps she hopes that women will invent a language system of their own, one that is specifically designed to express how woman see the world. It's unclear, however, precisely what form such a newly-designed female mode of expression might take.

THE SUBJUGATION OF WOMEN

Like many of Rich's poems, 'Our Whole Life' touches on the subjugation of women. The poem presents a male-dominated language that has arisen from a male-dominated civilisation. This is a world in which women are oppressed and kept in their place, much as the French colonial power kept the conquered Algerians in check for over a hundred years:

- Like the conquered Algerians, women are kept as second-class citizens in their own country.
- Women are forced to speak the language of their male oppressors, just as the Algerians were forced to speak the language of their French overlords.
- The burning Algerian man is utterly voiceless. He has no means of influencing the terrible events that have destroyed his life. And his opinion on these events will neither be sought nor listened to. Women, the poem implies, are similarly voiceless and helpless in a male-dominated society.

Presenting us with a grim view of white, Western males, the poem shows us how they oppress both women at home and subject peoples in their colonies overseas.

Trying to Talk with a Man

LINE BY LINE

Between 1951 and 1992, the US government conducted over 1,000 nuclear tests at various sites in the Nevada desert: 'Out in this desert we are testing bombs'. This series of explosions had a profound effect on the landscape in and around the test sites. The surface features or 'face' of the desert would be altered by the government's irresponsible actions: 'Coming to this desert we meant to change the face of'.

These detonations attracted a motley crew of interested parties: journalists, serious anti-nuclear campaigners, hippies, hangers-on and tourists from Las Vegas who simply wanted the thrill of seeing a mushroom cloud up close. The poet and her husband have journeyed into the desert in order to protest against such a scheduled explosion: 'Out in this desert we are testing bombs// that's why we came here.'

The desert

The desert is depicted as an incredibly arid environment. The only moisture present is an 'underground river' the speaker somehow senses beneath the desert floor: 'Sometimes I feel an underground river'. Perhaps she can faintly hear the water gushing beneath her feet, or perhaps she can sense the vibrations caused by the river as it flows deep underground.

The poet imagines the water travelling in a curve or 'locus', the course of the river veering at a sharp or an 'acute' angle as it travels beneath the landscape. She imagines that the course of the river traces the path of the sun, flowing from east to west across the condemned scenery of the desert: 'moving itself like a locus of the sun/ into this condemned scenery'.

The desert is almost devoid of vegetation. All that grows there are 'dull green succulents' (cacti and other similar spiny plants), whose hardiness and capacity for water-retention allows them to survive is this cruelest of landscapes.

The desert is filled with 'deformed cliffs', with rock formations that have been eroded by sandstorms and scorching desert winds until they have a bizarre and twisted appearance. It is also possible that damage caused by nuclear explosions has lent such cliff-faces their unnerving, alien appearance.

According to the poet, the desert is a place of 'condemned scenery'. This suggests that the desert is such an oppressive and inhospitable landscape that it might have been condemned or cursed by God. But the term 'condemned', of course, also suggests that the desert itself is scheduled for demolition, that it will be reduced to rubble by the seemingly endless nuclear tests.

The desert, it seems, is completely unpopulated. As they travel to the protest-site, the poet and her husband pass through a 'ghost town' and stop briefly to explore. A ghost town is a town completely abandoned by its former inhabitants.

Perhaps, in this instance, the townspeople left because they were threatened by the military activity going on nearby. Or perhaps they moved on because it was impossible to make a living in such an unforgiving desert environment.

Life before

The poet reflects on the life she shared with her husband, describing items and events that mattered a great deal to them, the personal moments that filled their relationship with meaning. She recalls going to see films in local cinemas. We can imagine the couple seeing their own passionate relationship reflected in the love stories portrayed on screen. They identified so strongly with these romantic movies that they felt they were starring in the films they watched: 'films we starred in/ playing in the neighbourhoods'.

She recalls the vinyl records she and her husband purchased over years, how they built up collections of soul music, of classical, of jazz: 'whole LP collections'. We can imagine the memories associated with each beloved album, how particular tracks will forever be linked with particular moments in their lives.

She recalls bakeries that sold 'dry, chocolate-filled Jewish cookies'. We can imagine Rich and her husband purchasing such treats for their three sons. Or perhaps they treated themselves to these delicious confections as they walked near their home in Central Park West after brunch on a sunny New York morning.

She describes romantic afternoons they spent 'on the river bank', where they pretended 'to be children'. Perhaps the couple went paddling, playfully splashing around in the water just as children might do. Or perhaps she means that she attempted to shut out all adult worries and concerns, to spending an evening living in a care-free almost child-like fashion.

Somewhat surprisingly, the speaker includes not only 'love-letters' but also 'suicide notes'. Both the poet and her husband, we sense, experienced their fair share of psychological trauma. At least one of them, it seems, has contemplated suicide so seriously that suicide notes have actually been written.

There is an especially jarring contrast between these two concepts – the language of 'love-letters' and that of 'suicide notes' – and yet the poet presents them side by side. She acknowledges that shared suffering was an essential part of the couple's relationship. They are bound by the challenges they endured and overcame together, just as they're bound by pleasant memories of walks along the riverbank.

Difficulties

Over time, it seems, the poet and her husband have gradually grown apart, the emotional distance between them increasing until they can no longer communicate on a deep and meaningful level. There is now a 'silence', the poet declares, at the heart of their relationship.

The speaker describes how a silence surrounds them as they travel through the desert: 'walking at noon … surrounded by a silence'. But she is not referring to the physical silence of the desert landscape, to the 'silence of the place'. Instead, she's referring to the silence that has appeared in the centre of their marriage. This is the dreadful emotional silence that they have brought with them into the desert: 'it came with us / and is familiar'.

The poet and her husband have spent a long time ignoring this emotional silence. They have focused on the hustle and bustle of everyday life, rather than on their emotional difficulties. They would engage in endless, trivial chitchat, concealing the fact that they had nothing meaningful to say to one another: 'and everything we were saying until now / was an effort to blot it out'.

In the emptiness of the desert, however, they are no longer able to 'blot out' this emotional silence. There is nothing out here to provoke such meaningless chitchat, no hustle and bustle to distract them from their predicament. Alone in this strange and haunting landscape, they must deal with their inability to communicate. They must directly confront the silence at the heart of their relationship: 'coming out here we are up against it'.

Waiting for the test

The poet and her husband reach the location from which they will witness the test taking place. They're probably in one of the semi-official observation posts set aside for members of the press, for representatives of NGOs and for protesters like the poet and her husband. In Nevada, such facilities were located a minimum of six miles from the test-site itself.

Yet there is an atmosphere of tension while those gathered in this installation wait for the explosion to occur. Nuclear detonations are unpredictable affairs, after all. There is always the possibility that the test could go horribly wrong and that those in the observation post, including the speaker and her husband, might suffer greatly. They might suffer tearing or 'laceration' caused by the fury of the blast. They might be left to die of 'thirst' in the desert's unforgiving landscape.

Perhaps understandably, then, the poet's husband apprehensively paces around the room, talking about the danger posed by the test and the various pieces of safety equipment present in the installation: 'You mention the danger/ and list the equipment'. The poet and her husband discuss how those present might tend each other's wounds if such an emergency did indeed occur: 'we talk of people caring for each other/ in emergencies'.

The end
The speaker says that she feels 'helpless'. There are probably several different types of helplessness involved here. She feels helpless when it comes to protecting herself or others should the test go wrong. She feels helpless, no doubt, when it comes to influencing the harmful nuclear policy of her government. She might even feel helpless (as we all do at times) before life's everyday challenges and difficulties.

The presence of the speaker's husband, however, does nothing to diminish her sense of vulnerability. She suspects, in fact, that she'd feel less helpless if he weren't around: 'Out here I feel more helpless/ with you than without you'. The presence of the poet's partner should make her feel nurtured and reassured. But instead it has the opposite effect, making her feel vulnerable and helpless.

The poet, in a most unusual turn of phrase, describes how her husband 'look[s] at me like an emergency'. The poet's husband, it seems, stares at her the way one might regard a serious and dangerous situation unfolding before one's very eyes. He looks at her as if their relationship brings danger and unpleasantness into his life, as if their marriage has become an ordeal to be survived.

As the husband paces the floor, the exit signs of the observation post are reflected in his eyes: 'they reflect signs that spell out EXIT'. This suggests the speaker's realisation that her marriage is over, that there is nothing that can be done to rescue her relationship. The only available option is to 'exit' the emotional mess that her marriage has become.

FOCUS ON STYLE

Form
The poem contains 39 lines, broken up into nine stanzas. The stanzas vary in length from one to seven lines. Strikingly, the first two stanzas consist of just one line each. This visually evokes the fact that although the speaker and her husband have come to the desert together – 'we came here' – in many ways, they are separate and isolated from each other.

Tone, Mood and Atmosphere
From the very first line, the poem's atmosphere is one of dread, danger and tension: 'Out in this desert we are testing bombs'. A tone of frustration and struggle is introduced with the image of the 'underground river/ forcing its way' between the couple. The poet uses the phrase 'condemned scenery' to refer not just to the desert but also, implicitly, to the battleground of her marriage.

There is a brief respite from imagery of struggle and dread in stanza 4, when the poet describes happier days with her partner: 'films we starred in'. However, even the pleasant atmosphere of this stanza contains an ominous detail: 'the language … of suicide notes'.

Stanzas 5 and 6 describe the oppressive, tense 'silence' that seems to follow this couple around, no matter where they are. The pace of the poem quickens in the final stanzas, as the poet's partner 'pace[s] the floor' furiously and talks about the 'danger' they might face in the desert. In these closing lines, the couple is framed as a ticking time bomb: 'as if we were testing anything else.'

The poem's lack of punctuation also adds to the tense atmosphere. There are only three full-stops in the poem – in lines 2, 7 and 39. From stanza 5 onwards, there is very little punctuation, and the poem unfolds as a torrent of imagery. This speeds up the pace of the poem, suggesting that the end is fast approaching for this couple.

Metaphor, Simile, Figures of Speech
There are several ways in which the desert landscape serves as a metaphor for the poet's relationship:

- The physical barrenness of the desert reflects the emotional barrenness that has crept into the couple's relationship.
- Like the desert, the couple's relationship has become distorted and 'deformed'.
- Like the desert, the couple's relationship is 'condemned' or destined to be destroyed.
- The unseen river that flows beneath the desert represents the underlying problems in their relationship. The fact that the river is 'underground' suggests that they don't talk about these problems, preferring to pretend ignore them.

The poet associates the river with understanding and suggests that it moves at an 'acute' angle. The poet says that the river moves at 'an acute angle of understanding'. This suggests that when the poet and her husband finally confront their issues, they will gain knowledge of a sharp and unpleasant nature.

Another striking metaphor is the poet's description of her husband's eyes as 'stars of a different magnitude'. This is quite a beautiful description, but it also suggests that his eyes are blazing with anger.

Imagery
Stanza 4 presents us with a series of images associated with the couple's life together. Compared to the harsh environment of the desert, their home life is cozy and carefree: 'LP collections, films we starred in … chocolate-filled Jewish cookies'. With one important exception (the reference to suicide notes), this stanza resembles a montage of their happier moments together. Contrasted with this are the images of the desert's arid, alien landscape, its ghost towns, 'deformed' cliffs and succulent plants.

THEMES

LOVE AND RELATIONSHIPS

'Trying to Talk With a Man' movingly depicts a failing relationship. Once, the poet's marriage was a happy one, filled with music and cookies, with movies and 'afternoons on the riverbank'. And even the couple's struggles, we sense, used to bring them closer together. Such togetherness, however, is now a thing of the past. Their relationship is now characterised by an emotional distance, by a terrible 'silence' at the heart of their marriage.

The couple, then, have come to the desert not only to protest against nuclear weapons, but also to confront this toxic silence that's eating away at their relationship. They feel, no doubt, that in the desert they'll be utterly free from any distractions, which will allow them to overcome such emotional distance and communicate in a meaningful manner. The emptiness of the desert will make it easier for them to have a full and frank discussion about the issues confronting their relationship.

Their journey, then, can be viewed as a last-ditch effort to rescue a failing relationship. For it's not only the military that will be 'testing bombs' in this desert landscape. The couple, in a metaphorical sense, are braced for a detonation of their own. Their conversation will be emotionally explosive, since it will involve a full and frank discussion about the state of their marriage. The couple will finally confront the silence at the heart of their relationship.

Both the poet and her husband, then, have developed extremely negative feelings about their relationship. Each has come to view the other as a source of emotional danger instead of emotional support. The poet, as we've seen, feels more rather than less vulnerable in her husband's presence. The husband, meanwhile, views the poet as if she were an emergency, as if she brings turmoil and uncertainty into his life.

The husband paces the room and talks about the dangers associated with the nuclear blast. But the poet realises that their relationship, too, is a source of danger: 'Talking about the danger/ as if it were not ourselves'. Their marriage has become a source of psychological and emotional tension, a most serious threat to the couple's well-being. They talk of 'people caring for each other/ in emergencies' but seem incapable of caring about each other anymore.

The drive into the desert was a final 'test' of themselves and of their relationship: 'as if we were testing anything else'. The poet hoped that in the space and silence of the desert they might have found a way to discuss their difficulties. This hope, however has proved a false one, for their difficulties, it seems, are too firmly embedded to be overcome. The exit sign reflected in her husband's eyes indicates the only way forward. All in all, this poem is a brilliant depiction of two people who know they shouldn't be together, but are as yet unable to say the words out loud.

PRIVILEGE AND OPPRESSION

The poem highlights the oppression involved in the nuclear programs pursued by wealthy, Western nations. The tests carried out by the US government in the Nevada desert oppress the region's people, altering the landscape, turning settlements into ghost towns and having untold long-term medical and environmental consequences. But the weapons being tested, of course, are also designed to oppress foreign populations, allowing, as they do, the US government to impose its will around the world. [Russia, France and Britain were also carrying out such programs at the time]. The poets use of the word 'we' in the opening line signals her awareness that, as an American citizen, she bears some responsibility for the actions her government is carrying out.

The poet and her husband enjoy a privileged life. We imagine a comfortable, one characterised by a reasonable level of luxury and leisure. Increasingly, however, they have begun to sacrifice more and more of their free time to campaigning against oppression in its various forms. Their hobbies and intellectual pursuits have begun to take a back seat to activism. The fight against their government's oppressive policies has begun to take over their lives: 'What we had to give up to get here'.

THE SUBJUGATION OF WOMEN

When the poet stands next to her husband in the observation post, she can feel heat radiating from his body. His temperature, we imagine, has been raised not only by the sultry desert conditions but also by the emotional stress he experiences as they wait for the test to commence. The poet, in a startling turn of phrase, compares this heat to 'power'.

- We can imagine how her husband's hot, musky, masculine smell might remind the poet of men in general and the power they wield over women.
- We might also imagine that the heat emanating from her husband's body reminds her of the terrible heat of an extremely powerful nuclear blast.
- The poet might be reminded how the masculine drive to dominate others led to the creation of nuclear weapons in the first place.
- Finally, the poet may be thinking that men use their privilege and power to oppress women in society just as wealthy countries their power to oppress less privileged populations over seas.

The poet compares her husband's eyes to stars of extraordinary brightness: 'your eyes are stars of a different magnitude'. We can imagine her husband's eyes flashing with intense emotion as he paces the floor of the observation post. We sense, however, that the poet sees her husband's eyes not as beautifully sparkling diamonds, but as raging furnaces of emotion. The furious glint in his eyes, like the heat emanating from his body, is associated with the power of men over women and with the imminent nuclear detonation. (The stars, it is important to note, are sustained by the nuclear reactions that take place deep within their cores).

ANALYSIS

Diving Into the Wreck

LINE BY LINE

This poem is concerned with gender, with how we are taught to identify ourselves as either male or female and to behave in the appropriate way.

But the poet does not believe that our sex determines our personality, that just because we are biologically identifiable as male or female we should think and act exclusively in either a masculine manner or a feminine one. Rather, the poet believes, the self at the moment of birth is essentially ungendered. As we grow, however, society teaches and conditions us to speak, walk, play, behave and dress in a particular manner. In doing so, a part of who we are, or who we potentially can be, is suppressed and ignored.

However, the poet imagines that, somewhere deep inside our unconscious minds, we possess a memory of what it was like to exist in this gender-neutral way. In 'Diving into the Wreck', she imagines journeying deep into her unconscious to discover and explore this memory. She presents this journey or exploration as a deep-sea dive.

The memory that the poet is seeking to find in the depths of the unconscious is like the wreck of a ship that lies far below the surface of the sea. The poet is hoping to access her unconscious mind and explore this memory of our lives as they were before the social construction of gender.

The Conscious and the Unconscious Mind
The conscious mind is where we spend most of our lives. It is the part of the mind that processes our immediate experiences, where we do our thinking and planning. The unconscious mind is the storehouse of all memories and past experiences, both those that have been repressed through trauma and those that have simply been consciously forgotten and no longer important to us. We cannot simply recover these memories at will.

The poet compares the earth's surface above the sea to the conscious mind. This is where we normally exist or dwell; it is our natural environment. The unconscious, then, is like the ocean, a realm that we rarely enter, if ever. It is the vast unknown aspect of our minds, just as the ocean is a vast and largely uncharted aspect of the world we inhabit.

1. The preparation
The diver has 'read the book of myths'. She has conducted all appropriate research, in order to ascertain where on the

surface of the ocean the wrecked ship sank. We can imagine her consulting history books, dusty maps, accounts of ancient voyages and tales told by sailors or pirates. All of this was done, of course, so that she will know the correct place to dive, if she is going to explore the wreck.

This represents the poet's research into the area of gender and sexuality. She has studied and analysed many stories in both the Western and Eastern traditions, everything from biblical narratives to fairy tales, from Indian folklore to modern cinema. All of this has been done so that the poet can understand how society constructs gender. But it has also given her some glimpses into what our original, ungendered consciousness might actually have been like.

The diver prepares by loading her camera with film and ensuring that her knife is sharp enough to deal with any emergencies that might arise. The camera represents the poet's determination not only to experience the unconscious mind, but also to recall what she experiences. The knife represents her awareness of the dangers that may lurk in her own unconscious mind. For such journeys into the depths of the self can often be disturbing or even traumatising.

The diver puts on her wetsuit, flippers and breathing apparatus. This equipment is necessary for a safe and successful dive. The wetsuit, in particular, is described as 'body-armor', suggesting the essential protection it offers. The diver's equipment represents the voice of the poet's therapists. We can imagine her reclining on her analyst's couch, listening to soothing, repetitive instructions. The analyst's voice will function like the diver's equipment, keeping her safe as she journeys down into the unconscious.

However, the diver's equipment makes her clumsy during her final preparations. The mask is described as 'awkward' and the flippers 'absurd'. We sense that the diver feels ridiculous, as she flip-flops around the deck of her ship. This represents how the speaker's mind loses sharpness and alertness as she enters a state of intense relaxation and suggestibility. Her mind, in a sense, becomes clumsy as she tunes into the sound of her analyst's voice.

The diver contrasts her situation with those encountered by Jacques Cousteau, the famous French diver and television personality. Cousteau, she says, always had an assiduous or 'hard-working team to assist him or back him up. The diver, however, must undertake her exploration alone. The poet's journey into the unconscious is also a solo one, because she is the only one who can explore the depths of her own mind.

The diver remarks how Cousteau's explorations typically took place in 'sun-flooded' Caribbean locations. But we sense that the diver's own descent will be made against the backdrop of a bleaker and more forbidding seascape. No doubt, this represents the poet's feelings of doubt and unease as she prepares to begin her own descent into the unconscious mind.

2. Climbing down

The diver mentions a ladder that hangs close to the side or the back of the ship. It is this ladder that she will use to descend from the ship's deck to the water. For any diver, such a ladder is a familiar and significant piece of equipment. We can imagine that it represents the link between the two worlds, the world above the surface of the ocean and the very different world beneath: 'We know what it is for,/ we who have used it'. But to those who have never dived, this ladder would seem a rather dull feature of the ship, just some 'sundry' equipment' that is hardly worth mentioning. The poet compares it to a piece of algae or seaweed. Unless you are a marine biologist, such sea vegetation may not seem very interesting. It is 'maritime floss', something for which we have little regard.

The ladder represents whatever it is that will enable the poet to make the transition from her conscious mind to her unconscious mind. Perhaps it is the analyst's words or her tone of voice. It could well be something that we know about but underestimate, something that will be fully appreciated only by those who have themselves undergone the kind of analysis that the poet is now experiencing.

The diver starts to climb down the ladder toward the surface of the ocean. To her, the descent seems interminable, as the ladder is hundreds of meters in length. It feels as if she is never going to reach the water. For a long time, she feels that she is still immersed in the oxygen-rich atmosphere and ordinary blue light of our surface world: I go down/ Rung after rung and still/ the oxygen immerses me/ the blue light/ the clear atoms/ of our human air'. This symbolises the gradual nature of the poet's transition from her conscious mind to her unconscious mind. The repeating of the phrase 'I go down' represents the slow but persistent nature of this transition.

The diver's flippers make the descent very awkward. It is very difficult for her to get a proper foothold and to move her feet from one rung to the next: 'My flippers cripple me'. Dressed in her full diving gear, the poet barely feels human anymore. She likens herself to some alien creature or 'insect' negotiating a device that has been specifically designed for human limbs: 'I crawl like an insect down the ladder'.

The diver's feelings of awkwardness represent the poet's discomfort as she makes the transition from her conscious mind to her unconscious mind. Her analyst is priming or preparing her to experience an aspect of her mind that is wholly unfamiliar to her.

3. Entering the water

Finally the diver reaches the bottom of the ladder and enters the ocean itself. At first the light in the watery realm is blue, because the diver is still close to the surface where the sun penetrates. As she swims downwards, however, her environment becomes increasingly dark, going from dark blue to green and eventually to black. Similarly, when the poet reaches her unconscious mind, she finds herself in an entirely new realm, one that is very remote from the everyday workings of consciousness.

The diver's initial response to being immersed in the dark depths of the ocean is one of panic. She feels as if she cannot breathe and that she is going to lose consciousness: 'I am blacking out'. But her breathing equipment does its job well, supplying her with the vital oxygen she needs: 'my mask is powerful/ it pumps my blood with power'.

This represents the poet's anxious feelings as she enters her unconscious mind. It is an aspect of herself with which she is entirely unfamiliar; as she allows her mind to make the transition, a moment of panic occurs. The analyst's voice acts like the diver's oxygen supply, however, and reassures her that she will be fine.

The diver describes how she must acclimatise to the underwater environment in which she finds herself. Similarly, the poet must acclimatise to the realm of the unconscious mind. The diver must move gently. Subtle changes of body position are the best way to navigate the deep element of this under-sea world. Similarly, the poet must remain relaxed and open as she journeys ever-deeper into herself.

The diver again emphasises how utterly alone she is. She has to figure out for herself how best to manoeuvre in the depths. She has no diving instructor or support staff to offer her guidance or assistance. This reminds us once again that the poet's inner journey is a solo one. Her analyst can help her transition to the unconscious mind, but after that she is on her own.

The diver describes the importance of staying focused. It's easy to get distracted by the weird and wonderful marine life that circulates amongst the depths. She describes, for instance, fish with ribbed or 'crenellated' fins darting amongst the coral reefs. However, she must ignore such exotic creatures. She must keep her eye on the prize and keep swimming downwards towards the wreck: 'I came to explore the wreck... I came to see the damage that was done'.

This represents the poet's determination not to become distracted while she is on her mental journey. As she explores her unconscious mind, she experiences many different, fascinating images and memories. But she cannot allow herself to dwell on these. There is only one mental state she is interested in exploring: the consciousness that she would have had in her earliest, ungendered state of existence.

The stories and accounts that the diver read when conducting her research in advance of the dive have given her a clear purpose and focus. They have inspired and motivated her to undertake this dive: 'The words are purposes'. And, as we already mentioned, the books and documents she has studied enabled her to determine the location of the wreck. As such, the 'words' are like 'maps'. The poet's research in the area of gender motivated her to undertake this very personal journey and to explore her unconscious. Her research has also given her a sense of what it is she is searching for and of where she might locate this pre-gendered self.

4. The diver reaches the wreck

Finally, the diver reaches the wreck. She moves the beam of her flashlight slowly along the side of the ship, illuminating section after section of what seems to be a vast vessel. The wreck, it seems, has been here for a long, long time. Generations of fish and seaweed have come and gone since it first landed on the ocean floor. It is 'something more permanent/ than fish or weed'.

- The diver sees 'evidence of damage', evidence that offers clues about the incident that caused the ship to sink in the first place.
- She notes how the swaying under-sea currents have gradually worn the ship down, thinning and eroding the timber structure.
- Due to such wear and tear, the ship seems 'threadbare'. Its outer layers have been stripped away, revealing the ship's 'ribs', the curved timber pieces that strengthen the exterior planking.
- According to the speaker, the wreck is haunted by deep-sea creatures. The term 'haunters' suggests that there is something ghostly or alien about the appearance of these creatures. But it also suggests that these strange creatures habitually flit about within the wreck's structure.
- These creatures are described as 'tentative', suggesting that they are unnerved by this diver's presence and that they approach her reluctantly, if they do so at all.
- The diver is convinced that the wreck still holds treasures that are waiting to be discovered. Such treasures, she believes, have 'prevailed' or survived for years or decades on the ocean floor.

To the diver, the wreck is an object of an unlikely but undeniable beauty. We can imagine the ship's worn hull as a vast sculpture on the ocean's floor, one carved into strange and beautiful shapes by the sea's currents.

The damage to the ship represents the damage that was done to the ungendered self early in life. Having been taught to identify as female and to behave accordingly, the poet's ungendered self has been sunk deep in her unconscious, where it has languished for decades. Neglected and forgotten, this mental state has gradually faded or weakened over time. However, just like the wreck of the ship, its form or shape is still recognisable and there is a certain beauty to it.

5. Preparing to enter the wreck

The diver's story, which has been realistic up until now, suddenly becomes very strange. Her body, it seems, splits in two. She becomes two different people: a mermaid and a merman. These strange creatures don't communicate. Instead, they orbit each other silently, swimming in circles outside the entrance to the wreck's hold.

The mermaid and the merman represent the feminine and masculine aspects of her being. From infancy, however, society has done its best to cover up the masculine aspect of her personality, as she was conditioned to speak, walk, play, behave and dress in a particular manner. Now, however, as she sits in the analyst's chair, she rediscovers this masculine aspect of herself where it has laid dormant in her mind for decades. She realises that the masculine and feminine aspects of her personality are equally valid and need to operate in harmony, just as the mermaid and merman dance in graceful circular patterns.

6. entering the Wreck
The mermaid and the merman swim into the wreck's hold. Inside they discover barrels that have been 'left to rot' as the wreck lay undiscovered for decades upon the ocean floor. The barrels are no longer neatly stacked, as they would have been when the ship first set sail. Instead, they are scattered around the hold, 'half-wedged' into various corners. The barrels contain great riches: copper, silver and vermeil, which is gold-plated bronze. This cargo has languished 'obscurely' or forgotten about, since the ship first sank.

The merman and the mermaid also see navigational instruments that the salt water has left 'half-destroyed'. They notice, for instance, a compass whose wood and metal components have been 'fouled' or rotted. They note the captain's log book, in which the captain would have recorded the ship's coordinates each day. This has been so eroded that it seems 'eaten' by the water. These instruments once 'held to a course', guiding and steering the ship across the ocean's surface. But now they languish uselessly on the ocean floor.

The diver, as we noted above, has split into two different creatures, a mermaid and a merman: 'I am she: I am he'. As these beings swim into the hold, they become one with the wreck itself:

- They fuse with the decks nearest the stern, which resemble the ship's face as it lies motionless on the ocean floor.
- They fuse with the planks of the hold, which are likened to the ship's breasts. These planks, as we've seen, still bear the weight of the ship's half rotten cargo: 'I am she: I am he ... whose breasts still bear the stress'.
- They fuse with the rotted navigational instruments, the 'fouled' compass and water-logged captain's log: 'we are the half-destroyed instruments'.

The ruined ship, as we've seen, represents the poet's earliest, ungendered self. The poet's first exploration of this earliest self is symbolised by the moment when the mermaid and the merman enter the wreck. The poet experiences a state of being where masculine and feminine become one, a state prior to all ordinary concepts of gender. This is represented by the mermaid and the merman becoming one with the wreck itself, fusing with the ship's planks and instruments.

7. A moment of healing
At the poem's conclusion, the diver remarks, almost with awe, how she has found her way back to this 'scene' or site of wreckage. She seems grateful for the tools and equipment that have helped her on her journey: 'a knife, a camera,/ a book of myths'. But she is no longer herself. She is now some strange combination of herself, the merman and the wreck itself: 'We are, I am, you are ... the one'.

This represents the poet's experience of a moment of healing within her psyche. She has found her 'way back' to her ungendered self, rediscovering a long-lost state of being. This has allowed her masculine and feminine selves to be unified or reconciled so that finally they are 'the one'.

The poet considers the different motivations that might lead someone to explore their unconscious and reconnect with their ungendered self. It could be 'cowardice' or 'courage' that leads us to this place. When she mentions 'cowardice' the poet might have in mind some retreat from the world; it is our inability to face up to or cope with the world as it is that leads us back here. Or perhaps it is 'courage', a brave effort to find a different way of being, to challenge what is taken and accepted as normal. The poet seems uncertain whether it was cowardice or courage that brought her to this point. But she seems untroubled by this; the important thing for her is that she has undertaken the journey and re-engaged with a valuable and important aspect of who she is: 'We are, I am, you are,/ by cowardice or courage/ the one who find our way/ back to this scene'.

FOCUS ON STYLE

Metaphor, Simile, Figures of Speech
As we have seen, the poem is an extended metaphor for the the exploration of the unconscious mind. The diver's descent deep into the ocean to find a wrecked ship represents the poet's journey deep into her unconscious mind to discover her ungendered self, the self she was before she was conditioned to think and behave in an exclusively female manner.

The poet uses a simile to describe the awkwardness of descending a ladder while wearing flippers. She likens herself to an insect in order to convey the awkward movement of her limbs in the diving gear as she attempts to negotiate the ladder into the water: 'I crawl like an insect down the ladder'.

The poet personifies the wreck, comparing the curved supporting timbers to 'ribs' which stand 'tall and proud' upon the ocean floor. The ship's back-most decks are likened to a face that forever gazes up towards the surface of the ocean. The ship's mid-section, where its precious cargo is stored, is likened to 'breasts' that must still bear the burden or 'stress' of the tragedy. The personification of the ship allows for a more personal and intimate relationship between the diver and the wreck she has come to explore. It is as if she is encountering someone about whom she has read and heard a great deal.

Imagery

The poet describes the wreck of the ship in some detail. She observes how the salt water and the constant movement of the water have gradually worn the ship down, thinning and damaging the timber structure. After so many years of wear from the ocean, the ship seems 'threadbare'. But the poet finds a particular beauty in the ship's form and appearance: 'this threadbare beauty'.

Many of the ship's outer layers have been stripped or destroyed, revealing the ship's 'ribs', the curved timber pieces that strengthen the exterior planking. The poet says that these ribs seem to be standing tall and proud, boldly asserting themselves among the fish and other creatures that move carefully around them: 'curving their assertion/ among the tentative haunters'. The poet uses another wonderful image to represent the different aspects of her personality reuniting. She compares the masculine aspect to a merman and the female aspect to a mermaid, who together conduct an underwater dance, circling each other before entering the hold of the ship fusing with the original state of being.

THEMES

GENDER

The poem is concerned with the idea of gender. According to the poet, gender is a social construct. The self, she believes, at birth is essentially un-gendered. However, society has decided that different types of behaviour are appropriate for the different sexes. Those of the female sex are expected to dress and behave one way, whilst those of the male sex are expected to dress and behave another way.

Very quickly, then, members of both sexes acquire behaviours that are reinforced and nurtured, whilst others are ignored or neglected. Over time, our personality or sense of identity is forged and, if we are of the male sex, we learn to identify with masculine values and if we are of the female sex we relate to the more feminine values. The consequence of this is that we each neglect a fundamental aspect of who we are.

The poet believes that somewhere deep in each of our unconscious minds there is a memory of what we were before we were conditioned to identify and behave according to either the masculine or feminine aspect of our being. We can locate and access this memory by undergoing some form of therapy or analysis.

The poet believes that our lives could be a whole lot richer if we allowed our complete or full personalities to develop and flourish, that there are possibilities of being we are neglecting. The poet imagines that the memory of her ungendered self might contain a wealth of 'treasures', ways of understanding that could open up whole new ways of being and experiencing life and the world.

However, because the memory has been long forgotten and neglected, confined to the depths of our unconscious mind, it has been diminished and tarnished. It is like the wreck of a ship that has languished for years on the ocean floor. Perhaps the poem suggests that we can never fully recapture what it is to live or understand ourselves in an ungendered way. Perhaps all we hope for is to draw some understanding or inspiration from what we discover here and use it to begin to forge a new way of being.

THIS IS POETRY — ADRIENNE RICH

From a Survivor

LINE BY LINE

In 1953 Rich married Alfred Conrad, an economist and social campaigner. Their marriage, which lasted for seventeen years, was subject to the ups and downs that affect any long-term relationship. In its final years, however, the union came under increasing strain. Eventually, in 1970, Rich left the family home. Shortly afterwards, her husband tragically took his own life.

'From a Survivor' was written in 1972, two years after her husband's death and nineteen years after she and her husband together undertook the 'pact' of marriage: 'Next year it would have been 20 years'. The poem reflects on their relationship and its tragic conclusion.

The poet thinks back to her wedding and the early years of her marriage, emphasising how she and her husband were like any other newly-married couple. For the 'pact' they made on their wedding day was no different to the vows undertaken by any other husband and wife: 'The pact that we made was the ordinary pact/ of men & women'.

The poet refers to the 'failures of the race', to the different faults and failings that affect the human species. We can, of course, imagine many different ways in which beings fail. Some types of failure are common to every member of the human race, while others are relatively rare. In this poem, Rich focuses on failures that affect marriages and that place such long-term relationships under stress:

- One partner might exhibit failures of patience and understanding that make him or her difficult to be around.
- One partner might exhibit failures of the body, enduring physical illness that makes the other partner's life extremely difficult.
- One partner might exhibit psychological failings, enduring mental illness that makes the other partner's life extremely difficult.
- One partner might exhibit failures of self-control and betray the marriage by sleeping with some else.

As they began married life, the poet and her husband knew that they would experience some of these failures. And they knew

ANALYSIS

The couple, as we've seen, believed that their marriage would be able to survive the pressure caused by any failures they might experience.. But in the end they were unable to 'resist' the strain such failures brought. The pressure on their relationship proved too much and, after seventeen years, they separated.

The poet seems shocked at the arrogance and ignorance that she and her husband exhibited at the beginning of their marriage: 'I don't know who we thought we were'. They were arrogant because they believed they were 'special' and capable of resisting life's various failures. They were ignorant because they simply didn't have a clue about the type and scope of the failures that lay in store.

The poet can't decide if she and husband were 'Lucky or unlucky' to be so ignorant and naive about the future. Maybe their naivety was a stroke of luck. Sometimes, after all, we're better off simply not knowing about the difficulties that lie in store for us; we're better off enjoying life while we can and dealing with such problems as they arise. Or maybe they were 'unlucky' in their ignorance, because it stopped them preparing for the failures that were coming down the track.

FOCUS ON STYLE

Form

'From a Survivor' is written in the prose-like style we associate with Rich's later work. It is formally loose, featuring lines of irregular length organised into irregular verse-paragraphs. There is no rhyme scheme. 'From a Survivor', then, contrasts with the regular, rhymed stanza of early poems like 'Storm Warnings' or 'The Uncle Speaks in the Drawing Room'.

Tone, Mood and Atmosphere

The poem's tone is matter-of-fact rather than flowery and poetic. There is a sense of defiance and resilience throughout, as the poet celebrates her own survivorhood, as well as a note of celebration at the poem's conclusion when the poet describes her new mindful existence.

Irony

There's a strong element of irony in line 9, where the poet describes how she and her husband, like every other couple, thought they were 'special'. Every couple thinks their relationship is one of the few that will prove immune to life's difficulties. And every couple is sadly mistaken. Ironically, then, thinking that we're special or different just makes us the same as everybody else.

that these mishaps and mistakes would place strain upon their marriage. But they were convinced, too, that their marriage would be able to survive such challenges.

For the poet and her husband believed that they were 'special'. They felt that they possessed an unusual mental toughness and resilience. They also thought that their 'personalities/ could resist' the failures that lay in store for them. They believed that they could easily deal with life's faults and failings, as well as with the strain that such challenges would place upon their marriage.

But the poet and her husband didn't realise the order or magnitude of the failures that lay in store for them. They didn't realise that human beings fail in ways that are terribly damaging to themselves, to their relationships and to those around them: 'we didn't know/ the race had failures of that order'. They didn't realise that they, like every other member of the human 'race', would share in the experience of these mishaps: 'and that were going to share them'

THEMES

LOVE AND RELATIONSHIPS
'From a Survivor' movingly recounts the story of a marriage. It begins with those early, heady days when the couple were convinced of their own specialness, when they believed their relationship would prove invulnerable to life's challenges. It takes us through their dawning awareness that such a view was desperately naive, that they, like everybody else, were destined to 'share' in the failings of the human race. The poem leads us inexorably, then, to the ultimate failure of the couple's marriage and its tragic aftermath.

The poem movingly reminds us how affection can survive the most traumatic break-up. The poet's marriage came to a most tragic and turbulent conclusion, she still retains a great deal of affection for her former husband. For instance, she can recall, with perfect clarity, what his body looked like: 'Your body is as vivid to me / as it ever was'. The intensity of such memories reminds us of the physical and sexual bond that existed between them at one time.

SUFFERING AND SURVIVAL
Like many of Rich's poems 'From a Survivor', deals the twin themes of suffering and survival. The poem highlights the suffering undergone by the poet and her husband as they contended with the failures of the race, with the stress that such failures placed upon their marriage and, ultimately, with the breakdown of the marriage itself.

As the poem's title suggests, the poet views herself as a 'survivor', as someone who experienced and outlived such suffering, who came through this terrible ordeal with her life and sanity intact. The same, alas, cannot be said of her husband whose suffering lead him, tragically, to take his own life.

The poet, we sense, grimly rejoices in her own resilience, in her own hard-won status as a survivor. But this is not the naive and ignorant attitude she exhibited as a newly-wed. Now she speaks as someone who has experienced more than her fair share of life's difficulties and has come out the other side. She is confident, then, that she's capable of handling whatever life throws at her, whatever mental and physical traumas she encounters. She knows that, no matter what happens, she will survive.

FORGING YOURSELF
Towards the end of their marriage, it seems, the couple discussed the possibility of radically changing their existences, of making what the poet describes as a great 'leap' into the unknown: 'the leap / we talked, too late, of making'. Such a leap would involve a complete alteration of their mindset and their approach to living. It would involve a new way of looking at the world, a new way of living with 'the failures of the race'.

In the two years since her husband's death, Rich has gone on to make such a leap, to change her life in such a fashion: 'which I live now'. Her new approach involves living life as a 'series' of moments, of living in the present rather than being constantly preoccupied with the future and the past. It involves seeing the extraordinary in the ordinary, seeing each moment as a wonderful gift, as something not only 'brief' but also 'amazing'.

Yet talk of this great change came 'too late' for the poet's husband. Perhaps he was too set in his ways, too locked into his pre-existing mindset, to contemplate such a change. or maybe he was too depressed, too overcome by suffering, to embrace such an optimistic vision of the world. In any event, before he could fully explore this possibility their marriage broke down and, tragically, he took his own life.

This, then, is the true calamity of her husband's death. His passing was an enormous waste because it denied him the opportunity of making 'the leap' from a life dominated by an unhappy marriage into a joyous and independent existence: 'you are wastefully dead / who might have made the leap'. Even as she celebrates her won survivorhood, then, she laments the tragic and pointless loss.

THE SUBJUGATION OF WOMEN
During the years of their marriage, the poet thought of her husband as an all-powerful, almost divine figure, regarding his body as the 'body of a god'. In the 1950s and 1960s, we should remind ourselves, marriage was a very unequal institution, and a woman was expected to respect and obey her husband and be guided by him in all things. The poet, it seems, internalised these values, coming to see her husband almost as her lord and master, granting him a great deal of 'power over [her] life'.

Since her marriage came to an end, the poet has been forced to make her own way in the world. In the intervening years, her confidence and self-belief have developed greatly. She has also developed a new, more feminist consciousness, one that emphasises equality and amity between the genders. Society, too, has changed over the intervening years; women are no longer expected to worship and obey the men in their lives. The 'pact/ of men and women in those days' isn't quite the same as it is today.

As a result of all these changes, the poet has a clearer understanding of who her husband was: 'my feeling for it is clearer'. She no longer thinks of him as an all-powerful figure with 'the body of a god'. Instead she understands that he was just an everyday human being, with normal abilities and limitations: 'I know what [his body] could and could not do'. She no longer feels capable of being dominated by him, or by any other man.

ANALYSIS

Power

LINE BY LINE

In this poem, Rich reflects on the life and death of Marie Curie (1867–1934), a Polish–French scientist. She was the first woman to win the Nobel Prize and the only person to win a Nobel in two different fields: physics and chemistry. She discovered the elements polonium and radium, developed the theory of radioactivity and invented a mobile X-ray unit that saved countless lives during World War I. She died at the age of 66 from aplastic anaemia, a rare disease caused by exposure to radiation throughout her life's work.

Lines 1 to 5

The poet mentions that an old bottle of 'tonic' was recently excavated from the earth. She doesn't say where exactly this happened, or how she heard about it; perhaps it was a brief report on the local TV news. This 'hundred-year-old' bottle, she says, emerged from the earth in a like-new condition, as if it had been just waiting to be discovered. She describes it as a living thing, subsisting in the soil of history: 'Living in the earth-deposits of our history'.

The bottle was unearthed by a 'backhoe' or mechanical digger from a 'crumbling flank of earth'. It was perfectly preserved and 'amber' in colour. The poet speculates that this tonic was supposed to cure 'fever' or 'melancholy', or to simply help a person get through a long winter: 'a tonic/ for living on this earth in the winters of this climate.' It's implied that this is a so-called cure-all, a bottle of quack medicine that is supposed to cure all ailments but in reality cures none.

Lines 6 to 13

In the third stanza, the poet shifts gears to discuss Marie Curie, the Nobel-winning scientist whose life she has been reading about. Perhaps the bottle of quack medicine has put her in mind of Curie, who was anything but a quack; perhaps the poet feels that Curie, like the tonic, has been lost in 'the earth-deposits of our history' by not getting enough credit for her incredible achievements.

The poet discusses the manner of Curie's death from exposure to radiation. As a scientist, she says, Curie must have known what the source of her sickness was: 'she must have known she suffered from radiation sickness'. There is an irony in the fact that even as Curie was making radiation safe for others' use – as X-rays, for example – it was destroying her own body: 'her body bombarded for years by the element/ she had purified'.

In lines 10 to 13, the poet paints a grim picture of Curie's fatal illness. The radiation poisoning caused 'cataracts on her eyes' and painful abrasions on her fingers: 'the cracked and suppurating skin of her finger-ends'. Cruelly, these wounds prevented her from doing the work she loved: 'she could no longer hold a test-tube or a pencil'. Extraordinarily, even though Curie knew what was making her sick, she 'denied it to the end'. Why?

Lines 14 to 17

In the final stanza, the poet attempts to understand why Curie, an extremely intelligent woman, denied that it was radioactivity that killed her. She depicts a proud Curie playing down her symptoms on her deathbed: 'She died a famous woman denying/ her wounds'. Curie, the poet suggests, was reluctant to publicly admit that 'her wounds came from the same source as her power'.

Here, the poet explores the complex duality of Curie's relationship with her work. Even as radioactivity made Curie a 'famous' icon of science and ensured her name would live on after her, it also destroyed her physical self. Even as Curie's genius gave her social, economic and political advantages not widely available to women at that time, it also led to her death.

The poet sees Curie as a sort of martyr to science, a woman who knew that her research was killing her but who proceeded nonetheless. Perhaps she didn't want to give rise to the idea that a woman couldn't or shouldn't be involved in potentially dangerous scientific research; so she publicly denied the cause of her illness. She wanted to die a 'famous woman', remembered for her achievements, rather than for the ironic tragedy of her death. In this strange way, Curie was trying to control the narrative of her life, to hold onto her 'power' for as long as she could.

It's clear that the poet sees Curie as a heroic and tragic figure, but perhaps there is also a commentary on the dangers of power in these closing lines. We can wield and direct power, we can even benefit from it, but we can never fully control it or prevent it from ultimately harming us.

FOCUS ON STYLE

Form

The poem consists of four stanzas, varying in length from one to eight lines. The most striking aspect of the poem's form is the large spaces between words, especially in the second and fourth stanzas. These spaces function like pauses; they slow down the pacing of the poem and give it a jagged, fragmented rhythm. The spaces make us stop and focus on certain words, such as 'amber' and 'perfect' in line 3.

Finally, the spaces suggest absences, as if certain words have been erased. This echoes the poem's theme of how certain items and figures get lost in history or in the earth, as the bottle of tonic does. It also suggests Curie's denial at the end of the poem, a denial that caused her to omit certain details of her story.

Metaphor, Simile, Figures of Speech

There is a striking example of personification in stanza 2: 'Today a backhoe divulged out of a crumbling flank of earth/ one bottle'. The word 'divulged' means to reveal information or tell a secret. Here, the poet personifies the mechanical digger, portraying it as revealing the bottle with a knowing or mischievous air, almost like a magician's trick.

Imagery

The image of the 'flank of earth' in stanza 2 is interesting. The word 'flank' refers to the side of the thigh, and is usually used in reference to horses and other animals. Here we visualise the earth as a huge animal, something with a life and mind of its own. There is also a certain parallel between the fragile, 'crumbling' earth and Marie Curie's deteriorating body: 'the cracked and suppurating skin of her finger-ends'.

THEMES

SUFFERING AND SURVIVAL

Marie Curie suffered greatly for her work, with her physical self being constantly 'bombarded' by the dangerous radiation she worked with on a daily basis. The poet gives us detailed descriptions of Curie's painful symptoms: 'the cataracts on her eyes/ the cracked and suppurating skin of her finger-ends'. The poet suggests that, although Curie knew the radiation was harming her, she continued her work nevertheless: 'she must have known she suffered from radiation sickness'.

Perhaps Curie felt that her work was more important than her health. She prioritised the survival of her research over the survival of her physical self: 'She died … denying/ her wounds'. However, her scientific discoveries and innovations did survive, and ensured her reputation: 'She died a famous woman'. Though she was weak at the end, she had created a legacy of great power. The poem suggests that real power has less to do with physical strength and more to do with influence and lasting impact.

Curie used her scientific genius to harness the power of dangerous radioactive substances: 'the element/ she had purified'. The poem suggests, however, that there is always a price when we dabble with power, even when our motivations are good. Power can never be fully controlled; to wield power is to be engaged in a constant struggle. At the end of her life, Curie wants to deny the fact that her illness and her life's work 'came from the same source'. To the poet, however, it makes perfect sense that suffering and power would be two sides of the same coin.

FORGING YOURSELF

Rich often celebrates strong women, especially figures who succeed in male-dominated environments. These women had to overcome prejudice and other obstacles in order to succeed in their chosen fields. Marie Curie is a prime example of this. She was a world-famous scientist in an era when women were not encouraged to even have a career, let alone a career as a Nobel-winning scientist.

Curie must have sacrificed a lot to pursue her research; she even sacrificed her life. She stubbornly refused, however, to publicly admit that her death was caused by exposure to radiation: 'It seems she denied to the end/ the source of the cataracts on her eyes'. She had fought so hard to achieve her goals and to become who she was that pride prevented her from admitting that her work killed her in the end: 'denying/ her wounds came from the same source as her power'.

THE SUBJUGATION OF WOMEN

Marie Curie is presented as a woman who gained real and lasting power. She gained professional power, becoming one of the most influential and authoritative figures in her field. In a sense, she gained political and economic power, because her discoveries had a profound impact on many different aspects of society. She also commanded power in a literal, physical sense, handling elements that were capable of emitting terrifying levels of energy.

The power wielded by Curie, then, massively outclasses the power enjoyed by the quack doctor. He was merely a con-artist who temporarily seduced and charmed his unwitting customers, but Marie Curie changed the world forever. Rich, therefore, shows how Marie Curie empowered herself, overcoming the subjugation to which women are routinely subjected. But her power came at a terrible price, her physical health destroyed by the toxic materials with which she worked. In this regard, Curie's career exemplifies the scarifices required by women as they empower themselves. She shows how hard women must struggle to succeed in what is still very much a 'man's world'.

William Butler Yeats

Themes

Nature

Yeats is well-known for his celebrations of the natural world. We see this in 'The Wild Swans at Coole', which captures the unique qualities of an Irish autumn evening: a crisp path underfoot, a haunting stillness in the twilight sky, trees in their multi-coloured beauty. The poem provides an especially memorable portrait of the 'mysterious' and 'beautiful' swans that drift on the still water. It also highlights the explosive power and force they exhibit as they 'mount/ And scatter', their wings thumping with the piercing regularity of a bell.

'The Lake Isle of Innisfree' is another of Yeats' best-loved nature poems. The island is depicted as a place of sublime tranquillity. It's a place of silence, devoid of any man-made sound. Peace, we're told, 'comes dropping' slowly from the banks of mist that cover the island each morning, drenching the grasses where the crickets are busy about their song. Yeats longs for a retreat to Innisfree. He imagines building a primitive hut on the island and growing his own food. There he will be free from the stresses and strains of modern living. He will have no access to news or media, to devices or technology. He will be out of the rat-race that constitutes modern urban living. We sense, however, that such a solitary, self-sufficient existence is destined to remain a fantasy for the poet.

Yeats' poetry explores how the natural world is in a constant state of flux and change. We see this, for instance, in 'Easter 1916', which emphasises how the natural world changes 'minute by minute'. The poem describes a constantly shifting landscape, where a stream evolves like a 'living' thing as it pulses along its course, where clouds tumble through the sky, where horses' hooves thunder and splash. 'Sailing to Byzantium' is another poem that emphasises the shifting nature of the natural world. The poem views the natural world as a kind of system that cycles through phases of birth, death and renewal. Every living thing is part of this system. Every living thing is 'begotten' or conceived, born, reproduces and eventually dies.

In 'The Stare's Nest by My Window' Yeats looks to the natural world as a source of hope and guidance. The poem, written during the Civil War, highlights the bitterness that has taken root in the Irish heart and the violence and chaos that rage throughout the country. Each stanza concludes with a plea to the honeybees to 'Come build in the empty house of the stare'. We must look to nature's positivity, energy and creativity, the poem suggests, if we are to reverse the damage that has been done to the soul of the Irish nation. The challenge for the Irish people is to follow nature's example. They must turn away from the path of destruction and begin to rebuild their homes, their shattered country and their trust in one another.

Youth and Age

Many of Yeats' poems lament the negative effects of ageing. We see this in 'The Wild Swans at Coole, for instance, where the poet has started to exhibit not only physical weakness and psychological exhaustion, but also a lessening of his good-looks and sexual opportunities. His heart is 'sore' as he contemplates his decline. The poem centres on the contrast between the poet, whose life has endured such changes, and the swans, who are presented as being utterly changeless. The swans, as we have seen, are 'unwearied' in body and mind, as they pursue lives of unbounded passion and sexual adventure.

'Sailing to Byzantium' provides another moving portrayal of the ageing process. The poet feels disgusted and constrained by his own body. In a shocking memorable phrase, he describes his body as a 'dying animal' to which he has been 'shackled'. The poem highlights how the elderly often consider themselves 'paltry', as in feeble and insignificant, and how in a world obsessed with youth and beauty, they all too often feel unsightly and unwanted, ridiculous or even invisible.

The poem draws a powerful contrast between youth and age, specifically between the elderly poet and the young people he observes at the height of the Irish summer. The young people are sexually attractive in their sexual prime. The poet's body, on the other hand, has been left 'tattered' by the ageing process. The young people enjoy lives of sexual opportunity, wandering the streets 'in one another's arms'. The aged poet too experiences sexual desire. But for him, alas, such opportunities are a thing of the past.

'Politics' is similar in this regard. The poet is entranced by a beautiful woman, but knows he's now too old to ever win her affections. There is real emotion in the poem's final lines, when he wishes that he could somehow be young again and hold the beautiful woman he so desires in his arms. The tragic reality, of course, is that is there is no turning back the clock. The poet's desire for youth must remain forever thwarted.

'In Memory of Eva Gore-Booth and Con Markievicz' is yet another poem that deals with the changes, both mental and physical, that will be wreaked on us by time's relentless march. Time, Yeats reminds us, is the enemy not only of physical beauty but also of innocence: 'The innocent and the beautiful/ Have no enemy but time'. Its passage begins to leave us not only weakened and decrepit on a physical level but cynical and embittered on a mental level too. The ravages of time are memorably personified as a 'raving autumn' that shears off the flowers on the wreath of youth and beauty. It turns Eva from a creature of gazelle-like beauty and elegance into a 'withered' and 'skeleton-gaunt' old woman. And each of us, sadly but inevitably, must suffer a similar transformation.

'An Acre of Grass' takes a somewhat different approach to growing old. Here we find the poet more accepting of the ageing process and even celebrating certain advantages that accompany it. He is no longer distracted by sexual desire: 'My temptation is quiet'. His mind has grown more mindful and serene. He likens the aged body to 'an old house' that barely contains any life: 'an old house/ Where nothing stirs but a mouse'. The poet's mind is now free to gain insight or understanding that was unavailable to him when he was young. Yeats describes the aged man's mind in terms of an 'eagle': 'An old man's eagle mind'. The comparison not only suggests the sharpness of the older man's mind but also that it is capable of soaring and gaining a perspective on life that is not available to the young.

War, Violence and Social Upheaval

'September 1913' presents a rather romantic or idealistic view of war and violence. It celebrates the military achievements of the Wild Geese on the continents, and the almost foolhardy courage of soldiers like Robert Emmett and John O'Leary who led tiny revolts against a vast imperial power. The poem emphasises the noble side of warfare, the idealism and self-sacrifice displayed by soldiers in the service of a cause. But it downplays the horror and bloodshed of the battlefield.

It could be argued that 'An Irish Airman Foresees His Death' presents a rather romantic view of war and violence. Yeats was always a scholar rather than a soldier. But he exhibited a lifelong fascination with men of action, with those who, like the airman, had the bravery to enter the field of battle, putting their lives on the line as they fought, died and killed. No doubt Yeats also admires how the airman is a person apart. The airman, unlike his fellow soldiers, has no truck with the propaganda of public men and politicians. He is unmoved by the great wave of patriotism that has swept across the continent. Instead, as we have seen, he fights for his own reasons.

'Easter 1916', on the other hand, displays a more complex attitude towards war and violence. Yeats celebrates the heroism and sacrifice of these men who fought and died for the Irish cause, describing how they will be venerated forever 'wherever green is worn'. But Yeats is also horrified and terrified by what has happened. Though he once lamented the absence of such heroics in modern Ireland, now that heroes have re-emerged Yeats is fearful of what this means for the future. He is quick to realise that the celebration of those who died in the Rising will spur others on to do the same. War and violence, he fears or suspects, will engulf Irish society. The beauty of the leaders' sacrifice is a 'terrible beauty' indeed.

'The Stare's Nest by My Window' also explores the horrors of war and violence. The poem, written during the Irish Civil War, presents a community and a country that has been ravaged by war. For two weeks, the conflict has created a claustrophobic sense of isolation, leaving people 'closed in' as it traps them in their homes. It has created a great sense of dread and uncertainty among the populace, who are able to discern 'no clear fact' about what's going on in the country or what the future holds. Violence and terror stalk the land, as men are shot dead, houses are destroyed and acts of inhumanity, like the dragging of the dead soldier's corpse, are carried out.

'Politics' is another poem that registers the horror of war. It was written in 1938, just as the Second World War was poised to break out across the continent of Europe. As Yeats puts it, 'war's alarms' were ringing throughout the world. The 'travelled man' and the politician seem deeply concerned about the coming catastrophe. The poet, however, finds himself distracted by the presence of a beautiful young woman. For a moment, romantic longing overtakes his fear of the coming storm.

'The Second Coming' is probably Yeats' greatest statement on the topic of war, violence and social upheaval. The poem was written in 1919, during the chaotic aftermath of the First World War. To Yeats, it seems that the entire world is filled with confusion and disorder. It seems that everywhere the voices of reason and moderation are silenced, while those of intolerance and extremism shout ever louder. Evil men pursue their goals relentlessly, while the good stand idly by. Civilisation itself seems on the verge of being swept away by a tide of bloodshed. Furthermore, the poem predicts that even greater destruction is on its way, represented by the pitiless beast that 'slouches towards Bethlehem to be born'.

Art and the Role of the Artist

Yeats presents art as a continuous practice, a craft or trade that must be perfected throughout the artist's life. His most famous declaration of this belief comes in 'Under Ben Bulben'. Future Irish poets, Yeats decrees, must 'learn [their] trade'. These aspiring bards must understand that poetry involves more than ideas and inspiration, that it requires practice, patience and determination. They must approach poetry the way an apprentice carpenter approaches the work bench, realising that they have a great deal to learn and that only hard work will grant them the mastery they desire.

'Sailing to Byzantium' presents a similar view of creativity. Despite his old age, the poet is determined to keep developing his craft. If anything, the nearness of death makes him all the more eager to reach his full artistic potential. The poem stresses that such improvement can be made only by studying the great artists of the past. Yeats, then, despite being an accomplished, Nobel prize-winning poet, recognises that he must still attend 'singing-school' in order that his soul can express itself with ever-greater clarity and purpose.

'An Acre of Grass' also emphasises the need for an artist to keep developing despite old age. Yeats declares his admiration for artists like Michelangelo, Shakespeare and William Blake, who continued, even in old age, to strive for artistic perfection. Yeats clearly wants to emulate the passion and energy exhibited by these past masters, who kept changing and developing until the very end of their lives. The artist, Yeats believes, should never feel satisfied or content with what they have already achieved. It is the artist's duty, even in old age, to remain restless and to constantly seek new ways to explore and reveal the truth.

If poetry is a 'trade', then it must serve a useful function. Like carpentry and tailoring it must be necessary to society. Poetry's function, as Yeats presents it in 'Under Ben Bulben', is to 'cast [his or her] mind on other days', to remember and write about the past. Will Ireland become just another identical outpost of capitalism, just another banal node in an international network of technology? Only the poets, according to Yeats, can prevent this from happening. Only they can remind Ireland as a whole of what it once was and can be again. Through their words, they can spur us on to be 'indomitable' in the face of modernity, to create a future that resembles the best aspects of our past.

'Swift's Epitaph' also emphasises the public or political role of the poet in society. There is a sense in this poem that Yeats believes it is the writer's duty to respond to public events, to criticise society and its leaders for their various faults and failings. The poem challenges writers to 'imitate' Swift if they dare. It asks them to have the courage to criticise society in their work, even if they might suffer as a result of speaking out.

'September 1913' is one poem where Yeats follows Swift's example, using his platform as an established writer to attack the network of powerful businessmen that ran Dublin society. Yeats was responding to two public events – the Dublin Lockout and the controversy surrounding the Hugh Lane bequest. Here the poet uses ridicule and irony in a savage takedown of Dublin's leading captains of industry. 'Easter 1916' is another poem where Yeats presents the artist as having a public role. The leaders of the Rising, he insists, must be remembered by the Irish people. He uses his poetic skills to contribute to this process, writing a 'verse' that will help to keep the leaders' names alive.

'Politics' raises a number of important questions about the political role of the poet. Is it self-centred of Yeats as a writer to assign more significance to his private anguish than to the looming disaster of war? Is it wrong for the poet or artist to focus on his or her personal relationships and problems when there is so much evil and suffering in the world? On the other hand, however, it is possible to regard Yeats' involvement with themes of the heart as arising not from self-obsession but from a desire to write about universal human experiences.

The theme of achieving immortality through art is another that occurs throughout Yeats' poetry. In 'In Memory', for instance, Yeats imagines himself protecting innocence and beauty by destroying time itself. He longs to somehow put a match to time's very fabric, so it will be consumed in a great and climbing 'conflagration': 'Arise and bid me strike a match/ And strike another till time catch.' Yeats feels he can undo time's march by immortalising, in poetry, the beauty and innocence of the girls. A truly skilful artist, therefore, can defeat time by recovering an event or person lost in the past – an evening in Lissadell and two girls in silk kimonos, for instance – and preserving it in a piece of art to be enjoyed by future generations.

'Sailing to Byzantium' is perhaps Yeats' most profound statement on the idea of attaining immortality through art. The poet, we sense, would have little interest in prolonging the life of his body through some revolutionary scientific method. Nor does he show any interest in the type of immortality associated with the Christian concept of heaven. Nor, as we've seen, is he taken with reincarnation. Instead he focuses on the type of artistic immortality enjoyed by Michelangelo and Shakespeare. He is determined that he will live on in the 'artifice of eternity', through the poems, plays and texts he has created over the course of his life. This is represented by the poet's soul inhabiting the magnificent golden bird created by the Grecian goldsmiths all those centuries ago.

Yeats and Ireland

The Ascendency

Yeats, as we have noted, was a great admirer of the Anglo-Irish Ascendancy, the class that dominated Irish society between the 17th and 19th centuries, and of which he himself was a member. He especially valued the formal, orderly way in which life was conducted on the estates and in the mansions of these wealthy Protestant landowners. In 'The Second Coming', for instance, Yeats describes how the Anglo-Irish lifestyle was full of 'ceremony'. And such a civilised, ceremonial existence, he believed, produced people who were 'innocent', who were fundamentally decent and morally upright.

Meanwhile, in 'In Memory' he praises Lissadell, one of the famous 'big houses' associated with the Anglo-Irish. Yeats praises that 'old Georgian mansion' for its impressive architecture, for its 'great windows open to the South'. But it's worth noting that Lissadell, like other Anglo-Irish mansions, although luxurious, was also a little austere. The Anglo-Irish didn't really go in for 'bling', instead creating simple but elegant environments.

Yeats also admired Anglo-Irish society not only because it valued art and creativity but also because it was open to new ideas. Both of these trends are embodied in the 'silk kimonos' worn by the Gore-Booth sisters on that long-ago evening in Lissadell. These gowns, which might be considered art objects in themselves, reflect Anglo-Irish openness to fresh thinking and foreign cultures.

'Under Ben Bulben' also celebrates Anglo-Irish culture, looking back to its heyday in the 18th and 19th centuries. Yeats presents the Ireland of that period as a place of almost medieval simplicity. The 'lords and ladies' of the ascendancy resided in their 'gay' mansions or relaxed by 'hard-riding' through the countryside. The Catholic 'peasantry' worked the land and drank porter in the taverns, content with the noble simplicity of their lot. The monks, cooped-up in their monasteries, got on with being holy.

By the time Yeats was writing, however, the heyday of the Anglo-Irish was long since past. Their power had waned throughout the nineteenth century and all but disappeared in the new Catholic Ireland that emerged after independence from Britain. In 'The Second Coming', Yeats laments how the last influence of the Anglo-Irish seems to be disappearing, as the War of Independence against British rule in Ireland was getting into full swing. Everywhere Yeats looked, then, he saw the 'ceremony' of the aristocratic lifestyle being swept away amid the bloodshed of war and revolution: 'The blood-dimmed tide is loosed, and everywhere/ The ceremony of innocence is drowned'.

'In Memory' uses another striking metaphor to describe this decline. Yeats compares Anglo-Irish civilisation to a gazebo, a small roofed structure that is used for outdoor entertaining and dining. Gazebos are often ornamental and elaborately-designed, suggesting the emphasis Anglo-Irish society placed not only on hospitality but also on art and on beautiful objects. But gazebos are relatively flimsy structures, reflecting how the Anglo-Irish dominance of Irish life proved to be fragile and fleeting. In the early decades of independence, the great Anglo-Irish families, once so prominent in Irish life, drifted to its margins or disappeared altogether. Their civilisation was torn down as easily as one might dismantle a gazebo.

The Decline of Irish Society

'September 1913' is one of many poems where Yeats laments the decline of Irish society. This poem draws a stark contrast between Ireland's heroic past and the sad reality of what it has become. Yeats declares that Ireland was once a 'Romantic' country, a place that valued artistry and imagination. It was a place that exhibited community and self-sacrifice, and one that valued risk-taking and adventure. But this 'Romantic Ireland is dead and gone'. It has been replaced by a soulless, materialistic culture, as exemplified by the powerful businessmen Yeats criticises in the poem.

A similar point is made in 'Easter 1916'. Yeats admits that he believed Ireland to be a ridiculous place, one of 'casual comedy' inhabited by clowns and fools that might very well have been wearing the 'motley' of the traditional court jester. Ireland, he felt, could produce nothing serious, nothing beautiful and nothing heroic. The shock of the 1916 Rising, however, has revised his opinion of the country.

'Under Ben Bulben' features another lament about the state of Irish society. In 1939, when Yeats wrote the poem, Ireland was becoming a place dominated by science and technology, by industry and commerce. These changes, Yeats feels, have made the Irish of today a rather 'base' lot. The 'sort now growing up' are devoid of morality, are incapable of feeling and are even physically inferior. Yeats, then, looks back with affection to this golden time before modernity, when gentleman and peasant alike were uncorrupted by the grubby influences of capitalism and materialism. This was also a time before science came to dominate mankind's view of the world, a time that Yeats, a spiritualist rather than a scientist in outlook, harks back to with the greatest of nostalgia.

Patriotism and Revolt

Yeats' poetry is marked by a profound meditation on the nature of patriotism and revolt. In 'September 1913', for instance, Yeats declares that Ireland has lost its patriotic values. At one time, the country produced individuals like Robert Emmet and Wolfe Tone, who were prepared to sacrifice everything for the causes they believed in. The Ireland of 1913, Yeats believes, is incapable of understanding such self-sacrifice. The idealism exhibited by Emmet and Tone would strike contemporary Ireland as alien and incomprehensible. Yeats imagines the old heroes somehow coming back to life, only to be treated with scorn by the businessmen who currently lead the country.

A similar point is made at the beginning of 'Easter 1916'. Yeats describes how he used to laugh behind the backs of nationalists like Pearse and Connolly when he met them on the streets of Dublin. These men were fervently convinced that Ireland could be roused to rebel against British rule. Yeats, on the other hand, felt that Ireland was no longer capable of producing the self-sacrifice and heroism necessary for rebellion.

However, Yeats is forced to concede that he was wrong. The rebel leaders not only had a dream but they acted on that dream to make it a reality, paying the ultimate price as they did so. Yeats accepts that these men and women made the ultimate sacrifice for their country and will be remembered as heroes. Wherever Irish people gather, wherever 'green is worn', people will recount their deeds with awe and admiration. The Rising, in Yeats' memorable phrase, has unleashed a 'terrible beauty'. It is beautiful because it involves heroism, honour and self-sacrifice. It is terrible because it involves bloodshed and destruction. Yeats, as he contemplates the future, feel that the coming years will be shaped by both this terror and this beauty.

This mediation on patriotism and revolt continues in 'The Stare's Nest by My Window', which was written during the Irish Civil War. Here Yeats exhibits a much more sceptical attitude towards patriotism and revolt. We sense that the closer Yeats came to the grim realities of guerrilla warfare, the less time he had for the 'fantasies' of freedom and martyrdom. Disagreements over Irish freedom, he suggests, aren't worth such terror and destruction, such loss of life and property.

In 'September 1913', Yeats suggested that the Irish people had forgotten the ideas of freedom and martyrdom that motivated the heroes of the past. In this poem, written ten years later, he argues the opposite. The Irish people, he claims, have not only remembered these ideas but have become obsessed with them. And their obsession with these dangerous 'fantasies' has poisoned their psyches, turning their hearts 'brutal'.

THIS IS POETRY — W.B. YEATS

The Lake Isle of Innisfree

LINE BY LINE

Stanza 1

The poem opens with a dramatic declaration of intent. It's as if the poet has suddenly made a decision. It's as if he's suddenly realised that he's had enough of modern living and that a change of direction is needed. And this new existence, he declares, will begin immediately, for he's going to stand up any minute now and embark on a new chapter in his life: 'I will arise and go now'. He even emphasises this intention by repeating it in Stanza 3.

Yeats declares his intention to go off and live on the island of Innisfree, a small uninhabited island on Lough Gill in County Sligo. He imagines he would live a very simple life once he gets there:
- He would live 'alone' in a clearing or glade upon the island.
- He would build his own cabin: 'And a small cabin build there'. This would be a very basic type of accommodation. It would be 'small'. It would be manufactured using the ancient 'wattle and daub' technique, which involves smearing mud over interwoven sticks and twigs.
- He would even produce his own food, keeping bees for their honey and growing rows of beans: 'Nine bean-rows will I have there, a hive for the honey-bee'.

Yeats, then, seems to imagine living 'off the grid', going without the amenities and conveniences of his time. He imagines a life without telephones and telegraphs, with no newspapers or postal service, without the primitive gas and electrical services that were available in 1890s Dublin and London.

Stanza 2

The poet imagines the great beauty of Innisfree, taking us through a day on the island from dawn to dusk to midnight:
- The poet would wake each day to the pleasant chirping sounds of crickets: 'where the cricket sings'.
- He uses a wonderful metaphor to describe the banks of mist that drift across the island each morning, comparing them to 'veils' that drift and disperse, momentarily obscuring the island's beauty as they pass: 'the veils of the morning'.
- Noon, too, is beautiful. Sunlight glitters on the heather that covers much of the island and gives it its name. ('Inis Fraoich', in Irish, means island of the heather). This glittering heather lends the whole place a 'purple glow'.
- Evenings on Innisfree are 'full' of the sound made by linnets (small brown finches common in the west of Ireland) as they flit around the island: 'And evening full of the linnet's wings'.
- Midnight, meanwhile, sees the starlight reflected on Lough Gill, so that its waters glitter and gleam: 'There midnight's all a glimmer'.

Stanza 3

The poet claims that the sound of Innisfree's beaches, of 'lake water lapping' on the island's shores, is always in his mind's ear. Like a catchy song he can't get out of his head, these 'low sounds' of water are 'always' present at the back of his mind.

ANALYSIS

They repeat over and over again, 'night and day'; we sense that the poet couldn't make them stop even if he wanted to.

These lines, then, emphasise the intensity of the poet's attachment to the little island. The lapping sound of its water echoes in the very 'core' of his heart, in the depths of his being or psyche. No matter where he goes, the sound of its waters is ever-present at the very centre of his mind, forming a kind of background music as he lives his life. But the thought of Innisfree, it seems, is especially important to the poet when he finds himself in an urban environment: 'While I stand on the roadway, or on the pavements grey'. We can imagine how the cold grey concrete makes him long for the island's beauty. We can imagine how the city's endless racket makes him long for that soothing, almost silent retreat.

Yeats, it's worth noting, was inspired to write the poem when he was living in London and was feeling homesick for his beloved Sligo. He was walking down Fleet Street, one of that city's busiest thoroughfares, when he saw a fountain in a shop window, which 'balanced a little ball upon its jet'. The trickling sound of the fountain reminded him of Innisfree's lapping waters and sparked the beginning of the poem.

FOCUS ON STYLE

Verbal Music
The poem contains many examples of assonance and alliteration. Assonance features in the second line, with its broad vowel sounds: 'a small cabin build there, of clay and wattles made'. It is also evident in line 7, where the repeated 'i' and 'o' sounds create a soft musical effect: 'midnight's all a glimmer, and noon a purple glow'. The repeated 'a' and 'o' sounds in line 10 have a similar musical quality: 'I hear lake water lapping with low sounds by the shore'. Combined with the alliteration of the 'l' sounds, these techniques make this line very pleasant to the ear.

Imagery
'The Lake Isle of Innisfree' is a poem of contrasting imagery. There is a stark difference between the imagery of the city and the imagery of Innisfree. The city is a drab and dull place, composed of roadways and 'pavements grey'. The island, in contrast, is alive with colour and sound. We can contrast the 'purple glow' of the heather with the 'pavements grey'. However, the city seems a very real place, while the island comes across as more of an imagined paradise.

Tone, Mood and Atmosphere
In his descriptions of Innisfree, Yeats creates a very peaceful, almost drowsy atmosphere. His days will be marked by the humming of bees and crickets. It is a place where 'peace comes dropping slow', where he can relax and be alone in nature. However, we also suspect that this is a highly idealised version of Innisfree. Were Yeats to actually go and try to live on the island by himself, the reality might be very different.

THEMES

NATURE

Nature's Beauty
This is one of Yeats' best-loved nature poems. Innisfree is depicted as a place of sublime tranquillity. It's a place of great silence, devoid of any man-made sound.

Innsisfree, then, is where the poet will discover the peace he so craves: 'And I shall have some peace there'. Yeats, in a wonderful turn of phrase, presents peace as a physical substance, 'dropping' in the form of dew to cover the entire island. Peace, we're told, 'comes dropping' slowly from the banks of mist that cover the island each morning, drenching the grasses where the crickets are busy about their song.

Getting Back to Nature
There are moments when each of us feels like escaping the 'rat race' that all-too-often constitutes modern living. We may feel, as Yeats suggests in Stanza 3, like trading in the cacophony of city living, with its endless traffic noise and car alarms, for a place of tranquillity where 'peace comes dropping slow'. We may feel, as Yeats does in this poem, that it's time to turn our backs on the stresses and strains of modern living, of exams and deadlines, and of career pressure and social obligations.

We may even fantasise about going off the grid completely, about living without media and devices, even without electricity. Some people even fantasise, as Yeats does here, about being completely self-sufficient, about growing their own food and building their own simple dwelling places.

Innisfree, as the poet describes it, is a place of fantasy, an idealised almost heavenly version of the actual island in County Sligo. It's a place where the poet can live out his dream of escape from modern life. But fantasy is the operative word. For we sense that Yeats, like most people, wouldn't last more than a week living alone and self-sufficiently upon Lough Gill. Think of the harsh winters, the difficulty of growing crops, the isolation, and the lack of warmth and electricity.

We sense, then, that the poet won't really follow through on this decision to 'arise and go'. We sense that this departure for Innisfree won't happen now and probably never will, and we also sense that that the poet isn't quite prepared to leave the modern world behind and embrace what today we'd describe today as a hippy or New Age lifestyle. However, such fantasies can be important. For the poet, this dream of the simple life serves as a comfort or escape when times get tough. When the rat race proves too draining, when he tires of the grey city pavements, he can always daydream about his bean rows on the island of Innisfree.

THIS IS POETRY

September 1913

The Dublin Municipal Gallery, named in honour of Hugh Lane and his gift to the Irish nation

LINE BY LINE

This poem was inspired by two different controversies that raged throughout 1913. The first involved Hugh Lane who was a nephew of Yeats' great friend Lady Gregory. Lane had accumulated an important collection of priceless French paintings, which he was prepared to donate to the city of Dublin on condition that Dublin Corporation provided a suitable gallery. The businessmen who ran the corporation, led by Ireland's most prominent capitalist William Martin Murphy, proved unwilling to provide public money for the gallery. They were also unwilling to contribute to a private fund set up to cover the gallery's cost.

Yeats was disgusted at the small-minded attitude exhibited by Dublin's business leaders, and he was distraught that such a priceless collection would be lost to Ireland forever.

The second controversy is known to history as the 'Dublin Lockout'. This was a massive industrial dispute. On the one side were thousands of ordinary workers – dockers, carters, labourers, tram and railway workers. On the other side were a group of wealthy businessmen who controlled most of the employment in Dublin and the surrounding area. William Martin Murphy again played a central role, emerging as the de facto leader of the employers.

Yeats, as a relatively privileged descendant of the Protestant landowning class, had little in common with the dockers and factory workers of inner city Dublin. But he showed himself to be a man of the people, using his platform as a famous writer to support the workers and their struggle for better paying conditions. He complained, in particular about the police brutality experienced by the workers throughout this long and bitter dispute.

Stanza 1

'September 1913', then, is a very public and political poem. Yeats was determined that it would reach a wide audience and published it in The Irish Times. It can be viewed as a political satire, a poem in which the poet uses mockery, irony and exaggeration in order to attack his or her political opponents. Here Yeats sets out to criticise and ridicule William Martin Murphy and his fellow business leaders.

These businessmen, Yeats declares, have 'come to sense'. They have achieved a deep and total understanding of the world. They've realised that 'men were born pray and save', that the only important things in life are praying to God and accumulating wealth. If they save enough money, they will ensure that they are secure in this world. And if they pray enough, they will ensure that their souls are secure in the next world.

These opening lines, however, are dripping with irony and sarcasm. For Yeats doesn't really believe that these businessmen have life all figured out. In fact, he regards their view of life as being very much mistaken and far too limited.

Yeats accuses these businessmen of accumulating wealth in a miserable and miserly fashion. They are so mean that they don't let a single penny, or even a half-penny, slip through their fingers as they 'add the halfpence to the pence'.

Yeats accuses these businessmen of praying in a soulless and mechanical fashion, describing how they count their prayers the same way they count their money. Their approach to prayer, then, resembles a business negotiation rather than genuine spirituality. They seem to believe that when they've added enough prayers to their account, God will guarantee them a place in heaven.

ANALYSIS

Yeats, in a brilliant turn of phrase, describes the businessmen's prayers as 'shivering'. This suggests that all their praying is motivated by fear, either of priests in this life, or of hell in the next, rather than out of a genuine desire to communicate with God.

> The phrase 'fumble in a greasy till' conjures up an especially vivid image. We imagine a greedy shopkeeper in his grubby, rundown little premises. We imagine him fumbling in his miserly haste to gather the last dirty little pennies from his till at the close of business.
>
> The businessmen that Yeats is criticising were captains of industry. They wore the finest clothes, ate the finest foods and socialised in the finest hotels and gentlemen's clubs around Dublin. But their penny-pinching, small-minded ways, Yeats suggests, makes them no better than the grubby shopkeeper described above.
>
> This comparison, then, is an especially devastating piece of criticism, one that very effectively takes these wealthy individuals down a peg or two.

Yeats feels that these businessmen have 'dried the marrow from the bone'. Their mean-spirited philosophy, in his opinion, sucks the goodness out of life and disregards everything that makes life worth living. Their emphasis on praying and saving doesn't leave space for art and heroism, beauty and love, things Yeats regarded as the highest aspects of human existence.

Stanza 2

In this stanza, Yeats refers to the patriots who fought and died for Irish freedom in the centuries leading up to 1913. He uses a wonderful simile to describe the fame achieved by these martyrs, declaring that their names have 'gone about the world like wind'. We can imagine the wind spreading stories of their courage to all four corners of the globe.

The businessmen of Dublin Corporation were children once. And during their childhood they looked up to these great historical figures. Yeats describes how they would stop playing whenever one of these patriots was mentioned by an adult. They would ask to hear more about the patriot in question, eager for tales of heroism and courage.

As adults, however, the businessmen have nothing in common with these patriots: 'Yet they were of a different kind'. For the patriots, unlike the businessmen, had little interest in money. Indeed, their lives were so consumed with the struggle for Irish freedom that they had no real opportunity to accumulate wealth: 'And what, God help us, could they save?' Nor were the patriot's interested in the grim, fearful brand of religion practised by the businessmen: 'But little time had they to pray'. Instead, their minds lay on higher things: heroism, honour and freedom.

Stanza 3

In this stanza, Yeats refers to several examples of heroism from Ireland's past:

- He mentions the 'Wild Geese'. These were soldiers who fought for Irish freedom in the 1690s. They were defeated and were forced into exile, where they served with great distinction in various European armies.
- He recalls Edward Fitzgerald and Wolfe Tone, who led a rebellion against British rule in 1798. Both died in prison while awaiting execution after the rebellion failed.
- He thinks of Robert Emmet who was executed after his own uprising failed in 1803.

The businessmen of Dublin Corporation, and other similar business leaders around the country, have created the new Ireland of 1913. And in doing so they have betrayed the legacy of patriots like Emmet and Fitzgerald. The businessmen, through their focus on praying and saving, have turned the country into a mean-spirited and materialistic place. This un-Romantic Ireland is not the Ireland the heroes fought and died to create: 'Was it … For this that all that blood was shed?'

Stana 4

In this stanza, Yeats wishes that he could 'turn the years again', that he could somehow reverse time's flow. By doing so, we could 'call' or summon Ireland's patriots from their graves. They would reappear just 'as they were' when they were alive, when they campaigned for Irish freedom all those years ago. What sort of reception, he wonders, would these patriots receive in the Ireland of 1913?

Yeats believes that the businessmen of Dublin Corporation would take a dim view of the resurrected patriots. They would look at the assembled heroes and come to the conclusion that every single one of them ('every mother's son') was utterly insane. The businessmen would claim that the patriots had been driven mad by their love of Ireland, just as a man might be driven mad by love for a beautiful woman: 'You'd cry, 'Some woman's yellow hair/ Has maddened every mother's son'.

The patriots, Yeats points out, willingly laid down their lives. Indeed, they did not think of their own lives as especially valuable or important: 'They weighed so lightly what they gave'. For they believed in a cause far greater than themselves. It's as if, having weighed their lives against their values and beliefs, they had concluded that their lives were less important. The heroes, therefore, don't belong in the Ireland of 1913, which is dominated by the businessmen of Dublin Corporation and others like them. This new Ireland is an individualistic and materialistic place, one incapable of appreciating the patriots' extraordinary self-sacrifice. The patriots, were they somehow to return, would only be mocked and misunderstood. Yeats concludes, therefore, that it's better to let the heroes rest in peace: 'But let them be, they're dead and gone/ They're with O'Leary in the grave'.

THEMES

YEATS AND IRELAND

In this poet Yeats laments the decline of Irish society. Yeats feels that the Ireland of 1913 is being shaped by the values of Murphy and his cronies in the Dublin Corporation, and by other materialistic business leaders throughout the land.

This poem draws a stark contrast between Ireland's heroic past and the sad reality of what it has become. Yeats declares that Ireland was once a 'Romantic' country. The word Romantic, as used here, suggests several different things:
- It suggests that Ireland was once a place that valued artistry and imagination, where images, songs and stories were valued by the people.
- It suggests that Ireland was once an idealistic place, one that exhibited community and self-sacrifice rather than miserly focus on self-enrichment.
- It suggests that Ireland was once a place that valued risk-taking and adventure. Now, however, it is a place where people play it safe, focusing on their prayer books and their bank accounts.

For Yeats, the values of Romantic Ireland were especially embodied by the great Irish patriot John O'Leary, who fought in the 1848 rebellion against British rule in Ireland. After this rising, he continued to campaign for Irish freedom, which led to him spending years in prison and in exile. He returned to Dublin in 1885, becoming a great friend and mentor to the young Yeats. But now O'Leary is 'dead and gone', having passed away in 1907. The Romantic Ireland he represented has passed away as well. It has been replaced by a soulless, materialistic culture, as exemplified by Murphy and his fellow business leaders.

The poem also tackles the theme of patriotism and revolution. There was a time when Ireland produced revolutionary patriots like Tone and Emmet. These were men who dreamed big and gave everything to make their dreams a reality. They were prepared to sacrifice everything for the causes they believed in – their wealth, their wellbeing and even their lives.

The Ireland of 1913, Yeats believes, is incapable of understanding such self-sacrifice. The idealism exhibited by Emmet and Tone would strike contemporary Ireland as alien and incomprehensible. Yeats imagines the old heroes somehow coming back to life, only to be treated with scorn by the businessmen who currently lead the country. But Yeats recognises that there was also something tragic about these men's lives. Their lives, he suggests, were marked by 'pain', as they invested year after thankless year into the impossible project of Irish freedom. 'Loneliness', too, was their lot. They were 'exiles' not only when sent abroad after defeat, but also in their own land, because their passionate beliefs alienated them from society at large.

Yeats stresses that the patriots were almost destined to fail, with the odds being stacked overwhelmingly against them. In a memorable turn of phrase, he describes how 'the hangman's rope was spun' for these heroes, as if their defeat and execution were pre-determined. There was almost suicidal element, therefore, about the patriots' efforts. They knew that failure and death were almost inevitable. But they fought anyway.

The middle classes are criticised for failing to understand the patriots' bravery, for regarding them as simply insane. But perhaps Yeats himself can't help suspecting that these heroes had been 'maddened' by their love for Ireland. Yeats says that the heroes 'weighed so lightly what they gave', referring to their patriotic willingness to lay down their lives for their cause. But is there a sense in which he believes that the heroes were a little too willing to die, that they weighed their lives too lightly?

ENERGY, PASSION, VITALITY

This poem celebrates the passion and conviction of certain heroic figures from Irish history, men such as Wolfe Tone and Robert Emmet who gave their lives in the pursuit of Irish independence. These men possessed a number of qualities that Yeats greatly admired. These were men who followed their own principles and instincts. They believed deeply in the idea that Ireland should be free of English rule and devoted their lives to bringing this about. They were not guided by the opinion of the masses and did not try to conform to anyone else's idea of what their lives ought to be. Instead, they let their principles and instincts guide them, believing in something greater than themselves.

These men were reckless, casually risking their lives for what they believed in. Though they knew that they were fated to die, that the odds were greatly stacked against them, they fought on regardless. As Yeats says, from the moment they began to fight, the 'hangman's rope was spun'. But these men seemed to place little stock in their own individual lives, believing that their causes and principles were worth dying for: 'They weighed so lightly what they gave'.

WAR, VIOLENCE AND SOCIAL UPHEAVAL

'September 1913' acknowledges the suffering endured by the patriots of Ireland's past. Many of them, as he notes, endured the loneliness and pain of being sent into exile. Many others suffered execution by the 'hangman's rope'. Overall, however, the poem presents a rather romantic or idealistic view of war and violence. It celebrates the military achievements of the Wild Geese on the continents, the almost foolhardy courage of soldiers like Robert Emmet and John O'Leary who led tiny revolts against a vast imperial power.

The poem emphasises the noble side of warfare, the idealism and self-sacrifice displayed by soldiers in the service of a cause. But it downplays the horror and bloodshed of the battlefield. In this regard, it can be contrasted with 'Easter 1916', which takes a less idealistic view of patriotic violence. It can also be contrasted with 'The Stare's Nest by My Window', where Yeats comes face to face with the terror and confusion of reality in a war zone.

The Wild Swans at Coole

LINE BY LINE

A walk in Coole Park

The poem is set in Coole Park, Co. Galway, which was the private estate and home of Lady Augusta Gregory. Lady Gregory was a major figure in Yeats' life. She helped him in discovering Ireland's heritage of myth and folklore. She collaborated with him on various projects, such as the founding of the Abbey Theatre, and she also provided the frequently cash-strapped poet with financial support. Yeats was a regular visitor to Coole Park, a place he found conducive to his writing.

This poem was written during one such visit to the estate. It is an October evening:
- The evening, according to the poet, is exceptionally 'still'. We imagine an evening without a puff of wind, the clouds static in the twilight sky,
- The woodland paths, according to the poet, are 'dry', which suggests a period of crisp, fine weather. We can imagine the pleasant crunching sound made by the poet's footsteps as he makes his way through the grounds.
- The trees in the park exhibit the beauty of autumn. We can imagine a multi-coloured array of browns, yellows and reds.

The poet comes to one of Coole Park's lakes. The evening is so still that the lake's surface is utterly un-rippled. Its surface resembles a mirror that perfectly reflects the twilight sky above. The lake is described as 'brimming', which suggests that gentle wavelets lap onto the stones around its edges.

The poet back then

As we mentioned above, the poet has been coming to Coole Park on a regular basis. Each time he visits, he takes the same walk around the estate's exquisite grounds, his route taking him past this lake 'among the stones'. He always pauses by this particular lake to count the swans that swim upon its surface. The poet remembers his 'first time' standing on the lake's rocky shore. It was 19 years ago, during his very first visit to Coole Park. That was the first time he attempted to count the swans on the lake's surface: 'The nineteenth autumn has come upon me/ Since I first made my count'.

On that occasion, however, the swans scattered and flew away before he could finish counting them. The poet still recalls the sound of the swans' wings as they circled above him in the 'twilight' nineteen years ago. The noise they produced was rhythmical and powerful, like the regular chiming of a bell: 'The bell-beat of their wings above my head'.

The poet now
Now we move back to the present day. The poet has come once more to the lake 'among the stones'. He pauses, as usual, to count the swans upon its surface. He manages, on this occasion, to complete his count, coming to a grand total of 59. The poet refers to the swans as 'brilliant'. The adjective 'brilliant' suggest that the swans are creatures of exceptional beauty. But it also suggests the extraordinary whiteness of their feathers. Watching these 'brilliant creatures', however, fills the poet with sorrow: 'And now my heart is sore'.

He finds himself thinking about the great changes that have occurred in the 19 years since he stood on this very lake shore and counted the swans for the very first time. And these changes, we sense, have not been for the better:

- The poet has aged physically. He is slower and weaker than he was on that first visit 19 years ago.
- The poet has grown psychologically exhausted over the past 19 years. He has been involved in any number of personal, political and financial struggles, enduring great disappointment and frustration.
- The poet has been unlucky in love. Yeats was famously infatuated with the great beauty Maud Gonne. But his pursuit of her proved unsuccessful. Now, as he enters middle age, he finds himself childless and unmarried.
- The poet's good looks have diminished. He no longer feels himself to be handsome or sexually attractive.

The poet describes how his footsteps were 'lighter' on that first visit to Coole Park. This of course suggests the physical changes the poet has experienced. He's now nearly two decades older and walks in a slower, more deliberate fashion. But it also suggests the psychological changes the poet has experienced. For over the past nineteen years he has become burdened by cares, regrets and disappointments. In the phrase 'All's changed', then, we hear the sigh of a man who fears that his best years are behind him.

The setting seems to correspond with the poet's feelings about his life. It is autumn, meaning the splendours of summer are passed and the bitterness of winter lies in wait. The poet, similarly, has entered the 'autumn' of his life. The splendours of youth are a distant memory and old age is fast approaching. Even the dryness of the woodland paths suggests the physical decline that accompanies the ageing process.

Contrast between the poet and the swans
The poet draws a sharp contrast between himself and the swans. The swans are 'Unwearied still'. They exhibit none of the physical decline that has affected the poet. They still have the strength to 'climb the air', to launch themselves skyward in a powerful and majestic fashion.

The swans are also 'Unwearied' in a psychological sense. 'Their hearts', unlike the heart of the poet, 'have not grown old'. They experience none of the mental exhaustion that has affected the poet, and they are unburdened by the cares and disappointments that weigh him down.

The swans, according to the poet, experience a rich and varied love life. A swan, he suggests, will have a passionate affair with one companion before moving on to the next. Each new affair will begin with flirtation and seduction, followed by a moment of sexual conquest. Each relationship is filled with passion and affection.

In this regard, the contrast between the poet and the swans couldn't be sharper. The swans exist in waters that are 'companionable', each swimming contentedly beside its current partner. The poet, in contrast, has no lover, wife or family. The swans enjoy lives of endless sexual opportunity. No matter where they go, they will experience passion and conquest: 'Passion or conquest, wander where they will,/ Attend upon them still'. The poet, by contrast, feels that his opportunities for love and passion have passed him by.

Will the swans depart?
The poet continues to watch the swans gliding on the lake's surface. He relishes this sight, emphasising its mystery and beauty: 'But now they drift on the still water,/ Mysterious, beautiful'. But he realises that the swans will not always be here. Sooner or later the colony will depart for some new home, leaving Coole Park behind forever. He imagines the swans arriving at some faraway 'lake' or 'pool', where they will build new nests for themselves among the rushes at the water's edge: 'Among what rushes will they build [?]'.

The poet imagines some future visit to Coole Park. He imagines walking by the lake only to discover that the swans have departed. He will no longer be able to enjoy the sight of these magnificent creatures. That privilege will now fall to others, those who live beside the swans' new home.

FOCUS ON STYLE

Form
This is a lyrical poem, comprising of five six-line stanzas. Each stanza follows the same rhyming scheme ABCBDD.

Verbal Music
There are several places where assonance and alliteration create a pleasant musical effect, reflecting the stillness of this fine October evening. We see this with the repeated 'i' sounds in 'drift on the still water' and 'Mirrors a still sky'.

A similar musical effect is created by the repeated 'a' and 'u' sounds in the poem's opening lines: 'autumn beauty' and 'woodland paths'.

There is an element of cacophony in the second stanza, where the clashing 't', 'k' and 'l' sounds suggest the rackett produced by the swans as they scatter screeching into the sky. Finally, the repeated broad vowel sounds in 'trod with a lighter tread' slow the pace of the verse, suggesting the poet's plodding, laborious gait.

Imagery

This poem is redolent with imagery of the natural world. Especially vivid is the image of the swans suddenly taking flight. Each mounts the air as though it were a horseman preparing to ride into battle. Yeats brilliantly captures the circular flight-path of the swans as they spiral upwards: 'scatter wheeling in great broken rings'.

The poem also features a memorable instance of personification. Personification occurs when an abstract concept is presented as if it were a person. In this instance, passion and conquest are presented as attendants or servants that follow the swans wherever they go: 'Passion or conquest, wander where they will,/ Attend upon them still'.

THEMES

NATURE

This is one of Yeats' best-loved nature poems. The poet captures the unique qualities of an Irish autumn evening: a crisp path underfoot, a haunting stillness in the twilight sky, trees in their multi-coloured beauty.

The poem especially celebrates swans, those most mysterious and beautiful creatures. Yeats shows us the swans in two very different states. He highlights their grace and serenity as they drift on the still water, and he also highlights the explosive power and force they exhibit as they 'mount/ And scatter', their wings thumping with the piercing regularity of a bell.

YOUTH AND AGE

The poet, as we've seen, laments the beginnings of middle age. He has started to exhibit not only physical weakness and psychological exhaustion, but also a lessening of his good looks and sexual opportunities. His heart is 'sore' as he contemplates his decline.

The poem centres on the contrast between the poet, whose life has endured such changes, and the swans, who are presented as being utterly changeless. The swans, as we have seen, are 'unwearied' in body and mind, as they pursue lives of unbounded passion and sexual adventure.

The end of the poem is almost unbearably sad. The poet, as we've seen, imagines that the swans will someday leave behind Coole Park. The park, then, will be deserted by the swans just as the poet will be deserted by the last of his vitality and good looks. The swans will be enjoyed by other people in the faraway places where they build their homes. Similarly, youth and vitality will be the preserve of the younger generation, as the poet sinks into old age.

THIS IS POETRY — W.B. YEATS

An Irish Airman Foresees His Death

LINE BY LINE

This is an example of a 'persona poem'. In such poems, the poet speaks not as him or herself, but takes on the voice of someone completely different. In this instance, Yeats speaks in the voice of an Irish pilot serving with the British armed forces in World War 1.

The poem was inspired by Major Robert Gregory, an Irish friend of Yeats who fought with the British Royal Flying Corps. He was shot down and killed in 1918, just before the end of that terrible conflict. Robert was the son of Lady Augusta Gregory, Yeats' great friend, supporter and collaborator. Yeats was a frequent visitor to the Gregory estate in Coole Park, Co. Galway, which inspired his famous poem 'The Wild Swans at Coole'.

The airman somehow knows in advance that he will die in battle: 'I know that I shall meet my fate'. He knows that his plane will be shot down 'Somewhere among the clouds above'. Despite this premonition, however, he still volunteers to fight. Why does he make this seemingly suicidal choice?

The airman claims that he has no affection for either side in the First World War, which saw Britain and her allies ranged against Germany and the other central powers. As a member of the Flying Corps, the airman flies on many missions against German forces, attacking enemy planes and ground positions. But he doesn't do so because he hates the German people: 'Those that I fight I do not hate'. His job as a member of the Flying Corps is to protect Britain and her interests in the world, especially to 'guard' the island of Britain itself from possible invasion. The airman carries out this task, flying in mission after mission aimed at making Britain more secure. But he does not do so out of any special love of the British people: 'Those that I guard I do not love'.

Nor did the airman volunteer in order to help his own people, the poor folk of Kiltartan in Co. Galway: 'My country is Kiltartan Cross,/ My countrymen Kiltartan's poor'. He knows that the result of the war will make no difference to them and to the rest of the Irish nation. The conflict – no matter how it ends – won't leave them any 'happier'. Nor will it bring them any great 'loss'.

He doesn't serve because he is required to do so by 'law'. Though Ireland was under British rule during the First World War, Irish people like the airman were not legally obliged to serve in the British army. Nor did he volunteer out of a sense of 'duty'. As an Irish person, he doesn't feel morally obliged to fight for Britain and her interests on the continent.

He is motivated neither by the speeches of politicians nor by by the cheers of the crowds that listened to them: 'Nor public men, nor cheering crowds'. We might think here of images and footage from the beginning of the war, which show a wave of patriotism sweeping across Europe. In London, Paris, Berlin and Vienna, thousands would gather to hear their leaders speak, each 'cheering crowd' convinced that right was on their country's side and that victory would be theirs. The airman, however, is unmoved by this mass patriotic hysteria.

So why does the airman fight? Why does he journey again and again into that 'tumult in the clouds', into the noise and confusion of aerial combat? Why did he volunteer, of his own free will, when he anticipates that doing so will lead to his death?

The airman describes how he was driven to volunteer by an 'impulse', by a strong and almost irresistible urge. According to the airman, the impulse driving him is one of 'delight':

- There's the delight that comes from the act of flying itself, from handling this magnificent piece of hardware and making it respond to one's slightest touch.
- There's the delight that comes from being so far above the world, from experiencing what might be described as a God's-eye view of creation. For the airman, operating at the dawn of aviation, such excitement must have been even more pronounced. For he was experiencing something few other humans ever had.
- There's the adrenaline rush that comes with all sport and competition, as the airman engages his German opponents in move and counter-move, in a noisy and chaotic game of three-dimensional chess.
- There's the thrill that comes from putting your life on the line. Again and again, soldiers and emergency responders report how they never feel more alive than in those moments when their deaths are a real possibility.

We often think that people who act on impulse behave in an unreflective and irrational manner. The airman, however, is adamant that he has not acted in such a way. He claims that he has assessed his life calmly and rationally, weighing up its every aspect: 'I balanced all, brought all to mind'. The conclusion he draws from this assessment is a bleak one. He regards his life up to this point as utterly pointless. All the years he's lived through were no more than a waste of time and energy: 'A waste of breath the years behind'. The years remaining to him seem equally futile: 'The years to come seemed waste of breath'. To the airman, then, life is a meaningless affair.

The airman views death in aerial combat as a fitting or appropriate end to the life he has lived: 'In balance with this life, this death'. This line is open to a number of interpretations. Perhaps the airman is simply suggesting that death offers him an escape from a life he finds pointless, dreary and depressing. Or perhaps he feels that going down in one final blaze of glory will 'balance out' or make up for the pointless waste of breath that was his life. It is also possible that the airman wants to die in aerial combat because that was the only place in which he truly feels alive. Such a death, therefore, would be a 'balanced' or appropriate conclusion to his life.

FOCUS ON STYLE

The poem is marked by a strong, propulsive rhythm. Repetition, too, features strongly, with repeated patterns of phrasing in lines 3 and 4 ('Those that... Those that...') as well as in lines 5 and 6 ('My country...My countrymen...') Similarly, the last four lines feature the repetition of 'all', 'balance', 'the years' and 'waste of 'breath'.

Rhythm, rhyme and repetition combine to lend the poem a relentless, driving music, one that echoes, perhaps, the sound of the airman's propellers rotating, or that evokes the thoughts swirling around and around his mind as he prepares for his final journey into battle.

THEMES

WAR, VIOLENCE AND SOCIAL UPHEAVAL

The poem was written at a time of extraordinary violence, when Europe witnessed the bloodiest and most destructive war it had ever seen. Yeats was always a scholar rather than a soldier. But he exhibited a lifelong fascination with men of action, with those who, like the airman, had the bravery to enter the field of battle, putting their lives on the line as they fought, died and killed.

No doubt Yeats also admires how the airman is a person apart. The airman, unlike his fellow soldiers, has no truck with the propaganda of public men and politicians. He is unmoved by the great wave of patriotism that has swept across the continent. Instead, as we have seen, he fights for his own reasons.

DEATH

Yeats, we sense, admires the airman's vitality and energy. The airman exhibits a reckless abandon, plunging almost joyfully into the terrifying melee of aerial combat, risking his life again and again in the chaotic 'tumult' of engagements with the enemy. There's a sense, then, in which the airman comes across as what today we would call a thrill-seeker or an adrenaline junkie, being someone who lives for the adventure of flight and the exhilaration of aerial combat. Like participants in various extreme sports, the airman takes 'delight' and pleasure in risking his life. We sense he only feels alive when he is involved in the chaos and 'tumult' of battle above the clouds. To the airman, life is only worth living when it's at its most intense.

But the airman, it must be noted, also exhibits a terrifying 'nihilism', which is the belief that everything in life is utterly pointless and without meaning. It is not surprising that he describes himself as being driven by a 'lonely impulse', given his depressing outlook on life. Many readers have taken issue with what might be described as the airman's 'suicidal tendencies' or 'death wish'. They also question his contemptuous disdain for everyday life. Can we endorse the airman's verdict that these things represent no more than a 'waste of breath'? Or can we reject his view of life as that of a 'lonely' individual whose only relief from depression comes in the thick of aerial combat?

THIS IS POETRY　　　W.B. YEATS

Easter 1916

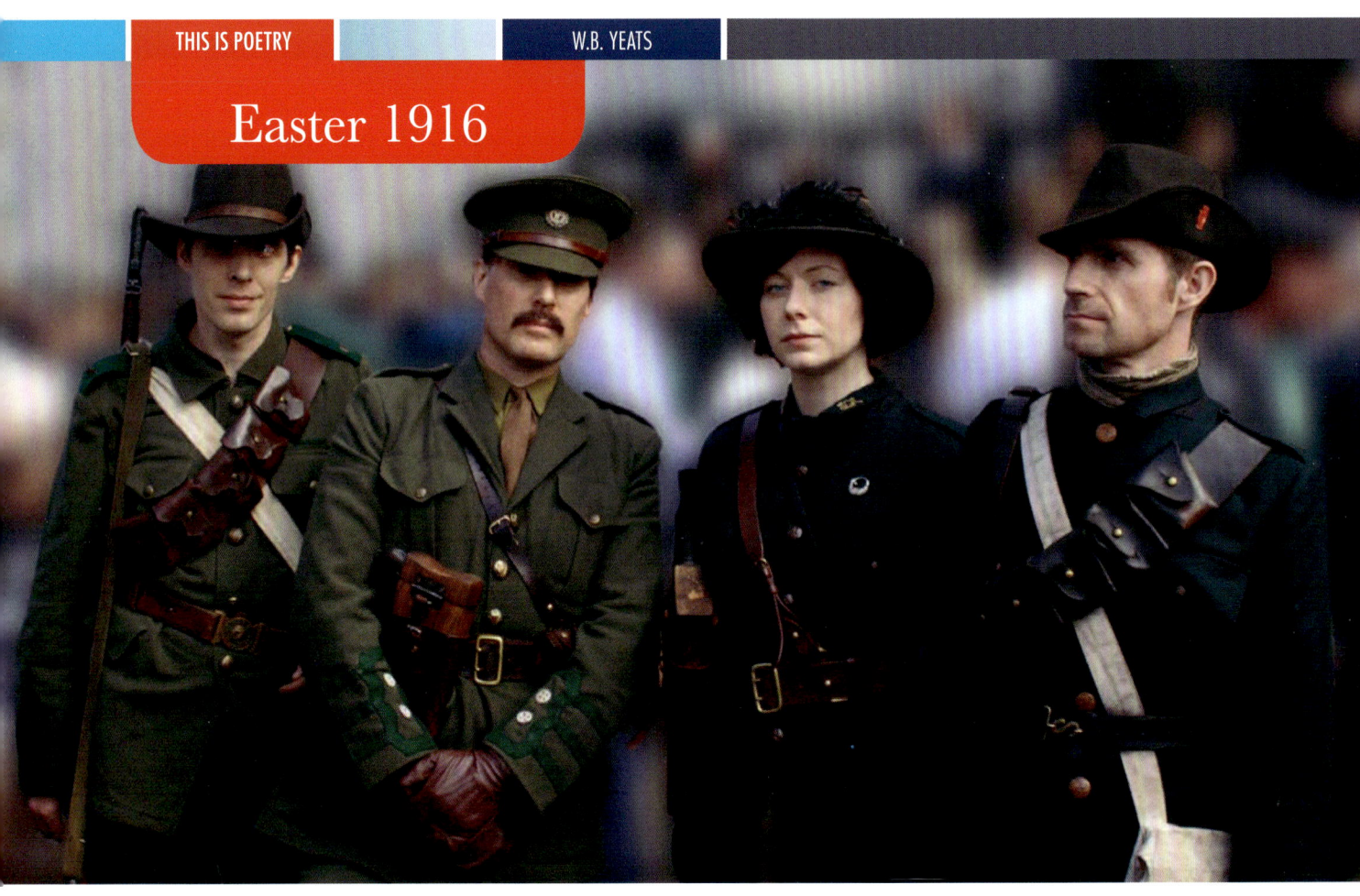

LINE BY LINE

The Easter Rising took place in Dublin between Monday 24 April and Saturday 29 April 1916. It was a rebellion against British rule in Ireland and was defeated after a swift British military response.

The Rising was planned in secret by seven men, mostly of the Irish Republican Brotherhood (IRB), who had formed a 'Military Council' to this end just after the outbreak of the First World War.

Yeats was absent from Dublin for the Rising but his response to it was intense: "I had no idea that any public event could so deeply move me," he wrote to Lady Gregory, "and I am very despondent about the future".

Section 1

Yeats recalls how he sometimes encountered the revolutionaries when walking through Dublin. He would run into them late in the afternoon, as they emerged from their various places of work around the city: 'I have met them at close of day/ Coming ... From counter or desk'.

These young men would have been barmen and shopkeepers, teachers and clerks. But they would have also been members of illegal organisations such as the IRB. They would meet regularly to discuss and plan the possibility of Irish independence being achieved by means of violent revolution. The passion and enthusiasm for their cause would be written on their faces, which the poet describes as 'vivid'.

Yeats would have known some of these people through their involvement in the theatre world or the arts. Others, he would have known just to see, perhaps from frequenting their shops or offices. He, like many people in Dublin, would have known that they were radicals, members of illegal organisations committed to revolution.

The poet would have been sympathetic to the revolutionaries' ultimate goal – Irish independence from Britain – but he did not believe that violence was the best means to achieve this. Although Yeats had in his youth flirted with the idea of revolution, he later came to believe that independence was best achieved through political means. And the possibility of this happening was very real. The Home Rule Act, intended to provide home rule for Ireland, had been passed by the British Parliament in 1914, but the implementation of it was postponed with the outbreak of the First World War. Home Rule would not have meant complete freedom from Britain, but it would have been a significant step towards this.

As such, Yeats believed that the 1916 rebels were misguided. But, more than this, he considered them to be naïve and foolish in their outlook and beliefs. What, he must have wondered, did they really think they were going to achieve? Ireland had been under British rule for over 800 years. The very buildings that the revolutionaries worked in were built by the British: 'grey nineteenth century houses'. The British empire at the time was the biggest empire the world had ever seen. There had been a number of attempts at violent revolution over the years, and every single one had utterly failed – both in terms of advancing the Irish cause and in terms of convincing the Irish public that violence was the best means of achieving independence.

Yeats never imagined that the revolutionaries he encountered on the streets would ever do or achieve anything of significance. He was quite sure that their talk of revolution was just that – talk. And if they ever did manage to organise a revolt, it would surely be a pathetic and embarrassing failure. He regarded the rebels as fools and clowns, who played at revolution but lacked the ability to make it a reality. He was sure that Ireland had become a place where 'motley', the colours of the jester, were worn.

The poet's contempt for the revolutionaries can be partly explained by the differences in their backgrounds. Yeats' family were members of the Protestant ascendancy, the landowning class that had dominated Ireland until the early 20th century. Although times were changing and the poet was by no means a wealthy man, Yeats' outlook and opinion of who he was were still defined in terms of this background.

Yeats had inherited enough money that he did not need to work, He socialised in the Gentlemen's clubs in Dublin, private clubs whose members would have all shared similar backgrounds to Yeats. The revolutionaries, in turn, were descendants of Irish Catholics, the very people whose land the Protestants had taken and held for centuries. These were men who had to work for a living and would socialise in the pubs around Dublin.

The poet could never imagine that the future political leaders of Ireland would come from the Catholic middle classes – he did not think they had the necessary qualities and intellect. Ireland's political leadership, both intellectual and political, would surely come only from the Protestant land-owning class as it always had. The idea that political power would come to rest in the hands of the shopkeepers and clerks who spoke excitedly about rising up against the British struck the poet as ridiculous.

And so, when the poet encountered these men as they came from their shops and offices after work, he would barely give them the time of day. More often than not, he would simply pass them with a 'nod of the head' or say something civil and perfunctory as they went by: 'polite meaningless words'. Occasionally, the poet would stop out of courtesy and have a brief chat. But again, nothing significant would be said apart from 'Polite meaningless words'. While he was chatting to them, he would be thinking about how he would later speak with scorn and ridicule of the encounter to some friend at a social club: 'a mocking tale or a gibe/ To please a companion/ Around the fire at the club'.

But then the Easter Rising took place and changed everything: 'All changed, changed utterly'. On Monday 24 April, the insurgents proclaimed an Irish Republic with Pearse as President and Connolly as commander in chief. They occupied positions around Dublin at the General Post Office, the Four Courts, the South Dublin Union, Boland's Mill, Stephen's Green and Jacobs' biscuit factory. Over the following week, the British deployed over 16,000 troops, artillery and naval gunboats in the city to suppress the Rising. In the week's fighting, about 450 people were killed and over 2,000 wounded. Sixteen of the rebel leaders were later executed.

Suddenly, therefore, the very people that Yeats had mocked and disparaged had acted with courage and conviction, risking and sacrificing their lives for the cause of Irish independence. They had staged an event that was momentous, that had earned the support and the sympathies of the Irish public. This forced the poet to re-evaluate and question many of his beliefs and convictions.

Yeats had to respect the manner in which these revolutionaries had put their lives on the line for their beliefs, but the whole idea of blood sacrifice and glorification of violence as a means of achieving political ends made him anxious and fearful for the future. The rebels had done something heroic and revealed a form of 'beauty' in dying for their cause, but the idea that an independent Ireland would be founded on violent insurrection was also 'terrible' and terrifying.

Section 2

Yeats was especially shocked and moved by the Rising because he knew some of those who were involved personally. He describes some of them, outlining what they did and how he felt about them prior to the Rising.

He begins with Constance Gore-Booth, someone that Yeats knew when she was a young lady. In 1894, the poet stayed at Lissadell, the home of the aristocratic Gore-Booth family in Sligo. He became friends with Constance and her sister Eva, and he greatly admired their beauty. Yeats recalls how 'beautiful' Constance looked when she was out riding with the hunt: 'When, young and beautiful,/ She rode to harriers'. He also remembers how delightful her voice sounded back then: 'What voice more sweet than hers'.

But when Constance later became involved in politics, Yeats was scornful and critical of her involvement. He believed that a beautiful, aristocratic lady such as Constance had no business involving herself in the grubby world of politics. Her intentions might have been good, but Yeats had little regard for her grasp of politics: 'That woman's days were spent/ In ignorant good-will'. Her involvement in politics, he believed, rendered her ugly. Her once 'sweet' voice 'grew shrill' when she engaged in political debates and arguments: 'Her nights in argument/ Until her voice grew shrill'.

Yeats describes two of the leaders of the rebellion, Pádraig Pearse and Thomas MacDonagh. Pearse had started his own school for boys in 1908: 'This man had kept a school'. Here the students were taught in English as well as Irish. Yeats also alludes to the fact that Pearse was poet, saying that he 'rode our winged horse' (Pegasus, a creature from Greek mythology, was a winged horse and a symbol of poetic inspiration).

Thomas MacDonagh was a friend of Pearse's and assisted him in running the school: 'This other his helper and friend'. MacDonagh was also a poet and dramatist and Yeats felt that he had real potential as a writer. He was 'coming into his force'. Yeats speculates that 'He might have won fame in the end' for his writing. He is described as 'sensitive' and his thoughts as 'so daring and sweet'.

Finally, Yeats describes Major John MacBride. In 1903 ,MacBride had married Maud Gonne, the lady that Yeats had loved and considered his muse. The marriage failed and there were accusations that MacBride had abused Maud Gonne and molested her daughter from a previous marriage. Yeats despised MacBride. He describes him as aggressive, drunken, and vain: 'A drunken, vainglorious lout', someone who had 'done most bitter wrong' to people that Yeats held dearly.

But that is who these people were and what the poet thought of them prior to their involvement in the Easter Rising. Now they have become heroes, and in the case of Pearse, MacDonagh and MacBride, martyrs for the cause of Irish independence. They have, therefore, 'been changed' and 'Transformed utterly'. It does not matter what Yeats once thought about these people – he might as well have 'dreamed' that MacBride was a 'lout' – the reality is that they will forever be remembered for their roles in the Rising. They are no longer part of the 'casual comedy' of Irish life; they have become detached from this petty world and have been elevated to the ranks of Wolfe Tone and Robert Emmet.

Section 3

Yeats considers the determination of the revolutionaries and the manner in which they were willing and able to devote their lives to a single cause: 'Hearts with one purpose alone'. Such steadfast commitment to a single cause strikes the poet as unnatural. How can people devote themselves to 'one purpose alone' in a world that is constantly transforming and changing?

Yeats compares life to a stream that is constantly flowing and, therefore, changing: 'the living stream'. He paints a picture of the surrounding landscape, which is also changing 'minute by minute'. The scene that the poet describes is full of movement and flux:
- A horse and rider come 'from the road' to cross the stream. When the horse enters the stream, it kicks and splashes the water as it crosses.
- Birds fly in different directions across the sky, through clouds that are 'tumbling' and changing and casting shadows on the ground that constantly shift and change.
- 'long-legged moor-hens dive' from the sky towards the stream and call out to the moorcocks.

It is a dynamic scene full of life and energy: 'Minute by minute they live'. But those who commit themselves and devote their entire lives to a single cause seem to be at odds with a world that is constantly moving and changing. It is as if they have been put under a spell that renders them oblivious and impervious to what is going on around them: 'Hearts with one purpose alone/ Through summer and winter seem/ Enchanted to a stone'.

Section 4

Yeats greatly fears that the Rising might instigate a new period in Irish history, one marked and defined by violent upheaval. He worries not only about the ensuing loss of life but also the toll that years of war, fighting and bloodshed will take on people. There can come a point when people stop caring, when they are no longer appalled at the notion of individuals sacrificing themselves for a cause: 'Too long a sacrifice/ Can make a stone of the heart'. And what amount of sacrifice is sufficient, the poet wonders, to achieve a goal such as Irish independence: 'O when may it suffice?'

The poet wonders if those who lost and sacrificed their lives in the Rising did so needlessly: 'Was it needless death after all'. As we mentioned above, the Home Rule Act had been passed by the British Parliament in 1914, but the implementation of it was postponed with the outbreak of the First World War. In 1916, this war still raged and many doubted that the bill would ever be implemented. But Yeats considers the possibility that England would keep its word. If this was to be the case, then the Rising would have been for nothing: 'Was it needless death after all?/ For England may keep faith'.

Yeats also considers the possibility that the rebels acted in a crazy, irrational manner, that they were 'bewildered' by their great love for Ireland and that this led them to take foolhardy action: 'what if excess of love/ Bewildered them till they died?' But ultimately he does not see any point in such reservation or surmise. It is impossible to know now what would have happened had the Rising not taken place, and it seems pointless to speculate whether the rebels acted rationally or irrationally. It is enough to know that they had a dream Ireland would be a sovereign country and they gave their lives to bring this about: 'enough/ To know they dreamed and are dead'.

Yeats knows that he is not in a position to say when or if such a sacrifice will lead to Irish independence. As a poet, all he can do is chronicle what has happened and record the names of those who selflessly sacrificed their lives for this cause: 'our part to murmur name upon name'. There is something soothing and loving about this act. Yeats likens the rebels to children who have been out running 'wild' and have now fallen asleep: 'When sleep at last has come/ On limbs that had run wild'. Those who recite the names of the rebels are likened to the mother who lovingly speaks the child's name as she soothes it

Dublin's General Post Office on fire after the 1916 Easter Rising

to sleep: 'To murmur name upon name,/ As a mother names her child'.

And so Yeats rounds the poem off by writing the names of some of those who died 'out in a verse': 'MacDonagh and MacBride/ And Connolly and Pearse'. He knows that, no matter what happens after, these individuals have become part of Irish history and will be remembered by Irish people all over the world: 'Wherever green is worn'. Their partaking in the Rising has transformed them into heroes and martyrs: 'Are changed, changed utterly'. By emulating the great Irish heroes of the past and sacrificing their lives for their country, these men have done something noble. Their actions, the poet knows, will inspire others to do the same: 'A terrible beauty is born'.

FOCUS ON STYLE

Form
The poem is composed of four stanzas: two comprising 16 lines and two comprising 24 lines. The rhyme scheme is made up of four-line rhyme units, i.e. ABAB CDCD EFEF etc. The poem's form and structure are deliberately symbolic, as the Easter Rising took place on the 24th day of the fourth month of 1916.

Metaphor, Simile, Figures of Speech
In stanza 3, Yeats uses the metaphor of the stream to represent life and the manner in which it is constantly moving and changing. He uses the metaphor of the stone to represent the revolutionaries' unwavering commitment to their cause: 'Hearts with one purpose alone … seem/ Enchanted to a stone'. The revolutionaries' hearts are like stones because they remain unaffected by the changes that are happening in the world around them, just as a stone lodged in a stream remains static and unchanged by the water's flow. Instead, it is the stone that affects the water, causing the stream to flow around it: 'To trouble the living stream.' This suggests the ripple effect that the revolutionaries' actions and courage had on the entire population.

In an effort to soften the tragedy of the revolutionaries' deaths, Yeats uses the metaphor of sleep: 'What is it but nightfall?' But he quickly dismisses the analogy, suggesting that there is no way to diminish the impact or the stark reality of what has happened.

Three of the poem's four stanzas end with the line, 'A terrible beauty is born', a refrain that captures the poet's conflicted feelings about what has happened. The phrase 'terrible beauty' is an oxymoron because it consists of two terms that we would normally consider contradictory. How can something be both beautiful and terrible? But for Yeats, the Rising and the manner in which the revolutionaries sacrificed their lives was a thing of beauty. There is something noble and heroic about the rebels' actions, and the poet believes that it signals the re-emergence of these qualities in a country that he had written off as shallow and farcical. However, their sacrifice is also 'terrible' because it involves violence and death, and Yeats fears that the Rising will provoke more bloodshed in the future.

THEMES

YEATS AND IRELAND

This is another poem in which Yeats talks about the decline of Irish society. Yeats believed that Ireland was a ridiculous place, one of 'casual comedy' that was inhabited by clowns and fools that might very well have been wearing the 'motley' of the traditional court jester. Yeats, as he indicated in 'September 1913', believed that Ireland had become a crass and materialistic culture. Ireland, he felt, could produce nothing serious, nothing beautiful and nothing heroic.

This poem also continues Yeats' meditation on patriotism and revolt. At the beginning of the poem, Yeats describes how he used to laugh behind the backs of nationalists like Pearse and Connolly when he met them on the streets of Dublin. These men were fervently convinced that Ireland could be roused to rebel against British rule. Yeats, on the other hand, felt that Ireland was no longer capable of producing the self-sacrifice and heroism necessary for rebellion (we see this in 'September 1913' where Yeats lamented that 'Romantic Ireland is dead and gone').

But Yeats is forced to concede that he was wrong. The rebel leaders not only had a dream, but they acted on that dream to make it a reality, paying the ultimate price as they did so: 'We know their dream; enough/ To know they dreamed and are dead'. They persuaded a small army to seize the centre of Dublin in defiance of the world's greatest empire, and in doing so utterly changed Ireland's political situation.

However, Yeats' undoubted admiration for the Rising leaders is tempered by a sense of unease:
- Perhaps the leaders were overly patriotic, experiencing an 'excess of love' for their country that drove them to extreme measures.
- He presents them as obsessives, who focused completely on 'one purpose alone'. Even when walking home from work, they had the 'vivid faces' of men on a mission, of people fired-up to make their 'one purpose' a reality.
- Many of the rebels had sacrificed a great deal in the years leading up to the Rising, devoting all their time and energy to the project of revolt. This sacrifice, Yeats believed, changed them as people, leaving them ruthless and unfeeling: 'Too long a sacrifice/ Can make a stone of the heart'.
- Yeats also suggests that their sacrifice might have all been for nothing. For Ireland might have gained a measure of independence anyway, without the Rising and all its attendant bloodshed and destruction: 'Was it needless death after all?'

Ultimately, however, Yeats accepts that these men and women have made the ultimate sacrifice for their country and will be remembered as heroes. Wherever Irish people gather, wherever 'green is worn', people will recount their deeds with an awe and admiration. It is the duty of Irish people, Yeats suggests, to keep their names alive, so that the story of their deeds is passed down to future generations.

The Rising, in Yeats' memorable phrase, has unleashed a 'terrible beauty'. It is beautiful because it involves heroism, honour and self-sacrifice. It is terrible because it involves bloodshed and destruction. Yeats, as he contemplates the future, feel that the coming years will be shaped by both this terror and this beauty.

NATURE

In the third section of the poem, Yeats describes how the world is in a constant state of flux, forever changing 'minute by minute'. He compares life to a 'stream' that is constantly moving and, therefore, changing: 'the living stream'. Yeats also captures the dramatic vibrancy of the natural world by describing a landscape that is constantly shifting. The different elements in the scene he describes impact on each other:
- The horses' hooves 'plashes' the water of the stream.
- The clouds tumble through the sky and create different, shifting shadows on the landscape below.

The poet contrasts this constant change with the singular commitment of the revolutionaries to their cause. He describes how 'Hearts with one purpose alone' are immune or oblivious to the fact that the world is constantly shifting and changing around them. He compares them to stones that lodge themselves in the stream and stubbornly refuse to move or change. In this regard, the revolutionaries strike the poet as unnatural. Ironically, however, the revolutionaries' singular commitment to their cause brings about great change in the world. By remaining immune to change and sticking to their purpose, they end up greatly disturbing or troubling 'the living stream'.

ART AND THE ROLE OF THE ARTIST

This is another poem where Yeats presents the artist as having a public role. The leaders of the Rising, he insists, must be remembered by the Irish people. He uses his poetic skills to contribute to this process, writing a 'verse' that will help to keep the leaders' names alive.

The Second Coming

ANALYSIS

LINE BY LINE

Anarchy loosed

Yeats wrote 'The Second Coming' in 1919, which was a time of chaos and uncertainty across Europe. The Great War, which had just ended, had torn the continent apart, leaving unprecedented disorder in its wake:

- Vast tracts of central Europe were left with no government, or with several competing governments, as old empires collapsed and new states arose from the ashes of war.
- In many cases, vital services provided by the state (such as policing, law and the provision of medical assistance) simply disappeared.
- Post-war food shortages put an end to the normal buying and selling of goods.
- Communist revolution added to political and social instability, most famously in Russia, but also in Germany, Hungary, Italy and elsewhere.
- To make matters worse, a vicious flu epidemic was raging across the continent, claiming millions of lives.

To Yeats, then, it seems like 'Things fall apart', that the entire structure of society is falling to pieces. The continent, he feels, has been plunged into 'anarchy', a state of complete disorder. In a brilliant turn of phrase, Yeats describes how anarchy has been 'loosed' or released, as if it were a pack of dogs that's now free to ravage the entire continent: 'Mere anarchy is loosed upon the world'.

The poet is also greatly troubled by what he sees as the rise of extremism. We often think of moderate political views as the 'centre'. More extreme or radical views, meanwhile, are associated with the left or the right. When Yeats looks at the world, he sees reasonable or sensible opinion giving way: 'the centre cannot hold'. Meanwhile, views he regards as worryingly extreme, or even dangerously crazy, seem to be gaining ground.

Yeats uses a metaphor from the sport of falconry to represent this chaos. In falconry a sportsman, known as a falconer, uses a trained falcon to hunt small animals and birds. Yeats depicts a falcon that has been released by its falconer and goes soaring into the air.

The bird's flight path forms the shape of a 'gyre', or upside-down cone, as it spirals upwards and outwards away from its master's hand: 'Turning and turning in the widening gyre'. Usually, the falconer controls the falcon by means of verbal commands. But on this occasion, the falcon has wheeled so far into the sky that it can no longer hear him: 'The falcon cannot hear the falconer'. The bird is out of control now, flying where it will.

The spiralling falcon serves as a powerful metaphor for current events. Just as the falconer has lost control of his falcon, so the voices of moderation have lost control of Europe's political scene. It seems to Yeats that there are no longer sensible people in charge; there are no longer rational people steering the governments of the world. Events, it seems to him, are quickly spinning out of control.

The bloody tide

1919 was also a time of great violence. The unprecedented slaughter of World War One was barely over when several terrible civil wars broke out across the continent. There were bloody conflicts in Russia, Greece and Germany for instance. Many other countries experienced lesser bouts of violence associated with riot, revolution and counter-revolution. Ireland, too, was wracked by the trauma of warfare, as the IRA fought for independence from British rule.

As he considers these events, Yeats feels that Europe is about to become an extremely violent place, a nightmarish zone of eternal war where once unimaginable bloodshed is now the norm. He uses a wonderfully vivid metaphor to describe this descent into butchery:
- He pictures a sea into which an enormous quantity of blood has flown.
- This blood had functioned as a kind of dye, so that the ocean's usually transparent waters have been dulled or dimmed.
- He imagines this gory ocean thrusting and sweeping forward in a great tidal wave to engulf the continent, or maybe the entire world: 'The blood-dimmed tide is loosed'.

Yeats' final complaint is that evil men seem to be full of strength, energy, and a sense of purpose. Good men, on the other hand, lack these qualities: 'The best lack all conviction, while the worst/ Are full of passionate intensity'.

Apocolypse and visions

Yeats, then, is greatly perturbed by the violence and chaos that characterise current events in Europe, from Dublin all the way to Moscow. But these disturbances, terrible as they are, strike him as mere omens of 'the Second Coming'; they seem to signal an event of even greater and more terrible consequence. 'Surely the Second Coming is at hand'. He imagines that the continent will soon face a disaster of truly apocalyptic proportions, a cataclysm that will make even the recently concluded First World War seem tame in comparison.

Throughout his life, Yeats was a great believer in mysticism and the occult. He was convinced that certain individuals, under the right conditions, were capable of extraordinary supernatural visions in which they witnessed past, present and future. We might think of these visions, often experienced during a trance-like state, as 'revelations' because they 'reveal' deep truths about the universe and the world.

'Spiritus Mundi' is a Latin term that literally means, 'world spirit'. We might think of it as a vast soul or consciousness that, according to Yeats, contains the memories of the entire universe. Mystics and prophets could at times 'tap into' Spiritus Mundi, especially when they entered a trance-like state. Artists, too, could commune with this 'world soul' when they permitted themselves to be guided by their unconscious rather than their conscious minds. To Yeats, Spiritus Mundi is the source of all images and symbols, 'a universal memory and a 'muse' of sorts that provides inspiration to the poet or writer'.

As he considers the dark direction of European society, Yeats feels that he himself is about to experience such a visionary moment: 'Surely some revelation is at hand'. Indeed, no sooner has Yeats considered this 'Second Coming' than his longed-for vision commences: 'The Second Coming! Hardly are those words out'. It's as if contemplating Europe's doom somehow triggers a supernatural capacity that has always lain dormant within him. The vision he experiences, however, is a not a pleasant one. For in this moment of revelation he witnesses a 'vast' entity, a creature that disturbs him greatly, that, as he puts it in a typically inventive turn of phrase, 'Troubles [his] sight'.

The beast

Yeats goes into some detail about the beast that dominates his vision. The phrase 'stony sleep' suggests that the beast is made out of stone, that it resembles a vast statue slowly coming to life. In many respects, it seems to resemble the statue of the sphinx at Giza in Egypt:
- It exists in a bleak desert landscape and is a grotesque mixture of man and animal: 'in sands of the desert/ A shape with lion body and the head of a man'.
- The expression on its all-too-human face is terrifying, suggesting that it is utterly incapable of any form of empathy or kindness: a 'gaze blank and pitiless as the sun'.
- The beast has been sleeping for 'twenty centuries' or two thousand years. But now its rest becomes 'vexed' or disturbed by a 'rocking cradle'. The cradle in question is almost certainly the world itself, which has been 'rocked' by the various upheavals referred to in the opening lines.
- It's as if the still-slumbering beast senses these dark happenings on an unconscious level and realises they serve as omens of its birth, that the time is quickly approaching when it must awaken and re-enter the world.

- The beast, having had its slumber disturbed in this fashion, experiences a state of nightmarish agitated sleep before finally awaking.
- The adjective 'rough' describes not only its harsh and unforgiving nature but also its stone surface, which has been left pock-marked, eroded and uneven by its two-thousand-year slumber in the desert.

The beast's thighs are described as 'slow', suggesting the difficulty with which its vast limbs (composed perhaps of granite or some other hard-wearing rock) creak into motion after such a long period of dormancy. It 'slouches' towards Bethlehem, suggesting that, after its long slumber, it's still moving in a rather stiff and ungainly fashion.

The beast's motion disturbs the 'desert birds' that have been roosting on its stony surface. The startled birds 'reel' away into the sky, outraged or 'indignant' that their resting place has suddenly started moving under them.

The end of the vision
Yeats believed that it's only in moments of revelation, like the one described in this poem, that we really see the universe for what it is. To Yeats, therefore, the end of his vision is like passing from light into darkness: 'The darkness drops again'. It's like a curtain has fallen across the great stage of the universe, obscuring his view of its mysteries.

The poet, however, has seen enough to learn something profound about the future: 'But now I know'. He knows that the beast's two-thousand-year-long slumber is at an end. He knows its time is coming: 'its hour come round at last'. According to Yeats, the beast will be 'born' in Bethlehem: 'what rough beast…/ Slouches towards Bethlehem to be born?'

Yeats was partial to occult and outlandish ideas. But not even he believed that an actual lion with the head of a man was going to suddenly appear in Bethlehem. Nor did he believe that this creature would be incarnated or born in the form of a human being. To him, the beast is instead a symbol, representing a wave of 'laughing, ecstatic destruction' that would soon be visited upon the world.

FOCUS ON STYLE

Metaphor, Simile, Figures of Speech
The falcon spinning out of control serves as a powerful metaphor for the chaotic nature of current events. Equally vivid is the metaphor of the 'blood-dimmed tide'. This tidal wave of blood-polluted water represents the violence Yeats sees 'everywhere' in 1919 and the even greater violence he believed was on the horizon.

A wonderful simile, meanwhile, is used to describe the creature's demeanour and facial expression. Yeats declares that it has a 'gaze blank and pitiless as the sun'. We can imagine the monster's face being as cruel and impassive as the scorching sun of the desert.

Imagery
The poem is dominated by the unforgettable 'vast image' of the sphinx-like creature awakening in the depths of the desert. We can visualise this enormous stone creature slowly stirring and flexing its stiff limbs before it 'slouches' off towards Bethlehem, its ultimate destination.

Equally vivid is the image of the birds that have been startled by the beast's awakening. 'all about it/ Reel shadows of the indignant desert birds'. The word 'Reel' suggests that there is something violent and frenzied about their movement. We can imagine the din of their angry cawing as they recoil through the air.

Personal Symbolism
The slow awakening of the 'vast' stone monster in 'sands of the desert' serves as a powerful personal symbol for the poet, representing the apocalyptic wave of destruction he believed the world would soon experience.

Verbal Music
'The Second Coming' has been compared to a dirge, which is a mournful, discordant song. Many of the lines in 'The Second Coming' are examples of cacophony, which is a grating mixture of sounds. A good example is the opening line, with its harsh, repeated 'i' sounds and the heavy stresses: 'Turning and turning in the widening gyre'. This discordant verbal music contributes to the sense of turmoil in the opening lines, with its description of the 'anarchy' that is consuming the world.

There is a change in the second stanza. The lines become more musical, the 's' alliteration has a calming effect, and the use of repetition slows down the frantic pace somewhat: 'Surely some revelation is at hand;/ Surely the Second Coming is at hand.' Lines 13 to 20, however, slowly build towards the poem's cacophonous ending: 'And what rough beast, its hour come round at last,/ Slouches towards Bethlehem to be born?' The harsh vowels of 'rough beast' and 'Slouches', as well as the heavy 'b' alliteration, brings the poem full circle and back to the turmoil of stanza 1.

Tone, Mood and Atmosphere
The poet's tone is full of urgency and conviction as Yeats tries to impress on the reader the dire state of the world: 'Things fall apart; the centre cannot hold'. There is a strong sense of menace and foreboding to lines such as 'The blood-dimmed tide is loosed'. With its use of the present tense – 'Mere anarchy is loosed upon the world' – the poem asserts that it is too late to reverse or undo the terrible future that awaits us.

THEMES

WAR, VIOLENCE AND SOCIAL UPHEAVAL

'The Second Coming' is Yeats' appalled and powerful reaction to a time of violence and chaos. To him it seems that the entire world is filled with confusion and disorder. It seems that everywhere the voices of reason and moderation are silenced, while those of intolerance and extremism shout ever louder. Evil men pursue their goals relentlessly, while the good stand idly by. Civilisation itself seems on the verge of being swept away by a tide of bloodshed. Furthermore, the poem predicts that even greater destruction is on its way, represented by the pitiless beast that 'Slouches toward Bethlehem to be born'.

'The Second Coming', though written in 1919, is a poem for our times. For in our age, too, it seems that 'things fall apart', that chaos and anarchy are everywhere. Each day the newspapers are so full of reports from 'small wars' around the world that it's easy to think we're drowning in a 'blood-dimmed tide'. Watch Sky News for even an hour and it's quite clear that evil is triumphing while good men do nothing. The worst are still 'full of passionate intensity', while the best, unfortunately, still lack all conviction. Given the state of the world today it's easy to think, sometimes, that some great beast of destruction is still out there waiting to be born, and that even now its hour is coming around.

Yeats' attitude to the impending catastrophe is somewhat unclear. He certainly presents the beast as being very unpleasant. As we've seen, he's appalled by the violence of 1919 and 'troubled' by the further upheaval the beast represents. But there's also a sense in which he seems fascinated and even excited by what this terrible creature promises.

Yeats was very unhappy with the current state of what he described as our 'scientific, democratic, fact-accumulating civilisation'. He believed that the 'laughing, ecstatic destruction' represented by the beast would change things forever. It would sweep away our tired, worn-out civilisation and give birth to a new era. Yeats looked forward to this new age. It would, he felt, be more in keeping with his own ideal society, being spiritual rather than scientific and aristocratic rather than democratic.

'The Second Coming', as we noted above, is greatly informed by Yeats' occult beliefs, especially by the ideas expounded in *A Vision*. This was a book Yeats wrote in response to his wife Georgie Hyde-Lees' automatic writing. Georgie would lapse into a trance and write page after page of mysterious statements, which she claimed were dictated to her by various spirit guides.

- In *A Vision*, Yeats outlines the occult notion that human history was divided into eras, each lasting roughly two thousand years.
- Our present era, which began with the birth of Chirst two thousand years ago, is soon due to expire.
- It will end, like all the eras before it, in a cataclysm of violence and destruction.
- This apocalypse is represented by the beast, with its terrible 'pitiless' gaze.
- This orgy of destruction, however, will clear the way for a new form of civilisation to arise, one that, as we noted, would be more in keeping with Yeats' ideal society.

Yeats' choice of Bethlehem as the beast's birthplace is highly symbolic. Just as Bethlehem was the place where the Christian era began with the birth of Christ, so it is the place where that era will end, with the coming of the beast. This almost blasphemous inversion of the Christmas nativity tale gives the conclusion of the poem real power, real shock value. Many early readers of the poem were horrified at the image of this rough, slouching monstrosity defiling the holy place of Christ's birth.

YEATS AND IRELAND

Yeats, as we have noted, was a great admirer of the Anglo-Irish Ascendancy, the class that dominated Irish society between the 17th and 19th centuries, and of which he himself was a member. He especially valued the formal, orderly way in which life was conducted on the estates and in the mansions of these wealthy Protestant landowners. To Yeats, then, this was a lifestyle full of 'ceremony'. And such a civilised, ceremonial existence, he believed, produced people who were 'innocent', fundamentally decent and morally upright.

In 1919, however, as Yeats was writing this poem, the War of Independence against British rule in Ireland was gaining traction. This war, and the Free State it produced, would greatly diminish the status of the Ascendancy class, which had already seen much of its influence evaporate over the preceding century.

Elsewhere in Europe, too, it seemed that the aristocratic way of life favoured by Yeats was under threat. The aristocracies of Germany and Russia, for instance, had all but vanished amid the chaos of the First World War. The new post-war world of democracy (not to mention socialism, communism and fascism) had little regard for such an existence. Everywhere Yeats looked, then, he saw the 'ceremony' of the aristocratic lifestyle being swept away amid the bloodshed of war and revolution: 'The blood-dimmed tide is loosed, and everywhere/ The ceremony of innocence is drowned'.

ANALYSIS

Sailing to Byzantium

The Suleymaniye Mosque in Istanbul

LINE BY LINE

The cycle of birth and death

This poem's opening stanza is all about the cycle of birth and death. This cycle applies to everything in nature. It encompasses mammals, or creatures of the 'flesh'. It encompasses birds, or 'fowl'. It encompasses the 'fish' that fill the seas. Every one of these creatures is 'begotten' or conceived through sexual activity. Then it is 'born'. Then, eventually, it 'dies'.

It is summer, a time when the 'begetting' phase of this cycle seems especially prominent. Every where the poet looks, he sees creatures of various types engaging in sexual activity:

- The 'birds in the trees' sing out their mating calls, their sweet tunes of flirtation and seduction.
- The seas are 'crowded' with throngs of mackerel that have gathered in their mating grounds at various points off the Irish coast.
- Salmon, too, are engaged in their mating season. They will then swim up river, leaping over falls and currents along the way, before spawning the next generation of their species.
- Summer, the poet suggests, is also the mating season for human beings. Everywhere he looks he sees young people in 'one another's arms', as they kiss, flirt or simply hold hands. Here the poet refers to the ancient (though perhaps unscientific) idea that human beings are more sexually active in the summer time.

All of nature, it seems to the poet, has been sexually active 'all summer long'. He has witnessed a festival of begetting, in which entire new generations of 'fish, flesh [and] fowl' have been conceived. Every creature, it seems to the poet, engages joyfully and willingly in sexual activity. And by doing so, they 'commend' or celebrate the cycle of birth and death, of which sexual activity is a crucial part.

The poet's attitude to this cycle

The poet himself, however, cannot 'commend' or celebrate this cycle of birth and death. There are several reasons for this.

- The poet is keenly aware that the cycle ends in the extinction of every creature. Each new generation is a 'dying generation'. No sooner is each creature conceived than the countdown to its death begins.
- Because the poet is an elderly man, moving gradually towards the end of his own life, this awareness of death is amplified.

- Because the poet is an elderly man, he is no longer sexually desirable. He could not, even if he wanted to, participate in the summer-long festival of begetting. The business of sexual reproduction, he suggests, must be left to the young: 'That is no country for old men'.

The poet, at this stage of his life, wants to focus on art rather than on sexuality. He especially wants to focus on the great artworks of the past, which he refers to as 'Monuments of unageing intellect'. This phrase suggests that great artworks, like monuments, are publicly available. Many artworks, after all, can be viewed by anyone who cares to do so. It suggests that great artworks, like monuments, are commemorative because when we engage with a great artwork, we remember its creator.

The frenzy of procreation described in the opening stanza is compared to a symphony or chorus. Each procreating creature is like one of the performers in this symphony. These creatures, Yeats suggests, are 'caught' or lost in the music they create; they are so absorbed in the pleasure and pursuit of sexuality that they forget about everything else.

It also suggests that great artworks, like monuments, are large and noticeable. Many great artworks exhibit a psychological vastness rather than a physical vastness. We might think of a play by Shakespeare or a miniature painting by Rembrandt, which doesn't take up much physical space, but reveals entire psychological worlds.

These artworks – whether they are films or poems, statues or songs – are described as 'unageing' because their ability to inspire us never grows old. Each individual artwork, Yeats suggests, possesses an 'intellect' of its own, a unique personality or intelligence. When we study a particular artwork then we engage with its 'intellect'. We develop our own conversation or relationship with the artwork in question. We need only think here of the intense bonds that people tend to form with their favourite songs, books or movies.

The poet's tattered body
Each human being, the poet believes, is composed of two distinct parts: a physical body and a non-physical soul. The body is doomed to waste away and die. The soul, on the other hand, is immortal. Our souls, according to tradition, are housed within our bodies. Each soul, Yeats suggests, wears its body like a 'mortal dress', a temporary garment it will cast off at the moment of death.

The poet laments how the ageing process has affected his own body, his own 'mortal dress'. Old age, he declares, has robbed his body of both its physical vigour and its good looks. The poet, in a striking turn of phrase, compares himself to a scarecrow: 'a tattered coat upon a stick'. This is a most revealing comparison:

- His body is 'tattered', its flesh, bones and sinews damaged by the ageing process.
- His body is withered to the point where it is stick-thin.
- His body, he feels, has come to resemble a scarecrow; it is both grotesque and ridiculous-looking.

The poet, therefore, is faced with the 'paltriness' of old age. He is faced with being physically 'paltry', with being pitiful or pathetic. He is faced with being socially 'paltry', with being negligible and insignificant. He is faced with being a 'thing', rather than a proper human being. For who, in a world dominated by youth and beauty, really cares about or even notices the old?

Focusing on the soul
Old age, then, is only bearable if we focus on the soul rather than the body.

- The soul, Yeats declares, must 'clap its hands and sing'. For Yeats, no doubt, this singing of the soul involves artistic expression: the creation of poems, plays and other texts.
- Our souls, Yeats says, must sing 'louder' as we approach death. This reflects Yeats' determination to keep improving his artistic practice. He wants to become better and better at writing as death approaches. He wants to create texts that explore the human condition with ever greater clarity and profundity, texts that will truly stand the test of time.
- The soul, Yeats insists, must attend 'singing school'; it must study and practice so it can sing with greater clarity and volume. This reflects Yeats' belief that artistic improvement can only be achieved by studying great artworks of the past. The word 'but', as used in line 7, means 'apart from', leading us to read the lines as follows: 'there is no singing school [apart from] studying [the great artworks of the past]'.

They poet, therefore, decides to make the long sea voyage to the ancient city of Byzantium. Given its imperial past, Byzantium is absolutely filled with extraordinary artworks, each one a monument to the 'magnificence' of the human soul that created it.

Byzantium is an old name for Istanbul, the capital of Turkey. In medieval times, Byzantium was a great military power and the centre of a Christian empire that lasted for nearly a thousand years. It was also an extraordinary centre of learning, one that inherited the wisdom of both Ancient Greece and the Roman Empire. It was especially famed for the skill of its artists and craftsmen, who created everything from enormous cathedrals to tiny but ingeniously crafted ornaments.

The mosaic
The poet has finally reached Byzantium and stands before one of the city's many extraordinary mosaics (a 'mosaic' is an image made from assembling small pieces of coloured glass and stone). This particular mosaic decorates a 'wall' somewhere in the city, perhaps in one of Byzantium's many palaces and cathedrals. It is hundreds of years old. Yeats describes how it shimmers with a 'gold' effect, suggesting the brightly coloured materials that were used in its construction.

The mosaic depicts 'sages' or men of great wisdom. God's presence surrounds the sages, taking the form of golden flames: they are 'standing in God's holy fire'. This miraculous blaze, however, doesn't harm the sages in any way. Instead, it fills them with vigour and intensity as if they were somehow sharing in the energy of God himself (it's been suggested that Yeats was inspired by a Byzantine mosaic depicting Moses and Elijah, two great sages or prophets from the Bible).

Yeats, as we noted above, believed that every great artwork had its own 'intellect' or personality. And the poet, it seems, is captivated by the intellect of this particular mosaic. He develops an extraordinary connection with this golden image. We can imagine him spending hours before the mosaic, returning to visit it again and again during his visit to Byzantium.

Yeats' connection with the mosaic is so powerful that the sages seem almost alive to him. He imagines that the sages could come to life and step out of the mosaic: 'Come from the holy fire'. He imagines that the sages could act as his mentors or instructors: 'be the singing-masters of my soul'. Under their guidance, Yeats' soul will learn to 'sing' better than it ever has done before. They would help him to create extraordinary texts that capture profound truths about time, reality and human existence.

> Yeats had a number of occult beliefs, which he detailed in his prose book *A Vision*. He believed that time is a stream that spirals in a 'gyre' or clockwise direction. He imagines the sages 'perning' or moving in a counter-clockwise direction, as if they were swimming against time's current. Eventually, the sages will make it all the way to the twentieth century and stand before the poet as alive as they ever were.
>
> Yeats, of course, doesn't believe that such time travel is possible, nor does he expect the sages will literally step from the mosaic. But this metaphor powerfully captures the intensity of the poet's relationship with the mosaic. It highlights how real the sages seem to him as he spends hours contemplating their golden forms.

Body and soul

Yeats calls on the sages to burn away his body using their 'holy fire'.

- He memorably refers to his body as a 'dying animal', suggesting that it is subhuman, disgusting and beneath contempt. He longs for this wretched, scarecrow-like body to be utterly burned up, utterly consumed away by the sages' miraculous flames.
- In particular, he wants the sages to eliminate his 'heart'. This refers not only to the organ itself, but to all bodily systems associated with love and sexuality. Yeats' heart is filled with sexual longing. But these are desires that he as an old man can't satisfy or act on. This preponderance of unsatisfied desire has left the heart 'sick' or dysfunctional. Yeats is, therefore, happy for it, along with the rest of his body, to be consumed away.

- Yeats' soul, then, would be liberated from the failing body in which it is currently confined.
- Yeats calls on the sages to 'gather' or carry his newly liberated soul and transport it into the 'artifice of eternity'.

Let's take a moment to unpack this phrase. The word 'artifice' refers to expert workmanship. It also refers to something that has been cunningly or skilfully designed. Yeats, then, has in mind here great artworks like the *Mona Lisa* and Michelangelo's *David*, which exhibit such extraordinary workmanship and design. These works are eternal in that they speak to people century after century.

The poet, then, longs for his soul to be gathered into one of these eternal artworks. It would reside forever within in some exquisite and unageing piece of craftsmanship.

The bird

The poet would like his soul to inhabit one such object in particular, a mechanical bird he has seen during his visit to Byzantium.

- The bird is hundreds of years old and was constructed during the heyday of the Byzantine Empire.
- The bird is made of gold that has been 'hammered' into shape by the gifted goldsmiths that constructed it. The goldsmiths are described as 'Grecian' because Byzantium was a Greek-speaking civilisation.
- The bird has been further decorated with gold varnish or 'enamelling'.
- The bird's body contains a carefully concealed set of pipes. Whenever the breeze passed through these pipes, it produced a sound like that of birdsong.

Yeats clearly takes great delight in this ingeniously constructed object that was created so long ago. He imagines a courtier placing it on an artificial golden branch, an extraordinary ornament that must have brought great joy and wonder to the 'lords and ladies' of the Byzantine court.

Or perhaps the bird was a gift for the emperor himself. Yeats imagines this precious object taking a place of honour beside the emperor's throne. It would serve as an amusement and a distraction from the cares of state. Its mechanical singing would serve to rouse the emperor if he started to doze off on a hot Byzantine afternoon.

THEMES

NATURE
The poem views the natural world as a kind of system that passes through phases of birth, death and renewal. Every living thing, be it fish, flesh or fowl, is part of this system. Every living thing is 'begotten' or conceived, born, reproduces and eventually dies. The bustling sexual activity of summer conducted by birds, fish and youthful human beings seems to 'commend' or celebrate this cycle. The poet has come to view this process of birth and death in a very negative way, for his own personal cycle is nearing its end.

The poet draws a sharp contrast between art and nature. Birds, animals and human beings are subject to the cycles of nature described above. They are temporary; they change and they die. Great works of art on the other hand are subject to no such cycle. These 'unageing' objects never change or decline. These great songs, paintings, poems and films – collectively referred to as the 'artifice of eternity' – last forever, speaking to generation after generation.

YOUTH AND AGE
This poem, then, draws a powerful contrast between youth and age, specifically between the elderly poet and the young people he observes at the height of the Irish summer.
- These young people are presented as sexually attractive. The aged poet, on the other hand, feels like he has lost his good looks. He thinks of himself as a wizened and grotesque scarecrow.
- The young people are in their physical prime. The poet's body, on the other hand, has been left tattered by the ageing process.
- The young people enjoy lives of sexual opportunity, wandering the streets 'in one another's arms'. The aged poet too experiences sexual desire. But for him, alas, such opportunities are a thing of the past. His heart is 'sick with desire' that he cannot satisfy.
- The lives of the young seem relaxed and carefree. Their only concern is love, romance and flirtation. The elderly poet on the other hand seems preoccupied with thoughts of mortality, ageing and decay.
- The ageing poet finds himself focusing more and more on 'monuments of unageing intellect', on the great artworks of the past. The young people, preoccupied with the 'sensual music' of procreation, care little about great works by past masters such as Shakespeare, Blake and Michelangelo.

The poem, then, provides a moving portrayal of the ageing process. It highlights how the elderly often consider themselves 'paltry', as in feeble and insignificant, how in a world obsessed with youth and beauty, they all too often feel unsightly and unwanted, ridiculous or even invisible.

The poet feels disgusted and constrained by his own body. In a shocking memorable phrase, he describes his body as a 'dying animal' to which he has been 'shackled'.

ART AND THE ROLE OF THE ARTIST
This is another poem in which Yeats presents art as a continuous practice, a craft or trade that must be perfected throughout the artist's life. Despite his old age, the poet is determined to keep growing as an artist. If anything, the nearness of death makes him all the more eager to reach his full artistic potential. The poem stresses that such improvement can be made only by studying the great artists of the past. Yeats, then, despite being an accomplished, Nobel prize-winning poet, recognises that he must still attend 'singing-school' in order that his soul can express itself with ever-greater clarity and purpose.

'Sailing to Byzantium' is also Yeats' most profound statement on the idea of attaining immortality through art. The poet, then, considers two different concepts of immortality. One is a form of reincarnation such as that envisaged by Buddhism and other Eastern religions. The soul would leave behind the body and the earthly plane of existence. It would be temporarily 'out of nature'. It would then rejoin the natural world, housing itself within some new person, bird or animal.

Yeats, however, rejects this form of immortality. The poet will not be re-born as any 'natural thing'. He is determined that his soul, 'once out of nature', will never rejoin the natural world. He will never again be subject to the cycles of birth and death that govern the natural world. His soul will never again be attached to such a 'dying animal'.

The poet instead is focused on the type of artistic immortality enjoyed by Michelangelo and Shakespeare. He uses an extraordinary set of metaphors to describe the process by which such immortality might be attained.

- The artist of today can only achieve greatness by studying the masterpieces of the past. This is represented by the sages stepping out of the mosaic to act as Yeats' mentors or 'singing-masters'.
- The artist must focus on the soul rather than the body. This is represented by the sages consuming the poet's body with their holy flame.
- The distractions of sex and sexuality in particular must be overcome. This is represented by the sages consuming away the poet's heart.
- The poet will live on through the poems, plays and texts he has created over the course of his life. This is represented by the poet's soul inhabiting the magnificent golden bird created by the Grecian goldsmiths all those centuries ago.

The poet would have little interest, we sense, in prolonging the life of his body through some revolutionary scientific method. Nor does he show any interest in the type of immortality associated with the Christian concept of heaven. Furthermore, as we've seen, he is not taken with reincarnation. Instead, he goes all-in on achieving the 'artifice of eternity'. And maybe he has succeeded. After all, we are still reading his works today.

The Stare's Nest by My Window

LINE BY LINE

This poem was written during the Irish Civil War of 1922 to 1923. This was an especially bitter conflict as former comrades turned against one another. Men who had fought the British side by side in the earlier War of Independence now took up arms to fight each other. Towns, villages and even families were split down the middle, as some took the 'pro-Treaty' side, associated in the popular imagination with Michael Collins, and some took the 'anti-Treaty' side, associated with Eamon de Valera.

When the civil war broke out, Yeats was staying at Thoor Ballylee, a 15th Century Norman tower in County Galway that he and his wife had recently renovated and moved into. For a time, Yeats was isolated by the guerrilla warfare that raged in the countryside around him and made travel impossible. This isolation was made worse when the anti-Treaty forces blew up the bridges and blocked the roads in the surrounding area.

Stanza 1
Yeats begins by considering the state of Thoor Ballylee. The mortar that binds its stone walls together has started to crumble: 'My wall is loosening'. If you pushed at one of the walls' stone components it might jiggle a little. Gaps have even begun to appear between one stone and the next.

Bees have colonised some of these cracks or 'crevices', using them as safe locations in which to construct their hives: 'The bees build in the crevices/ Of loosening masonry'. Other gaps have been used by birds as convenient nesting places. Their chicks have hatched, and the 'mother birds' bring food back to the tower for their young: 'and there/ The mother birds bring grubs and flies'.

One of the nests in the tower wall has been abandoned. Once a starling (a 'stare') had raised its young there. Now, however, this family of birds has moved on, leaving its 'house' or nest empty. Yeats wants a colony of bees to inhabit this gap in his tower wall, to build their hive and honeycomb in this empty crevice where the stare once nested: 'honey-bees,/ Come build in the empty house of the stare'.

Stanzas 2 and 3
Yeats considers the state of County Galway, gripped as it is by civil war. This bitter conflict has been raging for two weeks now: 'Some fourteen days of civil war'. During this time, the people of Galway have effectively become prisoners in their own homes: 'We are closed in'. They are afraid to stray very far, terrified of the violence that grips the countryside. Many roads have been closed off with 'A barricade of stone or of wood', making travel even more of an impossibility.

The civil war has visited death and destruction upon the countryside: men have been killed and houses burned down. There have been other even more brutal acts. One young soldier was beaten to death and had his bloody corpse dragged or 'trundled' down the road like a sack of grain: 'Last night they trundled down the road/ That dead young soldier in his blood'. These lines were inspired by an actual incident that took place near Yeats' home: a young soldier was beaten so badly that his mother could only recover his disembodied head for burial.

Nowadays, we get news updates from social media, from internet news sites, from television or from radio. At the time this poem was written, however, none of these things existed. There were only newspapers. Nor were there mobile phones, landlines or social media. People communicated by letters and by telegram.

The civil war, then, has brought the people of Galway great dread and great uncertainty: 'the key is turned/ On our uncertainty'. With the roads closed, the people of Galway had no newspapers, no letters and no clue about what was going on around the country.

They hear vague rumours about terrible events that are taking place: 'somewhere/ A man is killed, or a house burned'. But they have no solid and definite information, either about events in County Galway or in the country as a whole: 'no clear fact to be discerned'.

They didn't know what was happening up the road in Galway City, never mind in Wexford or Athlone. They didn't know if their friends and relatives around the country were still alive. They didn't know which side was winning the war, or was in control of the government in Dublin.

They didn't know how many farmhouses and villages were being burned down, or whose household would be next. We can imagine, then, how this 'uncertainty', and the swirl of rumour that accompanied it, added to the terror experienced by the people of Galway as the war raged on around them.

> The walls of Yeats' home aren't as stable or secure as they once were, a fact that's emphasised through the repetition of 'loosening' in lines 2 and 3. The walls that protect him from the outside world, then, become increasingly insecure as their masonry crumbles. Surprisingly, however, Yeats seems to welcome this 'loosening' of his defences. He seems happy that nature's creatures have made their homes among the walls' gaps. He chooses not to fill in the crevice where the stare once nested, instead hoping that bees will use it construct their hive.
>
> Perhaps this loosening of walls represents a loosening of attitudes. The minds of the Irish people have allowed their minds to be 'closed in' by certainties, by the conviction that their understanding of Irish freedom is the proper one. They have allowed their minds to be straitjacketed by the fantasies and obsessions outlined above.
>
> The Irish people must now relax and loosen these narrow-minded attitudes that have led them to a bloody civil war. If they do so, there is the possibility that a new attitude of forgiveness will slip into the national psyche just as the bees might slip into the tower wall. Forgiveness, the poem suggests, is as sweet as the honeycomb the bees construct, and it will serve as an antidote to the sour attitudes of hatred that have so gripped the national psyche.

Stanza 4

Yeats considers the state of the Irish psyche in the years leading up to the civil war. During this period, he suggests, the Irish people became obsessed with questions of nationhood, with what an independent Ireland meant and how it should be achieved. Ideas of freedom and martyrdom, of killing and dying for one's country came to predominate.

But these ideas, Yeats maintains, are mere 'fantasies'. 'Freedom' and 'martyrdom' can be considered fantasies in several different senses:

- They're abstract ideas rather than real things. When Yeats looks out from his tower, he sees the reality of everyday life: of real people in real homes trying to get on with real existence. But he also sees real terror, real violence and real destruction as people are shot to death and burned out of their homes. In light of such stark reality, notions like political freedom begin to seem very abstract, unreal and unimportant.
- 'Freedom' and 'martyrdom' are fantasies in the sense that they're obsessive preoccupations, goals or desires that the Irish people dwell on and return to again and again.
- The term 'fantasies' also suggests how the Irish people had developed an idealised concept of what 'freedom' and 'martyrdom' actually involved. They'd developed an idealised, almost comic book understanding of warfare, one that involved daring deeds and noble sacrifice, a million miles away from the grim reality of burning farmhouses and corpses 'trundled' down roads.

Yeats uses the strange but vivid metaphor of 'feeding the heart' to describe the country's obsession with these dangerous fantasies. To obsess about something, as Yeats puts it, is to feed it to your heart. In this instance, the Irish people have become obsessed with 'fantasies' of freedom and martyrdom and have fed their hearts with these dangerous notions: 'We had fed the heart on fantasies'.

The 'fare' or diet of fantasies has made the hearts of the Irish people 'brutal'. We might imagine here an organ that's become putrid and diseased, pumping bitter bile rather than life-giving blood. This is a powerful metaphor for the nation's corrupted psyche. A constant obsession has poisoned the minds of the Irish people, leaving them uncompromising and inflexible regarding what an independent Ireland would mean and how it should be achieved.

Corrupted hearts can now only find 'substance' or nourishment in hatred rather than in love: 'More substance in our enmities/ Than in our love'. This wonderfully suggests how the Irish people are now motivated more by hatred of their enemies than by love of their family and friends. It's as if they need enemies in order to thrive. And now, with the British gone, they've found the enmity they need in the form of antipathy to other Irish people, specifically those who have a different understanding of what Irish freedom means.

FOCUS ON STYLE

Imagery
'The Stare's Nest by My Window' can be described as a dialogue between images. On the one hand we have the beautiful, life-giving images of the building bees and the nesting birds. On the other, we have the horrific image of the dead solider 'trundled' down the road. The image of the 'loosening' tower walls serves as a symbol of reconciliation, as a bridge between the present horror of the civil war and a more positive future.

Verbal Music
A notable feature of this poem's soundscape is its use of repetition. Each stanza concludes with the same haunting refrain, as Yeats calls again and again on the bees to build in the starling's deserted nest. Each stanza broadens the horizons of the poet's meditation once more, from his tower home in stanza one, to his neighbours in County Galway in stanzas two and three, to the Irish people as a whole in stanza four.

At the end of each stanza, however, Yeats focuses in once more on his crumbling walls and the starling's empty nest, where he wants the bees to build. It's this image of hive-building, with all its sweetness and creativity, that he sees as an antidote to the poisonous and destructive mentality that has gripped the Irish people.

THEMES

WAR, VIOLENCE AND SOCIAL UPHEAVAL
'The Stare's Nest by My Window' presents a community and a country that has been ravaged by the horrors of war. For two weeks, the conflict has created a claustrophobic sense of isolation, leaving people 'closed in' as it traps them in their homes. It has created a great sense of dread and uncertainty among the populace, who are able to discern 'no clear fact' about what's going on in the country or what the future holds.

Violence and terror stalk the land, as men are shot dead, houses are destroyed and acts of inhumanity, like the dragging of the dead soldier's corpse, are carried out. The horror is amplified by that fact that Irish people are committing these acts against other Irish people, against neighbours and former friends, against people who had been close comrades in the struggle against British rule.

YEATS AND IRELAND
This poem continues Yeats' meditation on patriotism and revolt. 'September 1913' and 'Easter 1916' saw Yeats praise, in a cautious and qualified manner, those who fought and died for Ireland. In this poem, however, he has little time for the violence committed in Ireland's name. We sense that the closer Yeats came to the grim realities of guerrilla warfare, the less time he had for the 'fantasies' of freedom and martyrdom. Disagreements over Irish freedom, he suggests, aren't worth such terror and destruction, such loss of life and property.

In 'September 1913', Yeats suggested that the Irish people had forgotten the ideas of freedom and martyrdom that motivated the heroes of the past. In this poem, written ten years later, he argues the opposite. The Irish people, he claims, have not only remembered these ideas but have become obsessed with them. And their obsession with these dangerous 'fantasies' has poisoned their psyches, turning their hearts 'brutal'.

Now the notion of freedom means more to them than family, friendship or life itself. Many Irish people are willing to die to defend a particular concept of Irish freedom and are willing to kill those, including their former friends and comrades, who believe in a different concept. Now enmity and conflict nourish their souls rather than love, community and friendship.

NATURE
This poem, then, highlights the bitterness that has taken root in the Irish heart and the violence and chaos that rage throughout the country. Yet each stanza concludes with a plea to the honeybees to 'Come build in the empty house of the stare'. We must look to nature, the poem suggests, if we are to reverse the damage that has been done to the soul of the Irish nation:

- The sweetness of the bees' honey contrasts with the bitterness that has filled the hearts of the Irish people.
- Whereas the Irish people have become dedicated to destruction, the birds and bees that dwell in the tower walls are dedicated to building and creation.
- The Irish people willfully destroy life. The birds and bees, on the other hand, are dedicated to bringing new life into the world. They create nests and hives for their young to be born into and the mother birds bring food to keep their chicks alive.

The poem, then, celebrates the natural world, emphasising its positivity, energy and creativity. The challenge for the Irish people is to follow nature's example. They must turn away from the path of destruction and begin to rebuild their homes, their shattered country and their trust in one another.

In Memory of Eva Gore-Booth and Con Markievicz

LINE BY LINE

In 1894 Yeats stayed at Lissadell, the beautiful mansion of the aristocratic Gore-Booth family in Sligo. During his visit, Yeats became friendly with the daughters of the house, Constance and Eva. Yeats was greatly taken with these two fine-looking young women, especially Eva. For a while, he even considered asking for Eva's hand in marriage.

Yeats always looked back on his time at Lissadell with great affection. In 1916, twenty years after his stay, he wrote to Eva: 'Your sister and yourself, two beautiful girls among the great trees of Lissadell, are among the dear memories of my youth'. This poem was written in 1927, just months after the death of Constance. Eva had died the previous year.

A memory of Lissadell

Yeats fondly recalls a summer's evening spent with the sisters in their beautiful home. He recalls how the drawing room's 'Great windows' were open to the warmth: 'Great windows open to the south'. We can imagine how the 'light of evening' poured through these windows in fantastic golden shafts (these large sash windows can still be seen today and are south-facing to maximise their exposure to the sunlight).

He also, of course, has fond memories of the sisters themselves, remembering how both were 'beautiful'. Though Yeats recognised the beauty of both girls, he admired Eva in particular. He describes her as 'a gazelle', a small antelope famous for the graceful way it moves.

Yeats noted that both sisters wore silken Japanese dresses: 'Two girls in silk kimonos'. Such garments would have been extremely rare in the Ireland of the day. The girls' fondness for kimonos suggests not only that the girls were stylish but also that they were open to different cultures.

The girls' youthful beauty could not last, however. That summer, like all summers, inevitably gave way to autumn, causing the blooms and flowers to wither away. Similarly, the girls' youth gave way to middle age and then old age, causing their beauty to wither away. Yeats argues that their involvement with politics contributed to the decline of their good looks. Similarly, just as autumn strips away the foliage of summer, so the passage of time stripped away the sisters' beauty.

Constance's political campaigns

Constance was a member of the Irish Citizen Army and fought in the 1916 Rising, serving as a commander of the forces that occupied Stephen's Green. After the rebels' surrender, she was 'condemned to death' by the British authorities. However, the military court, reluctant to execute a woman, 'pardoned' her, commuting her sentence to life imprisonment. Constance, along with other rebel leaders, was released as part of an amnesty in 1917.

Yeats focuses on Constance's later years, between the end of the Irish Civil War in 1923 and her death in 1927. Constance had taken the losing anti-Treaty side in that terrible conflict and never quite made her peace with the Free State that emerged in its wake. In the years after the Civil War, she remained active in politics and vigorously opposed to the new regime, which in her opinion betrayed the ideals of the 1916 Rising.

Yeats takes a dim view of Constance's activities during this period. She spent her time, he says, 'conspiring', hatching various plots and plans with other opponents of the new Irish state. But in his opinion her fellow conspirators were 'ignorant' men and women, whose plots were destined never to get off the ground. Perhaps he thinks of them as being blinded by an extreme form of idealism. Or maybe, in his view, they were simply too stupid to get with the programme and accept the reality of the new Irish state.

Constance's final years, Yeats suggests, were 'lonely' ones. The implication is that her trenchant political views left her marginalised. She had, after all, fallen out with so many former friends and colleagues, regarding them as traitors for accepting the new Irish state. Where once she had been at the centre of Irish political life, now she occupied its fringes, pointlessly conspiring with a few fellow diehards. According to Yeats, Constance 'dragged out' these last few isolated years, as if they were a dull but necessary chore, as if, deep down, she couldn't wait for them to be over.

Eva's political campaigns

Eva, the younger Gore-Booth sister, also became active in the politics of her day. She settled in England and for twenty years was at the forefront of what became for her two overlapping struggles: the campaign for workers' rights and the struggle to win the right to vote for women. She was also committed to social work and spent much of her time voluntarily helping the poor workers of northern England.

Yeats, however, regards Eva as a hopeless idealist who dreams of bringing about a 'utopia', a perfect society that in practice can never be achieved. Yeats suggests that Eva and her fellow campaigners are very 'vague' about what their ideal society would actually be like. Theirs is a project, he suggests, that's long on ideals but short on detail. In fact, Yeats is so dismissive of Eva's political ideals that he doesn't even bother to engage with them or learn about them properly: 'I know not what the younger dreams–/ Some vague Utopia'.

Yeats considers Eva's appearance near the end of her life, when she seemed not only 'old' and 'withered' but also gaunt as a skeleton. Her shrivelled appearance, he says, was an 'image' of her political beliefs. This might suggest that Eva's devotion to her political struggle has 'withered' her gazelle-like beauty, leaving her gaunt and exhausted.

But it might also suggest Yeats' view of Eva's political beliefs. Perhaps Yeats viewed socialism and 'feminism' as withered belief systems. Once these ideas were powerful political forces, but now they're only shrivelled versions of their former selves, ideas that are irrelevant to the modern world and attract few new adherents.

Regrets

Many years have passed since that glorious summer's evening in Lisadell. There were many occasions over the intervening period when Yeats considered reaching out to one of the Gore-Booth sisters: 'Many a time I think to seek/ One or the other out'. He would have loved to arrange a meeting, to sit down with either Constance or Eva and talk about long ago times in Lisadell: 'and speak/ Of that old Georgian mansion'. However, we get the impression that he never quite got around to having this wonderful nostalgic conversation with the Gore-Booth sisters. Now, alas, both sisters have passed away and his chance is gone.

Yeats returns to the image of the beautiful girls in their silk kimonos, as lines 19 to 20 repeat lines 3 to 4 exactly. We read the same words and experience the same image. Now we see it differently, however, influenced by our knowledge of all that has happened: the sisters' decline and death as well as Yeats' failure to 'seek one or the other out' before they passed. The first time we encountered these lines they were energetic and celebratory. But now they reverberate with sadness.

'Dear Shadows'

In lines 21 to 30, Yeats speaks to the dead sisters directly. He addresses them as 'Dear Shadows' because he views them as shades or spirits residing in the afterlife. Now that they've passed on, he says, the sisters have realised the terrible mistake or 'folly' they committed while alive: 'Dear Shadows, now you know it all,/ All the folly'.

Their foolishness, Yeats maintains, was to involve themselves in political struggles and campaigns. They should never, he believes, have embroiled themselves in such a 'fight' against what they regarded as great 'wrongs' but that their opponents, naturally, regarded as right and appropriate: 'All the folly of a fight/ With a common wrong or right.'

Yeats seems to be playing on three separate meanings of the word 'common' here. He may be suggesting that political battles are 'common' because they affect the entire community. He may also be suggesting that the world of politics is 'common' in the sense that it is coarse and vulgar and quite unsuited to these beautiful aristocratic women. Finally, he may be suggesting that such political struggles are 'common' because they become commonplace in the lives of those who engage in them. They become everyday, gruelling struggles that suck up all the campaigner's time and energy.

Yeats regards the Gore-Booth sisters as paragons of innocence and beauty. Such people, he says, have only one adversary: 'The innocent and the beautiful/ Have no enemy but time'. For it is only the passage of time itself that can rob them of their fine qualities, of the virtues that set them apart from the rest of us. All their energies, therefore, should be devoted to their personal battle with time, towards retaining their innocence and beauty. Anything else, like the political campaigning undertaken by the Gore-Booth sisters for instance, is a mere distraction from this all-important struggle.

Indeed, involvement in political life, with all its exhausting and bitter conflicts, will only make the destructive work of time easier. Eva's efforts leave her utterly drained and withered like a skeleton. Constance, meanwhile, is reduced to a lonely, ignorant conspirator. It would be far better for the innocent and beautiful to avoid such communal battles and focus instead on staving off time's ravages for as long as they possibly can.

Setting time alight

Yeats concludes the poem by expressing an extraordinary desire. He wishes to do no less than destroy time itself and thereby prevent it from doing further damage to the innocence and beauty he so values. Specifically, he wants to set time on fire. He envisages striking match after match until the fabric of time itself somehow catches fire: 'Arise and bid me strike a match/ And strike another till time catch'.

Yeats imagines that this blaze or 'conflagration' will 'climb', rising the way fire does, laying waste to time as it goes. If this happens, if Yeats is successful in his mission to make time no more, he wants the sisters' shades to go running through the afterlife, spreading the good news.

Specifically, he wants them to inform the 'sages' of his staggering achievement. The term 'sages' refers to the spirits of the great thinkers and artists Yeats admired (included in their number, no doubt, are Michelangelo and William Blake, both mentioned in 'An Acre of Grass'). Yeats, it seems, imagines these great minds gathering in the afterlife, celebrating the Irish poet who'd put an end to time itself.

FOCUS ON STYLE

Verbal Music

The music of the poem's opening lines reflects the serenity and grandeur of that long-ago evening in Lissadell. Yeats uses assonance to achieve this. In lines 1 and 3, for example, the repetition of the 'i' sound creates a pleasant, euphonious effect: 'The light of evening Lissadell … two girls in silk kimonos'. A similar word music is generated in line 2, with its repeated broad-vowel sounds: 'Great windows open to the south'.

The slow, stately pace of line 2, courtesy of the proliferation of broad-vowel sounds, suggests the majesty and dignity of the Georgian mansion. Lines 5 to 6, however, shatter this pleasant music. Just as summer gives way to autumn, so the soothing music of lines 1 to 4 gives way to the harsh combination of sounds in lines 5 to 6. The words 'raving' and 'shears', in particular, contribute to this jarring effect.

Imagery

Yeats depicts the two sisters very vividly in this poem. He depicts them as wearing 'silk kimonos', traditional Japanese garments that would have been a rare sight in the Ireland of the early 20th century. This suggests that the sisters were stylish and perhaps a little eccentric. Yeats asserts that they were 'both/ Beautiful' and that Eva was particularly elegant: 'one a gazelle.'

However, Yeats depicts their political thinking as ruining their youthful beauty and innocence. Con is depicted as a lonely figure after participating in the 1916 Rising, with only 'the ignorant' for company. Eva, who had idealistic left-wing views that Yeats dismisses as dreaming of a 'vague Utopia', becomes old and haggard: 'withered old and skeleton-gaunt,/ An image of such politics.' In the second stanza, he laments the effects of time on the sisters: 'The innocent and the beautiful/ Have no enemy but time'.

Personal Symbolism

Yeats uses the image of a 'great gazebo' to describe Ireland. He, Eva and Con were all members of the Anglo-Irish ascendancy. They grew up in a society that believed Ireland to be a mere offshoot of Britain, the way a gazebo is an offshoot of a large house. He ruefully notes that it is families like theirs that built this idea of Ireland as a flimsy 'gazebo', unable to stand on its own: 'We the great gazebo built'.

Despite the fact that he, Eva and Con were nationalists, Yeats suggests they will get little thanks for it because of their privileged Anglo-Irish backgrounds. In fact, they will be seen as being complicit in the oppression of Ireland by Britain: 'They convicted us of guilt'. By the ordinary people of Ireland, they are seen as a relic of the past, something to be forgotten about, even destroyed. Yeats alludes to the destruction of Anglo-Irish mansions in the 1920s in the final line: 'Bid me strike a match and blow.'

THEMES

YEATS AND IRELAND

Yeats was a great admirer of the Anglo-Irish aristocracy, the Protestant land-owning class that dominated Irish society between the 18th and 20th centuries. In this poem he praises Lissadell, one of the famous 'big houses' associated with that class. Yeats praises that 'old Georgian mansion' for its impressive architecture, for its 'great windows open to the South'. But it's worth noting that Lissadell, like other Anglo-Irish mansions, although luxurious, was also a little austere. The Anglo-Irish didn't really go in for 'bling', instead creating simple but elegant environments.

Yeats also admired Anglo-Irish society not only because it valued art and creativity but because it was open to new ideas. Both of these trends are embodied in the 'silk kimonos' worn by the Gore-Booth sisters on that long-ago evening in Lissadell. These gowns, which might be considered art objects in themselves, reflect Anglo-Irish openness to fresh thinking and foreign cultures.

The poet, then, laments the passing of this cultured way of life. By the time Yeats wrote this poem, the heyday of the Anglo-Irish had long since past. Their power had waned throughout the nineteenth century and all but disappeared in the new Catholic Ireland that emerged after independence from Britain.

Yeats uses a most unusual metaphor to describe this passing, comparing Anglo-Irish civilisation to a gazebo, a small roofed structure that is used for outdoor entertaining and dining. Gazebos are often ornamental and elaborately-designed, suggesting the emphasis Anglo-Irish society placed not only on hospitality but also on art and on beautiful objects.

But gazebos are relatively flimsy structures, reflecting how the Anglo-Irish dominance of Irish life proved to be fragile and fleeting. During the struggle for independence, for instance, many Anglo-Irish mansions were burned down by the IRA. The Catholic middle classes, the dominant force in the newly-independent Ireland, 'convicted' the Anglo-Irish, regarding them as little more than collaborators with British oppression: 'They convicted us of guilt'. In the early decades of independence, the great Anglo-Irish families, once so prominent in Irish life, drifted to its margins or disappeared altogether. Their civilisation was torn down as easily as one might dismantle a gazebo.

YOUTH AND AGE

'In Memory' is a masterpiece of nostalgia in which Yeats deftly recreates a golden memory from his youth: two beautiful young women, a splendid mansion, the light of a summer's evening. There is something very moving about the poet's declaration that he often thought of 'seeking out' the sisters to reminisce with them about that long-ago time. Sadly, however, it seems that Yeats left it too late to meet up with the sisters and 'recall/ That table and the talk of youth'. Like many of us, he was simply too busy to find the time for chatting with old friends.

'In Memory', then, is another poem in which Yeats confronts the changes, both mental and physical, that will be wreaked on us by time's relentless march. Time, Yeats reminds us, is the enemy not only of physical beauty but also of innocence: 'The innocent and the beautiful/ Have no enemy but time'. Its passage begins to leave us not only weakened and decrepit on a physical level but also cynical and embittered on a mental one.

The ravages of time are memorably personified as a 'raving Autumn' that shears off the flowers on the wreath of youth and beauty. It turns Eva from a creature of gazelle-like beauty and elegance into a 'withered' and 'skeleton-gaunt' old woman. And each of us, sadly but inevitably, must suffer a similar transformation.

ART AND THE ROLE OF THE ARTIST

In this poem, just as in 'Sailing to Byzantium', Yeats considers the possibility of achieving immortality through art. Yeats imagines himself protecting innocence and beauty by destroying time itself. He longs to somehow put a match to time's very fabric, so it will be consumed in a great and climbing 'conflagration': 'Arise and bid me strike a match/ And strike another till time catch.'

Yeats, of course, doesn't think he can literally set time on fire. The act of putting a match to time is a metaphor for overcoming time's destruction through the power of art. Yeats feels he can undo time's march by immortalising, in poetry, the beauty and innocence of the girls. A truly skilful artist, therefore, can defeat time by recovering an event or person lost in the past – an evening in Lissadell and two girls in silk kimonos, for instance – and preserving it in a piece of art to be enjoyed by future generations.

Not surprisingly, many critics find Yeats' atitude to the sisters' political activity more than a little sexist. Yeats values women like the Gore-Booths for their physical appearance and their 'innocence' rather than for their abilities and achievements. He celebrates Constance's prettiness as a young girl rather than her courage in the 1916 rising, or her achievement in becoming one of the world's first female government ministers. He celebrates Eva's gazelle-like beauty, but not the selfless work she did on behalf of London's poor.

Critics argue that not only does Yeats make the sexist claim that beautiful, aristocratic women have no business in politics, but that he also unfairly devalues the sisters' social and political energy. He dismisses their political beliefs as the striving for 'Some vague Utopia' and an 'ignorant conspiracy'. By doing so, he shows his own ignorance of the good the sisters achieved. He also ignores their independence of mind and their selfless dedication to the various causes they supported.

THIS IS POETRY — W.B. YEATS

Swift's Epitaph

A scene from *Gulliver's Travels*, a work by Swift that has inspired artists and writers for hundreds of years

LINE BY LINE

Jonathan Swift (1667–1745) was a writer, a Protestant clergyman and, eventually, Dean of St Patrick's Cathedral in Dublin. Swift was born in Dublin, but his parents were English. Following his education at Trinity College, he spent a lot of time in England, where he moved in the world of the upper classes. He settled permanently in Dublin in 1714.

Like Yeats, Swift had a complex relationship with Ireland. He claimed to hate the country, but devoted a lot of his writing to defending Ireland. In particular, he defended the Irish economy, which was being unfairly exploited by the London government. He was also extremely generous to Dublin's poor, to whom he contributed one third of his own small income.

Swift is famous for the novel *Gulliver's Travels*, but he was also a poet and one of the greatest prose satirists in the English language. His other well-known works are *The Drapier Letters* and *A Modest Proposal*, a satire in which Swift argues (ironically) that it would make good economic sense for the children of the poor Irish to be raised on farms for consumption on the dinner tables of their English masters.

Swift implies that this would be no more difficult to justify than the economic system that allowed England to exploit Irish labour and trade. Swift is buried in St Patrick's Cathedral, where his epitaph is in Latin. Yeats' poem loosely translates the inscription into English.

The opening line tells us that Swift has gone to his rest and reward in the next life, after the struggles of this earthly existence. There, in the next world, he will be relieved from the righteous anger, the 'savage indignation' that prompted him to consistently speak out against the ills of society. His frustration and anger will no longer torment him – in effect, it will no longer cut his heart to pieces ('lacerate his breast').

In lines 4 and 5, Yeats addresses the reader directly, whom he describes as 'World-besotted traveller'. We are 'world-besotted' because we are obsessed with the things of this life, for example money, sex, and success. The word 'traveller' reminds us that we are not here forever. It reminds us that we are on a journey through life, a journey that will end when we, like Swift, have sailed into our rest.

Yeats concludes this short poem with a challenge to the reader, to us world-besotted travellers. He challenges us to imitate Swift: 'Imitate him if you dare … he/ Served human liberty'. Yeats implies that serving human liberty, as Swift did in his writings, is a risky business. Serving the cause of liberty, Yeats seems to suggest, may bring you only anger, frustration, ingratitude and the misunderstanding of the public. It will probably leave you with a lacerated breast!

ANALYSIS

An Acre of Grass

LINE BY LINE

The poem was written towards the end of the poet's life. Yeats had recently moved into Riversdale, an 18th-century farmhouse in Rathfarnham, a village near Dublin. The house came with a small plot of land, an 'acre of green grass'. Remarking on the move in a letter to a friend, Yeats wrote: 'At first I was unhappy, for everything made me remember the great rooms and the great trees of Coole, my home for nearly forty years, but now that the pictures are up I feel more content'.

The poet takes stock of his life

It is late at night and the poet seems to be sitting by himself, perhaps unable to sleep. He describes the stillness and quietness of the house. The only movement that the poet detects is that of a 'mouse': 'Where nothing stirs but a mouse'.

The poet takes stock of his life and what he is left with at this late stage. There is a sense that his life has been whittled down, and that very little now remains:

- This is someone who was a frequent guest at the grand houses and estates of the Irish Ascendency class. He is accustomed to 'great rooms' and vast private lands. Now his life is confined and restricted to an 'acre of grass'.
- This is someone who is well travelled, a world-famous poet and recipient of the Nobel Prize for Literature, someone who has played a prominent role in Irish cultural and political affairs. Now, all he has are his memories and framed pictures – only the 'picture' remains.
- This is a man who has devoted his entire life to his craft, who has spent countless hours labouring to produce poems that would stand the test of time. Now, his life's work is held or contained between the covers of a book. We can imagine the poet looking at a single hard-backed copy of his collected works and having a sense that his work is done.

The poet's body is also weakening: 'strength of body goes'. He no longer has the physical desires or appetites that he had as a younger man: 'My temptation is quiet'. The description of the house in which he now resides seems to serve as a perfect symbol or metaphor for his physical body. Like the house, the poet is 'old'. Nothing much now 'stirs' within him.

But the poet is not lamenting his lack of material wealth. There is a sense of acceptance that this is what he has. In

ART AND THE ROLE OF THE ARTIST

'Swift's Epitaph' emphasises the public or political role of the poet in society. This poem is Yeats' tribute to Swift. In middle age, Yeats began to regard Swift as one of his most important influences. Yeats admired not only Swift's skill as a writer, but also the courage and tenacity with which his writing opposed greed, stupidity and exploitation.

There is a sense in this poem that Yeats believes it is the writer's duty to respond to public events, to criticise society and its leaders for their various faults and failings. The poem challenges writers to 'imitate' Swift if they dare. It asks them to have the courage to criticise society in their work, even if they might suffer as a result of speaking out.

Yeats admires Swift because Swift was a man of conviction. He stood up for these beliefs even when it cost him dearly to do so. Swift acted as if he didn't care what others thought about him. Like the airman in 'An Irish Airman', he seemed to weigh very lightly the personal consequences of his actions. He acted because he was compelled to do so and did not let fear or failure or ridicule stand in his way. Yeats also admires the passion that Swift exhibited in his life and work. Swift's writing, even when it dealt with serious matters, was always marked by zest, energy and humour.

fact, we could say that he has all he needs to live comfortably and continue to work as a poet. The 'acre of grass' is ideal for getting fresh air and taking the exercise that the poet needs.

Nor does Yeats dwell on or lament the the fact that his body no longer affords him any pleasure. He is primarily concerned with creativity and his ongoing work as an artist. Rather than feeling proud and content about what he has achieved, the poet seems to be dissatisfied.

Making the 'truth known'

Yeats' desire or objective as a poet is to gain profound insight into the meaning of life, to achieve a deep understanding of the world. There is a sense in which he feels that his work, despite having devoted his life to it, has not yet achieved this.

Yeats hopes before he dies to arrive at some profound understanding of the world and to 'make the truth known'. He has traditionally used two different methods to fuel his poetic enterprise:

- He gives free reign to his thoughts, using what he calls 'loose imagination', in the hope that some interesting idea will arise.
- He meditates on the information that his mind receives each day, processing it and shaping it in such a way that it might lead to a poem. Yeats compares his mind to a 'mill' that processes the rough material it receives, the 'rag and bone' of daily life.

However, the poet feels that he needs something more than this if he is going to make the 'truth known' in the time that he has left.

The poet's appeal

Yeats considers the possibility that he will succumb to some form of frenzy or madness in his old age. He makes an appeal, perhaps to God, to allow this to happen: 'Grant me an old man's frenzy'. In this frenzied state, his mind will be greatly disturbed, and this will lead to profound understanding or insight. Yeats refers to two Shakespearean characters who experienced something like what he has in mind: Timon of Athens and Lear.

But the poet cannot be sure if he will be granted such a 'frenzy'. Therefore, he must take it upon himself to bring about the change that he needs to achieve the understanding he desires.

> **Timon** was an Ancient Greek philosopher who died in 399 BC. Shakespeare, in his play Timon of Athens, presents him as someone who devoted his life to his city, only to end up an outcast in his later years. The experience resulted in him acquiring a bitter understanding of life and humanity. Lear is the titular character from Shakespeare's King Lear. When he relinquishes control of his kingdom, dividing it up amongst his daughters, he suddenly realises what it is to be without power and respect. He wanders out into the world, goes insane and gains an insight into the sufferings of humanity.

Through a great effort of will, he must somehow 'remake' or refashion himself so that he becomes the kind of person he believes capable of gaining such profound insight or accessing such truth: 'Myself must I remake'.

Here Yeats cites the examples of William Blake and Michelangelo, two artists renowned for their ability to create great works even in old age. Yeats presents Blake as someone who kept pushing and pushing until he achieved the understanding he desired: 'beat upon the wall/ Till truth obeyed his call'. Michelangelo is described as having a brilliant, piercing mind that is capable of of penetrating insight and understanding: 'A mind Michel Angelo knew/ That can pierce the clouds'.

Yeats is hoping that in the time remaining he can somehow emulate Blake and Michelangelo and achieve the understanding he requires. There is a real sense of urgency in these closing lines. The poet knows that he cannot afford to be patient and complacent. He needs to get angry, to experience a rage that will disturb his mind and shake things up.

The poet believes that being old should not prevent this from happening. Rather, now that he is no longer distracted by physical desire or by any social duties, he is free to devote himself to this pursuit. Yeats compares the aged mind to an 'eagle', suggesting that the mind in old age is free to soar and gain a view or understanding of the world that is not possible to achieve when you are younger.

FOCUS ON STYLE

Yeats refers to the information that is received through the senses as the 'rag and bone' of the mind. Rag and bone is a term used to describe scraps or discarded items that someone would collect and try to sell for cash. Rag and bone men would spend their days searching for such scraps, in the hope that they might come across something valuable.

In a similar manner, the poet processes the day-to-day information that his mind receives, hoping to be inspired by it and convert it into a poem. Yeats compares the mind to a 'mill' or factory that processes and sorts the information it receives: 'the mill of the mind'.

The description of the 'old house' in which the poet lives is a metaphor for the poet's own decrepit body: 'an old house/ Where nothing stirs but a mouse.'

Yeats also uses the image of the eagle to represent the aged mind: 'An old man's eagle mind'. An eagle can soar into the air, gaining a wide perspective of the world. But it can also focus with extraordinary sharpness on any given object. An old man's mind, according to Yeats, can see life with a similarly broad perspective. Old people, after all, have lived and experienced more than younger people. An old man's mind also exhibits an eagle-like sharpness of focus because it is undistracted by the sexual desire and other frivolous concerns of youth.

THEMES

YOUTH AND AGE

Many of Yeats' poems lament the negative effects of ageing. 'An Acre of Grass', however, takes a different approach. The poet is accepting of the ageing process and even celebrates certain advantages that come with growing older. He is no longer distracted by sexual desire: 'My temptation is quiet'. His mind has grown more mindful and serene. He likens the aged body to 'an old house' that barely contains any life: 'an old house/ Where nothing stirs but a mouse'.

The poet's mind is now free to gain insight or understanding that was unavailable to him when he was young. Yeats describes the aged man's mind in terms of an 'eagle': 'An old man's eagle mind'. The comparison not only suggests the sharpness of the older man's mind but also that it is capable of soaring and gaining a perspective on life that is not available to the young.

ART AND THE ROLE OF THE ARTIST

This is another poem in which Yeats presents art as a continuous practice, a craft or trade that must be perfected throughout the artist's life. He admires artists like Michelangelo, William Shakespeare (who created the characters of Lear and Timon), and William Blake, who continued, even in old age, to strive for artistic perfection. Yeats clearly wants to emulate the passion and energy exhibited by these past masters, who kept changing and developing until the very end of their lives. The artist, Yeats believes, should never feel satisfied or content with what they have already achieved. It is the artist's duty, even in old age, to remain restless and to constantly seek new ways to explore and reveal the truth.

Yeats also presents the artist as a truth-seeker, someone who works to gain a profound understanding of the world, to break through the normal limits of the mind. Yeats compares such limits to walls or clouds that need to be somehow broken down, transgressed or pierced.

Yeats presents Blake as someone who kept pushing and pushing until he achieved the understanding he desired: 'beat upon the wall/ Till truth obeyed his call'. Michelangelo is described as having a brilliant, piercing mind that is capable of penetrating insight and understanding: 'A mind Michel Angelo knew/ That can pierce the clouds'.

from Under Ben Bulben

W.B. YEATS

LINE BY LINE

In this poem, Yeats addresses future Irish poets and offers them advice. Yeats presents poetry as a 'trade' that one must 'learn'. Poetry, according to this view, has much in common with other trades like carpentry, plumbing or silver-smithing.

Poetry, like all these professions, involves a particular set of skills and techniques, which are passed on from one generation of poets to the next. A poet, like any tradesman, must serve an apprenticeship, during which time he acquires these skills, methods and trade secrets.

The sort now growing up

Yeats is unimpressed at the direction that Irish society is taking. The population, in his view, is becoming increasingly 'base'.

- This term implies that the Irish people, increasingly, are devoid of morality and honour. Their hearts are 'unremembering' as if they no longer recall what decency and virtue actually are.
- The phrase 'unremembering hearts' also implies a different form of baseness, suggesting that they're incapable of subtle and complex emotions, the feelings involved, for instance, in contemplating Swift's poetry or Byzantine art.
- But their baseness also lies in their 'unremembering heads'. They have forgotten their country's heritage and traditions, its literature, its stories and its songs.
- We might even read the term 'base' as suggesting that the population is becoming physically inferior, as if these 'base' people are somehow ugly or deformed.

The Irish, then, are getting 'out of shape from toe to top', becoming more and more physically, intellectually and morally unfit.

Yeats suggests that these base qualities are growing more widespread with every passing generation because 'base' parents generate offspring who inherit their negative characteristics. With each generation, then, there are more and more of these ill-begotten children, these 'Base-born products of base beds'. Yeats cautions aspiring poets to avoid these base characters who form an increasingly large segment of the Irish population: 'Scorn the sort now growing up'. These 'out of shape' individuals, he advises, should never be used as a subject matter for poetry. But there's also a suggestion that poets should avoid associating with these 'base-born' masses, for fear, perhaps, that their negative qualities might rub off.

Proper sources of inspiration

Aspiring poets, Yeats advises, should stick to a specific range of subject matters, confining themselves to 'whatever is well made'. Poems should be inspired by beautiful objects, like the sculpted bird in 'Sailing to Byzantium', that have been 'well made' by gifted craftsmen. Or they should celebrate elements of the natural world, like birds, bees and flowers, that have been 'well made' by nature's processes. Or they should find inspiration in beautiful and noble people who have been 'well made' by a combination of genetics and upbringing.

In this regard, Yeats suggests the 'peasantry' as a fit subject matter for poetry. This refers to Ireland's poor farmers, especially those in the west of the country. These small farmers endured extreme poverty: living in tiny cottages without electricity, making their own clothes, working the same few stony acres for generation after generation, producing just enough to get by.

Another fit subject, according to Yeats, would be 'Hard-riding country gentlemen'. Here we imagine wealthy landowners dressed in the finest equestrian gear, powering through the countryside on thoroughbred steeds. Ireland's up-and-coming poets, Yeats suggests, should let themselves be inspired by such riders, by the force and motion they exhibit as they gallop through the countryside, by the grace and elegance of their prize animals.

Poets, according to Yeats, should also be inspired by Ireland's monks, taking inspiration from the 'holiness' and spirituality of their lives. Yeats, though by no means a conventional Christian, greatly admired how monks live in a way that is focused, disciplined and completely devoid of materialism. And he also venerated the learning and artistry associated with the monasteries of Ireland's past, which produced annals, chalices and fantastically illustrated volumes like The Book of Kells.

But poets can also find inspiration in less spiritual places, in the country's pubs for instance. Yeats, perhaps surprisingly, suggests a 'porter drinker' as a fitting subject matter: 'Porter drinker's randy laughter'. We might imagine here an exuberant and entertaining companion, someone full of life and energy, of laughter and talk, of stories and sexual desire.

The aristocrats of Ireland's past are another appropriate source of inspiration. Yeats describes these 'lords and ladies' as 'gay', which in this instance suggests that they were jovial and carefree. These aristocrats lived and died in a way that was energetic, exuberant and joyful. The term 'gay' also has connotations of vividness and bright colours, suggesting how these aristocrats valued art, design and beauty.

But these lords and ladies were also fierce warriors, commanding armies in a 'heroic' resistance to English rule in Ireland. Their struggle continued for 'seven centuries', from the 12th century to the 20th century. Time after time, these 'lords and ladies' were crushed and defeated, were 'beaten into the clay' by English oppression. But their descendants would always rise up again, continuing the struggle for generation after generation, so that their country might finally be free.

Looking to the past

Yeats concludes his advice to up-and-coming poets by urging them to look to history for inspiration: 'Cast your mind on other days'. For the things he values as sources of inspiration are increasingly things of the past. The peasantry, the gentlemen, the monks, the lord and ladies were rare in 1939 when Yeats wrote the poem and are even rarer in the Ireland of today.

The present and future, meanwhile, seem increasingly the province of the 'base' with their 'unremembering hearts and heads', who, as pointed out above, are under no circumstances to be considered fit subject matter for poetry.

Yeats' grave

Yeats imagines a time after his own death. He writes in the third person, as if he were an unnamed speaker contemplating the grave in which he has been laid (note how the speaker refers to the poet in the third person, using terms like 'Yeats' and 'his'). This anonymous onlooker describes Yeats' burial as a kind of homecoming:

- He has been buried in his beloved County Sligo, specifically under Ben Bulben, the famously distinctive mountain that from childhood haunted his imagination: 'Under bare Ben Bulben's head…Yeats is laid'.
- He has been buried in the grounds of a church with which he has a family connection. At some time in the past, one of his relatives worked as a minister in this very chapel: 'An ancestor was rector there/ Long years ago'.
- He has been buried near 'an ancient Cross', which symbolises his deep engagement with Ireland's history, heritage and mythology.
- His gravestone is manufactured from locally-sourced Sligo limestone, from 'limestone quarried near the spot'. Yeats has chosen this over marble, which was the material typically used in such monuments: 'No marble'.

Gravestones are typically carved with expressions like 'beloved uncle' or 'rest in peace' or 'here lies with God'. According to the speaker, however, Yeats' gravestone is marked with no such ordinary or 'conventional phrase'. The speaker describes how instead

> Unlike marble, a hard-wearing material that can last for decades or even centuries, limestone erodes relatively quickly. It's as if Yeats' choice of limestone reflects his desire to become one with the Sligo landscape. His headstone, he imagines, will be washed away by the rain, draining into the soil of the county he so loved.

Yeats requested that his monument be carved with a mysterious three-line poem: 'By his command these words are cut'.

FOCUS ON STYLE

Imagery

'Under Ben Bulben', like the best of Yeats' poetry, combines a powerful, logical argument with memorable images. In part V, the images flash by like a deck of cards being flicked at one corner: the monks, the hard-riding gentlemen, the porter drinkers, the lords and ladies. Part VI, in contrast, lingers on the single image of Yeats' burial place. The camera pans across every detail, from Ben Bulben in the distance to the cross by the roadside. The poem closes, fittingly for one of Yeats' final poetic statements, with the haunting image of the horseman.

Tone, Mood and Atmosphere

The poem's tone shifts between the sections. The tone in part V is premonitory and commanding, almost angry at times, as it issues decrees and condemnations. In part VI, however, the tone is one of calmness and detachment. There is a matter-of-factness to these lines that is in keeping with the lack of sentimentality that the poet urges us to have in our attitudes to life and death.

THEMES

ART AND THE ROLE OF THE ARTIST

This is another poem in which Yeats presents art as a continuous practice, a craft or trade that must be perfected throughout the artist's life. Future Irish poets, Yeats decrees, must 'learn [their] trade'. These aspiring bards must understand that poetry involves more than ideas and inspiration, that it requires practice, patience and determination. They must approach poetry the way an apprentice carpenter approaches the work bench, realising that they have a great deal to learn and that only hard work will grant them the mastery they desire.

'Under Ben Bulben' also explores the public or political role of the poet in society. If poetry is a 'trade', then it must serve a useful function. Like carpentry and tailoring it must be necessary to society. Poetry's function, as Yeats presents it here, is to 'cast [his or her] mind on other days', to remember and write about the past.

For seven centuries the 'Irishry' resisted English rule, proving themselves 'indomitable', impossible to overcome. But now they're in danger of succumbing to a new and more subtle foe, that of modernity. Will Ireland become just another identical outpost of capitalism, just another banal node in an international network of technology?

Only the poets, according to Yeats, can prevent this from happening. Only they can remind Ireland as a whole of what it once was and can be again. Through their words, they can spur us on to be 'indomitable' in the face of modernity, to create a future that resembles the best aspects of our past.

YEATS AND IRELAND

This is another poem in which Yeats laments what he saw as the decline of Irish society. In 1939, when Yeats wrote the poem, Ireland was becoming a place dominated by science and technology, industry and commerce. These changes, Yeats feels, have made the Irish of today a rather 'base' lot. The 'sort now growing up' are devoid of morality, incapable of feeling, and even physically inferior.

Yeats, then, looks back with affection to this golden time before modernity, when gentleman and peasant alike were uncorrupted by the grubby influences of capitalism and materialism. This was also a time before science came to dominate mankind's view of the world, a time that Yeats, a spiritualist rather than a scientist in outlook, harks back to with the greatest of nostalgia.

This is also a poem in which Yeats celebrates the revolutionary patriotism of Ireland's past. We see this in his mention of the lords and ladies who rose up again and again to challenge English rule over centuries of resistance.

The mention of the 'hard-riding country gentleman' reminds us of the Anglo-Irish, the Protestant landowners who dominated Irish life between the 17th and 20th centuries. Yeats felt great affection for this class, relishing the restrained and tasteful elegance of their mansions, admiring the formal, almost ceremonial, nature of their lifestyle and appreciating their devotion to art and culture.

> Many readers, perhaps understandably, have taken issue with Yeats' decrees about the appropriate subject matter for poetry. After all, why should a poet write about only what's 'well made'? Why can't she be inspired by things that are badly made, by images of horror and disgust? And who's to say what's well made anyway? Why can't we view soccer matches and computer terminals as fitting poetic material, instead of peasants and monks? Can we look to the future instead of always being stuck in the past?

The poem looks back to the heyday of the Anglo-Irish, long before his own time, in the 18th and early 19th centuries. Yeats presents the Ireland of that period as a place of almost medieval simplicity. The 'lords and ladies' of the ascendancy resided in their 'gay' mansions or relaxed by 'hard-riding' through the countryside. The Catholic 'peasantry' worked the land and drank porter in the taverns, content with the noble simplicity of their lot. The monks, cooped up in their monasteries, got on with being holy.

By the time Yeats wrote this poem, the heyday of the Anglo-Irish was long since past. Their power had waned throughout the nineteenth century and all but disappeared in the new Catholic Ireland that emerged after independence from Britain.

DEATH

Each of us who reads Yeats' famously enigmatic three-line inscription, whether on his headstone in Drumcliffe Churchyard or on the printed page, is a kind of horseman, a traveller on a journey through life. For all we can do is 'pass by' as we make our way from moment to moment, from year to year, and ultimately from the mysterious state before birth to the even more mysterious one that awaits us at our journey's end. The horse of time that carries us forward, relentlessly forward, will permit no pausing.

Yeats urges us to 'cast a cold eye' on this journey. We must assess our lives and the sum of our experience in a calm and coldly rational manner. We must be equally 'cold' about the reality of our own impending deaths, accepting that death, whether we like it or not, is our ultimate destination. For in such coldness, in such a purging of emotion, lies emotional freedom, an utter release from anxieties about life's failures and death's inevitability. We might even find ourselves laughing at the whole beautiful, ridiculous journey.

THIS IS POETRY   W.B. YEATS

Politics

LINE BY LINE

Yeats is in conversation with two wise, well-informed people:
- The first is a man who has travelled extensively throughout the world and, therefore, has a good understanding of the political and social affairs in different countries. Yeats says that this man speaks from experience, that he 'knows/ What he talks about'.
- The second is an experienced politician. Yeats says that the politician is 'learned', suggesting that he not only knows much about political affairs, but that he is a well-educated man who likely has a broad understanding of the world.

The conversation focuses on the political situation in Italy, Russia and Spain. In 1938, when Yeats wrote the poem, the situation in each of these countries was very grave as Europe was sliding towards World War Two. Russia was under the brutal rule of Stalin, who in 1938 was attempting to purge the country of all those he deemed a threat to his rule. Italy was ruled by fascist dictator Mussolini, while Spain was gradually being taken over by far-right forces led by General Franco. While all this was happening, Hitler, having just annexed Austria, was now pushing to take control of Czechoslovakia.

It is unsurprising, therefore, that the conversation between the poet, his well-travelled friend and the 'learned' politician centres around events in these countries and the growing possibility of war in Europe.

The poet knows that the men with whom he converses are knowledgeable and that their opinions are to be respected. He accepts that their predictions of approaching war are probably accurate: 'And maybe what they say is true/ Of war and war's alarms'.

Yet the poet cannot focus or 'fix his attention' on these urgent matters. All the while that they are talking, the poet is distracted by a beautiful young girl who is standing close by. He wishes he was young once again, so that he could be her lover: 'But O that I were young again/ And held her in my arms!'

THEMES

YOUTH AND AGE

Like many of Yeats' poems, 'Politics' laments the tragedy of old age. The poet is entranced by a beautiful woman, but knows he's now too old to ever win her affections. 'Politics', then, like 'Sailing to Byzantium' and 'An Acre of Grass', movingly depicts the restrictions and frustrations that come with growing older.

There is real emotion in the poem's final lines, when he wishes that he could somehow be young again and hold the beautiful woman he so desires in his arms. The tragic reality, of course, is that is there is no turning back the clock. The poet's desire for youth, and for this beautiful girl, must remain forever thwarted. This nostalgic lament for a vanished youth echoes both 'The Wild Swans at Coole' and 'In Memory of Eva Gore-Booth and Con Markiewicz'. All three poems find the poet yearning nostalgically for an earlier stage of his existence.

WAR, VIOLENCE AND SOCIAL UPHEAVAL

Yeats wrote this poem in 1938, a very dark time in the history of Europe. The Second World War was poised to break out over the continent like a terrible storm. As Yeats puts it, 'war's alarms' were ringing throughout the world. There is, then, a certain sense of dread in this poem. The 'travelled man' and the politician seem deeply concerned about the coming catastrophe. The poet, however, finds himself distracted by the presence of a beautiful young woman. For a moment romantic longing overtakes his fear of the coming storm. In this regard, 'Politics' is not unlike 'The Second Coming' and 'The Stare's Nest by My Window'. All three poems register a dread of the great violence, war and upheaval that marred the world during the last years of Yeats' life.

ART THE ROLE OF THE ARTIST

'Politics' is another poem that explores the public or political role of the poet in society. 'Politics' was inspired by an article by the writer Archibald MacLeish that criticised Yeats for failing to comment on political issues in his work. The poem contrasts a public catastrophe with private suffering. The public catastrophe is that of the impending war. The private suffering is that of the poet, as he endures the anguish of old age and the frustration of thwarted desire.

The poem suggests that this private tragedy is of more significance to Yeats as an artist than the public tragedy of war. He is unable to shift his attention from the beauty of the girl to important political matters. The poem seems to answer MacLeish by suggesting that poets are not obliged to write about 'public' matters of national importance. Instead, they should be free to deal with 'private' matters that will eventually affect us all, such as the delight and torture of romance and the decay and indignity of old age.

Therefore, although 'Politics' is a relatively simple poem, it raises a number of important questions. Is it self-centred of Yeats as a writer to assign more significance to his private anguish than to the looming disaster of war? Is it wrong for the poet or artist to focus on his or her personal relationships and problems when there is so much evil and suffering in the world? On the other hand, however, it is possible to regard Yeats' involvement with themes of the heart as arising not from self-obsession but from a desire to write about universal human experiences.

FOCUS ON STYLE

Form

The poem consists of twelve lines with no stanza breaks. It follows an ABCB DEFE GHIH rhyme scheme.

Tone, Mood and Atmosphere

Unusually for Yeats, the tone of 'Politics' is quite humorous, self-deprecating and tongue-in-cheek. Despite the fact that the poem references much of the political unrest in Europe at the time, Yeats insists he can't possibly focus on such serious issues when there is a beautiful girl standing in front of him: 'How can I, that girl standing there,/ My attention fix/ On … politics'.

There is also a wistful note to this poem. Whereas in 'The Stare's Nest by My Window' he praises the ability of the older man to focus on the serious issues in life, here he wants nothing more than to return to his youth: 'But O that I were young again/ And held her in my arms.'

THIS IS POETRY

How to Answer the Poetry Questions

I've been asked to write an essay in response to the following statement: 'I like (or do not like) to read the poetry of Derek Mahon'.

STAGE 1: PLANNING THE ANSWER

ESTABLISH A POINT OF VIEW
Firstly, I'm going to decide what my point of view is. I'm going to declare that I like the poetry of Derek Mahon for the following reasons:
- He doesn't just write about his feelings.
- He engages with the world beyond himself.
- He deals with real historic events.

This is one of the most important steps in the whole process. I have decided a point of view. I will not be rambling on vaguely about my attitude to Mahon's poetry. Everything in my answer will now relate to this point of view.

DECIDE WHICH POEMS TO TALK ABOUT
I am now going to decide which poems to talk about. It's good to talk about four to six poems in an answer. I'm going to talk about five: 'As it Should Be', 'After the *Titanic*', 'Rathlin', 'A Disused Shed in Co. Wexford' and 'Day Trip to Donegal'.

I'm going to quickly jot down the titles of these poems along with a couple of quotations from each poem that will relate to my point of view.

STRUCTURE THE ESSAY
Now I'm going to structure my essay. I'm going to write six paragraphs.
- The first paragraph, the introduction, will clearly state my point of view.
- The second paragraph will deal with 'As it Should Be' and 'After the *Titanic*'. I will focus on the fact that these poems are spoken by someone other than the poet himself.
- The third paragraph will deal with 'Antarctica', 'After the *Titanic*' and 'Rathlin'. I am going to focus on how these poems deal with individuals in extreme situations.
- My fourth paragraph will deal with 'A Disused Shed in Co. Wexford'. I am going to talk about how Mahon commemorates history's victims.
- My fifth paragraph will deal with 'Day Trip to Donegal'. I am going to focus on Mahon's compassion towards the natural world.
- The final paragraph will be the conclusion.

STAGE 2: WRITING THE ESSAY

WRITING THE INTRODUCTION
I'm going to write my introduction. This will state the point of view I came up with in the planning stage. I will also flesh this point out a little by emphasising what it is about Mahon's work that appeals to me:

> I must say I really liked the poetry of Derek Mahon. Whereas too many poets are content simply to just go on and on about their 'feelings', Mahon engages with the world beyond himself. His poems deal with history and its victims, detailing their plight in a way that I found to be both compassionate and truly moving. I also liked the way his work focuses on individuals from history who are trapped in extreme and desperate situations, whose minds are at the 'end of their tethers'. Paradoxically, perhaps, by shifting the focus away from himself and by avoiding the discussion of his own feelings, Mahon produces work that bristles with compassion, sympathy and empathy.in.

As you will see from introduction, I have clearly stated what my essay is going to be about. I have not gone into any great detail here. I did not attempt to describe what the different poems have to say about the topics I will be discussing throughout my essay. I simply made it clear to the reader what it is that I admire about Mahon's poetry.

WRITING THE BODY PARAGRAPHS
I see from my plan that my first body paragraph will deal with 'As it Should Be' and 'After the *Titanic*' and how these poems are spoken by someone other than the poet himself. So I'm going to start the paragraph with a topic sentence, a sentence declaring what the paragraph is going to be about:

> One of the things I most liked about his poems was the fact that so many of them are spoken by people other than the poet himself.

Every other sentence in this paragraph is going to relate to or expand on this topic sentence. If I find myself writing something that does not relate directly to this topic sentence, I know I've gone wrong. To complete this paragraph I am going to write a couple of sentences about how each of the poems illustrate the point that I am making.

> One of the things I most liked about his poems was the fact that so many of them are spoken by people other than the poet himself. In 'As it Should Be', for instance, we are brought into the mind of a cold-blooded killer who 'hunted the mad bastard/ Through bog, moorland, rock, to the starlit west'. Mahon allows us, chillingly, to see this brutal and murderous act from the perpetrator's point of view and to perhaps even begin to understand how his desire to protect his children might have led him to commit this crime. All he wanted, he declared, was for the community's children to 'grow up/ To a world with method in it'. 'After the *Titanic*' also surprises us by presenting that well-known tragedy from an unfamiliar point of view. Here, we are taken into the mind of Bruce Ismay, the ship's manager who was 'humbled at the inquiry' into that tragic incident and declared to be the villain of the piece. Mahon allows us to witness first hand the suffering and humiliation this man endured as his 'costly life' went 'thundering down' to the ocean's bottom, and I felt real emotion when he beseeched us to 'Include me in your lamentations'.

Note how every sentence I have written relates to my topic sentence. I don't wander off the point by talking about Mahon's love of nature or his experience of life in London as a freelance journalist.

Note how I don't fall into the trap of paraphrasing the poems, of telling the examiner everything that happened in each of them. I simple take two or three aspects that are relevant to my topic sentence.

Note also how I back up every point with a quote. The golden rule here is 'Always be quoting'!

Finally, note how the two poems are linked in the middle of the paragraph. Again, this is a skill that comes with practice.

I see that my next paragraph is going to deal with individuals who find themselves in extreme situations and I will be focusing on 'Antarctica', 'After the *Titanic*' and 'Rathlin'.

Once again, I start off with a simple topic sentence:

> Another feature of Mahon's poetry that appealed to me was its focus on individuals who are trapped in extreme situations.

Once again I am going to write a number of sentences that relate to this topic sentence. I'm going to make sure that nothing I write strays away from this topic.

> Another feature of Mahon's poetry that appealed to me was its focus on individuals who are trapped in extreme situations. He specialises in describing individuals who are psychologically on the edge, whose 'minds are at the ends of their tethers'. An obvious example of this is 'Antarctica', which depicts Captain Oates 'Goading his ghost into the howling snow' as he disappears into the frozen wilderness to die. 'After the *Titanic*', meanwhile, depicts Bruce Ismay in a psychologically extreme situation as his 'poor soul/ Screams out in the starlight', tormented by the memory of the deaths for which he was at least partly responsible. Psychological suffering is also movingly depicted in 'Rathlin', which describes the anguish of *Somhairle Bui* trapped powerless on the 'mainland' as he listens to the screams of his tribe being slaughtered on Rathlin island. Yet the most chilling depiction of a psychological desperation is surely that in 'Day Trip to Donegal', where the speaker dreams or hallucinates that he is 'alone far out at sea', adrift on a seething stormy ocean. I found the conclusion of this poem incredibly powerful, and I could almost see the speaker clinging to some kind of raft in the middle of an endless sea.

Note again how every sentence I have written relates to my topic sentence. I don't fall into the trap of paraphrasing the poems, of telling the examiner everything that happened in each of them. I simply take two or three aspects that are relevant to my topic sentence. I back up every point with a quote. The remainder of the body paragraphs will follow the same format outlined above.

WRITING THE CONCLUSION

The idea here is to sum up what I have said in the essay without repeating myself too much. I am going to bring the point of view I established in the introduction back in again. I am going to try and get personal. The first thing I am going to do is rewrite my point of view in slightly different language.

> Mahon's work is so powerful because it is dedicated to speaking out on behalf of these forgotten victims who have 'come so far in darkness and in pain'.

Now I am going to add a sentence that will make reference to some of the poems I have discussed in the essay.

> He refuses to abandon them to forgetfulness, whether they be the people of Rathlin, Pompeii and Treblinka, the hunted 'mad bastard' of 'As it Should Be' or poor old Bruce Ismay who each day is forced to 'drown again with all those dim/ Lost faces'.

Now I am going to add two or three more sentences that flesh out this point. I am going to try to make these as personal as possible.

THIS IS POETRY

> The triumph of his impersonal style is that it allows him to speak out on behalf of these people so movingly and with such effectiveness. His poems have given me a powerful and unforgettable insight into the lives and struggles of some of history's forgotten victims.

Note how the conclusion is short and does not ramble on and on repeating the points made in the essay. Note how the conclusion describes a personal response. Note how the conclusion is tied into the point of view established at the start of the essay.

If you are good at English, it can be good to finish with a flourish. This might involve using a memorable phrase, a quote from a famous writer or the poet under discussion, or some poetic sentence of your own.

THE SEVEN GOLDEN RULES

1. **Read the question carefully.** This sounds obvious but I can't stress how important it is.

2. **Establish a point of view.** Do this at the beginning of your planning stage. Remember that every sentence in your essay will relate to this point of view.

3. **Structure the essay carefully.** Determine what every paragraph is going to be about before you commence writing.

4. **Begin each paragraph with a topic sentence.** Every other sentence in the paragraph will relate to this sentence.

5. **Don't paraphrase.** Don't retell the story or the action of the poem – the examiner already knows this. Just identify the two or three elements of the poem that relate to your topic.

6. **Always be quoting.**

7. **Be aware of genre.** Are you being asked to write a straightforward essay or are you being asked to do something else like write a letter or give a short talk? If you are being asked to write a letter or a short talk, then the introduction and the conclusion of your piece will need to reflect this.

SEE NEXT PAGE FOR THE FULL ESSAY

SAMPLE ANSWER

Write an essay outlining the reasons why you like or dislike the poetry of Derek Mahon

I must say I really liked the poetry of Derek Mahon. Whereas too many poets are content simply to just go on and on about their 'feelings', Mahon engages with the world beyond himself. His poems deal with history and its victims, detailing their plight in a way that I found to be both compassionate and truly moving. I also liked the way his work focuses on individuals from history who are trapped in extreme and desperate situations, whose minds are at the 'end of their tethers'. Paradoxically, perhaps, by shifting the focus away from himself and by avoiding the discussion of his own feelings, Mahon produces work that bristles with compassion, sympathy and empathy.

One of the things I most liked about Mahon's poetry was the fact that so many of his poems are spoken by people other than the poet himself. In 'As it Should Be', for instance, we are brought into the mind of a cold-blooded killer who 'hunted the mad bastard/ Through bog, moorland, rock, to the starlit west'. Mahon allows us, chillingly, to see this brutal and murderous act from the perpetrator's point of view and to, perhaps, even begin to understand how his desire to protect his children might have led him to commit this crime. All he wanted, he declared, was for the community's children to 'grow up/ To a world with method in it'. 'After the *Titanic*' also surprises us by presenting that well-known tragedy from an unfamiliar point of view. Here, we are taken into the mind of Bruce Ismay, the ship's manager who was 'humbled at the inquiry' into that tragic incident and declared to be the villain of the piece. Mahon allows us to witness first-hand the suffering and humiliation this man endured as his 'costly life' went 'thundering down' to the ocean's bottom, and I felt real emotion when he beseeched us to 'Include me in your lamentations'.

Another feature of Mahon's poetry that appealed to me was its focus on individuals who are trapped in extreme situations. He specialises in describing individuals who are psychologically on the edge. An obvious example of this is 'Antarctica', which depicts Captain Oates 'Goading his ghost into the howling snow' as he disappears into the frozen wilderness to die. 'After the *Titanic*', meanwhile, depicts Bruce Ismay in a psychologically extreme situation as his 'poor soul/ Screams out in the starlight', tormented by the memory of the deaths for which he was at least partly responsible. Psychological suffering is also movingly depicted in 'Rathlin', which describes the anguish of Somhairle Bui trapped powerless on the 'mainland' as he listens to the screams of his tribe being slaughtered on Rathlin island. Yet the most chilling depiction of psychological desperation is surely that in 'Day Trip to Donegal', where the speaker dreams or hallucinates that he is 'alone far out at sea', adrift on a seething stormy ocean. I found the conclusion of this poem incredibly powerful, and I could almost see the speaker clinging to some kind of raft in the middle of an endless sea.

One of the most prominent features of Mahon's work is his overriding concern for the victims of history. This is perhaps at its most evident in 'A Disused Shed in Co. Wexford', where the mushrooms abandoned in a shed 'deep in the grounds of a burnt-out hotel' come to represent all the people who have suffered throughout history. Mahon presents them as a symbol for the 'Lost people of Treblinka and Pompeii' – the victims of both man-made conflicts, such as the holocaust, and natural disasters, like the destruction of Pompeii by the eruption of Vesuvius in 79 bc. A similar concern for history's victims is evident in 'Rathlin', where the speaker reflects on the massacre of the people of Somhairle Bui in the sixteenth century: 'Somhairle Bui, powerless on the mainland heard the screams of the Rathlin women/ Borne to him, seconds later, upon the wind'.

Mahon also shows compassion toward the non-human world. We see this in 'Day Trip to Donegal' where the speaker pities the 'writhing glimmer of fish' as they expire on the pier in 'attitudes of agony and heartbreak'. 'A Disused Shed in Co. Wexford', meanwhile, shows real compassion for the 'thousand mushrooms' who have endured a 'half century without visitors in the dark'.

Mahon's work is so powerful because it is dedicated to speaking out on behalf of these forgotten victims who have 'come so far in darkness and in pain'. He refuses to abandon them to forgetfulness, whether they be the people of Rathlin, Pompeii and Treblinka, the hunted 'mad bastard' of 'As it Should Be' or poor old Bruce Ismay who each day is forced to 'drown again with all those dim/ Lost faces'. The triumph of his impersonal style is that it allows him to speak out on behalf of these people so movingly and with such effectiveness. His poems have given me an unforgettable insight into the lives and struggles of some of history's forgotten victims.

UNSEEN POEM: SAMPLE ANSWER 1

Hotel Room 12th Floor

by Norman MacCaig

This morning I watched from here
a helicopter skirting like a damaged insect
the Empire State Building, that
jumbo size dentist's drill, and landing
on the roof of the PanAm skyscraper. [5]
But now midnight has come in
from foreign places. Its uncivilised darkness
is shot at by millions of lit windows, all
ups and acrosses.

But midnight is not
so easily defeated. I lie in bed, between
a radio and a television set, and hear
the wildest of warhoops continually ululating through [10]
the glittering canyons and gulches –
police cars and ambulances racing
to broken bones, the harsh screaming
from frozen coldwater flats, the blood
glazed on sidewalks.

The frontier is never [15]
somewhere else. And no stockades
can keep the midnight out.

Answer either Question 1 or Question 2

1. (a) Do you like the world that the poet describes in this poem? Give reasons for your answer supporting them by reference to the text. (10)

    (b) Choose a line or two that you find particularly appealing and explain why. (10)

OR

2. Write a personal response to the poem 'Back Yard'. (20)

(a) Do you like the world that the poet describes in this poem? Give reasons for your answer supporting them by reference to the text. (10)

I love the world that the poet presents in this poem. It is a magical and rather fantastical world, all coated in 'silver': 'All silver under your rain tonight'. Everything seems to have taken on a special glow or 'sheen' in the moon's light. The 'grass, catalpa and oak' and the 'cherry tree' in the neighbour's backyard are cast in a special light by the moon, beautifully transformed and altered. The poet's mood is also affected by the moon. He seems to be in a blissful state of mind, perfectly content and happy 'drinking white thoughts' that the moon inspires. Though he knows it is late, he cannot bring himself to leave this wonderful moment.

The world of the poem is also perfectly romantic. The poet thinks of others who may be appreciating the moon's special glow on this night. He imagines 'An Italian boy is sending songs to' the moon tonight 'from an accordion'. He also pictures a 'Polish boy' on a date with 'his best girl'. This couple will 'marry next month' but tonight they are out 'throwing' kisses to the moon. It seems that the world is unified on this night in its appreciation of the moon.

(b) Choose a line or two that you find particularly appealing and explain why. (10)

I like the lines: 'The clocks say I must go – I stay here sitting on the back porch/ drinking white thoughts you rain down'. The poet sets the world of convention and propriety against the romantic world of dreams and freedom. The 'clocks' seem to represent the restricted, ordered world of responsibility whereas the poet 'sitting on the back porch' seems to have entered a place free of duty and care. The line begins with the blunt demand of the 'clocks': 'The clocks say I must go'. The terse and matter-of-fact statement is set in stark contrast against the more poetic and gentle words that follow: 'I stay here sitting on the back porch/ drinking white thoughts you rain down'. The dash in the line neatly separates the two worlds and the way that the words 'I stay' stand alongside 'I must go' makes the poets decision all the more bold and satisfying: 'I must go – I stay'.

The poet suggests that the moon is inspiring him, feeding him 'thoughts' that are pure and joyous. It is as though the moon's rays are an intoxicating liquor that is making the poet tipsy. The image of him 'drinking white thoughts' calls to mind the term 'moonshine' that is used to describe certain illegally produced spirits. The poet by staying out upon his back porch seems to be rebelling against what is expected of him. It is late and he should be in bed, but he does not wish to act according to convention tonight.

Write a personal response to the poem 'Back Yard'. (20)

This is an inspiring and romantic poem that made me feel good when I read it. The poet conjures up a magical world that is all coated in the 'silver' light of the moon: 'the leaves of grass, catalpa and oak,/ All silver under your rain tonight'. It is a world of wonder and romance peopled with lovers and dreamers. The poet mentions an Italian accordion player, a young Polish couple and an elderly neighbour, each enthralled by the moon on this summer's night. The world of the poem seems to be blissfully innocent and good, devoid of troubles.

The poem contains some lovely imagery. The poet describes the effect of the moon's soft light upon his neighbour's cherry tree: 'a sheen/ that sits in a cherry tree in his back yard'. The soft sibilant 's' and 'ch' sounds corresponds with the tranquil atmosphere of the night. I also loved the way the poet introduces images of people in other countries far away who are sharing his pleasure on this night. The 'Italian boy' and the 'Polish boy' who 'is out with his best girl' introduce a wonderful international dimension to the poem.

I especially liked the lines 'The clocks say I must go – I stay sitting on the back porch/ drinking white thoughts you rain down'. The 'clocks' seem to represent the dull and tedious world of work and responsibility. Such a world stands in opposition to the world of romance and dream that the poet is part of on this summer's night. He knows that he ought to get to bed but he cannot resist the beauty of the moon's light and wishes to savour the moment for as long as he can. The moon's rays are like an intoxicating drink that the poet wants to keep on 'drinking'. They inspire sweet and pure thoughts ('white thoughts') that give the poet great pleasure.

PAST EXAM QUESTIONS

ELIZABETH BISHOP
2017: From the poetry of Elizabeth Bishop that you have studied, select the poems that, in your opinion, best demonstrate her skillful use of language and imagery to confront life's harsh realities. Justify your selection by demonstrating Bishop's skillful use of language and imagery to confront life's harsh realities in the poems you have chosen.

2019: "Bishop makes skillful use of a variety of poetic techniques to produce poems that are often analytical but rarely emotional." Discuss the extent to which you agree or disagree with the above statement. Develop your response with reference to the poems by Elizabeth Bishop on your course.

EMILY DICKINSON
2016: "Dickinson's use of an innovative style to explore intense experiences can both intrigue and confuse." Discuss this statement, supporting your answer with reference to the poetry of Emily Dickinson on your course.

2014: "The dramatic aspects of Dickinson's poetry can both disturb and delight readers." To what extent do you agree or disagree with the above statement? Support your answer with reference to both the themes and language found in the poetry of Emily Dickinson on your course.

JOHN DONNE
2006: Write an introduction to the poetry of John Donne for new readers. Your introduction should cover the following: - The ideas that were most important to him. - How you responded to his use of language and imagery. Refer to the poems by John Donne that you have studied.

2008: "John Donne uses startling imagery and wit in his exploration of relationships." Give your response to the poetry of John Donne in the light of this statement. Support your points with the aid of suitable reference to the poems you have studied.

PATRICK KAVANAGH
2010: In your opinion, is Kavanagh successful in achieving his desire to transform the ordinary world into something extraordinary? Support your answer with suitable reference to the poems on your course.

2012: "Aspects of Kavanagh's poetry could be seen as dated and irrelevant, but his unique poetic language has enduring appeal." Do you agree with this assessment of his poetry? Support your points with suitable reference to the poetry of Patrick Kavanagh on your course.

DEREK MAHON
2008: "Derek Mahon explores people and places in his own distinctive style." Write your response to this statement supporting your points with the aid of suitable reference to the poems you have studied.

2013: "Mahon uses language and imagery to transform personal observations into universal reflections." Write your response to this statement with reference to the poems by Derek Mahon on your course.

ADRIENNE RICH
2010: "Adrienne Rich explores the twin themes of power and powerlessness in a variety of interesting ways." Write a response to the poetry of Adrienne Rich in the light of this statement, supporting your points with suitable reference to the poems on your course.

2012: "Rich's poetry communicates powerful feelings through thought-provoking images and symbols." Write your response to this statement with reference to the poems by Adrienne Rich on your course.

WILLIAM BUTLER YEATS
2014: "Yeats uses evocative language to create poetry that includes both personal reflection and public commentary." Discuss this statement, supporting your answer with reference to both the themes and language found in the poetry of W. B. Yeats on your course.

2019: "Yeats's poetry is both intellectually stimulating and emotionally charged." Discuss the extent to which you agree or disagree with the above statement. Develop your response with reference to the themes and language evident in the poems by W. B. Yeats on your course.